SELECTED POEMS

WILLIAM BLAKE was born in Lond[...] [...]fession and an artist by vocation, he [...] power and originality who developed [...] which enabled him to design, inscri[...] publish his own verse. His *Songs of In[...]* was an expression of the deeply religiou[...] [...] which Isaiah Berlin would call 'the Counter-Enlightenment'. Blake, however, had sympathized with the American Revolution, and the French Revolution, that same year, inspired a phase of support for its secular assumptions. These views were expressed in his poems of the early 1790s: *America*, *Europe*, *Africa*, *Asia*, and the *Songs of Experience* which, in 1794, contradicted his previous lyrics. But Blake did not suppress his *Innocence* poems. Instead, he combined the two collections into a remarkable joint volume, *Songs of Innocence and of Experience Shewing the Two Contrary States of the Human Soul*, which demonstrated how it was possible to see the world in two radically different ways. By the end of the decade Blake had returned to the view that it was not political action but a change of heart, or spiritual awakening, that would build 'Jerusalem | In Englands green & pleasant Land'. Between 1800 and 1803 he lived in Sussex, developing an idiosyncratic mythology with which to dramatize this redemptive process, and, once back in London, expressed it in two long poems modelled on the Hebrew verse of the Old Testament: *Milton* and *Jerusalem*. Versatile as well as visionary, Blake also wrote striking poetry in other forms: ballads, narratives, comic and satirical verse, discursive poems, and verse epistles. William Blake died in 1827.

NICHOLAS SHRIMPTON is an Emeritus Fellow of Lady Margaret Hall, Oxford. He is the editor of Trollope's *An Autobiography*, *The Prime Minister*, and *The Warden* as well as Disraeli's *Sybil* for Oxford World's Classics. His other publications include *The Whole Music of Passion: New Essays on Swinburne* (1993), *Matthew Arnold: Selected Poems* (1998), and *Ruskin and 'War'* (2014).

OXFORD WORLD'S CLASSICS

*For over 100 years Oxford World's Classics have brought
readers closer to the world's great literature. Now with over 700
titles—from the 4,000-year-old myths of Mesopotamia to the
twentieth century's greatest novels—the series makes available
lesser-known as well as celebrated writing.*

*The pocket-sized hardbacks of the early years contained
introductions by Virginia Woolf, T. S. Eliot, Graham Greene,
and other literary figures which enriched the experience of reading.
Today the series is recognized for its fine scholarship and
reliability in texts that span world literature, drama and poetry,
religion, philosophy and politics. Each edition includes perceptive
commentary and essential background information to meet the
changing needs of readers.*

OXFORD WORLD'S CLASSICS

WILLIAM BLAKE

Selected Poems

Edited with an Introduction and Notes by
NICHOLAS SHRIMPTON

OXFORD

UNIVERSITY PRESS

Great Clarendon Street, Oxford, OX2 6DP,
United Kingdom

Oxford University Press is a department of the University of Oxford.
It furthers the University's objective of excellence in research, scholarship,
and education by publishing worldwide. Oxford is a registered trade mark of
Oxford University Press in the UK and in certain other countries

First published as an Oxford World's Classics paperback 2019

Impression:7

Published in the United States of America by Oxford University Press
198 Madison Avenue, New York, NY 10016, United States of America

British Library Cataloguing in Publication Data

Data available

Library of Congress Control Number: 2018957707

ISBN 978-0-19-880446-8

**Printed and bound in Great Britain by
Clays Ltd, Elcograf S.p.A.**

CONTENTS

x *Contents*

ABBREVIATIONS

Bentley (1978)	Bentley, G. E., Jr, ed., *William Blake's Writings*, Oxford, Clarendon Press, 2 volumes, 1978.
BR	Bentley, G. E., Jr, *Blake Records*, second edition, New Haven & London, Yale University Press, 2004.
E	Erdman, David V., ed., *The Complete Poetry & Prose of William Blake*, Berkeley, University of California Press, 1965, revised edition with a commentary by Harold Bloom 1982, reprinted 2008.
Gilchrist	Gilchrist, Alexander, *Life of William Blake, 'Pictor Ignotus'*, London, Macmillan, 2 volumes, 1863.
Johnson & Grant	Johnson, Mary Lynn, and John E. Grant, eds, *Blake's Poetry and Designs*, New York, W. W. Norton & Co., second edition, 2008.
N	Erdman, David V., ed., with the assistance of Donald K. Moore, *The Notebook of William Blake: A Photographic and Typographic Facsimile*, Oxford, Clarendon Press, 1973: a Notebook inherited from Blake's brother Robert in 1787, sometimes known as the Rossetti Manuscript or *Manuscript Notebook*. See next entry.
Nrev	Blake began to use the Notebook (see previous entry) for literary purposes in the early 1790s, initially working with the book 'reversed' and turned upside down: 'Nrev' (reversed) page numbers therefore follow each other in declining order, with the highest probably earliest in date. About 1799–1800 he started to use the book in the normal way, from the front: 'N' numbers therefore follow in a conventional, rising order, and represent a later phase of Blake's work.
Ostriker	Ostriker, Alicia, ed., *William Blake: The Complete Poems*, Harmondsworth, Penguin, 1977, repr. 1983.
Stevenson	Stevenson, W. H., ed., *Blake: The Complete Poems*, 1971, third edition, London & New York, Routledge, 2007.
Viscomi (1993)	*Blake and the Idea of the Book*, Princeton, Princeton University Press, 1993.

INTRODUCTION

WILLIAM BLAKE had many talents. By profession he was an engraver and a remarkable designer of printed books: his poems appeared in volumes which he not only wrote but also illustrated, engraved, printed, and published himself. By vocation he was a painter: trained at the Royal Academy Schools and, especially after 1808, chiefly committed to the making of pictures. His involvement in literature was, by comparison, occasional and, in his own view, probably of secondary importance. Though when 'Printed without the Writing' there was liable to be a 'Loss of some of the best things',[1] his publications seem, increasingly, to have been sold as exquisite sets of etchings or *livres d'artiste*: beautifully engraved and hand-coloured artefacts for collectors who valued books as physical objects. His longest poem, *Jerusalem*, was first (partially) published in the form of some 'Detached Specimens', or individual pages, shown at the annual exhibition of the Associated Painters in Water Colours in 1812, and not issued as a book until seven or eight years later.

Despite this preoccupation with the visual arts, Blake's greatest achievement was as a poet. Between 1769 and 1821 he created some of the most moving and memorable verse ever written in English. As a teenager, in the 1770s, he was, like Thomas Chatterton in the previous decade, a brilliantly precocious participant in the 'Preromantic' reinvention of English poetry. He performed his poems at Harriet Mathew's salon, saw them collected in the privately published *Poetical Sketches* of 1783, and included further snatches of song in his Menippean satire, 'An Island in the Moon'.[2] These early poems shared the contemporary enthusiasm for a rejection of the neo-classical rhyming couplet and the imitation, instead, of sixteenth- and seventeenth-century lyrics. Blake would develop this lyrical manner into the profoundly original *Songs of Innocence and of Experience* of 1794 and the poem now known as 'Jerusalem' which has become a popular alternative to the British national anthem.

---

[1] Blake's letter to Dawson Turner, 9 June 1818 (*E* 771).

[2] Mrs Anthony Mathew held literary and musical conversaziones in her house in Rathbone Place; her husband and John Flaxman sponsored the private publication of the poems which Blake performed there. 'An Island in the Moon' is an incomplete manuscript draft (now in the Fitzwilliam Museum) of some comic sketches of contemporary intellectual life in a manner derived from the (lost) work of the Greek Cynic Menippus.

He was also an important contributor to the ballad revival. Recommended by Joseph Addison in the *Spectator* in 1711 and provided with its models by Thomas Percy's *Reliques of Ancient English Poetry* in 1765, the imitation of ballads (whether late-medieval folk poems or popular 'broadside' verses) fulfilled a new demand for simplicity and directness. Simplicity of manner, that is, rather than of meaning: Blake's difficult and disturbing ballad 'The Mental Traveller' ranks with Coleridge's similarly obscure but engrossing 'The Rime of the Ancient Mariner', Wordsworth's 'The Idiot Boy', and Keats's 'La Belle Dame sans Merci' as one of the outstanding achievements in this major Romantic form.

The new poetry of the late eighteenth century had yet another ancient source: the Old Testament. The 'songs, hymns and prophecies of the Hebrew Bible' were, as Murray Roston argued in 1965, an even more important influence on Romantic practice than Elizabethan lyrics or medieval ballads. Here too Blake was a key figure. Roston calls him 'the culmination' of the 'concern with the visionary power and ethical insistence of Hebrew poetry' which had, in this analysis, played so important a part in the re-making of English verse.[3] Blake specifically identified just two of his so-called 'Prophetic Books' as prophecies: *America a Prophecy* (1793) and *Europe a Prophecy* (1794). But both the eight 'brief' epics written in the 1790s and the two 'diffuse' epics[4] on which he was at work between 1804 and 1820 clearly reflect the excited rediscovery of the poetic quality of the Bible ('Spiritual Verse' as Blake calls it in *Jerusalem* Plate 48) which had been prompted by Robert Lowth's lectures 'On the Sacred Poetry of the Hebrews' in the 1740s.[5] Isaiah, Ezekiel, and the Psalms were, it seemed, better models for inspired poetry than Homer, Virgil, or even Milton. Several poets in this period attempted the sublime epic or the 'prophetic' poem of indignant commentary on contemporary events. The orthodox manner of either Pope or Milton was, however, almost impossible to escape. Only Christopher Smart, in the 1760s, and William Blake managed to get back past Milton to create a convincing English equivalent of ancient Hebrew verse.

[3] Murray Roston, *Prophet and Poet: The Bible and the Growth of Romanticism* (London: Faber & Faber, 1965), 142 and 160.

[4] Milton's terms, used in *The Reason of Church-Government* (1642) of the Book of Job ('brief') and Homer, Virgil, and Tasso ('diffuse').

[5] Robert Lowth (1710–87) was an Anglican clergyman whose lectures as Oxford Professor of Poetry (1741–50) were delivered in Latin and not translated until 1787, though their content was echoed in Hugh Blair's lectures at Edinburgh University (1759–83) and summarized in Lowth's *Isaiah: A New Translation* (1778).

Blake was, in other words, a poet of exceptional skill and versatility—
though that versatility has, until recently, been obscured by the view
that the discussion of Romantic poetry in these generic or formal terms
was inappropriate. This, supposedly, was the era which saw 'a virtual
extinction of all the traditional genres'[6] and the rise, instead, of the concept of 'organic form'. Since the appearance of Stuart Curran's *Poetic
Form and British Romanticism* in 1986, however, critics have discovered
how useful generic concepts can be when seeking to understand the
poetic practice of this period. This is as true of Blake as it is of any of
his contemporaries. In this edition, therefore his poems are presented
in groups which reflect the genre or literary mode to which they belong:
lyrics, ballads, narrative poems, descriptive and discursive poems, comic
and satirical poems, epistolary poems, brief epics, and finally, his 'diffuse' sublime epics.[7] Within each category the texts are arranged in the
order in which they were written (in so far as that is known). But this is
not the straightforward march through Blake's career which has become
customary in editions of his work—for that the reader can turn to the
Chronology. Instead, the stress is on the formal categories which help
us to sense the ways in which he was possessed of literary, as well as
visual, artistry.

This is not meant to suggest that Blake's literary work lacks intellectual content. On the contrary, he was to a remarkable extent a poet of
ideas, despite the unpromising circumstances in which he grew up. Born
in London in 1757, Blake was unusual among the poets of his era in not
being a member of the upper, or upper-middle, classes. Sent to a drawing school when he was 10, and apprenticed to an engraver at the age of
14, he was, except as an artist, largely self-educated. This did not make
him, as some of his admirers would like to believe, a proletarian. Rather,
he came (like Shakespeare) from that most unfashionable of backgrounds:
the lower middle class. His father was a London shopkeeper who was
sufficiently prosperous to pay the premiums required to apprentice three
of his sons—William to the engraver James Basire in August 1772. The
eldest son, James, took over the haberdashery business at 28 Broad (now
Broadwick) Street after their father's death in 1784 and ran it until his
retirement at some point in the 1810s. When Blake needed a space in

[6] P. W. K. Stone, *The Art of Poetry 1750–1820: Theories of Poetic Composition and Style
in the Late Neo-Classic and Early Romantic Periods* (London: Routledge & Kegan Paul,
1967), 147.
[7] Blake also wrote some dramatic verse but that falls into a different category and is not
included in this edition.

which to stage a selling exhibition of his paintings, in 1809, he was able to use his own family's shop as a gallery.

This modest comfort did not, however, extend to the provision of university or even secondary education, other than a vocational training as a draughtsman. Given this, it can be a surprise to read Blake's own accounts of the range of his literary and philosophical interests. Writing to the sculptor John Flaxman in September 1800 he describes (in a passage of assured epistolary verse) the chief influences on his writing and thinking between 'childhood' (the 1760s) and 'the French Revolution' (1789):

> . . . Milton lovd me in childhood & shewd me his face
> Ezra came with Isaiah the Prophet, but Shakespeare in riper years gave me his
>   hand
> Paracelsus & Behmen appeard to me. terrors appeard in the Heavens above
> And in Hell beneath & a mighty & awful change threatened the Earth
> The American War began All its dark horrors passed before my face
> Across the Atlantic to France. Then the French Revolution commencd . . .
>
>   (p. 103).

A few years later he augmented this account in an annotation to the *Discourses* of Sir Joshua Reynolds:

> Burke's Treatise on the Sublime & Beautiful is founded on the Opinions of Newton & Locke on this Treatise Reynolds has grounded many of his assertions. in all his Discourses I read Burkes Treatise when very Young at the same time I read Locke on Human Understanding & Bacons Advancement of Learning on Every one of these Books I wrote my Opinions & on looking them over find that my Notes on Reynolds in this Book are exactly Similar. (*E* 660)

It seems improbable that this reading of Locke, Bacon, and Burke could have taken place above the haberdasher's shop. His discovery of such texts is more likely to have been at 31 Great Queen Street, Covent Garden, where he lived as an apprentice from 1772 to 1779. His master, James Basire, was principal engraver to both the Society of Antiquaries and the Royal Society. Basire's clients and friends were scholars and intellectuals who may well have suggested, or even lent, books to a clever and curious young member of the team of engravers working on their publications.

Milton, Ezra, Isaiah, Paracelsus, and Boehme ('Behmen') are a different matter. These writers could all have been part of the Christian culture of the household at 28 Broad Street. The Blakes were Nonconformists, that is Protestants who dissented from the doctrine and liturgy of the established Anglican Church. They would be buried in Bunhill Fields, the London cemetery for Nonconformists, and Henry Crabb Robinson, after talking to Blake's brother in 1809–10, noted that they belonged to 'einer dissentirenden Gemeinde' ('a dissenting community').[8] Unfortunately Crabb Robinson did not record which particular denomination of dissenters this was. We know that Blake's mother, Catherine Wright, was briefly a Moravian (a Pietist and ecumenical branch of the Lutheran Church): she and her first husband, Thomas Armitage, joined their London congregation in November 1750. But she left it again after Thomas's death in November 1751, and was no longer a Moravian when she married James Blake (the elder) in October 1752. It is possible that the family which she then joined were Baptists. In the present, imperfect state of our knowledge, however, my own guess is that they were Whitefieldian (that is, Calvinist) Methodists.[9] The boundary between Moravianism and Methodism was very permeable—John Cennick, who received the Armitages into the Moravian Church in 1750, had himself previously been a Whitefieldian Methodist minister—and William Blake's later attacks on a punitive God as 'Nobodaddy' (p. 96), like his rebarbative dismissal of the Calvinist theory of penal Atonement ('It is a horrible doctrine'),[10] have the lingering intensity of a teenage rebellion against a previously accepted truth.

Whichever branch of dissent they followed, the Blakes would have been part of a shared culture, based on a close study of the Bible but augmented by modern literary texts. Bunyan's *Pilgrim's Progress*, Milton's *Paradise Lost* and *Paradise Regained*, and the *Hymns and Spiritual Songs* and *Divine Songs for the Use of Children* by Isaac Watts were habitual reading in such households. There was also a lively tradition of spiritual enquiry which found expression in the works of William Law (an Anglican Nonjuror), Philip Doddridge (an Independent), and George Whitefield and John Wesley (the founders of the Calvinist and Arminian branches of Methodism). The translation of texts from other languages was another important part of this religious culture. Quite where Blake would have encountered the theological writings of Paracelsus is not clear, since they had not been published in English since the 1660s. But

---

[8] [Henry Crabb Robinson], 'Künstler, Dichter, und Religiöser Schwärmer', *Vaterländisches Museum*, II (1811), Hamburg, 107–31, here quoted from *BR* 583 and 599.

[9] George Whitefield (1714–70) and John Wesley (1703–91) were the founders of the Methodist movement. Both Protestants, their theological differences reflected those of the Anglican Church of which they were, technically, still members: Wesley was an Arminian but Whitefield a Calvinist.

[10] Crabb Robinson's diary for 7 December 1826 (*BR* 453).

Paracelsus (1493–1521) influenced Jakob Boehme (1575–1624) whose work Blake certainly knew since he praised the illustrations in the 'Law' edition of *The Works of Jacob Behmen* (1764–81).[11] Boehme, in turn, influenced Law's volumes of spiritual reflection and had clear effects on Blake's own thinking.

Even though he did not form part of Blake's early self-education, the most conspicuous figure here is the Swedish scientist and visionary Emanuel Swedenborg (1688–1772). By background a Lutheran, or Evangelical, Protestant, he began to claim direct contact with the spiritual world in the mid-1740s. His religious writings first appeared, in Latin, in 1749 and English translations soon followed. They were recommended by some Anglican clergymen, such as Jacob Duché, chaplain of an orphanage in Lambeth (where Blake lived in the 1790s), and Swedenborgian views were seen as entirely compatible with membership of other denominations. Blake sympathetically annotated a 1784 edition of Swedenborg's *A Treatise of Heaven and Hell* and a 1788 edition of *The Wisdom of Angels, concerning Divine Love and Divine Wisdom*, and in April 1789 he and his wife attended a meeting organized by a group of former Methodist preachers who had, since 1787, been seeking to establish a separate Swedenborgian church in London. Blake even signed their theological manifesto. But he then made hostile annotations ('Cursed Folly!') in a 1790 copy of *The Wisdom of Angels concerning the Divine Providence* and, between 1790 and 1793, produced a satirical attack on Swedenborg under the parodic title *The Marriage of Heaven and Hell*. Some of Blake's friends were Swedenborgians, as were some of his clients: the wealthy Swedenborgian–Anglican Charles Augustus Tulk, MP for Sudbury, certainly commissioned paintings from him. The need to accommodate the wishes of such customers might, indeed, explain why Blake's 1809 exhibition included a painting with a Swedenborgian topic: *The Spiritual Preceptor* ('This subject is taken from the visions of Emanuel Swedenborg', *E* 546). It does not, however, explain the fact that in Plate 48 of *Jerusalem* Blake chose to adopt a distinctively Swedenborgian canon of the Bible. Tulk's account of the matter was that Blake had told him that 'he had two different states; one in which he liked Swedenborg's writings, and one in which he disliked them'.[12]

---

[11] Law died in 1761, leaving the edition to be completed by others; for Blake's comments see *BR* 423–4.

[12] Letter to Garth Wilkinson quoted in J. Spilling, 'Blake the Visionary', *The New Church Magazine*, vi (1887), 210.

As this suggests, the religious culture in which Blake grew up was lively but complicated. He was clearly familiar with the ideas of a wide range of different sects, from the Protestant Antinomianism which had been part of the political discourse of the seventeenth-century Ranters to the Roman Catholic quietism of Madame Guyon (praised in *Jerusalem* Plate 72). The critic Jon Mee has called this ability to mix his theological vocabularies 'bricolage', while Jennifer Jesse has traced the way in which Blake adapted his terminology in order to address such different audiences as the 'Jews', 'Deists', and 'Christians' of the last three chapters of *Jerusalem*.[13] The Nonconformist background did have some negative consequences. Even if his family had wished it, William Blake could not have gone to university since the English universities were, at this date, exclusively Anglican institutions. Dissenting culture was also hostile to the visual arts. Here, Blake's mother's experience of Moravianism, brief though it was, may have been helpful to a boy with ambitions as an artist. Very unusually in the world of the dissenting sects, the Moravians approved of visual imagery and filled their Fetter Lane chapel with paintings.

The positive value of Blake's Nonconformist background was the intellectual energy with which dissenting Churches both absorbed and contested the great new cultural force of the era: the *Aufklärung* or Enlightenment. With its roots in the case made for inductive science by Francis Bacon, the Enlightenment was a movement developed in the philosophical and scientific writings of Descartes, Newton, Bayle, and Locke. It flowered in the work of the eighteenth-century French *philosophes*, Voltaire, Diderot, D'Alembert, Montesquieu, and Rousseau, and in the writings of their Scottish and German contemporaries. Descartes is usually seen as the origin of the Enlightenment's rationalism: John Locke's most significant publication on religion would, characteristically, be entitled *The Reasonableness of Christianity* (1695). Pierre Bayle's *Historical and Critical Dictionary*, in 1697, established another key characteristic of Enlightenment thought: its scepticism and rejection of dogma. Bacon, correspondingly, was the source of its empiricism: the view that knowledge arises only from observation and experiment. In 1690, Locke's *Essay Concerning Human Understanding* (which Blake read 'when very Young') gave this view its classic formulation, arguing that the mind, at birth, is:

[13] See Jon Mee, *Dangerous Enthusiasm: William Blake and the Culture of Radicalism in the 1790s* (Oxford: Clarendon Press, 1992) and Jennifer G. Jesse, *William Blake's Religious Vision* (Lanham: Lexington Books, 2013).

white Paper, void of all Characters, without any *Ideas*; How comes it to be furnished? . . . Whence has it all the materials of Reason and Knowledge? To this I answer, in one word, From *Experience*: In that, all our Knowledge is founded; and from that it ultimately derives it self.[14]

Dissenters, including Blake, welcomed the political ideas of the Enlightenment. The challenge to traditional authority, the demand for freedom of speech and opinion, and the concept of government by consent were all warmly endorsed by people who had been 'tolerated' since 1689 but denied full social and political rights. Some Nonconformists also adopted the movement's philosophical assumptions. Many Presbyterians, for example, gradually moved towards that most rational form of Protestant Christianity, Unitarianism. Most dissenters, however, drew a sharp distinction between the political and philosophical strands of Enlightenment thought. Some *philosophes*, after all, were atheists. Many more were Deists: believers in an absentee God who had created the universe, and established its natural laws, but then left it to its own devices.

Blake's response to such opinions was hostile. The Enlightenment ideal of reason is embodied in Urizen ('Your reason' in Blake's Cockney dialect), the malign deity who rules the fallen universe of his prophetic books. The scepticism encouraged by Pierre Bayle is mocked in witty couplets ('If the Sun & Moon should doubt | They'd immediately Go out')[15] and Chapter 3 of *Jerusalem* is directly addressed to the Deists: 'You, O Deists, profess yourselves the Enemies of Christianity, and you are so: you are also the enemies of the Human Race.' The most important aspect of Blake's response to the Enlightenment, however, was his treatment of its theory of knowledge. Here Blake's date of birth is significant. Though conventionally classified as a Romantic artist, he was actually a contemporary of Mozart. While Wordsworth's generation could treat the Enlightenment as a movement whose great achievements lay in the past, for Blake it was an immediately contemporary challenge. And while Coleridge could, after his visit to Germany in 1798–9, draw on the Idealist philosophical theories derived from Kant and developed by Schelling to cast doubt on empiricist assumptions, Blake could not. Instead, he used religious concepts, and the result is in some ways more easily grasped than the later, more abstract versions of Romantic thought.

Kantian philosophers undermined the empiricist view that all knowledge arises from sensory experience by arguing that we apprehend things,

---

[14] John Locke, *An Essay Concerning Human Understanding*, ed. Peter H. Nidditch (Oxford: Clarendon Press, 1975), 104.

[15] 'Auguries of Innocence', p. 80.

not directly, but only as they appear to us, under conditions (or necessary presuppositions) imposed by the structure of the human mind. Our world of appearances or 'phenomena' may, as a consequence, be quite different from reality: the world of 'noumena' or things as in themselves they really are. Blake makes the same point in a more concrete and traditional way. Reality is the universe which God originally created. But Adam and Eve transgressed and were cast out of Eden. What we now inhabit and apprehend is therefore the fallen world: a second-rate, imperfect version of reality. Far from being a source of truth, the natural world is a veil, or screen, which separates us from the real, or unfallen, universe. Blake's character Vala is, as her name suggests, a personification of that obscuring 'veil'.

How then can we apprehend the unfallen world? Blake's answer is that we do so, not with our senses, but with the imagination. This is a faculty which for Empiricists is real but trivial: the ability to picture things which do not exist. The account of the imagination developed during the Romantic period sees it very differently: as a profoundly significant cognitive capacity. When Wordsworth finds 'Imagination! Lifting up itself | Before the eye and progress of my Song' in Book Six of *The Prelude* (written by 1805 though not published until 1850), it is a power which offers 'visitings | Of awful promise, when the light of sense | Goes out in flashes that have shewn to us | The invisible world'. The imagination penetrates, that is, beyond the world apprehended by the senses to some deeper, more enduring truth.

Blake's version of this idea is, once again, more traditionally and literally religious. Where Wordsworth makes an unspecific gesture to 'the invisible world', and Kant speaks of 'the noumenal', Blake insists that the imagination gives us access to 'Eternity', the unfallen environment for which human beings were originally intended. As he does so, he aligns imagination (or 'Poetic Genius' as he calls it in his early work) with the 'inspiration' (2 Timothy 3.16) which allowed the authors of the Old Testament to communicate the word of God. At one level, this is an assertion of the kind of visionary poetry which Blake himself set out to write. At another, it is a theory of knowledge. His most famous poem, 'And did those feet in ancient time', is immediately followed by the quotation of a remark made by Moses in Numbers 11.29: 'Would to God that all the Lord's people were Prophets'. Building Jerusalem in England's green and pleasant land involves a general rejection of empiricism and a universal recovery of the capacity to apprehend the infinite.

Blake made an intellectual case for this theory in the three short prose texts now known as 'The 1788 Tractates'. Beginning with statements of the empiricist account of human understanding, they go on to insist that, 'He who sees the Infinite in all things sees God. He who sees the Ratio only sees himself only' (*E* 3). This is a modern, rationally argued version of St Paul's claim that 'the things which are seen are temporal; but the things which are not seen are eternal' (2 Corinthians 4.18) and Blake expresses it more strikingly in a commentary on his painting *The Last Judgment* in 1810: 'This world of Imagination is the World of Eternity it is the Divine bosom into which we shall all go after the death of the Vegetated body' (*E* 555). He also demonstrated it in his own life:

What it will be Questiond When the Sun rises do you not see a round disk of fire somewhat like a Guinea O no no I see an Innumerable company of the Heavenly host crying Holy Holy Holy is the Lord God Almighty I question not my Corporeal or Vegetative Eye any more than I would Question a Window concerning a Sight I look thro it & not with it. (*E* 565–6)

Not surprisingly, such behaviour led to accusations of madness. Blake's notes on a copy of Johann Spurzheim's *Observations on the Deranged Manifestations of the Mind* (1817) make it clear that this was not a psychological condition but an intellectual rejection of the philosophical assumptions of the Enlightenment:

Cowper came to me & said. O that I were insane always . . . You retain health & yet are as mad as any of us . . . mad as a refuge from unbelief—from Bacon Newton and Locke (*E* 662)

There is, however, a problem here. This profoundly religious man 'did not for the last forty years [of his life] attend any place of Divine worship',[16] and was a republican who sympathized with the French Revolution, despite its anti-clericism. This opponent of Enlightenment scepticism could write bitterly sceptical epigrams ('An answer to the parson'), and the man who believed, with St Paul, that 'we walk by faith, not by sight' (2 Corinthians 5.7) could make social and political statements which are clearly an exercise of the cognitive process which Locke called 'sensation' and 'reflection':

> I wander thro' each chartered street,
> Near where the chartered Thames does flow,
> And mark in every face I meet
> Marks of weakness, marks of woe.

Here, in his *Songs of Experience* (1794), Blake walks (or wanders), marks (by sight or sensation, not faith), and interprets (or reflects on) what he sees as 'weakness' and 'woe'.

[16] J. T. Smith, *Nollekens and His Times*, 1828 (*BR* 606–7).

There are simple answers to some of these apparent contradictions. Blake was not the only dissenter who avoided congregational worship and chose instead to follow Christ's instruction that you should, 'when thou prayest, enter into thy closet, and when thou hast shut thy door, pray to thy Father which is in secret' (Matthew 6.6). Dissenters were usually happy to adopt political attitudes associated with the Enlightenment, while the hostility to 'parsons', or Anglican clergymen, was a familiar Nonconformist attitude. As for reason, it was the dominance of the rational in 'the Age of Reason' that Blake objected to, not 'intellect' as such.[17] Empiricism is, however, a different matter and the fundamental reason why Blake can seem confusing is that he changed his mind about it. He did so, what's more, not once but twice—on the second occasion reverting to something which closely resembled his original beliefs. Statements made in the early 1790s can therefore contradict claims made either before or after that period.

Blake had read Locke and Bacon 'when very Young' and his satirical sketch, 'An Island in the Moon', written in the early to mid-1780s, contains some fiercely sceptical attacks on established authorities. But it also includes a discussion of Voltaire in which a character questions the French philosopher's scepticism ('a man may be a fool & make Queries but a man must have good sound sense to solve them', *E* 450), together with early drafts of three of the poems which would be collected as *Songs of Innocence* in 1789. That book, Blake's first major work as a poet, would be an expression of the deeply religious view of the world which he had absorbed from the Protestant culture of his childhood.

There had been some false starts. *Tiriel*, a narrative poem which Blake wrote and illustrated, but did not publish, in the late 1780s was influenced by the contemporary enthusiasm for Ossian, the ancient Gaelic bard supposedly discovered by James Macpherson. The exotic names of Ossian's characters and places, and the rhythmic prose which falls naturally into septenary (or seven-stress) verse lines, would leave a lasting mark on Blake's poetic practice. But this was not the way forward. Nor was *The Book of Thel* (engraved and printed in 1789), a philosophical narrative partly suggested by Milton's *Comus* and conducted with an uncharacteristic prettiness and delicacy.[18] Blake found his voice when he turned decisively to religious topics and to the ancient models found in Hebrew verse.

---

[17] 'God...is the intellectual fountain of Humanity', *Jerusalem* Plate 91.

[18] 'Blake first planned his idea of the beautiful book in the age of high rococo, the age of Watteau and Mozart', Northrop Frye, *Fearful Symmetry: A Study of William Blake* (Princeton: Princeton University Press, 1947; reprinted 1972), 358.

The first form in which he used it was the hymn. Retrieving three lyrics from 'An Island in the Moon', and another from some annotations made to a copy of *Poetical Sketches*, he assembled a collection of twenty-three poems which he illustrated, engraved, printed, and self-published as *Songs of Innocence*. In the Judaeo-Christian tradition, the hymn is found in the Psalms and Canticles of the Old Testament, and in the Latin hymns of the early Christian Church. Anglicans used translations of the Psalms but shunned original hymns until the 1830s. For Nonconformists, however, newly composed English hymns were an important mode of worship. Isaac Watts published his *Hymns and Spiritual Songs* in 1707, and John and Charles Wesley (chiefly Charles) wrote and published more than six thousand hymns.

For his *Songs of Innocence*, Blake drew on a particular sub-section of this flourishing literary mode: the children's hymn. This had its roots in a text by John Bunyan, first issued in 1686 as *A Book for Boys and Girls, or Country Rhimes for Children*.[19] In its frequent eighteenth-century reprints, this consisted, like adult emblem books, of a series of short, moralizing poems, each with a picture: a format which would be followed in Isaac Watts's *Divine Songs, attempted in easy language, for the use of children* (1715) and in Blake's illustrated *Songs*. The topics established in Bunyan's emblem book were also influential. Bunyan has poems on a fish, a swallow, a bee, a thief, a beggar, and a 'flint in water', just as Blake has a lamb, a blossom, a shepherd, and (in *Experience*) a tiger, and a clod and a pebble. Bunyan's 'The Pismire' is paralleled by Watts's 'The Ant, or Emmet' and Blake's 'A Dream' (with its lost 'Emmet'). Watts's 'The Fly' is a precedent for Blake's 'The Fly', while his 'Cradle Hymn' anticipates Blake's 'Cradle Song'. There is also a formal resemblance: Watts's use of the long metre, common metre, and short metre stanzas of Nonconformist hymnody (his poem 'The Hosanna' has stanzas in each of these metres, and identifies them for the reader) is echoed in Blake's metrical and stanzaic patterns.

Despite these similarities, *Songs of Innocence* is not, in a literal sense, a collection of children's hymns: the two dozen surviving copies of this expensive, hand-coloured book show no signs of the destructive treatment usual in the nursery.[20] Rather, it borrows the established format of the children's hymnbook in order to make an adult, philosophical

---

[19] Known after 1724 as *Divine Emblems: or, Temporal Things Spiritualized*.

[20] In October 1793 Blake priced the volume at '5s' (*E* 693). Though more copies may have been sold than now survive, Blake's income was derived from his work as a reproductive engraver and from commissions for paintings by a few loyal patrons, rather than from his little-known poetry.

statement. In a marginal note to the manuscript of *The Four Zoas* Blake will insist that, 'Innocence dwells with Wisdom, but never with Ignorance' (*E* 838) and what it signifies is perhaps best suggested by Kant's distinction between the Enlightenment and the mode of thought which it challenged or displaced, in his essay 'Was ist Aufklärung' ('What is Enlightenment?'):

Enlightenment is man's release from his self-incurred tutelage [German: Unmündigkeit]. Tutelage is man's inability to make use of his understanding without direction from another . . . Sapere aude! [Dare to know!] Have courage to use your own reason![21]

The religious riposte to this assertion is that the traditional willingness to receive 'direction' from the word of God is not cowardice but a proper humility, while the Enlightenment's belief in the autonomous power of human reason is arrogant and self-deluding. Blake's 'innocence' is a positive version of Kant's 'Unmündigkeit': a view of the universe which acknowledges the doctrine of the Fall and accepts the teaching (or 'tutelage') that there is a loving God who guides, protects, and judges his creation.

Parents protecting children and shepherds protecting sheep are Blake's images of that larger scheme. As that need for protection suggests, however, this remains a fallen world. Children are lost in woods or, more literally, orphaned, and services in St Paul's Cathedral are required to raise money for the charity schools which house them ('Holy Thursday'). But acts of charity provide—like Blake seeing angels where others saw the sun—a visionary glimpse of the divine reality:

> Beneath them sit the aged men, wise guardians of the poor;
> Then cherish pity, lest you drive an angel from your door.

In a fallen world there are also dirty and dangerous jobs to be done, such as sweeping chimneys. In this understanding, however, God gives those who do them a heavenly reward:

> And the Angel told Tom, if he'd be a good boy,
> He'd have God for his father, & never want joy.

This is not the sentimental reassurance customary in children's hymns, as a precisely calculated verbal usage in the final line of 'The Chimney Sweeper' makes clear: 'So if all do their duty they need not fear harm.'

---

[21] Immanuel Kant, 'Beantwortung der Frage: Was ist Aufklärung?' first published in the *Berlinische Monatsschrift*, December 1784.

The harm is real but they need not 'fear' it because it is a martyrdom which will win them a more enduring, posthumous consolation. The 'happy songs' sung by the figure 'Piping down the valleys wild' are a robust assertion of the view of the human condition which the Enlightenment was seeking to overthrow.

And then, even as Blake was printing the pages of the first copies of *Songs of Innocence*, the world suddenly changed. On 17 June 1789, the deputies of the French Third Estate declared themselves a National Assembly. The storming of the Bastille followed on 14 July and the Declaration of the Rights of Man on 26 August. Perhaps, instead of waiting for a posthumous reward, social problems could be solved by political action? Perhaps the Enlightenment's recommendation of natural rights, rather than religious truths, was correct? Perhaps the empirical analysis of physical experience was, after all, the best way to understand the world? In the early 1790s Blake certainly seemed to think so. The *Songs of Experience*, written from 1789 or 1790, and first published in 1794, are the product of a period in which Blake appears to have been won over to the philosophical claim that knowledge arises from sensation. This turn to the sceptical, empirical, and secular required a reconsideration of Innocence. In his Notebook, Blake began to draft lyrics which directly contested or contradicted songs which he had printed in 1789. These new lyrics would be advertised as *Songs of Experience* in October 1793 and printed in 1794.

Blake's attitude in the early 1790s was irreligious and it is most clearly expressed in a draft 'Motto to the Songs of Innocence & of Experience', written in his Notebook in 1792–3:

> The Good are attracted by Mens perceptions,
> And Think not for themselves;
> Till Experience teaches them to catch
> And to cage the Fairies & Elves
>
> And then the Knave begins to snarl
> And the Hypocrite to howl;
> And all his good Friends shew their private ends,
> And the Eagle is known from the Owl.

This celebration of 'Experience' is a direct attack on 'Unmündigkeit' and a vivid expression of the scepticism of the Enlightenment. But Blake did not, in practice, use this motto when he published the *Songs of Innocence and of Experience*, eighteen months later, in 1794 or 1795. Instead, he engraved a sub-title: *Shewing the Two Contrary States of the Human Soul*.

He had changed his mind again: both Innocence and Experience, he had come to think, were coherent ways of understanding the world, though they were 'contrary' or incompatible. Blake therefore presents two sets of poems, about the same things, from two radically different points of view. The adult, philosophically substantial status of the text is now obvious. Seen through the eyes of innocence, the Holy Thursday service is a manifestation of the moral intuition or divine commandment which prompts charity. Seen through the eyes of experience, it is a cynical demonstration of the social inequality which makes charity necessary in the first place. Seen through the eyes of innocence, God is a loving shepherd who protects his sheep ('The Lamb'). Seen through the eyes of experience ('The Tyger'), God is a sadist who deliberately created carnivores:

> Did he smile his work to see?
> Did he who made the Lamb make thee?

This poem echoes Pierre Bayle's sceptical thesis that the existence of evil cannot be reconciled with the goodness of an omnipotent God. Read together, 'The Lamb' and 'The Tyger' are a brilliant encapsulation of the issue which theologians call 'the problem of pain' or theodicy.[22]

Today we have internalized the secular assumptions of the Enlightenment so thoroughly that we find the *Experience* poems natural and the *Innocence* poems odd. Some critics have therefore suggested that the *Songs of Innocence* must be ironic or insincere. If they were ironic, however, they would merely be saying the same thing as *Experience* in a different way and the joint volume would not be the brilliant counterpointing of 'contrary' views which makes it so distinctive. Dante Gabriel Rossetti, in 1863, stood out against the modern tendency to prefer *Experience*: 'The first series is incomparably the more beautiful of the two . . . there can be no comparison between the first "Chimney Sweeper", which touches with such perfect simplicity the true pathetic chord of its subject, and the second, tinged merely with the commonplaces of social discontent.'[23] Subsequent critics have been more enthusiastic than Rossetti about the expression of 'social discontent' and have sometimes suggested that the way in which the 'Piper' of the 'Introduction' to *Innocence* 'stain'd the water clear' in order to write down his songs must mean that the poems are morally flawed. But this

---

[22] Leibniz coined the term in his *Essais de Théodicée sur la Bonté de Dieu* (1710), a response to the 'Rorarius' entry in Bayle's *Dictionary* ('The animal's soul has never sinned, and yet it is subjected to pain and misery').

[23] D. G. Rossetti in Alexander Gilchrist, *Life of William Blake* (London, 1863), 2.25.

is an over-ingenious misreading. The London guild of dyers and decor-
ators was, and still is, proud to be the Painter-Stainers Company, and
water dyed with vegetable juices is the pre-industrial, or Edenic, form
of ink. Innocence is as cogent a view of the universe as Experience and
it is Blake's ability to give powerful expression to genuinely 'contrary'
attitudes which makes this volume of simple but exquisite lyrics so
intellectually substantial.

Blake's secular and revolutionary views of the early 1790s were
expressed, without a qualifying contrary, in *The Marriage of Heaven
and Hell* and in his first 'prophetic' books: *Visions of the Daughters of
Albion* and *America a Prophecy* (both printed in 1793). *The Marriage* is
a prose text, not a poem, and its parodic function makes it hard to inter-
pret. Is Blake saying things which he believes? Or is he just performing
a comically distorted version of Swedenborg? The best clue comes in
Plate 22, where we are given 'the reason' why Swedenborg has failed:
'He conversed with Angels who are all religious, & conversed not with
Devils' (*E* 43). Swedenborg has only tested his ideas by discussing them
with like-minded, similarly virtuous people. Blake corrects that omission by providing a stream of shocking assertions, drawing, as he does
so, on his knowledge of Antinomianism (the belief that the Ten Commandments had been made redundant by the Gospel or, in its more
extreme form, that the Elect are predestined to be saved, irrespective of
their behaviour). There is an Antinomian flavour, too, about Blake's
campaign for free love, found in *Visions of the Daughters of Albion* and
in many of the Notebook poems of the early 1790s.

Antinomian politics are, however, a double-edged sword (oppressors,
as well as rebels, can claim to have been released from the old moral
prohibitions) and the revolutionary stance of *America* is more atheistical
than Antinomian. Beginning, at this time, to develop his own mytho-
logical system, Blake embodied the spirit of revolution in the figure of
Orc. When he is denounced by Albion's Angel (the British Church and
State) as a 'Blasphemous Demon, Antichrist, hater of Dignities; | Lover
of wild rebellion, and transgressor of Gods Law', Orc proudly replies,
'That stony law I stamp to dust: and scatter religion abroad | To the
four winds as a torn book, & none shall gather the leaves.' Not just the
'stony law' (or Ten Commandments), that is, but 'religion' as a whole.
The same note is heard in *Europe a Prophecy* (1794), where the oppression challenged by Orc's revolutionary arrival 'in the vineyards of red
France' is identified with the 'Eighteen hundred years' of the Christian
era. In *The Song of Los* (1795) Blake will add a beginning ('Africa') and
end ('Asia') to his sequence of poems about the loss and recovery of

freedom in the continents of the world. 'Africa' attributes the Fall, not to Eve's breach of God's commandment, but to God's invention of the prohibition in the first place. Religion in all its forms (Jewish, Greek, Hindu, Islamic, Norse, and even the New Testament 'Gospel' of 'Jesus') is to blame for the miserable condition from which revolutionary energy alone can rescue us.

As early as 1793, however, Blake was beginning to suggest that the empirical philosophy of 'five senses' (*Visions of the Daughters of Albion* Plate 5) was a delusion. In the final plate of 'Africa' the change would become conspicuous. As recently as 1791, in *The French Revolution* (printed as a set of proof sheets by Joseph Johnson but never published), Blake had praised Voltaire and Rousseau (*E* 298). Now, he insists that there is an 'Eternity' which has been 'obliterated & erased' by 'Newton & Locke', 'Rousseau & Voltaire'. Experience, it seems, is not the answer.

By 1795, in other words, Blake had ceased to believe, not just in the French Revolution, but in the secular and materialist philosophy on which it was based. The poem which articulates this disillusionment most clearly is *The Book of Ahania* (1795), in which the revolutionary figure is called Fuzon. Why not Orc? The answer is that Orc is associated with the successful American uprising, and that a different character was needed to represent a revolution which had turned violently on its own supporters: Danton, Saint-Just, and Robespierre were guillotined in the spring and early summer of 1794. David Erdman identified Fuzon with Robespierre.[24] Though this specific link may be too literal, the poem does appear to show the spirit, or ideology, of the French Revolution, first over-reaching itself ('I am God,' says Fuzon), and then lapsing into a new version of Urizenic tyranny. Blake was struggling to distinguish what was valid in Experience's criticism of the modern world from its failures—and to reconcile what remained with the philosophical assumptions of Innocence. That struggle is manifested in *The First Book of Urizen*.

Though issued with the date '1794' on its title-page, the eight surviving copies of this poem differ widely, suggesting that Blake wrestled with the problem over a considerable period. His answer involved the use of yet another of the religious doctrines with which he was familiar: Gnosticism, or the belief that the material universe had been created, not by the true Divine Being, but by an inferior 'Demiurge'. In the Bible and Milton the Fall occurs when Eve eats the apple. In Blake's

[24] David V. Erdman, *Blake: Prophet Against Empire*, 3rd edn (Princeton: Princeton University Press, 1977), 314–15.

'Africa' the Fall occurred, in an Antinomian manner, when God prohibited the eating of the apple. Now Blake pushes the Fall still further back. The true God is 'the will of the Immortal' or 'the Eternals' (plural, like the Hebrew 'Elohim'). Urizen is the Demiurge: a being who somehow separates himself from this immaterial condition ('Eternity') and creates the physical cosmos apprehended by Experience. Mundane authorities impose the laws of Urizen (or 'Nobodaddy'); established Churches worship him. Even art is compromised. Los, Blake's mythic embodiment of the creative artist, is sent by the Eternals to 'confine' Urizen. But he does so by giving form to the Urizenic universe and thus becomes complicit in the 'loss' of Eternity. His son, the revolutionary Orc, had once seemed to offer an escape. Now Orc is chained to a rock and it is the untrustworthy Fuzon who leads the attempt at an exodus.

Blake had solved his immediate problem. Though conventional religion was merely a demiurgic or Urizenic sham, Innocence was right to believe in God and to reject the claims of Experience to exclusive knowledge. But, if revolution would not work, how was mankind to be rescued from this catastrophe? Like Milton, who abandoned his plans for an epic based on British history in order to write *Paradise Lost*, Blake turned from the political and contingent to consider the problems of the human race at a deeper level, *sub specie aeternitatis*.

An awareness of the Antinomian politics of the seventeenth century (revived among the millenarian sects of the 1790s) may have helped with this shift. Then, too, political argument had been closely linked to theology and, though Blake's later doctrine would be Solifidian rather than Antinomian, his subsequent work is both socially concerned and profoundly religious. This stance was reinforced by a series of spiritual crises, described in his letters to Thomas Butts, which closely resemble the experience of being 'born again' customary in evangelical conversions. Combining the Swedenborgian idea that God is best understood as 'Jesus Christ in his Divine Humanity'[25] with a non-penal conception of the Atonement and an insistence that 'The Spirit of Jesus is continual forgiveness of Sin' (*Jerusalem* Plate 3), Blake's later poetry repeatedly asserts the Solifidian view that it is faith, and not good works, which saves us.[26] Without a prior acceptance that 'We are accounted righteous

---

[25] This phrase forms part of the resolutions signed by Blake at the First General Conference of the New Jerusalem Church in 1789.

[26] Antinomianism is an exaggeration of Solifidian doctrine into the claim that faith alone, without obedience to moral law, suffices for salvation. Solifidians hold that it remains 'necessary to do good works, not so that we can trust them to earn grace but because it is

before God, only for the merits of our Lord and Saviour Jesus Christ'[27] good works are futile—as the failure of the irreligious French revolutionaries had perhaps suggested.

This doctrine had been powerfully expressed by the Methodist leaders, John Wesley and George Whitefield. Though technically Anglicans until the 1780s, their criticisms of the established Church prefigured Blake's attack on it as 'Mystery' and they would be singled out for praise as 'Prophets' in *Milton* (Plate 20). Jesus, meanwhile, would become the key redemptive figure in both *Milton* and *Jerusalem*: the epigraph to Chapter 1 of *Jerusalem* is 'Jesus alone' (Matthew 17.8). It is His feet which may once have walked on 'Englands mountains green' and will do so again when, as Blake hopes, Jerusalem is established there. The problem was not institutional but fundamental. A profound change of heart and mind (or religious rebirth) was indispensable if the human condition was to be effectively ameliorated.

The difficulty in 1794, however, was artistic as well as philosophical. Urizen has split from 'the will of the Immortal'. Why? And how could one imagine, or dramatize, his reintegration? Blake would spend the next ten years trying to find answers to these questions in a long, complex, and unpublished text, initially called *Vala* and then (in an amendment to the draft title-page) *The Four Zoas*. The key development here is the introduction of 'Albion the Ancient Man'. Albion represents the human race in its divinely created form, and the Fall has once again been pushed back in time. Now it pre-dates Urizen's separation from the Eternals. Seduced by Vala, or the idea of the (not yet created) beauty of Nature (a motif more fully developed in Plate 43 of *Jerusalem*), Albion falls asleep, and it is this spiritual abdication which prompts Urizen to create and control a fallen world. While Albion sleeps, the four components of human consciousness (or 'Zoas') lose their 'Perfect Unity' and one of them, Urizen, is able to dominate the others: Tharmas (physical sensation), Luvah (the emotions), and Los (the imagination). The Fall is Albion's fault and we have both a reason for it (Vala's seduction) and a potential solution. An awakening from sleep is something which it is feasible to imagine and describe. It is also an appropriate analogy for the most significant religious event of the eighteenth century: the

the will of God' (Article 20.27 of the Lutheran Augsburg Confession; see notes to *Milton* Plate 11); though the ritual and dietary laws of the Old Testament have lapsed, the Ten Commandments are criticized only in so far as they encourage a doctrine of works.

[27] This is the view as it is formulated in Article 11 of the Thirty-Nine Articles of the Church of England; see Robert M. Ryan's chapter 'Blake's orthodoxy' in his *The Romantic Reformation* (Cambridge: Cambridge University Press, 1997), 50.

evangelical 'Great Awakening', led in America by Jonathan Edwards and George Whitefield and in Britain by Whitefield and Wesley. Blake has cleared the way for the two diffuse epics which he would spend the next sixteen years writing and engraving: *Milton* (1804–11) and *Jerusalem* (1804–20).

Blake's evolving myth of the Fall is found again in *Milton*, and Los's role is now more positive. Rather than simply giving form to Urizen, he is building the city of Golgonooza: an image of art as a barrier against the chaos and cruelty of the Urizenic world. The imaginative artist's role, it seems, is constantly to remind humanity of its 'loss' of paradise, and not allow us to lapse into an acceptance of the mundane assumptions of secular materialism. Golgonooza is, however, only a reminder of paradise and other things are needed to achieve redemption. One such thing is a prophetic summons to reform, in the manner of Isaiah or Ezekiel or, more recently, John Milton. Blake's immediate purpose in this poem is to update, or redefine the prophet's role and thus suggest how he himself will perform it. He does this, dramatically rather than literally, by bringing Milton back to earth to purge the faults which made his work, by 1804, no longer adequate. That done, Blake can assume Milton's re-tailored mantle and compose his own prophetic poem, *Jerusalem The Emanation of The Giant Albion*.

One reason why Blake may have believed that Milton's work was flawed was his failure to write an apocalypse. Despite its title, Milton's *Paradise Regained* is a drily argumentative text in which Christ (unlike Eve) resists the temptation of Satan and defeats him in debate. Blake wanted a modern equivalent of the Book of Revelation (what 'John in Patmos saw', *Milton* Plate 42).[28] In *Jerusalem* he supplied it, though not until the final chapter. First, we have three sections, addressed respectively to 'The Public', 'The Jews', and 'The Deists', in which Blake gives us the final version of his myth of the Fall. Then, thrillingly, he writes his apocalyptic account of 'The Breath Divine' waking Albion, bringing the four Zoas back into balance (so that 'every Man stood Fourfold'), restoring Jerusalem, and leading 'All Human Forms' into 'the Life of Immortality'. It is an astonishingly ambitious and deeply moving piece of poetry. It does, however, take us a long time to get there and the first three chapters are less assured. Addressed as they are to different audiences, they are sometimes repetitive, and Blake's decision to use his personal enemies as emblems of what is wrong with the fallen world

---

[28] Though written in Greek, Revelation is an imitation of the prophetic manner of the Hebrew Book of Daniel.

has a quality of subjective indignation which sits uneasily with the universal scope of the larger topic. Just as with Wordsworth's *Prelude* and *Excursion*, it is the preliminary poem, *Milton*, which is the masterpiece.

In generic terms, however, *Milton* is as much a challenge as *Jerusalem*, since neither poem is epic in the form in which we expect it. Rather than Homer, or Virgil, or even Milton, the model is the Hebrew poetry of the Old Testament, and the experience with which we should compare their effect upon us is that of reading Isaiah or Ezekiel. Robert Lowth's translation of Isaiah, in 1778, provided a convenient summary of his view (originally expressed in the 1740s) that Hebrew verse, with its 'true Enthusiasm' and structural principle of parallelism (rather than rhyme or metre), was the supreme model for modern writers. It also gave a practical demonstration of what prophetic poetry should look like, both in its 'Longer' verse lines ('A voice crieth: In the wilderness prepare ye the way of JEHOVAH! | Make straight in the desert a highway for our God!') and in the 'Shorter' ones ('Like a shepherd shall he feed his flock; | In his arm shall he gather up the lambs').[29] Blake used the 'Longer' line in *Visions of the Daughters of Albion*, *America*, *Europe* (predominantly), *The Four Zoas*, *Milton*, and *Jerusalem*, and the 'Shorter' line in *Africa*, *Asia*, *The First Book of Urizen*, *The Book of Ahania*, and *The Book of Los*. He seems also to have been aware of Thomas Howes's observation that prophets sacrifice 'chronologic order' to 'persuasion and argumentation'.[30] Modern scholars see the Book of Ezekiel as the work of a 'talented redactor of earlier fragments' and Isaiah as a gathering of chapters from different backgrounds, with 'First Isaiah' (chapters 1–39) originating from Judah in the eighth century BC, 'Second Isaiah' (chapters 40–66) from Babylon in the 540s, and 'Third Isaiah' (chapters 56–66) from Jerusalem after the return from exile.[31] This fragmentary quality was beginning to be noticed in the eighteenth century and its 'subordination of chronological order to thematic order . . . juxtaposition of episodes without proper transitions . . . digressions . . . combining of various genres, and . . . use of multiple perspectives'[32] were a model for Blake's epics. The narrative sequence of his 'Continental'

[29] Robert Lowth, *Isaiah. A New Translation* (London, J. Dodsley, 1778), pp. xxviii and 100–1 (translating Isaiah, chapter 40).

[30] Howes's views were summarized in William Newcome's translation of Ezekiel (Joseph Johnson, 1788).

[31] See J. Barton and J. Muddiman, eds., *The Oxford Bible Commentary* (Oxford: Oxford University Press, 2001), 534 and 433.

[32] Leslie Tannenbaum, 'The "still better order" of Blake's Rhetoric', in Don H. Bialostosky and Lawrence D. Needham, eds., *Rhetorical Traditions and British Romantic Literature* (Bloomington: Indiana University Press, 1995), 191.

prophecies, for example, runs 'Africa', *America*, *Europe*, 'Asia'. But they were published in the order *America*, *Europe*, 'Africa', 'Asia', and that prophetic disruption of 'chronologic order' is retained in this edition. Obscurity is a characteristic of the sublime and we should expect some-times, or even often, to be mystified. The man who wrote these poems was, in religion, an Enthusiastic or Methodistical Lutheran Protestant, in politics, a relatively radical Foxite Whig. It is the poetic inventiveness of his mode of expression which makes them seem so odd: the last line of *Jerusalem* insists that this lengthy text is not a treatise but a 'Song'.

In 1808, with *Milton* and *Jerusalem* still not finished, Blake decided to concentrate on his career as a painter. It was not a wise decision. Blake's visual style had been formed in the 1780s, under the influence of Fuseli, James Barry, and John Hamilton Mortimer, since when the avant-garde mode had shifted to the landscape painting of young men like Turner and Constable. Blake's paintings were old-fashioned and, with his engraving technique also deemed outdated, he became increasingly impoverished and obscure. He continued to work on his two Hebraic epics and still offered his earlier 'illuminated' poems for sale: by 1818 he was pricing his books at between two and ten guineas a copy, though he seems to have sold very few of them. But he wrote new poems too and these, like his paintings, were in a manner remembered from his eighteenth-century youth. In his Notebook he wrote witty squibs and epigrams, while his longer pieces used that characteristically Augustan technique, the couplet. Though written in iambic tetrameters, rather than pentameters, *For the Sexes: The Gates of Paradise* (*c*.1818) and 'The Everlasting Gospel' (*c*.1818–19) retain something of the polem-ical poise and verbal dexterity which Pope and Dryden brought to the form.

After the completion of *Jerusalem*, in 1820, Blake devoted much of his time to the elaborate colouring of one of the copies of the poem (Copy E). This concern with the book's visual appearance raises the important question of whether Blake's work should be received as a com-bination of word and image, rather than as the simply verbal medium customary for poets. W. J. T. Mitchell's study *Blake's Composite Art*, in 1978, is often assumed to have made the case for a 'unified interpretation' of the illuminated books. In fact, Mitchell's argument was a more sub-tle suggestion of 'an energetic rivalry, a dialogue or dialectic'[33] between Blake's words and images, and recent critics have been less interested in

---

[33] W. J. T. Mitchell, *Blake's Composite Art* (Princeton: Princeton University Press, 1978), 4.

their congruence than in the 'gap' between them.[34] Wonderful though they are, the images are probably better understood as decorations of the book than as illustrations of the text, and the words are certainly capable of standing—as they do in this edition—on their own. Blake's poetry is vigorous, versatile, original, intellectually substantial (even when the views expressed are eccentric or outdated), lyrically exquisite, and hauntingly memorable. T. S. Eliot rightly observed that Blake's verse has 'the unpleasantness of great poetry'.[35] It has the delightfulness of great poetry as well.

[34] Saree Makdisi, *Reading William Blake* (Cambridge: Cambridge University Press, 2015), 7.
[35] T. S. Eliot, 'Blake', in *The Sacred Wood* (London: Methuen, 1920), 137.

NOTE ON THE TEXT

Establishing a reliable text of Blake's verse is, at first sight, a straightforward matter. Almost all his poems survive in unique manuscript copies or in pages printed from stereotypes: sheets of metal on which the text has been permanently engraved. They were not, that is, repeatedly re-set in moveable type in ways which could introduce errors or allow the author to change his mind. Nor could authorial intention be compromised by the intervention of a publisher, since Blake performed that function for himself. He wrote his texts directly onto copper plates, in mirror writing and with an impervious fluid, then used nitric acid to eat away the metal around the words. Once this was done, the 'relief etched' copper plates would be printed on his private press: 'editions' in this context, means, as Joseph Viscomi has shown, batches of pages printed in the same session. Finally, he and his wife would gather and stitch pages from their stock into copies and sell them, unbound, to their customers, sometimes colouring the engraved decorations as they did so.

This represents an exceptional degree of authorial control over the text. But the results were less fixed than one might assume. Blake could remove words from the plate with an engraver's tool, or erase them from the printed page, or mask sections of text with slips of paper during the printing process. On a larger scale, he could add, omit, or rearrange pages whenever he gathered them into a copy. In this edition I take the view that Blake's revisions further complicated what were already complex poems, a process which can be made still more puzzling by the editorial construction of composite or eclectic texts. The content of each text here is therefore that of the earliest reliable copy, with the plate order and addition or omission of material guided by Bentley's bibliographic descriptions of those copies in *Blake Books* (1977) and checked against the photographic reproductions on the Blake Archive website (except for *Jerusalem*, where the early copies, A and C, are not yet thus available; fortunately Copy F repeats their arrangement). Material added later is not included. Apart from the correction of a single, obvious error in Copy C of *Songs of Innocence and of Experience*, these are the texts of actual copies of Blake's poems as a reader could have encountered them shortly after their first appearance. Where plate numbers in these early copies differ from the conventional numbers established (from later or composite texts) by G. E. Bentley, Jr, I have added the 'Bentley' number in parenthesis, thus: *Jerusalem* 29 (33). Texts of poems which survive only in manuscript have similarly been compared with the Blake Archive's images and with the photographic reproductions in D. F. McKenzie's reduced facsimile of the manuscript additions to *Poetical Sketches* (1968), Charles Ryskamp's facsimile of the Pickering Manuscript (1972), Erdman and Moore's facsimile of the Notebook (1973), and Michael Phillips's facsimile of 'An Island in the Moon' (1987).

The second major decision for an editor of Blake is whether to retain his idiosyncratic spelling and punctuation. Since the appearance of David Erdman's magisterial 'old spelling' edition of the complete works in 1965, it has become normal for critical and scholarly citation to be made from an unmodernized text. An unmodernized text is therefore what is presented here—literally, in the sense that it has, in practice, been made by removing the modernizing editorial interventions from the text established by Geoffrey Keynes in 1957 and reprinted by Oxford University Press in 1966. This has been compared with the Blake Archive's images and with printed facsimiles of the same or other copies: these orthographic details, though occasionally obscured by the way in which a plate has been inked or a page painted, remain the same from copy to copy. Readers will, I hope, enjoy the modest challenges presented by Blake's odd use of the full-stop or the need to decide when characters begin and finish speaking. Difficult readings (chiefly of punctuation) have been compared with the transcripts made by Erdman (1965, revised 1982), Erdman and Moore (1973), Bentley (1978), the editors of the six volumes of *The Illuminated Books of William Blake* (1991–5), and the editors of the Blake Archive: though I do not always share their judgements, I am grateful for their guidance. References to Blake's prose and to poems not included in this selection (most notably *The Four Zoas*, which Blake himself chose not to publish) are to the 2008 edition of David V. Erdman's *Complete Poetry and Prose of William Blake*. Short poems are line-numbered individually; long poems are line-numbered plate by plate. A plate and line reference without a prefixed title is to another plate within the same poem.

SELECT BIBLIOGRAPHY

Two indispensable sources of information, both available on-line, are the Blake Archive (www.blakearchive.org), edited by Morris Eaves, Robert N. Essick, and Joseph Viscomi, and the journal *Blake* (previously *Blake: An Illustrated Quarterly*) which can be accessed through the Blake Archive.

Life and Art

Bentley, G. E., Jr, *The Stranger from Paradise: A Biography of William Blake* (New Haven and London: Yale University Press, 2001).

Bentley, G. E., Jr, *Blake Records*, 2nd edn (New Haven and London: Yale University Press, 2004).

Bentley, G. E., Jr, 'Thomas Butts, White Collar Maecenas', *PMLA*, 71 (1956), 1052–66.

Bishop, Morchard, *Blake's Hayley: The Life, Works and Friendships of William Hayley* (London: Victor Gollancz, 1951).

Butlin, Martin, *The Paintings and Drawings of William Blake*, 2 vols (New Haven and London: Yale University Press), 1981.

Davies, Keri, and Marsha Keith Schuchard, 'Recovering the Lost Moravian History of William Blake's Family', *Blake* 38 (2004), 36–57.

Deck, Raymond H., Jr, 'New Light on C. A. Tulk, Blake's Nineteenth-Century Patron', *Studies in Romanticism*, 16 (1977), 217–36.

Essick, Robert N., *The Separate Plates of William Blake: A Catalogue* (Princeton: Princeton University Press, 1983).

Essick, Robert N., *William Blake's Commercial Book Illustrations: A Catalogue and Study of the Plates Engraved by Blake after Designs by Other Artists* (Oxford: Clarendon Press, 1991).

Gilchrist, Alexander, *The Life of William Blake, 'Pictor Ignotus'*, 2 vols (London: Macmillan, 1863).

Viscomi, Joseph, 'A "Green House" for Butts: New Information on Thomas Butts, His Residences, and Family', *Blake*, 30 (1996), 4–21.

Text, Publication and Reception History

Bentley, G. E., Jr, *Blake Books* (Oxford: Clarendon Press, 1977), and *Blake Books Supplement* (Oxford: Clarendon Press, 1995).

Dorfman, Deborah, *Blake in the 19th Century* (New Haven: Yale University Press, 1969).

Hoover, Suzanne R., 'William Blake in the Wilderness: A Closer Look at His Reputation, 1827–1863', in Paley and Phillips, eds, *William Blake: Essays in Honour of Sir Geoffrey Keynes*, 310–48.

Phillips, Michael, *William Blake: The Creation of the 'Songs': From Manuscript to Illuminated Printing* (London: The British Library, 2000).

Viscomi, Joseph, 'The Myth of Commissioned Illuminated Books: George Romney, Isaac D'Israeli, and "ONE HUNDRED AND SIXTY designs . . . of Blake's"', *Blake: An Illustrated Quarterly*, 23 (1989), 48–74.

Viscomi, Joseph, *Blake and the Idea of the Book* (Princeton: Princeton University Press, 1993).

Historical, Social, and Religious Context

Berlin, Isaiah, 'The Counter-Enlightenment', in Henry Hardy, ed., *Against the Current: Essays in the History of Ideas* (London: The Hogarth Press, 1979), 1–24.

Davies, J. G., *The Theology of William Blake* (Oxford: Clarendon Press, 1948).

Fischer, Kevin, *Converse in the Spirit: William Blake, Jacob Boehme, and the Creative Spirit* (Madison: Fairleigh Dickinson University Press, 2004).

Fisher, Peter F., 'Blake and the Druids', *Journal of English and Germanic Philology*, 58 (1959), 589–612.

Garrett, Clarke, *Respectable Folly: Millenarians and the French Revolution in France and England* (Baltimore and London: Johns Hopkins University Press, 1975).

Hirst, Désirée, *Hidden Riches: Traditional Symbolism from the Renaissance to Blake* (London: Eyre & Spottiswoode, 1964).

Jesse, Jennifer G., *William Blake's Religious Vision* (Lanham: Lexington Books, 2013).

Mee, Jon, *Romanticism, Enthusiasm and Regulation: Poetics and the Policing of Culture in the Romantic Period* (Oxford: Oxford University Press, 2003).

Morris, David B., *The Religious Sublime: Christian Poetry and Critical Tradition in 18th-Century England* (Lexington: University Press of Kentucky, 1972).

Morton, A. L., *The Everlasting Gospel: A Study in the Sources of William Blake* (London, Lawrence & Wishart, 1958).

Paley, Morton D., '"A New Heaven is Begun": Blake and Swedenborgianism', *Blake: An Illustrated Quarterly*, 12.2 (1979), 64–90.

Raine, Kathleen, *Blake and Tradition*, 2 vols (Princeton: Princeton University Press, 1968).

Roston, Murray, *The Bible and the Growth of Romanticism* (London: Faber & Faber, 1965).

Ryan, Robert, *The Romantic Reformation: Religious Politics in English Literature 1789–1824* (Cambridge: Cambridge University Press, 1997).

Ryan, Robert, 'Blake and Religion', in Morris Eaves, ed., *The Cambridge Companion to William Blake*, 150–68.

Worrall, David, 'Blake's *Jerusalem* and the Visionary History of Britain', *Studies in Romanticism*, 16 (1977), 189–216.

Criticism and Discussion

Bindman, David, *Blake as an Artist* (Oxford: Phaidon, 1977).

Bloom, Harold, *Blake's Apocalypse: A Study in Poetic Argument* (Garden City: Doubleday, 1963).

Bruder, Helen, *William Blake and the Daughters of Albion* (Basingstoke: Macmillan, 1997).

Damon, S. Foster, *A Blake Dictionary: The Ideas and Symbols of William Blake* (1965), revised, ed. Morris Eaves (Hanover: University Press of New England, 1988).

Damrosch, Leopold, Jr, *Symbol and Truth in Blake's Myth* (Princeton: Princeton University Press, 1980).

De Luca, Vincent Arthur, *Words of Eternity: Blake and the Poetics of the Sublime* (Princeton: Princeton University Press, 1991).

Eaves, Morris, *William Blake's Theory of Art* (Princeton: Princeton University Press, 1982).

Eaves, Morris, *The Counter-Arts Conspiracy: Art and Industry in the Age of Blake* (Ithaca: Cornell University Press, 1992).

Eaves, Morris, ed., *The Cambridge Companion to William Blake* (Cambridge: Cambridge University Press, 2003).

Eliot, T. S., 'Blake' in his *The Sacred Wood* (London: Methuen, 1920).

Erdman, David V., *Blake: Prophet against Empire: A Poet's Interpretation of the History of His Own Times* (Princeton: Princeton University Press, 1954; 3rd edn 1977).

Frye, Northrop, *Fearful Symmetry: A Study of William Blake* (Princeton: Princeton University Press, 1947).

Lincoln, Andrew, *Spiritual History: A Reading of William Blake's 'Vala' or 'The Four Zoas'* (Oxford: Clarendon Press, 1995).

Lowery, Margaret Ruth, *Windows of the Morning: A Critical Study of William Blake's 'Poetical Sketches' 1783* (New Haven: Yale University Press, 1940).

Makdisi, Saree, *William Blake and the Impossible History of the 1790s* (Chicago: Chicago University Press, 2003).

Makdisi, Saree, *Reading William Blake* (Cambridge: Cambridge University Press, 2015).

Matthews, Susan, '*Jerusalem* and Nationalism', in Stephen Copley and John Whale, eds, *Beyond Romanticism: New Approaches to Texts and Contexts 1780-1832* (London, Routledge, 1992), 79–100.

Matthews, Susan, *Blake, Sexuality and Bourgeois Politeness* (Cambridge: Cambridge University Press, 2011).

Mee, Jon, *Dangerous Enthusiasm: William Blake and the Culture of Radicalism in the 1790s* (Oxford: Clarendon Press, 1992).

Mitchell, W. J. T., *Blake's Composite Art: A Study of the Illuminated Poetry* (Princeton: Princeton University Press, 1978).

Myrone, Martin, *The Blake Book* (London: Tate Publishing, 2007).

Ostriker, Alicia, *Vision and Verse in William Blake* (Madison: University of Wisconsin Press, 1965).

Paley, Morton D., 'Cowper as Blake's Spectre', *Eighteenth-Century Studies*, 1 (1967–8), 236–52.

Paley, Morton D., 'William Blake, the Prince of the Hebrews, and the Woman

Clothed with the Sun', in Paley and Phillips, eds, *William Blake: Essays in Honour of Sir Geoffrey Keynes*, 260–93.

Paley, Morton D., 'The Truchsessian Gallery Revisited', *Studies in Romanticism*, 16 (1977), 165–76.

Paley, Morton D., *The Continuing City: William Blake's 'Jerusalem'* (Oxford: Clarendon Press, 1983).

Paley, Morton D., *The Traveller in the Evening: The Last Works of William Blake* (Oxford: Oxford University Press, 2004).

Paley, Morton D., and Michael Phillips, eds, *William Blake: Essays in Honour of Sir Geoffrey Keynes* (Oxford: Clarendon Press, 1973).

Sandler, Florence, 'The Iconoclastic Enterprise: Blake's Critique of Milton's Religion', *Blake Studies*, 5 (1972), 13–57.

Shrimpton, Nick, 'William Blake: Hell's Hymnbook', in R. T. Davies and B. G. Beatty, eds, *Literature of the Romantic Period 1750–1850* (Liverpool: Liverpool University Press, 1976), 19–35.

Swinburne, Algernon Charles, *William Blake: A Critical Essay* (London: Hotten, 1868).

Tannenbaum, Leslie, *Biblical Tradition in Blake's Early Prophecies: The Great Code of Art* (Princeton: Princeton University Press, 1982).

Tannenbaum, Leslie, 'Prophetic Form: The "still better order" of Blake's Rhetoric', in Don H. Bialostosky and Lawrence D. Needham, eds, *Rhetorical Traditions and British Romantic Literature* (Bloomington: Indiana University Press, 1995), 185–98.

Vogler, Thomas A., *Preludes to Vision* (Berkeley and Los Angeles: University of California Press, 1971).

Whittaker, Jason, *William Blake and the Myths of Britain* (Basingstoke: Macmillan, 1999).

Williams, Nicholas M., *Ideology and Utopia in the Poetry of William Blake* (Cambridge: Cambridge University Press, 1998).

Wittreich, Joseph Anthony, Jr, *Angel of Apocalypse: Blake's Idea of Milton* (Madison: University of Wisconsin Press, 1975).

Wright, Julia M., *Blake, Nationalism, and the Politics of Alienation* (Athens: Ohio University Press, 2003).

Editions, Facsimiles, and Reproductions

Bentley, G. E., Jr, *William Blake's Writings*, 2 vols (Oxford: Clarendon Press, 1978).

Bindman, David (General Editor), *The Illuminated Books of William Blake*, 6 vols (Princeton: The William Blake Trust/Princeton University Press, 1991–5; the individual volumes are: 1. *Jerusalem*, ed. Morton D. Paley; 2. *Songs of Innocence and of Experience*, ed. Andrew Lincoln; 3. *The Early Illuminated Books*, ed. Morris Eaves, Robert N. Essick, and Joseph Viscomi; 4. *The Continental Prophecies*, ed. D. W. Dörrbecker; 5. *Milton*, ed. Robert N. Essick and Joseph Viscomi; 6. *The Urizen Books*, ed. David Worrall).

Erdman, David V., *The Complete Poetry and Prose of William Blake* (Berkeley,

Los Angeles, and London: University of California Press, 1965, revised 1982, republished 2008).

Erdman, David V., with the assistance of Donald K. Moore, *The Notebook of William Blake: A Photographic and Typographic Facsimile* (Oxford: Clarendon Press, 1973).

Hamlyn, Robin, *William Blake, Poetical Sketches* (London: Tate Publishing, 2007).

Johnson, Mary Lynn, and John E. Grant, *Blake's Poetry and Designs* (New York: W. W. Norton & Co., 2008).

Keynes, Sir Geoffrey, *Blake: Complete Writings with Variant Readings* (London: Oxford University Press, 1972).

Keynes, Sir Geoffrey, *The Letters of William Blake with Related Documents*, 3rd edn (Oxford: Clarendon Press, 1980).

McKenzie, D. F., 'Blake *Poetical Sketches* (1783)', *Turnbull Library Record*, Vol. 1 (n.s.), 3 (March 1968), 4–8.

Myrone, Martin, ed., *Seen in My Visions: A Descriptive Catalogue of Pictures, William Blake* (London: Tate Publishing, 2009).

Ostriker, Alicia, ed., *William Blake: The Complete Poems* (Harmondsworth: Penguin Books, 1983).

Phillips, Michael, *An Island in the Moon: A Facsimile of the Manuscript Introduced, Transcribed and Annotated* (Cambridge: Cambridge University Press, 1986).

Ryskamp, Charles, *The Pickering Manuscript* (New York: Pierpont Morgan Library, 1972).

Stevenson, W. H., *Blake: The Complete Poems*, 3rd edn (London and New York: Routledge, 2007).

Genre, Genres, and Literary Modes

Curran, Stuart, *Poetic Form and British Romanticism* (Oxford: Oxford University Press, 1989).

Damrosch, Leopold, Jr, 'Blake, Burns, and the Recovery of Lyric', *Studies in Romanticism*, 21 (1982), 637–60.

Duff, David, *Romanticism and the Uses of Genre* (New York: Oxford University Press, 2009).

Groom, Nick, *The Making of Percy's Reliques* (Oxford: Oxford University Press, 1999).

Hosek, Chaviva, and Patricia Parker, eds, *Lyric Poetry: Beyond the New Criticism* (Ithaca: Cornell University Press, 1985).

Jones, Steven E., *Satire and Romanticism* (New York: St Martin's Press, 2000).

McLane, Maureen N., *Balladeering, Minstrelsy and the Making of British Romantic Poetry* (Cambridge: Cambridge University Press, 2008).

Overton, Bill, *The Eighteenth-Century British Verse Epistle* (Basingstoke: Palgrave Macmillan, 2007).

Rajan, Tilottama, and Julia M. Wright, eds, *Romanticism, History, and the Possibilities of Genre: Re-forming Literature 1789–1837* (Cambridge: Cambridge University Press, 1998).

Thain, Marion, ed., *The Lyric Poem, Formations and Transformations* (Cambridge: Cambridge University Press, 2013).

Tucker, Herbert, *Epic: Britain's Heroic Muse 1790–1910* (Oxford: Oxford University Press, 2008).

Wolfson, Susan, *Formal Charges: The Shaping of Poetry in British Romanticism* (Stanford: Stanford University Press, 1997).

A CHRONOLOGY OF WILLIAM BLAKE

Blake's life and work	*Historical and cultural background*
1737 James Blake 'gentleman' of Rotherhithe apprentices his son James to Francis Smith, haberdasher of Minories, London.	Frederick, Prince of Wales, leads opposition to George II and Walpole. Charles and John Wesley, *Psalms and Hymns*; Jonathan Edwards, *The Surprising Work of God in the Conversion of Many Hundred Souls*.
1738	Johnson, *London: A Poem*; Pope, *Poems and Imitations of Horace*. Wesley returns from Georgia, attends Moravian services in Fetter Lane chapel; experiences a spiritual awakening.
1739	Whitefield and Wesley begin field-preaching; 'Great Awakening' or religious revival in American colonies (to 1742). Hume, *Treatise of Human Nature*.
1740	Stukeley, *Stonehenge: a temple restor'd to the British druids*.
1741	Lowth's Oxford lectures on Hebrew poetry; Handel, *Messiah*.
1743	Blair, *The Grave*.
1744 James Blake the younger established as hosier and haberdasher at 5 Glasshouse Street, Westminster.	First Methodist Conference at Foundry Chapel, London. Akenside, *Pleasures of Imagination*; Warton, *The Enthusiast*; Berkeley, *Siris*.
1745	Young Pretender lands in Scotland; marches to Derby. Young, *The Complaint, or Night Thoughts*; Doddridge, *The Rise and Progress of Religion in the Soul*; Hogarth, *Marriage à la Mode*.
1746 Catherine Wright (from Nottinghamshire) marries Thomas Armitage (from Yorkshire), haberdasher and hosier of 28 Broad Street, Westminster, in St George's Chapel, Mayfair.	Young Pretender defeated at Culloden. Collins, *Odes*; Hervey, *Meditations and Contemplations*; Diderot, *Pensées philosophiques*.
1749	Swedenborg, *Arcana Coelestia* (to 1756); Law, *The Spirit of Prayer*.

Blake's life and work	*Historical and cultural background*
1750 Thomas and Catherine Armitage received into the Moravian congregation in Fetter Lane, Farringdon.	Rousseau, *Discours* (1750–4).
1751 Thomas Armitage dies; Catherine Armitage leaves Moravian congregation.	Frederick, Prince of Wales, dies. Diderot, ed., *L'Encyclopédie* (to 1772); Home (Lord Kames), *Principles of Natural Religion*.
1752 James Blake marries Catherine Armitage and moves to 28 Broad Street where he trades as a draper and hosier under the sign of the Woolpack & Peacock.	Law, *The Way to Divine Knowledge*; Birch, *Tillotson's Life and Sermons*.
1754	Lowth, *De Sacra Poesi Hebraeorum*; Cooke, *An Enquiry into the Patriarchal and Druidical Religion*.
1756	Mozart born.
1757 **William Blake born** (28 Nov.); baptized (11 Dec.) at St James's, Piccadilly.	Gray, *Odes*; Hume, 'The Natural History of Religion'. Horace Walpole sets up Strawberry Hill Press.
1758	Swedenborg, *Heaven and its Wonders, and Hell*.
1759	Voltaire, *Candide*; Young, *Conjectures on Original Composition*.
1760	Accession of George III. Macpherson, *Fragments of Ancient Poetry* (by 'Ossian', followed by *Fingal*, 1762, and *Temora*, 1763).
1761	William Ryland appointed Engraver to the King. Rousseau, *Julie, ou la Nouvelle Héloïse*.
1763	Smart, *A Song to David*.
1764	Voltaire, *Dictionnaire philosophique portatif*; Rousseau, *Émile*; Reid, *Enquiry into the Human Mind*; 'Law' edition of *The Works of Jacob Behmen* (to 1781); Percy, *Song of Solomon*. Mortimer, *St Paul preaching to the Ancient Britons*.
1765	Percy, *Reliques of Ancient English Poetry*; Smart, *Psalms of David*; Fuseli, *Painting and Sculpture of the Greeks* (trans. Winckelmann, 1755).

Blake's life and work	*Historical and cultural background*
*c.*1766 Blake reports a vision of angels on Peckham Rye Common.	Kant, *Träume eines Geistersehers* (attack on Swedenborg as a 'spook hunter'); Wright, *Lecture on the Orrery*.
1767 Attends Henry Pars's drawing school in the Strand.	Revenue Act imposes duties on imports to America; Mansfield verdict ends persecution of Dissenters. John and Charles Wesley, *Hymns for the Use of Families*; Runciman, *King Lear in the Storm*.
1768 Begins to view and collect prints at Abraham Langford's auction room, Covent Garden.	Wilkes MP for Middlesex but imprisoned; St George's Fields Massacre. Royal Academy founded with Reynolds as President. Wright, *The Air Pump*.
1769 Writes earliest of poems collected in *Poetical Sketches*: 'How sweet I roam'd from field to field'. Shakespeare's poems 'were favourite studies of Mr Blake's early days. So were Jonson's Underwoods and Miscellanies' (Malkin).	Chatterton, 'Ethelgar' and 'Elinoure and Juga'.
1770	James Beattie, *Essay on the Nature and Immutability of Truth in Opposition to Sophistry and Scepticism*.
1771	Arkwright's first cotton spinning mill, Derbyshire; Swedenborg visits London; London Unitarian Church founded; the King's engraver William Rylands made bankrupt. Swedenborg, *The True Christian Religion*; West, *Death of Wolfe*.
1772 Apprenticed to James Basire, engraver, of Great Queen Street, Covent Garden.	Mansfield's judgment in *Somerset's Case* establishes that slavery cannot exist in England.
1773 James Parker joins Blake as apprentice to Basire. Engraving of drawing of a centurion after Michelangelo (first state), later reworked as *Joseph of Arimathea Among the Rocks of Albion* (*c.*1810–20).	Boston Tea Party. James Martin becomes minister of Grafton St Baptist Chapel. Proposal by Reynolds and West for religious paintings in St Paul's rejected by Bishop of London as 'popery'. Goethe, *Götz von Berlichingen*; Reynolds, *Count Ugolino*.

Blake's life and work	Historical and cultural background
1774 Begins to draw tombs in Westminster Abbey for Basire's illustrations to Gough's *Sepulchral Monuments of Great Britain* (1786–96).	Wilkes becomes Lord Mayor of London. Bryant, *A New System of Ancient Mythology* (to 1776); Goethe, *Sorrows of Werther*; Roberts, *Judah Restored*; Reynolds, *James Beattie, or The Triumph of Truth*.
1775	American War of Independence (to 1783). Watt and Boulton, commercial steam engines.
1776	Smith, *The Wealth of Nations*; Gibbon, *Decline and Fall* (to 1788); Paine, *Common Sense*; Reynolds, *The Infant Samuel* and *The Child Baptist (St John)*; Barry, *The Phoenix, or, The Resurrection of Freedom*.
1777	British victory at Brandywine but defeat at Saratoga. Robert Lowth Bishop of London. Chatterton, *Poems*; Barry, *The Progress of Human Culture* (to 1783) and *Job reproved by his Friends*.
1778	France allies with American colonists. William Ryland's stipple or 'crayon' engraving technique used in Rogers, *A Collection of Prints in Imitation of Drawings*. Lowth, *Isaiah. A new translation*; West, *The Bard*.
1779 Completes apprenticeship and enters Royal Academy Schools (while also working as a commercial engraver); forms friendships with Flaxman, Stothard, and George Cumberland; moves back to 28 Broad Street. Twelve small watercolours illustrating English history: *Landing of Brutus, Lear and Cordelia, Non Angli Sed Angeli, Saint Augustine Converting King Ethelbert, Ordeal of Queen Emma, Death of Earl Goodwin, Search for the Body of Harold, Making of Magna Charta, Edward and Elenor, Black Prince, Penance of Jane Shore.*	Spain allies with American colonists; Countess of Huntingdon's Connection (Whitefieldian Methodists) become Nonconformists. Coalbrookdale cast-iron bridge. West's proposed paintings for a royal chapel at Windsor illustrating 'the history of revealed religion' approved by Anglican bishops (to 1801 though then rejected). Cowper, *Olney Hymns*.

Blake's life and work

Historical and cultural background

1780 Begins to engrave for the bookseller Joseph Johnson, chiefly after designs by Stothard. Present in crowd attacking Newgate Prison during Gordon Riots (June). His father votes for Fox in General Election (Oct.). Introduced to the salon of the Revd A. S. Mathew and his wife Harriet in Rathbone Place by John Flaxman, where he is heard to 'read and sing' his poems. May also attend gatherings of authors at Joseph Johnson's premises, 72 St Paul's Churchyard. *The Death of Earl Goodwin* (RA); *Glad Day* (later known as *The Dance of Albion*); watercolours of Shakespearian subjects; *Abraham and Isaac* (watercolour).

Dunning's motion, 'the influence of the crown has increased . . . and ought to be diminished', passed by Commons (Apr.); Gordon Riots (June: anti-Catholic protest against repeal of 1698 Popery Act); Charles James Fox MP for Westminster (to 1806); Society for Constitutional Information. Crabbe, *The Candidate*; Flaxman, *Sketch for a Monument to Chatterton* (RA).

1781 Etchings adapted from Raphael for *The Protestant's Family Bible*.

British defeat at Yorktown. Barbauld, *Hymns in Prose for Children*; Hayley, *Triumphs of Temper*; Kant, *Critique of Pure Reason*; Fuseli, *The Nightmare*.

1782 18 Aug.: marries Catherine Boucher at St Mary's, Battersea, and moves to rooms in Green Street, Leicester Square.

Henry Thornton MP for Southwark (to 1815); Barry made Professor of Painting at RA (to 1799). Cowper, *Poems*; Hayley, *Essay on Epic Poetry*; Rousseau, *Confessions* (to 1789); Romney, *Lady Hamilton as Circe*; Peters, *An Angel carrying the Spirit of a Child to Paradise*.

1783 *Poetical Sketches* (privately printed); commissioned to make a drawing for the collector John Hawkins who tries to raise a subscription to send him to study in Rome. May have attended Thomas Taylor's lectures on Plato at Flaxman's house. Engravings after Stothard for Ritson's *English Songs* and Ariosto's *Orlando Furioso*.

Fox–North coalition; Treaty of Versailles: American independence; Pitt the Younger PM (to 1801); the engraver William Ryland hanged at Tyburn. Rowland Hill opens Surrey Chapel, Blackfriars Road. Crabbe, *The Village*; Copley, *Death of Major Pierson*; Stubbs, *The Reapers*.

Blake's life and work	*Historical and cultural background*
1784 Father dies (July) and elder brother James takes over draper's business at 28 Broad Street. Partnership with James Parker, as Parker & Blake, printsellers and publishers, at 27 Broad Street. Writing 'An Island in the Moon' (*c*.1782–5) which includes drafts of three of the Innocence songs and comments on the relief-etching experiments of (probably) George Cumberland. *War unchained by an Angel* and *A Breach in a City* (RA). Engravings after Stothard and Collings for *The Wit's Magazine*.	Wesley ordains Methodist preachers for America; Flaxman joins newly founded (Swedenborgian) Theosophical Society; Hoffman, Tilloch, and George Cumberland experiment with stereotype printing. Charlotte Smith, *Elegiac Sonnets*; Blayney, *Jeremiah and Lamentations: a new translation*; Beaumarchais, *Marriage of Figaro*; Reynolds, *Mrs Siddons as the Tragic Muse*; West, *The Last Supper*; David, *Oath of the Horatii*.
1785 Leaves RA Schools; partnership with Parker dissolved (Autumn); moves to 28 Poland Street. Teaching his brother Robert to paint and engrave. Four drawings at RA (Apr.): *Joseph making himself known to his brethren*; *Joseph's brethren bowing before him*; *Joseph ordering Simeon to be bound*; and *The Bard, from Gray*.	Cowper, *The Task*; Paley, *Moral and Political Philosophy*; Wilkins translates the *Bhagavad-Gita*; Romney, *Macbeth and the Witches*.
1786 Winter: nurses his brother Robert. *The Complaint of Job* (sepia drawing and engraving); cover illustration for Commins's *An Elegy Set to Music*.	Jones identifies Sanskrit as root of European languages; Burns, *Poems Chiefly in Scottish Dialect*; Mozart, *Marriage of Figaro*.
1787 Robert dies of tuberculosis (Feb.); inherits Robert's sketchbook and uses it as a sketchbook and notebook *c*.1792–1818; develops a new technique for 'drawing on Copper' with impervious ink and relief-etching the image as a printing plate.	American Constitution; Porteus succeeds Lowth as Bishop of London; successive attempts (to 1790) by Dissenters to repeal the Test Act, with help from Fox. Lowth, *Lectures on the Sacred Poetry of the Hebrews* (1754 in Latin); Joel Barlow, *The Vision of Columbus* (as *The Columbiad*, 1804).

Blake's life and work

Historical and cultural background

Flaxman in Rome until 1794;
Blake becomes friends with
Fuseli.
c.1787: 'Song 1st by
a Shepherd', 'Song 2nd by
a Young Shepherd', and 'Song
3rd by an Old Shepherd'.
Relief etching after Robert
Blake, *The Approach of Doom*.

1788 *All Religions are One* and *There
is No Natural Religion* (first
relief-etched texts or 'Original
Stereotypes', probably only
proof sheets printed at this
stage).
c.1788–9, 'Tiriel' (MS and
associated illustrations).
Annotates copies of English
translations of Swedenborg's
Heaven and Hell (1784) and
Fuseli's translation of Lavater's
Aphorisms on Man (1788).
Engravings after Morland,
after Fuseli for Lavater's
Aphorisms, and after Hogarth's
Beggar's Opera, *Act III*.

George III's first bout of mental illness;
Regency crisis; Warren Hastings
impeached (trial to 1795); centenary of
British 'Glorious Revolution' of 1688;
Louis XVI summons Estates General
and lifts censorship.
Collins, 'Ode on Popular Superstitions
of the Highlands'; Wollstonecraft,
Original Stories; Mozart, *Jupiter*
symphony.

1789 *Songs of Innocence*.
The Book of Thel.
Annotates an English translation
of Swedenborg's *Divine Love
and Divine Wisdom* (1788);
attends general conference of
the Swedenborgian New
Jerusalem Church in Eastcheap
(Apr.) and signs its manifesto.
Prints sheets for at least 20
copies of *Songs of Innocence*
and (later in the year) several
copies of *Thel*.
Printing on both sides of the
paper and hand-colouring
(1789–93).
Engravings for Lavater's
Essays on Physiognomy.
Joseph of Arimathea Preaching
and *Charity* (early relief
etchings).

George III recovers; French Revolution:
National Assembly (17 June), fall of
Bastille (14 July), Declaration of the
Rights of Man (26 Aug.); Washington
first President of USA.
Price, 'On the Love of Our Country';
Bentham, *Principles of Morals and
Legislation*; Bowles, *Sonnets*.

Blake's life and work

Historical and cultural background

1790 Moves to 13 Hercules
Buildings, Lambeth (Autumn).
Annotates ('Cursed Folly!')
a copy of English translation of
Swedenborg's *Divine
Providence* (1790).
At work on *The Marriage of
Heaven and Hell* and on drafts of
poems for *Experience* (to 1793).
Prints sheets for further copies
of *Thel* and for several
(perhaps partial) copies of *The
Marriage of Heaven and Hell*.
Engraving after Fuseli for
Timon and Alcibiades;
watercolours of Shakespearian
subjects: *Oberon and Titania,
The Vision of Queen Katharine,
Lady Macbeth, Hamlet
Administering the Oath*.

Abolition of French nobility (19 June).
Joseph Proud, Baptist minister, joins
Swedenborgians.
Kant, *Critique of Judgement*; Ogden,
The Revolution, an Epic Poem; Burke,
Reflections on the Revolution in France
(Dec.).

1791 Subscribes to Cowper's Homer
translations.
*The French Revolution. A Poem,
in Seven Books. Book the First*
(page proofs, for Johnson).
Illustrations for 2nd edn of
Mary Wollstonecraft's *Original
Stories from Real Life*; engravings
after Fuseli for Darwin's *Botanic
Garden*, after Shackleton for
Hartley's *Observations on Man*,
and after Stedman for his
*Narrative of [an] expedition,
against the Revolted Negroes of
Surinam* (1796).

Albion Mills, Southwark, burnt down
(demolished 1809); Birmingham
anti-Jacobin riots destroy Priestley's
house and four Nonconformist chapels
(July); Austria and Prussia commit to
restoring French monarchy (Aug.); new
French constitution (Sept.).
Paine, *Rights of Man*, Part 1 (Feb.);
Burke, *Appeal from the New to the Old
Whigs* (Aug.); Darwin, *Loves of the
Plants*; Cowper, *Iliad* and *Odyssey*.
West, *Expulsion of Adam and Eve from
Paradise*.

1792 Blake's mother dies (Sept.).
'Motto to the Songs of
Innocence & of Experience'
(Notebook).
May have assisted Tom Paine's
escape from England (12 Sept.)
and have sketched him in the
Notebook, but after 'the Days
of Terror, in September '92
[the Paris massacres] and
subsequent defiance of kings
and of humanity', Blake 'tore

London Corresponding Society (Jan.);
war between France and Austria (Apr.);
George III's proclamation against
'tumultuous meetings and seditious
writings' (21 May); Louis XVI deposed
and imprisoned (Aug.); September
Massacres (of prisoners in Paris gaols on
orders of Paris Commune); French defeat
Prussians at Valmy (20 Sept.);
Convention replaces Assembly; French
Republic (21 Sept.); Whigs form 'Friends
of the Liberty of the Press' (22 Dec.).

Blake's life and work

Historical and cultural background

off his white cockade, and
assuredly never wore the red cap
again', though he remained 'a
republican' (Gilchrist, who may
be confusing the Terror of 1793
with the Massacres of 1792).
Engravings after Pars for
Stuart and Revett's *Antiquities
of Athens*; after King for
Hunter's *Transactions at Port
Jackson and Norfolk Island*.

Gillray, *A Voluptuary under the horrors of
Digestion* (July); More, *Village Politics*;
Rogers, *Pleasures of Memory*; Paine,
Rights of Man, Part 2; Wollstonecraft,
Vindication of the Rights of Woman; West
succeeds Reynolds as PRA; Romney, *The
Infant Shakespeare*, a portrait of *Tom
Paine*, and Milton drawings.

1793 *For Children The Gates of
Paradise* ('Published 17 May
1793').
*The Marriage of Heaven and
Hell* ('Published June 5: 1793').
June: 'I say I shant live five
years And if I live one it will be
a Wonder' (Notebook).
*Visions of the Daughters of Albion.
America a Prophecy.
To the Public*: prospectus, 10
Oct., announcing a new
'method of Printing' and
offering as 'on Sale', *Job* and
Edward and Elinor
(engravings), *America,
a Prophecy*; *Visions of the
Daughters of Albion*; *The Book
of Thel, a Poem*; *The Marriage
of Heaven and Hell*; *Songs of
Innocence*, and *Songs of
Experience* (books in
'Illuminated Printing'), and
The History of England, and
The Gates of Paradise (each
described as 'a small book of
engravings').
Prints sheets for copies of
*Visions of the Daughters of
Albion, For Children*, and
America.
Friendship with Thomas Butts.
The Complaint of Job
(engraving, 2nd state, Aug.);
larger versions of the 1779
watercolours of English history.

Louis XVI executed (21 Jan.); France
declares war on Britain and Holland
(1 Feb.); Jacobins rule through
Committee of Public Safety; Marat
assassinated (July); The Terror (Sept.);
Marie Antoinette and Girondin deputies
executed (Oct.); Festival of Reason in
deconsecrated Notre Dame (Nov.).
Godwin, *Political Justice*; Wordsworth,
Descriptive Sketches; David, *The Death of
Marat*.

Blake's life and work	*Historical and cultural background*
1794 *Songs of Innocence and of Experience Shewing the Two Contrary States of the Human Soul.* *Europe a Prophecy.* *The First Book of Urizen.* Prints sheets for *There is No Natural Religion, Marriage of Heaven and Hell, Songs of Experience, Europe,* and *The First Book of Urizen.* Begins to colour print, using a version of the à la poupée method (used for his illuminated books 1794–5, though images still finished in watercolour). Flaxman returns to London.	Danton executed (Apr.); Robespierre and Saint-Just executed (July); Habeas Corpus suspended (June; to July 1795); Whigs split; Portland Whigs join cabinet (July); Horne Tooke, Hardy, and Thelwall acquitted of treason (Nov.); famine in France. Godwin, *Caleb Williams*; Paley, *Evidences of Christianity*; Brothers, *Revealed Knowledge of the Prophecies and Times*; Paine, *Age of Reason*, Part 1; Hayley, *Milton*; Wordsworth's 'Salisbury Plain' (publ. 1842) uses Druidic Stonehenge as image of modern 'Oppression'.
1795 *The Song of Los* ('Africa' and 'Asia'). *The Book of Los.* *The Book of Ahania.* Prints sheets for *All Religions are One, There is No Natural Religion, Songs of Innocence, Thel, The Marriage of Heaven and Hell, America, Songs of Experience, Songs of Innocence and of Experience, Europe, The First Book of Urizen, The Song of Los, The Book of Ahania, The Book of Los,* creating a stock not augmented until 1802. The illuminated books now printed single-sided and hand-coloured in watercolour, though in brighter tones. John Gabriel Stedman stays with the Blakes (Aug.) and sends them a goose for Christmas. The 'Large Colour Prints' (dated 1795 though the known examples are on paper watermarked 1804): *Elohim Creating Adam*; *Satan Exulting over Eve*; *God Judging Adam*;	Directory replaces Convention (Sept.); Napoleon's 'whiff of grapeshot' crushes Paris uprising (Oct.); Directory rules in France (Nov., to 1799); George III's coach stoned after opening of Parliament (Oct.); British Treason and Sedition Acts (Dec.). Paine, *Age of Reason*, Part 2; Southey, *Joan of Arc*; Lewis, *The Monk*; More, *Cheap Repository Tracts* (to 1817); Goethe, *Wilhelm Meister*; Schiller, *Letters on Aesthetic Education*.

Blake's life and work	*Historical and cultural background*
	Lamech and His Two Wives; *Naomi Entreating Ruth and Orpah*; *Nebuchadnezzar*; *Newton*; *Pity*; *Hecate*; *The House of Death*; *The Good and Evil Angels*; *Christ Appearing to the Apostles after the Resurrection*.	
1796	Prints sheets for *The Large Book of Designs* and *The Small Book of Designs*. 537 watercolour illustrations to Young's *Night Thoughts* made *c*.1795–7; engravings for Cumberland's *Thoughts on Outline*; designs for Bürger's *Leonora* (engraved by Perry).	George Tierney MP for Southwark; Napoleon's Italian campaign; Spain declares war (Oct.); Pitt attempts peace negotiations (Oct.). Burke, *Letter on a Regicide Peace*; Watson, *Apology for the Bible*; Hayley, *Life of Milton* (2nd edn, praising his republicanism); Turner, *Fishermen at Sea*; Goya, *Los Capriccios*.
1797	Starts work on *Vala* (first title) or *The Four Zoas* (later title) and continues until *c*.1804; not engraved or published. Joseph Proud opens Swedenborgian church in Hatton Garden and invites Blake to join; Blake declines. Flaxman becomes ARA. 43 engraved illustrations to Young's *Night Thoughts*; engravings after Fuseli for Allen's *History of England*; commissioned by Flaxman to illustrate a copy of Gray's *Poems* with 116 watercolours; illustrations of the MS of *The Four Zoas* (to *c*.1804).	Battles of Cape St Vincent and Camperdown; naval mutinies at Spithead and the Nore (Apr.–May); Napoleon abolishes Venetian Republic. Wilberforce, *A Practical View of the Prevailing Religious System*. Gifford, *The Anti-Jacobin* (to 1799); Reynolds, *Works*; Radcliffe, *The Italian*; Ogden, *Emanuel; or, Paradise Regained*; Flaxman, *Sir William Jones writing from the Hindoo doctors*; Lawrence, *Satan Summoning his Legions*; West, *The Woman Clothed with the Sun*.
1798	Annotates a copy of Watson's *Apology for the Bible*, defending Paine's *Age of Reason* from Watson's attack (I 'believe the Bible & profess myself a Christian') and (at this date or shortly after) a 1798 edition of Bacon's *Essays*. Completes the watercolours for Ann Flaxman's copy of Gray's *Poems*. Engravings after Fuseli for Allen's *Roman History*.	French declare a Republic in Rome and conquer Switzerland. Napoleon invades Egypt; Battle of the Nile; Tierney fights duel with Pitt. Malthus, *Principle of Population*; Richard Watson, Bishop of Llandaff, *An Address to the People of Great Britain*; Barry, *A Letter to the Dilettanti Society*; Landor, *Gebir*; Wordsworth and Coleridge, *Lyrical Ballads*.

Blake's life and work

Historical and cultural background

1799   Thomas Butts commissions 50 'small Pictures from the Bible' in tempera, probably for his wife's school for girls in Great Marlborough Street (29 completed by Autumn 1800, the remainder between Nov. 1802 and May 1805).
23 Aug.: letter to Dr John Trusler in which he insists that 'This World is a World of IMAGINATION & Vision' and quotes a sentence from the first edition (1605) of Bacon's *The Advancement of Learning*.
Copy L of *Songs of Innocence and of Experience* (containing 'To Tirzah') acquired by 'JS'.
The Last Supper (RA); engraving after Opie for Boydell's *Shakespeare*.

French defeat at Acre; Napoleon returns to Europe; Consulate replaces Directory (effective end of French Revolution); Pitt introduces income tax; Joseph Johnson sentenced to six months for publishing Gilbert Wakefield's *Reply to the Bishop of Llandaff's Address*; Barry expelled from RA; Religious Tract Society.
Campbell, *Pleasures of Hope*; Sheridan *Pizarro*.

1800   2 July: writes to Cumberland that, 'I begin to Emerge from a deep pit of Melancholy, Melancholy without any real reason for it, a Disease which God keep you from'.
Sept.: moves to a cottage at Felpham, near Bognor, Sussex, with his wife and sister Catherine, at the invitation of William Hayley.
After a break of several years from illuminated printing, makes memoranda in Notebook about how to 'Engrave on Pewter' and 'Woodcut' on pewter and copper; these techniques used for *Little Tom the Sailor* and some plates in *Milton* and *Jerusalem*.
Paints more than 80 watercolours of biblical subjects for Butts (*c*.1800–5).
The Loaves and the Fishes (RA); illustrations for Hayley's *Little Tom the Sailor*; begins 18

Napoleon defeats Austrians at Marengo and Hohenlinden; 'Second Great Awakening' in American churches (to 1801).
Wordsworth, Preface to *Lyrical Ballads*; Bloomfield, *The Farmer's Boy*; Cottle, *Alfred*; West, *Joshua Passing the River Jordan with the Ark of the Covenant*; Girtin, *The White House*; Turner, *The Fifth Plague of Egypt*.

Blake's life and work   *Historical and cultural background*

'Heads of the Poets' paintings
for Hayley's library: *Homer,
Demosthenes, Cicero, Dante,
Chaucer, Camoens, Ercilla,
Tasso, Spenser, Shakespeare,
Milton, Dryden, Otway, Pope,
Voltaire, Klopstock, Cowper,
Thomas Alphonso Hayley*.
Flaxman becomes full RA.

1801 19 Oct.: writes to Flaxman,   Union of Great Britain and Ireland; Pitt
      'Peace opens the way to greater   resigns over George III's refusal of
      [works] still. The Kingdoms of   Catholic emancipation; Addington PM;
      this World are now become the   First Battle of Copenhagen; Catholic
      Kingdoms of God & his   Church restored in France; preliminary
      Christ, & we shall reign with   agreement for the Peace of Amiens
      him for ever & ever. The Reign   (1 Oct.).
      of Literature & the Arts   Southey, *Thalaba*; Pye, *Alfred*; Ogilvie,
      Commences.'   *Britannia*; Thelwall, *The Hope of Albion*
      Engraving for Fuseli's *Lectures*   (fragments); Todd's edition of Milton;
      on Painting; 8 watercolours of   Turner, *Dutch Boats in a Gale*.
      Milton's *Comus* for the Revd
      Joseph Thomas of Epsom;
      miniature of *Thomas Butts*.

1802 Learning Greek, Latin, and   Napoleon First Consul for life; Peace of
      Hebrew, probably taught by   Amiens (25 Mar.); first Factory Act.
      Hayley.   Paley, *Natural Theology*; *Edinburgh*
      22 Nov.: writes to Butts that,   *Review*; Scott, *Minstrelsy of the Scottish*
      'Tho I have been very unhappy   *Border*; Wordsworth, 'Milton! Thou
      I am so no longer I am again   should'st be living at this hour' (publ.
      Emerged into the light of Day   1807); Constable, *Dedham Vale*; Turner,
      I still & shall to Eternity Embrace *Ships bearing up for Anchorage*.
      Christianity and Adore him who
      is the Express image of God'.
      Prints sheets for copies of
      Songs of Innocence and *Songs of*
      Experience.
      Illustrations for Hayley's
      Ballads and *Life and*
      Posthumous Writings of William
      Cowper (1803).

1803 Apr.: writes to his brother   War with France resumes (May);
      James and to Butts to say that   Napoleon occupies Hanover (June) and
      he is returning to London,   stations army at Boulogne (Dec.).
      telling Butts that 'I can alone   William Owen [Pughe], *The Cambrian*
      carry on my visionary studies   *Biography . . . of Celebrated Men Among*
      in London unannoyed', adding   *the Ancient Britons*; Turner, *Calais Pier*;

Blake's life and work

that, 'I have in these three years composed an immense number of verses on One Grand Theme similar to Homers Iliad or Miltons Paradise Lost the Persons & Machinery intirely new'.

12 Aug.: Blake ejects John Scolfield from his Felpham garden; Scolfield charges Blake with sedition, claiming he had 'damned the King'.

Sept.: The Blakes move back to London, staying briefly with James before settling in rooms at 17 South Molton Street. *Satan Calling Up His Legions, an experiment Picture* (tempera on canvas; two versions, *c*.1795–1803); engravings after Maria Flaxman for Hayley's *The Triumphs of Temper* (13th edn) and Flaxman (of Ceres) for Hoare, *Academic Correspondence*.

1804 11 Jan.: Blake is tried and acquitted at Chichester Magistrates' Court.

Oct.: Views Count Truchsess's collection of paintings and writes to Hayley that 'on the day after', he was 'again enlightened with the light I enjoyed in my youth', but, 'have not been for twenty . . . years'.

Engraves title-pages for, and begins composition of, *Milton* (to 1811, with additional pages 1818) and *Jerusalem* (to 1820). Prints sheets for copies of *Songs* and sells one to the Revd Joseph Thomas for 'ten guineas'. Engraving for Hayley's *Life of Romney*; engravings after Flaxman for *The Iliad* and after Fuseli for Chalmers's *Shakespeare*.

Historical and cultural background

Norwich School of painters formed; Beethoven, *Eroica*.

Pitt PM (12 May); Napoleon Emperor (18 May); Spain joins war against Britain (Dec.).
Water Colour Society founded.
Krause, *Plan of a System of Philosophy* (panentheism); Ann and Jane Taylor, *Original Poems for Infant Minds*.

Blake's life and work	*Historical and cultural background*

1805 R. H. Cromek asks Blake to illustrate a new edition of Blair's *The Grave* but uses Schiavonetti to engrave them; Cromek's *Prospectus* describes Blake's designs as 'a high and original Effort of Genius' and lists 13 Royal Academicians and the connoisseur Thomas Hope as subscribers.
Blake designs frontispiece (engraved by Cromek) for Malkin's *A Father's Memoirs of His Child* (1806).
12 May: Blake records delivery to Butts of the last 12 of the 50 'small Pictures from the Bible' commissioned in 1799.
5 July and 7 Sept.: sells a set of the 'Large Colour Prints' to Butts.
Possible date of the 'Pickering' Manuscript (fair copy, on paper salvaged from the 1802 edition of Hayley's *Ballads*, of ten poems probably composed 1800–4).
20 watercolours to illustrate Blair's *The Grave*; further illustrations for a new edition of Hayley's *Ballads*; 19 Book of Job watercolours for Butts; *The Spiritual Form of Nelson guiding Leviathan*, *The Goats*, *The Spiritual Preceptor* (all tempera, *c.*1805–9).
Butts engages Blake as drawing master for his son, Thomas Butts, Jr (to 1809).

Napoleon moves army from Boulogne to the Rhine (Aug.); Battle of Ulm (20 Oct.); Battle of Trafalgar and death of Nelson (21 Oct.); Battle of Austerlitz (2 Dec.). West resigns as PRA (but resumes office 1806).
Barry, *Minerva turning from Scenes of Destruction and Violence to Religion and the Arts*; Scott, *Lay of the Last Minstrel*; Southey, *Madoc*; Beethoven, *Fidelio*; David, *Coronation of Napoleon*; Turner, *The Shipwreck*.

1806 Malkin's *A Father's Memoirs of his Child* contains a biographical account of Blake and prints six of his lyrics; reviews of the book are dismissive of Blake's verse ('divine Nonsensia', *British Critic*, Sept.; 'very inferior to Dr Watts', *Monthly Review*, Oct.) but some journals reprint poems.
9 Sept.: Copy E of *Songs of*

Pitt dies (22 Jan.); Grenville leads 'Ministry of All the Talents'; Fox dies (Sept.); Battle of Jena (Oct.); Berlin Decrees close European ports to British commerce (the 'Continental System'). Barry dies (22 Feb.); Arnim and Brentano, *Des Knaben Wunderhorn*; Ann and Jane Taylor, *Rhymes for the Nursery*; Turner, *The Battle of Trafalgar*; Ingres, *Napoleon I on his Imperial Throne*.

Blake's life and work   *Historical and cultural background*

Innocence and of Experience
(including 'To Tirzah')
assembled from sheets printed
in 1789, 1794, and 1795,
re-coloured, and sold to Butts.
Begins 6 watercolour
illustrations for a 2nd folio of
Shakespeare owned by Joseph
Thomas (to 1809); *The
Spiritual Form of Pitt guiding
Behemoth* (tempera, *c*.1806–9);
plans painting and engraving of
Chaucer's *Canterbury Pilgrims*;
claims Cromek steals the idea
(Cromek uses Stothard and
Schiavonetti to execute it).
A Vision of the Last Judgement
(watercolour).
Thomas Phillips paints Blake's
portrait.

1807 20 Jan.: 'between Two & Seven   Pittite Tories win General Election
in the Evening—Despair'   (June); Portland PM; Canning Foreign
(Notebook).   Secretary; Second Battle of Copenhagen
Apr.: Composes dedicatory   (Aug.); Orders in Council (blockade of
poem to Queen Charlotte for   European ports, to 1812); French invade
the Cromek edition of Blair's   Portugal; Slave Trade abolished in
The Grave (1808).   British Empire; Burdett succeeds Fox as
Thomas Phillips's portrait of   Westminster MP; Clapham Sect. Paine,
Blake exhibited at RA.   *Age of Reason*, Part 3.
William Owen Pughe   Wordsworth, *Poems in Two Volumes*;
commissions Blake to paint *The   Flaxman, monument to Reynolds
Ancient Britons*; Countess of   (St Paul's); Stothard, *Pilgrimage to
Egremont commissions a *Vision   Canterbury*; Turner, *Liber Studiorum*
of the Last Judgement* on   (to 1819).
recommendation of Ozias
Humphry.
Summer: 'Blake has eng[rave]d
60 plates of a new Prophecy'
(Cumberland's notebook;
Jerusalem is the only text with
more than 50 plates).
Perhaps prints sheets for a copy
of *America* and some proof
pages of *Jerusalem*.
Enoch (Blake's only lithograph);
two sets of 12 watercolours of
Milton's *Paradise Lost* (one for
Butts, one for Thomas).

	Blake's life and work	*Historical and cultural background*

1808   Jan.–Feb.: 'Description of
A Vision of the Last
Judgement. To Ozias
Humphry Esqr'.
July: Cromek's edition of
Blair's *The Grave* published;
Robert and Leigh Hunt
ridicule the designs in the
Examiner (28 Aug.) and
describe Blake as a 'Quack'.
19 Dec.: writes to Cumberland
that he would 'immediately
Engage in reviving my former
pursuits of printing if I had
not now so long been turned
out of the old channel into
a new one . . . my time . . . in
future must be devoted to
Designing & Painting'.
Jacob's Dream and *Christ in the
Sepulchre* (watercolours, RA);
Vision of the Last Judgement
(pen and watercolour, RA);
*Chaucer and the . . . Pilgrims on
their Journey to Canterbury*
(tempera); *The Holy Family*
(tempera).

Peninsular War to defend Portugal (to
1814), briefly suspended by the
Convention of Cintra armistice (Aug.).
Quarterly Review; Scott, *Marmion*;
Cottle, *The Fall of Cambria*; Goethe,
Faust.

1809   15 May: Exhibition at 28
Broad Street (meant to close 29
Sept. but still open June 1810),
of *The Ancient Britons*; *The
Spiritual Form of Nelson*; *The
Spiritual Form of Pitt*; *The
Canterbury Pilgrims*; *The Bard,
from Gray*; *A Subject from
Shakespeare* ('The Horse of
Intellect leaping from the cliffs
of Memory'); *The Goats*; *The
Spiritual Preceptor*; *Satan
calling up his Legions*; *The
Brahmins*; *The Body of Abel
found by Adam and Eve*;
*Soldiers casting lots for Christ's
Garments*; *Jacob's Dream*;
*Angels hovering over the body of
Jesus in the Sepulchre*; *Ruth*;
The Penance of Jane Shore.

Battle of Corunna and death of Sir John
Moore (Jan.); Battle of Talavera (July);
Battle of Wagram (July); Walcheren
Expedition (July–Dec.); Portland resigns
(Sept.); Perceval PM; Pall Mall lit by
gas.
Edward Davies, *Mythology and Rites of
the British Druids*; Coleridge, *The Friend*
(to 1810); *Quarterly Review*; Hayley, *Life
of Romney*; Turner, *Thomson's Aeolian
Harp*; Flaxman, monument to Nelson
(St Paul's, erected 1818); Caspar David
Friedrich, *Monk by the Sea*.

Blake's life and work

Historical and cultural background

May: *A Descriptive Catalogue of Pictures*, and *Blake's Chaucer*. Robert Hunt reviews Blake's exhibition (*Examiner*, 17 Sept.): 'the ebullitions of a distempered brain are mistaken for the sallies of genius'.

'Holy Thursday' (*Innocence*) reprinted in Priscilla Wakefield's *Perambulations in London* ('This uncommon scene is so well described in the following lines by Mr Blake'). Blake gives drawing lessons to William Seguier (later first Keeper of the National Gallery). *The Spiritual Form of Napoleon* (tempera, lost since 1882); *The Bard, from Gray* (tempera); *Mrs Butts* and *Thomas Butts Jnr.* (minatures); two sets of 6 watercolours of Milton's 'On the Morning of Christ's Nativity' (one for Butts, one for Thomas).

1810 23 May: 'found the Word Golden' (Notebook). 'For the Year 1810 Additions to Blakes Catalogue of Pictures &c' (Notebook: an account of *The Last Judgement*). 'Chaucer's Canterbury Pilgrims' (Notebook; later known as the *Public Address*): 'Let us teach Buonaparte . . . That it is not Arts that follow & attend upon Empire but Empire that attends upon & follows The Arts.' Sept.: article in *The Repository of Arts* remarks that Blake 'seems to have relinquished engraving, and to have cultivated the higher departments of designing and painting with great success'. At work (*c*.1810–27) on *The Last Judgement* (tempera,

Battle of Busaco (Sept.); Wellington entrenched at Torres Vedras. Wordsworth, 'The French Revolution as it appeared to Enthusiasts at its Commencement' (in *The Friend*; written 1805); Crabbe, *The Borough*; Scott, *Lady of the Lake*; Rogers, *Voyage of Columbus*; Southey, *Curse of Kehama*; Jane and Ann Taylor, *Hymns for Infant Minds*; Friedrich, *Abbey under Oak Trees*; 'Nazarene' painters in Rome.

Blake's life and work   *Historical and cultural background*

untraced since 1847); *Adam
Naming the Beasts, Eve Naming
the Birds, The Virgin and Child
in Egypt, Christ Blessing* (all
tempera on linen or canvas for
Butts); *The Canterbury Pilgrims*
(engraving, 8 Oct.).

1811 Probably completes *Milton* and   Prince of Wales becomes Regent (5 Feb.);
      prints copies A and B (together   Battle of Albuera (May).
      with sheets for copy C).   Austen, *Sense and Sensibility*; Goethe,
      Southey visits Blake and is   *Dichtung und Wahrheit*; West, *Christ
      shown 'a perfectly mad poem   Healing the Sick in the Temple*; Constable,
      called Jerusalem'.   *Dedham Vale: Morning*; Friedrich, *Winter
      Makes at least 33 further   Landscape with Church*.
      pictures for Butts between
      1811 and 1820.
      Jan.: Henry Crabb Robinson,
      'William Blake, Künstler,
      Dichter, und Religiöser
      Schwärmer' (*Vaterländisches
      Museum*, Hamburg).
      Prints sheets for copies of
      *Songs of Innocence.
      An Allegory of the Spiritual
      Condition of Man* (tempera);
      frontispiece and vignette for
      *The Prologue and Characters of
      Chaucer's Pilgrims* (Dec.).

1812 24 May: Wordsworth tells   Perceval (PM) assassinated (May); Tories
      Crabb Robinson that he   win General Election (Nov.); Liverpool
      considered Blake 'as having the   PM (to 1827); Luddite disturbances;
      elements of poetry—a   Napoleon invades Russia (June); Battle
      thousand times more than   of Borodino (Sept.); retreat from
      either Byron or Scott'.   Moscow (Oct.–Dec.).
      June: review in *The Lady's   Montgomery, *The World before the Flood*;
      Monthly Museum* describes   Byron, *Childe Harold*; Grimm, *Fairy
      Blake's pictures at the APWC   Tales*; Turner, *Snow Storm: Hannibal
      as 'too sublime for our   crossing the Alps*.
      comprehension' and only
      suitable for 'lovers of the
      Fuselian and the Angelesque'.
      Exhibits at the Associated
      Painters in Water Colours
      (three temperas, *The
      Canterbury Pilgrims, The
      Spiritual Form of Pitt*, and *The
      Spiritual Form of Nelson*, and

Blake's life and work	Historical and cultural background

'Detached Specimens of an original illuminated Poem, entitled *Jerusalem the Emanation of the Giant Albion*').

1813 June: Cumberland visits Blake in South Molton Street ('still poor still Dirty').
2nd edition of Cromek's edition of Blair's *The Grave* (with designs by Blake) published. Engraving after Phillips's portrait of Earl Spencer.

Leigh Hunt imprisoned (Feb.; to Feb. 1815) for libel of Prince Regent (*Examiner*, Mar. 1812); Prussia and Austria declare war on France; Battle of Leipzig (Oct.); French withdraw beyond Rhine; Wellington invades France (Oct.). Owen, *A New View of Society*; Shelley, *Queen Mab*; Austen, *Pride and Prejudice*; Wilkie, *Blind Man's Buff*.

1814 2nd edition of Wakefield's *Perambulations in London* (1809) with corrected text of 'Holy Thursday' (*Innocence*). Begins engravings after Flaxman for Hesiod's *Works Days and Theogony* (to 1817).

Prussians and Austrians reach Paris (31 Mar.); Battle of Toulouse; Napoleon abdicates (6 Apr.) and retires to Elba; Louis XVIII restored to throne; first Treaty of Paris (May); Joanna Southcote dies. Scott, *Waverley*; Southey, *Roderick*; Charlotte Dixon, *The Mount of Olives*; Wordsworth, *The Excursion*.

1815 20 Apr.: George Cumberland, Jr visits Blake: 'found him & his wife drinking Tea, durtyer than ever . . . he . . . shewed his large drawing in Water Colors of the last Judgement . . . his time is now intirely taken up with Etching & Engraving . . . Blake says he is fearful they will make too great a man of Napoleon and enable him to come to this Country—Mrs B says that if this Country does go to War our K–g ought to loose his head'.
8 watercolours of Milton's *Comus* and 6 watercolours of 'On the Morning of Christ's Nativity' for Butts; Spenser's *Faerie Queen* (watercolour); illustrations for Wedgwood catalogue (to 1816); engravings for *The Cyclopaedia* (to 1818). William Ensom's pen-and-ink portrait of Blake wins prize from Society for the Encouragement of Arts (30 May).

Napoleon escapes from Elba and returns to Paris (21 Mar.); Battle of Waterloo (18 June); allies re-enter Paris (July); second Peace of Paris; Napoleon to St Helena (Oct.).
Byron, *Hebrew Melodies*; Bowles, *Missionary of the Andes*; Scott, *Guy Mannering*; *Lord of the Isles*; Wordsworth, *Poems*; Friedrich, *Mountain with Rising Fog*; Ward, *Gordale Scar*.

Blake's life and work	*Historical and cultural background*
1816 July: Nancy Flaxman writes to her husband about being 'oblig'd to put up with B's odd humours'. The wealthy Swedenborgian-Anglican Charles Augustus Tulk begins to buy work from Blake. Autumn: Blake included in *A Biographical Dictionary of the Living Authors of Great Britain and Ireland* ('eccentric but very ingenious'). Copy BB of *Songs of Innocence and of Experience*, containing 'A Divine Image', bought by Robert Balmanno. 12 watercolours of Milton's *L'Allegro* and *Il Penseroso* for Butts (to 1820).	Economic recession and severe weather ('the year without a summer'); income tax abolished; government buys Elgin Marbles (June); Spa Field Riots (Dec.). Austen, *Emma*; Scott, *Old Mortality*; Peacock, *Headlong Hall*; Shelley, *Alastor*; Coleridge, *Christabel*; Constable, *The Wheatfield*.
1817 *The Judgement of Paris* (watercolour); 12 watercolours illustrating Milton's *Paradise Regained* (*c*.1816–20, bought by Linnell 1825); engravings for Flaxman's *Hesiod*.	Blanketeers march from Manchester (Mar.); Habeas Corpus suspended (to 1818); death of Princess Charlotte; Dulwich Gallery. Ricardo, *Political Economy*; *Blackwood's Magazine*; Keats, *Poems*; Moore, *Lalla Rookh*; Byron, *Manfred*; Constable, *Flatford Mill*; *A Cottage in a Cornfield*.
1818 6 Feb.: Coleridge reads C. A. Tulk's copy of *Songs of Innocence and of Experience* ('He is a man of Genius—and I apprehend a Swedenborgian—certainly a mystic'). Verse fragments in iambic tetrameter couplets for unfinished poem later known as 'The Everlasting Gospel'. Prints sheets for later copies of *Thel*, *Marriage*, *Visions*, *Songs of Innocence and of Experience*, *Urizen*, and additional pages for copies C and D of *Milton*; on 9 June writes to Dawson Turner offering to sell copies of these and (from stock) *America*, *Europe*, and the 'Large Colour Prints' of 1795. Removes 'Preface' (including 'And did those feet') from *Milton*.	Tories win General Election (July); Burdett's motion for universal male suffrage defeated; Church Building Act. Keats, *Endymion*; Shelley, *Revolt of Islam*; *Quarterly* and *Blackwood's* attack the 'Cockney School' of writers; Scott, *Heart of Midlothian*; Mary Shelley, *Frankenstein*; Isaac D'Israeli, *The Literary Character*; Constable, *Dedham Lock and Mill*.

Blake's life and work

Historical and cultural background

24 June: George Cumberland,
Jr introduces Blake to John
Linnell who asks him to
engrave his portrait of the
Baptist minister James Upton.
12 Sept.: Linnell introduces
Blake to Varley and Constable.
'Holy Thursday' (*Innocence*)
printed in a reissue of Jane and
Ann Taylor's *City Scenes*.

1819 7 Jan.: Isaac D'Israeli asks
a book dealer for a copy of
'Blake's Young'.
Starts to print sheets for copies
A, B, and C of *Jerusalem*.
30 Dec.: Linnell buys
Chapter 2 of *Jerusalem* (copy
C), probably adding Chapter 3
in December 1820 and the
'Balance' on 4 Feb. 1821.
Oct.: begins to draw 'Visionary
Heads' for John Varley; *The
Ghost of a Flea* (tempera);
makes designs and woodcuts for
Thornton's *The Pastorals of
Virgil* (3rd edn, 1821).

Peterloo massacre (Aug.); Six Acts.
Scott, *Ivanhoe*; Shelley, *The Cenci*;
Rogers, *Human Life*; Byron, *Don Juan*
(to 1824); Montgomery, *Greenland*.
Constable, *The White Horse*; Turner,
Ulysses Deriding Polyphemus; Géricault,
Raft of the Medusa.

1820 *Jerusalem* completed: mentioned
by 'Janus Weathercock'
(Thomas Griffith Wainewright)
in *London Magazine* (Sept.).
Prints sheets for two copies of
For the Sexes and three copies
of *Jerusalem*.
Sells his stock copies of
*America, Book of Thel, Europe,
Urizen, Marriage, Song of Los,
Songs of Innocence*, and *Songs of
Experience* to Edward Evans of
Great Queen Street who
advertises them in his July 1820
catalogue, coloured and
stitched, at 12 shillings each.
*Epitome of James Hervey's
Meditations among the Tombs*
(watercolour); engraving after
Villiers of *Mrs Harriet Quentin*
(mistress of Prince Regent;

Prince Regent becomes George IV
(Jan.); return (5 June) and trial (Aug.–
Nov.) of Queen Caroline; Cato Street
conspiracy; Tulk MP for Sudbury.
Shelley, *Prometheus Unbound*; Peacock,
The Four Ages of Poetry; Keats, *Lamia,
Isabella and Other Poems*; Southey, *Life of
Wesley*; Landseer, *Alpine Mastiffs*.

Blake's life and work	Historical and cultural background
1 June); *Laocoön* (etching); 'Old Parr when Young' (drawing).	

1821　Mark Martin, their South Molton Street landlord, retires to France; the Blakes move to 3 Fountain Court, Strand, where their landlord is Catherine's brother-in-law, Henry Banes. Blake sells his collection of Old Master prints to Colnaghi. Prints sheets for copies of *America*, *Songs of Innocence and of Experience*, *Europe*, and copies D and E of *Jerusalem*. Copies the 19 Book of Job watercolours made for Butts to produce set of 21 for Linnell (and adds 2 to the previous set); *The Sea of Time and Space*; woodcuts in Thornton's *Pastorals of Virgil*.

Riots at Queen Caroline's funeral. Schleiermacher, *The Christian Faith*; Byron, *Cain*; Shelley, *Adonais*; De Quincey, 'Confessions of an English Opium Eater'; Constable, *The Hay Wain*.

1822　28 June: Royal Academy awards £25 to 'William Blake an able Designer & Engraver laboring under great distress'. *On Homers Poetry [and] On Virgil*. *The Ghost of Abel*. Prints sheets for copies of *On Homers Poetry* and *The Ghost of Abel*. *The Man Sweeping the Interpreter's Parlour* (engraving).

Castlereagh (Foreign Secretary) commits suicide; Canning replaces him; Edward Irving begins to preach in London; Friedrich, *Lone Tree*; Wilkie, *Chelsea Pensioners reading the Waterloo Dispatch*.

1823　25 Mar.: Linnell commissions Blake to make the Book of Job engravings. Book of Job engravings (to 1826).

Gaols Act begins reform of prisons; Judgment of Death Act limits capital punishment. Ingres, *La Source*; Constable, *Salisbury Cathedral*.

1824　Linnell commissions Blake to make illustrations for Dante's *Divine Comedy*. Samuel Palmer introduced to Blake by Linnell. 'The Chimney-Sweeper' (*Innocence*) reprinted, with text supplied by Charles Lamb ('from a very rare and curious little work'), in James

Canning recognizes independence of South American republics; repeal of Seditious Meetings and Combination Acts; National Gallery founded; Byron dies. Hogg, *Confessions of a Justified Sinner*; Scott, *Redgauntlet*.

Blake's life and work   *Historical and cultural background*

Montgomery's *The Chimney-Sweeper's Friend, and Climbing-Boy's Album*. Watercolours of Dante's *Divine Comedy* and Bunyan's *Pilgrim's Progress* (both to 1827).

1825 'The Divine Image' and 'On Another's Sorrow' reprinted (anonymously) in the Swedenborgian journal *The Dawn of Light, and Theological Inspector* (Apr. and July). Prints sheets for copies of *Songs of Innocence and of Experience* and *For the Sexes*. T. F. Dibdin reports that Isaac D'Israeli 'possesses the largest collection of . . . the very extraordinary drawings of Mr Blake' [at this date, large but not the largest] and entertains visitors by displaying them in his drawing room; Dibdin comments that, 'at times . . . Mr Blake is himself no ordinary poet' (*The Library Companion*, 1824–5). *The Characters in Spenser's 'Faerie Queene'* (pen and watercolour).

    Commercial crisis; Stockton to Darlington railway. Bridgewater Lectures. Milton (d. 1674), *De Doctrina Christiana*; Macaulay, 'Milton'; Coleridge, *Aids to Reflection*; Constable, *The Leaping Horse*.

1826 Prints sheets for copies of *Songs of Innocence and of Experience*. *Illustrations of the Book of Job* (Mar.). Samuel Palmer, George Richmond, Francis Oliver Finch, Frederick Tatham, and Edward Calvert form a group of 'youthful disciples' of Blake, later termed 'The Ancients'.

    Tories win General Election (July); Niépce takes first true photograph; Tulk accused of heresy ('idealistic and gnostic notions') by fellow Swedenborgians; Flaxman dies (Dec.). Cooper, *Last of the Mohicans*; Scott, *Woodstock*; Disraeli, *Vivian Grey*.

1827 Prints sheets for *Marriage*, *Songs of Innocence and of Experience*, and one copy of *Jerusalem*. James Blake (brother) dies (22 Mar.) and is buried in Bunhill Fields.

    Canning succeeds Liverpool as PM (Apr.) but dies 8 Aug. Keble, *The Christian Year*; Clare, *Shepherd's Calendar*; Carlyle, *German Romance*; De Quincey, 'On Murder as one of the Fine Arts'; Beethoven dies; Constable, *The Cornfield*.

Blake's life and work	*Historical and cultural background*
At work on illustrated MS of Book of Genesis; designs and engraves calling card for George Cumberland (Apr.); colours several impressions of *The Ancient of Days* (originally the frontispiece of *Europe*). **William Blake dies** (12 Aug.) and is buried in Bunhill Fields (17 Aug.). Obituaries in the *Literary Gazette* (18 Aug.) and *Literary Chronicle* (1 Sept.). 11 Sept.: Catherine Blake moves to Cirencester Place as Linnell's housekeeper.	
1828 J. T. Smith, 'William Blake' in his *Nollekens and his Times*. Catherine Blake moves to Lisson Grove as Frederick Tatham's housekeeper.	
1829 Varley, *Zodiacal Physiognomy*. Tatham begins to sell works by Blake, initially on Catherine's behalf.	
1830 [C. A. Tulk], 'The Inventions of William Blake, Painter and Poet', *London University Magazine*. Allan Cunningham, 'William Blake' in his *Lives of the Most Eminent British Painters, Sculptors, and Architects*.	Lucas after Constable, *English Landscape Scenery* (mezzotints, to 1832).
1831 Catherine Blake (wife) dies and is buried in Bunhill Fields.	
1832 Frederick Tatham, MS 'Life of Blake', bound with copy E of *Jerusalem* which he was attempting to sell.	
1834 Isaac D'Israeli increases his collection to more than 160 plates with purchases at the Romney sale.	Benjamin Disraeli, *The Revolutionary Epick*.
1835	Browning, *Paracelsus*.
1836	Browning, 'Johannes Agricola'.

Blake's life and work	*Historical and cultural background*

1839 *Songs of Innocence and of Experience* republished (London, 9 July), with the dedicatory poem 'To the Queen' (1808), in an edition by the Swedenborgian, James John Garth Wilkinson; Browning is given a copy by his friend William Dow on 3 Aug.

1841 Catherine Blake (younger sister) dies; funeral service at All Souls, Marylebone.

1843 Ruskin buys a portfolio of Blake's drawings from the dealer Joseph Hogarth (acquired from Frederick Tatham) but returns it, fearing his father will not approve.

1845 Thomas Butts dies.

1847 British Museum acquires *Jerusalem* and *Visions of the Daughters of Albion*. Rossetti buys the Notebook from William Palmer.

1849 William Allingham discusses 'a new edition of Blake's poems' with the publisher Isaac Slater, but finds that the British Museum 'seem to have nothing of his'.

1852 First major sale of pictures from the Butts collection (Sotheby's, 26 Mar.).

1854 Auction of Joseph Hogarth's stock includes 78 pictures by Blake (7–30 July).

1856 British Museum acquires *Songs of Innocence and of Experience*, *Thel*, *America*, *Song of Los*.

1857 *Oberon and Titania on a Lily* and *The Vision of Queen Katharine* shown in Manchester Art-Treasures Exhibition.

Blake's life and work   *Historical and cultural background*

1859 British Museum acquires
      Milton and *Europe*.

1863 Gilchrist, *Life of William Blake
      'Pictor Ignotus'*, with a second
      volume of selected works,
      including poems from the
      'Pickering' Manuscript.

1865 Ruskin praises Blake as 'a
      beautiful soul' in his 'Cestus of
      Aglaia' articles (*Art Journal*,
      Jan.).
      B. M. Pickering acquires the
      'Pickering' MS.

1866 *Songs of Innocence and
      Experience with Other Poems*,
      ed. R. H. Shepherd (London,
      Pickering, 2nd edn 1868, 3rd
      edn 1874).

1868 Swinburne, *William Blake:
      A Critical Essay*.
      Poetical Sketches republished
      by Pickering.
      Marriage of Heaven and Hell
      republished in colour facsimile
      by Hotten.

1869 James Smetham, 'William
      Blake' (*London Quarterly
      Review*, Jan.).

1875 *Poetical Works*, ed.
      W. M. Rossetti (Aldine
      edition).

1876 Burlington Fine Arts Club
      exhibition of 333 items related
      to Blake.

1877 *Jerusalem* republished in
      facsimile by John Pearson.

1878 *David Delivered* and *An
      Epitome of Harvey's
      Meditations* presented to
      National Gallery by G. T. Saul
      (first Blake paintings in
      national collection).
      Frederick Tatham dies.

1880 2nd edn of Gilchrist, *Life of
      William Blake*.

Blake's life and work   *Historical and cultural background*

1882 National Gallery buys *The Spiritual Form of Pitt*.
John Linnell dies.

1884 *Body of Christ Borne to the Tomb* presented to National Gallery by F. T. Palgrave.
William Muir's facsimiles of *The Works of Wm. Blake* (to 1890).
The *Century Guild Hobby Horse* (1884–94) includes first letterpress printings of *The Marriage* (1887) and *Book of Los* (1890), Muir's facsimile of *Little Tom the Sailor*, and reproductions of *On Homer's Poetry [&] On Virgil* and three of the woodcuts for Thornton's *Virgil*.

1893 *The Four Zoas* first published in Ellis and Yeats, eds, *The Works of William Blake*.

1905 *Poetical Works*, ed. John Sampson.

1913 'Works by William Blake' exhibition at Tate Gallery.

1925 *The French Revolution* first published in *Poetical Works*, ed. John Sampson (2nd edn).

1926 'Samuel Palmer and Other Disciples of William Blake' exhibition at Victoria & Albert Museum.

SELECTED POEMS

LYRICS

Lyrics from *Poetical Sketches**

Song

How sweet I roam'd from field to field,*
  And tasted all the summer's pride,
'Till I the prince of love beheld,
  Who in the sunny beams did glide!

He shew'd me lilies for my hair,   5
  And blushing roses for my brow;
He led me through his gardens fair,
  Where all his golden pleasures grow.

With sweet May dews my wings were wet,
  And Phœbus fir'd my vocal rage;*   10
He caught me in his silken net,
  And shut me in his golden cage.

He loves to sit and hear me sing,
  Then, laughing, sports and plays with me;
Then stretches out my golden wing,   15
  And mocks my loss of liberty.

Song

My silks and fine array,*
  My smiles and languish'd air,
By love are driv'n away;
  And mournful lean Despair
Brings me yew to deck my grave: 5
Such end true lovers have.

His face is fair as heav'n,
   When springing buds unfold;
O why to him was't giv'n,
   Whose heart is wintry cold? 10
His breast is love's all worship'd tomb,
Where all love's pilgrims come.

Bring me an axe and spade,
   Bring me a winding sheet;
When I my grave have made, 15
   Let winds and tempests beat:
Then down I'll lie, as cold as clay.
True love doth pass away!

Song

Love and harmony combine,
And around our souls intwine,
While thy branches mix with mine,
And our roots together join.

Joys upon our branches sit, 5
Chirping loud, and singing sweet;
Like gentle streams beneath our feet
Innocence and virtue meet.

Thou the golden fruit dost bear,
I am clad in flowers fair; 10
Thy sweet boughs perfume the air,
And the turtle buildeth there.*

There she sits and feeds her young,
Sweet I hear her mournful song;
And thy lovely leaves among, 15
There is love: I hear his tongue.*

There his charming nest doth lay,
There he sleeps the night away;
There he sports along the day,
And doth among our branches play. 20

Song

I love the jocund dance,
  The softly-breathing song,
Where innocent eyes do glance,
  And where lisps the maiden's tongue.

I love the laughing vale,
  I love the echoing hill,   5
Where mirth does never fail,
  And the jolly swain laughs his fill.

I love the pleasant cot,
  I love the innocent bow'r,   10
Where white and brown is our lot,
  Or fruit in the mid-day hour.

I love the oaken seat,
  Beneath the oaken tree,
Where all the old villagers meet,   15
  And laugh our sports to see.*

I love our neighbours all,
  But, Kitty, I better love thee;
And love them I ever shall;
  But thou art all to me.   20

Song

Memory, hither come,
  And tune your merry notes;
And, while upon the wind
  Your music floats,
I'll pore upon the stream,   5
Where sighing lovers dream,
And fish for fancies as they pass
Within the watery glass.*

I'll drink of the clear stream,
  And hear the linnet's song;   10
And there I'll lie and dream
  The day along:

And, when night comes, I'll go
  To places fit for woe,
Walking along the darken'd valley   15
  With silent Melancholy.

Mad Song*

The wild winds weep,
  And the night is a-cold;
Come hither, Sleep,
  And my griefs infold*:
But lo! the morning peeps   5
  Over the eastern steeps,
And the rustling birds of dawn*
The earth do scorn.

Lo! to the vault
  Of paved heaven*   10
With sorrow fraught
  My notes are driven:
They strike the ear of night,
  Make weep the eyes of day;
They make mad the roaring winds,   15
  And with tempests play.

Like a fiend in a cloud,
  With howling woe,
After night I do croud,
  And with night will go;   20
I turn my back to the east,
From whence comforts have increas'd;
For light doth seize my brain
With frantic pain.

Song*

Fresh from the dewy hill, the merry year
Smiles on my head, and mounts his flaming car;*
Round my young brows the laurel wreathes a shade,
And rising glories beam around my head.

My feet are wing'd, while o'er the dewy lawn   5
I meet my maiden, risen like the morn:
Oh bless those holy feet, like angels' feet;
Oh bless those limbs, beaming with heav'nly light!

Like as an angel glitt'ring in the sky
In times of innocence and holy joy;   10
The joyful shepherd stops his grateful song
To hear the music of an angel's tongue.

So when she speaks, the voice of Heaven I hear:
So when we walk, nothing impure comes near;
Each field seems Eden, and each calm retreat;   15
Each village seems the haunt of holy feet.

But that sweet village, where my black-ey'd maid
Closes her eyes in sleep beneath night's shade,
Whene'er I enter, more than mortal fire
Burns in my soul, and does my song inspire.   20

Song

When early morn walks forth in sober grey,*
Then to my black ey'd maid I haste away;
When evening sits beneath her dusky bow'r,
And gently sighs away the silent hour,
The village bell alarms, away I go,   5
And the vale darkens at my pensive woe.

To that sweet village, where my black ey'd maid
Doth drop a tear beneath the silent shade,
I turn my eyes; and, pensive as I go,
Curse my black stars, and bless my pleasing woe.*   10

Oft when the summer sleeps among the trees,
Whisp'ring faint murmurs to the scanty breeze,
I walk the village round; if at her side
A youth doth walk in stolen joy and pride,
I curse my stars in bitter grief and woe,   15
That made my love so high, and me so low.

O should she e'er prove false, his limbs I'd tear,
And throw all pity on the burning air;

I'd curse bright fortune for my mixed lot,
And then I'd die in peace, and be forgot.   20

To the Muses

Whether on Ida's shady brow,*
   Or in the chambers of the East,*
The chambers of the sun, that now
   From antient melody have ceas'd;

Whether in Heav'n ye wander fair,   5
   Or the green corners of the earth,
Or the blue regions of the air,
   Where the melodious winds have birth;

Whether on chrystal rocks ye rove,
   Beneath the bosom of the sea   10
Wand'ring in many a coral grove,
   Fair Nine, forsaking Poetry!*

How have you left the antient love
   That bards of old enjoy'd in you!
The languid strings do scarcely move!   15
   The sound is forc'd, the notes are few!

Manuscript Poems from Ann Flaxman's copy of *Poetical Sketches**

Song 1ˢᵗ by a shepherd

Welcome stranger to this place,
Where joy doth sit on every bough,
Paleness flies from every face,
We reap not what we do not sow.

Innocence doth like a Rose   5
Bloom on every maidens cheek;

Honour twines around her brows,
The jewel Health adorns her neck.

Song 3rd by an old shepherd*

When silver snow decks Sylvio's cloaths
And jewel hangs at shepherds nose,
We can abide life's pelting storm
That makes our limbs quake, if our hearts be warm.

Whilst Virtue is our walking staff,   5
And truth a lantern to our path;
We can abide life's pelting storm
That makes our limbs quake, if our hearts be warm.

Blow boisterous Wind, stern Winter frown,
Innocence is a Winter's gown;   10
So clad, we'll abide life's pelting storm
That makes our limbs quake, if our hearts be warm.

* * *

[Plate 2]

Songs of Innocence and of Experience Shewing the Two Contrary States of the Human Soul*

[Plate 3]

SONGS OF INNOCENCE*

1789
The Author & Printer W Blake

[Plate 4]

Introduction

Piping down the valleys wild
Piping songs of pleasant glee*

On a cloud I saw a child.
And he laughing said to me.

Pipe a song about a Lamb:*   5
So I piped with merry chear,
Piper, pipe that song again—
So I piped, he wept to hear.

Drop thy pipe, thy happy pipe
Sing thy songs of happy chear,   10
So I sung the same again
While he wept with joy to hear

Piper sit thee down and write
In a book that all may read—
So he vanish'd from my sight   15
And I pluck'd a hollow reed

And I made a rural pen,
And I stain'd the water clear,*
And I wrote my happy songs,
Every child may joy to hear   20

[Plate 5 (25)]

Infant Joy

I have no name
I am but two days old.—
What shall I call thee?
I happy am
Joy is my name.—   5
Sweet joy befall thee!

Pretty joy!
Sweet joy but two days old.
Sweet joy I call thee;
Thou dost smile,   10
I sing the while
Sweet joy befall thee.

[Plate 6 (5)]

*The Shepherd**

How sweet is the Shepherds sweet lot,
From the morn to the evening he strays:
He shall follow his sheep all the day
And his tongue shall be filled with praise.

For he hears the lambs innocent call,   5
And he hears the ewes tender reply,
He is watchful while they are in peace,
For they know when their Shepherd is nigh.

[Plates 7–8 (16–17)]

*A Cradle Song**

Sweet dreams, form a shade,
O'er my lovely infants head.
Sweet dreams of pleasant streams,
By happy silent moony beams

Sweet sleep, with soft down.   5
Weave thy brows an infant crown.
Sweet sleep Angel mild,
Hover o'er my happy child.

Sweet smiles, in the night,
Hover over my delight.   10
Sweet smiles Mothers smiles
All the livelong night beguiles.

Sweet moans, dovelike sighs,
Chase not slumber from thy eyes.
Sweet moans, sweeter smiles,   15
All the dovelike moans beguiles.

Sleep sleep happy child,
All creation slept and smil'd.
Sleep sleep, happy sleep,
While o'er thee thy mother weep   20

Sweet babe in thy face,
Holy image I can trace.
Sweet babe once like thee.
Thy maker lay and wept for me*

Wept for me for thee for all,   25
When he was an infant small.
Thou his image ever see.
Heavenly face that smiles on thee,

Smiles on thee on me on all;
Who became an infant small,   30
Infant smiles are his own smiles,
Heaven & earth to peace beguiles.

[Plate 9 (8)]

*The Lamb**

Little Lamb, who made thee
Dost thou know who made thee
Gave thee life & bid thee feed.
By the stream & o'er the mead;
Gave thee clothing of delight.   5
Softest clothing wooly, bright;
Gave thee such a tender voice.
Making all the vales rejoice:
Little Lamb, who made thee
Dost thou know who made thee   10

Little Lamb, I'll tell thee,
Little Lamb, Ill tell thee;
He is called by thy name,
For he calls himself a Lamb:*
He is meek, & he is mild,   15
He became a little child:*
I a child, & thou a lamb,
We are called by his name,
Little Lamb God bless thee,
Little Lamb God bless thee.   20

[Plate 10 (11)]

*The Blossom**

    Merry Merry Sparrow
    Under leaves so green
    A happy Blossom
    Sees you swift as arrow
    Seek your cradle narrow   5
    Near my Bosom.

    Pretty Pretty Robin
    Under leaves so green
    A happy Blossom
    Hears you sobbing sobbing*   10
    Pretty Pretty Robin
    Near my Bosom.

[Plate 11 (24)]

*Nurse's Song**

When the voices of children are heard on the green
And laughing is heard on the hill,
My heart is at rest within my breast
And everything else is still

Then come home, my children, the sun is gone down   5
And the dews of night arise
Come come leave off play, and let us away
Till the morning appears in the skies

No no let us play, for it is yet day
And we cannot go to sleep   10
Besides in the sky, the little birds fly
And the hills are all coverd with sheep

Well well go & play till the light fades away
And then go home to bed
The little ones leaped & shouted & laugh'd   15
And all the hills echoed

[Plate 12 (19)]

Holy Thursday*

Twas on a Holy Thursday their innocent faces clean
The children walking two & two, in red & blue & green*
Grey headed beadles walkd before with wands as white as snow
Till into the high dome of Pauls they like Thames waters flow

O what a multitude they seemd, these flowers of London town   5
Seated in companies they sit with radiance all their own
The hum of multitudes was there, but multitudes of lambs
Thousands of little boys & girls raising their innocent hands

Now like a mighty wind they raise to heaven the voice of song*
Or like harmonious thunderings the seats of heaven among   10
Beneath them sit the aged men wise guardians of the poor
Then cherish pity, lest you drive an angel from your door*

[Plates 13–14 (6–7)]

The Ecchoing Green*

The Sun does arise,
And make happy the skies.
The merry bells ring,
To welcome the Spring.
The skylark and thrush,   5
The birds of the bush,
Sing louder around,
To the bells chearful sound.
While our sports shall be seen
On the Ecchoing Green.   10

Old John with white hair
Does laugh away care,
Sitting under the oak,
Among the old folk.
They laugh at our play,   15
And soon they all say,
Such, such were the joys.
When we all, girls & boys.

In our youth time were seen,
On the Ecchoing Green.   20

Till the little ones, weary
No more can be merry
The sun does descend,
And our sports have an end:
Round the laps of their mothers.   25
Many sisters and brothers,
Like birds in their nest.
Are ready for rest;
And sport no more seen,
On the darkening Green.   30

[Plate 15 (27)]

On Anothers Sorrow

Can I see anothers woe,
And not be in sorrow too.
Can I see anothers grief,
And not seek for kind relief.

Can I see a falling tear.   5
And not feel my sorrows share,
Can a father see his child,
Weep, nor be with sorrow fill'd.

Can a mother sit and hear.
An infant groan an infant fear—   10
No no never can it be,
Never never can it be.

And can he who smiles on all*
Hear the wren with sorrows small.
Hear the small birds grief & care   15
Hear the woes that infants bear—

And not sit beside the nest
Pouring pity in their breast.
And not sit the cradle near
Weeping tear on infants tear.   20

And not sit both night & day.
Wiping all our tears away.*
O! no never can it be.
Never never can it be.

He doth give his joy to all,   25
He becomes an infant small,
He becomes a man of woe*
He doth feel the sorrow too.

Think not. thou canst sigh a sigh,
And thy maker is not by.   30
Think not, thou canst weep a tear,
And thy maker is not near.

O! he gives to us his joy.*
That our grief he may destroy
Till our grief is fled & gone   35
He doth sit by us and moan

[Plates 16–17 (22–3)]

*Spring**

Sound the Flute!
Now it's mute.
Birds delight
Day and Night,
Nightingale   5
In the dale
Lark in Sky
Merrily
Merrily Merrily to welcome in the Year

Little Boy   10
Full of joy,
Little Girl
Sweet and small,
Cock does crow
So do you.   15
Merry voice
Infant noise
Merrily Merrily to welcome in the Year

Little Lamb
Here I am.   20
Come and lick
My white neck.
Let me pull
Your soft Wool.
Let me kiss   25
Your soft face
Merrily Merrily we welcome in the Year

[Plate 18 (53)]

*The School Boy**

I love to rise in a summer morn,
When the birds sing on every tree;
The distant huntsman winds his horn,
And the sky-lark sings with me.
O! what sweet company.   5

But to go to school in a summer morn,
O! it drives all joy away;
Under a cruel eye outworn.
The little ones spend the day,
In sighing and dismay.   10

Ah! then at times I drooping sit,
And spend many an anxious hour,
Nor in my book can I take delight,
Nor sit in learning's bower,
Worn thro' with the dreary shower.   15

How can the bird that is born for joy,
Sit in a cage and sing.
How can a child when fears annoy.
But droop his tender wing.
And forget his youthful spring.   20

O! father & mother, if buds are nip'd,
And blossoms blown away,
And if the tender plants are strip'd
Of their joy in the springing day,
By sorrow and cares dismay.   25

How shall the summer arise in joy.
Or the summer fruits appear.
Or how shall we gather what griefs destroy
Or bless the mellowing year.
When the blasts of winter appear.   30

[Plate 19 (18)]

The Divine Image*

To Mercy Pity Peace and Love.
All pray in their distress;
And to these virtues of delight
Return their thankfulness.

For Mercy Pity Peace and Love,   5
Is God our father dear:
And Mercy Pity Peace, and Love,
Is Man his child and care.

For Mercy has a human heart
Pity, a human face: 10
And Love, the human form divine,*
And Peace, the human dress.

Then every man of every clime,
That prays in his distress,
Prays to the human form divine   15
Love Mercy Pity Peace,

And all must love the human form.
In heathen, turk or jew,*
Where Mercy, Love, & Pity dwell
There God is dwelling too.   20

[Plate 20 (12)]

The Chimney Sweeper*

When my mother died I was very young,
And my Father sold me while yet my tongue,
Could scarcely cry weep weep weep weep,*
So your chimneys I sweep, & in soot I sleep.

There's little Tom Dacre, who cried when his head*   5
That curl'd like a lambs back, was shav'd, so I said.
Hush, Tom never mind it, for when your head's bare,
You know that the soot cannot spoil your white hair

And so he was quiet. & that very night.
As Tom was a sleeping he had such a sight,   10
That thousands of sweepers Dick, Joe, Ned & Jack
Were all of them lock'd up in coffins of black,

And by came an Angel who had a bright key
And he open'd the coffins & set them all free.
Then down a green plain leaping laughing they run   15
And wash in a river, and shine in the Sun.*

Then naked & white, all their bags left behind.
They rise upon clouds, and sport in the wind.
And the Angel told Tom, if he'd be a good boy,
He'd have God for his father & never want joy.   20

And so Tom awoke and we rose in the dark
And got with our bags & our brushes to work.
Tho' the morning was cold, Tom was happy & warm
So if all do their duty they need not fear harm.

[Plate 21 (15)]

*Laughing Song**

When the green woods laugh with the voice of joy
And the dimpling stream runs laughing by,
When the air does laugh with our merry wit,
And the green hill laughs with the noise of it.

When the meadows laugh with lively green   5
And the grasshopper laughs in the merry scene.
When Mary and Susan and Emily.
With their sweet round mouths sing Ha, Ha, He.

When the painted birds laugh in the shade
Where our table with cherries and nuts is spread   10
Come live & be merry, and join with me,
To sing the sweet chorus of Ha, Ha, He.

[Plates 22–3 (9–10)]

The Little Black Boy*

My mother bore me in the southern wild,
And I am black, but O! my soul is white.
White as an angel is the English child:
But I am black as if bereav'd of light.

My mother taught me underneath a tree   5
And sitting down before the heat of day,
She took me on her lap and kissed me,
And pointing to the east began to say,

Look on the rising sun: there God does live
And gives his light, and gives his heat away.   10
And flowers and trees and beasts and men receive
Comfort in morning joy in the noon day.

And we are put on earth a little space,
That we may learn to bear the beams of love.*
And these black bodies and this sunburnt face   15
Is but a cloud, and like a shady grove.

For when our souls have learn'd the heat to bear
The cloud will vanish we shall hear his voice.
Saying: come out from the grove my love & care.
And round my golden tent like lambs rejoice.   20

Thus did my mother say and kissed me.
And thus I say to little English boy.
When I from black and he from white cloud free,
And round the tent of God like lambs we joy:

I'll shade him from the heat, till he can bear,   25
To lean in joy upon our fathers knee.
And then I'll stand and stroke his silver hair,
And be like him and he will then love me.

[Plate 24 (54)]

The Voice of the Ancient Bard*

Youth of delight come hither.
And see the opening morn,

Image of truth new born.
Doubt is fled, & clouds of reason.
Dark disputes & artful teasing,   5
Folly is an endless maze,
Tangled roots perplex her ways,
How many have fallen there!
They stumble all night over bones of the dead:
And feel they know not what but care;   10
And wish to lead others when they should be led

[Plates 25–6 (20–1)]

*Night**

The sun descending in the west.
The evening star does shine.
The birds are silent in their nest,
And I must seek for mine,
The moon like a flower,   5
In heaven's high bower;
With silent delight,
Sits and smiles on the night.

Farewell, green fields and happy groves,
Where flocks have took delight;   10
Where lambs have nibbled, silent moves
The feet of angels bright;
Unseen they pour blessing,
And joy without ceasing,
On each bud and blossom,   15
And each sleeping bosom.

They look in every thoughtless nest
Where birds are cover'd warm;
They visit caves of every beast,
To keep them all from harm;   20
If they see any weeping,
That should have been sleeping
They pour sleep on their head
And sit down by their bed.

When wolves and tygers howl for prey   25
They pitying stand and weep;
Seeking to drive their thirst away,
And keep them from the sheep.
But if they rush dreadful;*
The angels most heedful,   30
Recieve each mild spirit.
New worlds to inherit.

And there the lions ruddy eyes,
Shall flow with tears of gold;
And pitying the tender cries,   35
And walking round the fold:
Saying: wrath, by his meekness
And by his health, sickness.
Is driven away,
From our immortal day.   40

And now beside thee bleating lamb.
I can lie down and sleep;*
Or think on him who bore thy name.
Grase after thee and weep.
For wash'd in life's river.*   45
My bright mane for ever.
Shall shine like the gold.
As I guard o'er the fold.

[Plate 27 (13)]

*The Little Boy lost**

Father, father, where are you going
O do not walk so fast.
Speak, father, speak to your little boy
Or else I shall be lost,

The night was dark, no father was there   5
The child was wet with dew.
The mire was deep, & the child did weep
And away the vapour flew*

[Plate 28 (14)]

*The Little Boy found**

The little boy lost in the lonely fen,
Led by the wand'ring light,
Began to cry, but God ever nigh,
Appeard like his father in white.

He kissed the child & by the hand led   5
And to his mother brought,
Who in sorrow pale, thro' the lonely dale
Her little boy weeping sought.

[Plate 29 (26)]

*A Dream**

Once a dream did weave a shade
O'er my Angel-guarded bed.
That an Emmet lost its way
Where on grass methought I lay.

Troubled wilder'd, and folorn,   5
Dark benighted travel-worn,
Over many a tangled spray,
All heart-broke I heard her say.

O, my children! do they cry,
Do they hear their father sigh.   10
Now they look abroad to see,
Now return and weep for me.

Pitying, I drop'd a tear;
But I saw a glow-worm near:
Who replied. What wailing wight   15
Calls the watchman of the night.

I am set to light the ground,
While the beetle goes his round:
Follow now the beetle's hum,
Little wanderer hie thee home.   20

[Plate 30 (29)]

SONGS OF EXPERIENCE*

1794
The Author & Printer W Blake

[Plate 31 (30)]

*Introduction*ature*

Hear the voice of the Bard!
Who Present, Past, & Future, sees
Whose ears have heard,
The Holy Word,*
That walk'd among the ancient trees.*   5

Calling the lapsed Soul
And weeping in the evening dew;
That might controll.
The starry pole;*
And fallen fallen light renew!   10

O Earth O Earth return!*
Arise from out the dewy grass;
Night is worn,
And the morn
Rises from the slumberous mass.   15

Turn away no more:
Why wilt thou turn away
The starry floor*
The watry shore
Is givn thee till the break of day.*   20

[Plate 32 (31)]

Earth's Answer

Earth raisd up her head.
From the darkness dread & drear.

Her light fled:
Stony dread!
And her locks cover'd with grey despair.   5

Prison'd on watry shore
Starry Jealousy does keep my den
Cold and hoar
Weeping o'er
I hear the Father of the ancient men   10

Selfish father of men
Cruel, jealous, selfish fear
Can delight,
Chain'd in night
The virgins of youth and morning bear.   15

Does spring hide its joy
When buds and blossoms grow?
Does the sower?
Sow by night?
Or the plowman in darkness plow?   20

Break this heavy chain
That does freeze my bones around
Selfish! vain!
Eternal bane!
That free Love with bondage bound.   25

[Plate 33 (48)]

*Infant Sorrow**

My mother groand! my father wept,
Into the dangerous world I leapt:
Helpless, naked, piping loud:
Like a fiend hid in a cloud.

Struggling in my fathers hands: 5
Striving against my swadling bands:
Bound and weary I thought best
To sulk upon my mothers breast.

[Plate 34 (51)]

A Little Girl Lost*

Children of the future Age.
Reading this indignant page;
Know that in a former time.
Love! sweet Love! was thought a crime.

In the Age of Gold,*   5
Free from winter's cold:
Youth and maiden bright.
To the holy light,
Naked in the sunny beams delight.

Once a youthful pair   10
Fill'd with softest care;
Met in garden bright.
Where the holy light,
Had just removd the curtains of the night.

There, in rising day.   15
On the grass they play:
Parents were afar;
Strangers came not near:
And the maiden soon forgot her fear.

Tired with kisses sweet   20
They agree to meet,
When the silent sleep
Waves o'er heaven's deep:
And the weary tired wanderers weep.

To her father white   25
Came the maiden bright:
But his loving look,
Like the holy book,
All her tender limbs with terror shook

Ona! pale and weak!   30
To thy father speak:
O the trembling fear!

O the dismal care!
That shakes the blossoms of my hoary hair

[Plate 35 (38)]

Nurses Song*

When the voices of children. are heard on the green
And whisprings are in the dale:
The days of my youth rise fresh in my mind,
My face turns green and pale.*

Then come home my children. the sun is gone down 5
And the dews of night arise
Your spring & your day. are wasted in play
And your winter and night in disguise.

[Plate 36 (41)]

The Angel*

I Dreamt a Dream! what can it mean?
And that I was a maiden Queen:
Guarded by an Angel mild;
Witless woe was ne'er beguil'd!

And I wept both night and day 5
And he wip'd my tears away
And I wept both day and night
And hid from him my heart's delight

So he took his wings and fled:
Then the morn blush'd rosy red: 10
I dried my tears, & arm'd my fears,
With ten thousand shields and spears.

Soon my Angel came again;
I was arm'd, he came in vain:
For the time of youth was fled 15
And grey hairs were on my head

[Plate 37 (39)]

The Sick Rose*

O Rose thou art sick.
The invisible worm.
That flies in the night
In the howling storm:

Has found out thy bed   5
Of crimson joy:
And his dark secret love
Does thy life destroy.

[Plate 38 (44)]

The Garden of Love

I went to the Garden of Love.
And saw what I never had seen:
A Chapel was built in the midst,
Where I used to play on the green.

And the gates of this Chapel were shut,   5
And Thou shalt not writ over the door;*
So I turn'd to the Garden of Love,
That so many sweet flowers bore,

And I saw it was filled with graves,
And tomb-stones where flowers should be: 10
And Priests in black gowns, were walking their rounds,
And binding with briars, my joys & desires.

[Plate 39 (45)]

The Little Vagabond*

Dear Mother, dear Mother, the Church is cold,
But the Ale-house is healthy & pleasant & warm:
Besides I can tell where I am use'd well,
Such usage in heaven will never do well.

But if at the Church they would give us some Ale.   5
And a pleasant fire, our souls to regale:
We'd sing and we'd pray all the live-long day:
Nor ever once wish from the Church to stray.

Then the Parson might preach & drink & sing.
And we'd be as happy as birds in the spring: 10
And modest dame Lurch, who is always at Church
Would not have bandy children nor fasting, nor birch

And God like a father rejoicing to see.
His children as pleasant and happy as he:
Would have no more quarrel with the Devil or the Barrel   15
But kiss him & give him both drink and apparel.

[Plate 40 (47)]

*The Human Abstract**

Pity would be no more,
If we did not make somebody Poor;
And Mercy no more could be.
If all were as happy as we;

And mutual fear brings peace;   5
Till the selfish loves increase.
Then Cruelty knits a snare,
And spreads his baits with care.

He sits down with holy fears.
And waters the ground with tears: 10
Then Humility takes its root
Underneath his foot.

Soon spreads the dismal shade
Of Mystery over his head;*
And the Catterpiller and Fly.   15
Feed on the Mystery.

And it bears the fruit of Deceit.
Ruddy and sweet to eat:
And the Raven his nest has made*
In its thickest shade.   20

The Gods of the earth and sea,
Sought thro' Nature to find this Tree
But their search was all in vain:
There grows one in the Human Brain

[Plates 41–2 (34–5)]

*The Little Girl Lost**

In futurity
I prophetic see.
That the earth from sleep.
(Grave the sentence deep)

Shall arise and seek   5
For her maker meek:
And the desart wild
Become a garden mild.

In the southern clime,
Where the summer's prime.   10
Never fades away;
Lovely Lyca lay.

Seven summers old
Lovely Lyca told,
She had wanderd long.   15
Hearing wild birds song.

Sweet sleep, come to me
Underneath this tree.
Do father, mother weep.—
'Where can Lyca sleep'.   20

Lost in desart wild
Is your little child.
How can Lyca sleep.
If her mother weep.

If her heart does ake.   25
Then let Lyca wake;
If my mother sleep,
Lyca shall not weep.

Frowning, frowning night,
O'er this desart bright.
Let thy moon arise.
While I close my eyes.

30

Sleeping Lyca lay:
While the beasts of prey,
Come from caverns deep,
View'd the maid asleep

35

The kingly lion stood
And the virgin view'd,
Then he gambold round
O'er the hallowd ground:

40

Leopards, tygers play,
Round her as she lay;
While the lion old,
Bow'd his mane of gold,

And her bosom lick,
And upon her neck,
From his eyes of flame,
Ruby tears there came;

45

While the lioness,
Loos'd her slender dress,
And naked they convey'd
To caves the sleeping maid.

50

[Plates 43–4 (35–6)]

The Little Girl Found

All the night in woe,
Lyca's parents go:
Over vallies deep.
While the desarts weep.

Tired and woe-begone.
Hoarse with making moan:
Arm in arm seven days.
They trac'd the desart ways.

5

Seven nights they sleep.
Among shadows deep: 10
And dream they see their child
Starv'd in desart wild.

Pale, thro' pathless ways
The fancied image strays.
Famish'd, weeping, weak   15
With hollow piteous shriek

Rising from unrest,
The trembling woman prest,
With feet of weary woe;
She could no further go.   20

In his arms he bore.
Her arm'd with sorrow sore:
Till before their way,
A couching lion lay.

Turning back was vain,   25
Soon his heavy mane.
Bore them to the ground;
Then he stalk'd around.

Smelling to his prey,
But their fears allay.   30
When he licks their hands:
And silent by them stands.

They look upon his eyes
Fill'd with deep surprise:
And wondering behold.   35
A Spirit arm'd in gold.

On his head a crown
On his shoulders down,
Flow'd his golden hair.
Gone was all their care.   40

Follow me he said,
Weep not for the maid;

In my palace deep.
Lyca lies asleep.

Then they followed,   45
Where the vision led;
And saw their sleeping child,
Among tygers wild.

To this day they dwell
In a lonely dell   50
Nor fear the wolvish howl,
Nor the lions growl.

[Plate 45 (50)]

*A Little Boy Lost**

Nought loves another as itself
Nor venerates another so.
Nor is it possible to Thought
A greater than itself to know:*

And Father, how can I love you,   5
Or any of my brothers more?
I love you like the little bird
That picks up crumbs around the door.

The Priest sat by and heard the child,
In trembling zeal he siez'd his hair: 10
He led him by his little coat:
And all admir'd the Priestly care.

And standing on the altar high.
Lo! what a fiend is here! said he:
One who sets reason up for judge   15
Of our most holy Mystery.*

The weeping child could not be heard,
The weeping parents wept in vain:
They strip'd him to his little shirt.
And bound him in an iron chain.   20

And burn'd him in a holy place.*
Where many had been burn'd before:
The weeping parents wept in vain.
Are such things done on Albions shore.

[Plate 46 (37)]

The Chimney Sweeper*

A little black thing among the snow:
Crying weep, weep, in notes of woe!
Where are thy father & mother? say?
They are both gone up to the church to pray.

Because I was happy upon the heath.*   5
And smil'd among the winters snow:
They clothed me in the clothes of death.
And taught me to sing the notes of woe.

And because I am happy. & dance & sing.
They think they have done me no injury: 10
And are gone to praise God & his Priest & King*
Who make up a heaven of our misery.

[Plate 47 (40)]

The Fly*

Little Fly
Thy summers play,
My thoughtless hand
Has brush'd away.

Am not I   5
A fly like thee?
Or art not thou
A man like me?

For I dance,
And drink & sing;   10
Till some blind hand
Shall brush my wing.

If thought is life
And strength & breath;
And the want   15
Of thought is death;

Then am I
A happy fly,
If I live,
Or if I die.   20

[Plate 48 (49)]

*A Poison Tree**

I was angry with my friend;
I told my wrath, my wrath did end.
I was angry with my foe:
I told it not, my wrath did grow.

And I waterd it in fears,   5
Night & morning with my tears:
And I sunned it with smiles,
And with soft deceitful wiles.

And it grew both day and night,
Till it bore an apple bright.   10
And my foe beheld it shine,
And he knew that it was mine.

And into my garden stole.
When the night had veil'd the pole;
In the morning glad I see,   15
My foe outstretchd beneath the tree.

[Plate 49 (46)]

*London**

I wander thro' each charter'd street.*
Near where the charter'd Thames does flow
And mark in every face I meet
Marks of weakness, marks of woe.

In every cry of every Man.   5
In every Infants cry of fear.
In every voice; in every ban.*
The mind-forg'd manacles I hear*

How the Chimney-sweepers cry
Every blackning Church appalls;   10
And the hapless Soldiers sigh
Runs in blood down Palace walls*

But most thro' midnight streets I hear
How the youthful Harlots curse
Blasts the new born Infants tear   15
And blights with plagues the Marriage hearse*

[Plate 50 (42)]

*The Tyger**

Tyger Tyger. burning bright,
In the forests of the night;
What immortal hand or eye.
Could frame thy fearful symmetry?*

In what distant deeps or skies.   5
Burnt the fire of thine eyes?
On what wings dare he aspire?
What the hand dare sieze the fire?

And what shoulder, & what art,
Could twist the sinews of thy heart?   10
And when thy heart began to beat.
What dread hand? & what dread feet?

What the hammer? what the chain,
In what furnace was thy brain?
What the anvil? what dread grasp.   15
Dare its deadly terrors clasp?

When the stars threw down their spears*
And water'd heaven with their tears:
Did he smile his work to see?
Did he who made the Lamb make thee?   20

Tyger Tyger! burning bright,
In the forests of the night:
What immortal hand or eye,
Dare frame thy fearful symmetry?

[Plate 51 (43)]

My Pretty Rose Tree

A flower was offerd to me;
Such a flower as May never bore.
But I said I've a Pretty Rose-tree.
And I passed the sweet flower o'er.

Then I went to my Pretty Rose-tree: 5
To tend her by day and by night.
But my Rose turnd away with jealousy:
And her thorns were my only delight.

*Ah! Sun-Flower**

Ah Sun-flower! weary of time.
Who countest the steps of the Sun:*
Seeking after that sweet golden clime
Where the travellers journey is done.

Where the Youth pined away with desire,   5
And the pale Virgin shrouded in snow:
Arise from their graves and aspire.
Where my Sun-flower wishes to go.

*The Lilly**

The modest Rose puts forth a thorn:
The humble Sheep, a threat'ning horn:
While the Lilly white, shall in Love delight,
Nor a thorn nor a threat stain her beauty bright

[Plate 52 (33)]

*Holy Thursday**

Is this a holy thing to see.
In a rich and fruitful land.
Babes reducd to misery.
Fed with cold and usurous hand?

Is that trembling cry a song?   5
Can it be a song of joy?
And so many children poor?
It is a land of poverty!

And their sun does never shine.
And their fields are bleak & bare.   10
And their ways are fill'd with thorns
It is eternal winter there.

For where-e'er the sun does shine
And where-e'er the rain does fall:
Babe can never hunger there,   15
Nor poverty the mind appall.

[Plate 53 (32)]

*The Clod & the Pebble**

Love seeketh not Itself to please.
Nor for itself hath any care;
But for another gives its ease.
And builds a Heaven in Hell's despair.

    So sung a little Clod of Clay,   5
    Trodden with the cattles feet;
    But a Pebble of the brook.
    Warbled out these metres meet.

Love seeketh only Self to please,
To bind another to Its delight;   10
Joys in anothers loss of ease.
And builds a Hell in Heaven's despite.

Poems Added to Later Copies of *Songs of Innocence and of Experience*

[Plate 52]

*To Tirzah**

Whate'er is Born of Mortal Birth,
Must be consumed with the Earth
To rise from Generation free:*
Then what have I to do with thee?*

The Sexes sprung from Shame & Pride   5
Blowd in the morn; in evening died
But Mercy changd Death into Sleep;
The Sexes rose to work & weep.

Thou, Mother of my Mortal part.
With cruelty didst mould my Heart.   10
And with false self-decieving tears.
Didst bind my Nostrils Eyes & Ears

Didst close my Tongue in senseless clay
And me to Mortal Life betray:
The Death of Jesus set me free.   15
Then what have I to do with thee?

[Plate b]

*A Divine Image**

Cruelty has a Human Heart
And Jealousy a Human Face
Terror. the Human Form Divine,
And Secrecy. the Human Dress.

The Human Dress is forged Iron,   5
The Human Form a fiery Forge,
The Human Face. a Furnace seal'd,
The Human Heart. its hungry Gorge.

Lyrics from *the Marriage of Heaven and Hell**

[Plate 2]

*The Argument**

Rintrah roars & shakes his fires in the burdend air;*
Hungry clouds swag on the deep*

Once meek, and in a perilous path,
The just man kept his course along
The vale of death.   5
Roses are planted where thorns grow,
And on the barren heath
Sing the honey bees.

Then the perilous path was planted:
And a river, and a spring   10
On every cliff and tomb;
And on the bleached bones*
Red clay brought forth.*

Till the villain left the paths of ease,
To walk in perilous paths, and drive   15
The just man into barren climes.

Now the sneaking serpent walks
In mild humility.
And the just man rages in the wilds
Where lions roam.   20

Rintrah roars & shakes his fires in the burdend air;
Hungry clouds swag on the deep.

[Plates 25–7]

*A Song of Liberty**

1. The Eternal Female groand! it was heard over all the Earth:*
2. Albions coast is sick silent; the American meadows faint!*

3. Shadows of Prophecy shiver along by the lakes and the rivers and mutter across the ocean, France rend down thy dungeon;*

4. Golden Spain burst the barriers of old Rome;

5. Cast thy keys O Rome into the deep down falling, even to eternity down falling,*

6. And weep*

7. In her trembling hands she took the new born terror howling;*

8. On those infinite mountains* of light now barr'd out by the atlantic sea, the new born fire stood before the starry king!*

9. Flag'd with grey brow'd snows and thunderous visages the jealous wings wav'd over the deep.

10. The speary hand burned aloft, unbuckled was the shield, forth went the hand of jealousy among the flaming hair. and hurl'd the new born wonder thro' the starry night.

11. The fire, the fire, is falling!

12. Look up! look up! O citizen of London enlarge thy countenance; O Jew, leave counting gold! return to thy oil and wine: O African! black African! (go. winged thought widen his forehead.)

13. The fiery limbs, the flaming hair, shot like the sinking sun into the western sea.

14. Wak'd from his eternal sleep, the hoary element roaring fled away;*

15. Down rushd beating his wings in vain the jealous king; his grey brow'd councellors, thunderous warriors, curl'd veterans. among helms, and shields, and chariots horses. elephants: banners, castles. slings and rocks,

16. Falling, rushing, ruining! buried in the ruins, on Urthona's dens.*

17. All night beneath the ruins, then their sullen flames faded emerge round the gloomy king,

18. With thunder and fire: leading his starry hosts thro' the waste wilderness he promulgates his ten commands, glancing his beamy eyelids over the deep in dark dismay,*

19. Where the son of fire in his eastern cloud, while the morning plumes her golden breast.

20. Spurning the clouds written with curses. stamps the stony law to dust, loosing the eternal horses* from the dens of night. crying Empire is no more! and now the lion & wolf shall cease.*

CHORUS

Let the Priests of the Raven of dawn. no longer in deadly black, with hoarse note curse the sons of joy. Nor his accepted brethren* whom.

tyrant, he calls free: lay the bound or build the roof. Nor pale religious letchery call that virginity. that wishes but acts not!

    For every thing that lives is Holy

Lyrics from the 'Notebook', *c*.1793–1811

    Silent Silent Night
    Quench the holy light
    Of thy torches bright

    For possessd of Day
    Thousand spirits stray   5
    That sweet joys betray

    Why should joys be sweet
    Used with deceit
    Nor with sorrows meet

    But an honest joy   10
    Does itself destroy
    For a harlot coy

         *   *   *

*The Wild Flowers Song**

    As I wandered the forest
    The green leaves among
    I heard a wild flower
    Singing a song

    I slept in the dark   5
    In the silent night
    I murmured my fears
    And I felt delight

    In the morning I went
    As rosy as morn   10

To seek for new Joy
But I met with scorn

* * *

Love to faults is always blind*
Always is to joy inclind
Lawless wingd & unconfined
And breaks all chains from every mind

Deceit to secrecy confind   5
Lawful cautious & refind
To every thing but interest blind
And forges fetters for the mind

* * *

Are not the joys of morning sweeter
Than the joys of night
And are the vigorous joys of youth
Ashamed of the light

Let age & sickness silent rob   5
The vineyards in the night
But those who burn with vigorous youth
Pluck fruits before the light

* * *

An old maid early eer I knew
Ought but the love that on me grew
And now Im coverd oer & oer
And wish that I had been a Whore

O I cannot cannot find   5
The undaunted courage of a Virgin Mind
For Early I in love was crost
Before my flower of love was lost

Morning*

To find the western path
Right thro the gates of Wrath
I urge my Way
Sweet Mercy leads me on

With soft repentant moan   5
I see the break of day

The war of swords & spears
Melted by dewy tears
Exhales on high
The Sun is freed from fears   10
And with soft grateful tears
Ascends the Sky

BALLADS*

Gwin, King of Norway*

Come, Kings, and listen to my song,
    When Gwin, the son of Nore,
Over the nations of the North
    His cruel sceptre bore:

The Nobles of the land did feed   5
    Upon the hungry Poor;
They tear the poor man's lamb, and drive
    The needy from their door!

The land is desolate; our wives
    And children cry for bread;   10
Arise, and pull the tyrant down;
    Let Gwin be humbled.

Gordred the giant rous'd himself*
    From sleeping in his cave;
He shook the hills, and in the clouds   15
    The troubl'd banners wave.

Beneath them roll'd, like tempests black,
    The num'rous sons of blood;
Like lions' whelps, roaring abroad,
    Seeking their nightly food.   20

Down Bleron's hills they dreadful rush,
    Their cry ascends the clouds;
The trampling horse, and clanging arms
    Like rushing mighty floods!

Their wives and children, weeping loud,   25
    Follow in wild array,
Howling like ghosts, furious as wolves
    In the bleak wintry day.

'Pull down the tyrant to the dust,
    'Let Gwin be humbled,'
They cry; and let ten thousand lives   30
    'Pay for the tyrant's head.'

From tow'r to tow'r the watchmen cry,
    'O Gwin, the son of Nore,
'Arouse thyself! the nations black,   35
    Like clouds, come rolling o'er!'

Gwin rear'd his shield, his palace shakes,
    His chiefs come rushing round;
Each, like an awful thunder cloud,
    With voice of solemn sound: 40

Like reared stones around a grave
    They stand around the King;
Then suddenly each seiz'd his spear,
    And clashing steel does ring.

The husbandman does leave his plow,   45
    To wade thro' fields of gore;
The merchant binds his brows in steel,
    And leaves the trading shore:

The shepherd leaves his mellow pipe,
    And sounds the trumpet shrill;   50
The workman throws his hammer down
    To heave the bloody bill.

Like the tall ghost of Barraton,
    Who sports in stormy sky,
Gwin leads his host as black as night,   55
    When pestilence does fly.

With horses and with chariots—
    And all his spearmen bold,
March to the sound of mournful song,
    Like clouds around him roll'd.   60

Gwin lifts his hand—the nations halt;
    'Prepare for war,' he cries——
Gordred appears!—his frowning brow
    Troubles our northern skies.

The armies stand, like balances 65
  Held in th' Almighty's hand;—
'Gwin, thou hast fill'd thy measure up,
  'Thou'rt swept from out the land.'

And now the raging armies rush'd,
  Like warring mighty seas; 70
The Heav'ns are shook with roaring war,
  The dust ascends the skies!

Earth smokes with blood, and groans, and shakes,
  To drink her childrens' gore,
A sea of blood; nor can the eye 75
  See to the trembling shore!

And on the verge of this wild sea
  Famine and death doth cry;
The cries of women and of babes
  Over the field doth fly. 80

The King is seen raging afar,
  With all his men of might;
Like blazing comets, scattering death
  Thro' the red fev'rous night.

Beneath his arm like sheep they die, 85
  And groan upon the plain;
The battle faints, and bloody men
  Fight upon hills of slain.

Now death is sick, and riven men
  Labour and toil for life; 90
Steed rolls on steed, and shield on shield,
  Sunk in this sea of strife!

The god of war is drunk with blood,
  The earth doth faint and fail;
The stench of blood makes sick the heav'ns; 95
  Ghosts glut the throat of hell!

O what have Kings to answer for,
  Before that awful throne!
When thousand deaths for vengeance cry,
  And ghosts accusing groan! 100

Like blazing comets in the sky,
That shake the stars of light,
Which drop like fruit unto the earth,
Thro' the fierce burning night;

Like these did Gwin and Gordred meet,   105
And the first blow decides;
Down from the brow unto the breast
Gordred his head divides!

Gwin fell; the Sons of Norway fled,
All that remain'd alive;   110
The rest did fill the vale of death,
For them the eagles strive.

The river Dorman roll'd their blood
Into the northern sea;
Who mourn'd his sons, and overwhelm'd   115
The pleasant south country.

[Quid the Cynic's First Song]*

When old corruption first begun
Adornd in yellow vest
He committed on flesh a whoredom
O what a wicked beast

2

From them a callow babe did spring   5
And old corruption smild
To think his race should never end
For now he had a child

3

He calld him Surgery & fed
The babe with his own milk   10
For flesh & he could neer agree
She would not let him suck

4

And this he always kept in mind
And formd a crooked knife

And ran about with bloody hands   15
To seek his mothers life

5

And as he ran to seek his mother
He met with a dead woman
He fell in love & married her
A deed which is not common   20

6

She soon grew pregnant & brought forth
Scurvy & spotted fever
The father grind and skipt about
And said I'm made for ever

7

For now I have procurd these imps   25
Ill try experiments
With that he tied poor scurvy down
& stopt up all its vents

8

And when the child began to swell
He shouted out aloud   30
Ive found the dropsy out & soon
Shall do the world more good

9

He took up fever by the neck
And cut out all its spots
And thro the holes which he had made   35
He first discovered guts

*   *   *

Fayette beheld the King & Queen*
In tears & iron bound
But mute Fayette wept tear for tear
And guarded them around

Let the Brothels of Paris be opened   5
With many an alluring dance
To awake the Physicians thro the city
Said the beautiful Queen of France

The King awoke on his couch of gold
As soon as he heard these tidings told   10
Arise & come both fife and drum
And the [Famine] shall eat both crust & crumb

The Queen of France just touchd this Globe
And the Pestilence darted from her robe
But our good Queen quite grows to the ground   15
And a great many suckers grow all around

Who will exchange his own fire side
For the steps of anothers door
Who will exchange his wheaten loaf
For the links of a dungeon floor   20

O who would smile on the wintry seas
Or Pity the stormy roar
Or who will exchange his new born child
For the dog at the wintry door

* * *

I asked a thief to steal me a peach*
He turned up his eyes
I ask'd a lithe lady to lie her down
Holy & meek she cries—

As soon as I went   5
An angel came.
He wink'd at the thief
And smild at the dame—

And without one word said
Had a peach from the tree   10
And still as a maid
Enjoy'd the lady.

* * *

Never pain to tell thy Love*
Love that never told can be
For the gentle wind does move
Silently invisibly

I told my love I told my love,   5
I told her all my heart

Trembling cold in ghastly fears
Ah she doth depart

Soon as she was gone from me
A traveller came by   10
Silently, invisibly
O, was no deny.

        *   *   *

I laid me down upon a bank
Where love lay sleeping
I heard among the rushes dank
Weeping Weeping

Then I went to the heath & the wild   5
To the thistles & thorns of the waste
And they told how they were beguild
Driven out & compelld to be chaste

        *   *   *

I saw a chapel all of gold
That none did dare to enter in
And many weeping stood without
Weeping mourning worshipping

I saw a serpent rise between   5
The white pillars of the door
And he forcd & forcd & forcd
Down the golden hinges tore

And along the pavement sweet
Set with pearls & rubies bright   10
All his slimy length he drew
Till upon the altar white

Vomiting his poison out
On the bread & on the wine
So I turnd into a sty   15
And laid me down among the swine

        *   *   *

I fear'd the fury of my wind
Would blight all blossoms fair & true
And my sun it shind & shind
And my wind it never blew

But a blossom fair or true   5
Was not found on any tree
For all blossoms grew & grew
Fruitless false tho fair to see

In a mirtle shade

Why should I be bound to thee
O my lovely mirtle tree
Love free love cannot be bound
To any tree that grows on ground

O how sick & weary I   5
Underneath my mirtle lie
Like to dung upon the ground
Underneath my mirtle bound

Oft my mirtle sighd in vain
To behold my heavy chain   10
Oft my father saw us sigh,
And laughd at our simplicity

So I smote him & his gore
Staind the roots my mirtle bore
But the time of youth is fled   15
And grey hairs are on my head

The Mental Traveller*

I traveld thro' a Land of Men
A Land of Men & Women too
And heard & saw such dreadful things
As cold Earth wanderers never knew

For there the Babe is born in joy   5
That was begotten in dire woe
Just as we Reap in joy the fruit
Which we in bitter tears did sow*

And if the Babe is born a Boy
He's given to a Woman Old*   10

Who nails him down upon a rock
Catches his Shrieks in Cups of gold

She binds iron thorns around his head
She pierces both his hands & feet
She cuts his heart out at his side   15
To make it feel both cold & heat

Her fingers number every Nerve
Just as a Miser counts his gold
She lives upon his shrieks & cries
And she grows young as he grows old   20

Till he becomes a bleeding youth
And she becomes a Virgin bright
Then he rends up his Manacles
And binds her down for his delight

He plants himself in all her Nerves   25
Just as a Husbandman his mould
And She becomes his dwelling place
And Garden fruitful seventy fold

An aged Shadow, soon he fades
Wandring round an Earthly Cot   30
Full filled all with gems & gold
Which he by industry had got

And these are the gems of the Human Soul
The rubies & pearls of a lovesick eye
The countless gold of the akeing heart   35
The martyrs groan & the lovers sigh

They are his meat they are his drink
He feeds the Beggar & the Poor
And the way faring Traveller
For ever open is his door   40

His grief is their eternal joy
They make the roofs & walls to ring
Till from the fire on the hearth
A little Female Babe does spring

And she is all of solid fire   45
And gems & gold that none his hand

Dares stretch to touch her Baby form
Or wrap her in his swaddling-band

But She comes to the Man she loves
If young or old or rich or poor   50
They soon drive out the aged Host
A Beggar at anothers door

He wanders weeping far away
Untill some other take him in
Oft blind & age-bent sore distrest   55
Untill he can a Maiden win

And to allay his freezing Age*
The Poor Man takes her in his arms
The Cottage fades before his sight
The Garden & its lovely Charms   60

The Guests are scatterd thro' the land
For the Eye altering alters all
The Senses roll themselves in fear
And the flat Earth becomes a Ball

The Stars Sun Moon all shrink away   65
A desart vast without a bound
And nothing left to eat or drink
And a dark desart all around

The honey of her Infant lips
The bread & wine of her sweet smile   70
The wild game of her roving Eye
Does him to Infancy beguile

For as he eats & drinks he grows
Younger & younger every day
And on the desart wild they both   75
Wander in terror & dismay

Like the wild Stag she flees away
Her fear plants many a thicket wild
While he pursues her night & day
By various arts of Love beguild   80

By various arts of Love & Hate
Till the wide desart planted oer

With Labyrinths of wayward Love
Where roams the Lion Wolf & Boar

Till he becomes a wayward Babe   85
And she a weeping Woman Old
Then many a Lover wanders here
The Sun & Stars are nearer rolld

The trees bring forth sweet Extacy
To all who in the desert roam   90
Till many a City there is Built
And many a pleasant Shepherds home

But when they find the frowning Babe
Terror strikes thro the region wide
They cry the Babe the Babe is Born   95
And flee away on Every side

For who dare touch the frowning form
His arm is witherd to its root
Lions Boars Wolves all howling flee
And every Tree does shed its fruit   100

And none can touch that frowning form
Except it be a Woman Old
She nails him down upon the Rock
And all is done as I have told

The Land of Dreams

Awake Awake my little Boy
Thou wast thy Mothers only joy
Why dost thou weep in thy gentle sleep
Awake thy Father does thee keep

O what Land is the Land of Dreams   5
What are its Mountains & what are its Streams
O Father I saw my Mother there
Among the Lillies by waters fair

Among the Lambs clothed in white
She walkd with her Thomas in sweet delight   10
I wept for joy like a dove I mourn
O when shall I again return

Dear Child I also by pleasant Streams
Have wanderd all Night in the Land of Dreams
But tho calm & warm the waters wide   15
I could not get to the other side

Father O Father what do we here
In this Land of unbelief & fear
The Land of Dreams is better far
Above the light of the Morning Star   20

*Mary**

Sweet Mary the first time she ever was there
Came into the Ball room among the Fair
The young Men & Maidens around her throng
And these are the words upon every tongue

An Angel is here from the heavenly Climes   5
Or again does return the Golden times
Her eyes outshine every brilliant ray
She opens her lips tis the Month of May

Mary moves in soft beauty & conscious delight
To augment with sweet smiles all the joys of the Night 10
Nor once blushes to own to the rest of the Fair
That sweet Love & Beauty are worthy our care

In the Morning the Villagers rose with delight
And repeated with pleasure the joys of the night
And Mary arose among Friends to be free   15
But no Friend from henceforward thou Mary shalt see

Some said she was proud some calld her a whore
And some when she passed by shut to the door
A damp cold came oer her her blushes all fled
Her lillies & roses are blighted & shed   20

O why was I born with a different Face
Why was I not born like this Envious Race
Why did Heaven adorn me with bountiful hand
And then set me down in an envious Land

To be weak as a Lamb & smooth as a dove   25
And not to raise Envy is calld Christian Love

But if you raise Envy your Merits to blame
For planting such spite in the weak & the tame

I will humble my Beauty I will not dress fine
I will keep from the Ball & my Eyes shall not shine   30
And if any Girls Lover forsakes her for me
I'll refuse him my hand & from Envy be free

She went out in Morning attird plain & neat
Proud Marys gone Mad said the Child in the Street
She went out in Morning in plain neat attire   35
And came home in Evening bespatterd with mire

She trembled & wept sitting on the Bed side
She forgot it was Night, & she trembled & cried
She forgot it was Night she forgot it was Morn
Her soft Memory imprinted with Faces of Scorn   40

With Faces of Scorn & with Eyes of disdain
Like foul Fiends inhabiting Marys mild Brain
She remembers no Face like the Human Divine
All Faces have Envy sweet Mary but thine

And thine is a Face of sweet Love in Despair   45
And thine is a Face of mild sorrow & care
And thine is a Face of wild terror & fear
That shall never be quiet till laid on its bier

The Crystal Cabinet

The Maiden caught me in the Wild
Where I was dancing merrily
She put me into her Cabinet
And Lockd me up with a golden Key

This Cabinet is formd of Gold   5
And Pearl & Crystal shining bright
And within it opens into a World
And a little lovely Moony Night*

Another England there I saw
Another London with its Tower   10
Another Thames & other Hills
And another pleasant Surrey Bower

Another Maiden like herself
Translucent lovely shining clear
Threefold each in the other closd   15
O what a pleasant trembling fear

O what a smile a threefold Smile
Filld me that like a flame I burnd
I bent to Kiss the lovely Maid
And found a Threefold Kiss returnd   20

I strove to sieze the inmost Form
With ardor fierce & hands of flame
But burst the Crystal Cabinet
And like a Weeping Babe became

A weeping Babe upon the wild   25
And Weeping Woman pale reclind
And in the outward air again
I filld with woes the passing Wind

*The Grey Monk**

I die I die the Mother said
My Children die for lack of Bread
What more has the merciless Tyrant said
The Monk sat down on the Stony Bed

The blood red ran from the Grey Monks side   5
His hands & feet were wounded wide
His Body bent his arms & knees
Like to the roots of ancient trees

His eye was dry no tear could flow
A hollow groan first spoke his woe   10
He trembled & shudderd upon the Bed
At length with a feeble cry he said

When God commanded this hand to write
In the studious hours of deep midnight
He told me the writing I wrote should prove   15
The Bane of all that on Earth I lovd

My Brother starvd between two Walls
His Childrens Cry my Soul appalls

I mockd at the wrack & griding chain
My bent body mocks their torturing pain   20

Thy Father drew his sword in the North
With his thousands strong he marched forth
Thy Brother has armd himself in Steel
To avenge the wrongs thy Children feel

But vain the Sword & vain the Bow   25
They never can work Wars overthrow
The Hermits Prayer & the Widows tear
Alone can free the World from fear

For a Tear is an Intellectual Thing
And a Sigh is the Sword of an Angel King   30
And the bitter groan of the Martyrs woe
Is an Arrow from the Almighties Bow

The hand of Vengeance found the Bed
To which the Purple Tyrant fled
The iron hand crushd the Tyrants head   35
And became a Tyrant in his Stead

Long John Brown & Little Mary Bell

Little Mary Bell had a Fairy in a Nut
Long John Brown had the devil in his Gut
Long John Brown lovd Little Mary Bell
And the Fairy drew the devil into the Nut-shell

Her Fairy skipd out & her Fairy skipd in   5
He laughd at the devil saying Love is a Sin
The devil he raged & the devil he was wroth
And the devil enterd into the Young Mans broth

He was soon in the Gut of the loving Young Swain
For John eat & drank to drive away Loves pain   10
But all he could do he grew thinner & thinner
Tho he eat & drank as much as ten Men for his dinner

Some said he had a Wolf in his stomach day & night
Some said he had the Devil & they guessd right

The fairy skipd about in his glory Joy & Pride 15
And he laughd at the devil till poor John Brown died

Then the Fairy skipd out of the old Nut shell
And woe & alack for Pretty Mary Bell
For the Devil crept in when the Fairy skipd out
And there goes Miss Bell with her fusty old Nut 20

William Bond

I wonder whether the Girls are mad
And I wonder whether they mean to kill
And I wonder if William Bond will die
For assuredly he is very ill

He went to Church in a May morning 5
Attended by Fairies one two & three
But the Angels of Providence drove them away
And he returnd home in Misery

He went not out to the Field nor Fold
He went not out to the Village nor Town 10
But he came home in a black black cloud
And took to his Bed & there lay down

And an Angel of Providence at his Feet
And an Angel of Providence at his Head
And in the midst a Black Black Cloud 15
And in the midst the Sick Man on his Bed

And on his Right hand was Mary Green
And on his Left hand was his Sister Jane
And their tears fell thro the black black Cloud
To drive away the sick mans pain 20

O William if thou dost another Love
Dost another Love better than poor Mary
Go & take that other to be thy Wife
And Mary Green shall her Servant be

Yes Mary I do another Love 25
Another I Love far better than thee
And Another I will have for my Wife
Then what have I to do with thee

For thou art Melancholy Pale
And on thy Head is the cold Moons shine   30
But she is ruddy & bright as day
And the sun beams dazzle from her eyne

Mary trembled & Mary chilld
And Mary fell down on the right hand floor
That William Bond & his Sister Jane   35
Scarce could recover Mary more

When Mary woke & found her Laid
On the Right hand of her William dear
On the Right hand of his loved Bed
And saw her William Bond so near   40

The Fairies that fled from William Bond
Danced around her Shining Head
They danced over the Pillow white
And the Angels of Providence left the Bed

I thought Love livd in the hot sun Shine   45
But O he lives in the Moony light*
I thought to find Love in the heat of day
But sweet Love is the Comforter of Night

Seek Love in the Pity of others Woe
In the gentle relief of anothers care   50
In the darkness of night & the winters snow
In the naked & outcast Seek Love there

NARRATIVE POEMS

*Fair Elenor**

The bell struck one, and shook the silent tower;
The graves give up their dead: fair Elenor
Walk'd by the castle gate, and looked in.
A hollow groan ran thro' the dreary vaults.

She shriek'd aloud, and sunk upon the steps   5
On the cold stone her pale cheek. Sickly smells
Of death, issue as from a sepulchre,
And all is silent but the sighing vaults.

Chill death withdraws his hand, and she revives;
Amaz'd, she finds herself upon her feet,   10
And, like a ghost, thro' narrow passages
Walking, feeling the cold walls with her hands.

Fancy returns, and now she thinks of bones,
And grinning skulls, and corruptible death,
Wrap'd in his shroud; and now fancies she hears   15
Deep sighs, and sees pale sickly ghosts gliding.

At length, no fancy, but reality
Distracts her. A rushing sound, and the feet
Of one that fled, approaches—Ellen stood,
Like a dumb statue, froze to stone with fear.   20

The wretch approaches, crying, 'The deed is done;
'Take this, and send it by whom thou wilt send;
'It is my life—send it to Elenor:—
'He's dead, and howling after me for blood!

'Take this', he cry'd; and thrust into her arms   25
A wet napkin, wrap'd about; then rush'd
Past, howling: she receiv'd into her arms
Pale death, and follow'd on the wings of fear.

They pass'd swift thro' the outer gate; the wretch,
Howling, leap'd o'er the wall into the moat,   30
Stifling in mud. Fair Ellen pass'd the bridge,
And heard a gloomy voice cry, 'Is it done?'

As the deer wounded, Ellen flew over
The pathless plain; as the arrows that fly
By night, destruction flies, and strikes in darkness.   35
She fled from fear, till at her house arriv'd.

Her maids await her; on her bed she falls,
That bed of joy, where erst her lord hath press'd:
'Ah, woman's-fear!' she cry'd; 'Ah, cursed duke!
'Ah, my dear lord! ah, wretched Elenor!   40

'My lord was like a flower upon the brows
'Of lusty May! Ah, life as frail as flower!
'O ghastly death! withdraw thy cruel hand,
'Seek'st thou that flow'r to deck thy horrid temples?

'My lord was like a star, in highest heav'n   45
'Drawn down to earth by spells and wickedness;
'My lord was like the opening eyes of day,
'When western winds creep softly o'er the flowers:

'But he is darken'd; like the summer's noon,
'Clouded; fall'n like the stately tree, cut down;   50
'The breath of heaven dwelt among his leaves.
'O Elenor, weak woman, fill'd with woe!'

Thus having spoke, she raised up her head,
And saw the bloody napkin by her side,
Which in her arms she brought; and now, tenfold   55
More terrified, saw it unfold itself.

Her eyes were fix'd; the bloody cloth unfolds,
Disclosing to her sight the murder'd head
Of her dear lord, all ghastly pale, clotted
With gory blood; it groan'd, and thus it spake: 60

'O Elenor, I am thy husband's head,*
'Who, sleeping on the stones of yonder tower,
'Was 'reft of life by the accursed duke!
'A hired villain turn'd my sleep to death!

'O Elenor, beware the cursed duke;   65
'O give not him thy hand now I am dead;
'He seeks thy love, who, coward, in the night,
'Hired a villain to bereave my life.'

She sat with dead cold limbs, stiffen'd to stone;
She took the gory head up in her arms;   70
She kiss'd the pale lips; she had no tears to shed;
She hugg'd it to her breast, and groan'd her last.

Blind-Man's Buff

When silver Snow decks Susan's cloaths,
And jewel hangs at th' shepherd's nose,*
The blushing bank is all my care,
With hearth so red, and walls so fair;
'Heap the sea-coal; come, heap it higher,   5
'The oaken log lay on the fire:'
The well-wash'd stools, a circling row,
With lad and lass, how fair the show!
The merry can of nut-brown ale,
The laughing jest, the love-sick tale,   10
'Till, tir'd of chat, the game begins,
The lasses prick the lads with pins;
Roger from Dolly twitch'd the stool,
She falling, kiss'd the ground, poor fool!
She blush'd so red, with side-long glance   15
At hob-nail Dick, who griev'd the chance.
But now for Blind-man's Buff they call;
Of each incumbrance clear the hall—
Jenny her silken kerchief folds,
And blear-ey'd Will the black lot holds;   20
Now laughing, stops, with 'Silence! hush!'
And Peggy Pout gives Sam a push.——
The Blind-man's arms, extended wide,
Sam slips between;—'O woe betide
'Thee, clumsy Will!'—but titt'ring Kate   25
Is pen'd up in the corner strait!
And now Will's eyes beheld the play,
He thought his face was t'other way.——
'Now, Kitty, now; what chance hast thou,

'Roger so near thee, Trips; I vow!' 30
She catches him—then Roger ties
His own head up—but not his eyes;
For thro' the slender cloth he sees,
And runs at Sam, who slips with ease
His clumsy hold; and, dodging round, 35
Sukey is tumbled on the ground!——
'See what it is to play unfair!
Where cheating is, there's mischief there.'
But Roger still pursues the chace,——
'He sees! he sees!' cries softly, Grace; 40
'O Roger, thou, unskill'd in art,
'Must, surer bound, go thro' thy part!'
Now Kitty, pert, repeats the rhymes,
And Roger turns him round three times;
Then pauses ere he starts——but Dick 45
Was mischief bent upon a trick:
Down on his hands and knees he lay,
Directly in the Blind-man's way——
Then cries out, 'Hem!' Hodge heard, and ran
With hood-wink'd chance—sure of his man: 50
But down he came.—Alas, how frail
Our best of hopes, how soon they fail!
With crimson drops he stains the ground;
Confusion startles all around!
Poor piteous Dick supports his head, 55
And fain would cure the hurt he made;
But Kitty hasted with a key,
And down his back they strait convey
The cold relief—the blood is stay'd,
And Hodge again holds up his head. 60
Such are the fortunes of the game,
And those who play should stop the same
By wholesome laws; such as all those*
Who on the blinded man impose,
Stand in his stead; as long a-gone 65
When men were first a nation grown;
Lawless they liv'd—till wantonness
And liberty began t'increase;
And one man lay in another's way,
Then laws were made to keep fair play. 70

The Golden Net

Three Virgins at the break of day
Whither young Man whither away
Alas for woe! alas for woe!
They cry & tears for ever flow
The one was Clothd in flames of fire   5
The other Clothd in iron wire
The other Clothd in tears & sighs
Dazling bright before my Eyes
They bore a Net of Golden twine
To hang upon the Branches fine   10
Pitying I wept to see the woe
That Love & Beauty undergo
To be consumd in burning Fires
And in ungratified Desires
And in tears clothd Night & day   15
Melted all my Soul away
When they saw my Tears a Smile
That did Heaven itself beguile
Bore the Golden Net aloft
As on downy Pinions soft   20
Over the Morning of my day
Underneath the Net I stray
Now intreating Burning Fire
Now intreating Iron Wire
Now intreating Tears & Sighs   25
O when will the morning rise

DESCRIPTIVE AND DISCURSIVE POETRY

To Spring*

O thou, with dewy locks, who lookest down
Thro' the clear windows of the morning; turn
Thine angel eyes upon our western isle,
Which in full choir hails thy approach, O Spring!

The hills tell each other, and the list'ning   5
Vallies hear; all our longing eyes are turned
Up to thy bright pavillions: issue forth,
And let thy holy feet visit our clime.

Come o'er the eastern hills, and let our winds
Kiss thy perfumed garments; let us taste   10
Thy morn and evening breath; scatter thy pearls
Upon our love-sick land that mourns for thee.

O deck her forth with thy fair fingers; pour
Thy soft kisses on her bosom; and put
Thy golden crown upon her languish'd head,*   15
Whose modest tresses were bound up for thee!*

To Summer

O thou, who passest thro' our vallies in
Thy strength, curb thy fierce steeds, allay the heat
That flames from their large nostrils! thou, O Summer,
Oft pitched'st here thy golden tent, and oft
Beneath our oaks hast slept, while we beheld   5
With joy, thy ruddy limbs and flourishing hair.

Beneath our thickest shades we oft have heard
Thy voice, when noon upon his fervid car

Rode o'er the deep of heaven; beside our springs
Sit down, and in our mossy vallies, on   10
Some bank beside a river clear, throw thy
Silk draperies off, and rush into the stream:
Our vallies love the Summer in his pride.

Our bards are fam'd who strike the silver wire:
Our youths are bolder than the southern swains: 15
Our maidens fairer in the sprightly dance:
We lack not songs, nor instruments of joy,
Nor echoes sweet, nor waters clear as heaven,
Nor laurel wreaths against the sultry heat.

To Autumn

O Autumn, laden with fruit, and stained
With the blood of the grape, pass not, but sit
Beneath my shady roof, there thou may'st rest,
And tune thy jolly voice to my fresh pipe;
And all the daughters of the year shall dance!   5
Sing now the lusty song of fruits and flowers.

'The narrow bud opens her beauties to
'The sun, and love runs in her thrilling veins;
'Blossoms hang round the brows of morning, and
'Flourish down the bright cheek of modest eve,   10
'Till clust'ring Summer breaks forth into singing,
'And feather'd clouds strew flowers round her head.

'The spirits of the air live on the smells
'Of fruit; and joy, with pinions light, roves round
'The gardens, or sits singing in the trees.'   15
Thus sang the jolly Autumn as he sat,
Then rose, girded himself, and o'er the bleak
Hills fled from our sight; but left his golden load.

To Winter

O Winter! bar thine adamantine doors:
The north is thine; there hast thou built thy dark

Deep-founded habitation. Shake not thy roofs,
Nor bend thy pillars with thine iron car.

He hears me not, but o'er the yawning deep   5
Rides heavy; his storms are unchain'd; sheathed
In ribbed steel, I dare not lift mine eyes;
For he hath rear'd his sceptre o'er the world.

Lo! now the direful monster, whose skin clings
To his strong bones, strides o'er the groaning rocks: 10
He withers all in silence, and in* his hand
Unclothes the earth, and freezes up frail life.

He takes his seat upon the cliffs; the mariner
Cries in vain. Poor little wretch! that deal'st
With storms; till heaven smiles, and the monster   15
Is driv'n yelling to his caves beneath mount Hecla.*

To the Evening Star

Thou fair-hair'd angel of the evening,
Now, whilst the sun rests on the mountains, light
Thy bright torch of love; thy radiant crown*
Put on, and smile upon our evening bed!
Smile on our loves; and, while thou drawest the   5
Blue curtains of the sky, scatter thy silver dew
On every flower that shuts its sweet eyes
In timely sleep. Let thy west wind sleep on
The lake; speak silence with thy glimmering eyes,
And wash the dusk with silver. Soon, full soon,   10
Dost thou withdraw; then the wolf rages wide,
And the lion glares thro' the dun forest:
The fleeces of our flocks are cover'd with
Thy sacred dew: protect them with thine influence.

To Morning

O holy virgin! clad in purest white,
Unlock heav'n's golden gates, and issue forth;
Awake the dawn that sleeps in heaven; let light

Rise from the chambers of the east, and bring*
The honied dew that cometh on waking day.   5
O radiant morning, salute the sun,
Rouz'd like a huntsman to the chace; and, with
Thy buskin'd feet, appear upon our hills.

[Obtuse Angle's Song]

To be or not to be
Of great capacity
Like Sir Isaac Newton
Or Locke or Doctor South*
Or Sherlock upon death*   5
Id rather be Sutton *

For he did build a house
For aged men & youth
With walls of brick and stone
He furnishd it within   10
With whatever he could win
And all his own

He drew out of the Stocks
His money in a box
And sent his servant   15
To Green the Bricklayer
And to the Carpenter
He was so fervent

The chimneys were three score
The windows many more   20
And for convenience
He sinks & gutters made
And all the way he pavd
To hinder pestilence

Was not this a good man   25
Whose life was but a span
Whose name was Sutton
As Locke or Doctor South
Or Sherlock upon Death
Or Sir Isaac Newton

* * *

A fairy skipd upon my knee*
Singing & dancing merrily
I said Thou thing of patches rings
Pins Necklaces & such like things
Disguiser of the Female Form   5
Thou paltry gilded poisnous worm
Weeping, he fell upon my thigh
And thus in tears did soft reply
Knowest thou not O Fairies Lord
How much by us Contemnd Abhorrd   10
Whatever hides the Female form
That cannot bear the Mental storm
Therefore in Pity still we give
Our lives to make the Female live
And what would turn into disease   15
We turn to what will joy & please

Soft Snow*

I walked abroad in a snowy day:
I ask'd the soft snow with me to play:
She play'd & she melted in all her prime,
And the winter call'd it a dreadful crime.

An ancient Proverb*

Remove away that blackning church
Remove away that marriage hearse
Remove away that man of blood
You'll quite remove the ancient curse

* * *

Why should I care for the men of thames
Or the cheating waves of charterd streams*
Or shrink at the little blasts of fear
That the hireling blows into my ear

Tho born on the cheating banks of Thames
Tho his waters bathed my infant limbs   5

The Ohio shall wash his stains from me*
I was born a slave but I go to be free*

* * *

    I heard an Angel singing
    When the day was springing
    Mercy Pity Peace
    Is the worlds release

    Thus he sung all day   5
    Over the new mown hay
    Till the sun went down
    And haycocks looked brown

    I heard a Devil curse
    Over the heath & the furze   10
    Mercy could be no more
    If there was nobody poor

    And pity no more could be
    If all were as happy as we
    At his curse the sun went down   15
    And the heavens gave a frown

* * *

O lapwing thou fliest around the heath*
Nor seest the net that is spread beneath
Why dost thou not fly among the corn fields
They cannot spread nets where a harvest yields

* * *

An answer to the parson*

Why of the sheep do you not learn peace
Because I don't want you to shear my fleece

* * *

    Thou hast a lap full of seed*
    And this is a fine country
    Why dost thou not cast thy seed
    And live in it merrily

    Shall I cast it on the sand   5
    And turn it into fruitful land

For on no other ground
Can I sow my seed
Without tearing up
Some stinking weed   10

* * *

Riches

The countless gold of a merry heart*
The rubies and pearls of a loving eye
The indolent never can bring to the mart
Nor the secret hoard up in his treasury

* * *

If you trap the moment before its ripe
The tears of repentence youll certainly wipe
But if once you let the ripe moment go
You can never wipe off the tears of woe

* * *

Eternity*

He who binds to himself a joy
Does the winged life destroy
But he who kisses the joy as it flies
Lives in eternity's sun rise

* * *

The sword sung on the barren heath
The sickle in the fruitful field
The sword he sung a song of death
But could not make the sickle yield

* * *

Abstinence sows sand all over
The ruddy limbs & flaming hair
But Desire Gratified
Plants fruits of life & beauty there

* * *

In a wife I would desire
What in whores is always found
lineaments of Gratified desire

* * *

The Question Answerd

What is it men in women do require
The lineaments of Gratified Desire
What is it women do in men require
The lineaments of Gratified Desire

* * *

Merlins prophecy*

The harvest shall flourish in wintry weather
When two virginities meet together

The King & the Priest must be tied in a tether
Before two virgins can meet together

* * *

Lacedemonian Instruction*

Come hither my boy tell me what thou seest there
A fool tangled in a religious snare

* * *

Motto to the Songs of Innocence
& of Experience*

The Good are attracted by Mens perceptions
And Think not for themselves
Till Experience teaches them to catch
And to cage the Fairies & Elves

And then the Knave begins to snarl
And the Hypocrite to howl

5

And all his good Friends shew their private ends
And the Eagle is known from the Owl

* * *

On the Virginity of the Virgin Mary & Johanna Southcott*

Whateer is done to her she cannot know
And if youll ask her she will swear it so
Whether tis good or evil none's to blame
No one can take the pride no one the shame

* * *

Mock on Mock on Voltaire Rousseau*
Mock on Mock on: tis all in vain!
You throw the sand against the wind
And the wind blows it back again

And every sand becomes a Gem   5
Reflected in the beams divine
Blown back they blind the mocking Eye
But still in Israels paths they shine*

The Atoms of Democritus*
And Newtons Particles of Light*   10
Are sands upon the Red sea shore
Where Israels tents do shine so bright

* * *

My Spectre around me night & day*
Like a Wild beast guards my way
My Emanation far within
Weeps incessantly for my Sin

A Fathomless & boundless deep   5
There we wander there we weep
On the hungry craving wind
My Spectre follows thee behind

He scents thy footsteps in the snow
Wheresoever thou dost go   10
Thro the wintry hail & rain
When wilt thou return again

Dost thou not in Pride & scorn
Fill with tempests all my morn
And with jealousies & fears   15
Fill my pleasant nights with tears

Seven of my sweet loves thy knife
Has bereaved of their life
Their marble tombs I built with tears
And with cold & shuddering fears   20

Seven more loves weep night & day
Round the tombs where my loves lay
And seven more loves attend each night
Around my couch with torches bright

And seven more Loves in my bed   25
Crown with wine my mournful head
Pitying & forgiving all
Thy transgressions great and small

When wilt thou return & view
My loves and them to life renew   30
When wilt thou return & live
When wilt thou pity as I forgive

Never Never I return
Still for Victory I burn
Living thee alone Ill have   35
And when dead Ill be thy Grave

Thro the Heavn & Earth & Hell
Thou shalt never never quell
I will fly & thou pursue
Night & Morn the flight renew   40

Till I turn from Female Love
And root up the Infernal Grove
I shall never worthy be
To Step into Eternity

And to end thy cruel mocks   45
Annihilate them on the rocks
And another form create
To be subservient to my Fate

Let us agree to give up Love
And root up the infernal grove 50
Then we shall return & see
The worlds of happy Eternity

& Throughout all Eternity
I forgive you you forgive me
As our dear Redeemer said 55
This the Wine & this the Bread

* * *

Grown old in Love from Seven till Seven times Seven*
I oft have wishd for Hell for Ease from Heaven

* * *

The Smile

There is a Smile of Love
And there is a Smile of Deceit
And there is a Smile of Smiles
In which these two Smiles meet

And there is a Frown of Hate 5
And there is a Frown of disdain
And there is a Frown of Frowns
Which you strive to forget in vain

For it sticks in the Hearts deep Core
And it sticks in the deep Back bone 10
And no smile that ever was smild
But only one Smile alone

That betwixt the Cradle & Grave
It only once Smild can be
But when it once is Smild 15
Theres an end to all Misery

* * *

Auguries of Innocence*

To see a World in a Grain of Sand
And a Heaven in a Wild Flower

Hold Infinity in the palm of your hand
And Eternity in an hour
A Robin Red breast in a Cage 5
Puts all Heaven in a Rage
A dove house filld with doves & Pigeons
Shudders Hell thro all its regions
A dog starvd at his Masters Gate
Predicts the ruin of the State 10
A Horse misusd upon the Road
Calls to Heaven for Human blood
Each outcry of the hunted Hare
A fibre from the Brain does tear
A Skylark wounded in the wing 15
A Cherubim does cease to sing
The Game Cock clipd & armd for fight*
Does the Rising Sun affright
Every Wolfs & Lions howl
Raises from Hell a Human Soul 20
The wild deer wandring here & there
Keeps the Human Soul from Care
The Lamb misusd breeds Public strife
And yet forgives the Butchers Knife
The Bat that flits at close of Eve 25
Has left the Brain that wont Believe
The Owl that calls upon the Night
Speaks the Unbelievers fright
He who shall hurt the little Wren
Shall never be belovd by Men 30
He who the Ox to wrath has movd
Shall never be by Woman lovd
The wanton Boy that kills the Fly
Shall feel the Spiders enmity
He who torments the Chafers sprite* 35
Weaves a Bower in endless Night
The Catterpiller on the Leaf
Repeats to thee thy Mothers grief
Kill not the Moth nor Butterfly
For the Last Judgment draweth nigh 40
He who shall train the Horse to War
Shall never pass the Polar Bar*
The Beggers Dog & Widows Cat

Feed them & thou wilt grow fat
The Gnat that sings his Summers song   45
Poison gets from Slanders tongue
The poison of the Snake & Newt
Is the sweat of Envys Foot
The Poison of the Honey Bee
Is the Artists Jealousy   50
The Princes Robes & Beggars Rags
Are Toadstools on the Misers Bags
A Truth thats told with bad intent
Beats all the Lies you can invent
It is right it should be so   55
Man was made for Joy & Woe
And when this we rightly know
Thro the World we safely go
Joy & Woe are woven fine
A Clothing for the soul divine   60
Under every grief & pine
Runs a joy with silken twine
The Babe is more than swadling Bands
Throughout all these Human Lands
Tools were made & Born were hands   65
Every Farmer Understands
Every Tear from Every Eye
Becomes a Babe in Eternity
This is caught by Females bright
And returnd to its own delight.   70
The Bleat the Bark Bellow & Roar
Are Waves that Beat on Heavens Shore
The Babe that weeps the Rod beneath
Writes Revenge in realms of death
The Beggars Rags fluttering in Air   75
Does to Rags the Heavens tear
The Soldier armd with Sword & Gun
Palsied strikes the Summers Sun
The poor Mans Farthing is worth more
Than all the Gold on Africs Shore   80
One Mite wrung from the Labrers hands
Shall buy & sell the Misers Lands
Or if protected from on high
Does that whole Nation sell & buy

He who mocks the Infants Faith   85
Shall be mock'd in Age & Death
He who shall teach the Child to Doubt
The rotting Grave shall neer get out
He who respects the Infants faith
Triumphs over Hell & Death   90
The Childs Toys & the Old Mans Reasons
Are the Fruits of the Two seasons
The Questioner who sits so sly
Shall never know how to Reply
He who replies to words of Doubt   95
Doth put the Light of Knowledge out
The Strongest Poison ever known
Came from Caesars Laurel Crown
Nought can deform the Human Race
Like to the Armours iron brace   100
When Gold & Gems adorn the Plow
To peaceful Arts shall Envy Bow
A Riddle or the Crickets Cry
Is to Doubt a fit Reply
The Emmets Inch & Eagles Mile   105
Make Lame Philosophy to smile
He who Doubts from what he sees
Will neer Believe, do what you Please
If the Sun & Moon should doubt
Theyd immediately Go out   110
To be in a Passion you Good may do
But no Good if a Passion is in you
The Whore & Gambler by the State
Licencd build that Nations Fate
The Harlots cry from Street to Street   115
Shall weave Old Englands winding Sheet
The Winners Shout, the Losers Curse
Dance before dead Englands Hearse
Every Night & every Morn
Some to Misery are Born   120
Every Morn & every Night
Some are Born to sweet delight
Some are Born to sweet delight
Some are Born to Endless Night
We are led to Believe a Lie   125
When we see not Thro' the Eye*

Which was Born in a Night to perish in a Night*
When the Soul Slept in Beams of Light
God Appears & God is Light
To those poor Souls who dwell in Night   130
But does a Human Form Display*
To those who Dwell in Realms of day

* * *

You don't believe I wont attempt to make ye
You are asleep I wont attempt to wake ye
Sleep on Sleep on while in your pleasant dreams
Of Reason you may drink of Lifes clear streams
Reason and Newton they are quite two things   5
For so the Swallow & the Sparrow sings

Reason says Miracle Newton says Doubt
Aye that's the way to make all Nature out
Doubt Doubt & don't believe without experiment
That is the very thing that Jesus meant   10
When he said Only Believe Believe & try
Try Try & never mind the Reason why

* * *

The Angel that presided oer my birth
Said Little creature formd for Joy & Mirth
Go love without the help of any King on Earth*

* * *

All Pictures thats Painted with Sense & with Thought
Are Painted by Madmen as sure as a Groat
For the Greater the Fool in the Pencil more blest
And when they are drunk they always paint best

They never can Rafael it Fuseli it or Blake it*   5
If they can't see an outline pray how can they make it
Where Men will draw outlines [begin] you to jaw them*
Madmen see outlines & therefore they draw them

* * *

You say their Pictures well Painted be
And yet they are Blockheads you all agree
Thank God I never was sent to school
To be Flogd into following the Style of a Fool

* * *

William Cowper Esqre*

For this is being a Friend just in the nick
Not when hes well but waiting till hes sick
He calls you to his help be you not movd
Untill by being Sick his wants are provd

You see him spend his Soul in Prophecy   5
Do you believe it a Confounded lie
Till some Bookseller & the Public Fame
Proves there is truth in his extravagant claim

For tis atrocious in a Friend you love
To tell you any thing that he cant prove   10
And tis most wicked in a Christian Nation
For any Man to pretend to Inspiration

*   *   *

I rose up at the dawn of day
Get thee away get thee away
Prayst thou for Riches away away
This is the Throne of Mammon grey

Said I this sure is very odd   5
I took it to be the Throne of God
For every Thing besides I have
It is only for Riches that I can crave

I have Mental Joy & Mental Health
And Mental Friends & Mental wealth   10
Ive a Wife I love & that loves me
Ive all But Riches Bodily

I am in Gods presence night & day
And he never turns his face away
The accuser of sins by my side does stand   15
And he holds my money bag in his hand

For my worldly things God makes him pay
And hed pay for more if to him I would pray
And so you may do the worst you can do
Be assurd Mr Devil I wont pray to you   20

Then If for Riches I must not Pray
God knows I little of Prayers need say

So as a Church is known by its Steeple
If I pray it must be for other People

He says if I do not worship him for a God   25
I shall eat coarser food & go worse shod
So as I don't value such things as these
You must do Mr Devil just as God please

                    *   *   *

Was I angry with Hayley who usd me so ill*
Or can I be angry with Felphams old Mill
Or angry with Flaxman or Cromek or Stothard*
Or poor Schiavonetti whom they to death botherd*
Or angry with Macklin or Boydel or Bowyer*   5
Because they did not say O what a Beau ye are
At a Friends errors Anger Shew
Mirth at the Errors of a Foe

                    *   *   *

[The Everlasting Gospel]*

[Preface]

[(a) Notebook N52]

I will tell you what Joseph of Arimathea*
Said to my Fairy was not it very queer
Pliny & Trajan what are You here*
Come listen to Joseph of Arimathea
Listen patient & when Joseph has done   5
Twill make a fool laugh & a Fairy Fun

[(b) Notebook N52]

What can be done with such desperate Fools
Who follow after the Heathen Schools
I was standing by when Jesus died
What I calld Humility they calld Pride   10

[(c) Notebook N52–4]

The Everlasting Gospel

Was Jesus Humble or did he
Give any Proofs of Humility
Boast of high Things with Humble tone
And give with Charity a Stone
When but a Child he ran away*   15
And left his Parents in Dismay.
When they had wanderd three days long
These were the words upon his tongue
No Earthly Parents I confess
I am doing my Fathers business*   20
When the rich learned Pharisee*
Came to consult him secretly
Upon his heart with Iron pen
He wrote Ye must be born again
He was too proud to take a bribe   25
He spoke with authority not like a Scribe*
He says with most consummate Art
Follow me I am meek & lowly of heart
As that is the only way to escape
The Misers net & the Gluttons trap   30
He who loves his Enemies betrays his Friends
This surely is not what Jesus intends
But the sneaking Pride of Heroic Schools
And the Scribes & Pharisees Virtuous Rules
For he acts with honest, triumphant Pride   35
And this is the cause that Jesus died
He did not die with Christian Ease
Asking pardon of his Enemies
If he had Caiphas would forgive*
Sneaking submission can always live   40
He had only to say that God was the devil
And the devil was God like a Christian Civil
Mild Christian regrets to the devil confess
For affronting him thrice in the Wilderness
He had soon been bloody Caesars Elf*   45
And at last he would have been Caesar himself
Like dr Priestly & Bacon & Newton*

Poor Spiritual Knowledge is not worth a button
For thus the Gospel Sr Isaac confutes
God can only be known by his Attributes*   50
And as to the Indwelling of the Holy Ghost*
Or of Christ & his Father its all a boast
And Pride & Vanity of Imagination
That disdains to follow this Worlds Fashion
To teach doubt & Experiment   55
Certainly was not what Christ meant
What was he doing all that time
From twelve years old to manly prime
Was he then Idle, or the Less
About his Fathers business   60
Or was his wisdom held in scorn
Before his wrath began to burn
In Miracles throughout the Land
That quite unnervd Lord Caiaphas hand
If he had been Antichrist Creeping Jesus*   65
Hed have done any thing to please us
Gone sneaking into Synagogues
And not usd the Elders & Priests like dogs
But Humble as a Lamb or Ass
Obeyd himself to Caiaphas   70
God wants not Man to Humble himself
This is the trick of the ancient Elf*
This is the Race that Jesus ran
Humble to God Haughty to Man
Cursing the Rulers before the People   75
Even to the temples highest Steeple
And when he Humbled himself to God
Then descended the Cruel Rod
If thou humblest thyself thou humblest me
Thou also dwellst in Eternity   80
Thou art a Man God is no more*
Thy own humanity learn to adore
For that is my Spirit of Life
Awake, arise to Spiritual Strife
And thy Revenge abroad display   85
In terrors at the Last Judgment Day
Gods Mercy & Long Suffering

Is but the Sinner to Judgment to bring
Thou on the Cross for them shalt pray
And take Revenge at the Last Day   90
Jesus replied & thunders hurld
I never will Pray for the World
Once a did so when I prayd in the Garden*
I wishd to take with me a Bodily Pardon
Can that which was of Woman born   95
In the absence of the Morn
When the Soul fell into Sleep
And Archangels round it weep
Shooting out against the Light
Fibres of a deadly night   100
Reasoning upon its own Dark Fiction
In Doubt which is Self Contradiction
Humility is only Doubt
And does the Sun & Moon blot out
Rooting over with thorns & stems   105
The buried Soul & all its Gems
This Lifes dim Windows of the Soul
Distorts the Heavens from Pole to Pole
And leads you to Believe a Lie
When you see with not thro the Eye*   110
That was born in a night to perish in a night
When the Soul slept in the beams of Light.

[(d) Notebook N54, added in margin]

Im sure This Jesus will not do
Either for Englishman or Jew

[(e) Notebook N48, added in margin]

This was Spoke by My Spectre to Voltaire Bacon &c

Did Jesus teach Doubt or did he   115
Give any lessons of Philosophy
Charge Visionaries with Deceiving
Or call Men wise for not Believing

[(f) Notebook N48–52]

Was Jesus Chaste or did he
Give any Lessons of Chastity   120
The morning blushd fiery red
Mary was found in Adulterous bed*
Earth groand beneath, & Heaven above
Trembled at discovery of Love
Jesus was sitting in Moses Chair*   125
They brought the trembling Woman There
Moses commands she be stoned to Death
What was the sound of Jesus breath
He laid his hand on Moses Law
The Ancient Heavens in Silent Awe   130
Writ with Curses from Pole to Pole
All away began to roll
The Earth trembling & Naked lay
In secret bed of Mortal Clay
On Sinai fell the hand Divine*   135
Putting back the bloody shrine
And she heard the breath of God
As she heard by Edens flood
Good & Evil are no more
Sinais trumpets cease to roar   140
Cease finger of God to Write
The Heavens are not clean in thy Sight
Thou art Good, & thou Alone
Nor may the sinner cast one stone
To be Good only is to be   145
A God or else a Pharisee
Thou Angel of the Presence Divine
That didst create this Body of Mine
Wherefore has thou writ these Laws
And Created Hells dark jaws   150
My Presence I will take from thee
A Cold Leper thou shalt be
Tho thou wast so pure & bright
That Heaven was Impure in thy Sight
Tho' thy Oath turnd Heaven Pale   155
Tho thy Covenant built Hells Jail*

Tho thou didst all to Chaos roll
With the Serpent for its soul
Still the breath Divine does move
And the breath Divine is Love   160
Mary Fear Not Let me see
The Seven Devils that torment thee
Hide not from my Sight thy Sin
That forgiveness thou maist win
Has no Man Condemned thee   165
No Man Lord! then what is he
Who shall Accuse thee. Come Ye forth
Fallen Fiends of Heavnly birth
That have forgot your Ancient love
And driven away my trembling Dove   170
You shall bow before her feet
You shall lick the dust for Meat
And tho you cannot Love but Hate
Shall be beggars at Loves Gate
What was thy love Let me see it   175
Was it love or Dark Deceit?
Love too long from Me has fled.
Twas dark deceit to Earn my bread
Twas Covet or twas Custom or*
Some trifle not worth caring for   180
That they may call a shame & Sin
Loves temple that God dwelleth in
And hide in secret hidden Shrine
The Naked Human form divine
And render that a Lawless thing   185
On which the Soul Expands its wing
But this O Lord this was my Sin
When first I let these Devils in
In dark pretence to Chastity
Blaspheming Love, blaspheming thee   190
Thence Rose Secret Adulteries
And thence did Covet also rise
My sin thou hast forgiven me
Canst thou forgive my Blasphemy
Canst thou return to this dark Hell   195
And in my burning bosom dwell
And canst thou Die that I may live

And canst thou Pity & forgive
Then Rolld the shadowy Man away
From the Limbs of Jesus to make them his prey   200
An Ever devouring appetite
Glittering with festering Venoms bright
Crying Crucify this cause of distress
Who don't keep the secrets of Holiness
All Mental Powers by Diseases we bind   205
But he heals the Deaf & the Dumb & the Blind
Whom God has afflicted for Secret Ends
He Comforts & Heals & calls them Friends
But, when Jesus was Crucified
Then was perfected his glittring pride   210
In three Nights he devourd his prey*
And still he devours the Body of Clay
For dust & Clay is the Serpents meat
Which never was made for Man to Eat

[(g) Notebook N100–1]

Was Jesus gentle or did he   215
Give any marks of Gentility
When twelve years old he ran away
And left his Parents in dismay
When after three days sorrow found
Loud as Sinai's trumpet sound   220
No Earthly Parents I confess
My Heavenly Fathers business
Ye understand not what I say
And angry force me to obey
Obedience is a duty then   225
And favour gains with God & Men
John from the Wilderness loud cried
Satan gloried in his Pride
Come said Satan, come away*
Ill soon see if youll obey   230
John for disobedience bled
But you can turn the stones to bread
Gods high king & Gods high Priest
Shall Plant their Glories in your breast

If Caiaphas you will obey   235
If Herod you with bloody Prey*
Feed with the Sacrifice & be
Obedient fall down, worship me
Thunders & lightnings broke around
And Jesus voice in thunders sound   240
Thus I sieze the Spiritual Prey
Ye smiters with disease, make way
I come Your King & God to sieze
Is God a smiter with disease
The God of this World raged in vain   245
He bound Old Satan in his Chain
And bursting forth his furious ire
Became a Chariot of fire
Throughout the land he took his course
And traced Diseases to their Source   250
He cursd the Scribe & Pharisee
Trampling down Hipocrisy
Where eer his Chariot took its way
There Gates of Death let in the Day
Broke down from every Chain & Bar   255
And Satan in his Spiritual War
Dragd at his Chariot wheels loud howld
The God of this World louder rolld
The Chariot Wheels & louder still
His voice was heard from Zions hill   260
And in his hand the Scourge shone bright
He scourgd the Merchant Canaanite*
From out the Temple of his Mind
And in his Body tight does bind
Satan & all his Hellish Crew   265
And thus with wrath he did subdue
The Serpent Bulk of Natures dross
Till He had naild it to the Cross
He took on Sin in the Virgins Womb
And put it off on the Cross & Tomb   270
To be Worshipd by the Church of Rome

[Epilogue]

[(h) Notebook N33]

The Vision of Christ that thou dost see
Is my Visions Greatest Enemy
Thine has a great hook nose like thine
Mine has a snub nose like to mine 275
Thine is the Friend of All Mankind,
Mine speaks in parables to the Blind
Thine loves the same world that mine hates
Thy Heaven doors are my Hell Gates
Socrates taught what Melitus* 280
Loathd as a Nations bitterest Curse
And Caiphas was in his own Mind
A benefactor to Mankind
Both read the Bible day & night
But thou readst black where I read white 285

* * *

For the Sexes: The Gates of Paradise

[Plate 2]

Mutual Forgiveness of each Vice
Such are the Gates of Paradise
Against the Accusers chief desire
Who walkd among the Stones of Fire
Jehovahs Finger Wrote the Law 5
Then Wept! Then rose in Zeal & Awe*
And the Dead Corpse from Sinais heat
Buried beneath his Mercy Seat
O Christians Christians! Tell me Why
You rear it on your Altars high 10

[Plate 19]

The Keys

The Catterpiller on the Leaf
Reminds thee of thy Mothers Grief

of the Gates

1 My Eternal Man set in Repose*
The Female from his darkness rose
And She found me beneath a Tree   15
A Mandrake & in her Veil hid me*
Serpent Reasonings us entice
Of Good & Evil: Virtue & Vice
2 Doubt Self Jealous Watry folly
3 Struggling thro Earths Melancholy   20
4 Naked in Air in Shame & Fear
5 Blind in Fire with shield & spear
Two Horn'd Reasoning Cloven Fiction*
In doubt which is Self contradiction
A dark Hermaphrodite We stood*   25
Rational Truth Root of Evil & Good
Round me flew the Flaming Sword
Round her snowy Whirlwinds roard
Freezing her Veil the Mundane Shell
6 I rent the Veil where the Dead dwell   30
When weary Man enters his Cave

[Plate 20]

He meets his Saviour in the Grave
Some find a Female Garment there
And some a Male, woven with care
Lest the Sexual Garments sweet   35
Should grow a devouring Winding sheet
7 One dies! Alas! The Living & Dead
One is slain & One is fled
8 In Vain-glory hatcht & nurst

By double Spectres Self Accurst 40
My Son! My Son! Thou treatest me
But as I have instructed thee
9 On the shadows of the Moon
Climbing thro Nights highest noon
10 In Times Ocean falling drownd 45
In Aged Ignorance profound
11 Holy & cold I clipd the Wings
Of all Sublunary Things
12 And in depths of my Dungeons
Closed the Father & the Sons 50
13 But when once I did descry
The Immortal Man that cannot Die
14 Thro evening shades I haste away
To close the Labours of my Day
15 The Door of Death I open found 55
And the Worm Weaving in the Ground
16 Thou'rt my Mother from the Womb
Wife, Sister, Daughter to the Tomb
Weaving to Dreams the Sexual strife
And weeping over the Web of Life 60

[Plate 21]

To The Accuser who is The God of This World

Truly My Satan thou art but a Dunce*
And dost not know the Garment from the Man
Every Harlot was a Virgin once
Nor canst thou ever change Kate into Nan 65

Tho thou art Worshipd by the Names Divine
Of Jesus & Jehovah: thou art still
The Son of Morn in weary Nights decline
The lost Travellers Dream under the Hill

COMIC AND SATIRICAL POETRY

An Anthem

[Suction] Lo the Bat with Leathern wing*
          Winking & blinking*
          Winking & blinking
          Winking & blinking
          Like Doctor Johnson   5

Quid   O ho Said Doctor Johnson
          To Scipio Africanus
          If you don't own me a Philosopher
          Ill kick your Roman Anus*

Suction   A ha To Doctor Johnson   10
          Said Scipio Africanus*
          Lift up my Roman Petticoat
          And kiss my Roman Anus
And the Cellar goes down with a Step (Grand Chorus*

[Quid the Cynic's Second Song]

      Hail Matrimony made of Love*
      To thy wide gates how great a drove
      On purpose to be yok'd do come
      Widows & maids & Youths also
      That lightly trip on beauty's toe   5
      Or sit on beauty's bum

      Hail fingerfooted lovely Creatures
      The females of our human Natures
      Formed to suckle all Mankind
      Tis you that come in time of need   10

Without you we should never Breed
Or any Comfort find

For if a Damsel's blind or lame
Or Nature's hand has crooked her frame
Or if she's deaf or is wall eyed   15
Yet if her heart is well inclined
Some tender lover she shall find
That panteth for a Bride

The universal Poultice this
To cure whatever is amiss   20
In damsel or in Widow gay
It makes them smile it makes them skip
Like Birds just cured of the pip
They chirp & hop away

Then come ye Maidens come ye Swains   25
Come & be eased of all your pains
In Matrimony's Golden cage—

[Tilly Lally's Song]

O I say you Joe*
Throw us the ball
Ive a good mind to go
And leave you all
I never saw such a bowler   5
To bowl the ball in a tansey*
And to clean it with my handkercher
Without saying a word

That Bills a foolish fellow   10
He has given me a black eye
He does not know how to handle a bat
Any more than a dog or a cat
He has knockd down the wicket
And broke the stumps   15
And runs without shoes to save his pumps

*   *   *

*To Nobodaddy**

Why art thou silent & invisible
Father of Jealousy
Why dost thou hide thyself in clouds
From every searching Eye

Why darkness & obscurity   5
In all thy words & laws
That none dare eat the fruit but from
The wily serpents jaws
Or is it because Secresy gains females loud applause

* * *

Her whole Life is an Epigram smack smooth & nobly pend
Platted quite neat to catch applause with a sliding noose at the end

* * *

When Klopstock England defied*
Uprose terrible Blake in his pride
For old Nobodaddy aloft
Farted & Belchd & coughd
Then swore a great oath that made heavn quake   5
And calld aloud to English Blake
Blake was giving his body ease
At Lambeth beneath the poplar trees
From his seat then started he
And turnd himself round three times three   10
The Moon at that sight blushd scarlet red
The stars threw down their cups and fled
And all the devils that were in hell
Answerd with a ninefold yell
Klopstock felt the intripled turn   15
And all his bowels began to churn
And his bowels turned round three times three
And lockd in his soul with a ninefold key
That from his body it neer could be parted
Till to the last trumpet it was farted   20
Then again old nobodaddy swore
He neer had seen such a thing before
Since Noah was shut in the ark
Since Eve first chose her hell fire spark

Since twas the fashion to go naked   25
Since the old anything was created
And so feeling he begd him to turn again
And ease poor Klopstocks nine fold pain
From pity then he redend round
And the spell unwound   30
If Blake could do this when he rose up from shite
What might he not do if he sat down to write

* * *

    The Hebrew Nation did not write it*
    Avarice & Chastity did shite it

* * *

    When a Man has Married a Wife
        he finds out whether
    Her knees & elbows are only
        glued together

* * *

    The Sussex Men are Noted Fools
    And weak is their brain pan
    I wonder if H— the painter*
    Is not a Sussex Man

*To H**

You think Fuseli is not a Great Painter Im Glad
This is one of the best compliments he ever had

*To F—**

I mock thee not tho I by thee am Mocked
Thou callst me Madman but I call thee Blockhead

*To Nancy F—**

How can I help thy Husbands copying Me
Should that make difference twixt me & Thee

* * *

Of Hs birth this was the happy lot*
His Mother on his Father him begot

* * *

Sir Joshua Praises Michael Angelo*
Tis Christian Mildness when Knaves Praise a Foe
But Twould be Madness all the World would say
Should Michael Angelo praise Sir Joshua
Christ usd the Pharisees in a rougher way   5

Advice of the Popes who succeeded the Age of Rafael

Degrade first the Arts if you'd Mankind degrade,
Hire Idiots to Paint with gold light & hot shade:
Give high Price for the worst, leave the best in disgrace,
And with Labours of Ignorance fill every place.

* * *

Some look. To see the sweet Outlines
And beauteous Forms that Love does wear
Some look. To find out Patches. Paint.
Bracelets & Stays & Powderd Hair

* * *

When France got free Europe 'twixt Fools & Knaves
Were Savage first to France, & after; Slaves

* * *

When Sr Joshua Reynolds died
All Nature was degraded;
The King dropd a tear into the Queens Ear;
And all his Pictures Faded.

* * *

When Nations grow Old. The Arts grow Cold
And Commerce settles on every Tree
And the Poor & the Old can live upon Gold
For all are Born Poor. Aged Sixty three

* * *

Hes a Blockhead who wants a proof of what he Can't Percieve
And he's a Fool who tries to make such a Blockhead believe

* * *

A Petty sneaking Knave I knew*
O Mr Cr— how do ye do

* * *

He has observd the Golden Rule*
Till hes become the Golden Fool

* * *

To the Royal Academy

A strange Erratum in all the Editions
Of Sir Joshua Reynoldss Lectures
Should be corrected by the Young Gentlemen
And the Royal Academy Directors

Instead of Michael Angelo
Read Rembrandt for it is fit
To make meer common honesty
In all that he has writ

5

* * *

P— loved me not as he lovd his Friends*
For he lovd them for gain to serve his Ends
He lovd me and for no Gain at all
But to rejoice & triumph in my fall

* * *

On H—ys Friendship*

When H—y finds out what you cannot do
That is the Very thing hell set you to
If you break not your Neck tis not his fault
But pecks of poisons are not pecks of salt
And when he could not act upon my wife
Hired a Villain to bereave my Life

* * *

Another [Epitaph]

I was buried near this Dike
That my Friends may weep as much as they like

A Pretty Epigram for the Entertainment of those Who have Paid Great Sums in the Venetian & Flemish Ooze

Nature & Art in this together Suit
What is Most Grand is always most Minute
Rubens thinks Tables Chairs & Stools are Grand
But Rafael thinks A Head a foot a hand

* * *

Rafael Sublime Majestic Graceful Wise
His Executive Power must I despise
Rubens Low Vulgar Stupid Ignorant
His power of Execution I must grant
Learn the Laboreous stumble of a Fool   5
Go send your Children to the Slobbering School

* * *

If I eer Grow to Mans Estate
O Give to me a Womans fate
May I govern all both great & small
Have the last word & take the wall

* * *

Blakes apology for his Catalogue

Having given great offence by writing in Prose
Ill write in verse as soft as Bartolloze*
Some blush at what others can see no crime in
But nobody sees any harm in Rhyming
Dryden in Rhyme cries Milton only plannd*   5
Every Fool shook his bells thoughout the land
Tom Cooke cut Hogarth down with his clean graving*

Thousands of Connoisseurs with joy ran raving
Thus Hayley on his Toilette seeing the Sope
Cries Homer is very much improvd by Pope*   10
Some say Ive given great Provision to my foes
And that now I lead my false friends by the nose
Flaxman & Stothard smelling a sweet savour
Cry Blakified Drawing spoils painter & Engraver
While I looking up to my Umbrella   15
Resolvd to be a very contrary fellow
Cry looking quite from Skumference to Center
No one can finish so high as the original Inventor
Thus Poor Schiavonetti died of the Cromek*
A thing that's tied around the Examiners neck   20
This is my sweet apology to my friends
That I may put them in mind of their latter Ends

VERSE EPISTLES
AND DEDICATIONS

*To Mrs Ann Flaxman [c.1798]**

A little Flower grew in a lonely Vale
Its form was lovely but its colours pale
One standing in the Porches of the Sun
When his Meridian Glories were begun
Leapd from the steps of fire & on the grass   5
Alighted where this little flower was
With hands divine he movd the gentle Sod
And took the Flower up in its native Clod
Then planting it upon a Mountains brow
'Tis you own fault if you don't flourish now   10

*To George Cumberland [1 September 1800]**

Dear Generous Cumberland nobly solicitous for a Friends welfare.
                                        Behold me
Whom your Friendship has Magnified: Rending the manacles of
                                        Londons Dungeon dark
I have rent the black net & escap'd. See My Cottage at Felpham in joy
Beams over the sea a bright light over France but the Web and the Veil
                                        I have left
Behind me at London resists every beam of light; hanging from   5
                                        heaven to Earth
Dropping with human gore. Lo! I have left it! I have torn it from
                                        my limbs
I shake my wings ready to take my flight! Pale, Ghastly pale; stands
                                        the City in fear*

To John Flaxman [12 September 1800]*

To My Dearest Friend John Flaxman, these lines
I bless thee O Father of Heaven & Earth that ever I saw Flaxmans face
Angels stand round my Spirit in Heaven. the blessed of Heaven are
                         my friends upon Earth
When Flaxman was taken to Italy. Fuseli was giv'n to me for a season*
And now Flaxman hath given me Hayley his friend to be mine. such   5
                         my lot upon Earth*
Now my lot in the Heavens is this; Milton lovd me in childhood &
                         shewd me his face
Ezra came with Isaiah the Prophet, but Shakespeare in riper years
                         gave me his hand*
Paracelsus & Behmen appeard to me. terrors appeard in the Heavens
                         above*
And in Hell beneath & a mighty & awful change threatened
                         the Earth
The American War began All its dark horrors passed before my face   10
Across the Atlantic to France. Then the French Revolution
                         commencd in thick clouds
And My Angels have told me. That Seeing such visions I could
                         not Subsist on the earth
But by my conjunction with Flaxman who knows how to forgive
                         Nervous Fear

To My dear Friend, Mrs Anna Flaxman
[14 September 1800]*

This Song to the flower of Flaxmans joy
To the blossom of hope for a sweet decoy
Do all that you can or all that you may
To entice him to Felpham & far away

Away to Sweet Felpham for heaven is there   5
The Ladder of Angels descends thro the air
On the Turret its spiral does softly descend*
Thro the village then winds at My Cot it does end

You stand in the village & look up to heaven
The precious stones glitter on flights seventy seven   10

And My Brother is there & My Friend & Thine*
Descend & Ascend with the Bread & the Wine

The Bread of sweet Thought & the Wine of Delight
Feeds the Village of Felpham by day & by night
And at his own door the blessd Hermit does stand   15
Dispensing Unceasing to all the whole Land

To Thomas Butts [2 October 1800]*

To my friend Butts I write
My first Vision of Light
On the yellow sands sitting
The Sun was Emitting
His Glorious beams   5
From Heavens high Streams
Over Sea over Land
My Eyes did Expand
Into regions of air
Away from all Care   10
Into regions of fire
Remote from desire
The Light of the Morning
Heavens Mountains adorning
In particles bright   15
The jewels of Light
Distinct shone & clear—
Amazd & in fear
I each particle gazed
Astonishd Amazed   20
For each was a Man
Human formd. Swift I ran
For they beckond to me
Remote by the Sea
Saying. Each grain of Sand   25
Every Stone on the Land
Each rock & each hill
Each fountain & rill
Each herb and each tree
Mountain hill Earth & Sea   30

Cloud Meteor & Star
Are Men Seen Afar
I stood in the Streams
Of Heavens bright beams
And Saw Felpham sweet   35
Beneath my bright feet
In soft Female charms
And in her fair arms
My Shadow I knew*   40
And my wifes shadow too
And My Sister & Friend.*
We like Infants descend
In our Shadows on earth
Like a weak mortal birth   45
My Eyes more & more
Like a Sea without shore
Continue Expanding
The Heavens commanding
Till the Jewels of light   50
Heavenly Men beaming bright
Appeard as One Man
Who Complacent began
My limbs to infold
In his beams of bright gold   55
Like dross purgd away
All my mire & my clay
Soft consumd in delight
In his bosom sun bright
I remaind. Soft he smild   60
And I heard his voice Mild
Saying This is My Fold
O thou Ram hornd with gold*
Who awakes from sleep
On the sides of the Deep   65
On the Mountains around
The roarings resound
Of the lion & wolf
The loud sea & deep gulf
These are guards of My Fold   70
O thou Ram hornd with gold
And the voice faded mild

I remaind as a Child
All I ever had known
Before me bright Shone   75
I saw you & your wife
By the fountains of Life
Such the Vision to me
Appeard on the Sea

To Mrs Butts [2 October 1800]*

Wife of the Friend of those I most revere.
Receive this tribute from a Harp sincere
Go on in Virtuous Seed sowing on Mold
Of Human Vegetation & Behold
Your Harvest Springing to Eternal life   5
Parent of Youthful Minds & happy Wife

To Thomas Butts [22 November 1802]

With happiness stretchd across the hills
In a cloud that dewy sweetness distills
With a blue sky spread over with wings
And a mild sun that mounts & sings
With trees & fields full of Fairy elves   5
And little devils who fight for themselves
Remembring the Verses that Hayley sung
When my heart knockd against the root of my tongue
With Angels planted in Hawthorn bowers
And God himself in the passing hours   10
With Silver Angels across my way
And Golden Demons that none can stay
With my Father hovering upon the wind
And my Brother Robert just behind
And my Brother John the evil one*   15
In a black cloud making his mone
Tho dead they appear upon my path
Notwithstanding my terrible wrath
They beg they intreat they drop their tears
Filld full of hopes filld full of fears   20

With a thousand Angels upon the Wind
Pouring disconsolate from behind
To drive then off & before my way
A frowning Thistle implores my stay
What to others a trifle appears   25
Fills me full of smiles or tears
For double the vision my Eyes do see
And a double vision is always with me
With my inward Eye 'tis an old Man grey
With my outward a Thistle across my way   30
'If thou goest back the thistle said
Thou art to endless woe betrayd
For here does Theotormon lower
And here is Enitharmons bower
And Los the terrible thus hath sworn*   35
Because thou backward dost return
Poverty Envy old age & fear
Shall bring thy Wife upon a bier
And Butts shall give what Fuseli gave
A dark black Rock & a gloomy Cave.'   40

I struck the Thistle with my foot
And broke him up from his delving root
'Must the duties of life each other cross'
'Must every joy be dung & dross'
Must my dear Butts feel cold neglect'   45
'Because I give Hayley his due respect'
'Must Flaxman look upon me as wild'
'And all my friends be with doubts beguild'
'Must my Wife live in my Sisters bane'
'Or my sister survive on my Loves pain'   50
'The curses of Los the terrible shade'
'And his dismal terrors make me afraid'
So I spoke & struck in my wrath
The old man weltering upon my path
Then Los appeard in all his power   55
In the Sun he appeard descending before
My face in fierce flames in my double sight
Twas outward a Sun inward Los in his might

'My hands are labourd day & night'
'And Ease comes never in my sight'   60

'My Wife has no indulgence given'
'Except what comes to her from heaven'
'We eat little we drink less'
'This Earth breeds not our happiness'
'Another Sun feeds our lifes streams'   65
'We are not warmed with thy beams'
'Thou measurest not the Time to me'
'Nor yet the Space that I do see'
'My Mind is not with thy light arrayd'
'Thy terrors shall not make me afraid'   70

When I had my defiance given
The Sun stood trembling in heaven
The Moon that glowd remote below
Became leprous & white as snow
And every Soul of men on the Earth   75
Felt affliction & sorrow & sickness & dearth
Los flamd in my path & the Sun was hot
With the bows of my Mind & the Arrows of Thought
My bowstring fierce with Ardour breathes
My arrows glow in their golden sheaves   80
My brothers & father march before
The heavens drop with human gore

Now I a fourfold vision see
And a fourfold vision is given to me
Tis fourfold in my supreme delight   85
And three fold in soft Beulahs night
And twofold Always. May God us keep
From Single vision & Newtons sleep*

To Thomas Butts [16 August 1803]

O why was I born with a different face
Why was I not born like the rest of my race
When I look each one starts! When I speak I offend
The I'm silent & passive & lose every Friend

Then my verse I dishonor. My pictures despise   5
My person degrade & my temper chastise
And the pen is my terror. The pencil my shame
All my Talents I bury, and Dead is my Fame

I am either too low or too highly prizd
When Elate I am Envy'd, When Meek I'm despisd   10

*To the Queen**

The Door of Death is made of Gold,
That Mortal Eyes cannot behold;
But, when the Mortal Eyes are clos'd,
And cold and pale the Limbs repos'd,
The Soul awakes; and, wond'ring, sees   5
In her mild Hand the golden Keys:
The Grave is Heaven's golden Gate,
And rich and poor around it wait;
O Shepherdess of England's Fold,
Behold this Gate of Pearl and Gold!   10

To dedicate to England's Queen
The Visions that my Soul has seen,
And, by Her kind permission, bring
What I have borne on solemn Wing,
From the vast regions of the Grave,   15
Before Her Throne my Wings I wave;
Bowing before my Sov'reign's Feet,
'The Grave produc'd these Blossoms sweet
'In mild repose from earthly strife;
'The Blossoms of Eternal Life!'   20

* * *

The Caverns of the Grave Ive seen*
And these I shewd to Englands Queen
But now the Caves of Hell I view
Who shall I dare to shew them to
What mighty Soul in Beautys form   5
Shall dauntless View the Infernal Storm
Egremonts Countess can control
The flames of Hell that round me roll
If she refuse I still go on
Till the Heavens & Earth are gone   10
Still admird by Noble minds
Followd by Envy on the winds
Re-engravd Time after Time

Ever in their youthful prime
My Designs unchangd remain   15
Time may rage but rage in vain
For above Times troubled Fountains
On the Great Atlantic Mountains*
In my Golden House on high
There they Shine Eternally   20

BRIEF EPIC

Visions of the Daughters of Albion*

The Eye sees more than the Heart knows.

[Plate 3]

THE ARGUMENT

I loved Theotormon
And I was not ashamed
I trembled in my virgin fears
And I hid in Leutha's vale!

I plucked Leutha's flower,*   5
And I rose up from the vale;
But the terrible thunders tore
My virgin mantle in twain.

[Plate 4]

VISIONS

Enslav'd, the Daughters of Albion weep; a trembling lamentation
Upon their mountains; in their valleys, sighs toward America.

For the soft soul of America, Oothoon wanderd in woe
Along the vales of Leutha seeking flowers to comfort her;
And thus she spoke to the bright Marygold of Leutha's vale   5

Art thou a flower! art thou a nymph! I see thee now a flower;
Now a nymph! I dare not pluck thee from thy dewy bed!

The Golden nymph replied; pluck thou my flower Oothoon
                                                        the mild
Another flower shall spring. because the soul of sweet delight
Can never pass away, She ceas'd, & closd her golden shrine.   10

Then Oothoon pluck'd the flower saying, I pluck thee from thy bed

Sweet flower. and put thee here to glow between my breasts
And thus I turn my face to where my whole soul seeks.

Over the waves she went in wing'd exulting swift delight;
And over Theotormons reign took her impetuous course.   15

Bromion rent her with his thunders. on his stormy bed *
Lay the faint maid, and soon her woes appalld his thunders hoarse

Bromion spoke. behold this harlot here on Bromions bed.
And let the jealous dolphins sport around the lovely maid: *
Thy soft American plains are mine, and mine thy north & south: 20
Stampt with my signet are the swarthy children of the sun;*
They are obedient, they resist not, they obey the scourge:
Their daughters worship terrors and obey the violent:

[Plate 5]

Now thou maist marry Bromions harlot, and protect the child
Of Bromions rage, that Oothoon shall put forth in nine moons time

Then storms rent Theotormons limbs: he rolld his waves around.
And folded his black jealous waters round the adulterate pair
Bound back to back in Bromions caves, terror & meekness dwell*   5

At entrance Theotormon sits, wearing the threshold hard
With secret tears; beneath him sound like waves on a desart shore
The voice of slaves beneath the sun, and children bought with money,
That shiver in religious caves beneath the burning fires
Of lust, that belch incessant from the summits of the earth   10

Oothoon weeps not, she cannot weep! her tears are locked up;
But she can howl incessant writhing her soft snowy limbs.
And calling Theotormons Eagles to prey upon her flesh.*

I call with holy voice! kings of the sounding air,
Rend away this defiled bosom that I may reflect,   15
The image of Theotormon on my pure transparent breast.

The Eagles at her call descend & rend their bleeding prey;
Theotormon severely smiles. her soul reflects the smile;
As the clear spring mudded with feet of beast, grows pure & smiles

The Daughters of Albion hear her woes, & eccho back her sighs.*   20

Why does my Theotormon sit weeping upon the threshold:
And Oothoon hovers by his side, perswading him in vain:

I cry arise O Theotormon for the village dog
Barks at the breaking day. the nightingale has done lamenting   25
The lark does rustle in the ripe corn, and the Eagle returns
From nightly prey, and lifts his golden beak to the pure east;
Shaking the dust from his immortal pinions to awake
The sun that sleeps too long. Arise my Theotormon I am pure.
Because the night is gone that clos'd me in its deadly black.   30
They told me that the night & day were all that I could see;
They told me that I had five senses to inclose me up.
And they inclos'd my infinite brain into a narrow circle,
And sunk my heart into the Abyss, a red round globe hot burning
Till all from life I was obliterated and erased.   35
Instead of morn arises a bright shadow, like an eye
In the eastern cloud: instead of night a sickly charnel house;
That Theotormon hears me not! to him the night and morn
Are both alike: a night of sighs, a morning of fresh tears;

[Plate 6]

And none but Bromion can hear my lamentations.

With what sense is it that the chicken shuns the ravenous hawk?
With what sense does the tame pigeon measure out the expanse?
With what sense does the bee form cells? have not the mouse & frog
Eyes and ears and sense of touch? yet are their habitations.   5
And their pursuits as different as their forms and as their joys:
Ask the wild ass why he refuses burdens: and the meek camel
Why he loves man: is it because of eye ear mouth or skin
Ask the blind worm the secrets of the grave, and why her spires   10
Love to curl round the bones of death! and ask the rav'nous snake
Where she gets poison: & the wing'd eagle why he loves the sun;
And then tell me the thoughts of man, that have been hid of old.

Silent I hover all the night, and all day could be silent
If Theotormon once would turn his loved eyes upon me;   15
How can I be defild when I reflect thy image pure?
Sweetest the fruit that the worm feeds on. & the soul prey'd
                                                on by woe
The new wash'd lamb ting'd with the village smoke & the bright swan
By the red earth of our immortal river: I bathe my wings,
And I am white and pure to hover round Theotormons breast.   20

Then Theotormon broke his silence, and he answered.

Tell me what is the night or day to one o'erflowd with woe?
Tell me what is a thought? & of what substance is it made?
Tell me what is a joy? & in what gardens do joys grow?
And in what rivers swim the sorrows? and upon what mountains   25

[Plate 7]

Wave shadows of discontent? and in what houses dwell the wretched
Drunken with woe forgotten. and shut up from cold despair,

Tell me where dwell the thoughts forgotten till thou call them forth
Tell me where dwell the joys of old! & where the ancient loves?
And when will they renew again & the night of oblivion past?   5
That I might traverse times & spaces far remote and bring
Comforts into a present sorrow and a night of pain
Where goest thou O thought! to what remote land is thy flight?
If thou returnest to the present moment of affliction
Wilt thou bring comforts on thy wings, and dews and honey   10
                                            and balm;
Or poison from the desart wilds, from the eyes of the envier.

Then Bromion said: and shook the cavern with his lamentation

Thou knowest that the ancient trees seen by thine eyes have fruit;
But knowest thou that trees and fruits flourish upon the earth
To gratify senses unknown? trees beasts and birds unknown: 15
Unknown, not unpercievd, spread in the infinite microscope,
In places yet unvisited by the voyager. and in worlds
Over another kind of seas, and in atmospheres unknown.
Ah! are there other wars, beside the wars of sword and fire!
And are there other sorrows, beside the sorrows of poverty?   20
And are there other joys, beside the joys of riches and ease?
And is there not one law for both the lion and the ox?*
And is there not eternal fire, and eternal chains?
To bind the phantoms of existence from eternal life?

Then Oothoon waited silent all the day and all the night,   25

[Plate 8]

But when the morn arose, her lamentation renewd,
The Daughters of Albion hear her woes, & eccho back her sighs.

O Urizen! Creator of men! mistaken Demon of heaven;
Thy joys are tears! thy labour vain to form men to thine image.
How can one joy absorb another? are not different joys   5
Holy, eternal, infinite! and each joy is a Love.

Does not the great mouth laugh at a gift? & the narrow eyelids mock
At the labour that is above payment, and wilt thou take the ape
For thy councellor? or the dog for a schoolmaster to thy children?
Does he who contemns poverty, and he who turns with abhorrence   10
From usury: feel the same passion or are they moved alike?
How can the giver of gifts experience the delights of the merchant?
How the industrious citizen the pains of the husbandman.
How different far the fat fed hireling with hollow drum;*
Who buys whole corn fields into wastes, and sings upon the heath: 15
How different their eye and ear! how different the world to them!
With what sense does the parson claim the labour of the farmer?*
What are his nets & gins & traps, & how does he surround him
With cold floods of abstraction, and with forests of solitude,
To build him castles and high spires, where kings & priests may dwell.   20
Till she who burns with youth, and knows no fixed lot; is bound
In spells of law to one she loathes: and must she drag the chain
Of life in weary lust! must chilling, murderous thoughts, obscure
The clear heaven of her eternal spring! to bear the wintry rage
Of a harsh terror driv'n to madness, bound to hold a rod   25
Over her shrinking shoulders all the day; & all the night
To turn the wheel of false desire: and longings that wake her womb
To the abhorred birth of cherubs in the human form
That live a pestilence & die a meteor & are no more.
Till the child dwell with one he hates, and do the deed he loaths   30
And the impure scourge force his seed into its unripe birth
Ere yet his eyelids can behold the arrows of the day.

Does the whale worship at thy footsteps as the hungry dog?
Or does he scent the mountain prey, because his nostrils wide
Draw in the ocean? does his eye discern the flying cloud   35
As the raven's eye? or does he measure the expanse like the vulture?
Does the still spider view the cliffs where eagles hide their young?
Or does the fly rejoice. because the harvest is brought in?
Does not the eagle scorn the earth & despise the treasures beneath?
But the mole knoweth what is there, & the worm shall tell it thee.   40
Does not the worm erect a pillar in the mouldering church yard?

[Plate 9]

And a palace of eternity in the jaws of the hungry grave
Over his porch these words are written. Take thy bliss O Man!
And sweet shall be thy taste & sweet thy infant joys renew!

In laps of pleasure; Innocence! honest, open, seeking   5
The vigorous joys of morning light; open to virgin bliss.
Who taught thee modesty, subtil modesty! child of night & sleep
When thou awakes. wilt thou dissemble all thy secret joys
Or wert thou not awake when all this mystery was disclos'd!
Then com'st thou forth a modest virgin knowing to dissemble   10
With nets found under thy night pillow, to catch virgin joy,
And brand it with the name of whore: & sell it in the night,
In silence, ev'n without a whisper, and in seeming sleep,
Religious dreams and holy vespers, light thy smoky fires:
Once were thy fires lighted by the eyes of honest morn   15
And does my Theotormon seek this hypocrite modesty!
This knowing, artful, secret. fearful, cautious, trembling hypocrite.
Then is Oothoon a whore indeed! and all the virgin joys
Of life are harlots: and Theotormon is a sick mans dream
And Oothoon is the crafty slave of selfish holiness.   20

But Oothoon is not so, a virgin fill'd with virgin fancies
Open to joy and to delight where ever beauty appears
If in the morning sun I find it; there my eyes are fix'd

[Plate 10]

In happy copulation; if in evening mild. wearied with work;*
Sit on a bank and draw the pleasures of this free born joy.

The moment of desire! the moment of desire! The virgin
That pines for man; shall awaken her womb to enormous joys
In the secret shadows of her chamber; the youth shut up from   5
The lustful joy, shall forget to generate, & create an amorous image
In the shadows of his curtains and in the folds of his silent pillow.*
Are not these the places of religion? the rewards of continence!
The self enjoyings of self denial? Why dost thou seek religion?
Is it because acts are not lovely, that thou seekest solitude,   10
Where the horrible darkness is impressed with reflections of desire.

Father of Jealousy, be thou accursed from the earth!
Why hast thou taught my Theotormon this accursed thing?
Till beauty fades from off my shoulders darken'd and cast out,
A solitary shadow wailing on the margin of non-entity.   15

I cry, Love! Love! Love! happy happy Love! free as the mountain
                                                          wind!
Can that be Love, that drinks another as a sponge drinks water?
That clouds with jealousy his nights, with weepings all the day:
To spin a web of age around him, grey and hoary! dark!
Till his eyes sicken at the fruit that hangs before his sight.   20
Such is self-love that envies all! a creeping skeleton
With lamplike eyes watching around the frozen marriage bed.

But silken nets and traps of adamant will Oothoon spread,
And catch for thee girls of mild silver, or of furious gold;
I'll lie beside thee on a bank & view their wanton play   25
In lovely copulation bliss on bliss, with Theotormon;*
Red as the rosy morning, lustful as the first born beam,
Oothoon shall view his dear delight, nor e'er with jealous cloud
Come in the heaven of generous love; nor selfish blightings bring.

Does the sun walk in glorious raiment, on the secret floor   30

[Plate 11]

Where the cold miser spreads his gold? or does the bright cloud drop
On his stone threshold? does his eye behold the beam that brings
Expansion to the eye of pity? or will he bind himself
Beside the ox to thy hard furrow? does not that mild beam blot
The bat, the owl, the glowing tyger, and the king of night.   5
The sea fowl takes the wintry blast. for a cov'ring to her limbs:
And the wild snake the pestilence to adorn him with gems & gold.
And trees. & birds. & beasts, & men. behold their eternal joy.
Arise you little glancing wings, and sing your infant joy!
Arise and drink your bliss. for every thing that lives is holy!   10

Thus every morning wails Oothoon. but Theotormon sits
Upon the margind ocean conversing with shadows dire,

The Daughters of Albion hear her woes, & eccho back her sighs.

THE END

America a Prophecy*

LAMBETH Printed by William Blake in the year 1793.

[Plate 3]

PRELUDIUM

The shadowy Daughter of Urthona stood before red Orc,
When fourteen suns had faintly journey'd o'er his dark abode;*
His food she brought in iron baskets, his drink in cups of iron;*
Crown'd with a helmet & dark hair the nameless female stood;
A quiver with its burning stores, a bow like that of night,   5
When pestilence is shot from heaven: no other arms she need:
Invulnerable tho' naked, save where clouds roll round her loins,
Their awful folds in the dark air: silent she stood as night;
For never from her iron tongue could voice or sound arise;
But dumb till that dread day when Orc assay'd his fierce embrace   10

Dark virgin; said the hairy youth. thy father stern abhorr'd;
Rivets my tenfold chains while still on high my spirit soars;
Sometimes an eagle screaming in the sky, sometimes a lion,
Stalking upon the mountains. & sometimes a whale I lash
The raging fathomless abyss, anon a serpent folding   15
Around the pillars of Urthona, and round thy dark limbs,
On the Canadian wilds I fold, feeble my spirit folds.*
For chaind beneath I rend these caverns; when thou bringest food
I howl my joy: and my red eyes seek to behold thy face
In vain! these clouds roll to & fro, & hide thee from my sight.   20

[Plate 4]

Silent as despairing love, and strong as jealousy,
The hairy shoulders rend the links, free are the wrists of fire;
Round the terrific loins he siez'd the panting, struggling womb;*
It joy'd: she put aside her clouds & smiled her first-born smile;
As when a black cloud shews its lightnings to the silent deep.   5

Soon as she saw the terrible boy, then burst the virgin cry.

I know thee, I have found thee, & I will not let thee go;
Thou art the image of God who dwells in darkness of Africa;
And thou art fall'n to give me life in regions of dark death.
On my American plains I feel the struggling afflictions   10
Endur'd by roots that writhe their arms into the nether deep:
I see a Serpent in Canada, who courts me to his love;
In Mexico an Eagle, and a Lion in Peru;
I see a Whale in the South-sea, drinking my soul away.
O what limb rending pains I feel. thy fire & my frost   15
Mingle in howling pains, in furrows by thy lightnings rent;
This is eternal death, and this the torment long foretold.*

[Plate 5]

A PROPHECY

The Guardian Prince of Albion burns in his nightly tent, *
Sullen fires across the Atlantic glow to America's shore:
Piercing the souls of warlike men, who rise in silent night,
Washington, Franklin, Paine & Warren, Gates, Hancock & Green;*
Meet on the coast glowing with blood from Albions fiery Prince.*   5

Washington spoke; Friends of America look over the Atlantic sea;
A bended bow is lifted in heaven, & a heavy iron chain
Descends link by link from Albions cliffs across the sea to bind
Brothers & sons of America, till our faces pale and yellow;
Heads deprest, voices weak, eyes downcast, hands work-bruis'd,*   10
Feet bleeding on the sultry sands, and the furrows of the whip
Descend to generations that in future times forget.—

The strong voice ceas'd; for a terrible blast swept over the heaving sea;
The eastern cloud rent: on his cliffs stood Albions wrathful Prince
A dragon form, clashing his scales at midnight he arose,*   15
And flam'd red meteors round the land of Albion beneath
His voice, his locks, his awful shoulders, and his glowing eyes,

[Plate 6]

Appear to the Americans upon the cloudy night.

Solemn heave the Atlantic waves between the gloomy nations
Swelling, belching from its deeps red clouds & raging fires;

Albion is sick. America faints! enrag'd the Zenith grew.
As human blood shooting its veins all round the orbed heaven   5
Red rose the clouds from the Atlantic in vast wheels of blood
And in the red clouds rose a Wonder o'er the Atlantic sea;
Intense! naked! a Human fire fierce glowing, as the wedge
Of iron heated in the furnace; his terrible limbs were fire
With myriads of cloudy terrors banners dark & towers   10
Surrounded: heat but not light went thro' the murky atmosphere

The King of England looking westward trembles at the vision

[Plate 7]

Albions Angel stood beside the Stone of night, and saw*
The terror like a comet, or more like the planet red
That once inclos'd the terrible wandering comets in its sphere.
Then Mars thou wast our center, & the planets three flew round*
Thy crimson disk; so e'er the Sun was rent from thy red sphere;   5
The Spectre glowd his horrid length staining the temple long*
With beams of blood; & thus a voice came forth. and shook the
                                                              temple:

[Plate 8]

The morning comes, the night decays, the watchmen leave their
                                                             stations;
The grave is burst, the spices shed, the linen wrapped up;*
The bones of death, the cov'ring clay, the sinews shrunk & dry'd.
Reviving shake, inspiring move, breathing! awakening!
Spring like redeemed captives when their bonds & bars are burst;   5
Let the slave grinding at the mill, run out into the field:*
Let him look up into the heavens & laugh in the bright air;
Let the inchained soul shut up in darkness and in sighing,
Whose face has never seen a smile in thirty weary years;
Rise and look out, his chains are loose, his dungeon doors are open   10
And let his wife and children return from the opressors scourge;
They look behind at every step & believe it is a dream.
Singing.The Sun has left his blackness, & has found a fresher
                                                              morning
And the fair Moon rejoices in the clear & cloudless night;
For Empire is no more, and now the Lion & Wolf shall cease.*   15

[Plate 9]

In thunders ends the voice. Then Albions Angel wrathful burnt
Beside the Stone of Night; and like the Eternal Lions howl
In famine & war. reply'd. Art thou not Orc, who serpent-form'd
Stands at the gate of Enitharmon to devour her children;
Blasphemous Demon, Antichrist, hater of Dignities;   5
Lover of wild rebellion. and transgressor of Gods Law;
Why dost thou come to Angels eyes in this terrific form?

[Plate 10]

The terror answerd: I am Orc. wreath'd round the accursed tree:*
The times are ended; shadows pass the morning gins to break:
The fiery joy, that Urizen perverted to ten commands,*
What night he led the starry hosts thro' the wide wilderness:
That stony law I stamp to dust: and scatter religion abroad   5
To the four winds as a torn book, & none shall gather the leaves:
But they shall rot on desart sands, & consume in bottomless deeps;
To make the desarts blossom, & the deeps shrink to their fountains,
And to renew the fiery joy, and burst the stony roof.
That pale religious letchery, seeking Virginity,   10
May find it in a harlot, and in coarse-clad honesty
The undefil'd tho' ravish'd in her cradle night and morn:*
For every thing that lives is holy, life delights in life;
Because the soul of sweet delight can never be defil'd.
Fires inwrap the earthly globe, yet man is not consum'd;   15
Amidst the lustful fires he walks: his feet become like brass,
His knees and thighs like silver. & his breast and head like gold.*

[Plate 11]

Sound! sound! my loud war-trumpets & alarm my Thirteen Angels!*
Loud howls the eternal Wolf! the eternal Lion lashes his tail!
America is darkend; and my punishing Demons, terrified
Crouch howling before their caverns deep like skins dry'd in the wind.
They cannot smite the wheat, nor quench the fatness of the earth.   5
They cannot smite with sorrows, nor subdue the plow and spade.
They cannot wall the city, nor moat round the castle of princes.
They cannot bring the stubbed oak to overgrow the hills.

For terrible men stand on the shores, & in their robes I see
Children take shelter from the lightnings: there stands Washington   10
And Paine and Warren with their foreheads reard toward the east
But clouds obscure my aged sight. A vision from afar!
Sound! sound! my loud war-trumpets & alarm my thirteen Angels!
Ah vision from afar! Ah rebel form that rent the ancient
Heavens; Eternal Viper, self-renew'd, rolling in clouds   15
I see thee in thick clouds and darkness on America's shore.
Writhing in pangs of abhorred birth; red flames the crest rebellious
And eyes of death; the harlot womb, oft opened in vain,
Heaves in enormous circles: now the times are return'd upon thee,
Devourer of thy parent, now thy unutterable torment renews.   20
Sound! sound! my loud war trumpets & alarm my thirteen Angels!
Ah terrible birth! a young one bursting! where is the weeping mouth?
And where the mother's milk? instead, those ever-hissing jaws
And parched lips drop with fresh gore; now roll thou in the clouds
Thy mother lays her length outstretch'd upon the shore beneath.   25
Sound! sound! my loud war-trumpets, & alarm my thirteen Angels!
Loud howls the eternal Wolf! the eternal Lion lashes his tail!

[Plate 12]

Thus wept the Angel voice & as he wept, the terrible blasts
Of trumpets blew a loud alarm across the Atlantic deep.
No trumpets answer; no reply of clarions or of fifes:
Silent the Colonies remain and refuse the loud alarm.

On those vast shady hills between America & Albions shore;   5
Now barr'd out by the Atlantic sea: call'd Atlantean hills:
Because from their bright summits you may pass to the Golden world
An ancient palace, archetype of mighty Emperies.
Rears its immortal pinnacles, built in the forest of God
By Ariston the king of beauty for his stolen bride,*   10

Here on their magic seats the thirteen Angels sat perturb'd,
For clouds from the Atlantic hover o'er the solemn roof.

[Plate 13]

Fiery the Angels rose, & as they rose deep thunder roll'd
Around their shores; indignant burning with the fires of Orc
And Bostons Angel cried aloud as they flew thro' the dark night.*

He cried: Why trembles honesty and like a murderer,
Why seeks he refuge from the frowns of his immortal station,   5
Must the generous tremble & leave his joy, to the idle, to the
                                        pestilence!
That mock him? who commanded this, what God, what Angel!
To keep the gen'rous from experience till the ungenerous
Are unrestraind performers of the energies of nature;
Till pity is become a trade, and generosity a science,   10
That men get rich by; & the sandy desart is giv'n to the strong
What God is he, writes laws of peace, & clothes him in a tempest
What pitying Angel lusts for tears, and fans himself with sighs
What crawling villain preaches abstinence & wraps himself
In fat of lambs? no more I follow, no more obedience pay.   15

[Plate 14]

So cried he, rending off his robe & throwing down his scepter.
In sight of Albions Guardian, and all the thirteen Angels*
Rent off their robes to the hungry wind, & threw their golden
                                        scepters
Down on the land of America. indignant they descended
Headlong from out their heav'nly heights, descending swift as fires   5
Over the land; naked & flaming are their lineaments seen
In the deep gloom, by Washington & Paine & Warren they stood
And the flame folded roaring fierce within the pitchy night
Before the Demon red, who burnt towards America,
In black smoke thunders and loud winds rejoicing in its terror   10
Breaking in smoky wreaths from the wild deep. & gath'ring thick
In flames as of a furnace on the land from North to South

[Plate 15]

What time the thirteen Governors that England sent convene
In Bernards house; the flames coverd the land, they rouze, they cry*
Shaking their mental chains, they rush in fury to the sea
To quench their anguish; at the feet of Washington down fall'n
They grovel on the sand and writhing lie. while all   5
The British soldiers thro' the thirteen states sent up a howl
Of anguish: threw their swords & muskets to the earth & ran
From their encampments and dark castles seeking where to hide

From the grim flames; and from the visions of Orc; in sight
Of Albions Angel; who enrag'd, his secret clouds open'd   10
From north to south, and burnt outstretchd on wings of wrath
                                                          cov'ring
The eastern sky, spreading his awful wings across the heavens;
Beneath him rolld his num'rous hosts, all Albions Angels camp'd
Darkend the Atlantic mountains & their trumpets shook the valleys
Arm'd with diseases of the earth to cast upon the Abyss,   15
Their numbers forty millions, must'ring in the eastern sky.*

[Plate 16]

In the flames stood & view'd the armies drawn out in the sky
Washington, Franklin, Paine, & Warren, Allen, Gates & Lee:*
And heard the voice of Albions Angel give the thunderous command
His plagues obedient to his voice flew forth out of their clouds*
Falling upon America, as a storm to cut them off   5
As a blight cuts the tender corn when it begins to appear.
Dark is the heaven above, & cold & hard the earth beneath;
And as a plague wind fill'd with insects cuts off man & beast;
And as a sea o'erwhelms a land in the day of an earthquake;

Fury! rage! madness! in a wind swept through America   10
And the red flames of Orc, that folded roaring, fierce, around
The angry shores, and the fierce rushing of th' inhabitants together;
The citizens of New-York close their books & lock their chests;
The mariners of Boston drop their anchors and unlade;
The scribe of Pensylvania casts his pen upon the earth;   15
The builder of Virginia throws his hammer down in fear.

Then had America been lost, o'erwhelm'd by the Atlantic,*
And Earth had lost another portion of the infinite!
But all rush together in the night in wrath and raging fire
The red fires rag'd! the plagues recoil'd! then rolld they back with fury 20

[Plate 17]

On Albions Angels: then the Pestilence began in streaks of red
Across the limbs of Albions Guardian, the spotted plague smote
                                                          Bristols
And the Leprosy Londons Spirit, sickening all their bands:*

The millions sent up a howl of anguish and threw off their
                                   hammerd mail,
And cast their swords & spears to earth, & stood a naked multitude.   5
Albions Guardian writhed in torment on the eastern sky
Pale quivring toward the brain his glimmering eyes, teeth chattering
Howling & shuddering, his legs quivering; convuls'd each
                                   muscle & sinew
Sick'ning lay Londons Guardian. and the ancient miter'd York*
Their heads on snowy hills, their ensigns sick'ning in the sky   10

The plagues creep on the burning winds driven by flames of Orc,
And by the fierce Americans rushing together in the night
Driven o'er the Guardians of Ireland and Scotland and Wales.
They spotted with plagues forsook the frontiers & their banners
                                   seard
With fires of hell, deform their ancient heavens with shame & woe.   15
Hid in his caves the Bard of Albion felt the enormous plagues.*
And a cowl of flesh grew o'er his head & scales on his back & ribs;
And rough with black scales all his Angels fright their ancient
                                   heavens
The doors of marriage are open, and the Priests in rustling scales
Rush into reptile coverts. hiding from the fires of Orc,   20
That play around the golden roofs in wreaths of fierce desire,
Leaving the females naked and glowing with the lusts of youth

For the female spirits of the dead pining in bonds of religion;
Run from their fetters reddening, & in long drawn arches sitting:
They feel the nerves of youth renew, and desires of ancient times.   25
Over their pale limbs as a vine when the tender grape appears*

[Plate 18]

Over the hills, the vales, the cities, rage the red flames fierce;
The Heavens melted from north to south; and Urizen who sat
Above all heavens in thunders wrap'd, emerg'd his leprous head
From out his holy shrine, his tears in deluge piteous
Falling into the deep sublime! flag'd with grey-brow'd snows   5
And thunderous visages, his jealous wings wav'd over the deep:
Weeping in dismal howling woe he dark descended howling
Around the smitten bands, clothed in tears & trembling
                                 shudd'ring cold.

His stored snows he poured forth, and his icy magazines
He open'd on the deep, and on the Atlantic sea white shiv'ring.   10
Leprous his limbs, all over white, and hoary was his visage.
Weeping in dismal howlings before the stern Americans
Hiding the Demon red with clouds & cold mists from the earth:
Till Angels & weak men twelve years should govern o'er the strong:*
And then their end should come, when France reciev'd the   15
                                                    Demons light.

Stiff shudderings shook the heav'nly thrones! France Spain & Italy,
In terror view'd the bands of Albion, and the ancient Guardians
Fainting upon the elements. smitten with their own plagues
They slow advance to shut the five gates of their law-built heaven*
Filled with blasting fancies and with mildews of despair*   20
With fierce disease and lust, unable to stem the fires of Orc;
But the five gates were consum'd, & their bolts and hinges melted
And the fierce flames burnt round the heavens, & round the
                                                    abodes of men

FINIS

Europe a Prophecy*

LAMBETH Printed by Will: Blake: 1794

[Plate 4]

PRELUDIUM

The nameless shadowy female rose from out the breast of Orc:
Her snaky hair brandishing in the winds of Enitharmon:
And thus her voice arose.

O mother Enitharmon wilt thou bring forth other sons?
To cause my name to vanish, that my place may not be found.   5
For I am faint with travel!*
Like the dark cloud disburdend in the day of dismal thunder.

My roots are brandish'd in the heavens, my fruits in earth beneath
Surge, foam and labour into life, first born & first consum'd!
Consumed and consuming!   10
Then why shouldst thou accursed mother bring me into life?

I wrap my turban of thick clouds around my lab'ring head:
And fold the sheety waters as a mantle round my limbs.
Yet the red sun and moon,
And all the overflowing stars rain down prolific pains.   15

[Plate 5]

Unwilling I look up to heaven! unwilling count the stars!
Sitting in fathomless abyss of my immortal shrine.
I sieze their burning power
And bring forth howling terrors, all devouring fiery kings.

Devouring & devoured roaming on dark and desolate mountains   5
In forests of eternal death, shrieking in hollow trees.
Ah mother Enitharmon!
Stamp not with solid form this vig'rous progeny of fires.

I bring forth from my teeming bosom myriads of flames,
And thou dost stamp them with a signet, then they roam abroad   10

And leave me void as death:
Ah! I am drown'd in shady woe, and visionary joy.

And who shall bind the infinite with an eternal band?
To compass it with swaddling bands? and who shall cherish it
With milk and honey?　　　　　　　　　　　　　　　　　　　15
I see it smile & I roll inward & my voice is past.

She ceast & rolld her shady clouds
Into the secret place.

[Plate 6]

A PROPHECY

　The deep of winter came:
　　What time the secret child
Descended thro' the orient gates of the eternal day:
War ceas'd, & all the troops like shadows fled to their abodes.*

Then Enitharmon saw her sons & daughters rise around.　　5
Like pearly clouds they meet together in the crystal house;*
And Los. possessor of the moon, joy'd in the peaceful night:*
Thus speaking while his num'rous sons shook their bright
　　　　　　　　　　　　　　　　　　　　　　fiery wings

Again the night is come
That strong Urthona takes his rest,　　　　　　　　　　　10
And Urizen unloos'd from chains
Glows like a meteor in the distant north
Stretch forth your hands and strike the elemental strings!
Awake the thunders of the deep,

[Plate 7]

The shrill winds wake!
Till all the sons of Urizen look out and envy Los:
Sieze all the spirits of life and bind
Their warbling joys to our loud strings
Bind all the nourishing sweets of earth　　　　　　　　　5
To give us bliss, that we may drink the sparkling wine of Los
And let us laugh at war,
Despising toil and care.

Because the days and nights of joy in lucky hours renew.
Arise, O Orc from thy deep den, 10
First born of Enitharmon, rise!
And we will crown thy head with garlands of the ruddy vine;
For now thou art bound;
And I may see thee in the hour of bliss, my eldest born.

The horrent Demon rose. surrounded with red stars of fire, 15
Whirling about in furious circles round the immortal fiend.

Then Enitharmon down descended into his red light,
And thus her voice rose to her children, the distant heavens

[Plate 8]

Now comes the night of Enitharmons joy!
Who shall I call? Who shall I send?
That Woman, lovely Woman! may have dominion*
Arise O Rintrah thee I call! & Palamabron thee.*
Go: tell the human race that Woman's love is Sin: 5
That an Eternal life awaits the worms of sixty winters
In an allegorical abode where existence hath never come:
Forbid all Joy, & from her childhood shall the little female
Spread nets in every secret path.
My weary eyelids draw towards the evening my bliss is yet but new. 10

[Plate 11]

Arise O Rintrah eldest born: second to none but Orc:
O lion Rintrah raise thy fury from thy forests black;
Bring Palamabron horned priest, skipping upon the mountains;
And silent Elynittria the silver bowed queen:
Rintrah, where hast thou hid thy bride! 5
Weeps she in desart shades?
Alas my Rintrah! bring the lovely jealous Ocalythron.

Arise my son! bring all thy brethren O thou king of fire.
Prince of the sun I see thee with thy innumerable race:
Thick as the summer stars: 10
But each ramping, his golden mane shakes.*
And thine eyes rejoice because of strength O Rintrah furious king.

[Plate 12]

Enitharmon slept,
Eighteen hundred years: Man was a Dream!*
The night of Nature and their harps unstrung:
She slept in middle of her nightly song.
Eighteen hundred years, a female dream!   5

Shadows of men in fleeting bands upon the winds:
Divide the heavens of Europe:
Till Albions Angel smitten with his own plagues fled with his bands*
The cloud bears hard on Albions shore:
Fill'd with immortal demons of futurity: 10
In council gather the smitten Angels of Albion
The cloud bears hard upon the council house; down rushing
On the heads of Albions Angels.

One hour they lay buried beneath the ruins of that hall;*
But as the stars rise from the salt lake, they arise in pain,   15
In troubled mists o'erclouded by the terrors of strugling times,

[Plate 13]

In thoughts perturb'd they rose from the bright ruins silent following
The fiery King, who sought his ancient temple serpent-form'd*
That stretches out its shady length along the Island white.
Round him roll'd his clouds of war; silent the Angel went,
Along the infinite shores of Thames to golden Verulam.*   5
There stand the venerable porches that high-towering rear
Their oak-surrounded pillars, form'd of massy stones, uncut
With tool; stones precious; such eternal in the heavens,
Of colours twelve. few known on earth, give light in the opake.
Plac'd in the order of the stars, when the five senses whelm'd   10
In deluge o'er the earth-born man; then turn'd the fluxile eyes
Into two stationary orbs, concentrating all things.
The ever-varying spiral ascents to the heavens of heavens
Were bended downward; and the nostrils golden gates shut
Turn'd outward, barr'd and petrify'd against the infinite.*   15

Thought chang'd the infinite to a serpent; that which pitieth:
To a devouring flame; and man fled from its face and hid
In forests of night; then all the eternal forests were divided

Into earths rolling in circles of space, that like an ocean rush'd
And overwhelmed all except this finite wall of flesh.   20
Then was the serpent temple form'd, image of infinite
Shut up in finite revolutions, and man became an Angel;
Heaven a mighty circle turning; God a tyrant crown'd.

Now arriv'd the ancient Guardian at the southern porch,
That planted thick with trees of blackest leaf, & in a vale   25
Obscure, inclos'd the Stone of Night; oblique it stood, o'erhung*
With purple flowers and berries red; image of that sweet south,
Once open to the heavens and elevated on the human neck,
Now overgrown with hair and coverd with a stony roof,
Downward 'tis sunk beneath th' attractive north, that round the feet   30
A raging whirlpool draws the dizzy enquirer to his grave.

[Plate 14]

    Albions Angel rose upon the Stone of Night.
    He saw Urizen on the Atlantic;
    And his brazen Book,
    That Kings & Priests had copied on Earth
    Expanded from North to South.   5

[Plate 15]

And the clouds & fires pale rolld round in the night of Enitharmon
Round Albions cliffs & Londons walls; still Enitharmon slept!
Rolling volumes of grey mist involve Churches, Palaces, Towers:
For Urizen unclasp'd his Book! feeding his soul with pity
The youth of England hid in gloom curse the paind heavens;   5
                           compell'd
Into the deadly night to see the form of Albions Angel
Their parents brought them forth, & aged ignorance preaches canting.
On a vast rock, perciev'd by those senses that are clos'd from thought:
Bleak, dark, abrupt, it stands & overshadows London city*
They saw his boney feet on the rock, the flesh consum'd in flames: 10
They saw the Serpent temple lifted above, shadowing the
                           Island white:
They heard the voice of Albions Angel howling in flames of Orc.
Seeking the trump of the last doom

Above the rest the howl was heard from Westminster
                        louder & louder;
The Guardian of the secret codes forsook his ancient mansion*   15
Driven out by the flames of Orc; his furr'd robes & false locks
Adhered and grew one with his flesh, and nerves & veins shot
                        thro' them
With dismal torment sick hanging upon the wind: he fled
Groveling along Great George Street thro' the Park gate;
                        all the soldiers
Fled from his sight: he drag'd his torments to the wilderness.   20

Thus was the howl thro Europe!
For Orc rejoic'd to hear the howling shadows
But Palamabron shot his lightnings trenching down his wide back
And Rintrah hung with all his legions in the nether deep

Enitharmon laugh'd in her sleep to see (O woman's triumph)   25
Every house a den. every man bound; the shadows are filld*
With spectres, and the windows wove over with curses of iron:
Over the doors Thou shalt not; & over the chimneys Fear is written:
With bands of iron round their necks, fasten'd into the walls
The citizens: in leaden gyves the inhabitants of suburbs   30
Walk heavy: soft and bent are the bones of villagers

Between the clouds of Urizen the flames of Orc roll heavy
Around the limbs of Albions Guardian. his flesh consuming.
Howlings & hissings. shrieks & groans. & voices of despair
Arise around him in the cloudy Heavens of Albion, Furious,   35

[Plate 16]

The red limb'd Angel siez'd in horror and torment;*
The Trump of the last doom; but he could not blow the iron tube!*
Thrice he assay'd presumptuous to awake the dead to Judgment.

A mighty Spirit leap'd from the land of Albion,
Nam'd Newton; he siez'd the Trump, & blow'd the enormous blast!*   5
Yellow as leaves of Autumn the myriads of Angelic hosts,
Fell thro' the wintry skies seeking their graves;
Rattling their hollow bones in howling and lamentation.

Then Enitharmon woke, nor knew that she had slept
And eighteen hundred years were fled   10

As if they had not been
She calld her sons & daughters
To the sports of night,
Within her crystal house;
And thus her song proceeds.   15

Arise, Ethinthus! tho' the earth-worm call*
Let him call in vain;
Till the night of holy shadows
And human solitude is past!

[Plate 17]

Ethinthus queen of waters, how thou shinest in the sky:
My daughter how do I rejoice! for thy children flock around
Like the gay fishes on the wave, when the cold moon drinks the dew,
Ethinthus! thou art sweet as comforts to my fainting soul:
For now thy waters warble round the feet of Enitharmon.   5

Manathu-Vorcyon! I behold thee flaming in my halls
Light of thy mothers soul! I see thy lovely eagles round;
Thy golden wings are my delight, & thy flames of soft delusion.

Where is my lureing bird of Eden! Leutha, silent love!
Leutha. the many coloured bow delights upon thy wings;   10
Soft soul of flowers Leutha!
Sweet smiling pestilence! I see thy blushing light;
Thy daughters many changing,
Revolve like sweet perfumes ascending O Leutha silken queen!

Where is the youthful Antamon. prince of the pearly dew,   15
O Antamon, why wilt thou leave thy mother Enitharmon?
Alone I see thee crystal form,
Floting upon the bosomd air;
With lineaments of gratified desire.
My Antamon the seven churches of Leutha seek thy love.   20

I hear the soft Oothoon in Enitharmons tents:
Why wilt thou give up womans secrecy my melancholy child?
Between two moments bliss is ripe:
O Theotormon robb'd of joy, I see thy salt tears flow
Down the steps of my crystal house.   25

Sotha & Thiralatha, secret dwellers of dreamful caves,
Arise and please the horrent fiend with your melodious songs.
Still all your thunders golden-hoofd, & bind your horses black.
Orc! smile upon my children!
Smile son of my afflictions. 30
Arise O Orc, and give our mountains joy of thy red light.

She ceas'd, for All were forth at sport beneath the solemn moon
Waking the stars of Urizen with their immortal songs,
That nature felt thro' all her pores the enormous revelry.
Till morning ope'd the eastern gate. 35
Then every one fled to his station. & Enitharmon wept.

But terrible Orc, when he beheld the morning in the east,

[Plate 18]

Shot from the heights of Enitharmon;
And in the vineyards of red France appear'd the light of his fury.*

The sun glow'd fiery red;
The furious terrors flew around!
On golden chariots raging, with red wheels dropping with blood; 5
The Lions lash their wrathful tails!
The Tigers couch upon the prey & suck the ruddy tide:
And Enitharmon groans & cries in anguish and dismay.

Then Los arose his head he reard in snaky thunders clad:
And with a cry that shook all nature to the utmost pole, 10
Call'd all his sons to the strife of blood.

FINIS

The Song of Los*

[*The Song of Los* Plate 3]

AFRICA*

I will sing you a song of Los. the Eternal Prophet:
He sung it to four harps at the tables of Eternity.
     In heart-formed Africa.
Urizen faded! Ariston shudderd!
     And thus the Song began   5

Adam stood in the garden of Eden:
And Noah on the mountains of Ararat:*
They saw Urizen give his Laws to the Nations
By the hands of the children of Los.*

Adam shudderd! Noah faded! black grew the sunny African*   10
 When Rintrah gave Abstract Philosophy to Brama in the East.*
  (Night spoke to the Cloud!
 Lo these Human form'd spirits, in smiling hypocrisy. War
 Against one another; so let them War on; slaves to the eternal
                            Elements)

Noah shrunk beneath the waters.   15
Abram fled in fires from Chaldea:*
Moses beheld upon Mount Sinai forms of dark delusion:*

To Trismegistus. Palamabron gave an abstract Law:
To Pythagoras Socrates & Plato.*

Times rolled on o'er all the sons of Har, time after time*   20
Orc on Mount Atlas howld, chain'd down with the Chain of Jealousy*
Then Oothoon hoverd over Judah & Jerusalem
And Jesus heard her voice (a man of sorrows) he recievd
A Gospel from wretched Theotormon.*

The human race began to wither. for the healthy built   25
Secluded places, fearing the joys of Love
And the disease'd only propagated;
So Antamon call'd up Leutha from her valleys of delight:
And to Mahomet a loose Bible gave. *

But in the North, to Odin, Sotha gave a Code of War. *   30
Because of Diralada, thinking to reclaim his joy.

[*The Song of Los* Plate 4]

These were the Churches: Hospitals: Castles: Palaces;
Like nets & gins & traps to catch the joys of Eternity
    And all the rest a desart;
Till, like a dream Eternity was obliterated & erased.

Since that dread day when Har and Heva fled.   5
Because their brethren & sisters liv'd in War & Lust;
And as they fled they shrunk
Into two narrow doleful forms:
Creeping in reptile flesh upon
The bosom of the ground: 10
And all the vast of Nature shrunk
Before their shrunken eyes.

Thus the terrible race of Los & Enitharmon gave
Laws & Religions to the sons of Har binding them more
And more to Earth: closing and restraining;   15
Till a Philosophy of Five Senses was complete
Urizen wept & gave it into the hands of Newton & Locke

    Clouds roll heavy upon the Alps round Rousseau & Voltaire:*
    And on the mountains of Lebanon round the deceased Gods
    Of Asia; & on the desarts of Africa round the Fallen Angels.   20
    The Guardian Prince of Albion burns in his nightly tent.

ASIA*

[*The Song of Los* Plate 6]

    The Kings of Asia heard
    The howl rise up from Europe!
    And each ran out from his Web;
    From his ancient woven Den;
    For the darkness of Asia was startled   5
    At the thick-flaming, thought-creating fires of Orc.

    And the Kings of Asia stood
    And cried in bitterness of soul.

Shall not the King call for Famine from the heath*
Nor the Priest, for Pestilence from the fen?   10
To restrain! to dismay! to thin!
The inhabitants of mountain and plain;
In the day of full-feeding prosperity;
And the night of delicious songs.

Shall not the Councellor throw his curb   15
Of Poverty on the laborious?
To fix the price of labour;
To invent allegoric riches:*

And the privy admonishers of men
Call for fires in the City   20
For heaps of smoking ruins,
In the night of prosperity & wantonness

To turn man from his path,
To restrain the child from the womb,

[*The Song of Los* Plate 7]

To cut off the bread from the city,
That the remnant may learn to obey.

That the pride of the heart may fail;
That the lust of the eyes may be quench'd:
That the delicate ear in its infancy   5
May be dull'd; and the nostrils clos'd up;
To teach mortal worms the path
That leads from the gates of the Grave.

    Urizen heard them cry;
And his shudd'ring, waving wings   10
Went enormous above the red flames
Drawing clouds of despair thro' the heavens
Of Europe as he went:
And his Books of brass, iron & gold
Melted over the land as he flew,   15
Heavy-waving, howling, weeping.

            And he stood over Judea;
            And stay'd in his ancient place;
            And stretch'd his clouds over Jerusalem.

For Adam, a mouldering skeleton   20
Lay bleach'd on the garden of Eden:
And Noah, as white as snow*
On the mountains of Ararat.

Then the thunders of Urizen bellow'd aloud
From his woven darkness above.   25

Orc raging in European darkness
Arose like a pillar of fire above the Alps
Like a serpent of fiery flame!
          The sullen Earth
                    Shrunk!   30

Forth from the dead dust, rattling bones to bones
Join: shaking convuls'd, the shivring clay breathes.
And all flesh naked stand; Fathers and Friends;
Mothers & Infants; Kings & Warriors:

The Grave shrieks with delight, & shakes   35
Her hollow womb, & clasps the solid stem;
Her bosom swells with wild desire:
And milk & blood & glandous wine,*
In rivers rush & shout & dance,
On mountain, dale and plain.   40

THE SONG OF LOS IS ENDED

Urizen Wept.

The First Book of Urizen*

LAMBETH. Printed by Will Blake 1794.

[Plate 2]

PRELUDIUM TO THE FIRST BOOK OF *URIZEN*

Of the primeval Priests assum'd power,
When Eternals spurn'd back his religion;
And gave him a place in the north,
Obscure. shadowy. void. solitary.

Eternals I hear your call gladly,   5
Dictate swift winged words. & fear not
To unfold your dark visions of torment.

[Plate 3]

CHAP: I

1. Lo, a shadow of horror is risen
In Eternity! Unknown, unprolific!
Self-closd, all-repelling; what Demon
Hath form'd this abominable void
This soul-shudd'ring vacuum? Some said   5
'It is Urizen'. But unknown, abstracted*
Brooding secret, the dark power hid.

2. Times on times he divided, & measur'd
Space by space in his ninefold darkness,
Unseen, unknown: changes appeard   10
Like desolate mountains rifted furious
By the black winds of perturbation

3. For he strove in battles dire
In unseen conflictions with shapes
Bred from his forsaken wilderness,   15
Of beast, bird, fish, serpent & element
Combustion, blast, vapour and cloud.

4. Dark revolving in silent activity:
Unseen in tormenting passions;

An activity unknown and horrible;   20
A self-contemplating shadow,
In enormous labours occupied

5. But Eternals beheld his vast forests
Age on ages he lay, clos'd, unknown,
Brooding shut in the deep; all avoid   25
The petrific, abominable chaos

6. His cold horrors silent, dark Urizen
Prepar'd: his ten thousands of thunders
Rang'd in gloom'd array stretch out across
The dread world, & the rolling of wheels   30
As of swelling seas, sound in his clouds
In his hills of stor'd snows, in his mountains
Of hail & ice; voices of terror,
Are heard, like thunders of autumn,
When the cloud blazes over the harvests   35

CHAP: II.

1. Earth was not: nor globes of attraction*
The will of the Immortal expanded
Or contracted his all flexible senses.
Death was not, but eternal life sprung

2. The sound of a trumpet the heavens   40
Awoke & vast clouds of blood roll'd
Round the dim rocks of Urizen, so nam'd
That solitary one in Immensity

3. Shrill the trumpet: & myriads of Eternity*

[Plate 4]

Muster around the bleak desarts
Now fill'd with clouds darkness & waters
That roll'd perplex'd lab'ring & utter'd
Words articulate, bursting in thunders
That roll'd on the tops of his mountains   5

4. From the depths of dark solitude, From
The eternal abode in my holiness,
Hidden, set apart, in my stern counsels

Reserv'd for the days of futurity,
I have sought for a joy without pain,   10
For a solid without fluctuation
Why will you die O Eternals?
Why live in unquenchable burnings?

5. First I fought with the fire; consum'd
Inwards, into a deep world within: 15
A void immense, wild dark & deep
Where nothing was; Nature's wide womb
And self balanc'd stretch'd o'er the void
I alone, even I! the winds merciless
Bound; but condensing in torrents   20
They fall & fall; strong I repell'd
The vast waves, & arose on the waters
A wide world of solid obstruction

6. Here alone I in books formd of metals*
Have written the secrets of wisdom   25
The secrets of dark contemplation
By fightings and conflicts dire.
With terrible monsters Sin-bred:
Which the bosoms of all inhabit;
Seven deadly Sins of the soul.*   30

7. Lo! I unfold my darkness: and on
This rock place with strong hand the Book
Of eternal brass, written in my solitude

8. Laws of peace, of love, of unity;
Of pity, compassion, forgiveness,   35
Let each chuse one habitation;
His ancient infinite mansion;
One command, one joy, one desire,
One curse, one weight, one measure,
One King, one God, one Law.*   40

CHAP: III.

1. The voice ended, they saw his pale visage
Emerge from the darkness; his hand
On the rock of eternity unclasping
The Book of brass. Rage siez'd the strong

2. Rage, fury, intense indignation   45
In cataracts of fire blood & gall
In whirlwinds of sulphurous smoke:
And enormous forms of energy;
All the seven deadly sins of the soul

[Plate 5]

In living creations appear'd
In the flames of eternal fury.

3. Sund'ring, dark'ning, thund'ring!
Rent away with a terrible crash
Eternity roll'd wide apart   5
Wide asunder rolling
Mountainous all around
Departing; departing: departing:
Leaving ruinous fragments of life
Hanging frowning cliffs & all between   10
An ocean of voidness unfathomable

4. The roaring fires ran o'er the heav'ns
In whirlwinds & cataracts of blood
And o'er the dark desarts of Urizen
Fires pour thro' the void on all sides   15
On Urizens self-begotten armies

5. But no light from the fires, all was darkness
In the flames of Eternal fury

6. In fierce anguish & quenchless flames
To the desarts and rocks he ran raging   20
To hide, but he could not: combining
He dug mountains & hills in vast strength
He piled them in incessant labour,
In howlings & pangs & fierce madness
Long periods in burning fires labouring   25
Till hoary, and age-broke, and aged.
In despair and the shadows of death.

7. And a roof vast petrific around,
On all sides he fram'd: like a womb;
Where thousands of rivers in veins   30

Of blood pour down the mountains to cool
The eternal fires beating without
From Eternals; & like a black globe
View'd by sons of Eternity, standing
On the shore of the infinite ocean   35
Like a human heart strugling & beating
The vast world of Urizen appear'd.

8. And Los, round the dark globe of Urizen*
Kept watch for Eternals to confine,
The obscure separation alone;   40
For Eternity stood wide apart

[Plate 6]

As the stars are apart from the earth

9. Los wept howling around the dark Demon:
And cursing his lot for in anguish
Urizen was rent from his side:
And a fathomless void for his feet;   5
And intense fires for his dwelling

10. But Urizen laid in a stony sleep
Unorganiz'd, rent from Eternity

11. The Eternals said: What is this? Death
Urizen is a clod of clay.   10

[Plate 10]

CHAP: IV

1. Ages on ages roll'd over him!
In stony sleep ages roll'd over him!
Like a dark waste stretching chang'able
By earthquakes riv'n, belching sullen fires
On ages roll'd ages in ghastly   5
Sick torment; around him in whirlwinds
Of darkness the eternal Prophet howl'd
Beating still on his rivets of iron
Pouring sodor of iron; dividing*
The horrible night into watches.   10

2. And Urizen (so his eternal name)
His prolific delight obscurd more & more
In dark secresy hiding in surging
Sulphureous fluid his phantasies.
The Eternal Prophet heavd the dark bellows   15
And turn'd restless the tongs; and the hammer
Incessant beat; forging chains new & new
Numb'ring with links, hours days & years

3. The eternal mind bounded began to roll
Eddies of wrath ceaseless round & round   20
And the sulphureous foam surging thick
Settled, a lake, bright, & shining clear
White as the snow on the mountains cold*

4. Forgetfulness, dumbness, necessity!
In chains of the mind locked up   25
Like fetters of ice shrinking together
Disorganiz'd, rent from Eternity.
Los beat on his fetters of iron:
And heated his furnaces & pour'd
Iron sodor and sodor of brass   30

5. Restless turnd the immortal inchain'd
Heaving dolorous! anguish'd! unbearable
Till a roof shaggy wild, inclos'd
In an orb, his fountain of thought.

6. In a horrible dreamful slumber;   35
Like the linked infernal chain;
A vast Spine writh'd in torment
Upon the winds; shooting pain'd
Ribs, like a bending cavern
And bones of solidness, froze   40
Over all his nerves of joy.
And a first Age passed over*
And a state of dismal woe.

[Plate 11]

7. From the caverns of his jointed Spine
Down sunk with fright a red

Round globe hot burning deep
Deep down into the Abyss:
Panting: Conglobing, Trembling 5
Shooting out ten thousand branches
Around his solid bones
And a second Age passed over
And a state of dismal woe

8. In harrowing fear rolling round; 10
His nervous brain shot branches
Round the branches of his heart
On high into two little orbs
And fixed in two little caves
Hiding carefully from the wind, 15
His Eyes beheld the deep,
And a third Age passed over:
And a state of dismal woe.

9. The pangs of hope began,
In heavy pain striving, struggling 20
Two Ears in close volutions.
From beneath his orbs of vision
Shot spiring out and petrified
As they grew. And a fourth Age passed
And a state of dismal woe. 25

10. In ghastly torment sick;
Hanging upon the wind;

[Plate 13]

Two Nostrils bent down to the deep.
And a fifth Age passed over,
And a state of dismal woe.

11. In ghastly torment sick;
Within his ribs bloated round,
A craving Hungry Cavern 5
Thence arose his channeld Throat,
And like a red flame a Tongue
Of thirst & of hunger appeard.
And a sixth Age passed over: 10
And a state of dismal woe

12. Enraged & stifled with torment
He threw his right Arm to the north
His left Arm to the south
Shooting out in anguish deep   15
And his Feet stampd the nether Abyss
In trembling & howling & dismay.
And a seventh Age passed over
And a state of dismal woe.

CHAP: V.

1. In terrors Los shrunk from his task   20
His great hammer fell from his hand
His fires beheld, and sickening
Hid their strong limbs in smoke.
For with noises ruinous loud;
With hurtlings & clashings & groans   25
The Immortal endurd his chains
Tho' bound in a deadly sleep

2. All the myriads of Eternity
All the wisdom & joy of life
Roll like a sea around him   30
Except what his little orbs
Of sight by degrees unfold

3. And now his eternal life
Like a dream was obliterated

4. Shudd'ring, the Eternal Prophet smote   35
With a stroke, from his north to south region
The bellows & hammer are silent now
A nerveless silence his prophetic voice
Siez'd; a cold solitude & dark void
The Eternal Prophet & Urizen clos'd   40

5. Ages on ages rolld over them
Cut off from life & light frozen
Into horrible forms of deformity
Los sufferd his fires to decay
Then he look'd back with anxious desire   45
But the space undivided by existence
Struck horror into his soul.

6. Los wept obscur'd with mourning
His bosom earthquak'd with sighs
He saw Urizen deadly black   50
In his chains bound & Pity began*

7. In anguish dividing & dividing
For pity divides the soul
In pangs eternity on eternity,
Life in cataracts pourd down his cliffs   55
The void shrunk the lymph into Nerves
Wandring wide on the bosom of night
And left a round globe of blood
Trembling upon the void.

[Plate 15]

Thus the Eternal Prophet was divided*
Before the death image of Urizen
For in changeable clouds and darkness
In a winterly night beneath
The Abyss of Los stretch'd immense   5
And now seen now obscurd to the eyes
Of Eternals the visions remote
Of the dark seperation appear'd.
As glasses discover Worlds
In the endless Abyss of space   10
So the expanding eyes of Immortals
Beheld the dark visions of Los,
And the globe of life blood trembling

[Plate 18]

8. The globe of life blood trembled
Branching out into roots:
Fibrous, writhing upon the winds;
Fibres of blood, milk and tears:
In pangs, eternity on eternity.   5
At length in tears & cries imbodied
A female form, trembling and pale
Waves before his deathy face.

9. All Eternity shudderd at sight
Of the first female now separate   10
Pale as a cloud of snow
Waving before the face of Los

10. Wonder, awe, fear, astonishment
Petrify the eternal myriads;
At the first female form now separate   15

[Plate 19]

They call'd her Pity, and fled

11. 'Spread a Tent with strong curtains around them
'Let cords & stakes bind in the Void
That Eternals may no more behold them'

12. They began to weave curtains of darkness   5
They erected large pillars round the Void
With golden hooks fasten'd in the pillars
With infinite labour the Eternals
A woof wove, and called it Science

CHAP: VI.

1. But Los saw the Female & pitied   10
He embrac'd her, she wept she refusd
In perverse and cruel delight
She fled from his arms, yet he followd

2. Eternity shudder'd when they saw,
Man begetting his likeness,   15
On his own divided image.

3. A time passed over, the Eternals
Began to erect the tent;
When Enitharmon, sick,
Felt a Worm within her womb.   20

4. Yet helpless it lay like a Worm
In the trembling womb
To be moulded into existence

5. All day the worm lay on her bosom
All night within her womb   25

The worm lay till it grew to a serpent
With dolorous hissings & poisons
Round Enitharmons loins folding,

6. Coild within Enitharmons womb
The serpent grew casting its scales   30
With sharp pangs the hissings began
To change to a grating cry,
Many sorrows and dismal throes
Many forms of fish, bird & beast
Brought forth an Infant form   35
Where was a worm before.

7. The Eternals their tent finished
Alarm'd with these gloomy visions
When Enitharmon groaning
Produc'd a man Child to the light.   40

8. A shriek ran thro' Eternity:
And a paralytic stroke;
At the birth of the Human shadow*

9. Delving earth in his resistless way:
Howling, the Child with fierce flames   45
Issu'd from Enitharmon.

10. The Eternal, closed the tent
They beat down the stakes the cords

[Plate 20]

Stretch'd for a work of eternity:
No more Los beheld Eternity.

11. In his hands he siez'd the infant
He bathed him in springs of sorrow
He gave him to Enitharmon.   5

CHAP: VII

1. They named the child Orc, he grew
Fed with milk of Enitharmon

2. Los awoke her; O sorrow & pain!
A tight'ning girdle grew,

Around his bosom. In sobbings   10
He burst the girdle in twain,
But still another girdle
Oppressd his bosom. In sobbings
Again he burst it. Again
Another girdle succeeds   15
The girdle was form'd by day;
By night was burst in twain.

3. These falling down on the rock
Into an iron Chain
In each other link by link lock'd   20

4. They took Orc to the top of a mountain*
O how Enitharmon wept!
They chain'd his young limbs to the rock
With the Chain of Jealousy
Beneath Urizens deathful shadow   25

5. The dead heard the voice of the child
And began to awake from sleep
All things. heard the voice of the child
And began to awake to life.

6. And Urizen craving with hunger   30
Stung with the odours of Nature
Explor'd his dens around

7. He form'd a line & a plummet
To divide the Abyss beneath.
He form'd a dividing rule: 35

8. He formed scales to weigh;
He formed massy weights;
He formed a brazen quadrant;
He formed golden compasses
And began to explore the Abyss   40
And he planted a garden of fruits

9. But Los encircled Enitharmon
With fires of Prophecy
From the sight of Urizen & Orc.

10. And she bore an enormous race   45

CHAP: VIII

1. Urizen explor'd his dens
Mountain, moor, & wilderness,
With a globe of fire lighting his journey
A fearful journey, annoy'd
By cruel enormities: forms   50

[Plate 23]

Of life on his forsaken mountains

2. And his world teemd vast enormities
Frightning; faithless; fawning
Portions of life; similitudes
Of a foot, or a hand, or a head   5
Or a heart, or an eye, they swam mischevous
Dread terrors! delighting in blood

3. Most Urizen sicken'd to see
His eternal creations appear
Sons & daughters of sorrow on mountains   10
Weeping! Wailing! first Thiriel appear'd
Astonish'd at his own existence
Like a man from a cloud born, & Utha
From the waters emerging, laments!
Grodna rent the deep earth howling   15
Amaz'd;! his heavens immense cracks
Like the ground parch'd with heat; then Fuzon
Flam'd out! first begotten, last born
All his eternal sons in like manner
His daughters from green herbs & cattle   20
From monsters & worms of the pit.

4. He in darkness clos'd, view'd all his race
And his soul sicken'd! he curs'd
Both sons & daughters; for he saw
That no flesh nor spirit could keep   25
His iron laws one moment.

5. For he saw that life liv'd upon death

[Plate 25]

The Ox in the slaughter house moans
The Dog at the wintry door*
And he wept, & he called it Pity
And his tears flowed down on the winds

6. Cold he wander'd on high, over their cities   5
In weeping & pain & woe
And where-ever he wanderd in sorrows
Upon the aged heavens,
A cold shadow followd behind him
Like a spiders web, moist, cold & dim   10
Drawing out from his sorrowing soul
The dungeon-like heaven dividing
Where ever the footsteps of Urizen
Walk'd over the cities in sorrow.

7. Till a Web dark & cold, throughout all   15
The tormented element stretch'd
From the sorrows of Urizens soul
And the Web is a Female in embrio
None could break the Web, no wings of fire.

8. So twisted the cords, & so knotted   20
The meshes: twisted like to the human brain

9. And all call'd it The Net of Religion

CHAP: IX

1. Then the Inhabitants of those Cities:
Felt their Nerves change into Marrow
And hardening Bones began   25
In swift diseases and torments
In throbbings & shootings & grindings
Thro' all the coasts; till weaken'd
The Senses inward rush'd, shrinking
Beneath the dark net of infection.   30

2. Till the shrunken eyes clouded over
Discernd not the woven hipocrisy
But the streaky slime in their heavens
Brought together by narrowing perceptions
Appeard transparent air; for their eyes   35
Grew small like the eyes of a man

And in reptile forms shrinking together
Of seven feet stature they remaind*

3. Six days they shrunk up from existence,
And on the seventh day they rested.   40
And they bless'd the seventh day, in sick hope*
And forgot their eternal life

4. And their thirty cities divided*
In form of a human heart
No more could they rise at will   45
In the infinite void, but bound down
To earth by their narrowing perceptions

[Plate 28]

They lived a period of years
Then left a noisom body
To the jaws of devouring darkness

5. And their children wept, & built
Tombs in the desolate places,   5
And form'd laws of prudence, and call'd them
The eternal laws of God

6. And the thirty cities remain,
Surrounded by salt floods, now call'd
Africa: its name was then Egypt.   10

7. The remaining sons of Urizen
Beheld their brethren shrink together
Beneath the Net of Urizen:
Perswasion was in vain
For the ears of the inhabitants   15
Were wither'd, & deafen'd, & cold!
And their eyes could not discern,
Their brethren of other cities.

8. So Fuzon call'd all together
The remaining children of Urizen: 20
And they left the pendulous earth:
They called it Egypt, & left it.*

9. And the salt ocean rolled englobd.

THE END OF THE FIRST BOOK OF URIZEN

The Book of Ahania*

LAMBETH Printed by W Blake 1795

[Plate 3]

CHAP: IST

1: Fuzon on a chariot iron-wing'd*
On spiked flames rose; his hot visage
Flam'd furious! sparkles his hair & beard
Shot down his wide bosom and shoulders
On clouds of smoke rages his chariot   5
And his right hand burns red in its cloud
Moulding into a vast globe his wrath
As the thunder-stone is moulded
Son of Urizens silent burnings

2: Shall we worship this Demon of smoke,   10
Said Fuzon, this abstract non-entity
This cloudy God seated on waters
Now seen, now obscur'd; King of sorrow?

3: So he spoke, in a fiery flame,
On Urizen frowning indignant,   15
The Globe of wrath shaking on high
Roaring with fury, he threw
The howling Globe: burning it flew
Lengthning into a hungry beam. Swiftly

4: Oppos'd to the exulting flam'd beam   20
The broad Disk of Urizen upheav'd
Across the Void many a mile.

5: It was forg'd in mills where the winter
Beats incessant; ten winters the disk
Unremitting endur'd the cold hammer.   25

6: But the strong arm that sent it, remember'd
The sounding beam; laughing it tore through
That beaten mass: keeping its direction
The cold loins of Urizen dividing.

7: Dire shriekd his invisible Lust   30
Deep groan'd Urizen! stretching his awful hand
Ahania (so name his parted soul)*
He siez'd on his mountains of Jealousy.
He groand anguishd, & called her Sin,
Kissing her and weeping over her;   35
Then hid her in darkness, in silence;
Jealous tho' she was invisible.

8: She fell down a faint shadow wandring
In chaos and circling dark Urizen,
As the moon anguishd circles the earth;   40
Hopeless! abhorrd! a death-shadow,
Unseen, unbodied, unknown,
The mother of Pestilence.

9. But the fiery beam of Fuzon
Was a pillar of fire to Egypt   45
Five hundred years wandring on earth*
Till Los siezd it and beat in a mass
With the body of the sun.

[Plate 4]

CHAP: II^D

1: But the forehead of Urizen gathering.
And his eyes pale with anguish, his lips
Blue & changing; in tears and bitter
Contrition he prepar'd his Bow.

2: Form'd of Ribs: that in his dark solitude   5
When obscur'd in his forests, fell monsters,
Arose. For his dire Contemplations
Rush'd down like floods from his mountains
In torrents of mud settling thick
With Eggs of unnatural production   10
Forthwith hatching; some howl'd on his hills
Some in vales; some aloft flew in air

3: Of these: an enormous dread Serpent
Scaled and poisonous horned
Approach'd Urizen even to his knees   15
As he sat on his dark rooted Oak.*

4: With his horns he push'd furious.
Great the conflict & great the jealousy
In cold poisons: but Urizen smote him

5: First he poison'd the rocks with his blood   20
Then polish'd his ribs, and his sinews
Dried; laid them apart till winter;
Then a Bow black prepar'd; on this Bow
A poisoned rock plac'd in silence:
He utter'd these words to the Bow.   25

6: O Bow of the clouds of secresy!
O nerve of that lust form'd monster!
Send this rock swift, invisible thro'
The black clouds, on the bosom of Fuzon

7: So saying, In torment of his wounds,   30
He bent the enormous ribs slowly;
A circle of darkness! then fixed
The sinew in its rest: then the Rock
Poisonous source! plac'd with art, lifting difficult
Its weighty bulk; silent the rock lay.   35

8: While Fuzon his tygers unloosing
Thought Urizen slain by his wrath.
I am God. said he. eldest of things!*

9: Sudden sings the rock, swift & invisible
On Fuzon flew, enter'd his bosom;   40
His beautiful visage, his tresses,
That gave light to the mornings of heaven
Were smitten with darkness, deform'd
And outstretch'd on the edge of the forest

10: But the rock fell upon the Earth,   45
Mount Sinai, in Arabia.*

CHAP: III:

1: The Globe shook; and Urizen seated
On black clouds his sore wound anointed
The ointment flow'd down on the void
Mix'd with blood; here the snake gets her poison   50

2: With difficulty & great pain; Urizen
Lifted on high the dead corse:

On his shoulders he bore it to where
A Tree hung over the Immensity

3: For when Urizen shrunk away   55
From Eternals, he sat on a rock
Barren; a rock which himself
From redounding fancies had petrified
Many tears fell on the rock,
Many sparks of vegetation;   60
Soon shot the pained root
Of Mystery under his heel:
It grew a thick tree; he wrote
In silence his book of iron:
Till the horrid plant bending its boughs   65
Grew to roots when it felt the earth
And again sprung to many a tree.

4: Amaz'd started Urizen! when
He beheld himself compassed round
And high roofed over with trees   70
He arose but the stems stood so thick
He with difficulty and great pain
Brought his Books, all but the Book

[Plate 5]

Of iron, from the dismal shade

5: The Tree still grows over the Void
Enrooting itself all around
An endless labyrinth of woe!

6: The corse of his first begotten   5
On the accursed Tree of Mystery:*
On the topmost stem of this Tree,
Urizen nail'd Fuzons corse.

CHAP: IV:

1. Forth flew the arrows of pestilence
Round the pale living Corse on the tree   10

2: For in Urizens slumbers of abstraction
In the infinite ages of Eternity:

When his Nerves of Joy melted & flow'd
A white Lake on the dark blue air
In perturb'd pain and dismal torment   15
Now stretching out, now swift conglobing.

3: Effluvia vapor'd above
In noxious clouds; these hover'd thick
Over the disorganiz'd Immortal.
Till petrific pain scurfd o'er the Lakes   20
As the bones of man, solid & dark

4: The clouds of disease hover'd wide
Around the Immortal in torment
Perching around the hurtling bones
Disease on disease, shape on shape,   25
Winged screaming in blood & torment.

5: The Eternal Prophet beat on his anvils
Enrag'd in the desolate darkness
He forg'd nets of iron around
And Los threw them around the bones   30

6: The shapes screaming flutter'd vain
Some combin'd into muscles & glands
Some organs for craving and lust
Most remain'd on the tormented void:
Urizens army of horrors.   35

7: Round the pale living Corse on the Tree
Forty years flew the arrows of pestilence

8: Wailing and terror and woe
Ran thro' all his dismal world:
Forty years all his sons & daughters   40
Felt their skulls harden; then Asia
Arose in the pendulous deep.

9: They reptilize upon the Earth.

10: Fuzon groand on the Tree.

CHAP: V

1: The lamenting voice of Ahania   45
Weeping upon the void.
And round the Tree of Fuzon:

Distant in solitary night
Her voice was heard, but no form
Had she: but her tears from clouds 50
Eternal fell round the Tree

2: And the voice cried: Ah, Urizen! Love!
Flower of morning! I weep on the verge
Of Non-entity; how wide the Abyss
Between Ahania and thee! 55

3: I lie on the verge of the deep.
I see thy dark clouds ascend
I see thy black forests and floods,
A horrible waste to my eyes!

4: Weeping I walk over rocks, 60
Over dens & thro' valleys of death
Why didst thou despise Ahania
To cast me from thy bright presence
Into the World of Loneness

5: I cannot touch his hand: 65
Nor weep on his knees, nor hear
His voice & bow, nor see his eyes
And joy, nor hear his footsteps, and
My heart leap at the lovely sound!
I cannot kiss the place 70
Whereon his bright feet have trod,

[Plate 6]

But I wander on the rocks
With hard necessity

6: Where is my golden palace
Where my ivory bed
Where the joy of my morning hour 5
Where the sons of eternity, singing

7: To awake bright Urizen my king!
To arise to the mountain sport,
To the bliss of eternal valleys.

8: To awake my king in the morn! 10
To embrace Ahanias joy

On the bredth of his open bosom:
From my soft cloud of dew to fall
In showers of life on his harvests

9: When he gave my happy soul   15
To the sons of eternal joy:
When he took the daughters of life
Into my chambers of love:

10: When I found babes of bliss on my beds.
And bosoms of milk in my chambers   20
Fill'd with eternal seed
O eternal births sung round Ahania
In interchange sweet of their joys.

11: Swell'd with ripeness & fat with fatness
Bursting on winds my odors,   25
My ripe figs and rich pomegranates
In infant joy at thy feet
O Urizen sported and sang;

12: Then thou with thy lap full of seed
With thy hand full of generous fire   30
Walked forth from the clouds of morning
On the virgins of springing joy,
On the human soul to cast
The seed of eternal science.

13: The sweat poured down thy temples   35
To Ahania return'd in evening
The moisture awoke to birth
My mothers-joys, sleeping in bliss.

14: But now alone over rocks, mountains
Cast out from thy lovely bosom: 40
Cruel jealousy! selfish fear!*
Self-destroying: how can delight,
Renew in these chains of darkness
Where bones of beasts are strown
On the bleak and snowy mountains   45
Where bones from the birth are buried
Before they see the light.

FINIS

DIFFUSE EPIC

[Plate 1]

Milton*

*A Poem in 2 Books**

The Author & Printer W Blake 1804
To Justify the Ways of God to Men*

[Plate 2]

PREFACE

Stolen and Perverted Writings of Homer & Ovid; of Plato & Cicero. which all Men ought to contemn: are set up by artifice against the Sublime of the Bible. but when the New Age is at leisure to Pronounce; all will be set right; & those Grand Works of the more ancient & consciously & professedly Inspired Men, will hold their proper rank. & the Daughters of Memory shall become the Daughters of Inspiration. Shakspeare & Milton were both curbd by the general malady & infection from the silly Greek & Latin slaves of the Sword*

Rouze up O Young Men of the New Age! set your foreheads against the ignorant Hirelings! For we have Hirelings in the Camp, the Court, & the University: who would if they could, for ever depress Mental & prolong Corporeal War. Painters! on you I call! Sculptors! Architects! Suffer not the fashonable Fools to depress your powers by the prices they pretend to give for contemptible works or the expensive advertizing boasts that they make of such works; believe Christ & his Apostles that there is a Class of Men whose whole delight is in Destroying. We do not want either Greek or Roman Models if we are but just & true to our own Imaginations, those Worlds of Eternity in which we shall live for ever; in Jesus our Lord.

And did those feet in ancient time.*
Walk upon Englands mountains green:*

And was the holy Lamb of God.
On Englands pleasant pastures seen!

And did the Countenance Divine.   5
Shine forth upon our clouded hills?
And was Jerusalem builded here.
Among these dark Satanic Mills?*

Bring me my Bow of burning gold;
Bring me my Arrows of desire: 10
Bring me my Spear: O clouds unfold:
Bring me my Chariot of fire!*

I will not cease from Mental Fight.
Nor shall my Sword sleep in my hand:*
Till we have built Jerusalem.*   15
In Englands green & pleasant Land

Would to God that all the Lords people were Prophets

Numbers XI. ch 29. v.

[Plate 3]

MILTON
BOOK THE FIRST

Daughters of Beulah! Muses who inspire the Poets Song *
Record the journey of immortal Milton thro' your Realms
Of terror & mild moony lustre, in soft sexual delusions
Of varied beauty, to delight the wanderer and repose
His burning thirst & freezing hunger! Come into my hand   5
By your mild power; descending down the Nerves of my
                                                    right arm
From out the Portals of my Brain, where by your ministry
The Eternal Great Humanity Divine, planted his Paradise
And in it caus'd the Spectres of the Dead to take sweet forms
In likeness of himself. Tell also of the False Tongue! vegetated   10
Beneath your land of shadows: of its sacrifices. and
Its offerings; even till Jesus, the image of the Invisible God
Became its prey; a curse, an offering, and an atonement,*
For Death Eternal. in the heavens of Albion, & before the Gates
Of Jerusalem his Emanation, in the heavens beneath Beulah*   15

Say first! what mov'd Milton, who walkd about in Eternity
One hundred years. pondring the intricate mazes of Providence*
Unhappy tho in heav'n, he obey'd, he murmur'd not. he was silent
Viewing his Sixfold Emanation scatter'd thro' the deep*
In torment! To go into the deep her to redeem & himself perish?   20
What cause at length mov'd Milton to this unexampled deed
A Bards prophetic Song! for sitting at eternal tables,
Terrific among the Sons of Albion in chorus solemn & loud
A Bard broke forth! all sat attentive to the awful man.

Mark well my words! they are of your eternal salvation;   25

Three Classes are Created by the Hammer of Los, & Woven

[Plate 4]

From Golgonooza the spiritual Four-fold London eternal*
In immense labours & sorrows, ever building, ever falling,
Thro Albions four Forests which overspread all the Earth,
From London Stone to Blackheath east; to Hounslow west;*
To Finchley north: to Norwood south: and the weights   5
Of Enitharmons Loom play lulling cadences on the winds of Albion*
From Caithness in the north. to Lizard-point & Dover in the south

Loud sounds the Hammer of Los, & loud his Bellows is heard
Before London to Hampsteads breadths & Highgates heights To
Stratford & old Bow: & across to the Gardens of Kensington   10
On Tyburns Brook: loud groans Thames beneath the iron Forge
Of Rintrah & Palamabron of Theotorm & Bromion. to forge the
                                                instruments
Of Harvest: the Plow & Harrow to pass over the Nations

The Surrey hills glow like the clinkers of the furnace:
                                Lambeths Vale*
Where Jerusalems foundations began; where they were   15
                                laid in ruins
Where they were laid in ruins from every Nation & Oak Groves
                                rooted
Dark gleams before the Furnace-mouth a heap of burning ashes.
When shall Jerusalem return & overspread all the Nations
Return: return to Lambeths Vale O building of human souls
Thence stony Druid Temples overspread the Island white,*   20
And thence from Jerusalems ruins .. from her walls of salvation

And praise: thro the whole Earth were rear'd from Ireland
To Mexico & Peru west, & east to China & Japan, till Babel
The Spectre of Albion frownd over the Nations in glory & war*
All things begin & end in Albions ancient Druid rocky shore*   25
But now the Starry Heavens are fled from the mighty limbs
                                                              of Albion

Loud sounds the Hammer of Los, loud turn the Wheels of
                                                          Enitharmon
Her Looms vibrate with soft affections, weaving the Web of Life
Out from the ashes of the Dead; Los lifts his iron Ladles
With molten ore: he heaves the iron cliffs in his rattling chains   30
From Hyde Park to the Alms-houses of Mile-end & old Bow
Here the Three Classes of Mortal Men take their fixd destinations,
And hence they overspread the Nations of the whole Earth & hence
The Web of Life is woven: & the tender sinews of life created
And the Three Classes of Men regulated by Los's Hammer   35
                                                          and woven

[Plate 5]

By Enitharmons Looms. & Spun beneath the Spindle of Tirzah
The first, The Elect from before the foundation of the World:
The second, The Redeemd. The Third. The Reprobate & Form'd*
To destruction from the mother's womb: follow with me my plow.

Of the first class was Satan: with incomparable mildness;   5
His primitive tyrannical attempts on Los: with most endearing love
He soft intreated Los to give to him Palamabrons station;
For Palamabron returnd with labour wearied every evening
Palamabron oft refus'd; and as often Satan offer'd
His service till by repeated offers and repeated intreaties   10
Los gave to him the Harrow of the Almighty; alas blamable
Palamabron fear'd to be angry lest Satan should accuse him of
Ingratitude, & Los believe the accusation thro Satans extreme
Mildness, Satan labour'd all day, it was a thousand years
In the evening returning terrified overlabourd & astonish'd   15
Embrac'd soft with a brothers tears Palamabron. who also wept

Mark well my words! they are of your eternal salvation

Next morning Palamabron rose; the horses of the Harrow
Were maddend with tormenting fury, & the servants of the Harrow*

The Gnomes, accus'd Satan. with indignation fury and fire.*   20
Then Palamabron reddening like the Moon in an eclipse,
Spoke, saying, You know Satans mildness and his self-imposition,
Seeming a brother, being a tyrant, even thinking himself a brother
While he is murdering the just; prophetic I behold
His future course thro' darkness and despair to eternal death   25
But we must not be tyrants also! he hath assum'd my place
For one whole day. under pretence of pity and love to me:
My horses hath he maddend! and my fellow servants injur'd:
How should he he know the duties of another? O foolish
                                            forbearance
Would I had told Los, all my heart! but patience O my friends,   30
All may be well: silent remain, while I call Los and Satan.

Loud as the wind of Beulah that unroots the rocks & hills
Palamabron call'd! and Los & Satan came before him
And Palamabron shew'd the horses & the servants. Satan wept,
And mildly cursing Palamabron, him accus'd of crimes   35
Himself had wrought. Los trembled; Satans blandishments almost
Perswaded the Prophet of Eternity that Palamabron
Was Satans enemy & that the Gnomes being Palamabron's friends
Were leagued together against Satan thro' ancient enmity.
What could Los do? how could he judge, when Satans   40
                                            self, believ'd
That he had not oppres'd the horses of the Harrow, nor the servants.

So Los said, Henceforth Palamabron, let each his own station
Keep: nor in pity false, nor in officious brotherhood, where
None needs, be active. Mean time Palamabrons horses
Rag'd with thick flames redundant, & the Harrow maddend   45
                                            with fury.
Trembling Palamabron stood; the strongest of Demons trembled:
Curbing his living creatures; many of the strongest Gnomes,
They bit in their wild fury, who also madden'd like wildest beasts

Mark well my words; they are of your eternal salvation

[Plate 6]

Mean while wept Satan before Los accusing Palamabron;
Himself exculpating with mildest speech, for himself believ'd
That he had not oppress'd nor injur'd the refractory servants.

But Satan returning to his Mills (for Palamabron had serv'd
The Mills of Satan as the easier task) found all confusion,   5
And back return'd to Los. not fill'd with vengeance but with tears.
Himself convinc'd of Palamabrons turpitude, Los beheld
The servants of the Mills drunken with wine and dancing wild.
With shouts and Palamabrons songs, rending the forests green
With ecchoing confusion, tho' the Sun was risen on high.   10

Then Los took off his left sandal placing it on his head.*
Signal of solemn mourning: when the servants of the Mills
Beheld the signal they in silence stood. tho' drunk with wine.
Los wept! But Rintrah also came, and Enitharmon on
His arm lean'd tremblingly observing all these things.   15

And Los said. Ye Genii of the Mills; the Sun is on high
Your labours call you! Palamabron is also in sad dilemma;
His horses are mad! his Harrow confounded! his companions
                                                        enragd.
Mine is the fault! I should have remember'd that pity divides
                                                        the soul
And man unmans: follow with me my Plow, this mournful day   20
Must be a blank in Nature; follow with me, and tomorrow again
Resume your labours, & this day shall be a mournful day

Wildly they follow'd Los and Rintrah, & the Mills were silent
They mourn'd all day this mournful day of Satan & Palamabron;
And all the Elect & all the Redeem'd mourn'd one toward another   25
Upon the mountains of Albion among the cliffs of the Dead.

They Plow'd in tears! incessant pourd Jehovahs rain & Molechs
Thick fires contending with the rain, thunder'd above rolling
Terrible over their heads; Satan wept over Palamabron
Theotormon & Bromion contended on the side of Satan   30
Pitying his youth and beauty; trembling at eternal death;
Michael contended against Satan in the rolling thunder
Thulloh the friend of Satan also reprovd him; faint their reproof.*

But Rintrah who is of the reprobate: of those Form'd to destruction
In indignation, for Satans soft dissimulation of friendship!   35
Flam'd above all the plowed furrows, angry red and furious.
Till Michael sat down in the furrow weary dissolv'd in tears
Satan, who drave the team beside him, stood angry & red
He smote Thulloh & slew him, & he stood terrible over Michael

Urging him to arise: he wept! Enitharmon saw his tears.   40
But Los hid Thulloh from her sight, lest she should die of grief
She wept; she trembled! she kissed Satan; she wept over Michael
She form'd a Space for Satan & Michael & for the poor infected
Trembling she wept over the Space, & clos'd it with a tender Moon

Los secret buried Thulloh, weeping disconsolate over the   45
                                        moony Space

But Palamabron called down a Great Solemn Assembly,
That he who will not defend Truth, may be compelled to
Defend a Lie, that he may be snared & caught & taken

[Plate 7]

And all Eden descended into Palamabrons tent
Among Albions Druids & Bards, in the caves beneath Albions
Death Couch, in the caverns of death, in the corner of the Atlantic.
And in the midst of the Great Assembly Palamabron pray'd:
O God protect me from my friends, that they have not power   5
                                        over me
Thou hast giv'n me power to protect myself from my bitterest enemies.

Mark well my words, they are of your eternal salvation

Then rose the Two Witnesses, Rintrah & Palamabron:
And Palamabron appeal'd to all Eden, and recievd
Judgment; and Lo; it fell on Rintrah and his rage: 10
Which now flam'd high & furious in Satan against Palamabron
Till it became a proverb in Eden. Satan is among the Reprobate.

Los in his wrath curs'd heaven & earth, he rent up Nations
Standing on Albions rocks among high-reard Druid temples
Which reach the stars of heaven & stretch from pole to pole,   15
He displacd continents, the oceans fled before his face
He alter'd the poles of the world, east, west & north & south
But he clos'd up Enitharmon from the sight of all these things

For Satan flaming with Rintrahs fury hidden beneath his own
                                        mildness
Accus'd Palamabron before the Assembly of ingratitude! of malice;   20
He created Seven deadly Sins drawing out his infernal scroll,
Of Moral laws and cruel punishments upon the clouds of Jehovah

To pervert the Divine voice in its entrance to the earth
With thunder of war & trumpets sound, with armies of disease
Punishments & deaths musterd & number'd; Saying I am God alone 25
There is no other! let all obey my principles of moral individuality
I have brought them from the uppermost innermost recesses
Of my Eternal Mind, transgressors I will rend off for ever,
As now I rend this accursed Family from my covering.

Thus Satan rag'd amidst the Assembly! and his bosom grew 30
Opake against the Divine Vision; the paved terraces of
His bosom inwards shone with fires, but the stones becoming opake!
Hid him from sight. in an extreme blackness and darkness,
And there a World of deeper Ulro was open'd, in the midst
Of the Assembly. In Satans bosom a vast unfathomable Abyss. 35
Astonishment held the Assembly in an awful silence; and tears
Fell down as dews of night, & a loud solemn universal groan
Was utter'd from the east & from the west & from the south
And from the north; and Satan stood opake immeasurable
Covering the east with solid blackness, round his hidden heart 40
With thunders utterd from his hidden wheels; accusing loud
The Divine Mercy, for protecting Palamabron in his tent,

Rintrah rear'd up walls of rocks and pourd rivers & moats
Of fire round the walls: columns of fire guard around
Between Satan and Palamabron in the terrible darkness. 45

And Satan not having the Science of Wrath, but only of Pity:
Rent them asunder, and wrath was left to wrath, & pity to pity,
He sunk down, a dreadful Death, unlike the slumbers of Beulah

The Separation was terrible; the Dead was repos'd on his Couch
Beneath the Couch of Albion, on the seven mountains of Rome 50
In the whole place of the Covering Cherub. Rome, Babylon & Tyre.*
His Spectre raging furious descended into its Space

[Plate 9]

He set his face against Jerusalem to destroy the Eon of Albion*

But Los hid Enitharmon from the sight of all these things.
Upon the Thames whose lulling harmony repos'd her soul:
Where Beulah lovely terminates in rocky Albion:
Terminating in Hyde Park. on Tyburns awful brook. 5

And the Mills of Satan were separated into a moony Space
Among the rocks of Albions Temples, and Satans Druid sons
Offer the Human Victims throughout all the Earth, and Albions
Dread Tomb immortal on his Rock. overshadowd the whole Earth:
Where Satan, making to himself Laws from his own identity.   10
Compell'd others to serve him in moral gratitude & submission,
Being call'd God, setting himself above all that is called God;
And all the Spectres of the Dead, calling themselves Sons of God,
In his Synagogues worship Satan under the Unutterable Name

And it was enquir'd: Why in a Great Solemn Assembly   15
The Innocent should be condemn'd for the Guilty? Then an
                                        Eternal rose*

Saying: If the Guilty should be condemn'd, he must be an Eternal
                                                       Death
And one must die for another throughout all Eternity.
Satan is fall'n from his station & never can be redeem'd
But must be new Created continually moment by moment   20
And therefore the Class of Satan shall be calld the Elect. & those
Of Rintrah the Reprobate. & those of Palamabron the Redeem'd
For he is redeem'd from Satans Law. the wrath falling on Rintrah;
And therefore Palamabron dared not to call a solemn Assembly
Till Satan had assum'd Rintrahs wrath in the day of mourning   25
In a feminine delusion of false pride self-deciev'd.

So spake the Eternal and confirm'd it with a thunderous oath

But when Leutha (a Daughter of Beulah) beheld Satans
                                        condemnation
She down descended into the midst of the Great Solemn Assembly
Offering herself a Ransom for Satan, taking on her, his Sin   30

Mark well my words, they are of your eternal salvation!

And Leutha stood glowing with varying colours, immortal,
                                        heart-piercing
And lovely: & her moth-like elegance shone, over the Assembly

At length standing upon the golden floor of Palamabron
She spoke: I am the Author of this Sin! by my suggestion   35
My Parent power Satan has committed this transgression.
I loved Palamabron & I sought to approach his Tent,
But beautiful Elynittria with her silver arrows repelld me.

[Plate 10]

For her light is terrible to me. I fade before her immortal beauty.
O wherefore doth a Dragon-Form forth issue from my limbs
To sieze her new born son? Ah me! the wretched Leutha!
This to prevent. entering the doors of Satans brain night
                                                    after night
Like sweet perfumes I stupified the masculine perceptions   5
And kept only the feminine awake. hence rose, his soft
Delusory love to Palamabron: admiration join'd with envy
Cupidity unconquerable! my fault, when at noon of day
The Horses of Palamabron call'd for rest and pleasant death:
I sprang out of the breast of Satan. over the Harrow beaming   10
In all my beauty: that I might unloose the flaming steeds
As Elynittria used to do; but too well those living creatures
Knew that I was not Elynittria. and they brake the traces
But me, the servants of the Harrow saw not; but as a bow
Of varying colours on the hills; terribly rag'd the horses.   15
Satan astonishd and with power above his own controll
Compell'd the Gnomes to curb the horses, & to throw banks of sand
Around the fiery flaming Harrow in labyrinthine forms.
And brooks between to intersect the meadows in their course.
The Harrow cast thick flames: Jehovah thunderd above: 20
Chaos & ancient night fled from beneath the fiery Harrow:
The Harrow cast thick flames & orb'd us round in concave fires
A Hell of our own making, see, its flames still gird me round
Jehovah thunder'd above: Satan in pride of heart
Drove the fierce Harrow among the constellations of Jehovah   25
Drawing a third part in the fires as stubble north & south
To devour Albion and Jerusalem the Emanation of Albion
Driving the Harrow in Pitys paths. 'twas then, with our dark fires
Which now gird round us (O eternal torment) I form'd the Serpent
Of precious stones & gold turn'd poisons on the sultry wastes   30
The Gnomes in all that day spar'd not; they curs'd Satan bitterly.
To do unkind things in kindness! with power armd. to say
The most irritating things in the midst of tears and love
These are the stings of the Serpent! thus did we by them; till thus
They in return retaliated, and the Living Creatures maddend.   35
The Gnomes labour. I weeping hid in Satans inmost brain;
But when the Gnomes refus'd to labour more, with blandishments
I came forth from the head of Satan! back the Gnomes recoil'd.

And call'd me Sin, and for a sign portentous held me. Soon
Day sunk and Palamabron return'd, trembling I hid myself. 40
In Satans inmost Palace of his nervous fine wrought Brain:
For Elynittria met Satan with all her singing women.
Terrific in their joy & pouring wine of wildest power
They gave Satan their wine indignant at the burning wrath.
Wild with prophetic fury his former life became like a dream 45
Cloth'd in the Serpents folds, in selfish holiness demanding purity
Being most impure, self-condemn'd to eternal tears, he drove
Me from his inmost Brain & the doors clos'd with thunder's sound
O Divine Vision who didst create the Female: to repose
The Sleepers of Beulah; pity the repentant Leutha, My 50

[Plate 11]

Sick Couch bears the dark shades of Eternal Death infolding
The Spectre of Satan. he furious refuses to repose in sleep
I humbly bow in all my Sin before the Throne Divine,
Not so the Sick-one; Alas what shall be done him to restore?
Who calls the Individual Law, Holy: and despises the Saviour. 5
Glorying to involve Albions Body in fires of eternal War

Now Leutha ceas'd: tears flow'd: but the Divine Pity supported her.

All is my fault! We are the Spectre of Luvah the murderer
Of Albion; O Vala! O Luvah! O Albion! O lovely Jerusalem
The Sin was begun in Eternity. and will not rest to Eternity 10
Till two Eternitys meet together, Ah! lost! lost! lost! for ever!

So Leutha spoke. But when she saw that Enitharmon had
Created a New Space to protect Satan from punishment:
She fled to Enitharmons Tent & hid herself. Loud raging
Thunderd the Assembly dark & clouded. and they ratify'd 15
The kind decision of Enitharmon & gave a Time to the Space,
Even Six Thousand years: and sent Lucifer for its Guard.*
But Lucifer refus'd to die & in pride he forsook his charge
And they elected Molech, and when Molech was impatient
The Divine hand found the Two Limits: first of Opacity, then of 20
           Contraction
Opacity was named Satan, Contraction was named Adam.
Triple Elohim came: Elohim wearied fainted: they elected Shaddai.
Shaddai angry. Pahad descended: Pahad terrified. they sent Jehovah

And Jehovah was leprous; loud he call'd. stretching his hand
                                                    to Eternity
For then the Body of Death was perfected in hypocritic holiness.   25
Around the Lamb. a Female Tabernacle woven in Cathedron's Looms
He died as a Reprobate, he was Punish'd as a Transgressor;
Glory! Glory! Glory! to the Holy Lamb of God
I touch the heavens as an instrument to glorify the Lord!
The Elect shall meet the Redeem'd. on Albions rocks they   30
                                                    shall meet
Astonish'd at the Transgressor, in him beholding the Saviour.
And the Elect shall say to the Redeemd. We behold it is of Divine
Mercy alone! of Free Gift and Election that we live.
Our Virtues & Cruel Goodnesses, have deserv'd Eternal Death.*
Thus they weep upon the fatal Brook of Albions River.   35

But Elynittria met Leutha in the place where she was hidden.
And threw aside her arrows and laid down her sounding Bow:
She sooth'd her with soft words & brought her to Palamabrons bed
In moments new created for delusion, interwoven round about,
In dreams she bore the shadowy Spectre of Sleep. & namd   40
                                                    him Death.
In dreams she bore Rahab the mother of Tirzah & her sisters,
In Lambeths vales: in Cambridge & in Oxford, places of Thought
Intricate labyrinths of Times and Spaces unknown. that Leutha lived
In Palamabrons Tent. and Oothoon was her charming guard.

The Bard ceas'd. All consider'd and a loud resounding murmur   45
Continu'd round the Halls: and much they question'd the immortal
Loud voicd Bard, and many condemn'd the high toned Song
Saying Pity and Love are too venerable for the imputation
Of Guilt. Others said. If it is true! if the acts have been perform'd
Let the Bard himself witness. Where hadst thou this terrible Song   50

The Bard replied. I am Inspired! I know it is Truth! for I Sing

[Plate 12]

According to the inspiration of the Poetic Genius
Who is the eternal all-protecting Divine Humanity
To whom be Glory & Power & Dominion Evermore Amen*

Then there was murmuring in the Heavens of Albion
Concerning Generation & the Vegetative power & concerning   5

The Lamb the Saviour: Albion trembled to Italy Greece & Egypt
To Tartary & Hindostan & China & to Great America
Shaking the roots & fast foundations of the Earth in doubtfulness
The loud voic'd Bard terrify'd took refuge in Miltons bosom

Then Milton rose up from the heavens of Albion ardorous!   10
The whole Assembly wept prophetic, seeing in Miltons face
And in his lineaments divine the Shades of Death & Ulro
He took off the robe of the promise, & ungirded himself from
                                                    the oath of God

And Milton said, I go to Eternal Death! The Nations still
Follow after the detestable Gods of Priam; in pomp*   15
Of warlike selfhood.contradicting and blaspheming.
When will the Resurrection come; to deliver the sleeping body
From corruptibility; O when, Lord Jesus wilt thou come?
Tarry no longer; for my soul lies at the gates of death.
I will arise and look forth for the morning of the grave.   20
I will go down to the sepulcher to see if morning breaks!
I will go down to self annihilation and eternal death,
Lest the Last Judgment come & find me unannihilate
And I be siez'd & giv'n into the hands of my own Selfhood
The Lamb of God is seen thro' mists & shadows, hov'ring   25
Over the sepulchers in clouds of Jehovah & winds of Elohim
A disk of blood, distant; & heav'ns & earths roll dark between
What do I here before the Judgment? without my Emanation?
With the daughters of memory, & not with the daughters of
                                                    inspiration*
I in my Selfhood am that Satan: I am that Evil One!   30
He is my Spectre! in my obedience to loose him from my Hells
To claim the Hells, my Furnaces, I go to Eternal Death.

And Milton said, I go to Eternal Death! Eternity shudder'd
For he took the outside course, among the graves of the dead
A mournful shade, Eternity shudderd at the image of eternal death   35

Then on the verge of Beulah he beheld his own Shadow:
A mournful form double; hermaphroditic: male & female*
In one wonderful body, and he enterd into it
In direful pain for the dread shadow, twenty-seven fold
Reachd to the depths of direst Hell, & thence to Albions land: 40
Which is this earth of vegetation on which now I write.

The Seven Angels of the Presence wept over Milton's Shadow!*

Milton

[Plate 14]

As when a man dreams, he reflects not that his body sleeps,
Else he would wake; so seem'd he entering his Shadow: but
With him the Spirits of the Seven Angels of the Presence
Entering; they gave him still perceptions of his Sleeping Body:
Which now arose and walk'd with them in Eden, as an Eighth   5
Image Divine tho' darken'd; and tho walking as one walks
In sleep: and the Seven comforted and supported him.

Like as a Polypus that vegetates beneath the deep!*
They saw his Shadow vegetated underneath the Couch
Of death: for when he enterd into his Shadow: Himself: 10
His real and immortal Self; was as appeard to those
Who dwell in immortality, as One sleeping on a couch
Of gold; and those in immortality gave forth their Emanations
Like Females of sweet beauty, to guard round him & to feed
His lips with food of Eden in his cold and dim repose!   15
But to himself he seem'd a wanderer lost in dreary night.

Onwards his Shadow kept its course among the Spectres; call'd
Satan, but swift as lightning passing them. startled the shades
Of Hell beheld him in a trail of light as of a comet
That travels into Chaos: so Milton went guarded within.   20

The nature of infinity is this: That every thing, has its
Own Vortex; and when once a traveller thro Eternity,*
Has passd that Vortex, he percieves it roll backward behind
His path, into a globe itself infolding: like a sun:
Or like a moon, or like a universe of starry majesty.   25
While he keeps onwards in his wondrous journey on the earth
Or like a human form, a friend with whom he livd benevolent.
As the eye of man views both the east & west encompassing
Its vortex; and the north & south, with all their starry host;
Also the rising sun & setting moon he views surrounding   30
His corn-fields and his valleys of five hundred acres square,
Thus is the earth one infinite plane, and not as apparent
To the weak traveller confin'd beneath the moony shade.
Thus is the heaven a vortex passd already, and the earth
A vortex not yet pass'd by the traveller thro' Eternity.   35

First Milton saw Albion upon the Rock of Ages,*
Deadly pale outstretchd and snowy cold, storm coverd:

A Giant form of perfect beauty outstretchd on the rock
In solemn death. the Sea of Time & Space thunderd aloud
Against the rock, which was inwrapped with the weeds of death   40
Hovering over the cold bosom, in its vortex Milton bent down
To the bosom of death, what was underneath soon seem'd above.
A cloudy heaven mingled with stormy seas in loudest ruin;
But as a wintry globe descends precipitant thro' Beulah bursting,
With thunders loud and terrible: so Miltons shadow fell,   45
Precipitant loud thundring into the Sea of Time & Space.

Then first I saw him in the Zenith as a falling star.*
Descending perpendicular, swift as the swallow or swift;
And on my left foot falling on the tarsus, enterd there;*
But from my left foot a black cloud redounding spread   50
                              over Europe.

Then Milton knew that the Three Heavens of Beulah were
                              beheld
By him on earth in his bright pilgrimage of sixty years*

[Plate 16]

In those three females whom his Wives, & those three whom his
                              Daughters
Had represented and containd, that they might be resum'd
By giving up of Selfhood: & they distant view'd his journey
In their eternal spheres, now Human. tho' their Bodies
                              remain clos'd
In the dark Ulro till the Judgment: also Milton knew: they and   5
Himself was Human, tho' now wandering thro Death's Vale
In conflict with those Female forms, which in blood & jealousy
Surrounded him, dividing & uniting without end or number.

He saw the cruelties of Ulro, and he wrote them down
In iron tablets: and his Wives & Daughters names were these   10
Rahab and Tirzah, & Milcah & Malah & Noah & Hoglah.*
They sat rang'd round him as the rocks of Horeb round the land
Of Canaan: and they wrote in thunder smoke and fire
His dictate; and his body was the Rock Sinai, that body*
Which was on earth born to corruption: & the six Females   15
Are Hor & Peor & Bashan & Abarim & Lebanon & Hermon
Seven rocky masses terrible in the Desarts of Midian.

But Miltons Human Shadow continu'd journeying above
The rocky masses of The Mundane Shell; in the Lands
Of Edom & Aram & Moab & Midian & Amalek.   20

The Mundane Shell, is a vast Concave Earth: an immense*
Hardend shadow of all things upon our Vegetated Earth
Enlarg'd into dimension & deform'd into indefinite space
And Ancient Night; & Purgatory. It is a cavernous Earth   25
Of labyrinthine intricacy twenty–seven–folds of opakeness
And finishes where the lark mounts; here Milton journeyed
In that Region calld Midian among the Rocks of Horeb
For travellers from Eternity, pass outward to Satans seat
But travellers to Eternity pass inward to Golgonooza.   30

Los the Vehicular terror beheld him, & divine Enitharmon
Call'd all her daughters, Saying. Surely to unloose my bond
Is this Man come! Satan shall be unloosd upon Albion

Los heard in terror Enitharmons words: in fibrous strength
His limbs shot forth like roots of trees against the forward path   35
Of Milton's journey. Urizen beheld the immortal Man

[Plate 17]

And he also darkend his brows: freezing dark rocks between
The footsteps, and infixing deep the feet in marble beds:
That Milton labourd with his journey. & his feet bled sore
Upon the clay now chang'd to marble; also Urizen rose.
And met him on the shores of Arnon; & by the streams of the brooks*   5

Silent they met. and silent strove among the streams of Arnon
Even to Mahanaim, when with cold hand Urizen stoop'd down
And took up water from the river Jordan: pouring on
To Miltons brain the icy fluid from his broad cold palm.
But Milton took of the red clay of Succoth. moulding it with care   10
Between his palms; and filling up the furrows of many years
Beginning at the feet of Urizen, and on the bones
Creating new flesh on the Demon cold, and building him,
As with new clay a Human form in the Valley of Beth Peor.

Four Universes round the Mundane Egg remain Chaotic   15
One to the North. named Urthona; One to the South, named Urizen;
One to the East, named Luvah: One to the West, named Tharmas

They are the Four Zoa's that stood around the Throne Divine!*
But when Luvah assum'd the World of Urizen to the South;
And Albion was slain upon his mountains, & in his tent;   20
All fell towards the Center in dire ruin, sinking down.
And in the South remains a burning fire; in the East a void.
In the West, a world of raging waters; in the North a solid,
Unfathomable! without end, But in the midst of these,
Is built eternally the Universe of Los and Enitharmon: 25
Towards which Milton went, but Urizen oppos'd his path.

The Man and Demon strove many periods, Rahab beheld
Standing on Carmel; Rahab and Tirzah trembled to behold
The enormous strife, one giving life, the other giving death
To his adversary, and they sent forth all their sons & daughters   30
In all their beauty to entice Milton across the river,

The Twofold form Hermaphroditic: and the Double-sexed:
The Female-male & the Male-female, self-dividing stood
Before him in their beauty, & in cruelties of holiness!
Shining in darkness, glorious upon the deeps of Entuthon.   35

Saying. Come thou to Ephraim! behold the Kings of Canaan!
The beautiful Amalekites, behold the fires of youth
Bound with the Chain of Jealousy by Los & Enitharmon;
The banks of Cam: cold learnings streams: Londons dark-frowning
                                                             towers;
Lament upon the winds of Europe in Rephaims Vale.   40
Because Ahania rent apart into a desolate night,
Laments! & Enion wanders like a weeping inarticulate voice
And Vala labours for her bread & water among the Furnaces
Therefore bright Tirzah triumphs! putting on all beauty,
And all perfection, in her cruel sports among the Victims.   45
Come bring with thee Jerusalem with songs on the Grecian Lyre!
In Natural Religion, in experiments on Men,
Let her be Offerd up to Holiness! Tirzah numbers her;
She numbers with her fingers every fibre ere it grow;
Where is the Lamb of God? where is the promise of his coming?   50
Her shadowy Sisters form the bones, even the bones of Horeb:
Around the marrow! and the orbed scull around the brain:
His Images are born for War! for Sacrifice to Tirzah:
To Natural Religion! to Tirzah the Daughter of Rahab the Holy!*
She ties the knot of nervous fibre, into a white brain!   55

She ties the knot of bloody veins, into a red hot heart!
Within her bosom Albion lies embalmd, never to awake
Hand is become a rock! Sinai & Horeb, is Hyle & Coban:
Scofield* is bound in iron armour before Reubens Gate!*
She ties the knot of milky seed into two lovely Heavens, 60

[Plate 18]

Two yet but one: each in the other sweet reflected: these
Are our Three Heavens beneath the shades of Beulah. land of rest!
Come then to Ephraim & Manasseh O beloved-one!
Come to my ivory palaces O beloved of thy mother!
And let us bind thee in the bands of War & be thou King 5
Of Canaan and reign in Hazor where the Twelve Tribes meet.

So spoke they as in one voice! Silent Milton stood before
The darkend Urizen; as the sculptor silent stands before
His forming image; he walks round it patient labouring.
Thus Milton stood forming bright Urizen, while his Mortal part 10
Sat frozen in the rock of Horeb: and his Redeemed portion,
Thus form'd the Clay of Urizen; but within that portion
His real Human walkd above in power and majesty
Tho darkend; and the Seven Angels of the Presence attended him.

O how can I with my gross tongue that cleaveth to the dust. 15
Tell of the Four-fold Man. in starry numbers fitly orderd
Or how can I with my cold hand of clay! But thou O Lord
Do with me as thou wilt! for I am nothing, and vanity:
If thou chuse to elect a worm, it shall remove the mountains.
For that portion namd the Elect, the Spectrous body of Milton: 20
Redounding from my left foot into Los's Mundane space,
Brooded over his Body in Horeb against the Resurrection
Preparing it for the Great Consummation; red the Cherub on Sinai
Glow'd, but in terrors folded round his clouds of blood.

Now Albions sleeping Humanity began to turn upon his Couch; 25
Feeling the electric flame of Miltons awful precipitate descent.
Seest thou the little winged fly. smaller than a grain of sand?
It has a heart like thee; a brain open to heaven & hell,
Withinside wondrous & expansive: its gates are not clos'd,
I hope thine are not: hence it clothes itself in rich array; 30
Hence thou art cloth'd with human beauty O thou mortal man

Seek not thy heavenly father then beyond the skies:
There Chaos dwells & ancient Night & Og & Anak old:*
For every human heart has gates of brass & bars of adamant,
Which few dare unbar because dread Og & Anak guard the gates   35
Terrific! and each mortal brain is walld and moated round
Within: and Og & Anak watch here; here is the Seat
Of Satan in its Webs; for in brain and heart and loins
Gates open behind Satans Seat to the City of Golgonooza
Which is the spiritual fourfold London in the loins of Albion   40

Thus Milton fell thro Albions heart, travelling outside of Humanity
Beyond the Stars in Chaos in Caverns of the Mundane Shell.

But many of the Eternals rose up from eternal tables
Drunk with the Spirit, burning round the Couch of death they stood
Looking down into Beulah! wrathful, fill'd with rage!   45
They rend the heavens round the Watchers in a fiery circle:
And round the Shadowy Eighth: the Eight close up the Couch
Into a tabernacle, and flee with cries down to the Deeps:
Where Los opens his three wide gates, surrounded by raging fires;
They soon find their own place & join the Watchers of the Ulro.   50

Los saw them and a cold pale horror cover'd o'er his limbs
Pondering he knew that Rintrah & Palamabron might depart:
Even as Reuben & as Gad; gave up himself to tears.
He sat down on his anvil-stock; and leand upon the trough,
Looking into the black water, mingling it with tears,   55

At last when desperation almost tore his heart in twain
He recollected an old Prophecy in Eden recorded,
And often sung to the loud harp at the immortal feasts
That Milton of the Land of Albion should up ascend
Forwards from Ulro from the Vale of Felpham; and set free*   60
Orc from his Chain of Jealousy, he started at the thought

[Plate 19]

And down descended into Udan-Adan; it was night:*
And Satan sat sleeping upon his Couch in Udan Adan:
His Spectre slept, his Shadow woke: when one sleeps th'other wakes

But Milton entering my Foot: I saw in the nether*
Regions of the Imagination; also all men on Earth,   5

And all in Heaven, saw in the nether regions of the Imagination
In Ulro beneath Beulah, the vast breach of Milton's descent.
But I knew not that it was Milton, for man cannot know
What passes in his members till periods of Space & Time
Reveal the secrets of Eternity: for more extensive   10
Than any other earthly things are Mans earthly lineaments.

And all this Vegetable World appeard on my left Foot,
As a bright sandal formd immortal of Precious stones & gold:
I stooped down & bound it on to walk forward thro' Eternity.

There is in Eden a sweet River, of milk & liquid pearl,   15
Namd Ololon; on whose mild banks dwelt those who Milton drove*
Down into Ulro: and they wept in long resounding song
For seven days of eternity, and the rivers living banks
The mountains waild! & every plant that grew, in solemn sighs
                                                              lamented.

When Luvahs bulls each morning drag the sulphur Sun out   20
                                                    of the Deep
Harnessd with starry harness black & shining kept by black slaves
That work all night at the starry harness. Strong and vigorous
They drag the unwilling Orb: at this time all the Family
Of Eden heard the lamentation, and Providence began,
But when the clarions of day sounded they drownd the   25
                                                lamentations
And when night came, all was silent in Ololon: & all refusd to lament
In the still night fearing lest they should others molest,

Seven mornings Los heard them, as the poor bird within the shell
Hears its impatient parent bird: and Enitharmon heard them:
But saw them not, for the blue Mundane Shell inclosd them in.   30
And they lamented that they had in wrath & fury & fire
Driven Milton into the Ulro: for now they knew too late
That it was Milton the Awakener! they had not heard the Bard.
Whose song calld Milton to the attempt; and Los heard these
                                                        laments,

He heard them call in prayer all the Divine Family;   35
And he beheld the Cloud of Milton stretching over Europe.

But all the Family Divine collected as Four Suns
In the Four Points of heaven East, West & North & South
Enlarging and enlarging till their Disks approachd each other:

And when they touch'd closed together Southward in One Sun   40
Over Ololon: and as One Man, who weeps over his brother,
In a dark tomb, so all the Family Divine wept over Ololon.

Saying, Milton goes to Eternal Death! so saying they groan'd in spirit
And were troubled! and again the Divine Family groaned in spirit!

And Ololon said, Let us descend also, and let us give   45
Ourselves to death in Ulro among the Transgressors,
Is Virtue a Punisher? O no! how is this wondrous thing:
This World beneath, unseen before; this refuge from the wars
Of Great Eternity! unnatural refuge! unknown by us till now:
Or are these the pangs of repentance: let us enter into them   50

Then the Divine Family said. Six Thousand Years are now
Accomplish'd in this World of Sorrow; Miltons Angel knew
The Universal Dictate: and you also feel this Dictate.
And now you know this World of Sorrow, and feel Pity. Obey
The Dictate! Watch over this World, and with your brooding wings   55
Renew it to Eternal Life: Lo! I am with you alway
But you cannot renew Milton he goes to Eternal Death

So spake the Family Divine as One Man, even Jesus
Uniting in One with Ololon & the appearance of One Man
Jesus the Saviour appeard coming in the Clouds of Ololon: 60

[Plate 20]

Tho' driven away with the Seven Starry Ones into the Ulro
Yet the Divine Vision remains Every-where For-ever. Amen.
And Ololon lamented for Milton with a great lamentation.

While Los heard indistinct in fear, what time I bound my sandals
On; to walk forward thro' Eternity, Los descended to me: 5
And Los behind me stood; a terrible flaming Sun: just close
Behind my back; I turned round in terror, and behold.
Los stood in that fierce glowing fire; & he also stoop'd down
And bound my sandals on in Udan-Adan; trembling I stood
Exceedingly with fear & terror, standing in the Vale   10
Of Lambeth: but he kissed me and wishd me health.
And I became One Man with him arising in my strength.
Twas too late now to recede. Los had enterd into my soul:
His terrors now posses'd me whole! I arose in fury & strength.

I am that Shadowy Prophet who Six Thousand Years ago*   15
Fell from my station in the Eternal bosom. Six Thousand Years
Are finishd. I return! both Time & Space obey my will.
I in Six Thousand Years walk up and down; for not one Moment
Of Time is lost, nor one Event of Space unpermanent
But all remain: every fabric of Six Thousand Years   20
Remains permanent: tho' on the Earth where Satan
Fell, and was cut off all things vanish & are seen no more
They vanish not from me & mine, we guard them first & last
The generations of men run on in the tide of Time
But leave their destind lineaments permanent for ever & ever.   25
So spoke Los as we went along to his supreme abode

Rintrah and Palamabron met us at the Gate of Golgonooza
Clouded with discontent, & brooding in their minds terrible
                                                          things
They said. O Father most beloved! O merciful Parent!
Pitying and permitting evil, tho strong & mighty to destroy.   30
Whence is this Shadow terrible? wherefore dost thou refuse
To throw him into the Furnaces: knowest thou not that he
Will unchain Orc? & let loose Satan. Og. Sihon & Anak.
Upon the Body of Albion? for this he is come! behold it written
Upon his fibrous left Foot black! most dismal to our eyes   35
The Shadowy Female shudders thro' heaven in torment
                                                    inexpressible:
And all the Daughters of Los prophetic wail; yet in deceit.
They weave a new Religion from new Jealousy of Theotormon!
Miltons Religion is the cause; there is no end to destruction!
Seeing the Churches at their Period in terror & despair: 40
Rahab created Voltaire: Tirzah created Rousseau:
Asserting the Self-righteousness against the Universal Saviour,*
Mocking the Confessors & Martyrs, claiming Self-righteousness;
With cruel Virtue: making War upon the Lambs Redeemed;
To perpetuate War & Glory, to perpetuate the Laws of Sin: 45
They perverted Swedenborgs Visions in Beulah & in Ulro;
To destroy Jerusalem as a Harlot & her Sons as Reprobates;
To raise up Mystery the Virgin Harlot Mother of War.
Babylon the Great, the Abomination of Desolation:
O Swedenborg! strongest of men, the Samson shorn by   50
                                               the Churches!
Shewing the Transgresors in Hell, the proud Warriors in Heaven:

Heaven as a Punisher & Hell as One under Punishment;
With Laws from Plato & his Greeks to renew the Trojan Gods,
In Albion; & to deny the value of the Saviours blood,
But then I rais'd up Whitefield, Palamabron raisd up Westley,*   55
And these are the cries of the Churches before the two Witnesses,
Faith in God the dear Saviour who took on the likeness of men:
Becoming obedient to death, even the death of the Cross
The Witnesses lie dead in the Street of the Great City
No Faith is in all the Earth: the Book of God is trodden   60
                              under Foot:
He sent his two Servants, Whitefield & Westley; were they Prophets
Or were they Idiots or Madmen? shew us Miracles!

[Plate 22]

Can you have greater Miracles than these? Men who devote
Their lifes whole comfort to intire scorn & injury & death
Awake, thou sleeper on the Rock of Eternity Albion awake
The trumpet of Judgment hath twice sounded; all Nations
                              are awake
But thou art still heavy and dull: Awake Albion awake!   5
Lo Orc arises on the Atlantic. Lo his blood and fire
Glow on Americas shore: Albion turns upon his Couch
He listens to the sounds of War, astonishd and confounded:
He weeps into the Atlantic deep, yet still in dismal dreams
Unwaken'd! and the Covering Cherub advances from the East: 10
How long shall we lay dead in the Street of the great City
How long beneath the Covering Cherub give our Emanations
Milton will utterly consume us & thee our beloved Father
He hath enterd into the Covering Cherub, becoming one with
Albion's dread Sons, Hand. Hyle & Coban surround him as   15
A girdle; Gwendolen & Conwenna as a garment woven
Of War & Religion: let us descend & bring him chained
To Bowlahoola O father most beloved: O mild Parent!*
Cruel in thy mildness, pitying and permitting evil
Tho strong and mighty to destroy, O Los our beloved Father!   20

Like the black storm, coming out of Chaos, beyond the stars:
It issues thro the dark & intricate caves of the Mundane Shell
Passing the planetary visions, & the well adorned Firmament
The Sun rolls into Chaos & the stars into the Desarts;

And then the storms become visible, audible & terrible,   25
Covering the light of day & rolling down upon the mountains,
Deluge all the country round. Such is a vision of Los;
When Rintrah & Palamabron spake: and such his stormy face
Appeard as does the face of heaven, when cover'd with thick storms
Pitying and loving tho in frowns of terrible perturbation   30

But Los dispersd the clouds even as the strong winds of Jehovah.
And Los thus spoke. O noble Sons, be patient yet a little
I have embracd the falling Death, he is become One with me
O Sons we live not by wrath. by mercy alone we live!
I recollect an old Prophecy in Eden recorded in gold; and oft   35
Sung to the harp: That Milton of the land of Albion.
Should up ascend forward from Felphams Vale & break the Chain
Of Jealousy from all its roots; be patient therefore O my Sons
These lovely Females form sweet night and silence and secret
Obscurities to hide from Satans Watch-Fiends. Human loves   40
And graces; lest they write them in their Books, & in the Scroll
Of mortal life, to condemn the accused: who at Satans Bar
Tremble in Spectrous Bodies continually day and night
While on the Earth they live in sorrowful Vegetations
O when shall we tread our Wine-presses in heaven; and Reap   45
Our wheat with shoutings of joy, and leave the Earth in peace
Remember how Calvin and Luther in fury premature*
Sow'd War and stern division between Papists & Protestants
Let it not be so now: O go not forth in Martyrdoms & Wars
We were plac'd here by the Universal Brotherhood & Mercy   50
With powers fitted to circumscribe this dark Satanic death
And that the Seven Eyes of God may have space for Redemption,
But how this is as yet we know not. and we cannot know;
Till Albion is arisen: then patient wait a little while,
Six Thousand years are passd away the end approaches fast;   55
This mighty one is come from Eden, he is of the Elect.
Who died from Earth & he is returnd before the Judgment,
                                        This thing
Was never known that one of the holy dead should willing return
Then patient wait a little while till the Last Vintage is over:
Till we have quenchd the Sun of Salah in the Lake of   60
                              Udan-Adan
O my dear Sons! leave not your Father, as your brethren left me
Twelve Sons successive fled away in that thousand years of sorrow

[Plate 23]

Of Palamabron's Harrow, & of Rintrahs wrath & fury;
Reuben & Manazzoth & Gad & Simeon & Levi,
And Ephraim & Judah were Generated. because
They left me, wandering with Tirzah: Enitharmon wept
One thousand years, and all the Earth was in a wat'ry deluge   5
We call'd him Menassheh because of the Generations of Tirzah
Because of Satan; & the Seven Eyes of God continually
Guard round them, but I the Fourth Zoa am also set
The Watchman of Eternity, the Three are not! & I am preserved
Still my four mighty ones are left to me in Golgonooza   10
Still Rintrah fierce, and Palamabron mild & piteous
Theotormon filld with care, Bromion loving Science*
You, O my Sons still guard round Los. O wander not & leave me
Rintrah, thou well rememberest when Amalek & Canaan
Fled with their Sister Moab into that abhorred Void   15
They became Nations in our sight beneath the hands of Tirzah,
And Palamabron thou rememberest when Joseph an infant;
Stolen from his nurses cradle wrapd in needle-work
Of emblematic texture, was sold to the Amalekite,
Who carried him down into Egypt where Ephraim & Menassheh   20
Gatherd my Sons together in the Sands of Midian
And if you also flee away and leave your Fathers side,
Following Milton into Ulro, altho your power is great
Surely you also shall become poor mortal vegetations
Beneath the Moon of Ulro: pity then your Fathers tears   25
When Jesus raisd Lazarus from the Grave I stood & saw
Lazarus, who is the Vehicular Body of Albion the Redeemd
Arise into the Covering Cherub who is the Spectre of Albion
By martyrdoms to suffer: to watch over the Sleeping Body.
Upon his Rock beneath his Tomb. I saw the Covering Cherub   30
Divide Four-fold into Four Churches when Lazarus arose
Paul, Constantine, Charlemaine, Luther; behold, they stand
                                                    before us*
Stretchd over Europe & Asia. come O Sons, come, come away
Arise O Sons give all your strength against Eternal Death
Lest we are vegetated, for Cathedrons Looms weave only Death*   35
A Web of Death: & were it not for Bowlahoola & Allamanda
No Human Form but only a Fibrous Vegetation
A Polypus of soft affections without Thought or Vision

Must tremble in the Heavens & Earths thro all the Ulro space
Throw all the Vegetated Mortals into Bowlahoola   40
But as to this Elected Form who is returnd again
He is the Signal that the Last Vintage now approaches
Nor Vegetation may go on till all the Earth is reapd

So Los spoke. Furious they descended to Bowlahoola & Allamanda
Indignant, unconvincd by Loss arguments & thunders rolling   45
They saw that wrath now swayd and now pity absorbd him
As it was, so it remain'd & no hope of an end.

Bowlahoola is namd Law by mortals, Tharmas founded it:
Because of Satan, before Luban in the City of Golgonooza.
But Golgonooza is namd Art & Manufacture by mortal men.   50

In Bowlahoola Los's Anvils stand & his Furnaces rage;
Thundering the Hammers beat & the Bellows blow loud
Living self moving mourning lamenting & howling incessantly
Bowlahoola thro all its porches feels, tho' too fast founded
Its pillars & porticoes to tremble at the force   55
Of mortal or immortal arm: and softly lilling flutes
Accordant with the horrid labours make sweet melody.
The Bellows are the Animal Lungs: the Hammers the Animal Heart
The Furnaces the Stomach for digestion. terrible their fury
Thousands & thousands labour. thousands play on instruments   60
Stringed or fluted to ameliorate the sorrows of slavery
Loud sport the dancers in the dance of death, rejoicing in carnage
The hard dentant Hammers are lulld by the flutes lula lula
The bellowing Furnaces blare by the long sounding clarion
The double drum drowns howls & groans, the shrill fife.   65
                              shrieks & cries:
The crooked horn mellows the hoarse raving serpent, terrible but
                              harmonious
Bowlahoola is the Stomach in every individual man.

Los is by mortals nam'd Time Enitharmon is nam'd Space
But they depict him bald & aged who is in eternal youth
All powerful and his locks flourish like the brows of morning   70
He is the Spirit of Prophecy the ever apparent Elias
Time is the mercy of Eternity; without Times swiftness
Which is the swiftest of all things; all were eternal torment:
All the Gods of the Kingdoms of Earth labour in Los's Halls.
Every one is a fallen Son of the Spirit of Prophecy   75
He is the Fourth Zoa, that stood around the Throne Divine.

[Plate 24]

But the Wine-press of Los is eastward of Golgonooza before
                    the Seat
Of Satan. Luvah laid the foundation & Urizen finish'd it in
                    howling woe.
How red the sons & daughters of Luvah: here they tread the grapes.
Laughing & shouting drunk with odours many fall oerwearied
Drownd in the wine is many a youth & maiden: those around   5
Lay them on skins of Tygers & of the spotted Leopard & the
                    Wild Ass
Till they revive, or bury them in cool grots, making lamentation.

This Wine-press is call'd War on Earth, it is the Printing-Press
Of Los; and here he lays his words in order above the mortal brain
As cogs are formd in a wheel to turn the cogs of the adverse wheel.   10

Timbrels & violins sport round the Wine-presses; the little Seed;
The sportive Root. the Earth-worm, the gold Beetle: the wise
                    Emmet;
Dance round the Wine-presses of Luvah: the Centipede is there:
The ground Spider with many eyes: the Mole clothed in velvet
The ambitious Spider in his sullen web; the lucky golden Spinner; 15
The Earwig armd: the tender Maggot emblem of immortality:
The Flea: Louse: Bug: the Tape-Worm: all the Armies of Disease:
Visible or invisible to the slothful vegetating Man.
The slow Slug: the Grasshopper that sings & laughs & drinks:
Winter comes, he folds his slender bones without a murmur.   20
The cruel Scorpion is there: the Gnat: Wasp: Hornet & the
                    Honey Bee:
The Toad & venomous Newt; the Serpent clothd in gems & gold;
They throw off their gorgeous raiment: they rejoice with loud jubilee
Around the Wine-presses of Luvah, naked & drunk with wine.

There is the Nettle that stings with soft down; and there   25
The indignant Thistle: whose bitterness is bred in his milk:
Who feeds on contempt of his neighbour: there all the idle Weeds
That creep around the obscure places, shew their various limbs.
Naked in all their beauty dancing—round the Wine-presses.

But in the Wine-presses the Human grapes sing not, nor dance   30
They howl & writhe in shoals of torment; in fierce flames consuming,
In chains of iron & in dungeons circled with ceaseless fires.

In pits & dens & shades of death: in shapes of torment & woe.
The plates & screws & wracks & saws & cords & fires & cisterns
The cruel joys of Luvahs Daughters lacerating with knives   35
And whips their Victims & the deadly sport of Luvahs Sons.

They dance around the dying, & they drink the howl & groan
They catch the shrieks in cups of gold, they hand them to one
                                                              another:
These are the sports of love, & these the sweet delights of
                                                    amorous play
Tears of the grape, the death sweat of the cluster the last sigh   40
Of the mild youth who listens to the lureing songs of Luvah

But Allamanda calld on Earth Commerce. is the Cultivated land
Around the City of Golgonooza in the Forests of Entuthon;
Here the Sons of Los labour against Death Eternal; through all
The Twenty-seven Heavens of Beulah in Ulro Seat of Satan,   45
Which is the False Tongue beneath Beulah: it is the Sense of Touch:
The Plow goes forth in tempests & lightnings & the Harrow cruel
In blights of the east; the heavy Roller follows in howlings of woe.

Urizens sons here labour also; & here are seen the Mills
Of Theotormon on the verge of the Lake of Udan-Adan: 50
These are the starry voids of night & the depths & caverns of earth
These Mills are oceans, clouds & waters ungovernable in their fury
Here are the stars created & the seeds of all things planted
And here the Sun & Moon recieve their fixed destinations

But in Eternity the Four Arts: Poetry, Painting, Music,   55
And Architecture which is Science: are the Four Faces of Man.
Not so in Time & Space: there Three are shut out, and only
Science remains thro Mercy: & by means of Science, the Three
Become apparent in Time & Space, in the Three Professions
Poetry in Religion: Music, Law: Painting, in Physic & Surgery: 60
That Man may live upon Earth till the time of his awaking,
And from these Three, Science derives every Occupation of Men.
And Science is divided into Bowlahoola & Allamanda.

[Plate 25]

Loud shout the Sons of Luvah at the Wine-presses as Los descended
With Rintrah & Palamabron in his fires of resistless fury.

The Wine-press on the Rhine groans loud, but all its central beams*
Act more terrific in the central Cities of the Nations
Where Human Thought is crushd beneath the iron hand of Power.   5
There Los puts all into the Press. the Opressor & the Opressed
Together, ripe for the Harvest & Vintage & ready for the Loom,

They sang at the Vintage. This is the Last Vintage! & Seed
Shall no more be sown upon Earth. till all the Vintage is over
And all gatherd in, till the Plow has passd over the Nations   10
And the Harrow & heavy thundering Roller upon the mountains

And loud the Souls howl round the Porches of Golgonooza
Crying O God deliver us to the Heavens or to the Earths.
That we may preach righteousness & punish the sinner with death
But Los refused till all the Vintage of Earth was gathered in.   15

And Los stood & cried to the Labourers of the Vintage in voice of awe.

Fellow Labourers! The Great Vintage & Harvest is now upon Earth
The whole extent of the Globe is explored: Every scatterd Atom*
Of Human Intellect now is flocking to the sound of the Trumpet
All the Wisdom which was hidden in caves & dens, from ancient   20
Time; is now sought out from Animal & Vegetable & Mineral
The Awakener is come. outstretchd over Europe: the Vision of God is
                                                            fulfilled
The Ancient Man upon the Rock of Albion Awakes,
He listens to the sounds of War astonishd & ashamed;
He sees his Children mock at Faith and deny Providence   25
Therefore you must bind the Sheaves not by Nations or Families
You shall bind them in Three Classes; according to their Classes
So shall you bind them. Separating What has been Mixed
Since Men began to be Wove into Nations by Rahab & Tirzah
Since Albions Death & Satans Cutting-off from our awful Fields;   30
When under pretence to benevolence the Elect Subdud All.
From the Foundation of the World. The Elect is one Class; You
Shall bind them separate: they cannot Believe in Eternal Life
Except by Miracle & a New Birth. The other two Classes;
The Reprobate who never cease to Believe, and the Redeemd,   35
Who live in doubts & fears perpetually tormented by the Elect
These you shall bind in a twin-bundle for the Consummation
But the Elect must be saved fires of Eternal Death,
To be formed into the Churches of Beulah that they destroy not
                                                        the Earth

For in every Nation & every Family the Three Classes are born   40
And in every Species of Earth, Metal, Tree, Fish, Bird & Beast.
We form the Mundane Egg. that Spectres coming by fury or amity*
All is the same, & every one remains in his own energy
Go forth Reapers with rejoicing. you sowed in tears
But the time of your refreshing cometh, only a little moment   45
Still abstain from pleasure & rest. in the labours of eternity
And you shall Reap the whole Earth, from Pole to Pole! from
                                                   Sea to Sea

Begining at Jerusalems Inner Court, Lambeth ruin'd and given
To the detestable Gods of Priam, to Apollo; and at the Asylum*
Given to Hercules, who labour in Tirzahs Looms for bread   50
Who set Pleasure against Duty: who Create Olympic crowns
To make Learning a burden & the Work of the Holy Spirit: Strife.
The Thor & cruel Odin who first reard the Polar Caves*
Lambeth mourns calling Jerusalem, she weeps & looks abroad
For the Lords coming, that Jerusalem may overspread all Nations   55
Crave not for the mortal & perishing delights, but leave them
To the weak, and pity the weak as your infant care; Break not
Forth in your wrath lest you also are vegetated by Tirzah
Wait till the Judgement is past, till the Creation is consumed
And then rush forward with me into the glorious spiritual   60
Vegetation; the Supper of the Lamb & his Bride; and the*
Awaking of Albion our friend and ancient companion.

So Los spoke. But lightnings of discontent broke on all sides round
And murmurs of thunder rolling heavy long & loud over the
                                                   mountains
While Los calld his Sons around him to the Harvest & the Vintage.   65

Thou seest the Constellations in the deep & wondrous Night
They rise in order and continue their immortal courses
Upon the mountain & in vales with harp & heavenly song
With flute & clarion; with cups & measures filld with foaming wine
Glittring the streams reflect the Vision of beatitude,   70
And the calm Ocean joys beneath & smooths his awful waves!

[Plate 26]

These are the Sons of Los, & these the Labourers of the Vintage
Thou seest the gorgeous clothed Flies that dance & sport in summer

Upon the sunny brooks & meadows: every one the dance.
Knows in its intricate mazes of delight artful to weave:
Each one to sound his instruments of music in the dance, 5
To touch each other & recede; to cross & change & return
These are the Children of Los; thou seest the Trees on mountains
The wind blows heavy. loud they thunder thro' the darksom sky
Uttering prophecies & speaking instructive words to the sons
Of men: These are the Sons of Los! These the Visions of Eternity 10
But we see only as it were the hem of their garments.
When with our vegetable eyes we view these wondrous Visions

There are Two Gates thro which all Souls descend, One Southward
From Dover Cliff to Lizard Point. the other toward the North
Caithness & rocky Durness, Pentland & John Groats House 15

The Souls descending to the Body. wail on the right hand
Of Los; & those deliverd from the Body. on the left hand
For Los against the east his force continually bends
Along the Valleys of Middlesex from Hounslow to Blackheath
Lest those Three Heavens of Beulah should the Creation destroy. 20
And lest they should descend before the north & south Gates,
Groaning with pity, he among the wailing Souls laments.

And these the Labours of the Sons of Los in Allamanda;
And in the City of Golgonooza: & in Luban: & around
The Lake of Udan-Adan in the Forests of Entuthon Benython* 25
Where Souls incessant wail, being piteous Passions & Desires
With neither lineament nor form, but like to wat'ry clouds
The Passions & Desires descend upon the hungry winds
For such alone Sleepers remain, meer passion & appetite:
The Sons of Los clothe them & feed & provide houses & fields 30

And every Generated Body in its inward form
Is a garden of delight & a building of magnificence,
Built by the Sons of Los in Bowlahoola & Allamanda
And the herbs & flowers & furniture & beds & chambers
Continually woven in the Looms of Enitharmons Daughters 35
In bright Cathedrons golden Dome with care & love & tears
For the various Classes of Men are all markd out determinate
In Bowlahoola; & as the Spectres choose their affinities
But not by Natural, but by Spiritual power alone. Because 40
The Natural power continually seeks & tends to Destruction

Ending in Death:which would of itself be Eternal Death.
And all are Class'd by Spiritual, & not by Natural power,

And every Natural Effect has a Spiritual Cause, and Not
A Natural: for a Natural Cause only seems, it is a Delusion   45
Of Ulro: & a ratio of the perishing Vegetable Memory.

[Plate 27]

Some Sons of Los surround the Passions with porches of
                                                    iron & silver
Creating form & beauty around the dark regions of sorrow.
Giving to airy nothing a name and a habitation*
Delightful: with bounds to the Infinite putting off the Indefinite
Into most holy forms of Thought: (such is the power of inspiration)   5
They labour incessant; with many tears & afflictions:
Creating the beautiful House for the piteous sufferer.

Others; Cabinets richly fabricate of gold & ivory;
For Doubts & fears unform'd & wretched & melancholy
The little weeping Spectre stands on the threshold of Death   10
Eternal; and sometimes two Spectres like lamps quivering
And often malignant they combat (heart-breaking sorrowful &
                                                    piteous)
Antamon takes them into his beautiful flexible hands,
As the Sower takes the seed, or as the Artist his clay
Or fine wax, to mould artful a model for golden ornaments.   15
The soft hands of Antamon draw the indelible line:
Form immortal with golden pen; such as the Spectre admiring
Puts on the sweet form; then smiles Antamon bright thro
                                                    his windows
The Daughters of beauty look up from their Loom & prepare.
The integument soft for its clothing with joy & delight.   20

But Theotormon & Sotha stand in the Gate of Luban anxious
Their numbers are seven million & seven thousand & seven
                                                    hundred
They contend with the weak Spectres, they fabricate soothing
                                                    forms
The Spectre refuses. he seeks cruelty. they create the crested Cock
Terrified the Spectre screams & rushes in fear into their Net   25
Of kindness & compassion & is born a weeping terror.

Or they create the Lion & Tyger in compassionate thunderings
Howling the Spectres flee: they take refuge in Human lineaments.

The Sons of Ozoth within the Optic Nerve stand fiery glowing
And the number of his Sons is eight millions & eight. 30
They give delights to the man unknown; artificial riches
They give to scorn, & their possessors to trouble & sorrow & care,
Shutting the sun, & moon, & stars. & trees, & clouds, & waters,
And hills, out from the Optic Nerve & hardening it into a bone
Opake, and like the black pebble on the enraged beach. 35
While the poor indigent is like the diamond which tho cloth'd
In rugged covering in the mine, is open all within
And in his hallowd center holds the heavens of bright eternity
Ozoth here builds walls of rocks against the surging sea
And timbers crampt with iron cramps bar in the joys of life 40
From fell destruction in the Spectrous cunning or rage. He Creates
The speckled Newt, the Spider & Beetle, the Rat & Mouse.
The Badger & Fox: they worship before his feet in trembling fear.

But others of the Sons of Los build Moments & Minutes
        & Hours
And Days & Months & Years & Ages & Periods; wondrous 45
        buildings
And every Moment has a Couch of gold for soft repose.
(A Moment equals a pulsation of the artery)
And between every two Moments stands a Daughter of Beulah
To feed the Sleepers on their Couches with maternal care.
And every Minute has an azure Tent with silken Veils. 50
And every Hour has a bright golden Gate carved with skill.
And every Day & Night has Walls of brass & Gates of adamant.
Shining like precious stones & ornamented with appropriate signs:
And every Month, a silver paved Terrace builded high:
And every Year, invulnerable Barriers with high Towers, 55
And every Age is Moated deep with Bridges of silver & gold.
And every Seven Ages is Incircled with a Flaming Fire.
Now Seven Ages is amounting to Two Hundred Years
Each has its Guard, each Moment Minute Hour Day
        Month & Year.
All are the work of Fairy hands of the Four Elements 60
The Guard are Angels of Providence on duty evermore
Every Time less than a pulsation of the artery
Is equal in its period & value to Six Thousand Years.

[Plate 28]

For in this Period the Poets Work is Done: and all the Great
Events of Time start forth & are concievd in such a Period
Within a Moment: a Pulsation of the Artery.

The Sky is an immortal Tent built by the Sons of Los
And every Space that a Man views around his dwelling-place.   5
Standing on his own roof, or in his garden on a mount
Of twenty-five cubits in height. such space is his Universe;
And on its verge the Sun rises & sets. the Clouds bow
To meet the flat Earth & the Sea in such an orderd Space:
The Starry heavens reach no further but here bend and set   10
On all sides & the two Poles turn on their valves of gold:
And if he move his dwelling-place. his heavens also move.
Where'er he goes & all his neighbourhood bewail his loss:
Such are the Spaces called Earth & such its dimension:
As to that false appearance which appears to the reasoner.   15
As of a Globe rolling thro' Voidness, it is a delusion of Ulro
The Microscope knows not of this nor the Telescope, they alter
The ratio of the Spectators Organs, but leave Objects untouch'd
For every Space larger than a red Globule of Mans blood,
Is visionary: and is created by the Hammer of Los   20
And every Space smaller than a Globule of Mans blood, opens
Into Eternity of which this vegetable Earth is but a shadow;
The red Globule is the unwearied Sun by Los created
To measure Time and Space to mortal Men, every morning.
Bowlahoola & Allamanda are placed on each side   25
Of that Pulsation & that Globule, terrible their power.

But Rintrah & Palamabron govern over Day & Night
In Allamanda & Entuthon Benython where Souls wail:
Where Orc incessant howls burning in fires of Eternal Youth.
Within the vegetated mortal Nerves; for every Man born is joined   30
Within into One mighty Polypus. and this Polypus is Orc.

But in the Optic vegetative Nerves Sleep was transformed
To Death in old time by Satan the father of Sin & Death
And Satan is the Spectre of Orc & Orc is the generate Luvah

But in the Nerves of the Nostrils. Accident being formed   35
Into Substance & Principle, by the cruelties of Demonstration
It became Opake & Indefinite; but the Divine Saviour,

Formed it into a Solid by Loss Mathematic power.
He named the Opake Satan: he named the Solid Adam

And in the Nerves of the Ear. (for the Nerves of the Tongue   40
              are closed)
On Albions Rock Los stands creating the glorious Sun each
              morning
And when unwearied in the evening he creates the Moon
Death to delude, who all in terror at their splendor leaves
His prey while Los appoints, & Rintrah & Palamabron guide
The Souls clear from the Rock of Death. that Death himself   45
              may wake
In his appointed season when the ends of heaven meet.

Then Los conducts the Spirits to be Vegetated into
Great Golgonooza, free from the four iron pillars of Satan's Throne,
(Temperance, Prudence, Justice, Fortitude, the four pillars
              of tyranny)
That Satan's Watch-Fiends touch them not before they Vegetate.   50

But Enitharmon and her Daughters take the pleasant charge.
To give them to their lovely heavens till the Great Judgment Day
Such is their lovely charge. But Rahab & Tirzah pervert
Their mild influences, therefore the Seven Eyes of God walk round
The Three Heavens of Ulro, where Tirzah & her Sisters   55
Weave the black Woof of Death upon Entuthon Benython
In the Vale of Surrey where Horeb terminates in Rephaim.
The stamping feet of Zelophehads Daughters are coverd with
              Human Gore*
Upon the treddles of the Loom, they sing to the winged shuttle:
The River rises above his banks to wash the Woof: 60
He takes it in his arms: he passes it in strength thro his current
The veil of human miseries is woven over the Ocean
From the Atlantic to the Great South Sea. the Erythrean.*

Such is the World of Los the labour of six thousand years.
Thus Nature is a Vision of the Science of the Elohim.   65

END OF THE FIRST BOOK.

[Plate 29]

WILLIAM

Milton

[Plate 30]

MILTON

BOOK THE SECOND

There is a place where Contrarieties are equally True
This place is called Beulah, It is a pleasant lovely Shadow*
Where no dispute can come. Because of those who Sleep,
Into this place the Sons & Daughters of Ololon descended
With solemn mourning into Beulahs moony shades & hills   5
Weeping for Milton: mute wonder held the Daughters of Beulah
Enrapturd with affection sweet and mild benevolence

Beulah is evermore Created around Eternity; appearing
To the Inhabitants of Eden. around them on all sides.
But Beulah to its Inhabitants appears within each district   10
As the beloved infant in his mothers bosom round incircled
With arms of love & pity & sweet compassion, But to
The Sons of Eden the moony habitations of Beulah,
Are from Great Eternity a mild & pleasant Rest.

And it is thus Created. Lo the Eternal Great Humanity   15
To whom be Glory & Dominion Evermore Amen
Walks among all his awful Family seen in every face
As the breath of the Almighty, such are the words of man to man
In the great Wars of Eternity. in fury of Poetic Inspiration
To build the Universe stupendous: Mental forms Creating   20

But the Emanations trembled exceedingly, nor could they
Live, because the life of Man was too exceeding unbounded
His joy became terrible to them they trembled & wept
Crying with one voice. Give us a habitation & a place
In which we may be hidden under the shadow of wings   25
For if we who are but for a time, & who pass away in winter
Behold these wonders of Eternity we shall consume
But you, O our Fathers & Brothers, remain in Eternity
But grant us a Temporal Habitation, do you speak
To us; we will obey your words as you obey Jesus   30
The Eternal who is blessed for ever & ever. Amen

So spake the lovely Emanations: & there appeard a pleasant
Mild Shadow above: beneath: & on all sides round,

[Plate 31]

Into this pleasant Shadow all the weak & weary
Like Women & Children were taken away as on wings
Of dovelike softness, & shadowy habitations prepared for them
But every Man returnd & went still going forward thro'
The Bosom of the Father in Eternity on Eternity   5
Neither did any lack or fall into Error without
A Shadow to repose in all the Days of happy Eternity

Into this pleasant Shadow Beulah. all Ololon descended
And when the Daughters of Beulah heard the lamentation
All Beulah wept. for they saw the Lord coming in the Clouds.   10
And the Shadows of Beulah terminate in rocky Albion—

And all Nations wept in affliction Family by Family
Germany wept towards France & Italy: England wept & trembled
Towards America: India rose up from his golden bed:
As one awakend in the night: they saw the Lord coming   15
In the Clouds of Ololon with Power & Great Glory!

And all the Living Creatures of the Four Elements, wail'd
With bitter wailing: these in the aggregate are named Satan
And Rahab: they know not of Regeneration, but only
                                        of Generation
The Fairies, Nymphs, Gnomes & Genii of the Four Elements*   20
Unforgiving & unalterable: these cannot be Regenerated
But must be Created, for they know only of Generation
These are the Gods of the Kingdoms of the Earth: in
                                        contrarious
And cruel opposition: Element against Element, opposed in War
Not Mental, as the Wars of Eternity, but a Corporeal Strife   25
In Los's Halls continual labouring in the Furnaces of
                                        Golgonooza
Orc howls on the Atlantic: Enitharmon trembles; All Beulah weeps

Thou hearest the Nightingale begin the Song of Spring:
The Lark sitting upon his earthy bed: just as the morn
Appears; listens silent: then springing from the waving Corn-field! 30
                                        loud
He leads the Choir of Day! trill, trill, trill, trill,
Mounting upon the wings of light into the Great Expanse.
Reecchoing against the lovely blue & shining heavenly Shell:

His little throat labours with inspiration; every feather
On throat & breast & wings vibrates with the effluence Divine   35
All Nature listens silent to him & the awful Sun
Stands still upon the Mountain looking on this little Bird
With eyes of soft humility, & wonder love & awe,
Then loud from their green covert all the Birds begin their Song
The Thrush, the Linnet & the Goldfinch, Robin & the Wren   40
Awake the Sun from his sweet reverie upon the Mountain:
The Nightingale again assays his song & thro' the day,
And thro the night warbles luxuriant: every Bird of Song
Attending his loud harmony with admiration & love.
This is a Vision of the lamentation of Beulah over Ololon!   45

Thou percievest the Flowers put forth their precious Odours!
And none can tell how from so small a center comes such sweets
Forgetting that within that Center Eternity expands
Its ever during doors. that Og & Anak fiercely guard
First eer the morning breaks joy opens in the flowery bosoms   50
Joy even to tears, which the Sun rising dries: first the Wild
                                                              Thyme
And Meadow-sweet downy & soft waving among the reeds.
Light springing on the air lead the sweet Dance: they wake
The Honeysuckle sleeping on the Oak: the flaunting beauty
Revels along upon the wind; the White-thorn lovely May   55
Opens her many lovely eyes: listening the Rose still sleeps
None dare to wake her. soon she bursts her crimson curtaind bed
And comes forth in the majesty of beauty; every Flower:
The Pink, the Jessamine, the Wall-flower, the Carnation
The Jonquil, the mild Lilly opes her heavens! every Tree,   60
And Flower & Herb soon fill the air with an innumerable Dance
Yet all in order sweet & lovely, Men are sick with Love!
Such is a Vision of the lamentation of Beulah over Ololon

[Plate 32]

And the Divine Voice was heard in the Songs of Beulah Saying:
When I first Married you, I gave you all my whole Soul
I thought that you would love my loves & joy in my delights
Seeking for pleasures in my pleasures O Daughter of Babylon
Then thou wast lovely, mild & gentle, now thou art terrible   5
In jealousy & unlovely in my sight. because thou hast cruelly

Cut off my loves in fury till I have no love left for thee
Thy love depends on him thou lovest, & on his dear loves
Depend thy pleasures which thou hast cut off by jealousy
Therefore I shew my Jealousy & set before you Death. 10
Behold Milton descended to Redeem the Female Shade
From Death Eternal; such your lot, to be continually Redeem'd
By death & misery of those you love & by Annihilation
When the Sixfold Female percieves that Milton annihilates
Himself; that seeing all his loves by her cut off: he leaves 15
Her also: intirely abstracting himself from Female loves
She shall relent in fear of death; She shall begin to give
Her maidens to her husband: delighting in his delight.
And then & then alone begins the happy Female joy
As it is done in Beulah, & thou, O Virgin Babylon Mother of 20
Whoredoms
Shalt bring Jerusalem in thine arms in the night watches; and
No longer turning her a wandering Harlot in the streets
Shalt give her into the arms of God your Lord & Husband.

Such are the Songs of Beulah, in the Lamentations of Ololon.

[Plate 33]

ROBERT*

[Plate 34]

And all the Songs of Beulah sounded comfortable notes
To comfort Ololons lamentation, for they said
Are you the Fiery Circle that late drove in fury & fire
The Eight Immortal Starry-Ones down into Ulro dark
Rending the Heavens of Beulah with your thunders & lightnings 5
And can you thus lament & can you pity & forgive?
Is terror changd to pity O wonder of Eternity;

And the Four States of Humanity in its Repose,
Were shewed them. First of Beulah a most pleasant Sleep
On Couches soft, with mild music, tended by Flowers of Beulah 10
Sweet Female forms, winged or floating in the air spontaneous
The Second State is Alla & the third State Al-Ulro;
But the Fourth State is dreadful; it is named Or-Ulro:

The First State is in the Head, the Second is in the Heart:
The Third in the Loins & Seminal Vessels & the Fourth   15
In the Stomach & Intestines terrible. deadly, unutterable.
And he whose Gates are opend in those Regions of his Body
Can from those Gates view all these wondrous Imaginations

But Ololon sought the Or-Ulro & its fiery Gates   20
And the Couches of the Martyrs: & many Daughters of Beulah
Accompany them down to the Ulro with soft melodious tears
A long journey & dark thro Chaos in the track of Miltons course
To where the Contraries of Beulah War beneath Negations Banner

Then view'd from Miltons Track they see the Ulro: a vast Polypus   25
Of living fibres down into the Sea of Time & Space growing
A self-devouring monstrous Human Death Twenty-seven fold
Within it sit Five Females & the nameless Shadowy Mother
Spinning it from their bowels with songs of amorous delight
And melting cadences that lure the Sleepers of Beulah down   30
The River Storge (which is Arnon) into the Dead Sea:*
Around this Polypus Los continual builds the Mundane Shell

Four Universes round the Universe of Los remain Chaotic
Four intersecting Globes. & the Egg form'd World of Los
In midst; stretching from Zenith to Nadir, in midst of Chaos,   35
One of these Ruind Universes is to the North named Urthona,
One to the South this was the glorious World of Urizen.
One to the East, of Luvah: One to the West; of Tharmas.
But when Luvah assumed the World of Urizen in the South
All fell towards the Center sinking downward in dire Ruin   40

Here in these Chaoses the Sons of Ololon took their abode
In Chasms of the Mundane Shell which open on all sides round
Southward & by the East within the Breach of Miltons descent
To watch the time, pitying, & gentle to awaken Urizen
They stood in a dark land of death of fiery corroding waters   45
Where lie in evil death the Four Immortals pale and cold
And the Eternal Man even Albion upon the Rock of Ages
Seeing Miltons Shadow, some Daughters of Beulah trembling
Returnd, but Ololon remain'd before the Gates of the Dead

And Ololon looked down into the Heavens of Ulro in fear   50
They said. How are the Wars of Man which in Great Eternity
Appear around in the External Spheres of Visionary Life

Here renderd Deadly within the Life & Interior Vision
How are the Beasts & Birds & Fishes. & Plants & Minerals
Here fixd into a frozen bulk subject to decay & death   55
Those Visions of Human Life & Shadows of Wisdom &
                                                  Knowledge

[Plate 35]

Are here frozen to unexpansive deadly destroying terrors
And War & Hunting: the Two Fountains of the River of Life*
Are become Fountains of bitter Death & of corroding Hell
Till Brotherhood is changd into a Curse & a Flattery
By Differences between Ideas, that Ideas themselves, (which are   5
The Divine Members) may be slain in offerings for sin
O dreadful Loom of Death! O piteous Female forms compelld
To weave the Woof of Death. On Camberwell Tirzahs Courts
Malahs on Blackheath, Rahab & Noah, dwell on Windsors heights
Where once the Cherubs of Jerusalem spread to Lambeths Vale   10
Milcah's Pillars shine from Harrow to Hampstead where Hoglah
On Highgates heights magnificent Weaves over trembling Thames
To Shooters Hill and thence to Blackheath the dark Woof! Loud
Loud roll the Weights & Spindles over the whole Earth let down
On all sides round to the Four Quarters of the World, eastward on   15
Europe to Euphrates & Hindu, to Nile & back in Clouds
Of Death across the Atlantic to America North & South

So spake Ololon in reminiscence astonishd, but they
Could not behold Golgonooza without passing the Polypus
A wondrous journey not passable by Immortal feet, & none   20
But the Divine Saviour can pass it without annihilation.
For Golgonooza cannot be seen till having passd the Polypus
It is viewed on all sides round by a Four-fold Vision
Or till you become Mortal & Vegetable in Sexuality
Then you behold its mighty Spires & Domes of ivory & gold   25

And Ololon examined all the Couches of the Dead.
Even of Los & Enitharmon & all the Sons of Albion
And his Four Zoas terrified & on the verge of Death
In midst of these was Miltons Couch, & when they saw Eight
Immortal Starry-Ones, guarding the Couch in flaming fires   30
They thunderous utterd all a universal groan, falling down

Prostrate before the Starry Eight asking with tears forgiveness
Confessing their crime with humiliation and sorrow,

O how the Starry Eight rejoic'd to see Ololon descended:
And now that a wide road was open to Eternity,   35
By Ololons descent thro Beulah to Los & Enitharmon.

For mighty were the multitudes of Ololon, vast the extent
Of their great sway, reaching from Ulro to Eternity
Surrounding the Mundane Shell outside in its Caverns
And through Beulah and all silent forbore to contend   40
With Ololon for they saw the Lord in the Clouds of Ololon

There is a Moment in each Day that Satan cannot find
Nor can his Watch Fiends find it, but the Industrious find
This Moment & it multiply, & when it once is found
It renovates every Moment of the Day if rightly placed   45
In this Moment Ololon descended to Los & Enitharmon
Unseen beyond the Mundane Shell Southward in Miltons track

Just in this Moment when the morning odours rise abroad
And first from the Wild Thyme, stands a Fountain in a rock*
Of crystal flowing into two Streams, one flows thro Golgonooza   50
And thro Beulah to Eden beneath Los's western Wall
The other flows thro the Aerial Void & all the Churches
Meeting again in Golgonooza beyond Satans Seat

The Wild Thyme is Los's Messenger to Eden, a mighty Demon
Terrible deadly & poisonous his presence in Ulro dark   55
Therefore he appears only a small Root creeping in grass
Covering over the Rock of Odours his bright purple mantle
Beside the Fount above the Larks nest in Golgonooza
Luvah slept here in death & here is Luvahs empty Tomb
Ololon sat beside this Fountain on the Rock of Odours.   60

Just at the place to where the Lark mounts, is a Crystal Gate
It is the enterance of the First Heaven named Luther: for
The Lark is Loss Messenger thro the Twenty-seven Churches*
That the Seven Eyes of God who walk even to Satans Seat
Thro all the Twenty-seven Heavens, may not slumber nor sleep   65
But the Larks Nest is at the Gate of Los, at the eastern
Gate of wide Golgonooza & the Lark is Los's Messenger

[Plate 36]

When on the highest lift of his light pinions he arrives
At that bright Gate. another Lark meets him & back to back
They touch their pinions tip tip: and each descend
To their respective Earths & there all night consult with Angels
Of Providence & with the Eyes of God all night in slumbers   5
Inspired; & at the dawn of day send out another Lark
Into another Heaven to carry news upon his wings
Thus are the Messengers dispatchd till they reach the Earth again
In the East Gate of Golgonooza. & the Twenty-eighth bright
Lark, met the Female Ololon descending into my Garden*   10
Thus it appears to Mortal eyes & those of the Ulro Heavens
But not thus to Immortals, the Lark is a mighty Angel.

For Ololon step'd into the Polypus within the Mundane Shell
They could not step into Vegetable Worlds without becoming
The enemies of Humanity except in a Female Form   15
And as One Female. Ololon and all its mighty Hosts
Appear'd: a Virgin of twelve years nor time nor space was
To the perception of the Virgin Ololon but as the
Flash of lightning but more quick the Virgin in my Garden
Before my Cottage stood for the Satanic Space is delusion   20

For when Los joind with me he took me in his firy whirlwind
My Vegetated portion was hurried from Lambeths shades
He set me down in Felphams Vale & prepard a beautiful
Cottage for me that in three years I might write all these Visions*
To display Natures cruel holiness: the deceits of Natural Religion 25
Walking in my Cottage Garden, sudden I beheld
The Virgin Ololon & address'd her as a Daughter of Beulah

Virgin of Providence fear not to enter into my Cottage
What is thy message to thy friend? What am I now to do
Is it again to plunge into deeper affliction? behold me   30
Ready to obey, but pity thou my Shadow of Delight*
Enter my Cottage, comfort her, for she is sick with fatigue

[Plate 37]

The Virgin answerd. Knowest thou of Milton who descended
Driven from Eternity; him I seek! terrified at my Act
In Great Eternity which thou knowest! I come him to seek

So Ololon utterd in words distinct the anxious thought
Mild was the voice, but more distinct than any earthly   5
That Miltons Shadow heard & condensing all his Fibres
Into a strength impregnable of majesty & beauty infinite
I saw he was the Covering Cherub & within him Satan
And Rahab, in an outside which is fallacious! within
Beyond the outline of Identity, in the Selfhood deadly   10
And he appeard the Wicker Man of Scandinavia in whom*
Jerusalems children consume in flames among the Stars

Descending down into my Garden, a Human Wonder of God
Reaching from heaven to earth a Cloud & Human Form
I beheld Milton with astonishment & in him beheld   15
The Monstrous Churches of Beulah, the Gods of Ulro dark
Twelve monstrous dishumanizd terrors Synagogues of Satan.
A Double Twelve & Thrice Nine: such their divisions.

And these their Names & their Places within the Mundane Shell

In Tyre & Sidon I saw Baal & Ashtaroth. In Moab Chemosh   20
In Ammon, Molech: loud his Furnaces rage among the Wheels
Of Og, & pealing loud the cries of the Victims of Fire:
And pale his Priestesses infolded in Veils of Pestilence, border'd
With War: Woven in Looms of Tyre & Sidon by beautiful
                                                    Ashtaroth.

In Palestine Dagon, Sea Monster! worshipd o'er the Sea.   25
Thammuz in Lebanon & Rimmon in Damascus curtaind
Osiris: Isis: Orus: in Egypt: dark their Tabernacles on Nile
Floating with solemn songs, & on the Lakes of Egypt nightly
With pomp, even till morning break & Osiris appear in the sky
But Belial of Sodom & Gomorrha, obscure Demon of Bribes   30
And secret Assasinations, not worshipd nor adord; but
With the finger on the lips & the back turnd to the light
And Saturn Jove & Rhea of the Isles of the Sea remote
These Twelve Gods, are the Twelve Spectre Sons of the
                                            Druid Albion

And these the names of the Twenty-seven Heavens & their   35
                                            Churches
Adam, Seth, Enos, Cainan, Mahalaleel, Jared, Enoch.
Methuselah, Lamech: these are Giants mighty, Hermaphroditic
Noah, Shem, Arphaxad, Cainan the second, Salah, Heber,
Peleg. Reu, Serug, Nahor, Terah, these are the Female-Males

A Male within a Female hid as in an Ark & Curtains.   40
Abraham, Moses, Solomon, Paul. Constantine, Charlemaine
Luther, these seven are the Male-Females, the Dragon Forms
Religion hid in War, a Dragon red & hidden Harlot*

All these are seen in Miltons Shadow who is the Covering
                                                              Cherub
The Spectre of Albion in which the Spectre of Luvah inhabits   45
In the Newtonian Voids between the Substances of Creation

For the Chaotic Voids outside of the Stars are measured by
The Stars, which are the boundaries of Kingdoms, Provinces
And Empires of Chaos invisible to the Vegetable Man
The Kingdom of Og, is in Orion: Sihon is in Ophiucus   50
Og has Twenty-seven Districts: Sihons Districts Twenty-one
From Star to Star, Mountains & Valleys, terrible dimension
Stretchd out, compose the Mundane Shell, a mighty Incrustation
Of Forty-eight deformed Human Wonders of the Almighty
With Caverns whose remotest bottoms meet again beyond   55
The Mundane Shell in Golgonooza, but the Fires of Los, rage
In the remotest bottoms of the Caves. that none can pass
Into Eternity that way, but all descend to Los
To Bowlahoola & Allamanda & to Entuthon Benython

The Heavens are the Cherub, the Twelve Gods are Satan   60

[Plate 39]

And the Forty-eight Starry Regions are Cities of the Levites
The Heads of the Great Polypus, Four-fold twelve enormity
In mighty & mysterious comingling enemy with enemy
Woven by Urizen into Sexes from his mantle of years
And Milton collecting all his fibres into impregnable strength   5
Descended down a Paved work of all kinds of precious stones
Out from the eastern sky; descending down into my Cottage
Garden: clothed in black. severe & silent he descended.

The Spectre of Satan stood upon the roaring sea & beheld
Milton within his sleeping Humanity! trembling & shuddring   10
He stood upon the waves a Twenty-seven fold mighty Demon
Gorgeous & beautiful: loud roll his thunders against Milton
Loud Satan thunderd, loud & dark upon mild Felpham shore
Not daring to touch one fibre he howld round upon the Sea.

I also stood in Satans bosom & beheld its desolations!   15
A ruind Man: a ruind building of God not made with hands;
Its plains of burning sand, its mountains of marble terrible;
Its pits & declivities flowing with molten ore & fountains
Of pitch & nitre; its ruind palaces & cities & mighty works;
Its furnaces of affliction in which his Angels & Emanations   20
Labour with blackend visages among its stupendous ruins
Arches & pyramids & porches colonades & domes:
In which dwells Mystery Babylon, here is her secret place
From hence she comes forth on the Churches in delight
Here is her Cup filld with its poisons, in these horrid vales   25
And here her scarlet Veil woven in pestilence & war:
Here is Jerusalem bound in chains, in the Dens of Babylon*

In the Eastern porch of Satans Universe Milton stood & said

Satan! my Spectre! I know my power thee to annihilate
And be a greater in thy place, & be thy Tabernacle   30
A covering for thee to do thy will, till one greater comes
And smites me as I smote thee & becomes my covering
Such are the Laws of thy false Heavns! but Laws of Eternity
Are not such: know thou: I come to Self Annihilation
Such are the Laws of Eternity that each shall mutually   35
Annihilate himself for others good, as I for thee
Thy purpose & the purpose of thy Priests & of thy Churches
Is to impress on men the fear of death; to teach
Trembling & fear, terror, constriction; abject selfishness
Mine is to teach Men to despise death & to go on   40
In fearless majesty annihilating Self. laughing to scorn
Thy Laws & terrors, shaking down thy Synagogues as webs
I come to discover before Heavn & Hell the Self righteousness
In all its Hypocritic turpitude. opening to every eye
These wonders of Satans holiness shewing to the Earth   45
The Idol Virtues of the Natural Heart, & Satans Seat
Explore in all its Selfish Natural Virtue & put off
In Self annihilation all that is not of God alone:*
To put off Self & all I have ever & ever Amen

Satan heard! Coming in a cloud with trumpets & flaming fire   50
Saying I am God the judge of all, the living & the dead
Fall therefore down & worship me, submit thy supreme
Dictate, to my eternal Will & to my dictate bow

I hold the Balances of Right & Just & mine the Sword
Seven Angels bear my Name & in those Seven I appear   55
But I alone am God & I alone in Heav'n & Earth
Of all that live dare utter this, others tremble & bow

[Plate 40]

Till All Things become One Great Satan, in Holiness
Oppos'd to Mercy, and the Divine Delusion Jesus, be no more

Suddenly around Milton on my Path, the Starry Seven
Burnd terrible! my Path became a solid fire, as bright
As the clear Sun & Milton silent came down on my Path   5
And there went forth from the Starry limbs of the Seven: Forms
Human; with Trumpets innumerable, sounding articulate
As the Seven spake; and they stood in a mighty Column of Fire
Surrounding Felphams Vale, reaching to the Mundane Shell, Saying

Awake, Albion awake! reclaim thy Reasoning Spectre. Subdue   10
Him to the Divine Mercy. Cast him down into the Lake
Of Los, that ever burneth with fire, ever & ever Amen!
Let the Four Zoa's awake from Slumbers of Six Thousand Years

Then loud the Furnaces of Los were heard! & seen as Seven Heavens
Stretching from south to north over the mountains of Albion   15

Satan heard; trembling round his Body, he incircled it
He trembled with exceeding great trembling & astonishment
Howling in his Spectre round his Body hungring to devour
But fearing for the pain for if he touches a Vital,
His torment is unendurable; therefore he cannot devour: 20
But howls round it as a lion round his prey continually
Loud Satan thunderd, loud & dark upon mild Felphams Shore
Coming in a Cloud with Trumpets & with Fiery Flame
An awful Form eastward from midst of a bright Paved-work
Of precious stones by Cherubim surrounded: so permitted   25
(Lest he should fall apart in his Eternal Death) to imitate
The Eternal Great Humanity Divine surrounded by
His Cherubim & Seraphim in ever happy Eternity
Beneath sat Chaos: Sin on his right hand Death on his left
And Ancient Night spread over all the heavn his Mantle of Laws   30
He trembled with exceeding great trembling & astonishment

Then Albion rose up in the Night of Beulah on his Couch
Of dread repose seen by the visionary eye; his face is toward
The east, toward Jerusalems Gates: groaning he sat above
His rocks. London & Bath & Legions & Edinburgh*   35
Are the four pillars of his Throne; his left foot near London
Covers the shades of Tyburn; his instep from Windsor
To Primrose Hill stretching to Highgate & Holloway
London is between his knees; its basements fourfold
His right foot stretches to the sea on Dover cliffs, his heel   40
On Canterburys ruins; his right hand covers lofty Wales
His left Scotland; his bosom girt with gold involves
York, Edinburgh, Durham & Carlisle & on the front
Bath, Oxford, Cambridge, Norwich; his right elbow
Leans on the Rocks of Erins Land, Ireland, ancient nation   45
His head bends over London: he sees his embodied Spectre
Trembling before him with exceeding great trembling & fear
He views Jerusalem & Babylon, his tears flow down.
He movd his right foot to Cornwall, his left to the Rocks of Bognor*
He strove to rise to walk into the Deep, but strength failing   50
Forbad & down with dreadful groans he sunk upon his Couch
In moony Beulah, Los, his strong Guard walks round beneath the
                                                              Moon

Urizen faints in terror striving among the Brooks of Arnon
With Miltons Spirit: as the Plowman or Artificer or Shepherd
While in the labours of his Calling sends his Thought abroad   55
To labour in the ocean or in the starry heaven. So Milton
Labourd in Chasms of the Mundane Shell. tho here before
My Cottage midst the Starry Seven, where the Virgin Ololon
Stood trembling in the Porch: loud Satan thunderd on the stormy Sea
Circling Albions Cliffs in which the Four-fold World resides   60
Tho seen in fallacy outside; a fallacy of Satans Churches

[Plate 42]

Before Ololon Milton stood & percievd the Eternal Form
Of that mild Vision; wondrous were their acts, by me unknown
Except remotely; and I heard Ololon say to Milton

I see thee strive upon the Brooks of Arnon. there a dread
And awful Man I see, oercoverd with the mantle of years,   5

I behold Los & Urizen. I behold Orc & Tharmas!
The Four Zoa's of Albion, & thy Spirit with them striving
In Self annihilation giving thy life to thy enemies
Are those who contemn Religion & seek to annihilate it
Become in their Femine portions, the causes & promoters   10
Of these Religions, how is this thing? this Newtonian Phantasm,
This Voltaire & Rousseau: this Hume & Gibbon & Bolingbroke*
This Natural Religion! this impossible absurdity
Is Ololon the cause of this? O where shall I hide my face
These tears fall for the little-ones: the Children of Jerusalem   15
Lest they be annihilated in thy annihilation,

No sooner she had spoke but Rahab Babylon appeard
Eastward upon the Paved work across Europe & Asia
Glorious as the midday Sun in Satans bosom glowing:
A Female hidden in a Male, Religion hidden in War   20
Namd Moral Virtue: cruel two-fold Monster shining bright
A Dragon red & hidden Harlot which John in Patmos saw*

And all beneath the Nations innumerable of Ulro
Appeard, the Seven Kingdoms of Canaan & Five Baalim
Of Philistea, into Twelve divided, calld after the Names   25
Of Israel: as they are in Eden. Mountain River & Plain
City & sandy Desert intermingled beyond mortal ken

But turning toward Ololon in terrible majesty Milton
Replied. Obey thou the Words of the Inspired Man
All that can be annihilated must be annihilated   30
That the Children of Jerusalem may be saved from slavery
There is a Negation, & there is a Contrary
The Negation must be destroyd to redeem the Contraries
The Negation is the Spectre; the Reasoning Power in Man
This is a false Body: an Incrustation over my Immortal   35
Spirit; a Selfhood which must be put off & annihilated alway
To cleanse the Face of my Spirit by Self-examination,

[Plate 43]

To bathe in the Waters of Life; to wash off the Not Human
I come in Self-annihilation & the grandeur of Inspiration
To cast off Rational Demonstration by Faith in the Saviour
To cast off the rotten rags of Memory by Inspiration

To cast off Bacon. Locke & Newton from Albions covering   5
To take off his filthy garments, & clothe him with Imagination
To cast aside from Poetry, all that is not Inspiration
That it no longer shall dare to mock with the aspersion of Madness
Cast on the Inspired, by the tame high finisher of paltry Blots,
Indefinite, or paltry Rhymes; or paltry Harmonies,   10
Who creeps into State Government like a catterpiller to destroy
To cast off the idiot Questioner who is always questioning,
But never capable of answering; who sits with a sly grin
Silent plotting when to question, like a thief in a cave;
Who publishes doubt & calls it knowledge; whose Science   15
                                          is Despair
Whose pretence to knowledge is Envy: whose whole Science is
To destroy the wisdom of ages to gratify ravenous Envy.
That rages round him like a Wolf day & night without rest
He smiles with condescension; he talks of Benevolence & Virtue
And those who act with Benevolence & Virtue, they murder time on 20
                                                      time

These are the destroyers of Jerusalem. these are the murderers
Of Jesus, who deny the Faith & mock at Eternal Life:
Who pretend to Poetry that they may destroy Imagination:
By imitation of Natures Images drawn from Remembrance
These are the Sexual Garments, the Abomination of Desolation 25
Hiding the Human Lineaments as with an Ark & Curtains*
Which Jesus rent: & now shall wholly purge away with Fire
Till Generation is swallow'd up in Regeneration.

Then trembled the Virgin Ololon & replyd in clouds of despair
Is this our Femine Portion the Six-fold Miltonic Female   30
Terribly this Portion trembles before thee O awful Man
Altho' our Human Power can sustain the severe contentions
Of Friendship, our Sexual cannot: but flies into the Ulro.
Hence arose all our terrors in Eternity! & now remembrance
Returns upon us! are we Contraries O Milton, Thou & I   35
O Immortal! how were we led to War the Wars of Death
Is this the Void Outside of Existence, which if enterd into

[Plate 44]

Becomes a Womb? & is this the Death Couch of Albion
Thou goest to Eternal Death & all must go with thee

So saying, the Virgin divided Six-fold & with a shriek
Dolorous that ran thro all Creation a Double Six-fold
                                  Wonder:
Away from Ololon she divided & fled into the depths   5
Of Miltons Shadow as a Dove upon the stormy Sea.

Then as a Moony Ark Ololon descended to Felphams Vale
In clouds of blood, in streams of gore, with dreadful thunderings
Into the Fires of Intellect that rejoic'd in Felphams Vale
Around the Starry Eight: with one accord the Starry Eight   10
                                  became
One Man Jesus the Saviour. wonderful! round his limbs
The Clouds of Ololon folded as a Garment dipped in blood
Written within & without in woven letters: & the Writing
Is the Divine Revelation in the Litteral expression:
A Garment of War, I heard it namd the Woof of   15
                        Six Thousand Years

And I beheld the Twenty-four Cities of Albion
Arise upon their Thrones to Judge the Nations of the Earth
And the Immortal Four in whom the Twenty-four appear
                        Four-fold
Arose around Albions body: Jesus wept & walked forth
From Felphams Vale clothed in Clouds of blood, to enter into   20
Albions Bosom, the bosom of death & the Four surrounded him
In the Column of Fire in Felphams Vale; then to their mouths
                        the Four
Applied their Four Trumpets & them sounded to the Four winds

Terror struck in the Vale I stood at that immortal sound
My bones trembled. I fell outstretchd upon the path   25
A moment, & my Soul returnd into its mortal state
To Resurrection & Judgment in the Vegetable Body
And my sweet Shadow of Delight stood trembling by my side

Immediately the Lark mounted with a loud trill from
                        Felphams Vale
And the Wild Thyme from Wimbletons green & impurpled Hills   30
And Los & Enitharmon rose over the Hills of Surrey
Their clouds roll over London with a south wind, soft Oothoon
Pants in the Vales of Lambeth weeping oer her Human Harvest
Los listens to the Cry of the Poor Man: his Cloud
Over London in volume terrific, low bended in anger,   35

Rintrah & Palamabron view the Human Harvest beneath
Their Wine-presses & Barns stand open; the Ovens are prepard
The Waggons ready: terrific Lions & Tygers sport & play
All Animals upon the Earth, are prepard in all their strength

[Plate 45]

To go forth to the Great Harvest & Vintage of the Nations

FINIS

Jerusalem
The Emanation of The Giant Albion*

1804 Printed by W. Blake Sᵗʰ Molton Sᵗ·

[Plate 3]*

SHEEP   To the Public   GOATS

After my three years slumber* on the banks of the Ocean, I again display my Giant forms to the Public: My former Giants & Fairies having reciev'd the highest reward possible; the [*love*] and [*friendship*] of those with whom to be connected is to be *blessed*: I cannot doubt that this more consolidated & extended Work will be as kindly received—The Enthusiasm of the following Poem, the Author hopes [*no Reader will think presumptuousness or arrogance when he is reminded that the Ancients entrusted their love to their Writing, to the full as enthusiastically as I have who Acknowledge mine for my Saviour and Lord; for they were wholly absorb'd in their Gods.*] I also hope the Reader will be with me, wholly One in Jesus our Lord, who is the God [*of Fire*] and Lord [*of Love*] to whom the Ancients look'd and saw his day afar off, with trembling & amazement.

The Spirit of Jesus is continual forgiveness of Sin; he who waits to be righteous before he enters into the Saviours kingdom, the Divine Body; will never enter there. I am perhaps the most sinful of men! I pretend not to holiness; yet I pretend to love, to see, to converse with daily as man with man, & the more to have an interest in the Friend of Sinners. Therefore, [*Dear*] Reader, [*forgive*] what you do not approve, & [*love*] me for this energetic exertion of my talent.

> Reader! [*lover*] of books! [*lover*] of heaven,
> And of that God from whom [*all books are given*]
> Who in mysterious Sinais awful cave,
> To Man the wond'rous art of writing gave,
> Again he speaks in thunder and in fire!   5
> Thunder of Thought, & flames of fierce desire:
> Even from the depths of Hell his voice I hear,
> Within the unfathomd caverns of my Ear.
> Therefore I print; nor vain my types shall be:

Heaven, Earth & Hell, henceforth shall live in harmony   10

Of the Measure, in which the following Poem is written

We who dwell on Earth can do nothing of ourselves, every thing is conducted by Spirits, no less than Digestion or Sleep. [*to Note the last words of Jesus* Εδοθη μοι πασα εξουσια εν ουρανω και επι γης.]*

When this Verse was first dictated to me I consider'd a Monotonous Cadence like that used by Milton & Shakspeare & all writers of English Blank Verse, derived from the modern bondage of Rhyming; to be a necessary and indispensible part of Verse. But I soon found that in the mouth of a true Orator such monotony was not only awkward, but as much a bondage as rhyme itself. I therefore have produced a variety in every line, both of cadences & number of syllables. Every word and every letter is studied and put into its fit place: the terrific numbers are reserved for the terrific parts the mild & gentle, for the mild & gentle parts. and the prosaic, for inferior parts; all are necessary to each other. Poetry, Fetter'd. Fetters the Human Race. Nations are Destroy'd or Flourish, in proportion as Their Poetry Painting and Music, are Destroy'd or Flourish! The Primeval State of Man, was Wisdom, Art, and Science.

[Plate 4]

Μονος ὁ Ιεςους*

JERUSALEM CHAP: I

Of the Sleep of Ulro! and of the passage through *
Eternal Death! and of the awaking to Eternal Life

This theme calls me in sleep night after night, & ev'ry morn
Awakes me at sun-rise; then I see the Saviour over me
Spreading his beams of love & dictating the words of this mild song.*   5

Awake! awake O sleeper of the land of shadows, wake! expand!
I am in you and you in me, mutual in love divine:
Fibres of love from man to man thro Albions pleasant land.
In all the dark Atlantic vale down from the hills of Surrey
A black water accumulates, return Albion! return!   10
Thy brethren call thee, and thy fathers, and thy sons,
Thy nurses and thy mothers, thy sisters and thy daughters
Weep at thy souls disease, and the Divine Vision is darkend:

Thy Emanation that was wont to play before thy face,
Beaming forth with her daughters into the Divine bosom   15
Where hast thou hidden thy Emanation lovely Jerusalem
From the vision and fruition of the Holy-one?
I am not a God afar off, I am a brother and friend;
Within your bosoms I reside, and you reside in me:
Lo! we are One; forgiving all Evil; Not seeking recompense!   20
Ye are my members O ye sleepers of Beulah, land of shades!

But the perturbed Man away turns down the valleys dark;

Phantom of the over heated brain! shadow of immortality!
Seeking to keep my soul a victim to thy Love! which binds
Man the enemy of man into deceitful friendships: 25
Jerusalem is not! her daughters are indefinite:
By demonstration, man alone can live, and not by faith.*
My mountains are my own, and I will keep them to myself!
The Malvern and the Cheviot, the Wolds Plinlimmon & Snowdon
Are mine. here will I build my Laws of Moral Virtue!   30
Humanity shall be no more: but war & princedom & victory!

So spoke Albion in jealous fears, hiding his Emanation
Upon the Thames and Medway, rivers of Beulah: dissembling
His jealousy before the throne divine, darkening. cold!

[Plate 5]

The banks of the Thames are clouded! the ancient porches of Albion
                                                            are
Darken'd! they are drawn thro' unbounded space, scatter'd upon
The Void in incoherent despair! Cambridge & Oxford & London
Are driven among the starry Wheels, rent away and dissipated,
In Chasms & Abysses of sorrow, enlarg'd without dimension, terrible   5
Albions mountains run with blood. the cries of war & of tumult
Resound into the unbounded night, every Human perfection
Of mountain & river & city. are small & wither'd & darken'd
Cam is a little stream! Ely is almost swallowd up!
Lincoln & Norwich stand trembling on the brink of Udan-Adan!   10
Wales and Scotland shrink themselves to the west and to the north!
Mourning for fear of the warriors in the Vale of Entuthon-Benython*
Jerusalem is scatterd abroad like a cloud of smoke thro'
                                        non-entity!

Moab & Ammon & Amalek & Canaan & Egypt & Aram
Recieve her little-ones for sacrifices and the delights of cruelty   15

Trembling I sit day and night, my friends are astonish'd at me.
Yet they forgive my wanderings, I rest not from my great task!
To open the Eternal Worlds, to open the immortal Eyes
Of Man inwards into the Worlds of Thought: into Eternity
Ever expanding in the Bosom of God. the Human Imagination   20
O Saviour pour upon me thy Spirit of meekness & love:
Annihilate the Selfhood in me, be thou all my life!
Guide thou my hand which trembles exceedingly upon the rock of
                                                                        ages,
While I write of the building of Golgonooza, & of the terrors of
                                                                Entuthon:
Of Hand & Hyle & Coban, of Kwantok, Peachey, Brereton, Slayd &   25
                                                                Hutton,
Of the terrible sons & daughters of Albion. and their Generations.

Scofield. Kox, Kotope and Bowen, revolve most mightily upon*
The Furnace of Los: before the eastern gate bending their fury.
They war, to destroy the Furnaces, to desolate Golgonooza:
And to devour the Sleeping Humanity of Albion in rage & hunger.   30
They revolve into the Furnaces Southward & are driven forth
                                                                Northward
Divided into Male and Female forms time after time.
From these Twelve all the Families of England spread abroad.

The Male is a Furnace of beryll; the Female is a golden Loom.
I behold them, and their rushing fires overwhelm my Soul   35
In London's darkness, and my tears fall day and night
Upon the Emanations of Albion's Sons, the Daughters of Albion,
Names anciently remember'd, but now contemn'd as fictions
Although in every bosom they controll our Vegetative powers.

These are united into Tirzah and her Sisters, on Mount Gilead.*   40
Cambel & Gwendolen & Conwenna & Cordella & Ignoge.
And these united into Rahab in the Covering Cherub on Euphrates
Gwiniverra & Gwinefred, & Gonorill & Sabrina beautiful,
Estrild, Mehetabel & Ragan, lovely Daughters of Albion
They are the beautiful Emanations of the Twelve Sons of Albion   45

The Starry Wheels revolv'd heavily over the Furnaces;
Drawing Jerusalem in anguish of maternal love,
Eastward a pillar of a cloud with Vala upon the mountains

Howling in pain, redounding from the arms of Beulahs Daughters,
Out from the Furnaces of Los above the head of Los.   50
A pillar of smoke writhing afar into Non-Entity, redounding
Till the cloud reaches afar outstretch'd among the Starry Wheels
Which revolve heavily in the mighty Void above the Furnaces

O what avail the loves & tears of Beulahs lovely Daughters
They hold the Immortal Form in gentle bands & tender tears   55
But all within is open'd into the deeps of Entuthon Benython
A dark and unknown night, indefinite, unmeasurable, without end.
Abstract Philosophy warring in enmity against Imagination
(Which is the Divine Body of the Lord Jesus, blessed for ever).
And there Jerusalem wanders with Vala upon the mountains,   60
Attracted by the revolutions of those Wheels, the Cloud of smoke
Immense. and Jerusalem & Vala weeping in the Cloud
Wander away into the Chaotic Void, lamenting with her Shadow
Among the Daughters of Albion, among the Starry Wheels;
Lamenting for her children, for the sons & daughters of Albion   65

Los heard her lamentations in the deeps afar! his tears fall
Incessant before the Furnaces, and his Emanation divided in pain,
Eastward toward the Starry Wheels. But Westward, a black Horror.

[Plate 6]

His Spectre driv'n by the Starry Wheels of Albions sons, black and*
Opake divided from his back; he labours and he mourns!

For as his Emanation divided, his Spectre also divided
In terror of those starry wheels: and the Spectre stood over Los
Howling in pain: a blackning Shadow, blackning dark & opake   5
Cursing the terrible Los: bitterly cursing him for his friendship
To Albion, suggesting murderous thoughts against Albion.

Los rag'd and stamp'd the earth in his might & terrible wrath!
He stood and stampd the earth! then he threw down his hammer
in rage &
In fury; then he sat down and wept, terrified! Then arose   10
And chaunted his song, labouring with the tongs and hammer:
But still the Spectre divided, and still his pain increas'd!

In pain the Spectre divided: in pain of hunger and thirst:
To devour Los's Human Perfection, but when he saw that Los

[Plate 7]

Was living: panting like a frighted wolf and howling
He stood over the Immortal. in the solitude and darkness:
Upon the darkning Thames, across the whole Island westward.
A horrible Shadow of Death, among the Furnaces: beneath
The pillar of folding smoke; and he sought by other means.   5
To lure Los: by tears, by arguments of science & by terrors:
Terrors in every Nerve, by spasms & extended pains:
While Los answer'd unterrified to the opake blackening Fiend

And thus the Spectre spoke: Wilt thou still go on to destruction?
Till thy life is all taken away by this deceitful Friendship?*   10
He drinks thee up like water! like wine he pours thee
Into his tuns: thy Daughters are trodden in his vintage
He makes thy Sons the trampling of his bulls, they are plow'd
And harrowd for his profit, lo! thy stolen Emanation
Is his garden of pleasure! all the Spectres of his Sons mock thee   15
Look how they scorn thy once admired palaces! now in ruins
Because of Albion! because of deceit and friendship! For Lo!
Hand has peopled Babel & Nineveh! Hyle. Ashur & Aram!
Cobans son is Nimrod: his son Cush is adjoind to Aram,
By the Daughter of Babel, in a woven mantle of pestilence & war.   20
They put forth their spectrous cloudy sails; which drive their
                                                    immense
Constellations over the deadly deeps of indefinite Udan-Adan
Kox is the Father of Shem & Ham & Japheth. he is the Noah
Of the Flood of Udan-Adan. Hutn is the Father of the Seven
From Enoch to Adam; Schofield is Adam who was New-   25
Created in Edom. I saw it indignant, & thou art not moved!*
This has divided thee in sunder: and wilt thou still forgive?
O! thou seest not what I see! what is done in the Furnaces.
Listen, I will tell thee what is done in moments to thee unknown:
Luvah was cast into the Furnaces of affliction and sealed,*   30
And Vala fed in cruel delight, the Furnaces with fire:
Stern Urizen beheld; urgd by necessity to keep
The evil day afar, and if perchance with iron power
He might avert his own despair: in woe & fear he saw
Vala incircle round the Furnaces where Luvah was clos'd: 35
With joy she heard his howlings & forgot he was her Luvah,
With whom she liv'd in bliss in times of innocence & youth!
Vala comes from the Furnace in a cloud, but wretched Luvah

Is howling in the Furnaces, in flames among Albions Spectres,
To prepare the Spectre of Albion to reign over thee O Los.   40
Forming the Spectres of Albion according to his rage:
To prepare the Spectre sons of Adam, who is Scofield: the Ninth
Of Albions sons, & the father of all his brethren in the Shadowy
Generation. Cambel & Gwendolen wove webs of war & of
Religion, to involve all Albions sons, and when they had   45
Involv'd Eight; their webs roll'd outwards into darkness
And Scofield the Ninth remain on the outside of the Eight
And Kox, Kotope, & Bowen, One in him, a Fourfold Wonder
Involv'd the Eight—Such are the Generations of the Giant Albion
To separate a Law of Sin, to punish thee in thy members.   50

Los answer'd: Altho' I know not this! I know far worse than this:
I know that Albion hath divided me. and that thou O my Spectre,
Hast just cause to be irritated: but look stedfastly upon me:
Comfort thyself in my strength the time will arrive,
When all Albions injuries shall cease, and when we shall   55
Embrace him tenfold bright. rising from his tomb in immortality.
They have divided themselves by Wrath. they must be united by
Pity: let us therefore take example & warning O my Spectre,
O that I could abstain from wrath! O that the Lamb
Of God would look upon me and pity me in my fury.   60
In anguish of regeneration! in terrors of self annihilation:
Pity must join together those whom wrath has torn in sunder.
And the Religion of Generation, which was meant for the destruction
Of Jerusalem, become her covering, till the time of the End.
O holy Generation! [*Image*] of regeneration!   65
O point of mutual forgiveness between Enemies!
Birthplace of the Lamb of God incomprehensible!
The Dead despise & scorn thee, & cast thee out as accursed:
Seeing the Lamb of God in thy gardens & thy palaces:
Where they desire to place the Abomination of Desolation.*   70
Hand sits before his furnace: scorn of others & furious pride:
Freeze round him to bars of steel & to iron rocks beneath
His feet: indignant self-righteousness like whirlwinds of the north:

[Plate 8]

Rose up against me thundering from the Brook of Albions River
From Ranelagh & Strumbolo, from Cromwells gardens & Chelsea

The place of wounded Soldiers. but when he saw my Mace*
Whirld round from heaven to earth, trembling he sat; his cold
Poisons rose up: & his sweet deceits coverd them all over   5
With a tender cloud. As thou art now; such was he O Spectre
I know thy deceit & thy revenges, and unless thou desist
I will certainly create an eternal Hell for thee. Listen!
Be attentive! be obedient! Lo the Furnaces are ready to recieve thee.
I will break thee into shivers! & melt thee in the furnaces of death   10
I will cast thee into forms of abhorrence & torment if thou
Desist not from thine own will, & obey not my stern command!
I am closd up from my children! my Emanation is dividing
And thou my Spectre art divided against me. But mark
I will compell thee to assist me in my terrible labours. To beat   15
These hypocritic Selfhoods on the Anvils of bitter Death
I am inspired: I act not for myself: for Albions sake
I now am what I am: a horror and an astonishment
Shuddring the heavens to look upon me: Behold what cruelties
Are practised in Babel & Shinar, & have approachd to   20
                                   Zions Hill*

While Los spoke, the terrible Spectre fell shuddring before him
Watching his time with glowing eyes to leap upon his prey
Los opend the Furnaces in fear. the Spectre saw to Babel & Shinar
Across all Europe & Asia. he saw the tortures of the Victims,
He saw now from the outside what he before saw & felt from within   25
He saw that Los was the sole, uncontrolld Lord of the Furnaces
Groaning he kneeld before Los's iron-shod feet on London Stone,
Hungring & thirsting for Los's life yet pretending obedience.
While Los pursud his speech in threatnings loud & fierce.

Thou art my Pride & Self-righteousness; I have found thee out: 30
Thou art reveald before me in all thy magnitude & power
Thy Uncircumcised pretences to Chastity must be cut in sunder!
Thy holy wrath & deep deceit cannot avail against me
Nor shalt thou ever assume the triple-form of Albions Spectre
For I am one of the living: dare not to mock my inspired fury   35
If thou wast cast forth from my life! if I was dead upon the
                                   mountains

Thou mightest be pitied & lovd: but now I am living; unless
Thou abstain ravening I will create an eternal Hell for thee.
Take thou this Hammer & in patience heave the thundering Bellows

Take thou these Tongs: strike thou alternate with me: 40
                           labour obedient
Hand & Hyle & Koban: Skofeld, Kox & Kotope, labour mightily
In the Wars of Babel & Shinar, all their Emanations were
Condensd. Hand has absorbd all his Brethren in his might
All the infant Loves & Graces were lost, for the mighty Hand

[Plate 9]

Condens'd his Emanations into hard opake substances;
And his infant thoughts & desires, into cold, dark, cliffs of death.
His hammer of gold he siez'd; and his anvil of adamant.
He siez'd the bars of condens'd thoughts, to forge them:
Into the sword of war! into the bow and arrow: 5
Into the thundering cannon and into the murdering gun
I saw the limbs form'd for exercise, contemn'd! & the beauty of
Eternity, look'd upon as deformity, & loveliness as a dry tree:
I saw disease forming a Body of Death around the Lamb
Of God, to destroy Jerusalem. & to devour the body of Albion   10
By war and stratagem to win the labour of the husbandman:

Awkwardness arm'd in steel: folly in a helmet of gold:
Weakness with horns & talons: ignorance with a rav'ning beak!
Every Emanative joy forbidden as a Crime:
And the Emanations buried alive in the earth with pomp   15
                           of religion:
Inspiration deny'd; Genius forbidden by laws of punishment:
I saw terrified; I took the sighs & tears & bitter groans:
I lifted them into my Furnaces; to form the spiritual sword.*
That lays open the hidden heart: I drew forth the pang
Of sorrow red hot: I workd it on my resolute anvil: 20
I heated it in the flames of Hand, & Hyle & Coban
Nine times: Gwendolen & Cambel & Gwineverra

Are melted into the gold, the silver, the liquid ruby,
The crysolite, the topaz, the jacinth, & every precious stone.
Loud roar my Furnaces and loud my hammer is heard: 25
I labour day and night, I behold the soft affections
Condense beneath my hammer into forms of cruelty
But still I labour in hope, tho' still my tears flow down.
That he who will not defend Truth, may be compelld to defend

A Lie: that he may be snared and caught and snared and taken   30
That Enthusiasm and Life may not cease: arise Spectre arise!

Thus they contended among the Furnaces with groans & tears;
Groaning the Spectre heavd the bellows, obeying Los's frowns;
Till the Spaces of Erin were perfected in the furnaces*
Of affliction, and Los drew them forth, compelling the harsh   35
                                                          Spectre.

[Plate 10]

Into the Furnaces & into the valleys of the Anvils of Death
And into the mountains of the Anvils & of the heavy Hammers
Till he should bring the Sons & Daughters of Jerusalem to be
The Sons & Daughters of Los that he might protect them from
Albions dread Spectres; storming, loud, thunderous & mighty   5
The Bellows & the Hammers move compell'd by Los's hand.

And this is the manner of the Sons of Albion in their strength
They take the Two Contraries which are calld Qualities, with which
Every Substance is clothed, they name them Good & Evil
From them they make an Abstract. which is a Negation*   10
Not only of the Substance from which it is derived
A murderer of its own Body: but also a murderer
Of every Divine Member: it is the Reasoning Power
An Abstract objecting power, that Negatives every thing
This is the Spectre of Man; the Holy Reasoning Power   15
And in its Holiness is closed the Abomination of Desolation

Therefore Los stands in London building Golgonooza—
Compelling his Spectre to labours mighty; trembling in fear
The Spectre weeps. but Los unmovd by tears or threats remains

I must Create a System, or be enslav'd by another Mans*   20
I will not Reason & Compare: my business is to Create

So Los, in fury & strength: in indignation & burning wrath
Shuddring the Spectre howls. his howlings terrify the night
He stamps around the Anvil, beating blows of stern despair
He curses Heaven & Earth, Day & Night & Sun & Moon   25
He curses Forest Spring & River, Desart & sandy Waste
Cities & Nations, Families & Peoples, Tongues & Laws
Driven to desperation by Los's terrors & threatning fears

Los cries, Obey my voice & never deviate from my will
And I will be merciful to thee: be thou invisible to all   30
To whom I make thee invisible, but chief to my own Children
O Spectre of Urthona: Reason not against their dear approach*
Nor them obstruct with thy temptations of doubt & despair
O Shame O strong & mighty Shame I break thy brazen fetters
If thou refuse, thy present torments will seem southern breezes   35
To what thou shalt endure if thou obey not my great will

The Spectre answer'd. Art thou not ashamd of those thy Sins
That thou callest thy Children? lo the Law of God commands
That they be offered upon his Altar; O cruelty & torment
For thine are also mine! I have kept silent hitherto.   40
Concerning my chief delight: but thou hast broken silence
Now I will speak my mind! Where is my lovely Enitharmon*
O thou my enemy, where is my Great Sin? She is also thine
I said: now is my grief at worst: incapable of being
Surpassed: but every moment it accumulates more & more   45
It continues accumulating to eternity! the joys of God advance
For he is Righteous: he is not a Being of Pity & Compassion*
He cannot feel Distress: he feeds on Sacrifice & Offering:
Delighting in cries & tears & clothed in holiness & solitude
But my griefs advance also, for ever & ever without end   50
O that I could cease to be! Despair! I am Despair
Created to be the great example of horror & agony: also my
Prayer is vain I called for compassion: compassion mockd
Mercy & pity threw the grave stone over me & with lead
And iron, bound it over me for ever: Life lives on my   55
Consuming: & the Almighty hath made me his Contrary
To be all evil, all reversed & for ever dead: knowing
And seeing life, yet living not; how can I then behold
And not tremble; how can I be beheld & not abhorrd

So spoke the Spectre shuddring, & dark tears ran down his   60
                                                    shadowy face
Which Los wiped off, but comfort none could give! or beam
                                                    of hope.
Yet ceasd he not from labouring at the roarings of his Forge
With iron & brass Building Golgonooza in great contendings
Till his Sons & Daughters came forth from the Furnaces
At the sublime Labours for Los. compelld the invisible Spectre   65

[Plate 11]

To labours mighty, with vast strength, with his mighty chains.
In pulsations of time, & extensions of space, like Urns of Beulah,
With great labour upon his anvils, & in his ladles the Ore
He lifted, pouring it into the clay ground prepar'd with art;
Striving with Systems to deliver Individuals from those Systems:			5
That whenever any Spectre began to devour the Dead,
He might feel the pain as if a man gnawd his own tender nerves,

Then Erin came forth from the Furnaces, & all the Daughters
							of Beulah
Came from the Furnaces, by Los's mighty power for Jerusalems
Sake: walking up and down among the Spaces of Erin:				10
And the Sons and Daughters of Los came forth in perfection lovely!
And the Spaces of Erin reach'd from the starry heighth, to the
							starry depth.

Los wept with exceeding joy & all wept with joy together!
They feard they never more should see their Father, who
Was built in from Eternity, in the Cliffs of Albion.				15

But when the joy of meeting was exhausted in loving embrace;
Again they lament. O what shall we do for lovely Jerusalem?
To protect the Emanations of Albions mighty ones from cruelty?
Sabrina & Ignoge begin to sharpen their beamy spears
Of light and love: their little children stand with arrows of gold:			20
Ragan is wholly cruel Scofield is bound in iron armour!
He is like a mandrake in the earth before Reubens gate:*
He shoots beneath Jerusalems walls to undermine her foundations;
Vala is but thy Shadow, O thou loveliest among women!
A shadow animated by thy tears O mournful Jerusalem!			25

[Plate 12]

Why wilt thou give to her a Body whose life is but a Shade?
Her joy and love, a shade, a shade of sweet repose:
But animated and vegetated, she is a devouring worm:
What shall we do for thee O lovely mild Jerusalem?

And Los said. I behold the finger of God in terrors!				5
Albion is dead! his Emanation is divided from him!
But I am living! yet I feel my Emanation also dividing

Such thing was never known! O pity me, thou all-piteous-one!
What shall I do! or how exist, divided from Enitharmon?
Yet why despair! I saw the finger of God go forth   10
Upon my Furnaces, from within the Wheels of Albions Sons:
Fixing their Systems, permanent: by mathematic power
Giving a body to Falsehood that it may be cast off for ever.
With Demonstrative Science piercing Apollyon with his own bow!
God is within, & without! he is even in the depths of Hell!   15

Such were the lamentations of the Labourers in the Furnaces:

And they appeard within & without incircling on both sides
The Starry Wheels of Albions Sons, with Spaces for Jerusalem:
And for Vala the shadow of Jerusalem: the ever mourning shade:
On both sides, within & without beaming gloriously!   20

Terrified at the sublime Wonder, Los stood before his Furnaces,
And they stood around, terrified with admiration at Erins Spaces
For the Spaces reachd from the starry heighth, to the starry
                                                          depth;
And they builded Golgonooza: terrible eternal labour!

What are those golden builders doing? where was the   25
                                        burying-place
Of soft Ethinthus? near Tyburns fatal Tree? is that
Mild Zions hills most ancient promontory; near mournful
Ever weeping Paddington? is that Calvary and Golgotha?*
Becoming a building of pity and compassion? Lo!
The stones are pity, and the bricks, well wrought affections: 30
Enameld with love & kindness, & the tiles engraven gold
Labour of merciful hands: the beams & rafters are forgiveness:
The mortar & cement of the work, tears of honesty: the nails,
And the screws & iron braces, are well wrought blandishments,
And well contrived words, firm fixing, never forgotten,   35
Always comforting the remembrance: the floors, humility,
The cielings, devotion: the hearths, thanksgiving:
Prepare the furniture O Lambeth in thy pitying looms!*
The curtains, woven tears & sighs, wrought into lovely forms
For comfort, there the secret furniture of Jerusalems chamber   40
Is wrought: Lambeth! the Bride the Lambs Wife loveth thee:
Thou art one with her & knowest not of self in thy supreme joy
Go on, builders in hope: tho Jerusalem wanders far away,
Without the gate of Los: among the dark Satanic wheels.

Fourfold the Sons of Los in their divisions: and fourfold   45
The great City of Golgonooza: fourfold toward the north*
And toward the south fourfold, & fourfold toward the east & west
Each within other toward the four points: that toward
Eden, and that toward the World of Generation,
And that toward Beulah, and that toward Ulro;   50
Ulro is the space of the terrible starry wheels of Albions sons:
But that toward Eden is walled up, till time of renovation:
Yet it is perfect in its building, ornaments & perfection.

And the Four Points are thus beheld in Great Eternity
West, the Circumference: South, the Zenith: North,   55
The Nadir: East, the Center, unapproachable for ever.
These are the four Faces towards the Four Worlds of Humanity
In every Man. Ezekiel saw them by Chebars flood.*
And the Eyes are the South, and the Nostrils are the East.
And the Tongue is the West, and the Ear is the North.   60

And the North Gate of Golgonooza, toward Generation;
Has four sculpturd Bulls terrible, before the Gate of iron.
And iron the Bulls: and that which looks toward Ulro,
Clay bak'd & enamel'd, eternal glowing as four furnaces:
Turning upon the Wheels of Albions sons with enormous   65
                                            power,
And that toward Beulah four, gold, silver, brass, & iron:

[Plate 13]

And that toward Eden. four, form'd of gold, silver, brass, & iron.

The South, a golden Gate, has four Lions terrible, living!
That toward Generation, four, of iron carv'd wondrous:
That toward Ulro, four, clay bak'd, laborious workmanship
That toward Eden, four; immortal gold, silver, brass & iron.   5

The Western Gate fourfold, is closd: having four Cherubim
Its guards, living, the work of elemental hands, laborious task!
Like Men, hermaphroditic, each winged with eight wings
That towards Generation, iron; that toward Beulah, stone:
That toward Ulro, clay: that toward Eden, metals.   10
But all clos'd up till the last day, when the graves shall yield
                                            their dead

The Eastern Gate. Fourfold: terrible & deadly its ornaments:
Taking their forms from the Wheels of Albions sons; as cogs
Are formd in a wheel, to fit the cogs of the adverse wheel.

That toward Eden, eternal ice, frozen in seven folds   15
Of forms of death: and that toward Beulah, stone:
The seven diseases of the earth are carved terrible.
And that toward Ulro, forms of war; seven enormities;
And that toward Generation, seven generative forms.

And every part of the City is fourfold; & every inhabitant, fourfold.   20
And every pot & vessel & garment & utensil of the houses,
And every house, fourfold; but the third Gate in every one
Is closd as with a threefold curtain of ivory & fine linen & ermine.
And Luban stands in middle of the City. a moat of fire,
Surrounds Luban, Los's Palace & the golden Looms of Cathedron,   25

And sixty-four thousand Genii, guard the Eastern Gate:
And sixty-four thousand Gnomes, guard the Northern Gate:
And sixty-four thousand Nymphs, guard the Western Gate:
And sixty-four thousand Fairies, guard the Southern Gate:

Around Golgonooza lies the land of death eternal! a Land   30
Of pain and misery and despair and ever brooding melancholy;
In all the Twenty-seven Heavens, numberd from Adam to Luther;*
From the blue Mundane Shell. reaching to the Vegetative Earth.

The Vegetative Universe. opens like a flower from the Earth's center:
In which is Eternity. It expands in Stars to the Mundane Shell   35
And there it meets Eternity again, both within and without,
And the abstract Voids between the Stars are the Satanic Wheels.

There is the Cave; the Rock; the Tree; the Lake of Udan Adan;
The Forest, and the Marsh, and the Pits of bitumen deadly:
The Rocks of solid fire: the Ice valleys: the Plains   40
Of burning sand: the rivers, cataract & Lakes of Fire:
The Islands of the fiery Lakes: the Trees of Malice; Revenge;
And black Anxiety; and the Cities of the Salamandrine men:*
(But whatever is visible to the Generated Man,
Is a Creation of mercy & love, from the Satanic Void.)   45
The land of darkness flamed but no light & no repose:
The land of snows of trembling, & of iron hail incessant:
The land of earthquakes: and the land of woven labyrinths:
The land of snares & traps & wheels & pit-falls & dire mills:

The Voids, the Solids, & the land of clouds & regions of waters: 50
With their inhabitants: in the Twenty-seven Heavens beneath Beulah:
Self-righteousnesses conglomerating against the Divine Vision:
A Concave Earth wondrous, Chasmal, Abyssal, Incoherent!
Forming the Mundane Shell: above; beneath: on all sides
                                                    surrounding
Golgonooza: Los walks round the walls night and day.   55

He views the City of Golgonooza, & its smaller Cities:
The Looms & Mills & Prisons & Work-houses of Og & Anak:
The Amalekite: the Canaanite: the Moabite; the Egyptian:
And all that has existed in the space of six thousand years:*
Permanent, & not lost not lost nor vanishd, & every little act,   60
Word, work. & wish, that has existed, all remaining still
In those Churches ever consuming & ever building by the Spectres
Of all the inhabitants of Earth wailing to be Created:
Shadowy to those who dwell not in them, meer possibilities:
But to those who enter into them they seem the only substances   65
For every thing exists & not one sigh nor smile nor tear,

[Plate 14]

One hair nor particle of dust, not one can pass away.

He views the Cherub at the Tree of Life. also the Serpent, *
Orc the first born, coild in the south: the Dragon Urizen:
Tharmas the Vegetated Tongue even the Devouring Tongue:*
A threefold region, a false brain: a false heart: 5
And false bowels: altogether composing the False Tongue,
Beneath Beulah: as a watry flame revolving every way
And as dark roots and stems: a Forest of affliction, growing
In seas of sorrow. Los also views the Four Females:
Ahania, and Enion, and Vala. and Enitharmon lovely.   10
And from them all the lovely beaming Daughters of Albion.
Ahania & Enion & Vala, are three evanescent shades:
Enitharmon is a vegetated mortal Wife of Los:
His Emanation, yet his Wife till the sleep of Death is past.

Such are the Buildings of Los! & such are the Woofs of   15
                                                    Enitharmon!

And Los beheld his Sons, and he beheld his Daughters:
Every one a translucent Wonder: a Universe within,

Increasing inwards, into length and breadth, and heighth:
Starry & glorious: and they every one in their bright loins:
Have a beautiful golden gate which opens into the vegetative   20
                                                              world:
And every one a gate of rubies & all sorts of precious stones
In their translucent hearts, which opens into the vegetative world
And every one a gate of iron dreadful and wonderful
In their translucent heads. which opens into the vegetative world;
And every one has the three regions Childhood: Manhood: &   25
                                                              Age.
But the gate of the tongue: the western gate in them is clos'd,
Having a wall builded against it. and thereby the gates
Eastward & Southward & Northward are incircled with flaming
                                                              fires.
And the North is Breadth, the South is Height & Depth:
The East is Inwards,: & the West is Outwards every way.   30

And Los beheld the mild Emanation Jerusalem eastward bending
Her revolutions toward the Starry Wheels in maternal anguish
Like a pale cloud, arising from the arms of Beulahs Daughters:
In Entuthon Benythons deep Vales beneath Golgonooza.

[Plate 15]

And Hand & Hyle rooted into Jerusalem by a fibre
Of strong revenge & Skofeld Vegetated by Reubens Gate
In every Nation of the Earth till the Twelve Sons of Albion
Enrooted into every Nation: a mighty Polypus growing
From Albion over the whole Earth: such is my awful Vision.   5

I see the Four-fold Man. The Humanity in deadly sleep
And its fallen Emanation. The Spectre & its cruel Shadow.
I see the Past, Present & Future, existing all at once
Before me; O Divine Spirit sustain me on thy wings!
That I may awake Albion from his long & cold repose.   10
For Bacon & Newton sheathd in dismal steel. their terrors hang
Like iron scourges over Albion, Reasonings like vast Serpents
Infold around my limbs, bruising my minute articulations

I turn my eyes to the Schools & Universities of Europe
And there behold the Loom of Locke whose Woof rages dire   15
Washd by the Water-wheels of Newton. black the cloth*

In heavy wreathes folds over every Nation; cruel Works
Of many Wheels I view, wheel without wheel, with cogs tyrannic
Moving by compulsion each other: not as those in Eden: which
Wheel within Wheel, in freedom revolve in harmony & peace.   20

I see in deadly fear in London Los raging round his Anvil
Of death: forming an Ax of gold: the Four Sons of Los
Stand round him cutting the Fibres from Albions hills
That Albions Sons may roll apart over the Nations
While Reuben enroots his brethren in the narrow Canaanite*   25
From the Limit Noah to the Limit Abram in whose Loins
Reuben in his Twelve-fold majesty & beauty shall take refuge
As Abraham flees from Chaldea shaking his goary locks
But first Albion must sleep, divided from the Nations

I see Albion sitting upon his Rock in the first Winter   30
And thence I see the Chaos of Satan & the World of Adam
When the Divine Hand went forth on Albion in the mid Winter
And at the place of Death when Albion sat in Eternal Death
Among the Furnaces of Los in the Valley of the Son of Hinnom

[Plate 16]

Hampstead Highgate Finchley Hendon Muswell hill: rage loud
Before Bromions iron Tongs & glowing Poker reddening fierce
Hertfordshire glows with fierce Vegetation! in the Forests
The Oak frowns terrible, the Beech & Ash & Elm enroot
Among the Spiritual fires: loud the Corn-fields thunder along   5
The Soldiers fife; the Harlots shriek; the Virgins dismal groan
The Parents fear: the Brothers jealousy: the Sisters curse
Beneath the Storms of Theotormon & the thund'ring Bellows
Heaves in the hand of Palamabron who in Londons darkness
Before the Anvil. watches the bellowing flames: thundering   10
The Hammer loud rages in Rintrahs strong grasp swinging loud
Round from heaven to earth down falling with heavy blow
Dead on the Anvil, where the red hot wedge groans in pain
He quenches it in the black trough of his Forge; Londons River
Feeds the dread Forge, trembling & shuddering along the Valleys   15

Humber & Trent roll dreadful before the Seventh Furnace
And Tweed & Tyne anxious give up their Souls for Albions sake
Lincolnshire Derbyshire Nottinghamshire Leicestershire

From Oxfordshire to Norfolk on the Lake of Udan Adan
Labour within the Furnaces, walking among the Fires   20
With Ladles huge & iron Pokers over the Island white.

Scotland pours out his Sons to labour at the Furnaces
Wales gives his Daughters to the Looms; England: nursing Mothers
Gives to the Children of Albion & to the Children of Jerusalem
From the blue Mundane Shell even to the Earth of Vegetation   25
Throughout the whole Creation, which groans to be deliverd
Albion groans in the deep slumbers of Death upon his Rock.

Here Los fixd down the Fifty-two Counties of England & Wales
The Thirty-six of Scotland & the Thirty-four of Ireland
With mighty power, when they fled out at Jerusalems Gate   30
Away from the Conflict of Luvah & Urizen, fixing the Gates
In the Twelve Counties of Wales & thence Gates looking every way
To the Four Points: conduct to England & Scotland & Ireland
And thence to all the Kingdoms & Nations & Families of the Earth
The Gate of Reuben in Carmarthenshire: the Gate of Simeon in*   35
Cardiganshire: & the Gate of Levi in Montgomeryshire
The Gate of Judah Merionethshire: the Gate of Dan Flintshire
The Gate of Napthali, Radnorshire: the Gate of Gad Pembrokeshire
The Gate of Asher, Carnarvonshire the Gate of Issachar
                                        Brecknokshire
The Gate of Zebulun, in Anglesea & Sodor. so is Wales divided.   40
The Gate of Joseph, Denbighshire: the Gate of Benjamin
                                        Glamorganshire
For the protection of the Twelve Emanations of Albions Sons

And the Forty Counties of England are thus divided in the Gates
Of Reuben Norfolk, Suffolk. Essex, Simeon Lincoln, York
                                        Lancashire
Levi. Middlesex Kent Surrey. Judah Somerset Glouster Wiltshire,   45
Dan. Cornwal Devon Dorset, Napthali, Warwick Leicester
                                        Worcester
Gad. Oxford Bucks Harford. Asher, Sussex Hampshire Berkshire
Issachar, Northampton Rutland Nottgham. Zebulun Bedford
                                        Huntgn Camb
Joseph Stafford Shrops Heref. Benjamin, Derby Cheshire
                                        Monmouth;
And Cumberland Northumberland Westmoreland & Durham are   50
Divided in the the Gates of Reuben, Judah Dan & Joseph

And the Thirty-six Counties of Scotland. divided in the Gates
Of Reuben Kincard Haddntn Forfar, Simeon Ayr Argyll Banff
Levi Edinburgh Roxbro Ross. Judah, Abrdeen Berwik Dumfries
Dan Bute Caitnes Clakmanan. Napthali Nairn Invernes Linlithgo   55
Gad Peebles Perth Renfru. Asher Sutherlan Sterling Wigtoun
Issachar Selkirk Dumbartn Glasgo. Zebulun Orkney Shetland Skye
Joseph Elgin Lanerk Kinros, Benjamin Kromarty Murra Kirkubriht
Governing all by the sweet delights of secret amorous glances
In Enitharmons Halls builded by Los & his mighty Children   60

All things acted on Earth are seen in the bright Sculptures of
Los's Halls & every Age renews its powers from these Works
With every pathetic story possible to happen from Hate or
Wayward Love & every sorrow & distress is carved here
Every Affinity of Parents Marriages & Friendships are here   65
In all their various combinations wrought with wondrous Art
All that can happen to Man in his pilgrimage of seventy years
Such is the Divine Written Law of Horeb & Sinai:
And such the Holy Gospel of Mount Olivet & Calvary:

[Plate 17]

His Spectre divides & Los in fury compells it to divide:
To labour in the fire, in the water, in the earth, in the air.
To follow the Daughters of Albion as the hound follows the scent
Of the wild inhabitant of the forest. to drive them from his own:
To make a way for the Children of Los to come from the Furnaces   5
But Los himself against Albions Sons his fury bends, for he
Dare not approach the Daughters openly lest he be consumed
In the fires of their beauty & perfection & be Vegetated beneath
Their Looms. in a Generation of death & resurrection to
                                                           forgetfulness
They wooe Los continually to subdue his strength: he continually   10
Shews them his Spectre: sending him abroad over the four points
                                                            of heaven
In the fierce desires of beauty & in the tortures of repulse! He is
The Spectre of the Living pursuing the Emanations of the Dead.
Shuddring they flee: they hide in the Druid Temples in cold chastity:
Subdued by the Spectre of the Living & terrified by undisguis'd   15
                                                             desire.

For Los said: Tho' my Spectre is divided: as I am a Living Man
I must compell him to obey me wholly! that Enitharmon may not
Be lost: & lest he should devour Enitharmon: Ah me!
Piteous image of my soft desires & loves: O Enitharmon!
I will compell my Spectre to obey: I will restore to thee thy   20
                                              Children.
No one bruises or starves himself to make himself fit for labour!

Tormented with sweet desire for these beauties of Albion
They would never love my power if they did not seek to destroy
Enitharmon: Vala would never have sought & loved Albion
If she had not sought to destroy Jerusalem; such is that false   25
And Generating Love: a pretence of love to destroy love:
Cruel hipocrisy, unlike the lovely delusions of Beulah:
And cruel forms, unlike the merciful forms of Beulahs Night

They know not why they love nor wherefore they sicken & die
Calling that Holy Love: which is Envy Revenge & Cruelty   30
Which separated the stars from the mountains; the mountains
                                              from Man
And left Man. a little grovelling Root, outside of Himself.
Negations are not Contraries! Contraries mutually Exist:
But Negations Exist Not: Exceptions & Objections & Unbeliefs
Exist not: nor shall they ever be Organized for ever & ever: 35
If thou separate from me, thou art a Negation: a meer
Reasoning & Derogation from me, an Objecting & cruel Spite
And Malice & Envy: but my Emanation, Alas! will become
My Contrary: O thou Negation, I will continually compell
Thee to be invisible to any but whom I please, & when   40
And where & how I please, and never! never! shalt thou be
                                              Organized
But as a distorted & reversed Reflexion in the Darkness
And in the Non Entity: nor shall that which is above
Ever descend into thee: but thou shalt be a Non Entity for ever
And if any enter into thee, thou shalt be an Unquenchable Fire   45
And he shall be a never dying Worm, mutually tormented by
Those that thou tormentest, a Hell & Despair for ever & ever.

So Los in secret with himself communed, & Enitharmon heard
In her darkness & was comforted: yet still she divided away
In gnawing pain from Los's bosom in the deadly Night;   50
First as a red Globe of blood trembling beneath his bosom

Suspended over her he hung: he infolded her in his garments
Of wool: he hid her from the Spectre, in shame & confusion of
Face; in terrors & pains of Hell & Eternal Death; the
Trembling Globe shot forth Self-living & Los howld over it: 55
Feeding it with his groans & tears day & night without ceasing:
And the Spectrous Darkness from his back divided in temptations,
And in grinding agonies in threats: stiflings: & direful strugglings.

Go thou to Skofield: ask him if he is Bath or if he is Canterbury*
Tell him to be no more dubious: demand explicit words   60
Tell him: I will dash him into shivers, where & at what time
I please: tell Hand & Skofield they are my ministers of evil
To those I hate; for I can hate also as well as they!

[Plate 18]

From every-one of the Four Regions of Human Majesty,
There is an Outside spread Without, & an Outside spread Within
Beyond the Outline of Identity both ways, which meet in One:
An orbed Void of doubt, despair, hunger, & thirst & sorrow.
Here the Twelve Sons of Albion, join'd in dark Assembly,   5
Jealous of Jerusalems children, asham'd of her little-ones
(For Vala produc'd the Bodies. Jerusalem gave the Souls)
Became as Three Immense Wheels, turning upon one-another
Into Non-Entity, and their thunders hoarse appall the Dead
To murder their own Souls, to build a Kingdom among the Dead   10

Cast! Cast ye Jerusalem forth! The Shadow of delusions!
The Harlot daughter! Mother of pity and dishonourable forgiveness
Our Father Albions sin and shame! But father now no more!
With transgressors meeting in brotherhood around the table,   15
Or in the porch or garden. No more the sinful delights
Of age and youth, and boy and girl and animal and herb,
And river and mountain, and city & village, and house & family,
Beneath the Oak & Palm. beneath the Vine and Fig-tree.
In self-denial!—But War and deadly contention, Between   20
Father and Son, and light and love! All bold asperities
Of Haters met in deadly strife, rending the house & garden
The unforgiving porches, the tables of enmity, and beds
And chambers of trembling & suspition, hatreds of age & youth
And boy & girl, & animal & herb, & river & mountain   25

And city & village, and house & family. That the Perfect.
May live in glory, redeem'd by Sacrifice of the Lamb
And of his children, before sinful Jerusalem. To build
Babylon the City of Vala, the Goddess Virgin-Mother.
She is our Mother! Nature! Jerusalem is our Harlot-Sister   30
Return'd with Children of pollution, to defile our House,
With Sin and Shame. Cast! Cast her into the Potters field.*
Her little-ones. She must slay upon our Altars: and her aged
Parents must be carried into captivity, to redeem her Soul
To be for a Shame & a Curse, and to be our Slaves for ever   35

So cry Hand & Hyle the eldest of the fathers of Albions
Little-ones; to destroy the Divine Saviour; the Friend of Sinners,
Building Castles in desolated places, and strong Fortifications.
Soon Hand mightily devour'd & absorb'd Albions Twelve Sons.
Out from his bosom a mighty Polypus, vegetating in darkness,*   40
And Hyle & Coban were his two chosen ones for Emissaries
In War: forth from his bosom they went and return'd.
Like Wheels from a great Wheel reflected in the Deep.
Hoarse turn'd the Starry Wheels. rending a way in Albions Loins
Beyond the Night of Beulah. In a dark & unknown Night.   45
Outstretch'd his Giant beauty on the ground in pain & tears;*

[Plate 19]

His Children exil'd from his breast pass to and fro before him
His birds are silent on his hills, flocks die beneath his branches
His tents are fall'n! his trumpets, and the sweet sound of his harp
Are silent on his clouded hills, that belch forth storms & fire.
His milk of Cows, & honey of Bees. & fruit of golden harvest,   5
Is gather'd in the scorching heat, & in the driving rain:
Where once he sat he weary walks in misery and pain:
His Giant beauty and perfection fallen into dust:
Till, from within his witherd breast grown narrow with his woes:
The corn is turn'd to thistles & the apples into poison: 10
The birds of song to murderous crows, his joys to bitter groans!
The voices of children in his tents, to cries of helpless infants!
And self-exiled from the face of light & shine of morning,
In the dark world a narrow house! he wanders up and down,
Seeking for rest and finding none! and hidden far within,   15
His Eon weeping in the cold and desolated Earth.*

All his Affections now appear withoutside: all his Sons,
Hand, Hyle & Coban. Guantok, Peachey, Brereton, Slayd & Hutton,
Scofeld, Kox, Kotope & Bowen; his Twelve Sons: Satanic Mill!
Who are the Spectres of the Twenty-four, each Double-form'd: 20
Revolve upon his mountains groaning in pain: beneath
The dark incessant sky, seeking for rest and finding none:
Raging against their Human natures, ravning to gormandize
The Human majesty and beauty of the Twentyfour.
Condensing them into solid rocks with cruelty and abhorrence   25
Suspition & revenge, & the seven diseases of the Soul
Settled around Albion and around Luvah in his secret cloud
Willing the Friends endur'd for Albions sake, and for
Jerusalem his Emanation shut within his bosom;
Which hardend against them more and more; as he builded onwards   30
On the Gulph of Death in self-righteousness, that roll'd
Before his awful feet, in pride of virtue for victory;
And Los was roofd in from Eternity in Albions Cliffs
Which stand upon the ends of Beulah, and withoutside, all
Appear'd a rocky form against the Divine Humanity   35

Albions Circumference was clos'd: his Center began darkning
Into the Night of Beulah, and the Moon of Beulah rose
Clouded with storms: Los his strong Guard, walkd round
                                         beneath the Moon
And Albion fled inward among the currents of his rivers.

He found Jerusalem upon the River of his City soft repos'd   40
In the arms of Vala, assimilating in one with Vala
The Lilly of Havilah: and they sang soft thro' Lambeths vales,*
In a sweet moony night & silence that they had created
With a blue sky spread over with wings and a mild moon,
Dividing & uniting into many female forms: Jerusalem   45
Trembling! then in one comingling in eternal tears,
Sighing to melt his Giant beauty, on the moony river.

[Plate 20]

But when they saw Albion fall'n upon mild Lambeths vale:
Astonish'd! Terrified! they hover'd over his Giant limbs.
Then thus Jerusalem spoke, while Vala wove the veil of tears:
Weeping in pleadings of Love, in the web of despair.

Wherefore hast thou shut me into the winter of human life   5
And clos'd up the sweet regions of youth and virgin innocence:
Where we live, forgetting error, not pondering on evil:
Among my lambs & brooks of water, among my warbling birds:
Where we delight in innocence before the face of the Lamb:
Going in and out before him in his love and sweet affection.   10

Vala replied weeping & trembling, hiding in her veil*

When winter rends the hungry family and the snow falls:
Upon the ways of men hiding the paths of man and beast,
Then mourns the wanderer: then he repents his wanderings & eyes
The distant forest: then the slave groans in the dungeon of stone.   15
The captive in the mill of the stranger, sold for scanty hire.
They view their former life: they number moments over and over;
Stringing them on their remembrance as on a thread of sorrow.
Thou art my sister and my daughter! thy shame is mine also!
Ask me not of my griefs! thou knowest all my griefs.   20

Jerusalem answer'd with soft tears over the valleys.

O Vala, what is Sin? that thou shudderest and weepest
At sight of thy once lov'd Jerusalem! What is Sin but a little
Error & fault that is soon forgiven; but mercy is not a Sin
Nor pity nor love nor kind forgiveness! O! if I have Sinned   25
Forgive & pity me; O! unfold thy Veil in mercy & love!

Slay not my little ones, beloved Virgin daughter of Babylon
Slay not my infant loves & graces, beautiful daughter of Moab
I cannot put off the human form I strive but strive in vain
When Albion rent thy beautiful net of gold and silver twine;   30
Thou hadst woven it with art, thou hadst caught me in the bands
Of love; thou refusedst to let me go: Albion beheld thy beauty
Beautiful thro' our Love's comeliness, beautiful thro' pity.
The Veil shone with thy brightness in the eyes of Albion,
Because it inclosd pity & love; because we lov'd one-another!   35
Albion lov'd thee! he rent thy Veil! he embrac'd thee! he lov'd thee!
Astonish'd at his beauty & perfection, thou forgavest his furious love
I redounded from Albions bosom in my virgin loveliness.
The Lamb of God reciev'd me in his arms he smil'd upon us:
He made me his Bride & Wife: he gave thee to Albion.   40
Then was a time of love: O why is it passed away!

Then Albion broke silence and with groans reply'd

[Plate 21]

O Vala! O Jerusalem! do you delight in my groans
You O lovely forms, you have prepared my death-cup:
The disease of Shame covers me from head to feet: I have no hope
Every boil upon my body is a separate & deadly Sin,
Doubt first assaild me, then Shame took possession of me   5
Shame divides Families. Shame hath divided Albion in sunder!
First fled my Sons, & then my Daughters, then my Wild Animations
My Cattle next, last ev'n the Dog of my Gate, the Forests fled
The Corn:fields, & the breathing Gardens outside separated
The Sea; the Stars: the Sun: the Moon: drivn forth by my disease   10
All is Eternal Death unless you can weave a chaste
Body over an unchaste Mind! Vala! O that thou wert pure!
That the deep wound of Sin might be clos'd up with the Needle.
And with the Loom: to cover Gwendolen & Ragan with costly Robes
Of Natural Virtue, for their Spiritual forms without a Veil   15
Wither in Luvahs Sepulcher. I thrust him from my presence
And all my Children followd his loud howlings into the Deep.
Jerusalem! dissembler Jerusalem! I look into thy bosom:
I discover thy secret places: Cordella! I behold
Thee whom I thought pure as the heavens in innocence & fear: 20
Thy Tabernacle taken down, thy secret Cherubim disclosed
Art thou broken? Ah me Sabrina, running by my side:
In childhood what wert thou? unutterable anguish! Conwenna
Thy cradled infancy is most piteous, O hide, O hide!
Their secret gardens were made paths to the traveler: 25
I knew not of their secret loves with those I hated most,
Nor that their every thought was Sin & secret appetite
Hyle sees in fear, he howls in fury over them, Hand sees
In jealous fear: in stern accusation with cruel stripes
He drives them thro' the Streets of Babylon before my face: 30
Because they taught Luvah to rise into my clouded heavens
Battersea and Chelsea mourn for Cambel & Gwendolen!
Hackney and Holloway sicken for Estrild & Ignoge!
Because the Peak, Malvern & Cheviot Reason in Cruelty
Penmaenmawr & Dhinas-bran Demonstrate in Unbelief   35
Manchester & Liverpool are in tortures of Doubt & Despair
Malden & Colchester Demonstrate: I hear my Childrens voices
I see their piteous faces gleam out upon the cruel winds
From Lincoln & Norwich, from Edinburgh & Monmouth

I see them distant from my bosom scourgd along the roads   40
Then lost in clouds; I hear their tender voices! clouds divide
I see them die beneath the whips of the Captains! they are taken
In solemn pomp into Chaldea across the bredths of Europe
Six months they lie embalmd in silent death: warshipped
Carried in Arks of Oak before the armies in the spring*   45
Bursting their Arks they rise again to life: they play before
The Armies: I hear their loud cymbals & their deadly cries
Are the Dead cruel? are those who are infolded in moral Law
Revengeful? O that Death & Annihilation were the same!

Then Vala answerd spreading her scarlet Veil over Albion   50

[Plate 22]

Albion thy fear has made me tremble; thy terrors have surrounded me
Thy Sons have naild me on the Gates piercing my hands & feet:
Till Skofields Nimrod the mighty Huntsman Jehovah came
With Cush his Son & took me down. He in a golden Ark,
Bears me before his Armies tho my shadow hovers here   5
The flesh of multitudes fed & nourisd me in my childhood
My morn & evening food were prepard in Battles of Men
Great is the cry of the Hounds of Nimrod along the Valley
Of Vision, they scent the odor of War in the Valley of Vision.
All Love is lost! terror succeeds & Hatred instead of Love   10
And stern demands of Right & Duty instead of Liberty
Once thou wast to me the loveliest Son of heaven; but now
Where shall I hide from thy dread countenance & searching eyes
I have looked into the secret Soul of him I loved
And in the dark recesses found Sin & can never return,   15

Albion again utterd his voice beneath the silent Moon

I brought Love into light of day to pride in chaste beauty
I brought Love into light & fancied Innocence is no more

Then spoke Jerusalem O Albion! my Father Albion
Why wilt thou number every little fibre of my Soul   20
Spreading them out before the Sun like stalks of flax to dry?
The Infant Joy is beautiful, but its anatomy
Horrible ghast & deadly! nought shalt thou find in it
But dark despair & everlasting brooding melancholy!

Then Albion turnd his face toward Jerusalem & spoke   25

Hide thou Jerusalem in impalpable voidness, not to be
Touchd by the hand nor seen with the eye: O Jerusalem,
Would thou wert not & that thy place might never be found
But come O Vala with knife & cup! drain my blood
To the last drop! then hide me in thy Scarlet Tabernacle   30
For I see Luvah whom I slew. I behold him in my Spectre
As I behold Jerusalem in thee O Vala dark and cold

Jerusalem then stretchd her hand toward the Moon & spoke

Why should Punishment Weave the Veil with Iron Wheels of War
When Forgiveness might it Weave with Wings of Cherubim   35

Loud groand Albion from mountain to mountain & replied

[Plate 23]

Jerusalem! Jerusalem! deluding shadow of Albion!
Daughter of my phantasy! unlawful pleasure! Albions curse!
I came here with intention to annihilate thee! But
My soul is melted away. inwoven within the Veil
Hast thou again knitted the Veil of Vala, which I for thee   5
Pitying rent in ancient times. I see it whole and more
Perfect and shining with beauty! But thou! O wretched Father!

Jerusalem reply'd, like a voice heard from a sepulcher:
Father! once piteous! Is Pity. a Sin? Embalm'd in Vala's bosom
In an Eternal Death for. Albions sake, our best beloved.   10
Thou art my Father & my Brother: Why hast thou hidden me,
Remote from the divine Vision: my Lord and Saviour.

Trembling stood Albion at her words in jealous dark despair

He felt that Love and Pity are the same; a soft repose!
Inward complacency of Soul: a Self-annihilation!   15

I have erred! I am ashamed! and will never return more:
I have taught my children sacrifices of cruelty: what shall
                                          I answer?
I will hide it from Eternals! I will give myself for my Children!
Which way soever I turn, I behold Humanity and Pity!

He recoil'd: he rush'd outwards; he bore the Veil whole away   20
His fires redound from his Dragon Altars in Errors returning

He drew the Veil of Moral Virtue. woven for Cruel Laws,
And cast it into the Atlantic Deep, to catch the Souls of the Dead.
He stood between the Palm tree & the Oak of weeping
Which stand upon the edge of Beulah; and there Albion sunk   25
Down in sick pallid languor! These were his last words, relapsing!
Hoarse from his rocks, from caverns of Derbyshire & Wales
And Scotland, utter'd from the Circumference into Eternity.

Blasphemous Sons of Feminine delusion! God in the dreary Void
Dwells from Eternity, wide separated from the Human Soul   30
But thou deluding Image, by whom imbu'd the Veil I rent
Lo, here is Valas Veil whole. for a Law. a Terror & a Curse!
And therefore God takes vengeance on me: from my clay-cold bosom
My children wander trembling victims of his Moral Justice.
His snows fall on me and cover me, while in the Veil I fold   35
My dying limbs. Therefore O Manhood, if thou art aught
But a meer Phantasy, hear dying Albions Curse!
May God who dwells in this dark Ulro & voidness, vengeance take,
And draw thee down into this Abyss of sorrow and torture,
Like me thy Victim. O that Death & Annihilation were the same!   40

[Plate 24]

What have I said? What have I done? O all-powerful Human Words!
You recoil back upon me in the blood of the Lamb slain in his
                                                        Children
Two bleeding Contraries equally true are his Witnesses against me
We reared mighty Stones: we danced naked around them:
Thinking to bring Love into light of day, to Jerusalems shame: 5
Displaying our Giant limbs to all the winds of heaven! Sudden
Shame siezd us, we could not look on one-another for abhorrence.
                                                        the Blue
Of our immortal Veins & all their Hosts fled from our Limbs,
And wanderd distant in a dismal Night clouded & dark:
The Sun fled from the Britons forehead: the Moon from   10
                                              his mighty loins:
Scandinavia fled with all his mountains filld with groans.

O what is Life & what is Man. O what is Death? Wherefore
Are you my Children, natives in the Grave to where I go
Or are you born to feed the hungry ravenings of Destruction

To be the sport of Accident! to waste in Wrath & Love, a weary   15
Life, in brooding cares & anxious labours, that prove but chaff.
O Jerusalem. Jerusalem I have forsaken thy Courts
Thy Pillars of ivory & gold: thy Curtains of silk & fine
Linen: thy Pavements of precious stones: thy Walls of pearl
And gold, thy Gates of Thanksgiving thy Windows of Praise: 20
Thy Clouds of Blessing; thy Cherubims of Tender-mercy
Stretching their Wings sublime over the Little-ones of Albion
O Human Imagination O Divine Body I have Crucified
I have turned my back upon thee into the Wastes of Moral Law:
There Babylon is builded in the Waste, founded in Human   25
                                         desolation.
O Babylon thy Watchman stands over thee in the night
Thy severe Judge all the day long proves thee O Babylon
With provings of destruction, with giving thee thy hearts desire.
But Albion is cast forth to the Potter his Children to the Builders
To build Babylon because they have forsaken Jerusalem   30
The Walls of Babylon are Souls of Men: her Gates the Groans
Of Nations: her Towers are the Miseries of once happy Families.
Her Streets are paved with Destruction, her Houses built with
                                         Death
Her Palaces with Hell & the Grave; her Synagogues with Torments
Of ever-hardening Despair squard & polishd with cruel skill   35
Yet thou wast lovely as the summer cloud upon my hills
When Jerusalem was thy hearts desire in times of youth & love.
Thy Sons came to Jerusalem with gifts. she sent them away
With blessings on their hands & on their feet, blessings of gold,
And pearl & diamond: thy Daughters sang in her Courts: 40
They came up to Jerusalem; they walked before Albion
In the Exchanges of London every Nation walkd
And London walkd in every Nation mutual in love & harmony
Albion coverd the whole Earth, England encompassd the Nations,
Mutual each within others bosom in Visions of Regeneration;   45
Jerusalem coverd the Atlantic Mountains & the Erythrean,
From bright Japan & China to Hesperia France & England.*
Mount Zion lifted his head in every Nation under heaven:
And the Mount of Olives was beheld over the whole Earth:
The footsteps of the Lamb of God were there: but now no more   50
No more shall I behold him, he is closd in Luvahs Sepulcher.
Yet why these smitings of Luvah, the gentlest mildest Zoa?
If God was Merciful this could not be: O Lamb of God

Thou art a delusion and Jerusalem is my Sin! O my Children
I have educated you in the crucifying cruelties of Demonstration   55
Till you have assum'd the Providence of God & slain your Father
Dost thou appear before me, who liest dead in Luvahs Sepulcher
Dost thou forgive me! thou who wast Dead & art Alive?
Look not so merciful upon me O thou Slain Lamb of God
I die! I die in thy arms tho Hope is banishd from me,   60

Thundring the Veil rushes from his hand Vegetating Knot by
Knot, Day by Day, Night by Night; loud roll the indignant Atlantic
Waves & the Erythrean, turning up the bottoms of the Deeps

[Plate 25]

And there was heard a great lamenting in Beulah: all the Regions
Of Beulah were moved as the tender bowels are moved: & they said:

Why did you take Vengeance O ye Sons of the mighty Albion?
Planting these Oaken Groves: Erecting these Dragon Temples
Injury the Lord heals but Vengeance cannot be healed: 5
As the Sons of Albion have done to Luvah: so they have in him
Done to the Divine Lord & Saviour. who suffers with those that
                                                                                    suffer:
For not one sparrow can suffer, & the whole Universe not suffer also,
In all its Regions, & its Father & Saviour not pity and weep.
But Vengeance is the destroyer of Grace & Repentance in the bosom   10
Of the Injurer: in which the Divine Lamb is cruelly slain;
Descend O Lamb of God & take away the imputation of Sin
By the Creation of States & the deliverance of Individuals Evermore
                                                                                    Amen

Thus wept they in Beulah over the Four Regions of Albion
But many doubted & despaird & imputed Sin & Righteousness   15
To Individuals & not to States, and these Slept in Ulro.

[Plate 26]

[*An image of* 'HAND' *in flames before* 'JERUSALEM' *with the words:*]
SUCH VISIONS HAVE/APPEARD TO ME/AS I MY ORDERD
RACE HAVE RUN/JERUSALEM/IS NAMED/LIBERTY/
AMONG THE SONS/ OF ALBION

[Plate 27]

TO THE JEWS.

Jerusalem the Emanation of the Giant Albion! Can it be? Is it a Truth that the Learned have explored? Was Britain the Primitive Seat of the Patriarchal Religion? if it is true: my title-page is also True, that Jerusalem was & is the Emanation of the Giant Albion. It is True. and cannot be controverted. Ye are united, O ye Inhabitants of Earth, in One Religion. The Religion of Jesus: the most Ancient, the Eternal: & the Everlasting Gospel—The Wicked will turn it to Wickedness, the Righteous to Righteousness. Amen! Huzza! Selah!

'All things Begin & End in Albions Ancient Druid Rocky Shore.'

Your Ancestors derived their origin from Abraham, Heber, Shem and Noah. who were Druids: as the Druid Temples (which are the Patriarchal Pillars & Oak Groves) over the whole Earth witness to this day.

You have a tradition, that Man anciently contain'd in his mighty limbs all things in Heaven & Earth: this you recieved from the Druids.

'But now the Starry Heavens are fled from the mighty limbs of Albion'

Albion was the Parent of the Druids; & in his Chaotic State of Sleep Satan & Adam & the whole World was Created by the Elohim.*

The fields from Islington to Marybone,
To Primrose Hill and Saint Johns Wood:
     Were builded over with pillars of gold,
And there Jerusalems pillars stood.

Her Little-ones ran on the fields   5
The Lamb of God among them seen
     And fair Jerusalem his Bride:
Among the little meadows green.

Pancrass & Kentish-town repose
Among her golden pillars high: 10
     Among her golden arches which
Shine upon the starry sky.

The Jew's-harp-house & the Green Man;*
The Ponds where Boys to bathe delight:
     The fields of Cows by Willans farm: 15
Shine in Jerusalems pleasant sight.

She walks upon our meadows green:
The Lamb of God walks by her side:

And every English Child is seen,
Children of Jesus & his Bride.   20

Forgiving trespasses and sins
Lest Babylon with cruel Og,*
With Moral & Self-righteous Law
Should Crucify in Satans Synagogue!*

What are those golden Builders doing   25
Near mournful ever-weeping Paddington*
Standing above that mighty Ruin
Where Satan the first victory won.

Where Albion slept beneath the Fatal Tree,
And the Druids golden Knife,   30
Rioted in human gore,
In Offerings of Human Life

They groan'd aloud on London Stone,*
They groan'd aloud on Tyburns Brook
Albion gave his deadly groan,   35
And all the Atlantic Mountains shook

Albions Spectre from his Loins
Tore forth in all the pomp of War!
Satan his name: in flames of fire
He stretch'd his Druid Pillars far.   40

Jerusalem fell from Lambeth's Vale,
Down thro Poplar & Old Bow;
Thro Malden & acros the Sea,
In War & howling death & woe,

The Rhine was red with human blood: 45
The Danube rolld a purple tide:*
On the Euphrates Satan stood:
And over Asia stretch'd his pride.

He witherd up sweet Zions Hill,
From every Nation of the Earth;   50
He witherd up Jerusalems Gates,
And in a dark Land gave her birth.

He witherd up the Human Form,
By laws of sacrifice for sin:

Till it became a Mortal Worm: 55
But O! translucent all within.

The Divine Vision still was seen
Still was the Human Form, Divine
    Weeping in weak & mortal clay
O Jesus still the Form was thine.   60

    And thine the Human Face & thine
The Human Hands & Feet & Breath
    Entering thro' the Gates of Birth
And passing thro' the Gates of Death

    And O thou Lamb of God, whom I   65
Slew in my dark self-righteous pride:*
    Art thou returnd to Albions Land!
And is Jerusalem thy Bride?

    Come to my arms & never more
Depart; but dwell for ever here: 70
    Create my Spirit to thy Love:
Subdue my Spectre to thy Fear.

    Spectre of Albion! warlike Fiend!
In clouds of blood & ruin roll'd:
    I here reclaim thee as my own   75
My Self-hood! Satan! armd in gold.

    Is this thy soft Family-Love
Thy cruel Patriarchal pride
    Planting thy Family alone
Destroying all the World beside,   80

    A man's worst enemies are those
Of his own house & family;
    And he who makes his law a curse,
By his own law shall surely die.

    In my Exchanges every Land   85
Shall walk, & mine in every Land,
    Mutual shall build Jerusalem:
Both heart in heart & hand in hand

If Humility is Christianity; you O Jews are the true Christians; If your
tradition that Man contained in his Limbs, all Animals, is True & they

were separated from him by cruel Sacrifices; and when compulsory
cruel Sacrifices had brought Humanity into a Feminine Tabernacle. in
the loins of Abraham & David: the Lamb of God, the Saviour became
apparent on Earth as the Prophets had foretold? The Return of Israel
is a Return to Mental Sacrifice & War. Take up the Cross O Israel &
follow Jesus.

[Plate 28]

JERUSALEM.
CHAP: 2.

Every ornament of perfection, and every labour of love,
In all the Garden of Eden, & in all the golden mountains
Was become an envied horror, and a remembrance of jealousy:
And every Act a Crime, and Albion the punisher & judge.

And Albion spoke from his secret seat and said   5

All these ornaments are crimes, they are made by the labours
Of loves: of unnatural consanguinities and friendships
Horrid to think of when enquired deeply into; and all
These hills & valleys are accursed witnesses of Sin
I therefore condense them into solid rocks. stedfast!   10
A foundation and certainty and demonstrative truth:
That Man be separate from Man, & here I plant my seat.
Cold snows drifted around him: ice cover'd his loins around
He sat by Tyburns brook, and underneath his heel, shot up:
A deadly Tree, he nam'd it Moral Virtue, and the Law*   15
Of God who dwells in Chaos hidden from the human sight.

The Tree spread over him its cold shadows, (Albion groand)
They bent down. they felt the earth, and again enrooting
Shot into many a Tree! an endless labyrinth of woe!

From willing sacrifice of Self. to sacrifice of (miscall'd) Enemies   20
For Atonement: Albion began to erect twelve Altars,
Of rough unhewn rocks. before the Potters Furnace
He nam'd them Justice. and Truth. And Albions Sons
Must have become the first Victims, being the first transgressors
But they fled to the mountains to seek ransom: building A Strong   25
Fortification against the Divine Humanity and Mercy,
In Shame & Jealousy to annihilate Jerusalem!

[Plate 29 (33)]

Turning his back to the Divine Vision. his Spectrous
Chaos before his face appeard: an Unformed Memory.

Then spoke the Spectrous Chaos to Albion darkning cold
From the back & loins where dwell the Spectrous Dead

I am your Rational Power O Albion & that Human Form   5
You call Divine, is but a Worm seventy inches long
That creeps forth in a night & is dried in the morning sun
In fortuitous concourse of memorys accumulated & lost
It plows the Earth in its own conceit, it overwhelms the Hills
Beneath its winding labyrinths, till a stone of the brook   10
Stops it in midst of its pride among its hills & rivers
Battersea & Chelsea mourn. London & Canterbury tremble
Their place shall not be found as the wind passes over
The ancient Cities of the Earth remove as a traveller
And shall Albions Cities remain when I pass over them   15
With my deluge of forgotten remembrances over the tablet

So spoke the Spectre to Albion. he is the Great Selfhood
Satan: Worshipd as God by the Mighty Ones of the Earth
Having a white Dot calld a Center from which branches out
A Circle in continual gyrations. this became a Heart   20
From which sprang numerous branches varying their motions
Producing many Heads three or seven or ten. & hands & feet
Innumerable at will of the unfortunate contemplator
Who becomes his food such is the way of the Devouring Power

And this is the cause of the appearance in the frowning Chaos 25
Albions Emanation which he had hidden in Jealousy
Appeard now in the frowning Chaos prolific upon the Chaos
Reflecting back to Albion in Sexual Reasoning Hermaphroditic*

Albion spoke. Who art thou that appearest in gloomy pomp
Involving the Divine Vision in colours of autumn ripeness   30
I never saw thee till this time. nor beheld life abstracted
Nor darkness immingled with light on my furrowd field
Whence camest thou: who art thou O loveliest? the Divine
                                                          Vision
Is as nothing before thee. faded is all life and joy

Vala replied in clouds of tears Albions garment embracing   35

I was a City & a Temple built by Albions Children.
I was a Garden planted with beauty I allured on hill & valley
The River of Life to flow against my walls & among my trees
Vala was Albions Bride & Wife in great Eternity
The loveliest of the daughters of Eternity when in day-break   40
I emanated from Luvah over the Towers of Jerusalem
And in her Courts among her little Children offering up
The Sacrifice of fanatic love! why loved I Jerusalem:
Why was I one with her, embracing in the Vision of Jesus
Wherefore did I loving create love, which never yet   45
Immingled God & Man, when thou & I, hid the Divine Vision
In cloud of secret gloom which behold, involve me round about
Know me now Albion: look upon me I alone am Beauty
The Imaginative Human Form is but a breathing of Vala
I breathe him forth into the Heaven from my secret Cave   50
Born of the Woman to obey the Woman O Albion the mighty
For the Divine appearance is Brotherhood, but I am Love

[Plate 30 (34)]

Elevate into the Region of Brotherhood with my red fires

Art thou Vala? replied Albion. image of my repose
O how I tremble! how my members pour down milky fear!
A dewy garment covers me all over, all manhood is gone:
At thy word & at thy look death enrobes me about   5
From head to feet, a garment of death & eternal fear
Is not that Sun thy husband & that Moon thy glimmering Veil?
Are not the Stars of heaven thy Children! art thou not Babylon?
Art thou Nature Mother of all! is Jerusalem thy Daughter
Why have thou elevate inward: O dweller of outward chambers   10
From grot & cave beneath the Moon dim region of death
Where I laid my Plow in the hot noon. where my hot team fed
Where implements of War are forged, the Plow to go over the
                                                          Nations
In pain girding me round like a rib of iron in heaven! O Vala
In Eternity they neither marry nor are given in marriage   15
Albion the high Cliff of the Atlantic is become a barren Land

Los stood at his Anvil: he heard the contentions of Vala—
He heavd his thundring Bellows upon the valleys of Middlesex
He opend his Furnaces before Vala. then Albion frownd in anger

On his Rock: ere yet the Starry Heavens were fled away   20
From his awful Members. and thus Los cried aloud
To the Sons of Albion & to Hand the eldest Son of Albion

I hear the screech of Childbirth loud pealing. & the groans
Of Death. in Albions clouds dreadful utterd over all the Earth
What may Man be? who can tell! but what may Woman be?   25
To have power over Man from Cradle to corruptible Grave.
There is a Throne in every Man, it is the Throne of God
This Woman has claimd as her own & Man is no more!
Albion is the Tabernacle of Vala & her Temple
And not the Tabernacle & Temple of the Most High   30
O Albion, why wilt thou Create a Female Will?*
To hide the most evident God in a hidden covert, even
In the shadows of a Woman & a secluded Holy Place
That we may pry after him as after a stolen treasure
Hidden among the Dead & mured up from the paths of life   35
Hand! art thou not Reuben enrooting thyself into Bashan
Till thou remainest a vaporous Shadow in a Void! O Merlin!
Unknown among the Dead where never before Existence came
Is this the Female Will O ye lovely Daughters of Albion. To
Converse concerning Weight & Distance in the Wilds of Newton & 40
                                                        Locke

So Los spoke, standing on Mam-Tor looking over Europe & Asia*
The Graves thunder beneath his feet from Ireland to Japan

Reuben slept in Bashan like one dead in the valley
Cut off from Albions mountains & from all the Earths summits
Between Succoth & Zaretan beside the Stone of Bohan   45
While the Daughters of Albion divided Luvah into three Bodies
Los bended his Nostrils down to the Earth, then sent him over
Jordan to the Land of the Hittite: every-one that saw him
Fled! they fled at his horrible Form: they hid in caves
And dens, they looked on one-another & became what they beheld 50

Reuben return'd to Bashan, in despair he slept on the Stone.
Then Gwendolen divided into Rahab & Tirza in Twelve Portions
Los rolled his Eyes into two narrow circles, then sent him
Over Jordan; all terrified fled; they became what they beheld

If Perceptive Organs vary: Objects of Perception seem to vary: 55
If the Perceptive Organs close: their Objects seem to close also:

Consider this O mortal Man,: O worm of sixty winters said Los
Consider Sexual Organization & hide thee in the dust.

[Plate 31 (35)]

Then the Divine hand found the Two Limits, Satan and Adam,
In Albions bosom: for in every Human bosom those Limits stand.
And the Divine voice came from the Furnaces, as multitudes without
Number! the voices of the innumerable multitudes of Eternity.
And the appearance of a Man was seen in the Furnaces: 5
Saving those who have sinned from the punishment of the Law,
(In pity of the punisher whose state is eternal death,)
And keeping them from Sin by the mild counsels of his love.

Albion goes to Eternal Death: In Me all Eternity.
Must pass thro' condemnation, and awake beyond the Grave: 10
No individual can keep these Laws, for they are death
To every energy of man, and forbid the springs of life;
Albion hath enterd the State Satan! Be permanent O State!
And be thou for ever accursed! that Albion may arise again:
And be thou created into a State! I go forth to Create   15
States: to deliver Individuals evermore! Amen.

So spoke the voice from the Furnaces, descending into Non-Entity

[Plate 32 (36)]

Reuben return'd to his place, in vain he sought beautiful Tirzah
For his Eyelids were narrowd. & his Nostrils scented the ground
And Sixty Winters Los raged in the Divisions of Reuben:
Building the Moon of Ulro. plank by plank & rib by rib
Reuben slept in the Cave of Adam, and Los folded his Tongue   5
Between Lips of mire & clay, then sent him forth over Jordan
In the love of Tirzah he said Doubt is my food day & night—
All that beheld him fled howling and gnawed their tongues
For pain: they became what they beheld In reasonings Reuben
                                                            returned
To Heshbon. disconsolate he walkd thro Moab & he stood   10
Before the Furnaces of Los in a horrible dreamful slumber,
On Mount Gilead looking toward Gilgal: and Los bended
His Ear in a spiral circle outward; then sent him over Jordan.

The Seven Nations fled before him they became what they beheld
Hand, Hyle & Coban fled: they became what they beheld   15
Gwantock & Peachy hid in Damascus beneath Mount Lebanon
Brereton & Slade in Egypt. Hutton & Skofeld & Kox
Fled over Chaldea in terror in pains in every nerve
Kotope & Bowen became what they beheld, fleeing over the Earth
And the Twelve Female Emanations fled with them, agonizing.   20

Jerusalem trembled seeing her Children drivn by Loss Hammer
In the visions of the dreams of Beulah on the edge of Non-Entity
Hand stood between Reuben & Merlin. as the Reasoning Spectre
Stands between the Vegetative Man & his Immortal Imagination

And the Four Zoa's clouded rage East & West & North & South   25
They change their situations, in the Universal Man.
Albion groans, he sees the Elements divide before his face.
And England who is Brittannia divided into Jerusalem & Vala*
And Urizen assumes the East, Luvah assumes the South
In his dark Spectre ravening from his open Sepulcher   30

And the Four Zoa's who are the Four Eternal Senses of Man*
Became Four Elements separating from the Limbs of Albion
These are their names in the Vegetative Generation

And Accident & Chance were found hidden in Length Bredth &
                                                    Highth
And they divided into Four ravening deathlike Forms   35
Fairies & Genii & Nymphs & Gnomes of the Elements.
These are States Permanently Fixed by the Divine Power
The Atlantic Continent sunk round Albions cliffy shore
And the Sea poured in amain upon the Giants of Albion
As Los bended the Senses of Reuben Reuben is Merlin   40
Exploring the Three States of Ulro: Creation; Redemption.
                                                    & Judgment
And many of the Eternal Ones laughed after their manner

Have you known the Judgment that is arisen among the
Zoa's of Albion? where a Man dare hardly to embrace
His own Wife; for the terrors of Chastity that they call   45
By the name of Morality, their Daughters govern all
In hidden deceit! they are Vegetable, only fit for burning,
Art & Science cannot exist but by Naked Beauty displayd

Then those in Great Eternity who contemplate on Death
Said thus. What seems to Be: Is: To those to whom   50
It seems to Be. & is productive of the most dreadful
Consequences to those to whom it seems to Be: even of
Torments, Despair, Eternal Death; but the Divine Mercy
Steps beyond and Redeems Man in the Body of Jesus Amen
And Length Bredth Highth again Obey the Divine Vision   55
                                        Hallelujah

[Plate 33 (37)]

And One stood forth from the Divine family & said

I feel my Spectre rising upon me! Albion! arouze thyself!
Why dost thou thunder with frozen Spectrous wrath against us?
The Spectre is, in Giant Man; insane, and most deform'd.
Thou wilt certainly provoke my Spectre against thine in fury!   5
He has a Sepulcher hewn out of a Rock ready for thee:
And a Death of Eight thousand years forg'd by thyself, upon
The point of his Spear! if thou persistest to forbid with Laws
Our Emanations, and to attack our secret supreme delights

So Los spoke: But when he saw pale death in Albions feet,   10
Again he join'd the Divine Body, following merciful;
While Albion fled more indignant: revengeful covering

[Plate 34 (38)]

His face and bosom with petrific hardness, and his hands
And feet, lest any should enter his bosom & embrace
His hidden heart; his Emanation wept & trembled within him:
Uttering not his jealousy, but hiding it as with
Iron and steel, dark and opake. with clouds & tempests brooding: 5
His strong limbs shudderd upon his mountains high and dark.

Turning from Universal Love, petrific as he went,
His cold against the warmth of Eden rag'd with loud
Thunders of deadly war (the fever of the human soul)
Fires and clouds of rolling smoke! but mild the Saviour follow'd him.   10
Displaying the Eternal Vision! the Divine Similitude!
In loves and tears of brothers, sisters, sons, fathers and friends
Which if Man ceases to behold, he ceases to exist:

Saying, Albion! Our wars are wars of life, & wounds of love,
With intellectual spears, & long winged arrows of thought: 15
Mutual in one anothers love and wrath all renewing
We live as One Man; for contracting our infinite senses*
We behold multitude; or expanding: we behold as one,
As One Man all the Universal Family; and that One Man
We call Jesus the Christ: and he in us, and we in him,   20
Live in perfect harmony in Eden the land of life.
Giving, recieving, and forgiving each others trespasses.
He is the Good shepherd, he is the Lord and master:
He is the Shepherd of Albion, he is all in all,
In Eden: in the garden of God: and in heavenly Jerusalem.   25
If we have offended, forgive us, take not vengeance against us,

Thus speaking; the Divine Family follow Albion:
I see them in the Vision of God upon my pleasant valleys.

I behold London; a Human awful wonder of God!
He says: Return, Albion, return! I give myself for thee: 30
My Streets are my, Ideas of Imagination.
Awake Albion, awake! and let us awake up together.
My Houses are Thoughts: my Inhabitants; Affections,
The children of my thoughts, walking within my blood-vessels,
Shut from my nervous form which sleeps upon the verge of Beulah   35
In dreams of darkness. while my vegetating blood in veiny pipes,
Rolls dreadful thro' the Furnaces of Los, and the Mills of Satan.
For Albions sake, and for Jerusalem thy Emanation
I give myself, and these my brethren give themselves for Albion.

So spoke London, immortal Guardian! I heard in Lambeths shades: 40
In Felpham I heard and saw the Visions of Albion
I write in South Molton Street, what I both see and hear*
In regions of Humanity, in Londons opening streets.
I see thee awful Parent Land in light, behold I see!
Verulam! Canterbury! venerable parent of men,*   45
Generous immortal Guardian golden clad! for Cities
Are Men, fathers of multitudes, and Rivers & Mountins
Are also Men; every thing is Human. mighty! sublime!
In every bosom a Universe expands, as wings
Let down at will around, and call'd the Universal Tent.   50
York, crown'd with loving kindness. Edinburgh, cloth'd
With fortitude as with a garment of immortal texture
Woven in looms of Eden. in spiritual deaths of mighty men

Who give themselves in Golgotha, Victims to Justice; where
There is in Albion a Gate of Precious stones and gold   55
Seen only by Emanations, by vegetations viewless,
Bending across the road of Oxford Street; it from Hyde Park
To Tyburns deathful shades, admits the wandering souls*
Of multitudes who die from Earth: this Gate cannot be found

[Plate 35 (39)]

By Satans Watch-fiends tho' they search numbering every grain
Of sand on Earth every night, they never find this Gate.
It is the Gate of Los. Withoutside is the Mill, intricate, dreadful
And fill'd with cruel tortures; but no mortal man can find the Mill
Of Satan, in his mortal pilgrimage of seventy years   5
For Human beauty knows it not: nor can Mercy find it! But
In the Fourth region of Humanity, Urthona namd
Mortality begins to roll the billows of Eternal Death
Before the Gate of Los. Urthona here is named Los.
And here begins the System of Moral Virtue, named Rahab.   10
Albion fled thro' the Gate of Los. and he stood in the Gate.

Los was the friend of Albion who most lov'd him. In
                                        Cambridgeshire*
His eternal station, he is the twenty-eighth, & is four-fold.
Seeing Albion had turn'd his back against the Divine Vision,
Los said to Albion. Whither fleest thou? Albion reply'd.   15

I die! I go to Eternal Death! the shades of death
Hover within me & beneath. and spreading themselves outside
Like rocky clouds, build me a gloomy monument of woe:
Will none accompany me in my death? or be a Ransom for me
In that dark Valley? I have girded round my cloke. and on my feet   20
Bound these black shoes of death, & on my hands, death's iron
                                        gloves:
God hath forsaken me, & my friends are become a burden
A weariness to me, & the human footstep is a terror to me.

Los answerd, troubled: and his soul was rent in twain:
Must the Wise die for an Atonement? does Mercy endure   25
                                        Atonement?
No! It is Moral Severity, & destroys Mercy in its Victim.
So speaking, not yet infected with the Error & Illusion,

[Plate 36 (40)]

Los shudder'd at beholding Albion, for his disease
Arose upon him pale and ghastly: and he call'd around
The Friends of Albion: trembling at the sight of Eternal Death*
The four appear'd with their Emanations in fiery
Chariots: black their fires roll beholding Albions House of   5
                                                    Eternity
Damp couch the flames beneath and silent, sick, stand shuddering
Before the Porch of sixteen pillars: weeping every one
Descended and fell down upon their knees round Albions knees,
Swearing the Oath of God! with awful voice of thunders round
Upon the hills & valleys, and the cloudy Oath roll'd far and wide   10

Albion is sick! said every Valley, every mournful Hill
And every River: our brother Albion is sick to death.
He hath leagued himself with robbers! he hath studied the arts
Of unbelief! Envy hovers over him! his Friends are his abhorrence!
Those who give their lives for him are despised!   15
Those who devour his soul, are taken into his bosom!
To destroy his Emanation is their intention:
Arise! awake O Friends of the Giant Albion
They have perswaded him of horrible falsehoods!
They have sown errors over all his fruitful fields!   20

The Twenty-four heard! they came trembling on watry chariots.*
Borne by the Living Creatures of the third procession
Of Human Majesty, the Living Creatures wept aloud, as they
Went along Albions road. till they arriv'd at Albions House.

O! how the torments of Eternal Death waited on Man: 25
And the loud-rending bars of the Creation ready to burst:
That the wide world might fly from its hinges. & the immortal
                                                    mansion
Of Man for ever be possess'd by monsters of the deeps:
And Man himself become a Fiend, wrap'd in an endless curse,
Consuming and consum'd for-ever in flames of Moral Justice.   30

For had the Body of Albion fall'n down and from its dreadful ruins
Let loose the enormous Spectre on the darkness of the deep,
At enmity with the Merciful & fill'd with devouring fire,
A nether-world must have recievd the foul enormous spirit,
Under pretence of Moral Virtue, fill'd with Revenge and Law.   35

There to eternity chain'd down, and issuing in red flames
And curses, with his mighty arms brandish'd against the heavens
Breathing cruelty blood & vengeance, gnashing his teeth with pain
Torn with black storms, & ceaseless torrents of his own
                        consuming fire:
Within his breast his mighty Sons chaind down & fill'd with   40
                        cursings:
And his dark Eon, that once fair crystal form divinely clear:
Within his ribs producing serpents whose souls are flames of fire.
But glory to the Merciful-One. for he is of tender mercies!
And the Divine Family wept over him as One Man.

And these the Twenty-four in whom the Divine Family   45
Appear'd; and they were One in Him, A Human Vision!
Human Divine, Jesus the Saviour, blessed for ever and ever.

Selsey, true friend! who afterwards submitted to be devour'd*
By the waves of Despair. whose Emanation rose above
The flood and was nam'd Chichester. lovely mild & gentle! Lo!   50
Her lambs bleat to the sea-fowls' cry, lamenting still for Albion

Submitting to be call'd the son of Los the terrible vision:
Winchester stood devoting himself for Albion: his tents
Outspread with abundant riches, and his Emanations
Submitting to be call'd Enitharmons daughters and be born   55
In vegetable mould: created by the Hammer and Loom
In Bowlahoola & Allamanda where the Dead wail night & day.*

(I call them by their English names: English, the rough basement,
Los built the stubborn structure of the Language, acting against
Albions melancholy, who must else have been a Dumb despair.)   60

Gloucester and Exeter and Salisbury and Bristol: and benevolent

[Plate 37 (41)]

Bath who is Legions: he is the Seventh, the physician and*
The poisoner: the best and worst in Heaven and Hell:
Whose Spectre first assimilated with Luvah in Albions mountains
A triple octave he took, to reduce Jerusalem to twelve
To cast Jerusalem forth upon the wilds to Poplar & Bow: 5
To Malden & Canterbury in the delights of cruelty:
The Shuttles of death sing in the sky to Islington & Pancrass

Round Marybone to Tyburns River, weaving black melancholy as a
                                                             net,
And despair as meshes closely wove over the west of London,
Where mild Jerusalem sought to repose in death & be no more.   10
She fled to Lambeths mild Vale and hid herself beneath
The Surrey Hills where Rephaim terminates: her Sons are siez'd
For victims of sacrifice; but Jerusalem cannot be found! Hid
By the Daughters of Beulah: gently snatch'd away: and hid in Beulah

There is a Grain of Sand in Lambeth that Satan cannot find   15
Nor can his Watch Fiends find it: tis translucent & has many Angles
But he who finds it will find Oothoons palace, for within
Opening into Beulah every angle is a lovely heaven
But should the Watch Fiends find it, they would call it Sin
And lay its Heavens & their inhabitants in blood of punishment   20
Here Jerusalem & Vala were hid in soft slumberous repose
Hid from the terrible East. shut up in the South & West.

The Twenty-eight trembled in Deaths dark caves, in cold despair*
They kneeld around the Couch of Death in deep humiliation
And tortures of self condemnation, while their Spectres ragd within, 25
The Four Zoa's in terrible combustion clouded rage
Drinking the shuddering fears & loves of Albions Families
Destroying by selfish affections the things that they most admire
Drinking & eating. & pitying & weeping, as at a trajic scene.
The soul drinks murder & revenge, & applauds its own holiness   30

They saw Albion endeavouring to destroy their Emanations.

[Plate 38 (43)]

They saw their Wheels rising up poisonous against Albion
Urizen, cold & scientific: Luvah pitying & weeping
Tharmas. indolent & sullen: Urthona, doubting & despairing
Victims to one another & dreadfully plotting against each other
To prevent Albion walking about in the Four Complexions.*   5

They saw America clos'd out by the Oaks of the western shore;
And Tharmas dash'd on the Rocks of the Altars of Victims in Mexico.
If we are wrathful, Albion will destroy Jerusalem with rooty Groves
If we are merciful, ourselves must suffer destruction on his Oaks:
Why should we enter into our Spectres. to behold our own   10
                                                   corruptions
O God of Albion descend! deliver Jerusalem from the Oaken Groves!

Then Los grew furious raging: Why stand we here trembling around
Calling on God for help; and not ourselves in whom God dwells
Stretching a hand to save the falling Man: are we not Four
Beholding Albion upon the Precipice ready to fall into Non-Entity: 15
Seeing these Heavens & Hells conglobing in the Void. Heavens over
                                                                Hells
Brooding in holy hypocritic lust, drinking the cries of pain
From howling victims of Law: building Heavens Twenty-seven-fold.
Swell'd & bloated General Forms, repugnant to the Divine-
Humanity, who is the Only General and Universal Form 20
To which all Lineaments tend & seek with love & sympathy
All broad & general principles belong to benevolence
Who protects minute particulars, every one in their own identity.
But here the affectionate touch of the tongue is closd in by deadly
                                                                teeth
And the soft smile of friendship & the open dawn of benevolence 25
Become a net & a trap, & every energy renderd cruel,
Till the existence of friendship & benevolence is denied:
The wine of the Spirit & the vineyards of the Holy-One.
Here: turn into poisonous stupor & deadly intoxication:
That they may be condemnd by Law & the Lamb of God be slain! 30
And the two Sources of Life in Eternity Hunting and War,
Are become the Sources of dark & bitter Death & of corroding Hell:
The open heart is shut up in integuments of frozen silence
That the spear that lights it forth may shatter the ribs & bosom
A pretence of Art. to destroy Art! a pretence of Liberty 35
To destroy Liberty. a pretence of Religion to destroy Religion
Oshea and Caleb fight: they contend in the valleys of Peor*
In the terrible Family Contentions of those who love each other:
The Armies of Balaam weep—no women come to the field
Dead corses lay before them, & not as in Wars of old. 40
For the Soldier who fights for Truth, calls his enemy his brother:
They fight & contend for life, & not for eternal death!
But here the Soldier strikes, & a dead corse falls at his feet
Nor Daughter nor Sister nor Mother come forth to embosom
                                                        the Slain!
But Death! Eternal Death! remains in the Valleys of Peor. 45
The English are scatterd over the face of the Nations: are these
Jerusalem's children? Hark! hear the Giants of Albion cry at night
We smell the blood of the English! we delight in their blood on our
                                                            Altars!

The living & the dead shall be ground in our rumbling Mills
For bread of the Sons of Albion: of the Giants Hand & Scofield   50
Scofeld & Kox are let loose upon my Saxons! they accumulate
A World in which Man is by his Nature the Enemy of Man,
In pride of Selfhood unwieldy stretching out into Non Entity
Generalizing Art & Science till Art & Science is lost.
Bristol & Bath, listen to my words, & ye Seventeen: give ear!*   55
It is easy to acknowledge a man to be great & good while we
Derogate from him in the trifles & small articles of that goodness;
Those alone are his friends, who admire his minutest powers.
Instead of Albions lovely mountains & the curtains of Jerusalem
I see a Cave, a Rock, a Tree deadly and poisonous, unimaginative: 60
Instead of the Mutual Forgivenesses, the Minute Particulars, I see
Pits of bitumen ever burning: artificial Riches of the Canaanite
Like Lakes of liquid lead: instead of heavenly Chapels, built
By our dear Lord: I see Worlds crusted with snows & ice;
I see a Wicker Idol woven round Jerusalems children. I see*   65
The Canaanite, the Amalekite, the Moabite, the Egyptian:
By Demonstrations the cruel Sons of Quality & Negation.
Driven on the Void in incoherent despair into Non Entity
I see America closd apart, & Jerusalem driven in terror
Away from Albions mountains, far away from Londons spires!   70
I will not endure this thing! I alone withstand to death,
This outrage! Ah me! how sick & pale you all stand round me!
Ah me! pitiable ones! do you also go to deaths vale?
All you my Friends & Brothers! all you my beloved Companions!
Have you also caught the infection of Sin & stern Repentance?   75
I see Disease arise upon you! yet speak to me and give
Me some comfort: why do you all stand silent? I alone
Remain in permanent strength. Or is all this goodness & pity, only
That you may take the greater vengeance in your Sepulcher,

So Los spoke. Pale they stood around the House of Death: 80
In the midst of temptations & despair: among the rooted Oaks:
Among reared Rocks of Albions Sons, at length they rose

[Plate 39 (44)]

With one accord in love sublime, & as on Cherubs wings
They Albion surround with kindest violence to bear him back

Against his will thro Los's Gate to Eden: Four-fold; loud!
Their Wings waving over the bottomless Immense: to bear
Their awful charge back to his native home: but Albion dark,   5
Repugnant; rolld his Wheels backward into Non-Entity
Loud roll the Starry Wheels of Albion into the World of Death
And all the Gate of Los, clouded with clouds redounding from
Albions dread Wheels, stretching out spaces immense between
That every little particle of light & air, became Opake   10
Black & immense, a Rock of difficulty & a Cliff
Of black despair; that the immortal Wings labourd against
Cliff after cliff, & over Valleys of despair & death:
The narrow Sea between Albion & the Atlantic Continent:
Its waves of pearl became a boundless Ocean bottomless,   15
Of grey obscurity, filld with clouds & rocks & whirling waters
And Albions Sons ascending & descending in the horrid Void.

But as the Will must not be bended but in the day of Divine
Power: silent calm & motionless, in the mid-air sublime,
The Family Divine hover around the darkend Albion.   20

Such is the nature of the Ulro: that whatever enters:
Becomes Sexual & is Created, and Vegetated, and Born.
From Hyde Park spread their vegetating roots beneath Albion
In dreadful pain the Spectrous Uncircumcised Vegetation.
Forming a Sexual Machine: an Aged Virgin Form.   25
In Erins Land toward the north, joint after joint & burning
In love & jealousy immingled, & calling it Religion
And feeling the damps of death they with one accord
                                         delegated Los,
Conjuring him by the Highest that he should Watch over them
Till Jesus shall appear: & they gave their power to Los   30
Naming him the Spirit of Prophecy, calling him Elijah*

Strucken with Albions disease they become what they behold;
They assimilate with Albion in pity & compassion;
Their Emanations return not: their Spectres rage in the Deep
The Slumbers of Death came over them around the Couch   35
                                         of Death
Before the Gate of Los & in the depths of Non Entity
Among the Furnaces of Los; among the Oaks of Albion.

Man is adjoind to Man by his Emanative portion:
Who is Jerusalem in every individual Man: and her

Shadow is Vala, builded by the Reasoning power in Man   40
O search & see: turn your eyes inward: open O thou World
Of Love & Harmony in Man: expand thy ever lovely Gates.

They wept into the deeps a little space; at length was heard
The voice of Bath, faint as the voice of the Dead in the House
                                                              of Death

[Plate 40 (45)]

Bath, healing City! whose wisdom in midst of Poetic*
Fervor: mild spoke thro' the Western Porch, in soft gentle tears

O Albion mildest Son of Eden! clos'd is thy Western Gate
Brothers of Eternity! this Man whose great example
We all admir'd & lov'd, whose all benevolent countenance, seen   5
In Eden, in lovely Jerusalem, drew even from envy
The tear: and the confession of honesty, open & undisguis'd
From mistrust and suspition. The Man is himself become
A piteous example of oblivion, To teach the Sons
Of Eden, that however great and glorious; however loving   10
And merciful the Individuality; however high
Our palaces and cities, and however fruitful are our fields
In Selfhood, we are nothing: but fade away in mornings breath.
Our mildness is nothing: the greatest mildness we can use
Is incapable and nothing! none but the Lamb of God can heal   15
This dread disease: none but Jesus! O Lord descend and save.
Albions Western Gate is clos'd: his death is coming apace!
Jesus alone can save him; for alas we none can know
How soon his lot may be our own. When Africa in sleep
Rose in the night of Beulah, and bound down the Sun & Moon   20
His friends cut his strong chains, & overwhelm'd his dark
Machines in fury & destruction, and the Man reviving repented
He wept before his wrathful brethren, thankful & considerate
For their well timed wrath. But Albions sleep is not
Like Africa's; and his machines are woven with his life   25
Nothing but mercy can save him! nothing but mercy interposing
Lest he should slay Jerusalem in his fearful jealousy
O God descend! gather our brethren, deliver Jerusalem
But that we may omit no office of the friendly spirit
Oxford, take thou these leaves of the Tree of Life: with eloquence* 30

That thy immortal tongue inspires; present them to Albion:
Perhaps he may recieve them, offerd from thy loved hands.

So spoke, unhear'd by Albion, the merciful Son of Heaven
To those whose Western Gates were open, as they stood weeping,
Around Albion: but Albion heard him not; obdurate! hard!   35
He frown'd on all his Friends, counting them enemies in his sorrow

And the Seventeen conjoinining with Bath, the Seventh:
In whom the other Ten shone manifest, a Divine Vision!
Assimilated and embrac'd Eternal Death for Albions sake.
And these the names of the Eighteen combining with those Ten   40

[Plate 41 (46)]

Bath, mild Physician of Eternity, mysterious power
Whose springs are unsearchable & knowledg infinite.
Hereford, ancient Guardian of Wales, whose hands
Builded the mountain palaces of Eden. stupendous works!*
Lincoln, Durham & Carlisle, Councellors of Los.   5
And Ely, Scribe of Los, whose pen no other hand
Dare touch! Oxford, immortal Bard! with eloquence
Divine, he wept over Albion: speaking the words of God
In mild perswasion: bringing leaves of the Tree of Life.

Thou art in Error Albion. the Land of Ulro: 10
One Error not remov'd. will destroy a human Soul
Repose in Beulahs night, till the Error is remov'd
Reason not on both sides. Repose upon our bosoms
Till the Plow of Jehovah. and the Harrow of Shaddai
Have passed over the Dead, to awake the Dead to Judgment.   15
But Albion turn'd away refusing comfort.

Oxford trembled while he spoke, then fainted in the arms
Of Norwich, Peterboro, Rochester, Chester awful, Worcester,
Litchfield. Saint Davids. Landaff, Asaph. Bangor. Sodor,
Bowing their heads devoted: and the Furnaces of Los   20
Began to rage. thundering loud the storms began to roar
Upon the Furnaces, and loud the Furnaces rebellow beneath

And these the Four in whom the twenty-four appear'd four-fold:
Verulam. London. York. Edinburgh. mourning one towards another
Alas!—The time will come, when a mans worst enemies   25

Shall be those of his own house and family: in a Religion
Of Generation, to destroy, by Sin and Atonement, happy Jerusalem,
The Bride and Wife of the Lamb. O God thou art Not an Avenger!

[Plate 42]

Thus Albion sat, studious of others in his pale disease:
Brooding on evil: but when Los opend the Furnaces before him:
He saw that the accursed things were his own affections,
And his own beloveds: then he turn'd sick! his soul died within him
Also Los sick & terrified beheld the Furnaces of Death   5
And must have died, but the Divine Saviour descended
Among the infant loves & affections, and the Divine Vision wept
Like evening dew on every herb upon the breathing ground

Albion spoke in his dismal dreams; O thou deceitful friend
Worshipping mercy & beholding thy friend in such affliction: 10
Los! thou now discoverest thy turpitude to the heavens.
I demand righteousness & justice. O thou ingratitude!
Give me my Emanations back food for my dying soul!
My daughters are harlots! my sons are accursed before me.
Enitharmon is my daughter: accursed with a father's curse!   15
O! I have utterly been wasted! I have given my daughters to devils

So spoke Albion in gloomy majesty, and deepest night
Of Ulro rolld round his skirts from Dover to Cornwall.

Los answerd, Righteousness & justice I give thee in return
For thy righteousness! but I add mercy also, and bind   20
Thee from destroying these little ones: am I to be only
Merciful to thee and cruel to all that thou hatest
Thou wast the Image of God surrounded by the Four Zoa's
Three thou hast slain: I am the Fourth, thou canst not destroy me.
Thou art in Error; trouble me not with thy righteousness.   25
I have innocence to defend and ignorance to instruct:
I have no time for seeming; and little arts of compliment,
In morality and virtue: in self-glorying and pride.
There is a limit of Opakeness, and a limit of Contraction:
In every Individual Man. and the limit of Opakeness,   30
Is named Satan: and the limit of Contraction is named Adam,
But when Man sleeps in Beulah, the Saviour in Mercy takes
Contraction's Limit, and of the Limit he forms Woman: That

Himself may in process of time be born Man to redeem
But there is no Limit of Expansion! there is no Limit of   35
                        Translucence.
In the bosom of Man for ever from eternity to eternity.
Therefore I break thy bonds of righteousness; I crush thy messengers!
That they may not crush me and mine: do thou be righteous,
And I will return it: otherwise I defy thy worst revenge:
Consider me as thine enemy: on me turn all thy fury   40
But destroy not these little ones, nor mock the Lords anointed:
Destroy not by Moral Virtue, the little ones whom he hath chosen!
The little ones whom he hath chosen in preference to thee.
He hath cast thee off for ever; the little ones he hath anointed!
Thy Selfhood is for ever accursed from the Divine presence   45

So Los spoke: then turn'd his face & wept for Albion.

Albion replied. Go! Hand & Hyle! sieze the abhorred friend:
As you Have siezd the Twenty-four rebellious ingratitudes;
To atone for you, for spiritual death! Man lives by deaths of Men
Bring him to justice before heaven here upon London stone,   50
Between Blackheath & Hounslow. between Norwood & Finchley
All that they have is mine: from my free genrous gift.
They now hold all they have: ingratitude to me!
To me their benefactor, calls aloud for vengeance deep.

Los stood before his Furnaces awaiting the fury of the Dead: 55
And the Divine hand was upon him, strengthening him mightily.

The Spectres of the Dead cry out from the deeps beneath
Upon the hills of Albion; Oxford groans in his iron furnace
Winchester in his den & cavern; they lament against
Albion: they curse their human kindness & affection   60
They rage like wild beasts in the forests of affliction
In the dreams of Ulro they repent of their human kindness.

Come up, build Babylon, Rahab is ours & all her multitudes
With her, in pomp and glory of victory. Depart
Ye twenty-four, into the deeps! let us depart to glory!   65

Their Human majestic Forms sit up upon their Couches
Of death: they curb their Spectres as with iron curbs
They enquire after Jerusalem in the regions of the dead,
With the voices of dead men, low, scarcely articulate,
And with tears cold on their cheeks they weary repose.   70

O when shall the morning of the grave appear, and when
Shall our salvation come? we sleep upon our watch
We cannot awake! and our Spectres rage in the forests
O God of Albion where art thou! pity the watchers!

Thus mourn they, Loud the Furnaces of Los thunder upon   75
The clouds of Europe & Asia. among the Serpent Temples!

And Los drew his Seven Furnaces around Albions Altars
And as Albion built his frozen Altars, Los built the Mundane
                                                        Shell,
In the Four Regions of Humanity East & West & North & South,
Till Norwood & Finchley & Blackheath & Hounslow, coverd the   80
                                                        whole Earth.
This is the Net & Veil of Vala, among the Souls of the Dead.

[Plate 43 (29)]

Then the Divine Vision like a silent Sun appeard above
Albions dark rocks: setting behind the Gardens of Kensington
On Tyburns River in clouds of blood: where was mild Zion Hills
Most ancient promontory. and in the Sun. a Human Form
                                                        appeard
And thus the Voice Divine went forth upon the rocks of Albion   5

I elected Albion for my glory: I gave to him the Nations,
Of the whole Earth. He was the Angel of my Presence: and all
The Sons of God were Albions Sons: and Jerusalem was my joy.
The Reactor hath hid himself thro envy. I behold him.*
But you cannot behold him till he be reveald in his System   10
Albions Reactor must have a Place prepard: Albion must Sleep
The Sleep of Death. till the Man of Sin & Repentance be reveald,
Hidden in Albions Forests he lurks: he admits of no Reply
From Albion: but hath founded his Reaction into a Law
Of Action, for Obedience to destroy the Contraries of Man   15
He hath compelld Albion to become a Punisher & hath possessd
Himself of Albions Forests & Wilds! and Jerusalem is taken!
The City of the Woods in the Forest of Ephratah is taken!*
London is a stone of her ruins; Oxford is the dust of her walls!
Sussex & Kent are her scatterd garments! Ireland her holy place! 20
And the murderd bodies of her little ones are Scotland and Wales
The Cities of the Nations are the smoke of her consummation

The Nations are her dust! ground by the chariot wheels
Of her lordly conquerors, her palaces levelld with the dust
I come that I may find a way for my banished ones to return   25
Fear not O little Flock I come! Albion shall rise again.

So saying, the mild Sun inclosd the Human Family.

Forthwith from Albion's dark'ning locks came two Immortal forms,*
Saying We alone are escaped. O merciful Lord and Saviour,
We flee from the interiors of Albions hills and mountains!   30
From his Valleys Eastward: from Amalek Canaan & Moab;
Beneath his vast ranges of hills surrounding Jerusalem.
Albion walkd on the steps of fire before his Halls
And Vala walkd with him in dreams of soft deluding slumber.
He looked up & saw the Prince of Light with splendor faded   35
Then Albion ascended mourning into the porches of his Palace
Above him rose a Shadow from his wearied intellect:
Of living gold, pure, perfect, holy: in white linen pure he hoverd
A sweet entrancing self-delusion a watry vision of Albion
Soft exulting in existence; all the Man absorbing!   40

Albion fell upon his face prostrate before the watry Shadow
Saying O Lord, whence is this change: thou knowest I am nothing!
And Vala trembled & coverd her face! & her locks were spread on the
                                                        pavement

We heard, astonishd at the Vision & our hearts trembled within us:
We heard the voice of slumberous Albion. and thus he spake.   45
Idolatrous to his own Shadow words of eternity uttering:

O I am nothing when I enter into judgment with thee!
If thou withdraw thy breath I die & vanish into Hades
If thou dost lay thine hand upon me behold I am silent:
If thou withhold thine hand! I perish like a fallen leaf!   50
O I am nothing: and to nothing must return again:
If thou withdraw thy breath. Behold, I am oblivion.

He ceasd: the shadowy voice was silent: but the cloud hoverd over
                                                        their heads
In golden wreathes. the sorrow of Man; & the balmy drops fell down.
And lo! that son of Man that Shadowy Spirit of mild Albion: 55
Luvah descended from the cloud; in terror Albion rose:
Indignant rose the awful Man, & turn'd his back on Vala.

We heard the voice of Albion starting from his sleep:

Whence is this voice crying Enion; that soundeth in my ears?*
O cruel pity! O dark deceit; can love seek for dominion?   60

And Luvah strove to gain dominion over Albion*
They strove together above the Body where Vala was inclosd
And the dark Body of Albion left prostrate upon the crystal pavement,
Coverd with boils from head to foot: the terrible smitings of Luvah.

Then frownd the fallen Man, and put forth Luvah from his presence   65
Saying. Go and Die the Death of Man, for Vala the sweet wanderer.
I will turn the volutions of your ears outward, and bend your nostrils
Downward, and your fluxile eyes englob'd roll round in fear:
Your withring lips and tongue shrink up into a narrow circle,
Till into narrow forms you creep: go take your fiery way: 70
And learn what tis to absorb the Man you Spirits of Pity & Love.

They heard the voice and fled swift as the winters setting sun.
And now the human blood foamd high. the Spirits Luvah & Vala
Went down the Human Heart where Paradise & its joys abounded,
In jealous fears & fury & rage, & flames roll round their fervid feet: 75
And the vast form of Nature like a serpent playd before them
And as they fled in folding fires & thunders of the deep:
Vala shrunk in like the dark sea that leaves its slimy banks
And from her bosom Luvah fell far as the east and west.
And the vast form of Nature like a serpent rolld between   80
Whether of Jerusalems or Valas ruins congenerated we know not:
All is confusion: all is tumult, & we alone are escaped.
So spoke the fugitives; they joind the Divine Family. trembling,

[Plate 44 (30)]

And the Two that escaped; were the Emanation of Los & his
Spectre: for whereever the Emanation goes, the Spectre
Attends her as her Guard, & Los's Emanation is named
Enitharmon. & his Spectre is named Urthona: they knew
Not where to flee: they had been on a visit to Albions Children   5
And they strove to weave a Shadow of the Emanation
To hide themselves: weeping & lamenting for the Vegetation
Of Albions Children. fleeing thro Albions vales in streams of gore

Being not irritated by insult bearing insulting benevolences
They percieved that corporeal friends are spiritual enemies   10

They saw the Sexual Religion in its embryon Uncircumcision
And the Divine hand was upon them bearing them thro darkness
Back safe to their Humanity as doves to their windows:
Therefore the Sons of Eden praise Urthonas Spectre in Songs
Because he kept the Divine Vision in time of trouble.   15

They wept & trembled: & Los put forth his hand & took them in.
Into his Bosom: from which Albion shrunk in dismal pain;
Rending the fibres of Brotherhood & in Feminine Allegories
Inclosing Los: but the Divine Vision appeard with Los
Following Albion into his Central Void among his Oaks.   20

And Los prayed and said. O Divine Saviour arise
Upon the Mountains of Albion as in ancient time. Behold!
The Cities of Albion seek thy face, London groans in pain
From Hill to Hill & the Thames laments along the Valleys
The little Villages of Middlesex & Surrey hunger & thirst   25
The Twenty-eight Cities of Albion stretch their hands to thee:
Because of the Opressors of Albion in every City & Village:
They mock at the Labourer's limbs! they mock at his starvd Children.
They buy his Daughters that they may have power to sell his Sons:
They compell the Poor to live upon a crust of bread by soft mild arts: 30
They reduce the Man to want: then give with pomp & ceremony.
The praise of Jehovah is chaunted from lips of hunger & thirst!
Humanity knows not of Sex: wherefore are Sexes in Beulah?
In Beulah the Female lets down her beautiful Tabernacle;
Which the Male enters magnificent between her Cherubim: 35
And becomes One with her mingling condensing in Self-love
The Rocky Law of Condemnation & double Generation, & Death.
Albion hath enter'd the Loins the place of the Last Judgment;
And Luvah hath drawn the Curtains around Albion in Vala's bosom
The Dead awake to Generation! Arise O Lord, & rend the Veil!   40

So Los in lamentations followd Albion. Albion coverd.

[Plate 45 (31)]

His western heaven with rocky clouds of death & despair.

Fearing that Albion should turn his back against the Divine Vision
Los took his globe of fire to search the interiors of Albions
Bosom, in all the terrors of friendship. entering the caves

Of despair & death, to search the tempters out, walking among   5
Albions rocks & precipices! caves of solitude & dark despair,
And saw every Minute Particular of Albion degraded & murderd
But saw not by whom; they were hidden within in the minute
                                                       particulars
Of which they had possessd themselves; and there they take up
The articulations of a mans soul, and laughing throw it down   10
Into the frame. then knock it out upon the plank, & souls are bak'd
In bricks to build the pyramids of Heber & Terah. But Los
Searchd in vain: closd from the minutia he walkd, difficult.
He came down from Highgate thro Hackney & Holloway towards
                                                       London
Till he came to old Stratford & thence to Stepney & the Isle   15
Of Leuthas Dogs, thence thro the narrows of the Rivers side*
And saw every minute particular, the jewels of Albion,
                                                       running down
The kennels of the streets & lanes as if they were abhorrd.
Every Universal Form. was become barren mountains of Moral
Virtue: and every Minute Particular hardend into grains of sand: 20
And all the tendernesses of the soul cast forth as filth & mire,
Among the winding places of deep contemplation intricate
To where the Tower of London frownd dreadful over Jerusalem:
A building of Luvah builded in Jerusalems eastern gate to be
His secluded Court: thence to Bethlehem where was builded*   25
Dens of despair in the house of bread: enquiring in vain
Of stones and rocks he took his way, for human form was none:
And thus he spoke, looking on Albions City with many tears
What shall I do! what could I do, if I could find these Criminals
I could not dare to take vengeance; for all things are so constructed   30
And builded by the Divine hand, that the sinner shall always escape,
And he who takes vengeance alone is the criminal of Providence;
If I should dare to lay my finger on a grain of sand
In way of vengeance; I punish the already punishd: O whom
Should I pity if I pity not the sinner who is gone astray!   35
O Albion, if thou takest vengeance; if thou revengest thy wrongs
Thou art for ever lost! What can I do to hinder the Sons
Of Albion from taking vengeance? or how shall I them perswade.

So spoke Los, travelling thro darkness & horrid solitude:
And he beheld Jerusalem in Westminster & Marybone,   40
Among the ruins of the Temple: and Vala who is her Shadow,

Jerusalems Shadow bent northward over the Island white.
At length he sat on London Stone, & heard Jerusalems voice.

Albion I cannot be thy Wife. thine own Minute Particulars,
Belong to God alone. and all thy little ones are holy   45
They are of Faith & not of Demonstration: wherefore is Vala
Clothd in black mourning upon my rivers currents, Vala awake!
I hear thy shuttles sing in the sky, and round my limbs
I feel the iron threads of love & jealousy & despair.

Vala reply'd: Albion is mine: Luvah gave me to Albion   50
And now recieves reproach & hate. Was it not said of old
Set your Son before a man & he shall take you & your sons
For slaves: but set your Daughter before a man & She
Shall make him & his sons & daughters your slaves for ever:
And is this Faith? Behold the strife of Albion & Luvah   55
Is great in the east. their spears of blood rage in the eastern heaven
Urizen is the champion of Albion, they will slay my Luvah:
And thou O harlot daughter! daughter of despair art all
This cause of these shakings of my towers on Euphrates.
Here is the House of Albion, & here is thy secluded place   60
And here we have found thy sins: & hence we turn thee forth.
For all to avoid thee: to be astonishd at thee for thy sins:
Because thou art the impurity & the harlot: & thy children!
Children of whoredoms: born for Sacrifice: for the meat & drink
Offering: to sustain the glorious combat & the battle & war   65
That Man may be purified by the death of thy delusions.

So saying she her dark threads cast over the trembling River:
And over the valleys; from the hills of Hertfordshire to the hills
Of Surrey across Middlesex & across Albions House
Of Eternity! pale stood Albion at his eastern gate,   70

[Plate 46 (32)]

Leaning against the pillars. & his disease rose from his skirts
Upon the Precipice he stood, ready to fall into Non-Entity.

Los was all astonishment & terror: he trembled sitting on the Stone
Of London: but the interiors of Albions fibres & nerves were hidden
From Los, astonishd he beheld only the petrified surfaces!   5
And saw his Furnaces in ruins, for Los is the Demon of the Furnaces,

He saw also the Four Points of Albion reversd inwards
He siezd his Hammer & Tongs, his iron Poker & his Bellows,
Upon the valleys of Middlesex, Shouting loud for aid Divine.

In stern defiance came from Albions bosom Hand, Hyle, Koban,   10
Gwantok, Peachy. Brertun, Slaid, Huttn, Skofeld, Kock, Kotope,
Bowen: Albions Sons: they bore him a golden couch into the porch
And on the Couch reposd his limbs, trembling from the bloody field.
Rearing their Druid Patriarchal rocky Temples around his limbs.
(All things begin & end, in Albions Ancient Druid Rocky Shore.)   15

[Plate 47]

From Camberwell to Highgate where the mighty Thames shudders
                                                                        along,
Where Los's Furnaces stand, where Jerusalem & Vala howl:
Luvah tore forth from Albions Loins, in fibrous veins. in rivers
Of blood over Europe: a Vegetating Root in grinding pain.
Animating the Dragon Temples, soon to become that Holy Fiend   5
The Wicker Man of Scandinavia in which cruelly consumed*
The Captives reard to heaven howl in flames among the stars
Loud the cries of War on the Rhine & Danube with Albions Sons,
Away from Beulahs hills & vales break forth the Souls of the Dead,
With cymbal, trumpet, clarion; & the scythed chariots of Britain.   10

And the Veil of Vala, is composed of the Spectres of the Dead

Hark! the mingling cries of Luvah with the Sons of Albion
Hark! & Record the terrible wonder! that the Punisher
Mingles with his Victims Spectre, enslaved and tormented
To him whom he has murderd, bound in vengeance & enmity   15
Shudder not. but Write, & the hand of God will assist you!
Therefore I write Albions last words: Hope is banish'd from me.

[Plate 48]

These were his last words. and the merciful Saviour in his arms
Reciev'd him, in the arms of tender mercy, and repos'd
The pale limbs of his Eternal Individuality
Upon the Rock of Ages. Then, surrounded with a Cloud:
In silence the Divine Lord builded with immortal labour,   5

Of gold & jewels a sublime Ornament, a Couch of repose,
With Sixteen pillars: canopied with emblems & written verse.
Spiritual Verse, order'd & measur'd, from whence time shall reveal.
The Five books of the Decalogue, the books of Joshua & Judges.
Samuel, a double book & Kings, a double book, the Psalms &   10
                                                      Prophets
The Four-fold Gospel, and the Revelations everlasting*
Eternity groan'd & was troubled, at the image of Eternal Death!

Beneath the bottoms of the Graves, which is Earth's central joint,
There is a place where Contrarieties are equally true:
(To protect from the Giant blows in the sports of intellect,   15
Thunder in the midst of kindness, & love that kills its beloved:
Because Death is for a period, and they renew tenfold.)
From this sweet Place Maternal Love awoke Jerusalem
With pangs she forsook Beulah's pleasant lovely shadowy Universe
Where no dispute can come; created for those who Sleep.   20

Weeping was in all Beulah, and all the Daughters of Beulah
Wept for their Sister the Daughter of Albion. Jerusalem:
When out of Beulah the Emanation of the Sleeper descended
With solemn mourning out of Beulahs moony shades and hills:
Within the Human Heart, whose Gates closed with solemn sound.   25

And this the manner of the terrible Separation
The Emanations of the grievously afflicted Friends of Albion
Concenter in one Female form an Aged pensive Woman.*
Astonish'd! lovely! embracing the sublime shade: the Daughters of
                                                      Beulah
Beheld her with wonder! With awful hands she took   30
A Moment of Time, drawing it out with many tears & afflictions
And many sorrows: oblique across the Atlantic Vale
Which is the Vale of Rephaim dreadful from East to West,
Where the Human Harvest waves abundant in the beams of Eden
Into a Rainbow of jewels and gold, a mild Reflection from   35
Albions dread Tomb. Eight thousand and five hundred years
In its extension. Every two hundred years has a door to Eden
She also took an Atom of Space, with dire pain opening it a Center
Into Beulah: trembling the Daughters of Beulah dried
Her tears. she ardent embrac'd her sorrows. occupied in labours   40
Of sublime mercy in Rephaims Vale. Perusing Albions Tomb
She sat: she walk'd among the ornaments solemn mourning.

The Daughters attended her shudderings, wiping the death sweat.
Los also saw her in his seventh Furnace, he also terrified
Saw the finger of God go forth upon his seventh Furnace: 45
Away from the Starry Wheels to prepare Jerusalem a place.
When with a dreadful groan the Emanation mild of Albion
Burst from his bosom in the Tomb like a pale snowy cloud,
Female and lovely, struggling to put off the Human form
Writhing in pain. The Daughters of Beulah in kind arms reciev'd   50
Jerusalem: weeping over her among the Spaces of Erin.
In the Ends of Beulah, where the Dead wail night & day.

And thus Erin spoke to the Daughters of Beulah, in soft tears

Albion the Vortex of the Dead! Albion the Generous!
Albion the mildest son of Heaven! The Place of Holy Sacrifice!   55
Where Friends Die for each other: will become the Place,
Of Murder & Unforgiving. Never-awaking Sacrifice of Enemies
The Children must be sacrific'd! (a horror never known
Till now in Beulah.) unless a Refuge can be found
To hide them from the wrath of Albions Law that freezes sore   60
Upon his Sons & Daughters, self-exiled from his bosom
Draw ye Jerusalem away from Albions Mountains
To give a Place for Redemption, let Sihon and Og
Remove Eastward to Bashan and Gilead, and leave

[Plate 49]

The secret coverts of Albion & the hidden places of America
Jerusalem Jerusalem! why wilt thou turn away
Come ye O Daughters of Beulah, lament for Og & Sihon
Upon the Lakes of Ireland from Rathlin to Baltimore:
Stand ye upon the Dargle from Wicklow to Drogheda   5
Come & mourn over Albion the White Cliff of the Atlantic
The Mountain of Giants: all the Giants of Albion are become
Weak: witherd: darkend: & Jerusalem is cast forth from Albion.
They deny that they ever knew Jerusalem, or ever dwelt in Shiloh
The Gigantic roots & twigs of the vegetating Sons of Albion   10
Filld with the little-ones are consumed in the Fires of their Altars
The vegetating Cities are burned & consumed from the Earth:
And the Bodies in which all Animals & Vegetations, the Earth &
                                                                  Heaven

Were contain in the All Glorious Imagination are witherd & darkend.
The golden Gate of Havilah, and all the Garden of God, 15
Was caught up with the Sun in one day of fury and war:
The Lungs, the Heart, the Liver, shrunk away far distant from Man
And left a little slimy substance floating upon the tides.
In one night the Atlantic Continent was caught up with the Moon,
And became an Opake Globe far distant clad with moony beams, 20
The Visions of Eternity, by reason of narrowed perceptions,
Are become weak Visions of Time & Space, fix'd into furrows of
                                                    death;
Till deep dissimulation is the only defence an honest man has left
O Polypus of Death O Spectre over Europe and Asia
Withering the Human Form by Laws of Sacrifice for Sin 25
By Laws of Chastity & Abhorrence I am wither'd up.
Striving to Create a Heaven in which all shall be pure & holy
In their Own Selfhoods, in Natural Selfish Chastity to banish Pity
And dear Mutual Forgiveness; & to become One Great Satan
Inslavd to the most powerful Selfhood: to murder the Divine 30
                                                    Humanity
In whose sight all are as the dust & who chargeth his Angels with
                                                    folly:
Ah! weak & wide astray! Ah shut in narrow doleful form!
Creeping in reptile flesh upon the bosom of the ground!
The Eye of Man, a little narrow orb, closd up & dark.
Scarcely beholding the Great Light; conversing with the ground. 35
The Ear, a little shell, in small volutions shutting out
True Harmonies, & comprehending great, as very small:
The Nostrils, bent down to the earth & clos'd with senseless flesh.
That odours cannot them expand, nor joy on them exult:
The Tongue, a little moisture fills, a little food it cloys, 40
A little sound it utters, & its cries are faintly heard.
Therefore they are removed: therefore they have taken root

In Egypt & Philistea: in Moab & Edom & Aram:
In the Erythrean Sea their Uncircumcision in Heart & Loins
Be lost for ever & ever. then they shall arise from Self, 45
By Self Annihilation into Jerusalems Courts & into Shiloh
Shiloh the Masculine Emanation among the Flowers of Beulah
Lo Shiloh dwells over France, as Jerusalem dwells over Albion
Build & prepare a Wall & Curtain for Americas shore!
Rush on: Rush on. Rush on! ye vegetating Sons of Albion 50

The Sun shall go before you in Day: the Moon shall go
Before you in Night. Come on! Come on! Come on! The Lord
Jehovah is before, behind, above, beneath, around
He has builded the arches of Albions Tomb binding the Stars
In merciful Order, bending the Laws of Cruelty to Peace.   55
He hath placed Og & Anak, the Giants of Albion for their Guards:
Building the Body of Moses in the Valley of Peor: the Body
Of Divine Analogy; and Og & Sihon in the tears of Balaam
The Son of Beor, have given their power to Joshua & Caleb.
Remove from Albion, far remove these terrible surfaces.   60
They are beginning to form Heavens & Hells in immense
Circles; the Hells for food to the Heavens; food of torment,
Food of despair: they drink the condemnd Soul & rejoice
In cruel holiness, in their Heavens of Chastity & Uncircumcision
Yet they are blameless & Iniquity must be imputed only   65
To the State they are enterd into that they may be deliverd:*
Satan is the State of Death, & not a Human existence:
But Luvah is named Satan, because he has enterd that State.
A World where Man is by Nature the enemy of Man
Because the Evil is Created into a State. that Men   70
May be deliverd time after time evermore. Amen.
Learn therefore O Sisters to distinguish the Eternal Human
That walks about among the stones of fire in bliss & woe
Alternate! from those States or Worlds in which the Spirit travels:
This is the only means to Forgiveness of Enemies   75
Therefore remove from Albion these terrible Surfaces
And let wild seas & rocks close up Jerusalem away from

[Plate 50]

The Atlantic Mountains where Giants dwelt in Intellect;
Now given to stony Druids, and Allegoric Generation
To the Twelve Gods of Asia, the Spectres of those who Sleep:*
Sway'd by a Providence oppos'd to the Divine Lord Jesus:
A murderous Providence! A Creation that groans, living on Death.   5
Where Fish & Bird & Beast & Man & Tree & Metal & Stone
Live by Devouring, going into Eternal Death continually:
Albion is now possess'd by the War of Blood! the Sacrifice
Of envy Albion is become, and his Emanation cast out:
Come Lord Jesus, Lamb of God descend! for if; O Lord!   10

If thou hadst been here, our brother Albion had not died.
Arise sisters! Go ye & meet the Lord, while I remain—
Behold the foggy mornings of the Dead on Albion's cliffs!
Ye know that if the Emanation remains in them:
She will become an Eternal Death, an Avenger of Sin   15
A Self-righteousness: the proud Virgin-Harlot! Mother of War!
And we also & all Beulah, consume beneath Albions curse.

So Erin spoke to the Daughters of Beulah. Shuddering
With their wings they sat in the Furnace, in a night
Of stars, for all the Sons of Albion appeard distant stars,   20
Ascending and descending into Albions sea of death.
And Erins lovely Bow enclos'd the Wheels of Albions Sons.

Expanding on wing, the Daughters of Beulah replied in sweet
                                                    response

Come O thou Lamb of God and take away the remembrance of Sin
To Sin & to hide the Sin in sweet deceit.is lovely!!   25
To Sin in the open face of day is cruel & pitiless! But
To record the Sin for a reproach: to let the Sun go down
In a remembrance of the Sin: is a Woe & a Horror!
A brooder of an Evil Day, and a Sun rising in blood
Come then O Lamb of God and take away the remembrance of Sin   30

END OF CHAP: 2ᵈ

[Plate 52]

Rahab is an Eternal	TO THE DEISTS.	{The Spiritual States of
State}		the Soul are all Eternal/
		Distinguish between the
		Man, & his present State

He never can be a Friend to the Human Race who is the Preacher of
Natural Morality or Natural Religion. he is a flatterer who means to
betray. to perpetuate Tyrant Pride & the Laws of that Babylon which he
Foresees shall shortly be destroyed. with the Spiritual and not the
Natural Sword: He is in the State named Rahab: which State must be
put off before he can be the Friend of Man.

You O Deists profess yourselves the Enemies of Christianity. and
you are so: you are also the Enemies of the Human Race & of Universal

Nature. Man is born a Spectre or Satan & is altogether an Evil, & requires a New Selfhood continually & must continually be changed into his direct Contrary. But your Greek Philosophy (which is a remnant of Druidism) teaches that Man is Righteous in his Vegetated Spectre:* an Opinion of fatal & accursed consequence to Man. as the Ancients saw plainly by Revelation to the intire abrogation of Experimental Theory. and many believed what they saw, and Prophecied of Jesus.

Man must & will have Some Religion; if he has not the Religion of Jesus, he will have the Religion of Satan, & will erect the Synagogue of Satan. calling the Prince of this World, God and destroying all who do not worship Satan under the Name of God. Will any one say, Where are those who worship Satan under the Name of God! Where are they? Listen! Every Religion that Preaches Vengeance for Sin is the Religion of the Enemy & Avenger; and not of the Forgiver of Sin, and their God is Satan, Named by the Divine Name Your Religion O Deists: Deism, is the Worship of the God of this World by the means of what you call Natural Religion and Natural Philosophy, and of Natural Morality or Self-Righteousness, the Selfish Virtues of the Natural Heart. This was the Religion of the Pharisees who murderd Jesus. Deism is the same & ends in the same.

Voltaire Rousseau Gibbon Hume. charge the Spiritually Religious with Hypocrisy! but how a Monk or a Methodist either, can be a Hypocrite, I cannot concieve. We are Men of like passions with others & pretend not to be holier than others: therefore, when a Religious Man falls into Sin, he ought not to be calld a Hypocrite: this title is more properly to be given to a Player who falls into Sin; whose profession is Virtue & Morality & the making Men Self-Righteous. Foote* in calling Whitefield, Hypocrite: was himself one: for Whitefield pretended not to be holier than others: but confessed his Sins before all the World; Voltaire! Rousseau! You cannot escape my charge that you are Pharisees & Hypocrites, for you are constantly talking of the Virtues of the Human Heart, and particularly of your own, that you may accuse others, & especially the Religious, whose errors you by this display of pretended Virtue, chiefly design to expose. Rousseau thought Men Good by Nature: he found them Evil & found no friend. Friendship cannot exist without Forgiveness of Sins continually. The Book written by Rousseau calld his Confessions is an apology & cloke for his sin & not a confession.

But you also charge the poor Monks & Religious with being the causes of War: while you acquit & flatter the Alexanders & Caesars, the

Lewis's & Fredericks:* who alone are its causes & its actors. But the Religion of Jesus, Forgiveness of Sin, can never be the cause of a War nor of a single Martyrdom.

Those who Martyr others or who cause War are Deists, but never can be Forgivers of Sin. The Glory of Christianity is To Conquer by Forgiveness. All the Destruction, therefore, in Christian Europe has arisen from Deism, which is Natural Religion—

I saw a Monk of Charlemaine*
Arise before my sight
　I talkd with the Grey Monk as we stood
In beams of infernal light

Gibbon arose with a lash of steel　　　　5
And Voltaire with a wracking wheel
　The Schools in clouds of learning rolld
Arose with War in iron & gold.

Thou lazy Monk they sound afar
In vain condemning glorious War　　　　10
　And in your Cell you shall ever dwell
Rise War, & bind him in his Cell,

The blood. red ran from the Grey Monks side
His hands & feet were wounded wide
　His body bent, his arms & knees　　　　15
Like to the roots of ancient trees

When Satan first the black bow bent
And the Moral Law from the Gospel rent
　He forgd the Law into a Sword
And spilld the blood of mercys Lord.　　　20

Titus! Constantine! Charlemaine!*
O Voltaire! Rousseau! Gibbon! Vain
　Your Grecian Mocks & Roman Sword
Against this image of his Lord!

For a Tear is an Intellectual thing!　　　25
And a Sigh is the Sword of an Angel King
　And the bitter groan of a Martyrs woe
Is an Arrow from the Almighties Bow

[Plate 53]

JERUSALEM

CHAP. 3.

But Los, who is the Vehicular Form of strong Urthona
Wept vehemently over Albion where Thames currents spring
From the rivers of Beulah; pleasant river! soft, mild, parent stream
And the roots of Albions Tree enterd the Soul of Los
As he sat before his Furnaces clothed in sackcloth of hair   5
In gnawing pain dividing him from his Emanation;
Inclosing all the Children of Los time after time.
Their Giant forms condensing into Nations & Peoples & Tongues
Translucent the Furnaces, of Beryll & Emerald immortal:
And Seven-fold each within other: incomprehensible   10
To the Vegetated Mortal Eye's perverted & single vision
The Bellows are the Animal Lungs. the Hammers, the Animal Heart
The Furnaces, the Stomach for Digestion; terrible their fury
Like seven burning heavens rang'd from South to North

Here on the banks of the Thames. Los builded Golgonooza.*   15
Outside of the Gates of the Human Heart, beneath Beulah
In the midst of the rocks of the Altars of Albion. In fears
He builded it. in rage & in fury, It is the Spiritual Fourfold
London: continually building & continually decaying desolate!
In eternal labours: loud the Furnaces & loud the Anvils   20
Of Death thunder incessant around the flaming Couches of
The Twentyfour Friends of Albion and round the awful Four
For the protection of the Twelve Emanations of Albions Sons
The Mystic Union of the Emanation in the Lord; Because
Man divided from his Emanation is a dark Spectre   25
His Emanation is an ever-weeping melancholy Shadow
But she is made receptive of Generation thro' mercy
In the Potters Furnace, among the Funeral Urns of Beulah
From Surrey hills, thro' Italy and Greece. to Hinnoms vale,

[Plate 54]

In Great Eternity, every particular Form gives forth or Emanates
Its own peculiar Light & the Form is the Divine Vision
And the Light is his Garment This is Jerusalem in every Man

A Tent & Tabernacle of Mutual Forgiveness Male & Female
                                            Clothings.
And Jerusalem is called Liberty among the Children of Albion   5

But Albion fell down a Rocky fragment from Eternity hurld
By his own Spectre. who is the Reasoning Power in every Man
Into his own Chaos which is the Memory between Man & Man

The silent broodings of deadly revenge springing from the
All powerful parental affection. fills Albion from head to foot   10
Seeing his Sons assimilate with Luvah, bound in the bonds
Of spiritual Hate. from which springs Sexual Love as iron chains:
He tosses like a cloud outstretchd among Jerusalems Ruins
Which overspread all the Earth, he groans among his ruind porches

But the Spectre like a hoar frost & a Mildew rose over Albion   15
Saying, I am God O Sons of Men! I am your Rational Power!
Am I not Bacon & Newton & Locke who teach Humility to Man!
Who teach Doubt & Experiment & my two Wings, Voltaire: Rousseau.
Where is that Friend of Sinners! that Rebel against my Laws!
Who teaches Belief to the Nations, & an unknown Eternal Life   20
Come hither into the Desart & turn these stones to bread.
Vain Foolish Man! wilt thou believe without Experiment?
And build a World of Phantasy upon my Great Abyss!
A World of Shapes in craving lust & devouring appetite

So spoke the hard cold constrictive Spectre he is named Arthur*   25
Constricting into Druid Rocks round Canaan Agag &
                                            Aram & Pharoh

Then Albion drew England into his bosom in groans & tears
But she stretchd out her starry Night in Spaces against him. like
A long Serpent, in the Abyss of the Spectre which augmented
The Night with Dragon wings coverd with stars & in the Wings   30
Jerusalem & Vala appeard: & above between the Wings magnificent
The Divine Vision dimly appeard in clouds of blood weeping.

[Plate 55]

When those who disregard all Mortal Things, saw a Mighty-One
Among the Flowers of Beulah still retain his awful strength
They wonderd; checking their wild flames & Many gathering
Together into an Assembly; they said, let us go down

And see these changes! Others said, If you do so prepare   5
For being driven from our fields; what have we to do with the Dead
To be their inferiors or superiors we equally abhor;
Superior, none we know: inferior none: all equal share
Divine Benevolence & joy, for the Eternal Man
Walketh among us, calling us his Brothers & his Friends: 10
Forbidding us that Veil which Satan puts between Eve & Adam:
By which the Princes of the Dead enslave their Votaries
Teaching them to form the Serpent of precious stones & gold
To sieze the Sons of Jerusalem & plant them in One Mans Loins
To make One Family of Contraries: that Joseph may be sold   15
Into Egypt: for Negation; a Veil the Saviour born & dying rends.

But others said: Let us to him who only Is, & who
Walketh among us, give decision. bring forth all your fires!

So saying, an eternal deed was done: in fiery flames
The Universal Concave raged, such thunderous sounds as never   20
Were sounded from a mortal cloud, nor on Mount Sinai old
Nor in Havilah where the Cherub rolld his redounding flame.

Loud! loud! the Mountains lifted up their voices, loud the Forests
Rivers thunderd against their banks, loud Winds furious fought
Cities & Nations contended in fires & clouds & tempests.   25
The Seas raisd up their voices & lifted their hands on high
The Stars in their courses fought, the Sun! Moon! Heaven! Earth.
Contending for Albion & for Jerusalem his Emanation
And for Shiloh, the Emanation of France & for lovely Vala.

Then far the greatest number were about to make a Separation   30
And they Elected Seven, calld the Seven Eyes of God;
Lucifer, Molech. Elohim, Shaddai, Pahad, Jehovah, Jesus.
They namd the Eighth. he came not, he hid in Albions Forests*
But first they said: (& their Words stood in Chariots in array
Curbing their Tygers with golden bits & bridles of silver & ivory)   35

Let the Human Organs be kept in their perfect Integrity
At will Contracting into Worms, or Expanding into Gods
And then behold! what are these Ulro Visions of Chastity
Then as the moss upon the tree: or dust upon the plow:
Or as the sweat upon the labouring shoulder: or as the chaff   40
Of the wheat-floor or as the dregs of the sweet wine-press
Such are these Ulro Visions, for tho we sit down within

The plowed furrow. listning to the weeping clods till we
Contract or Expand Space at will: or if we raise ourselves
Upon the chariots of the morning. Contracting or Expanding Time!   45
Every one knows, we are One Family: One Man blessed for ever

Silence remaind & every one resumd his Human Majesty
And many conversed on these things as they labourd at the furrow
Saying: It is better to prevent misery, than to release from misery
It is better to prevent error, than to forgive the criminal: 50
Labour well the Minute Particulars, attend to the Little-ones:
And those who are in misery cannot remain so long
If we do but our duty: labour well the teeming Earth.

They Plow'd in tears, the trumpets sounded before the golden Plow
And the voices of the Living Creatures were heard in the clouds of   55
                                                    heaven
Crying; Compell the Reasoner to Demonstrate with unhewn
                                              Demonstrations
Let the Indefinite be explored. and let every Man be Judged
By his own Works, Let all Indefinites be thrown into
                                              Demonstrations
To be pounded to dust & melted in the Furnaces of Affliction:
He who would do good to another, must do it in Minute Particulars   60
General Good is the plea of the scoundrel hypocrite & flatterer:
For Art & Science cannot exist but in minutely organized Particulars
And not in generalizing Demonstrations of the Rational Power,
The Infinite alone resides in Definite & Determinate Identity
Establishment of Truth depends on destruction of Falsehood   65
                                              continually
On Circumcision: not on Virginity, O Reasoners of Albion

So cried they at the Plow. Albions Rock frowned above
And the Great Voice of Eternity rolled above terrible in clouds
Saying Who will go forth for us! & Who shall we send before our
                                              face?

[Plate 56]

Then Los heaved his thund'ring Bellows on the Valley of Middlesex
And thus he chaunted his Song: the Daughters of Albion reply.

What may Man be? who can tell! But what may Woman be?
To have power over Man from Cradle to corruptible Grave.*

He who is an Infant, and whose Cradle is a Manger   5
Knoweth the Infant sorrow: whence it came, and where it goeth:
And who weave it a Cradle of the grass that withereth away.
This World is all a Cradle for the erred wandering Phantom:
Rock'd by Year, Month, Day & Hour; and every two Moments
Between. dwells a Daughter of Beulah. to feed the Human Vegetable   10
Entune: Daughters of Albion. your hymning Chorus mildly!
Cord of affection thrilling extatic on the iron Reel:
To the golden Loom of Love! to the moth-labourd Woof
A Garment and Cradle weaving for the infantine Terror:
For fear; at entering the gate into our World of cruel   15
Lamentation: it flee back & hide in Non-Entitys dark wild
Where dwells the Spectre of Albion: destroyer of Definite Form.
The Sun shall be a Scythed Chariot of Britain: the Moon; a Ship
In the British Ocean! Created by Los's Hammer; measured out
Into Days & Nights & Years & Months, to travel with my feet   20
Over these desolate rocks of Albion: O daughters of despair;
Rock the Cradle, and in mild melodies tell me where found
What you have enwoven with so much tears & care? so much
Tender artifice: to laugh: to weep: to learn: to know;
Remember! recollect! what dark befel in wintry days   25

O it was lost for ever! and we found it not: it came
And wept at our wintry Door: Look! look! behold! Gwendolen
Is become a Clod of Clay! Merlin is a Worm of the Valley!

Then Los uttered with Hammer & Anvil: Chaunt! revoice!
I mind not your laugh: and your frown I not fear! and   30
You must my dictate obey from your gold-beam'd Looms; trill
Gentle to Albions Watchman, on Albion's mountains; reeccho,
And rock the Cradle while! Ah me! Of that Eternal Man
And of the cradled Infancy in his bowels of compassion:
Who fell beneath his instruments of husbandry & became   35
Subservient to the clods of the furrow! the cattle and even
The emmet and earth-Worm are his superiors & his lords.

Then the response came warbling from trilling Looms in Albion
We Women tremble at the light therefore! hiding fearful
The Divine Vision with Curtain & Veil & fleshly Tabernacle   40
Los utter'd, swift as the rattling thunder upon the mountains
Look back into the Church Paul! Look! Three Women around
The Cross; O Albion why didst thou a Female Will Create?

[Plate 57]

And the voices of Bath & Canterbury & York & Edinburgh. Cry
Over the Plow of Nations in the strong hand of Albion thundering
along
Among the Fires of the Druid & the deep black rethundering Waters
Of the Atlantic which poured in impetuous loud, loud. louder &
louder.
And the Great Voice of the Atlantic howled over the Druid Altars: 5
Weeping over his Children in Stone-henge in Malden & Colchester.
Round the Rocky Peak of Derbyshire London Stone & Rosamonds
Bower*

What is a Wife & what is a Harlot? What is a Church & What
Is a Theatre? are they Two & not One? can they Exist Separate?
Are not Religion & Politics the Same Thing? Brotherhood is Religion   10
O Demonstrations of Reason Dividing Families in Cruelty & Pride!

But Albion fled from the Divine Vision. with the Plow of Nations
enflaming,
The Living Creatures madden and Albion fell into the Furrow, and
The Plow went over him & the Living was Plowed in among the Dead
But his Spectre rose over the starry Plow. Albion fled beneath the   15
Plow
Till he came to the Rock of Ages. & he took his Seat upon the Rock.

Wonder siezd all in Eternity! to behold the Divine Vision. open
The Center into an Expanse, & the Center rolled out into an Expanse.

[Plate 58]

In beauty the Daughters of Albion divide & unite at will
Naked & drunk with blood Gwendolen dancing to the timbrel
Of War: reeling up the Street of London she divides in twain
Among the Inhabitants of Albion. the People fall around.
The Daughters of Albion. divide & unite in jealousy & cruelty.   5
The Inhabitants of Albion at the Harvest & the Vintage
Feel their Brain cut round beneath the temples shrieking
Bonifying into a Scull, the Marrow exuding in dismal pain
They flee over the rocks bonifying: Horses; Oxen: feel the knife.
And while the Sons of Albion by severe War & Judgment, bonify   10
The Hermaphroditic Condensations are divided by the Knife
The obdurate Forms are cut asunder by Jealousy & Pity.

Rational Philosophy and Mathematic Demonstration
Is divided in the intoxications of pleasure & affection
Two Contraries War against each other in fury & blood,   15
And Los fixes them on his Anvil, incessant his blows:
He fixes them with strong blows, placing the stones & timbers.
To Create a World of Generation from the World of Death:
Dividing the Masculine & Feminine: for the comingling
Of Albions & Luvahs Spectres was Hermaphroditic*   20

Urizen wrathful strode above directing the awful Building:
As a Mighty Temple; delivering Form out of confusion.
Jordan sprang beneath its threshold bubbling from beneath
Its pillars: Euphrates ran under its arches: white sails
And silver oars reflect on its pillars, & sound on its echoing   25
Pavements: where walk the Sons of Jerusalem who remain
                                        Ungenerate
But the revolving Sun and Moon pass thro its porticoes,
Day & night, in sublime majesty & silence they revolve
And shine glorious within! Hand & Koban archd over the Sun
In the hot noon. as he traveld thro his journey; Hyle &   30
                                        Skofield
Archd over the Moon at midnight & Los Fix'd them there,
With his thunderous Hammer; terrified the Spectres rage & flee
Canaan is his portico; Jordan is a fountain in his porch;
A fountain of milk & wine to relieve the traveler:
Egypt is the eight steps within. Ethiopia supports his pillars.   35
Lybia & the Lands unknown. are the ascent without;
Within is Asia & Greece, ornamented with exquisite art:
Persia & Media are his halls: his inmost hall is Great Tartary.
China & India & Siberia are his temples for entertainment
Poland & Russia & Sweden. his soft retired chambers   40
France & Spain & Italy & Denmark & Holland & Germany
Are the temples among his pillars. Britain is Los's Forge;
America North & South are his baths of living waters.

Such is the Ancient World of Urizen in the Satanic Void
Created from the Valley of Middlesex by Londons River   45
From Stone-henge and from London Stone, from Cornwall to
                                        Cathnes
The Four Zoa's rush around on all sides in dire ruin
Furious in pride of Selfhood the terrible Spectres of Albion
Rear their dark Rocks among the Stars of God: stupendous

Works! A World of Generation continually Creating out of   50
The Hermaphroditic Satanic World of rocky destiny,

[Plate 59]

And formed into Four precious stones. for enterance from Beulah

For the Veil of Vala which Albion cast into the Atlantic Deep
To catch the Souls of the Dead: began to Vegetate & Petrify
Around the Earth of Albion among the Roots of his Tree
This Los formed into the Gates & mighty Wall, between the Oak   5
Of Weeping & the Palm of Suffering beneath Albions Tomb.
Thus in process of time it became the beautiful Mundane Shell.*
The Habitation of the Spectres of the Dead, & the Place
Of Redemption & of awaking again into Eternity

For Four Universes round the Mundane Egg remain Chaotic   10
One to the North: Urthona: One to the South: Urizen;
One to the East: Luvah: One to the West, Tharmas;
They are the Four Zoas that stood around the Throne Divine
Verulam: London: York & Edinburgh: their English names
But when Luvah assumed the World of Urizen Southward   15
And Albion was slain upon his Mountains & in his Tent.
All fell towards the Center, sinking downwards in dire ruin,
In the South remains a burning Fire: in the East. a Void
In the West, a World of raging Waters: in the North:
                    solid Darkness
Unfathomable without end: but in the midst of these   20
Is Built eternally the sublime Universe of Los & Enitharmon

And in the North Gate, in the West of the North. toward Beulah
Cathedrons Looms are builded. and Los's Furnaces in the South
A wondrous golden Building immense with ornaments sublime
Is bright Cathedrons golden Hall, its Courts, Towers &   25
                    Pinnacles

And one Daughter of Los sat at the fiery Reel & another
Sat at the shining Loom with her Sisters attending round
Terrible their distress, & their sorrow cannot be utterd
And another Daughter of Los sat at the Spinning Wheel
Endless their labour, with bitter food. void of sleep,   30
Tho hungry they labour: they rouze themselves anxious
Hour after hour labouring at the whirling Wheel

Many Wheels & as many lovely Daughters sit weeping
Yet the intoxicating delight that they take in their work
Obliterates every other evil; none pities their tears   35
Yet they regard not pity & they expect no one to pity
For they labour for life & love, regardless of any one
But the poor Spectres that they work for, always incessantly

They are mockd by every one that passes by. they regard not
They labour; & when their Wheels are broken by scorn & malice   40
They mend them sorrowing with many tears & afflictions.
Other Daughters Weave on the Cushion & Pillow, Network fine
That Rahab & Tirzah may exist & live & breathe & love
Ah, that it could be as the Daughters of Beulah wish!

Other Daughters of Los, labouring at Looms less fine   45
Create the Silk-worm & the Spider & the Catterpiller
To assist in their most grievous work of pity & compassion
And others Create the wooly Lamb & the downy Fowl
To assist in the work: the Lamb bleats: the Sea-fowl cries
Men understand not the distress & the labour & sorrow   50
That in the Interior Worlds is carried on in fear & trembling
Weaving the shuddring fears & loves of Albions Families
Thunderous rage the Spindles of iron. & the iron Distaff
Maddens in the fury of their hands, Weaving in bitter tears
The Veil of Goats-hair & Purple & Scarlet & fine twined Linen   55

[Plate 60]

The clouds of Albions Druid Temples rage in the eastern heaven
While Los sat terrified beholding Albions Spectre who is Luvah*
Spreading in bloody veins in torments over Europe & Asia;
Not yet formed but a wretched torment unformed & abyssal
In flaming fire; within the Furnaces the Divine Vision appeard   5
On Albions hills: often walking from the Furnaces in clouds
And flames among the Druid Temples & the Starry Wheels
Gatherd Jerusalems Children in his arms & bore them like
A Shepherd in the night of Albion which overspread all the Earth

I gave thee liberty and life O lovely Jerusalem   10
And thou hast bound me down upon the Stems of Vegetation
I gave thee Sheep-walks upon the Spanish Mountains Jerusalem
I gave thee Priams City and the Isles of Grecia lovely!

I gave thee Hand & Scofield & the Counties of Albion:
They spread forth like a lovely root into the Garden of God: 15
They were as Adam before me: united into One Man,
They stood in innocence & their skiey tent reachd over Asia
To Nimrods Tower to Ham & Canaan walking with Mizraim
Upon the Egyptian Nile, with solemn songs to Grecia
And sweet Hesperia even to Great Chaldea & Tesshina   20
Following thee as a Shepherd by the Four Rivers of Eden
Why wilt thou rend thyself apart, Jerusalem?
And build this Babylon & sacrifice in secret Groves,
Among the Gods of Asia: among the fountains of pitch & nitre
Therefore thy Mountains are become barren Jerusalem!   25
Thy Valleys, Plains of burning sand. thy Rivers: waters of death
Thy Villages die of the Famine and thy Cities
Beg bread from house to house, lovely Jerusalem
Why wilt thou deface thy beauty & the beauty of thy little-ones
To please thy Idols, in the pretended chastities of Uncircumcision   30
Thy Sons are lovelier than Egypt or Assyria; wherefore
Dost thou blacken their beauty by a Secluded place of rest.
And a peculiar Tabernacle. to cut the integuments of beauty
Into veils of tears and sorrows O lovely Jerusalem!
They have perswaded thee to this, therefore their end shall come   35
And I will lead thee thro the Wilderness in shadow of my cloud
And in my love I will lead thee, lovely Shadow of Sleeping Albion,

This is the Song of the Lamb, sung by Slaves in evening time.

But Jerusalem faintly saw him, closd in the Dungeons of Babylon
Her Form was held by Beulahs Daughters. but all within unseen   40
She sat at the Mills, her hair unbound, her feet naked
Cut with the flints: her tears run down, her reason grows like
The Wheel of Hand, incessant turning day & night without rest
Insane she raves upon the winds hoarse, inarticulate:
All night Vala hears. she triumphs in pride of holiness   45
To see Jerusalem deface her lineaments with bitter blows
Of despair. while the Satanic Holiness triumphd in Vala
In a Religion of Chastity & Uncircumcised Selfishness
Both of the Head & Heart & Loins. clos'd up in Moral Pride.

But the Divine Lamb stood beside Jerusalem. oft she saw   50
The lineaments Divine & oft the Voice heard, & oft she said:

O Lord & Saviour, have the Gods of the Heathen pierced thee?
Or hast thou been pierced in the House of thy Friends?
Art thou alive! & livest thou for evermore? or art thou
Not: but a delusive shadow, a thought that liveth not.   55
Babel mocks saying, there is no God nor Son of God
That thou O Human Imagination. O Divine Body art all
A delusion. but I know thee O Lord when thou arisest upon
My weary eyes even in this dungeon & this iron mill.
The Stars of Albion cruel rise: thou bindest to sweet influences: 60
For thou also sufferest with me altho I behold thee not;
And altho I sin & blaspheme thy holy name. thou pitiest me;
Because thou knowest I am deluded by the turning mills.
And by these visions of pity & love because of Albions death.

Thus spake Jerusalem, & thus the Divine Voice replied.   65

Mild Shade of Man. pitiest thou these Visions of terror & woe!
Give forth thy pity & love. fear not! lo I am with thee always.
Only believe in me that I have power to raise from death
Thy Brother who Sleepeth in Albion: fear not trembling Shade

[Plate 61]

Behold: in the Visions of Elohim Jehovah, behold Joseph & Mary
And be comforted O Jerusalem in the Visions of Jehovah Elohim

She looked & saw Joseph the Carpenter in Nazareth & Mary
His espoused Wife. And Mary said, If thou put me away from thee
Dost thou not murder me? Joseph spoke in anger & fury. Should I   5
Marry a Harlot & an Adulteress? Mary answerd, Art thou more
                                                               pure*
Than thy Maker who forgiveth Sins & calls again Her that is Lost
Tho She hates. he calls her again in love. I love my dear Joseph
But he driveth me away from his presence. yet I hear the voice
                                                           of God
In the voice of my Husband. tho he is angry for a moment, he   10
                                                        will not
Utterly cast me away. if I were pure, never could I taste the sweets
Of the Forgivess of Sins! if I were holy! I never could behold the
                                                             tears
Of love! of him who loves me in the midst of his anger in furnace of
                                                              fire.

Ah my Mary: said Joseph: weeping over & embracing her closely in.
His arms: Doth he forgive Jerusalem & not exact Purity from   15
           her who is
Polluted. I heard his voice in my sleep & his Angel in my dream:
Saying, Doth Jehovah Forgive a Debt only on condition that it shall
Be Payed? Doth he Forgive Pollution only on conditions of Purity
That Debt is not Forgiven! That Pollution is not Forgiven
Such is the Forgiveness of the Gods, the Moral Virtues of the   20
Heathen, whose tender Mercies are Cruelty. But Jehovahs
           Salvation
Is without Money & without Price, in the Continual Forgiveness of
           Sins
In the Perpetual Mutual Sacrifice in Great Eternity! for behold!
There is none that liveth & Sinneth not! And this is the Covenant
Of Jehovah: If you Forgive one-another, so shall Jehovah Forgive   25
           You:
That He Himself may Dwell among You. Fear not then to take
To thee Mary thy Wife, for she is with Child by the Holy Ghost

Then Mary burst forth into a Song! she flowed like a River of
Many Streams in the arms of Joseph & gave forth her tears of joy
Like many waters, and Emanating into gardens & palaces upon   30
Euphrates & to forests & floods & animals wild & tame from
Gihon to Hiddekel. & to corn fields & villages & inhabitants
Upon Pison & Arnon & Jordan. And I heard the voice among
The Reapers Saying, Am I Jerusalem the lost Adulteress? or am I
Babylon come up to Jerusalem? And another voice answerd Saying   35
Does the voice of my Lord call me again? am I pure thro his Mercy
And Pity. Am I become lovely as a Virgin in his sight, who am
Indeed a Harlot drunken with the Sacrifice of Idols does he
Call her pure as he did in the days of her Infancy when She
Was cast out to the loathing of her person. The Chaldean took   40
Me from my Cradle. The Amalekite stole me away upon his Camels
Before I had ever beheld with love the Face of Jehovah; or known
That there was a God of Mercy: O Mercy O Divine Humanity!
O Forgiveness & Pity & Compassion! If I were Pure I should never
Have known Thee; If I were Unpolluted I should never have   45
Glorified thy Holiness, or rejoiced in thy great Salvation.

Mary leaned her side against Jerusalem, Jerusalem received
The Infant into her hands in the Visions of Jehovah. Times passed on

Jerusalem fainted over the Cross & Sepulcher She heard the
voice

Wilt thou make Rome thy Patriarch Druid & the Kings of   50
Europe his

Horsemen? Man in the Resurrection changes his Sexual
Garments at will

Every Harlot was once a Virgin: every Criminal an Infant Love:

[Plate 62]

Repose on me till the morning of the Grave. I am thy life.

Jerusalem replied. I am an outcast: Albion is dead:
I am left to the trampling foot & the spurning heel!
A Harlot I am calld. I am sold from street to street!
I am defaced with blows & with the dirt of the Prison!   5
And wilt thou become my Husband O my Lord & Saviour?
Shall Vala bring thee forth! shall the Chaste be ashamed also?
I see the Maternal Line, I behold the Seed of the Woman!
Cainah & Ada & Zillah & Naamah Wife of Noah.
Shuahs daughter & Tamar & Rahab the Canaanites: 10
Ruth the Moabite, & Bathsheba of the daughters of Heth
Naamah the Ammonite, Zibeah the Philistine. & Mary
These are the Daughters of Vala, Mother of the Body of death
But I thy Magdalen behold thy Spiritual Risen Body*
Shall Albion arise? I know he shall arise at the Last Day!   15
I know that in my flesh I shall see God: but Emanations
Are weak. they know not whence they are, nor whither tend.

Jesus replied. I am the Resurrection & the Life.*
I Die & pass the limits of possibility, as it appears
To individual perception. Luvah must be Created   20
And Vala; for I cannot leave them in the gnawing Grave.
But will prepare a way for my banished-ones to return
Come now with me into the villages. walk thro all the cities.
Tho thou art taken to prison & judgment, starved in the streets
I will command the cloud to give thee food & the hard rock   25
To flow with milk & wine, tho thou seest me not a season
Even a long season & a hard journey & a howling wilderness:
Tho' Valas cloud hide thee & Luvahs fires follow thee!
Only believe & trust in me, Lo. I am always with thee;

So spoke the Lamb of God while Luvahs Cloud reddening above   30
Burst forth in streams of blood upon the heavens & dark night
Involvd Jerusalem. & the Wheels of Albions Sons turnd hoarse
Over the Mountains & the fires blaz'd on Druid Altars
And the Sun set in Tyburns Brook where Victims howl & cry.

But Los beheld the Divine Vision among the flames of the Furnaces   35
Therefore he lived & breathed in hope. but his tears fell incessant
Because his Children were closd from him apart: & Enitharmon
Dividing in fierce pain: also the Vision of God was closd in clouds
Of Albions Spectres, that Los in despair oft sat & often ponderd
On Death Eternal, in fierce shudders upon the mountains of Albion   40
Walking: & in the vales in howlings fierce, then to his Anvils
Turning, anew began his labours, tho in terrible pains!

[Plate 63]

Jehovah stood among the Druids in the Valley of Annandale*
When the Four Zoas of Albion. the Four Living Creatures, the
                                    Cherubim
Of Albion tremble before the Spectre, in the starry Harness of
                                      the Plow
Of Nations. And their Names are Urizen & Luvah & Tharmas &
                                      Urthona

Luvah slew Tharmas, the Angel of the Tongue & Albion brought   5
                                      him
To Justice in his own City of Paris, denying the Resurrection*
Then Vala the Wife of Albion, who is the Daughter of Luvah
Took vengeance Twelve-fold among the Chaotic Rocks of the
                                      Druids
Where the Human Victims howl to the Moon & Thor & Friga
Dance the dance of death contending with Jehovah among the   10
                                      Cherubim.
The Chariot Wheels filled with Eyes rage along the howling Valley
In the Dividing of Reuben & Benjamin bleeding from Chesters
                                      River

The Giants & the Witches & the Ghosts of Albion dance with
Thor & Friga, & the Fairies lead the Moon along the Valley of
                                      Cherubim
Bleeding in torrents from Mountain to Mountain. a lovely Victim   15

And Jehovah stood in the Gates of the Victim. & he appeared
A weeping Infant in the Gates of Birth in the midst of Heaven
The Cities & Villages of Albion became Rock & Sand Unhumanized
The Druid Sons of Albion & the Heavens a Void around
                                        unfathomable
No Human Form but Sexual & a little weeping Infant pale   20
                                        reflected
Multitudinous in the Looking Glass of Enitharmon, on all sides
Around in the clouds of the Female. on Albions Cliffs of the Dead

Such the appearance in Cheviot: in the Divisions of Reuben

When the Cherubim hid their heads under their wings in deep
                                        slumbers
When the Druids demanded Chastity from Woman & all was lost.   25

How can the Female be Chaste O thou stupid Druid Cried Los
Without the Forgiveness of Sins in the merciful clouds of Jehovah
And without the Baptism of Repentance to wash away Calumnies. and
The Accusations of Sin that each may be Pure in their Neighbours
                                        sight
O when shall Jehovah give us Victims from his Flocks & Herds   30
Instead of Human Victims by the Daughters of Albion & Canaan

Then laugh'd Gwendolen & her laughter shook the Nations &
                                        Familys of
The Dead beneath Beulah from Tyburn to Golgotha. and from
Ireland to Japan. furious her Lions & Tygers & Wolves sport before
Los on the Thames & Medway. London & Canterbury groan   35
                                        in pain

Los knew not yet what was done: he thought it was all in Vision
In Visions of the Dreams of Beulah among the Daughters of
                                        Albion
Therefore the Murder was put apart in the Looking-Glass of
                                        Enitharmon

He saw in Vala's hand the Druid Knife of Revenge & the Poison Cup
Of Jealousy, and thought it a Poetic Vision of the Atmospheres   40
Till Canaan rolld apart from Albion across the Rhine: along the
                                        Danube
And all the Land of Canaan suspended over the Valley of Cheviot
From Bashan to Tyre & from Troy to Gaza of the Amalekite
And Reuben fled with his head downwards among the Caverns

[Plate 64]

Of the Mundane Shell which froze on all sides round Canaan on
The vast Expanse: where the Daughters of Albion Weave the Web
Of Ages & Generations. folding & unfolding it like a Veil of
                                                    Cherubim
And sometimes it touches the Earths summits & sometimes
                                                    spreads
Abroad into the Indefinite Spectre, who is the Rational Power.   5

Then All the Daughters of Albion became One before Los:
                                    even Vala!
And she put forth her hand upon the Looms in dreadful howlings
Till she vegetated into a hungry Stomach & a devouring Tongue.
Her Hand is a Court of Justice, her Feet: two Armies in Battle
Storms & Pestilence: in her Locks: & in her Loins Earthquake.   10
And Fire. & the Ruin of Cities & Nations & Families & Tongues

She cries: The Human is but a Worm, & thou O Male: Thou art
Thyself Female, a Male: a breeder of Seed: a Son & Husband: & Lo.
The Human Divine is Womans Shadow, a Vapor in the summers
                                                    heat
Go assume Papal dignity thou Spectre, thou Male Harlot! Arthur*   15
Divide into the Kings of Europe in times remote O Woman-born
And Woman-nourishd & Woman-educated & Woman-scorn'd!

Wherefore art thou living? said Los. & Man cannot live in thy
                                                    presence
Art thou Vala the Wife of Albion O thou lovely Daughter of Luvah
All Quarrels arise from Reasoning. the secret Murder, and   20
The violent Man-slaughter. these are the Spectres double Cave
The Sexual Death living on accusation of Sin & Judgment
To freeze Love & Innocence into the gold & silver of the Merchant
Without Forgiveness of Sin Love is Itself Eternal Death

Then the Spectre drew Vala into his bosom magnificent terrific   25
Glittering with precious stones & gold. with Garments of blood
                                                    & fire
He wept in deadly wrath of the Spectre, in self-contradicting agony
Crimson with Wrath & green with Jealousy dazling with Love
And Jealousy immingled & the purple of the violet darkend deep
Over the Plow of Nations thundring in the hand of Albions   30
                                    Spectre

A dark Hermaphrodite they stood frowning upon Londons River
And the Distaff & Spindle in the hands of Vala with the Flax of
Human Miseries turnd fierce with the Lives of Men along the Valley
As Reuben fled before the Daughters of Albion Taxing the Nations*

Derby Peak yawnd a horrid Chasm at the Cries of Gwendolen. & at   35
The stamping feet of Ragan upon the flaming Treddles of her Loom
That drop with crimson gore with the Loves of Albion & Canaan
Opening along the Valley of Rephaim, weaving over the Caves of
                                                              Machpelah*

[Plate 65]

To decide Two Worlds with a great decision: a World of Mercy. and
A World of Justice: the World of Mercy for Salvation
To cast Luvah into the Wrath, and Albion into the Pity
In the Two Contraries of Humanity & in the Four Regions.

For in the depths of Albions bosom in the eastern heaven,*   5
They sound the clarions strong! they chain the howling Captives!
They cast the lots into the helmet: they give the oath of blood in
                                                              Lambeth
They vote the death of Luvah, & they naild him to Albions Tree in
                                                              Bath!
They staind him with poisonous blue, they inwove him in cruel roots
To die a death of Six thousand years bound round with vegetation   10
The sun was black & the moon rolld a useless globe thro Britain!

Then left the Sons of Urizen the plow & harrow, the loom
The hammer & the chisel, & the rule & compasses; from London
                                                              fleeing
They forg'd the sword on Cheviot, the chariot of war & the battle-ax,
The trumpet fitted to mortal battle. & the flute of summer in   15
                                                              Annandale
And all the Arts of Life. they changd into the Arts of Death in
                                                              Albion.
The hour-glass contemnd because its simple workmanship.
Was like the workmanship of the plowman. & the water wheel.
That raises water into cisterns. broken & burnd with fire:
Because its workmanship. was like the workmanship of the shepherd.   20
And in their stead. intricate wheels invented. wheel without wheel:
To perplex youth in their outgoings, & to bind to labours in Albion

Of day & night the myriads of eternity that they may grind
And polish brass & iron hour after hour laborious task!*
Kept ignorant of its use, that they might spend the days of wisdom   25
In sorrowful drudgery, to obtain a scanty pittance of bread:
In ignorance to view a small portion & think that All,
And call it Demonstration: blind to all the simple rules of life.

Now: now the battle rages round thy tender limbs O Vala.
Now smile among thy bitter tears: now put on all thy beauty   30
Is not the wound of the sword sweet! & the broken bone delightful?
Wilt thou now smile among the scythes when the wounded groan in
                                                        The field?
We were carried away in thousands from London; & in tens*
Of thousands from Westminster & Marybone in ships closd up:
Chaind hand & foot, compelld to fight under the iron whips   35
Of our captains; fearing our officers more than the enemy.
Lift up thy blue eyes Vala & put on thy sapphire shoes:
O melancholy Magdalen behold the morning over Malden break;
Gird on thy flaming zone, descend into the sepulcher of Canterbury.
Scatter the blood from thy golden brow. the tears from thy silver locks: 40
Shake off the waters from thy wings! & the dust from thy white
                                                        garments
Remember all thy feigned terrors on the secret couch of Lambeths
                                                        Vale
When the sun rose in glowing morn. with arms of mighty hosts
Marching to battle who was wont to rise with Urizens harps
Girt as a sower with his seed to scatter life abroad over Albion: 45
Arise O Vala!, bring the bow of Urizen: bring the swift arrows
                                                        of light.
How rag'd the golden horses of Urizen, compelld to the chariot of
                                                        love!
Compelld to leave the plow to the ox, to snuff up the winds of
                                                        desolation
To trample the corn fields in boastful neighings: this is no gentle
                                                        harp
This is no warbling brook, nor shadow of a mirtle tree: 50
But blood and wounds and dismal cries, and shadows of the oak:
And hearts laid open to the light, by the broad grizly sword:
And bowels hid in hammerd steel rip'd quivering on the ground.
Call forth thy smiles of soft deceit: call forth thy cloudy tears:
We hear thy sighs in trumpets shrill when morn shall blood renew.   55

So sang the Spectre Sons of Albion round Luvahs Stone of Trial:
Mocking and deriding at the writhings of their Victim on
                                                    Salisbury:
Drinking his Emanation in intoxicating bliss rejoicing in Giant
                                                    dance;
For a Spectre has no Emanation but what he imbibes from
                                                    decieving
A Victim! Then he becomes her Priest & she his Tabernacle.   60
And his Oak Grove, till the Victim rend the woven Veil.
In the end of his sleep when Jesus calls him from his grave

Howling the Victims on the Druid Altars yield their souls
To the stern Warriors: lovely sport the Daughters round their
                                                    Victims;
Drinking their lives in sweet intoxication. hence arose from Bath   65
Soft deluding odours, in spiral volutions intricately winding
Over Albions mountains. a feminine indefinite cruel delusion.
Astonishd: terrified & in pain & torment. Sudden they behold
Their own Parent the Emanation of their murderd Enemy
Become their Emanation and their Temple and Tabernacle   70
They knew not. this Vala was their beloved Mother Vala Albions
                                                    Wife.

Terrified at the sight of the Victim: at his distorted sinews!
The tremblings of Vala vibrate thro' the limbs of Albions Sons:
While they rejoice over Luvah in mockery & bitter scorn:
Sudden they become like what they behold in howlings & deadly   75
                                                    pain
Spasms smite their features, sinews & limbs: pale they look on one
                                                    another.
They turn, contorted: their iron necks bend unwilling towards
Luvah: their lips tremble: their muscular fibres are crampd &
                                                    smitten
They become like what they behold! Yet immense in strength &
                                                    power,

[Plate 66]

In awful pomp & gold, in all the precious unhewn stones of Eden
They build a stupendous Building on the Plain of Salisbury; with
                                                    Chains*

Of rocks round London Stone: of Reasonings: of unhewn
                                        Demonstrations
In labyrinthine arches. (Mighty Urizen the Architect.) thro' which
The Heavens might revolve & Eternity be bound in their chain.   5
Labour unparallell'd! a wondrous rocky World of cruel destiny
Rocks piled on rocks reaching the stars: stretching from
                                        pole to pole.
The Building is Natural Religion & its Altars Natural Morality
A building of eternal death: whose proportions are eternal despair
Here Vala stood turning the iron Spindle of destruction   10
From heaven to earth: howling! invisible! but not invisible
Her Two Covering Cherubs afterwards named Voltaire &
                                        Rousseau:
Two frowning Rocks: on each side of the Cove & Stone of
                                        Torture:*
Frozen Sons of the feminine Tabernacle of Bacon, Newton &
                                        Locke.
For Luvah is France: the Victim of the Spectres of Albion.   15

Los beheld in terror: he pour'd his loud storms on the Furnaces:
The Daughters of Albion clothed in garments of needle work
Strip them off from their shoulders and bosoms, they lay aside
Their garments; they sit naked upon the Stone of trial.
The Knife of flint passes over the howling Victim: his blood   20
Gushes & stains the fair side of the fair Daugters of Albion.
They put aside his curls; they divide his seven locks upon
His forehead: they bind his forehead with thorns of iron
They put into his hand a reed, they mock, Saying: Behold
The King of Canaan whose are seven hundred chariots of iron!   25
They take off his vesture whole with their Knives of flint:
But they cut asunder his inner garments: searching with
Their cruel fingers for his heart, & there they enter in pomp.
In many tears; & there they erect a temple & an altar;
They pour cold water on his brain in front, to cause.   30
Lids to grow over his eyes in veils of tears: and caverns
To freeze over his nostrils. while they feed his tongue from cups
And dishes of painted clay. Glowing with beauty & cruelty:
They obscure the sun & the moon; no eye can look upon them.

Ah! alas! at the sight of the Victim. & at sight of those who are   35
                                        smitten,
All who see. become what they behold. their eyes are coverd

With veils of tears and their nostrils & tongues shrunk up
Their ear bent outwards. as their Victim, so are they, in the pangs
Of unconquerable fear! amidst delights of revenge Earth-shaking!
And as their eye & ear shrunk, the heavens shrunk away   40
The Divine Vision became First a burning flame. then a column
Of fire, then an awful fiery wheel surrounding earth & heaven:
And then a globe of blood wandering distant in an unknown night:
Afar into the unknown night the mountains fled away:
Six months of mortality; a summer: & six months of mortality; a   45
                                                    winter:*

The Human form began to be alterd by the Daughters of Albion
And the perceptions to be dissipated into the Indefinite.
                                                    Becoming
A mighty Polypus nam'd Albion's Tree: they tie the Veins
And Nerves into two knots: & the Seed into a double knot:
They look forth: the Sun is shrunk; the Heavens are shrunk   50
Away into the far remote: and the Trees & Mountains witherd
Into indefinite cloudy shadows in darkness & separation.
By Invisible Hatreds adjoind, they seem remote and separate
From each other; and yet are a Mighty Polypus in the Deep!
As the Mistletoe grows on the Oak, so Albions Tree on Eternity;   55
                                                    Lo!

He who will not comingle in Love must be adjoind by Hate

They look forth from Stone-henge! from the Cove round London
                                                    Stone

They look on one another: the mountain calls out to the mountain:
Plinlimmon shrunk away: Snowdon trembled: the mountains
Of Wales & Scotland beheld the descending War: the routed flying: 60
Red run the streams of Albion: Thames is drunk with blood:
As Gwendolen cast the shuttle of war: as Cambel returnd the beam.
The Humber & the Severn: are drunk with the blood of the slain:
London feels his brain cut round: Edinburghs heart is
                                            circumscribed!
York & Lincoln hide among the flocks, because of the griding   65
                                                    Knife.

Worcester & Hereford: Oxford & Cambridge reel & stagger,
Overwearied with howling: Wales & Scotland alone sustain the fight!
The inhabitants are sick to death: they labour to divide into Days
And Nights, the uncertain Periods: and into Weeks & Months.
                                                    In vain

They send the Dove & Raven: & in vain the Serpent over the   70
                                        mountains.
And in vain the Eagle & Lion over the four-fold wilderness.
They return not; but generate in rocky places desolate.
They return not; but build a habitation separate from Man.
The Sun forgets his course like a drunken man; he hesitates,
Upon the Cheselden hills, thinking to sleep on the Severn*   75
In vain: he is hurried afar into an unknown Night
He bleeds in torrents of blood as he rolls thro heaven above
He chokes up the paths of the sky; the Moon is leprous as snow!
Trembling & descending down seeking to rest upon high Mona:
Scattering her leprous snows in flakes of disease over Albion.   80
The Stars flee remote: the heaven is iron, the earth is sulphur,
And all the mountains & hills shrink up like a withering gourd,
As the Senses of Men shrink together under the Knife of flint.
In the hands of Albions Daughters among the Druid Temples.

[Plate 67]

By those who drink their blood & the blood of their Covenant

And the Twelve Daughters of Albion united in Rahab & Tirzah
A Double Female: and they drew out from the Rocky Stones
Fibres of Life to Weave, for every Female is a Golden Loom
The Rocks are opake hardnesses covering all Vegetated things.   5
And as they Wove & Cut from the Looms, in various divisions
Stretching over Europe & Asia from Ireland to Japan
They divided into many lovely Daughters to be counterparts
To those they Wove, for when they Wove a Male, they divided
Into a Female to the Woven Male, in opake hardness   10
They cut the Fibres from the Rocks groaning in pain they Weave;
Calling the Rocks Atomic Origins of Existence: denying Eternity
By the Atheistical Epicurean Philosophy of Albions Tree
Such are the Feminine & Masculine when separated from Man
They call the Rocks Parents of Men. & adore the frowning Chaos   15
Dancing around in howling pain clothed in the bloody Veil.
Hiding Albions Sons within the Veil, closing Jerusalems
Sons without; to feed with their Souls the Spectres of Albion
Ashamed to give Love openly to the piteous & merciful Man
Counting him an imbecile mockery: but the Warrior   20
They adore: & his revenge cherish with the blood of the Innocent

They drink up Dan & Gad, to feed with milk Skofeld & Kotope
They strip off Josephs Coat & dip it in the blood of battle*

Tirzah sits weeping to hear the shrieks of the dying: her Knife
Of flint is in her hand: she passes it over the howling Victim   25
The Daughters Weave their Work in loud cries over the Rock
Of Horeb; still eyeing Albions Cliffs eagerly siezing & twisting
The threads of Vala & Jerusalem running from mountain to
                                                        mountain
Over the whole Earth: loud the Warriors rage in Beth Peor
Beneath the iron whips of their Captains & consecrated   30
                                                        banners
Loud the Sun & Moon rage in the conflict: loud the Stars
Shout in the night of battle & their spears grow to their hands
With blood weaving the deaths of the Mighty into a Tabernacle
For Rahab & Tirzah; till the Great Polypus of Generation covered
                                                        the Earth

In Verulam the Polypus's Head, winding around his bulk   35
Thro Rochester and Chichester, & Exeter & Salisbury,
To Bristol: & his Heart beat strong on Salisbury Plain
Shooting out Fibres round the Earth, thro Gaul & Italy
And Greece & along the Sea of Rephaim into Judea
To Sodom & Gomorrha: thence to India, China & Japan   40
The Twelve Daughters in Rahab & Tirzah have circumscribd
                                                        the Brain
Beneath & pierced it thro the midst with a golden pin.
Blood hath staind her fair side beneath her bosom.

O thou poor Human Form! said she. O thou poor child of woe!
Why wilt thou wander away from Tirzah: why me compel to bind   45
                                                        thee
If thou dost go away from me I shall consume upon these Rocks
These fibres of thine eyes that used to beam in distant heavens
Away from me: I have bound down with a hot iron.
These nostrils that expanded with delight in morning skies
I have bent downward with lead melted in my roaring furnaces   50
Of affliction; of love: of sweet despair: of torment unendurable
My soul is seven furnaces. incessant roars the bellows
Upon my terribly flaming heart, the molten metal runs
In channels thro my fiery limbs: O love! O pity! O fear!
O pain! O the pangs. the bitter pangs of love forsaken   55

Ephraim was a wilderness of joy where all my wild beasts ran
The River Kanah wander'd by my sweet Manassehs side
To see the boy spring into heavens sounding from my sight!
Go Noah fetch the girdle of strong brass, heat it red-hot:
Press it around the loins of this ever expanding cruelty   60
Shriek not so my only love; I refuse thy joys: I drink
Thy shrieks because Hand & Hyle are cruel & obdurate to me

[Plate 68]

O Skofield why art thou cruel? Lo Joseph is thine! to make
You One: to weave you both in the same mantle of skin
Bind him down Sisters, bind him down on Ebal. Mount of cursing:
Malah, come forth from Lebanon: & Hoglah from Mount Sinai:
Come, circumscribe this tongue of sweets, & with a screw of iron   5
Fasten this ear into the rock: Milcah, the task is thine
Weep not so, Sisters: weep not so! our life depends on this
Or mercy & truth are fled away from Shechem & Mount Gilead
Unless my beloved is bound upon the Stems of Vegetation

And thus the Warriors cry. in the hot day of Victory, in Songs.   10

Look: the beautiful Daughter of Albion sits naked upon the Stone
Her panting Victim beside her: her heart is drunk with blood
Tho her brain is not drunk with wine: she goes forth from Albion
In pride of beauty: in cruelty of holiness: in the brightness
Of her tabernacle. & her ark & secret place. the beautiful Daughter   15
Of Albion. delights the eyes of the Kings, their hearts & the
Hearts of their Warriors glow hot before Thor & Friga. O Molech!
O Chemosh! O Bacchus! O Venus! O Double God of Generation
The Heavens are cut like a mantle around from the Cliffs of Albion
Across Europe; across Africa; in howlings & deadly War   20
A sheet & veil & curtain of blood is let down from Heaven
Across the hills of Ephraim & down Mount Olivet to
The Valley of the Jebusite: Molech rejoices in heaven,
He sees the Twelve Daughters naked upon the Twelve Stones
Themselves condensing to rocks & into the Ribs of a Man   25
Lo they shoot forth in tender Nerves across Europe & Asia
Lo they rest upon the Tribes, where their panting Victims lie
Molech rushes into the Kings in love to the beautiful Daughters
But they frown & delight in cruelty. refusing all other joy

Bring your Offerings, your first begotten: pamperd with milk   30
                                                        & blood
Your first born of seven years old! be they Males or Females:
To the beautiful Daughters of Albion! they sport before the Kings
Clothed in the skin of the Victim! Blood! human blood: is the life
And delightful food of the Warrior: the well fed Warriors flesh
Of him who is slain in War: fills the Valleys of Ephraim with   35
Breeding Women walking in pride & bringing forth under green
                                                        trees

With pleasure, without pain, for their food is blood of the Captive
Molech rejoices thro the Land from Havilah to Shur: he rejoices
In moral law & its severe penalties: loud Shaddai & Jehovah
Thunder above: when they see the Twelve panting Victims   40
On the Twelve Stones of Power. & the beautiful Daughters of
                                                        Albion*
If you dare rend their Veil with your Spear; you are healed of Love!
From the Hills of Camberwell & Wimbledon: from the Valleys
Of Walton & Esher: from Stone-henge & from Maldens Cove
Jerusalems Pillars fall in the rendings of fierce War   45
Over France & Germany: upon the Rhine & Danube
Reuben & Benjamin flee: they hide in the Valley of Rephaim
Why trembles the Warriors limbs when he beholds thy beauty
Spotted with Victims blood: by the fires of thy secret tabernacle
And thy ark & holy place: at thy frowns: at thy dire revenge   50
Smitten as Uzzah of old: his armour is softend; his spear
And sword faint in his hand. from Albion across Great Tartary*
O beautiful Daughter of Albion: cruelty is thy delight
O Virgin of terrible eyes, who dwellest by Valleys of springs
Beneath the Mountains of Lebanon, in the City of Rehob in   55
                                                        Hamath
Taught to touch the harp: to dance in the Circle of Warriors
Before the Kings of Canaan: to cut the flesh from the Victim
To roast the flesh in fire: to examine the Infants limbs
In cruelties of holiness: to refuse the joys of love: to bring
The Spies from Egypt. to raise jealousy in the bosoms of the   60
                                                        Twelve
Kings of Canaan: then to let the Spies depart to Meribah Kadesh*
To the place of the Amalekite; I am drunk with unsatiated love
I must rush again to War: for the Virgin has frownd & refusd
Sometimes I curse & sometimes bless thy fascinating beauty
Once Man was occupied in intellectual pleasures & Energies   65

But now my soul is harrowd with grief & fear & love & desire
And now I hate & now I love, & Intellect is no more:
There is no time for any thing but the torments of love & desire
The Feminine & Masculine Shadows, soft, mild & ever varying,
In beauty: are Shadows now no more, but Rocks in Horeb   70

[Plate 69]

Then all the Males conjoined into One Male, & every one
Became a ravening eating Cancer growing in the Female
A Polypus of Root, of Reasoning Doubt Despair & Death.
Going forth & returning from Albions Rocks to Canaan:
Devouring Jerusalem from every Nation of the Earth.   5

Envying stood the enormous Form, at variance with Itself
In all its Members: in eternal torment of love & jealousy:
Drivn forth by Los time after time from Albions cliffy shore,
Drawing the free loves of Jerusalem into infernal bondage;
That they might be born in contentions of Chastity & in   10
Deadly Hate between Leah & Rachel, Daughters of Deceit &
                                        Fraud:
Bearing the Images of various Species of Contention
And Jealousy & Abhorrence & Revenge & deadly Murder.
Till they refuse liberty to the Male; & not like Beulah
Where every Female delights to give her maiden to her husband*   15
The Female searches sea & land for gratifications to the
Male Genius: who in return clothes her in gems & gold
And feeds her with the food of Eden, hence all her beauty beams
She Creates at her will a little moony night & silence
With Spaces of sweet gardens & a tent of elegant beauty: 20
Closed in by a sandy desart & a night of stars shining.
And a little tender moon & hovering angels on the wing.
And the Male gives a Time & Revolution to her Space
Till the time of love is passed in ever varying delights
For All Things Exist in the Human Imagination   25
And thence in Beulah they are stolen by secret amorous theft,
Till they have had Punishment enough to make them commit Crimes
Hence rose the Tabernacle in the Wilderness & all its Offerings.
From Male & Female Loves in Beulah & their Jealousies
But no one can consummate Female bliss in Los's World without   30
Becoming a Generated Mortal, a Vegetating Death

And now the Spectres of the Dead awake in Beulah: all
The Jealousies become Murderous: uniting together in Rahab
A Religion of Chastity, forming a Commerce to sell Loves,
With Moral Law, an Equal Balance, not going down with decision   35
Therefore the Male severe & cruel filld with stern Revenge:
Mutual Hate returns & mutual Deceit & mutual Fear.

Hence the Infernal Veil grows in the disobedient Female:
Which Jesus rends & the whole Druid Law removes away
From the Inner Sanctuary: a False Holiness hid within the Center,   40
For the Sanctuary of Eden, is in the Camp in the Outline.
In the Circumference: & every Minute Particular is Holy:
Embraces are Cominglings: from the Head even to the Feet:
And not a pompous High Priest entering by a Secret Place.

Jerusalem pined in her inmost soul over Wandering Reuben   45
As she slept in Beulahs Night hid by the Daughters of Beulah

[Plate 70]

And this the form of mighty Hand sitting on Albions cliffs
Before the face of Albion, a mighty threatning Form.

His bosom wide & shoulders huge overspreading wondrous
Bear Three strong sinewy Necks & Three awful & terrible Heads*
Three Brains in contradictory council brooding incessantly.   5
Neither daring to put in act its councils, fearing each-other.
Therefore rejecting Ideas as nothing & holding all Wisdom
To consist in the agreements & disagreents of Ideas.
Plotting to devour Albions Body of Humanity & Love.

Such Form the aggregate of the Twelve Sons of Albion took;   10
                                                     & such
Their appearance when combind: but often by birth-pangs & loud
                                                     groans
They divide to Twelve: the key-bones & the chest dividing in pain
Disclose a hideous orifice; thence issuing the Giant-brood
Arise as the smoke of the furnace, shaking the rocks from sea to sea.
And there they combine into Three Forms, named Bacon &   15
                                              Newton & Locke,
In the Oak Groves of Albion which overspread all the Earth.

Imputing Sin & Righteousness to Individuals; Rahab
Sat, deep within him hid: his Feminine Power unreveal'd
Brooding Abstract Philosophy. to destroy Imagination, the Divine-
Humanity A Three-fold Wonder: feminine: most beautiful: 20
                                        Three-fold
Each within other. On her white marble & even Neck, her Heart
Inorb'd and bonified: with locks of shadowing modesty, shining
Over her beautiful Female features. soft flourishing in beauty
Beams mild, all love and all perfection, that when the lips
Recieve a kiss from Gods or Men, a threefold kiss returns   25
From the press'd loveliness: so her whole immortal form three-fold
Three-fold embrace returns: consuming lives of Gods & Men
In fires of beauty melting them as gold & silver in the furnace
Her Brain enlabyrinths the whole heaven of her bosom & loins
To put in act what her Heart wills; O who can withstand her power   30
Her name is Vala in Eternity: in Time her name is Rahab

The Starry Heavens all were fled from the mighty limbs of Albion

[Plate 71]

And above Albions Land was seen the Heavenly Canaan
As the Substance is to the Shadow: and above Albions Twelve Sons
Were seen Jerusalems Sons: and all the Twelve Tribes spreading
Over Albion. As the Soul is to the Body, so Jerusalems Sons,
Are to the Sons of Albion: and Jerusalem is Albions Emanation   5

What is Above is Within. for every-thing in Eternity is translucent!
The Circumference is Within: Without, is formed the Selfish Center
And the Circumference still expands going forward to Eternity.
And the Center has Eternal States! these States we now explore.

And these the Names of Albions Twelve Sons. & of his Twelve   10
                                        Daughters
With their Districts. Hand dwelt in Selsey & had Sussex & Surrey
And Kent & Middlesex: all their Rivers & their Hills. of flocks &
                                        herds:
Their Villages Towns Cities Sea-Ports Temples sublime Cathedrals;
All were his Friends & their Sons & Daughters intermarry in
                                        Beulah
For all are Men in Eternity. Rivers Mountains Cities Villages.   15

All are Human & when you enter into their Bosoms you walk
In Heavens & Earths; as in your own Bosom you bear your Heaven
And Earth, & all you behold, tho it appears Without it is Within
In your Imagination of which this World of Mortality is but
                                                    a Shadow.

Hyle dwelt in Winchester comprehending Hants Dorset Devon   20
                                                    Cornwall.
Their Villages Cities Sea Ports, their Corn fields & Gardens spacious
Palaces. Rivers & Mountains. and between Hand & Hyle arose
Gwendolen & Cambel who is Boadicea: they go abroad & return
Like lovely beams of light from the mingled affections of the
                                                    Brothers
The Inhabitants of the whole Earth rejoice in their beautiful light.   25

Coban dwelt in Bath. Somerset Wiltshire Gloucestershire,
Obeyd his awful voice Ignoge is his lovely Emanation;
She adjoind with Gwantokes Children, soon lovely Cordella arose.
Gwantoke forgave & joyd over South Wales & all its Mountains.

Peachey had North Wales Shropshire Cheshire & the Isle of Man.   30
His Emanation is Mehetabel terrible & lovely upon the Mountains

Brertun had Yorkshire Durham Westmoreland & his Emanation
Is Ragan, she adjoin'd to Slade, & produced Gonorill far beaming.

Slade had Lincoln Stafford Derby Nottingham & his lovely
Emanation Gonorill rejoices over hills & rocks & woods & rivers.   35

Huttn had Warwick Northampton Bedford Buckingham
Leicester & Berkshire: & his Emanation is Gwinefred beautiful

Skofeld had Ely Rutland Cambridge Huntingdon Norfolk
Suffolk Hartford & Essex: & his Emanation is Gwinevera
Beautiful, she beams towards the east. all kinds of precious stones 40
And pearl, with instruments of music in holy Jerusalem

Kox had Oxford Warwick Wilts: his Emanation is Estrild:
Joind with Cordella she shines southward over the Atlantic.

Kotope had Hereford Stafford Worcester, & his Emanation
Is Sabrina joind with Mehetabel she shines west over America   45

Bowen had all Scotland, the Isles, Northumberland & Cumberland
His Emanation is Conwenna, she shines a triple form

Over the north with pearly beams gorgeous & terrible
Jerusalem & Vala rejoice in Bowen & Conwenna.

But the Four Sons of Jerusalem that never were Generated   50
Are Rintrah and Palamabron and Theotormon and Bromion. They
Dwell over the Four Provinces of Ireland in heavenly light
The Four Universities of Scotland, & in Oxford & Cambridge &
                                                        Winchester

But now Albion is darkened & Jerusalem lies in ruins:
Above the Mountains of Albion. above the head of Los.   55

And Los shouted with ceaseless shoutings & his tears poured down
His immortal cheeks, rearing his hands to heaven for aid Divine!
But he spoke not to Albion: fearing lest Albion should turn his
                                                        Back
Against the Divine Vision: & fall over the Precipice of
                                    Eternal Death.
But he receded before Albion & before Vala weaving the Veil   60
With the iron shuttle of War among the rooted Oaks of Albion;
Weeping & shouting to the Lord day & night; and his Children
Wept round him as a flock silent Seven Days of Eternity

[Plate 72]

And the Thirty-two Counties of the Four Provinces of Ireland
Are thus divided: The Four Counties are in the Four Camps
Munster South in Reubens Gate, Connaut West in Josephs Gate
Ulster North in Dans Gate, Leinster East in Judahs Gate

For Albion in Eternity has Sixteen Gates among his Pillars   5
But the Four towards the West were Walled up & the Twelve
That front the Four other Points were turned Four Square
By Los for Jerusalems sake & called the Gates of Jerusalem
Because Twelve Sons of Jerusalem fled successive thro the Gates
But the Four Sons of Jerusalem who fled not but remaind   10
Are Rintrah & Palamabron & Theotormon & Bromion
The Four that remain with Los to guard the Western Wall
And these Four remain to guard the Four Walls of Jerusalem
Whose foundations remain in the Thirty-two Counties of Ireland
And in Twelve Counties of Wales & in the Forty Counties   15
Of England & in the Thirty-six Counties of Scotland

And the names of the Thirty-two Counties of Ireland are these
Under Judah & Issachar & Zebulun are Lowth Longford
Eastmeath Westmeath Dublin Kildare Kings County
Queens County Wicklow Catherloh Wexford Kilkenny   20
And those under Reuben & Simeon & Levi are these
Waterford Tipperary Cork Limerick Kerry Clare
And those under Ephraim, Manasseh & Benjamin are these
Galway Roscommon Mayo Sligo Leitrim
And those under Dan Asher & Napthali are these   25
Donnegal Antrim Tyrone Fermanagh Armagh Londonderry
Down Managhan Cavan. These are the Land of Erin

All these Center in London & in Golgonooza. from whence
They are Created continually East & West & North & South
And from them are Created all the Nations of the Earth   30
Europe & Asia & Africa & America, in fury Fourfold!

And Thirty-two the Nations: to dwell in Jerusalems Gates
O Come ye Nations Come ye People Come up to Jerusalem
Return Jerusalem & dwell together as of old! Return
Return; O Albion let Jerusalem overspread all Nations   35
As in the times of old! O Albion awake! Reuben wanders
The Nations wait for Jerusalem. they look up for the Bride

France Spain Italy Germany Poland Russia Sweden Turkey
Arabia Palestine Persia Hindostan, China Tartary Siberia
Egypt Lybia Ethiopia Guinea Caffraria Negroland Morocco   40
Congo Zaara Canada Greenland Carolina Mexico
Peru Patagonia Amazonia Brazil. Thirty-two Nations
And under these Thirty-two Classes of Islands in the Ocean
All the Nations Peoples & Tongues throughout all the Earth

And the Four Gates of Los surround the Universe Within and   45
Without; & whatever is visible in the Vegetable Earth. the same
Is visible in the Mundane Shell: reversd in mountain & vale
And a Son of Eden was set over each Daughter of Beulah to guard
In Albions Tomb the wondrous Creation: & the Four-fold Gate
Towards Beulah is to the South Fenelon, Guion, Teresa,   50
Whitefield & Hervey, guard that Gate; with all the gentle Souls*
Who guide the great Wine-press of Love; Four precious stones that
                                                          Gate:

[Plate 73]

Such are Cathedrons golden Halls: in the City of Golgonooza

And Los's Furnaces howl loud; living: self-moving: lamenting
With fury & despair. & they stretch from South to North
Thro all the Four Points: Lo! the Labourers at the Furnaces
Rintrah & Palamabron, Theotormon & Bromion. loud labring   5
With the innumerable multitudes of Golgonooza, round the Anvils
Of Death. But how they came forth from the Furnaces & how long
Vast & severe the anguish eer they knew their Father; were
Long to tell & of the iron rollers, golden axle-trees & yokes
Of brass, iron chains & braces & the gold. silver & brass   10
Mingled or separate: for swords; arrows; cannons; mortars
The terrible ball: the wedge: the loud sounding hammer of
                                            destruction
The sounding flail to thresh, the winnow to winnow kingdoms,
The water wheel & mill of many innumerable wheels resistless
Over the Fourfold Monarchy from Earth to the Mundane Shell.*   15

Perusing Albions Tomb in the starry characters of Og & Anak:
To Create the lion & wolf the bear: the tyger & ounce:
To Create the wooly lamb & downy fowl & scaly serpent
The summer & winter: day & night: the sun & moon & stars
The tree: the plant: the flower: the rock: the stone: the metal: 20
Of Vegetative Nature: by their hard restricting condensations.

Where Luvahs World of Opakeness grew to a period: It
Became a Limit. a Rocky hardness without form & void
Accumulating without end: here Los who is of the Elohim
Opens the Furnaces of affliction in the Emanation   25
Fixing the Sexual into an ever-prolific Generation
Naming the Limit of Opakeness Satan & the Limit of Contraction
Adam, who is Peleg & Jokta: & Esau & Jacob: & Saul & David

Voltaire insinuates that these Limits are the cruel work of God
Mocking the Remover of Limits & the Resurrection of the Dead   30
Setting up Kings in wrath: in holiness of Natural Religion
Which Los with his mighty Hammer demolishes time on time
In miracles & wonders in the Four-fold Desart of Albion
Permanently Creating to be in Time Reveald & Demolishd
Satan Cain Tubal Nimrod Pharoh Priam Bladud Belin   35
Arthur Alfred the Norman Conqueror Richard John

And all the Kings & Nobles of the Earth & all their Glories
These are Created by Rahab & Tirzah in Ulro: but around
These, to preserve them from Eternal Death Los Creates
Adam Noah Abraham Moses Samuel David Ezekiel   40

Dissipating the rocky forms of Death by his thunderous Hammer
As the Pilgrim passes while the Country permanent remains
So Men pass on: but States remain permanent for ever*

The Spectres of the Dead howl round the porches of Los
In the terrible Family feuds of Albions cities & villages   45
To devour the Body of Albion, hungring & thirsting & ravning
The Sons of Los clothe them & feed, & provide houses & gardens
And every Human Vegetated Form in its inward recesses
Is a house of pleantness & a garden of delight Built by the
Sons & Daughters of Los in Bowlahoola & in Cathedron   50

From London to York & Edinburgh the Furnaces rage terrible
Primrose Hill is the mouth of the Furnace & the Iron Door;

[Plate 74]

The Four Zoa's clouded rage; Urizen stood by Albion
With Rintrah and Palamabron and Theotormon and Bromion
These Four are Verulam & London & York & Edinburgh
And the Four Zoa's are Urizen & Luvah & Tharmas & Urthona
In opposition deadly, and their Wheels in poisonous   5
And deadly stupor turn'd against each other loud & fierce
Entering into the Reasoning Power, forsaking Imagination
They became Spectres; & their Human Bodies were reposed
In Beulah, by the Daughters of Beulah with tears & lamentations

The Spectre is the Reasoning Power in Man; & when separated   10
From Imagination and closing itself as in steel, in a Ratio
Of the Things of Memory. It thence frames Laws & Moralities
To destroy Imagination! the Divine Body, by Martyrdoms & Wars

Teach me O Holy Spirit the Testimony of Jesus! let me
Comprehend wonderous things out of the Divine Law   15
I behold Babylon in the opening Streets of London, I behold
Jerusalem in ruins wandering about from house to house
This I behold the shudderings of death attend my steps
I walk up and down in Six Thousand Years: their Events are present
                                                      before me

To tell how Los in grief & anger. whirling round his Hammer on   20
                                                             high
Drave the Sons & Daughters of Albion from their ancient mountains
They became the Twelve Gods of Asia Opposing the Divine Vision

The Sons of Albion are Twelve: the Sons of Jerusalem Sixteen
I tell how Albions Sons by Harmonies of Concords & Discords
Opposed to Melody, and by Lights & Shades, opposed to Outline*   25
And by Abstraction opposed to the Visions of Imagination
By cruel Laws divided Sixteen into Twelve Divisions
How Hyle roofd Los in Albions Cliffs by the Affections rent
Asunder & opposed to Thought, to draw Jerusalems Sons
Into the Vortex of his Wheels. therefore Hyle is called Gog   30
Age after age drawing them away towards Babylon
Babylon, the Rational Morality deluding to death the little ones
In strong temptations of stolen beauty; I tell how Reuben slept
On London Stone & the Daughters of Albion ran around admiring
His awful beauty: with Moral Virtue, the fair deceiver; offspring   35
Of Good & Evil, they divided him in love upon the Thames & sent
Him over Europe in streams of gore out of Cathedrons Looms
How Los drave them from Albion & they became Daughters of
                                                          Canaan
Hence Albion was calld the Canaanite & all his Giant Sons.
Hence is my Theme. O Lord my Saviour open thou the Gates   40
And I will lead forth thy Words, telling how the Daughters
Cut the Fibres of Reuben, how he rolld apart & took Root
In Bashan. terror-struck Albions Sons look toward Bashan
They have divided Simeon he also rolld apart in blood*
Over the Nations till he took Root beneath the shining Looms   45
Of Albions Daughters in Philistea by the side of Amalek
They have divided Levi: he hath shot out into Forty eight Roots
Over the Land of Canaan: they have divided Judah
He hath took Root in Hebron, in the Land of Hand & Hyle
Dan: Napthali: Gad: Asher: Issachar: Zebulun: roll apart   50
From all the Nations of the Earth to dissipate into Non Entity

I see a Feminine Form arise from the Four terrible Zoas
Beautiful but terrible struggling to take a form of beauty
Rooted in Shechem: this is Dinah. the youthful form of Erin
The Wound I see in South Molton Street & Stratford place*   55
Whence Joseph & Benjamin rolld apart away from the Nations
In vain they rolld apart; they are fix'd into the Land of Cabul*

[Plate 75]

And Rahab Babylon the Great hath destroyed Jerusalem
Bath stood upon the Severn with Merlin & Bladud & Arthur*
The Cup of Rahab in his hand: her Poisons Twenty-seven-fold

And all her Twenty-seven Heavens now hid & now reveal'd
Appear in strong delusive light of Time & Space drawn out   5
In shadowy pomp by the Eternal Prophet created evermore
For Los in Six Thousand Years walks up & down continually
That not one Moment of Time be lost, & every revolution
Of Space he makes permanent in Bowlahoola & Cathedron.

And these the names of the Twenty-seven Heavens & their Churches   10
Adam, Seth, Enos, Cainan, Mahalaleel, Jared, Enoch,
Methuselah, Lamech; these are the Giants mighty, Hermaphroditic
Noah, Shem, Arphaxad, Cainan the Second, Salah, Heber,
Peleg, Reu. Serug, Nahor, Terah: these are the Female Males:
A Male within a Female hid as in an Ark & Curtains.   15
Abraham, Moses, Solomon, Paul, Constantine, Charlemaine.
Luther. these Seven are the Male Females: the Dragon Forms
The Female hid within a Male: thus Rahab is reveald
Mystery Babylon the Great: the Abomination of Desolation
Religion hid in War: a Dragon red & hidden Harlot   20
But Jesus breaking thro' the Central Zones of Death & Hell
Opens Eternity in Time & Space; triumphant in Mercy

Thus are the Heavens formd by Los within the Mundane Shell
And where Luther ends Adam begins again in Eternal Circle
To awake the Prisoners of Death; to bring Albion again   25
With Luvah into light eternal. in his eternal day.

But now the Starry Heavens are fled from the mighty limbs
                                                    of Albion

[Plate 77]

TO THE CHRISTIANS

Devils are   I give you the end of a golden string,
False Religions   Only wind it into a ball:
   'Saul Saul'   It will lead you in at Heavens gate,
'Why persecutest thou me,*   Built in Jerusalems wall.

We are told to abstain from fleshly desires that we may lose no time from the Work of the Lord. Every moment lost, is a moment that cannot be redeemed every pleasure that intermingles with the duty of our station is a folly unredeemable & is planted like the seed of a wild flower among our wheat. All the tortures of repentance. are tortures of self-reproach on account of our leaving the Divine Harvest to the Enemy, the struggles of intanglement with incoherent roots. I know of no other Christianity and of no other Gospel than the liberty both of body & mind to exercise the Divine Arts of Imagination Imagination, the real & eternal World of which this Vegetable Universe is but a faint shadow & in which we shall live in our Eternal or Imaginative Bodies, when these Vegetable Mortal Bodies are no more. The Apostles knew of no other Gospel. What were all their spiritual gifts? What is the Divine Spirit? is the Holy Ghost any other than an Intellectual Fountain? What is the Harvest of the Gospel & its Labours? What is that Talent which it is a curse to hide? What are the Treasures of Heaven which we are to lay up for ourselves, are they any other than Mental Studies & Performances? What are all the Gifts of the Gospel. are they not all Mental Gifts? Is God a Spirit who must be worshipped in Spirit & in Truth and are not the Gifts of the Spirit Every-thing to Man? O ye Religious discountenance every one among you who shall pretend to despise Art & Science! I call upon you in the Name of Jesus! What is the Life of Man but Art & Science? is it Meat & Drink? is not the Body more than Raiment? What is Mortality but the things relating to the Body which Dies? What is Immortality but the things relating to the Spirit which Lives Eternally! What is the Joy of Heaven but Improvement in the things of the Spirit? What are the Pains of Hell but Ignorance, Bodily Lust, Idleness & devastation of the things of the Spirit Answer this to yourselves, & expel from among you those who pretend to despise the labours of Art & Science, which alone are the labours of the Gospel: Is not this plain & manifest to the thought? Can you think at all & not pronounce heartily! That to Labour in Knowledge. is to Build up Jerusalem: and to Despise Knowledge, is to Despise Jerusalem & her Builders. And remember: He who despises & mocks a Mental Gift in another; calling it pride & selfishness & sin; mocks Jesus the giver of every Mental Gift, which always appear to the ignorance-loving Hypocrite, as Sins. but that which is a Sin in the sight of cruel Man, is not so in the sight of our kind God. Let every Christian as much as in him lies engage himself openly & publicly before all the World in some Mental pursuit for the Building up of Jerusalem

I stood among my valleys of the south*
And saw a flame of fire, even as a Wheel
Of fire surrounding all the heavens: it went
From west to east, against the current of
Creation and devourd all things in its loud   5
Fury & thundering course round heaven & earth
By it the Sun was rolld into an orb:
By it the Moon faded into a globe.
Travelling thro the night: for from its dire
And restless fury, Man himself shrunk up   10
Into a little root a fathom long.
And I asked a Watcher & a Holy-One
Its Name? he answerd. It is the Wheel of Religion
I wept & said. Is this the law of Jesus
This terrible devouring sword turning every way   15
He answerd; Jesus died because he strove
Against the current of this Wheel: its Name
Is Caiaphas, the dark Preacher of Death
Of sin, of sorrow & of punishment;
Opposing Nature! It is Natural Religion   20
But Jesus is the bright Preacher of Life
Creating Nature from this fiery Law,
By self-denial & forgiveness of Sin:
Go therefore, cast out devils in Christs name
Heal thou the sick of spiritual disease   25
Pity the evil, for thou art not sent
To smite with terror & with punishments
Those that are sick. like to the Pharisees
Crucifying & encompassing sea & land
For proselytes to tyranny & wrath.   30
But to the Publicans & Harlots go!*
Teach them True Happiness. but let no curse
Go forth out of thy mouth to blight their peace
For Hell is opend to Heaven; thine eyes beheld
The dungeons burst & the Prisoners set free.   35

England! awake! awake! awake!
    Jerusalem thy Sister calls!
Why wilt thou sleep the sleep of death?
    And close her from thy ancient walls.

Thy hills & valleys felt her feet,   5
    Gently upon their bosoms move:
Thy gates beheld sweet Zions ways;
    Then was a time of joy and love.

And now the time returns again:
    Our souls exult & Londons towers   10
Recieve the Lamb of God to dwell
    In Englands green & pleasant bowers.

[Plate 78]

JERUSALEM. C 4

The Spectres of Albions Twelve Sons revolve mightily
Over the Tomb & over the Body: ravning to devour
The Sleeping Humanity. Los with his mace of iron
Walks round: loud his threats, loud his blows fall
On the rocky Spectres, as the Potter breaks the potsherds;   5
Dashing in pieces Self-righteousnesses: driving them from Albions
Cliffs: dividing them into Male & Female forms in his Furnaces
And on his Anvils: lest they destroy the Feminine Affections
They are broken. Loud howl the Spectres in his iron Furnace

While Los laments at his dire labours, viewing Jerusalem,   10
Sitting before his Furnaces clothed in sackcloth of hair;
Albions Twelve Sons surround the Forty-two Gates of Erin.*
In terrible armour, raging against the Lamb & against Jerusalem,
Surrounding them with armies to destroy the Lamb of God.
They took their Mother Vala, and they crown'd her with gold: 15
They nam'd her Rahab, & gave her power over the Earth
The Concave Earth round Golgonooza in Entuthon Benython.
Even to the stars exalting her Throne, to build beyond the Throne
Of God and the Lamb, to destroy the Lamb & usurp the Throne
                                                of God
Drawing their Ulro Voidness round the Four-fold Humanity   20

Naked Jerusalem lay before the Gates upon Mount Zion
The Hill of Giants, all her foundations levelld with the dust:

Her Twelve Gates thrown down: her children carried into captivity
Herself in chains: this from within was seen in a dismal night

Outside, unknown before in Beulah. & the twelve gates were fill'd   25
With blood; from Japan eastward to the Giants causeway, west*
In Erins Continent: and Jerusalem wept upon Euphrates banks
Disorganizd; an evanescent shade, scarce seen or heard among
Her childrens Druid Temples dropping with blood wanderd weeping!
And thus her voice went forth in the darkness of Philisthea.*   30

My brother & my father are no more! God hath forsaken me
The arrows of the Almighty pour upon me & my children
I have sinned and am an outcast from the Divine Presence!

[Plate 79]

My tents are fall'n! my pillars are in ruins! my children dashd
Upon Egypts iron floors & the marble pavements of Assyria;
I melt my soul in reasonings among the towers of Heshbon;
Mount Zion is become a cruel rock & no more dew
Nor rain: no more the spring of the rock appears: but cold   5
Hard & obdurate are the furrows of the mountain of wine & oil:
The mountain of blessing is itself a curse & an astonishment;
The hills of Judea are fallen with me into the deepest hell
Away from the Nations of the Earth, & from the Cities of the
                                                            Nations;
I walk to Ephraim. I seek for Shiloh: I walk like a lost sheep   10
Among precipices of despair: in Goshen I seek for light
In vain, and in Gilead for a physician and a comforter.
Goshen hath followd Philistea: Gilead hath joind with Og!
They are become narrow places in a little and dark land:
How distant far from Albion! his hills & his valleys no more   15
Recieve the feet of Jerusalem: they have cast me quite away:
And Albion is himself shrunk to a narrow rock in the midst of
                                                            the sea!
The plains of Sussex & Surrey. their hills of flocks & herds
No more seek to Jerusalem nor to the sound of my Holy-ones.
The Fifty-two Counties of England are hardend against me   20
As if I was not their Mother, they despise me & cast me out
London coverd the whole Earth. England encompassd the Nations:
And all the Nations of the Earth were seen in the Cities of Albion:
My pillars reachd from sea to sea: London beheld me come
From my east & from my west; he blessed me and gave   25
His children to my breasts. his sons & daughters to my knees

His aged parents sought me out in every city & village:
They discernd my countenance with joy. they shewd me to their
                                                                    sons
Saying Lo Jerusalem is here! she sitteth in our secret chambers
Levi and Judah & Issachar: Ephram, Manasseh, Gad and Dan   30
Are seen in our hills & valleys: they keep our flocks & herds:
They watch them in the night: and the Lamb of God appears
                                                                    among us.
The river Severn stayd his course at my command:
Thames poured his waters into my basons and baths:
Medway mingled with Kishon: Thames recievd the heavenly   35
                                                                    Jordan
Albion gave me to the whole Earth to walk up & down; to pour
Joy upon every mountain; to teach songs to the shepherd &
                                                                    plowman
I taught the ships of the sea to sing the songs of Zion.
Italy saw me in sublime astonishment: France was wholly mine:
As my garden & as my secret bath; Spain was my heavenly couch: 40
I slept in his golden hills: the Lamb of God met me there.
There we walked as in our secret chamber among our little ones
They looked upon our loves with joy: they beheld our secret joys:
With holy raptures of adoration rapd sublime in the Visions of
                                                                    God:
Germany; Poland & the North wooed my footsteps they found   45
My gates in all their mountains & my curtains in all their vales
The furniture of their houses was the furniture of my chamber
Turkey & Grecia saw my instrments of music, they arose
They siezd the harp: the flute: the mellow horn of Jerusalems joy
They sounded thanksgivings in my courts: Egypt & Lybia heard   50
The swarthy sons of Ethiopia stood round the Lamb of God
Enquiring for Jerusalem: he led them up my steps to my altar:
And thou, America! I once beheld thee but now behold no more
Thy golden mountains where my Cherubim & Seraphim rejoicd
Together among my little-ones. But now my Altars run with blood!   55
My fires are corrupt! my incense is a cloudy pestilence
Of seven diseases! Once a continual cloud of salvation. rose
From all my myriads; once the Four-fold World rejoicd among
The pillars of Jerusalem, between my winged Cherubim:
But now I am closd out from them in the narrow passages   60
Of the valleys of destruction. into a dark land of pitch & bitumen.
From Albions Tomb afar and from the four-fold wonders of God

Shrunk to a narrow doleful form in the dark land of Cabul;
There is Reuben & Gad & Joseph & Judah & Levi, closd up
In narrow vales: I walk & count the bones of my beloveds   65
Along the Valley of Destruction, among these Druid Temples
Which overspread all the Earth in patriarchal pomp & cruel pride
Tell me O Vala thy purposes; tell me wherefore thy shuttles
Drop with the gore of the slain; why Euphrates is red with blood
Wherefore in dreadful majesty & beauty outside appears   70
Thy Masculine from thy Feminine, hardening against the heavens
To devour the Human! Why dost thou weep upon the wind among
These cruel Druid Temples: O Vala! Humanity is far above
Sexual organization; & the Visions of the Night of Beulah
Where Sexes wander in dreams of bliss among the Emanations   75
Where the Masculine & Feminine are nurs'd into Youth & Maiden
By the tears & smiles of Beulahs Daughters till the time of Sleep is
                                                                        past.
Wherefore then do you realize these nets of beauty & delusion
In open day to draw the souls of the Dead into the light.
Till Albion is shut out from every Nation under Heaven.   80

[Plate 80]

Encompassd by the frozen Net and by the rooted Tree
I walk weeping in pangs of a Mothers torment for her Children:
I walk in affliction: I am a worm, and no living soul!
A worm going to eternal torment! raisd up in a night
To an eternal night of pain. lost! lost! lost! for ever!   5
Beside her Vala howld upon the winds in pride of beauty
Lamenting among the timbrels of the Warriors: among the Captives
In cruel holiness, and her lamenting songs were from Arnon
And Jordan to Euphrates. Jerusalem followd trembling
Her children in captivity. listening to Valas lamentation   10
In the thick cloud & darkness. & the voice went forth from
The cloud. O rent in sunder from Jerusalem the Harlot daughter!
In an eternal condemnation in fierce burning flames
Of torment unendurable: and if once a Delusion be found
Woman must perish & the Heavens of Heavens remain no more   15

My Father gave to me command to murder Albion
In unreviving Death; my Love, my Luvah orderd me in night
To murder Albion the King of Men. he fought in battles fierce*

He conquerd Luvah my beloved: he took me and my Father,
He slew them: I revived them to life in my warm bosom   20
He saw them issue from my bosom dark in Jealousy
He burnd before me: Luvah framd the Knife & Luvah gave
The Knife into his daughters hand! such thing was never known
Before in Albions land. that one should die a death never to be
                                                          reviv'd:
For, in our battles we the Slain men view with pity and love: 25
We soon revive them in the secret of our tabernacles
But I Vala, Luvahs daughter, keep his body embalmd in moral laws
With spices of sweet odours of lovely jealous stupefaction:
Within my bosom. lest he arise to life & slay my Luvah
Pity me then O Lamb of God! O Jesus pity me!   30
Come into Luvahs Tents and seek not to revive the Dead!

So sang she: and the Spindle turnd furious as she sang:
The Children of Jerusalem the Souls of those who sleep
Were caught into the flax of her Distaff: & in her Cloud
To weave Jerusalem a body according to her will   35
A Dragon form on Zion Hills most ancient promontory

The Spindle turnd in blood & fire: loud sound the trumpets
Of war: the cymbals play loud before the Captains
With Cambel & Gwendolen in dance and solemn song
The Cloud of Rahab vibrating with the Daughters of Albion   40
Los saw terrified melted with pity & divided in wrath
He sent them over the narrow seas in pity and love
Among the Four Forests of Albion which overspread all the Earth
They go forth & return swift as a flash of lightning.
Among the tribes of warriors: among the Stones of power!   45
Against Jerusalem they rage thro all the Nations of Europe*
Thro Italy & Grecia. to Lebanon & Persia & India.

The Serpent Temples thro the Earth, from the wide Plain of
                                                          Salisbury
Resound with cries of Victims, shouts & songs & dying groans
And flames of dusky fire. to Amalek. Canaan and Moab   50
And Rahab like a dismal and indefinite hovering Cloud
Refusd to take a definite form, she hoverd over all the Earth
Calling the definite sin: defacing every definite form;
Invisible, or Visible. stretch'd out in length or spread in breadth:
Over the Temples drinking groans of victims weeping in pity,   55
And joying in the pity, howling over Jerusalems walls.

Hand slept on Skiddaws top: drawn by the love of beautiful*
Cambel: his bright beaming Counterpart, divided from him
And her delusive light beamd fierce above the Mountain,
Soft: invisible: drinking his sighs in sweet intoxication: 60
Drawing out fibre by fibre; returning to Albions Tree
At night: and in the morning to Skiddaw: she sent him over
Mountainous Wales into the Loom of Cathedron fibre by fibre:
He ran in tender nerves across Europe to Jerusalems Shade;
To weave Jerusalem a Body repugnant to the Lamb.   65

Hyle on East Moor in rocky Derbyshire, rav'd to the Moon
For Gwendolen: she took up in bitter tears his anguishd heart
That, apparent to all in Eternity. glows like the Sun in the breast:
She hid it in his ribs & back: she hid his tongue with teeth
In terrible convulsions pitying & gratified drunk with pity   70
Glowing with loveliness before him. becoming apparent
According to his changes; she roll'd his kidneys round
Into two irregular forms: and looking on Albions dread Tree,
She wove two vessels of seed, beautiful as Skiddaws snow;
Giving them bends of self interest & selfish natural virtue: 75
She hid them in his loins; raving he ran among the rocks.
Compelld into a shape of Moral Virtue against the Lamb.
The invisible lovely one giving him a form according to
His Law a form against the Lamb of God opposd to Mercy
And playing in the thunderous Loom in sweet intoxication   80
Filling cups of silver & crystal with shrieks & cries. with groans
And dolorous sobs: the wine of lovers in the Wine-press of Luvah

O sister Cambel said Gwendolen, as their long beaming light
Mingled above the Mountain what shall we do to keep
These awful forms in our soft bands: distracted with trembling   85

[Plate 81]

I have mock'd those who refused cruelty & I have admired
The cruel Warrior. I have refused to give love to Merlin the piteous.
He brings to me the Images of his Love & I reject in chastity
And turn them out into the streets for Harlots to be food
To the stern Warrior. I am become perfect in beauty over my   5
                                                           Warrior
For Men are caught by Love: Woman is caught by Pride

That Love may only be obtaind in the passages of Death.
Let us look! let us examine! is the Cruel become an Infant
Or is he still a cruel Warrior? look Sisters. look! O piteous
I have destroyd Wandring Reuben who strove to bind my Will   10
I have stripd off Josephs beautiful integument for my Beloved.
The Cruel-one of Albion: to clothe him in gems of my Zone
I have named him Jehovah of Hosts. Humanity is become
A weeping Infant in ruind lovely Jerusalems folding Cloud.

In Heaven Love begets Love! but Fear is the Parent of Earthly   15
                                                          Love!
And he who will not bend to Love must be subdud by Fear,

[Plate 82]*

I have heard Jerusalems groans; from Vala's cries & lamentations
I gather our eternal fate: Outcasts from life and love:
Unless we find a way to bind these awful Forms to our
Embrace we shall perish annihilate, discoverd our Delusions.
Look I have wrought without delusion: Look! I have wept!   5
And given soft milk mingled together with the spirits of flocks
Of lambs and doves, mingled together in cups and dishes
Of painted clay; the mighty Hyle is become a weeping infant;
Soon shall the Spectres of the Dead follow my weaving threads.

The Twelve Daughters of Albion attentive listen in secret shades   10
On Cambridge and Oxford beaming soft, uniting with Rahabs
                                                          cloud
While Gwendolen spoke to Cambel turning soft the spinning reel:
Or throwing the wingd shuttle; or drawing the cords with softest
                                                          songs
The golden cords of the Looms animate beneath their touches soft,
Along the Island white. among the Druid Temples, while Gwendolen   15
Spoke to the Daughters of Albion standing on Skiddaws top.

So saying she took a Falsehood & hid it in her left hand:
To entice her Sisters away to Babylon on Euphrates.
And thus she closed her left hand and utterd her Falsehood:
Forgetting that Falsehood is prophetic, she hid her hand behind   20
                                                          her,
Upon her back behind her loins & thus utter'd her Deceit

I heard Enitharmon say to Los! Let the Daughters of Albion
Be scatterd abroad and let the name of Albion be forgotten:
Divide them into three; name them Amalek Canaan & Moab:
Let Albion remain a desolation without an inhabitant: 25
And let the Looms of Enitharmon & the Furnaces of Los
Create Jerusalem. & Babylon & Egypt & Moab & Amalek.
And Helle & Hesperia & Hindostan & China & Japan.
But hide America, for a Curse an Altar of Victims & a Holy Place.
See Sisters Canaan is pleasant, Egypt is as the Garden of Eden: 30
Babylon is our chief desire. Moab our bath in summer:
Let us lead the stems of this Tree let us plant it before Jerusalem
To judge the Friend of Sinners to death without the Veil:
To cut her off from America. to close up her secret Ark:
And the fury of Man exhaust in War! Woman permanent remain   35
See how the fires of our loins point eastward to Babylon
Look, Hyle is become an infant Love: look behold! see him lie!
Upon my bosom. look! here is the lovely wayward form
That gave me sweet delight by his torments beneath my Veil;
By the fruit of Albions Tree I have fed him with sweet milk   40
By contentions of the mighty for Sacrifice of Captives:
Humanity the Great Delusion: is chang'd to War & Sacrifice;
I have naild his hands on Beth Rabbim & his feet on Heshbons
                                                                                           Wall:
O that I could live in his sight: O that I could bind him to my arm.
So saying: She drew aside her Veil from Mam-Tor to Dovedale   45
Discovering her own perfect beauty to the Daughters of Albion
And Hyle a winding Worm beneath [*her Loom upon the scales.*
Hyle was become a winding Worm:] & not a weeping Infant.
Trembling & pitying she screamd & fled upon the wind:
Hyle was a winding Worm and herself perfect in beauty;   50
The desarts tremble at his wrath: they shrink themselves in fear.

Cambel trembled with jealousy: she trembled! she envied!
The envy ran thro Cathedrons Looms into the Heart
Of mild Jerusalem. to destroy the Lamb of God. Jerusalem
Languishd upon Mount Olivet. East of mild Zions Hill   55

Los saw the envious blight above his Seventh Furnace
On Londons Tower on the Thames: he drew Cambel in wrath,
Into his thundering Bellows, heaving it for a loud blast!
And with the blast of his Furnace upon fishy Billingsgate.*
Beneath Albions fatal Tree before the Gate of Los:*   60

Shewd her the fibres of her beloved to ameliorate
The envy; loud she labourd in the Furnace of fire,
To form the mighty form of Hand according to her will.
In the Furnaces of Los & in the Wine-press, treading day & night
Naked among the human clusters: bringing wine of anguish   65
To feed the afflicted in the Furnaces: she minded not
The raging flames, tho' she returnd [*consumd day after day
A redning skeleton in howling woe:*] instead of beauty
Deformity: she gave her beauty to another: bearing abroad
Her struggling torment in her iron arms: and like a chain.   70
Binding his wrists & ankles with the iron arms of love.

Gwendolen saw the Infant in her sisters arms; she howld
Over the forests with bitter tears, and over the winding Worm
Repentant: and she also in the eddying wind of Los's Bellows
Began her dolorous task of love in the Wine-press of Luvah   75
To form the Worm into a form of love by tears & pain.
The Sisters saw! trembling ran thro their Looms! softening mild
Towards London: then they saw the Furnaces opend & in tears
Began to give their souls away in the Furnaces of affliction.

Los saw & was comforted at his Furnaces uttering thus his voice.   80
I know I am Urthona keeper of the Gates of Heaven,
And that I can at will expatiate in the Gardens of bliss;
But pangs of love draw me down to my loins, which are
Become a fountain of veiny pipes: O Albion! my brother!

[Plate 83]

Corruptibility appears upon thy limbs, and never more
Can I arise and leave thy side, but labour here incessant
Till thy awaking! yet alas I shall forget Eternity!
Against the Patriarchal pomp and cruelty, labouring incessant
I shall become an Infant horror. Enion! Tharmas! friends   5
Absorb me not in such dire grief: O Albion. my brother!
Jerusalem hungers in the desart! affection to her children!
The scorn'd and contemnd youthful girl, where shall she fly?
Sussex shuts up her Villages. Hants, Devon & Wilts
Surrounded with masses of stone in orderd forms. determine then* 10
A form for Vala and a form for Luvah. here on the Thames
Where the Victim nightly howls beneath the Druids knife:

A Form of Vegetation, nail them down on the stems of Mystery:
O when shall the Saxon return with the English, his redeemed
                                                    brother!*
O when shall the Lamb of God descend among the Reprobate!   15
I woo to Amalek to protect my fugitives Amalek trembles:
I call to Canaan & Moab in my night watches, they mourn:
They listen not to my cry, they rejoice among their warriors
Woden and Thor and Friga wholly consume my Saxons:
On their enormous Altars built in the terrible north: 20
From Irelands rocks to Scandinavia Persia and Tartary:
From the Atlantic Sea to the universal Erythrean.
Found ye London! enormous City! weeps thy River?
Upon his parent bosom lay thy little ones O Land
Forsaken. Surrey and Sussex are Enitharmons Chamber.   25
Where I will build her a Couch of repose & my pillars
Shall surround her in beautiful labyrinths: Oothoon!
Where hides my child? in Oxford hidest thou with Antamon?
In graceful hidings of error: in merciful deceit
Lest Hand the terrible destroy his Affection, thou hidest her: 30
In chaste appearances for sweet deceits of love & modesty
Immingled, interwoven, glistening to the sickening sight.
Let Cambel and her Sisters sit within the Mundane Shell:
Forming the fluctuating Globe according to their will.
According as they weave the little embryon nerves & veins   35
The Eye, the little Nostrils, & the delicate Tongue & Ears
Of labyrinthine intricacy: so shall they fold the World
That whatever is seen upon the Mundane Shell, the same
Be seen upon the Fluctuating Earth woven by the Sisters.
And sometimes the Earth shall roll in the Abyss & sometimes   40
Stand in the Center & sometimes stretch flat in the Expanse.
According to the will of the lovely Daughters of Albion.
Sometimes it shall assimilate with mighty Golgonooza:
Touching its summits: & sometimes divided roll apart.
As a beautiful Veil so these Females shall fold & unfold   45
According to their will the outside surface of the Earth
An outside shadowy Surface superadded to the real Surface;
Which is unchangeable for ever & ever Amen: so be it!
Separate Albions Sons gently from their Emanations
Weaving bowers of delight on the current of infant Thames   50
Where the old Parent still retains his youth as I alas!*

Retain my youth eight thousand and five hundred years.*
The labourer of ages in the Valleys of Despair;
The land is markd for desolation & unless we plant
The seeds of Cities & of Villages in the Human bosom   55
Albion must be a rock of blood: mark ye the points
Where Cities shall remain & where Villages for the rest!
It must lie in confusion till Albions time of awaking.
Place the Tribes of Llewellyn in America for a hiding place!
Till sweet Jerusalem emanates again into Eternity   60
The night falls thick: I go upon my watch: be attentive:
The Sons of Albion go forth; I follow from my Furnaces:
That they return no more: that a place be prepard on Euphrates
Listen to your Watchmans voice: sleep not before the Furnaces
Eternal Death stands at the door. O God, pity our labours.   65

So Los spoke. to the Daughters of Beulah while his Emanation
Like a faint rainbow waved before him in the awful gloom
Of London City on the Thames from Surrey Hills to Highgate:
Swift turn the silver spindles, & the golden weights play soft
And lulling harmonies beneath the Looms, from Caithness in the   70
                                                            north
To Lizard-point & Dover in the south: his Emanation
Joy'd in the many weaving threads in bright Cathedrons Dome*
Weaving the Web of life for Jerusalem. the Web of life
Down flowing into Entuthons Vales, glistens with soft affections.

While Los arose upon his Watch. and down from Golgonooza   75
Putting on his golden sandals to walk from mountain to
                                                  mountain,
He takes his way, girding himself with gold & in his hand
Holding his iron mace: The Spectre remains attentive
Alternate they watch in night: alternate labour in day
Before the Furnaces laboring. while Los all night watches   80
The stars rising & setting, & the meteors & terrors of night.
With him went down the Dogs of Leutha at his feet
They lap the water of the trembling Thames then follow swift
And thus he heard the voice of Albions daughters on Euphrates.
Our Father Albions land: O it was a lovely land! & the Daughters of   85
                                                            Beulah
Walked up and down in its green mountains: but Hand is fled
Away: & mighty Hyle: & after them Jerusalem is gone. Awake

[Plate 84]

Highgates heights & Hampsteads, to Poplar Hackney & Bow:
To Islington & Paddington & the Brook of Albions River
We builded Jerusalem as a City & a Temple; from Lambeth
We began our Foundations; lovely Lambeth! O lovely Hills
Of Camberwell, we shall behold you no more in glory & pride   5
For Jerusalem lies in ruins & the Furnaces of Los are builded
                                                              there
You are now shrunk up to a narrow Rock in the midst of the Sea
But here we build Babylon on Euphrates. compelld to build
And to inhabit. our Little-ones to clothe in armour of the gold
Of Jerusalems Cherubims & to forge them swords of her Altars   10
I see London blind & age-bent begging thro the Streets*
Of Babylon, led by a child. his tears run down his beard
The voice of Wandering Reuben ecchoes from street to street
In all the Cities of the Nations Paris Madrid Amsterdam
The Corner of Broad Street weeps; Poland Street languishes   15
To Great Queen Street & Lincolns Inn all is distress & woe.*

The night falls thick Hand comes from Albion in his strength
He combines into a Mighty-one the Double Molech & Chemosh
Marching thro Egypt in his fury the East is pale at his course
The Nations of India, the Wild Tartar that never knew Man   20
Starts from his lofty places & casts down his tents & flees away
But we woo him all the night in songs, O Los come forth O Los
Divide us from these terrors & give us power them to subdue
Arise upon thy Watches let us see thy Globe of fire
On Albions Rocks & let thy voice be heard upon Euphrates.   25

Thus sang the Daughters in lamentation, uniting into One
With Rahab as she turnd the iron Spindle of destruction.*
Terrified at the Sons of Albion they took the Falsehood which
Gwendolen hid in her left hand. it grew & grew till it

[Plate 85]

Became a Space & an Allegory around the Winding Worm
They namd it Canaan & built for it a tender Moon
Los smild with joy thinking on Enitharmon, & he brought
Reuben from his twelvefold wandrings & led him into it
Planting the Seeds of the Twelve Tribes & Moses & David   5

And gave a Time & Revolution to the Space, Six Thousand Years
He calld it Divine Analogy, for in Beulah the Feminine
Emanations Create Space, the Masculine Create Time, & plant
The Seeds of beauty in the Space listning to their lamentation
Los walks upon his ancient Mountains in the deadly darkness   10
Among his Furnaces directing his laborious Myriads watchful
Looking to the East: & his voice is heard over the whole Earth
As he watches the Furnaces by night & directs the labourers

And thus Los replies upon his Watch: the Valleys listen silent:
The Stars stand still to hear: Jerusalem & Vala cease to mourn: 15
His voice is heard from Albion: the Alps & Appenines
Listen: Hermon & Lebanon bow their crowned heads
Babel & Shinar look toward the Western Gate, they sit down
Silent at his voice: they view the red Globe of fire in Los's hand
As he walks from Furnace to Furnace directing the Labourers   20
And this is the Song of Los. the Song that he sings on his Watch

O lovely mild Jerusalem! O Shiloh of Mount Ephraim!
I see thy Gates of precious stones! thy Walls of gold & silver
Thou art the soft reflected Image of the Sleeping Man
Who, stretchd on Albions rocks reposes amidst his Twenty-eight   25
Cities: where Beulah lovely terminates, in the hills & valleys of
                                                            Albion
Cities not yet embodied in Time and Space: plant ye
The Seeds O Sisters in the bosom of Time & Spaces womb
To spring up for Jerusalem: lovely Shadow of Sleeping Albion
Why wilt thou rend thyself apart & build an Earthly Kingdom   30
To reign in pride & to opress & to mix the Cup of Delusion
O thou that dwellest with Babylon! Come forth O lovely-one

[Plate 86]

I see thy Form O lovely mild Jerusalem, Wingd with Six Wings
In the opacous Bosom of the Sleeper. lovely Three-fold
In Head & Heart & Reins three Universes of love & beauty*
Thy forehead bright: Holiness to the Lord, with Gates of pearl
Reflects Eternity beneath thy azure wings of feathery down   5
Ribbd delicate & clothd with featherd gold & azure & purple
From thy white shoulders shadowing, purity in holiness!
Thence featherd with soft crimson of the ruby bright as fire

Spreading into the azure Wings which like a canopy
Bends over thy immortal Head in which Eternity dwells   10
Albion beloved Land; I see thy mountains & thy hills
And valleys & thy pleasant Cities Holiness to the Lord
I see the Spectres of thy Dead O Emanation of Albion.

Thy Bosom white, translucent, coverd with immortal gems
A sublime ornament not obscuring the outlines of beauty   15
Terrible to behold for thy extreme beauty & perfection
Twelve-fold here all the Tribes of Israel I behold
Upon the Holy Land: I see the River of Life & Tree of Life
I see the New Jerusalem descending out of Heaven*
Between thy Wings of gold & silver featherd immortal   20
Clear as the rainbow, as the cloud of the Suns tabernacle

Thy Reins, coverd with Wings translucent sometimes covering
And sometimes spread abroad, reveal the flames of holiness
Which like a robe covers: & like a Veil of Seraphim
In flaming fire unceasing burns from Eternity to Eternity   25
Twelvefold I there behold Israel in her Tents
A Pillar of a Cloud by day: a Pillar of fire by night
Guides them: there I behold Moab & Ammon & Amalek
There, Bells of silver round thy knees living articulate
Comforting sounds of love & harmony & on thy feet   30
Sandals of gold & pearl, & Egypt & Assyria before me
The Isles of Javan, Philistea. Tyre and Lebanon

Thus Los sings upon his Watch walking from Furnace to Furnace.
He siezes his Hammer every hour, flames surround him as
He beats: seas roll beneath his feet, tempests muster   35
Around his head. the thick hail stones stand ready to obey
His voice in the black cloud, his Sons labour in thunders
At his Furnaces; his Daughters at their Looms sing woes
His Emanation separates in milky fibres agonizing
Among the golden Looms of Cathedron sending fibres of love   40
From Golgonooza with sweet visions for Jerusalem. wanderer.

Nor can any consummate bliss without being Generated
On Earth; of those whose Emanations weave the loves
Of Beulah for Jerusalem & Shiloh. in immortal Golgonooza
Concentering in the majestic form of Erin in eternal tears   45
Viewing the Winding Worm on the Desarts of Great Tartary
Viewing Los in his shudderings, pouring balm on his sorrows

So dread is Los's fury that none dare him to approach
Without becoming his Children in the Furnaces of affliction

And Enitharmon like a faint rainbow waved before him   50
Filling with Fibres from his loins which reddend with desire
Into a Globe of blood beneath his bosom trembling in darkness
Of Albions clouds. he fed it, with his tears & bitter groans
Hiding his Spectre in invisibility from the timorous Shade
Till it became a separated cloud of beauty grace & love   55
Among the darkness of his Furnaces dividing asunder till
She separated stood before him a lovely Female weeping
Even Enitharmon separated outside, & his Loins closed
And heal'd after the separation: his pains he soon forgot:
Lured by her beauty outside of himself in shadowy grief.   60
Two Wills they had; Two Intellects: & not as in times of old.

Silent they wanderd hand in hand like two Infants wandring
From Enion in the desarts, terrified at each others beauty
Envying each other yet desiring in all devouring Love,

[Plate 87]

Repelling weeping Enion blind & age-bent into the fourfold
Desarts. Los first broke silence & began to utter his love

O lovely Enitharmon: I behold thy graceful forms
Moving beside me till intoxicated with the woven labyrinth
Of beauty & perfection my wild fibres shoot in veins   5
Of blood thro all my nervous limbs. soon overgrown in roots
I shall be closed from thy sight. sieze therefore in thy hand
The small fibres as they shoot around me draw out in pity
And let them run on the winds of thy bosom: I will fix them
With pulsations, we will divide them into Sons & Daughters   10
To live in thy Bosoms translucence as in an eternal morning

Enitharmon answerd. No! I will sieze thy Fibres & weave
Them: not as thou wilt but as I will, for I will Create
A round Womb beneath my bosom lest I also be overwoven
With Love; be thou assured I never will be thy slave   15
Let Mans delight be Love; but Womans delight be Pride
In Eden our loves were the same here they are opposite
I have Loves of my own I will weave them in Albions Spectre.

Cast thou in Jerusalems shadows thy Loves! silk of liquid
Rubies Jacinths Crysolites: issuing from thy Furnaces, While   20
Jerusalem divides thy care: while thou carest for Jerusalem
Know that I never will be thine: also thou hidest Vala
From her these fibres shoot to shut me in a Grave.
You are Albions Victim, he has set his Daughter in your path

[Plate 88]

Los answerd sighing like the Bellows of his Furnaces

I care not! the swing of my Hammer shall measure the starry round
When in Eternity Man converses with Man they enter
Into each others Bosom (which are Universes of delight)
In mutual interchange. and first their Emanations meet   5
Surrounded by their Children. if they embrace & comingle
The Human Four-fold Forms mingle also in thunders of Intellect
But if the Emanations mingle not; with storms & agitations
Of earthquakes & consuming fires they roll apart in fear
For Man cannot unite with Man but by their Emanations   10
Which stand both Male & Female at the Gates of each Humanity
How then can I ever again be united as Man with Man
While thou my Emanation refusest my Fibres of dominion.
When Souls mingle & join thro all the Fibres of Brotherhood
Can there be any secret joy on Earth greater than this?   15

Enitharmon answerd: This is Womans World, nor need she any
Spectre to defend her from Man. I will Create secret places
And the masculine names of the places Merlin & Arthur.
A triple Female Tabernacle for Moral Law I weave
That he who loves Jesus may loathe terrified, Female love   20
Till God himself become a Male subservient to the Female.

She spoke in scorn & jealousy, alternate torments; and
So speaking she sat down on Sussex shore singing lulling
Cadences. & playing in sweet intoxication among the glistening
Fibres of Los: sending them over the Ocean eastward into   25
The realms of dark death; O perverse to thyself, contrarious
To thy own purposes; for when she began to weave
Shooting out in sweet pleasure her bosom in milky Love
Flowd into the aching fibres of Los, yet contending against him
In pride sending his Fibres over to her objects of jealousy   30

In the little lovely Allegoric Night of Albions Daughters
Which stretchd abroad expanding east & west & north & south,
Thro' all the World of Erin & of Los & all their Children

A sullen smile broke from the Spectre in mockery & scorn
Knowing himself the author of their divisions & shrinkings, 35
                                                      gratified
At their contentions. he wiped his tears he washd his visage.

The Man who respects Woman shall be despised by Woman
And deadly cunning & mean abjectness only, shall enjoy them
For I will make their places of joy & love, excrementitious,
Continually building. continually destroying in Family feuds 40
While you are under the dominion of a jealous Female
Unpermanent for ever because of love & jealousy.
You shall want all the Minute Particulars of Life

Thus joyd the Spectre in the dusky fires of Los's Forge, eyeing
Enitharmon who at her shining Looms sings lulling cadences 45
While Los stood at his Anvil in wrath the victim of their love
And hate: dividing the Space of Love with brazen Compasses
In Golgonooza & in Udan-Adan & in Entuthon of Urizen

The blow of his Hammer is Justice. the swing of his Hammer Mercy
The force of Los's Hammer is eternal Forgiveness; but 50
His rage or his mildness were vain, she scatterd his love on the
                                                              wind
Eastward into her own Center, creating the Female Womb
In mild Jerusalem around the Lamb of God. Loud howl
The Furnaces of Los! loud roll the Wheels of Enitharmon
The Four Zoa's in all their faded majesty burst out in fury 55
And fire. Jerusalem took the Cup which foamd in Vala's hand
Like the red Sun upon the mountains in the bloody day
Upon the Hermaphroditic Wine-presses of Love & Wrath.

[Plate 89]

Tho divided by the Cross & Nails & Thorns & Spear
In cruelties of Rahab & Tirzah permanent endure
A terrible indefinite Hermaphroditic form
A Wine-press of Love & Wrath double Hermaphroditic
Twelvefold in Allegoric pomp in selfish holiness 5

The Pharisaion, the Grammateis, the Presbuterion,
The Archiereus, the Iereus, the Saddusaion: double*
Each withoutside of the other, covering eastern heaven

Thus was the Covering Cherub reveald majestic image
Of Selfhood, Body put off. the Antichrist accursed   10
Coverd with precious stones. a Human Dragon terrible
And bright. stretchd over Europe & Asia gorgeous
In three nights he devourd the rejected corse of death

His Head dark, deadly, in its Brain incloses a reflexion
Of Eden all perverted; Egypt on the Gihon many tongued   15
And many mouthd: Ethiopia. Lybia, the Sea of Rephaim
Minute Particulars in slavery I behold among the brick-kilns
Disorganizd, & there is Pharoh in his iron Court:*
And the Dragon of the River & the Furnaces of iron.
Outwoven from Thames & Tweed & Severn awful streams   20
Twelve ridges of Stone frown over all the Earth in tyrant pride*
Frown over each River stupendous Works of Albions Druid Sons
And Albions Forests of Oaks coverd the Earth from Pole to Pole

His Bosom wide reflects Moab & Ammon on the River
Pison, since calld Arnon, there is Heshbon beautiful   25
The Rocks of Rabbath on the Arnon & the Fish-pools of Heshbon
Whose currents flow into the Dead Sea by Sodom & Gomorra
Above his Head high arching Wings black filld with Eyes
Spring upon iron sinews from the Scapulæ & Os Humeri.*
There Israel in bondage to his Generalizing Gods   30
Molech & Chemosh. & in his left breast is Philistea
In Druid Temples over the whole Earth with Victims Sacrifice,
From Gaza to Damascus Tyre & Sidon & the Gods
Of Javan thro the Isles of Grecia & all Europes Kings
Where Hiddekel pursues his course among the rocks   35
Two Wings spring from his ribs of brass, starry, black as night
But translucent their blackness as the dazling of gems

His Loins inclose Babylon on Euphrates beautiful
And Rome in sweet Hesperia, there Israel scatterd abroad
In martyrdoms & slavery I behold: ah vision of sorrow!   40
Inclosed by eyeless Wings, glowing with fire as the iron
Heated in the Smiths forge, but cold the wind of their dread fury

But in the midst of a devouring Stomach, Jerusalem
Hidden within the Covering Cherub as in a Tabernacle

Of threefold workmanship in allegoric delusion & woe   45
There the Seven Kings of Canaan & Five Baalim of Philistea
Sihon & Og the Anakim & Emim Nephilim & Gibborim
From Babylon to Rome & the Wings spread from Japan
Where the Red Sea terminates the World of Generation & Death
To Irelands farthest rocks where Giants builded their Causeway   50
Into the Sea of Rephaim. but the Sea oerwhelmd them all.

A Double Female now appear'd within the Tabernacle,
Religion hid in War, a Dragon red & hidden Harlot*
Each within other. but without a Warlike Mighty-one
Of dreadful power sitting upon Horeb pondering dire   55
And mighty preparations mustering multitudes innumerable
Of warlike sons among the sands of Midian & Aram
For multitudes of those who sleep in Alla descend
Lured by his warlike symphonies of tabret pipe & harp
Burst the bottoms of the Graves & Funeral Arks of Beulah   60
Wandering in that unknown Night beyond the silent Grave
They become One with the Antichrist & are absorbd in him

[Plate 90]

The Feminine separates from the Masculine & both from Man.
Ceasing to be His Emanations, Life to Themselves assuming:
And while they circumscribe his Brain. & while they circumscribe
His Heart, & while they circumscribe his Loins! a Veil & Net
Of Veins of red Blood grows around them like a scarlet robe.   5
Covering them from the sight of Man like the woven Veil of Sleep
Such as the Flowers of Beulah weave to be their Funeral Mantles
But dark: opake! tender to touch, & painful: & agonizing
To the embrace of love, & to the mingling of soft fibres
Of tender affection. that no more the Masculine mingles   10
With the Feminine. but the Sublime is shut out from the Pathos
In howling torment. to build stone walls of separation, compelling
The Pathos, to weave curtains of hiding secresy from the torment.

Bowen & Conwenna stood on Skiddaw cutting the Fibres
Of Benjamin from Chesters River: loud the River; loud the Mersey   15
And the Ribble. thunder into the Irish sea, as the Twelve Sons
Of Albion drank & imbibed the Life & eternal Form of Luvah
Cheshire & Lancashire & Westmoreland groan in anguish

As they cut the fibres from the Rivers he sears them with hot
Iron of his Forge & fixes them into Bones of chalk & Rock   20
Conwenna sat above: with solemn cadences she drew
Fibres of life out from the Bones into her golden Loom
Hand had his Furnace on Highgates heights & it reachd*
To Brockley Hills across the Thames: he with double Boadicea*
In cruel pride cut Reuben apart from the Hills of Surrey   25
Comingling with Luvah & with the Sepulcher of Luvah
For the Male is a Furnace of beryl: the Female is a golden Loom

Los cries: No Individual ought to appropriate to Himself
Or to his Emanation, any of the Universal Characteristics
Of David or of Eve, of the Woman. or of the Lord.   30
Of Reuben or of Benjamin, of Joseph or Judah or Levi
Those who dare appropriate to themselves Universal Attributes
Are the Blasphemous Selfhoods & must be broken asunder
A Vegetated Christ & a Virgin Eve, are the Hermaphroditic
Blasphemy, by his Maternal Birth he is that Evil-One   35
And his Maternal Humanity must be put off Eternally
Lest the Sexual Generation swallow up Regeneration
Come Lord Jesus, take on thee the Satanic Body of Holiness

So Los cried in the Valleys of Middlesex in the Spirit of
                                         Prophecy
While in Selfhood Hand & Hyle & Bowen & Skofeld appropriate   40
The Divine Names: seeking to Vegetate the Divine Vision
In a corporeal & ever dying Vegetation & Corruption
Mingling with Luvah in One. they become One Great Satan

Loud scream the Daughters of Albion beneath the Tongs &
                                         Hammer
Dolorous are their lamentations in the burning Forge   45
They drink Reuben & Benjamin as the iron drinks the fire
They are red hot with cruelty: raving along the Banks of Thames
And on Tyburns Brook among the howling Victims in loveliness
While Hand & Hyle condense the Little-ones & erect them into
A mighty Temple even to the stars: but they Vegetate   50
Beneath Los's Hammer, that Life may not be blotted out.

For Los said: When the Individual appropriates Universality
He divides into Male & Female: & when the Male & Female,
Appropriate Individuality, they become an Eternal Death.
Hermaphroditic worshippers of a God of cruelty & law!   55

Your Slaves & Captives; you compell to worship a God of Mercy,*
These are the Demonstrations of Los. & the blows of my mighty
                                                          Hammer

So Los spoke. And the Giants of Albion terrified & ashamed
With Los's thunderous Words, began to build trembling rocking
                                                          Stones*
For his Words roll in thunders & lightnings among the Temples   60
Terrified rocking to & fro upon the earth, & sometimes
Resting in a Circle in Malden or in Strathness or Dura.
Plotting to devour Albion & Los the friend of Albion
Denying in private: mocking God & Eternal Life: & in Public
Collusion, calling themselves Deists, Worshipping the Maternal   65
Humanity: calling it Nature, and Natural Religion

But still the thunder of Los peals loud & thus the thunders cry
These beautiful Witchcrafts of Albion, are gratifyd by Cruelty

[Plate 91]

It is easier to forgive an Enemy than to forgive a Friend:*
The man who permits you to injure him, deserves your vengeance:
He also will recieve it: go Spectre! obey my most secret desire:
Which thou knowest without my speaking: Go to these Fiends of
                                                          Righteousness
Tell them to obey their Humanities, & not pretend Holiness;   5
When they are murderers: as far as my Hammer & Anvil permit
Go, tell them that the Worship of God, is honouring his gifts
In other men: & loving the greatest men best, each according
To his Genius: which is the Holy Ghost in Man; there is no other
God than that God who is the intellectual fountain of Humanity;   10
He who envies or calumniates: which is murder & cruelty,
Murders the Holy-one: Go tell them this & overthrow their cup,
Their bread, their altar-table, their incense & their oath:
Their marriage & their baptism, their burial & consecration:
I have tried to make friends by corporeal gifts but have only   15
Made enemies: I never made friends but by spiritual gifts;
By severe contentions of friendship & the burning fire of thought.
He who would see the Divinity must see him in his Children
One first, in friendship & love; then a Divine Family, & in the midst
Jesus will appear; so he who wishes to see a Vision; a perfect Whole 20

Must see it in its Minute Particulars; Organized & not as thou
O Fiend of Righteousness pretendest; thine is a Disorganized
And snowy cloud: brooder of tempests & destructive War
You smile with pomp & rigor: you talk of benevolence & virtue!
I act with benevolence & virtue & get murderd time after time: 25
You accumulate Particulars, & murder by analyzing, that you
May take the aggregate; & you call the aggregate Moral Law:
And you call that swelld & bloated Form; a Minute Particular.
But General Forms have their vitality in Particulars: & every
Particular is a Man; a Divine Member of the Divine Jesus.   30

So Los cried at his Anvil in the horrible darkness weeping!

The Spectre builded stupendous Works, taking the Starry Heavens
Like to a curtain & folding them according to his will
Repeating the Smaragdine Table of Hermes to draw Los down*
Into the Indefinite, refusing to believe without demonstration   35
Los reads the Stars of Albion! the Spectre reads the Voids
Between the Stars; among the arches of Albions Tomb sublime
Rolling the Sea in rocky paths: forming Leviathan
And Behemoth; the War by Sea enormous & the War
By Land astounding: erecting pillars in the deepest Hell.   40
To reach the heavenly arches; Los beheld undaunted furious
His heavd Hammer; he swung it round & at one blow,
In unpitying ruin driving down the pyramids of pride
Smiting the Spectre on his Anvil & the integuments of his Eye
And Ear unbinding in dire pain, with many blows   45
Of strict severity self-subduing, & with many tears labouring.

Then he sent forth the Spectre all his pyramids were grains
Of sand, & his pillars: dust on the flys wing: & his starry
Heavens; a moth of gold & silver mocking his anxious grasp
Thus Los alterd his Spectre & every Ratio of his Reason   50
He alterd time after time, with dire pain & many tears
Till he had completely divided him into a separate space.

Terrified Los sat to behold trembling & weeping & howling
I care not whether a Man is Good or Evil; all that I care
Is whether he is a Wise Man or a Fool, Go! put off Holiness   55
And put on Intellect: or my thundrous Hammer shall drive thee
To wrath which thou condemnest: till thou obey my voice

So Los terrified cries: trembling & weeping & howling! Beholding

[Plate 92]

What do I see! The Briton Saxon Roman Norman amalgamating
In my Furnaces into One Nation the English: & taking refuge
In the Loins of Albion. The Canaanite united with the fugitive
Hebrew. whom she divided into Twelve. & sold into Egypt
Then scatterd the Egyptian & Hebrew to the four Winds: 5
This sinful Nation Created in our Furnaces & Looms is Albion

So Los spoke. Enitharmon answerd in great terror in Lambeths Vale

The Poets Song draws to its period, & Enitharmon is no more.
For if he be that Albion I can never weave him in my Looms
But when he touches the first fibrous thread. like filmy dew 10

My Looms will be no more & I annihilate vanish for ever
Then thou wilt Create another Female according to thy Will.

Los answered swift as the shuttle of gold. Sexes must vanish & cease
To be when Albion arises from his dread repose O lovely
                 Enitharmon:
When all their Crimes. their Punishments their Accusations of 15
                 Sin:
All their Jealousies Revenges. Murders. hidings of Cruelty in
                 Deceit
Appear only in the Outward Spheres of Visionary Space and Time.
In the shadows of Possibility by Mutual Forgiveness forevermore
And in the Vision & in the Prophecy. that we may Foresee & Avoid
The terrors of Creation & Redemption & Judgment. Beholding 20
                 them
Displayd in the Emanative Visions of Canaan in Jerusalem & in
                 Shiloh
And in the Shadows of Remembrance. & in the Chaos of the Spectre
Amalek. Edom. Egypt. Moab. Ammon. Ashur. Philistea. around
                 Jerusalem,
Where the Druids reard their Rocky Circles to make permanent
                 Remembrance
Of Sin. & the Tree of Good & Evil sprang from the Rocky Circle 25
                 & Snake
Of the Druid. along the Valley of Rephaim from Camberwell to
                 Golgotha
And framed the Mundane Shell Cavernous in Length, Bredth &
                 Highth

[Plate 93]

Enitharmon heard. She raisd her head like the mild Moon

O Rintrah! O Palamabron. What are your dire & awful purposes
Enitharmons name is nothing before you: you forget all my
　　　　　　　　　　　　　　　Love!
The Mothers love of obedience is forgotten & you seek a Love
Of the pride of dominion. that will Divorce Ocalythron &　　　5
　　　　　　　　　　　　　　　Elynittria
Upon East Moor in Derbyshire & along the Valleys of Cheviot
Could you Love me, Rintrah, if you Pride not in my Love
As Reuben found Mandrakes in the field & gave them to his
　　　　　　　　　　　　　　　Mother*
Pride meets with Pride upon the Mountains in the stormy day
In that terrible Day of Rintrahs Plow & of Satans driving the　　10
　　　　　　　　　　　　　　　Team.*
Ah! then I heard my little ones weeping along the Valley!
Ah! then I saw my beloved ones fleeing from my Tent
Merlin was like thee Rintrah among the Giants of Albion
Judah was like Palamabron: O Simeon! O Levi! ye fled away
How can I hear my little ones weeping along the Valley　　　15
Or how upon the distant Hills see my beloveds Tents.

Then Los again took up his speech as Enitharmon ceast

Fear not, my Sons this Waking Death. he is become One with me
Behold him here! We shall not Die! we shall be united in Jesus.
Will you suffer this Satan this Body of Doubt that Seems but Is　20
　　　　　　　　　　　　　　　Not
To occupy the very threshold of Eternal Life. if Bacon. Newton.
　　　　　　　　　　　　　　　Locke
Deny a Conscience in Man & the Communion of Saints & Angels
Contemning the Divine Vision & Fruition. Worshiping the Deus
Of the Heathen. The God of This World. & the Goddess Nature
Mystery Babylon the Great. The Druid Dragon & hidden　　25
　　　　　　　　　　　　　　　Harlot
Is it not that Signal of the Morning which was told us in the
　　　　　　　　　　　　　　　Beginning

Thus they converse upon Mam-Tor. the Graves thunder under their
　　　　　　　　　　　　　　　feet

[Plate 94]

Albion cold lays on his Rock: storms & snows beat round him.
Beneath the Furnaces & the starry Wheels & the Immortal Tomb
Howling winds cover him: roaring seas dash furious against him
In the deep darkness broad lightnings glare long thunders roll

The weeds of Death inwrap his hands & feet blown incessant   5
And washd incessant by the for-ever restless sea-waves foaming
                                                              abroad
Upon the white Rock. England a Female Shadow as deadly damps*
Of the Mines of Cornwall & Derbyshire lays upon his bosom heavy
Moved by the wind in volumes of thick cloud returning folding
                                                              round
His loins & bosom unremovable by swelling storms & loud   10
                                                            rending
Of enraged thunders. Around them the Starry Wheels of their
                                                        Giant Sons
Revolve: & over them the Furnaces of Los, & the Immortal Tomb
                                                           around
Erin sitting in the Tomb. to watch them unceasing night and day
And the Body of Albion was closed apart from all Nations.

Over them the famishd Eagle screams on boney Wings and around   15
Them howls the Wolf of famine deep heaves the Ocean black
                                                        thundering
Around the wormy Garments of Albion: then pausing in deathlike
                                                            silence

Time was Finished! The Breath Divine Breathed over Albion
Beneath the Furnaces & starry Wheels and in the Immortal Tomb
And England who is Brittannia awoke from Death on Albions   20
                                                           bosom*
She awoke pale & cold she fainted seven times on the Body of Albion

O pitious Sleep O pitious Dream! O God O God awake I have slain
In Dreams of Chastity & Moral Law I have Murdered Albion! Ah!
In Stone-henge & on London Stone & in the Oak Groves of Malden
I have Slain him in my Sleep with the Knife of the Druid O England 25
O all ye Nations of the Earth behold ye the Jealous Wife
The Eagle & the Wolf & Monkey & Owl & the King & Priest were
                                                            there

[Plate 95]

Her voice pierc'd Albions clay cold ear. he moved upon the Rock
The Breath Divine went forth upon the morning hills. Albion mov'd
Upon the Rock, he opend his eyelids in pain; in pain he mov'd
His stony members, he saw England. Ah! shall the Dead live again

The Breath Divine went forth over the morning hills Albion rose   5
In anger: the wrath of God breaking, bright flaming on all sides
                                                                  around
His awful limbs: into the Heavens he walked clothed in flames
Loud thundring, with broad flashes of flaming lightning & pillars
Of fire, speaking the Words of Eternity in Human Forms, in
                                                                  direful
Revolutions of Action & Passion. thro the Four Elements   10
                                                         on all sides
Surrounding his awful Members. Thou seest the Sun in
                                                     heavy clouds
Struggling to rise above the Mountains, in his burning hand
He takes his Bow, then chooses out his arrows of flaming gold
Murmuring the Bowstring breathes with ardor! clouds roll round
                                                                  the
Horns of the wide Bow, loud sounding winds sport on the mountain   15
                                                                  brows
Compelling Urizen to his Furrow; & Tharmas to his Sheepfold;
And Luvah to his Loom: Urthona he beheld mighty labouring at
His Anvil, in the Great Spectre Los unwearied labouring &
                                                         weeping*
Therefore the Sons of Eden praise Urthonas Spectre in songs
Because he kept the Divine Vision in time of trouble.   20

As the Sun & Moon lead forward the Visions of Heaven & Earth
England who is Brittannia, enterd Albions bosom rejoicing.
Rejoicing in his indignation! adoring his wrathful rebuke.
She who adores not your frowns will only loathe your smiles

[Plate 96]

As the Sun & Moon lead forward the Visions of Heaven & Earth
England who is Brittannia entered Albions bosom rejoicing

Then Jesus appeared standing by Albion as the Good Shepherd
By the lost Sheep that he hath found & Albion knew that it

Was the Lord the Universal Humanity. & Albion saw his Form   5
A Man. & they conversed as Man with Man, in Ages of Eternity
And the Divine Appearance was the likeness & similitude of Los

Albion said. O Lord, what can I do: my Selfhood cruel
Marches against thee deceitful, from Sinai & from Edom
Into the Wilderness of Judah to meet thee in his pride   10
I behold the Visions of my deadly Sleep of Six Thousand Years
Dazling around thy skirts like a Serpent of precious stones & gold
I know it is my Self: O my Divine Creator & Redeemer

Jesus replied Fear not Albion unless I die thou canst not live*
But if I die I shall arise again & thou with me   15
This is Friendship & Brotherhood without it Man Is Not

So Jesus spoke: the Covering Cherub coming on in darkness
Overshadowd them & Jesus said Thus do Men in Eternity
One for another to put off, by forgiveness, every sin

Albion replyd. Cannot Man exist without Mysterious   20
Offering of Self for Another, is this Friendship & Brotherhood
I see thee in the likeness & similitude of Los my Friend

Jesus said. Wouldest thou love one who never died
For thee or ever die for one who had not died for thee
And if God dieth not for Man & giveth not himself   25
Eternally for Man Man could not exist. for Man is Love:
As God is Love: every kindness to another is a little Death
In the Divine Image nor can Man exist but by Brotherhood

So saying. the Cloud overshadowing divided them asunder
Albion stood in terror: not for himself but for his Friend   30
Divine, & Self was lost in the contemplation of faith
And wonder at the Divine Mercy & at Los's sublime honour

Do I sleep amidst danger to Friends! O my Cities & Counties
Do you sleep! rouze up! rouze up. Eternal Death is abroad

So Albion spoke & threw himself into the Furnaces of affliction   35
All was a Vision. all a Dream: the Furnaces became
Fountains of Living Waters flowing from the Humanity Divine*
And all the Cities of Albion rose from their Slumbers, and All
The Sons & Daughters of Albion on soft clouds Waking from Sleep
Soon all around remote the Heavens burnt with flaming fires   40
And Urizen & Luvah & Tharmas & Urthona arose into

Albions Bosom: Then Albion stood before Jesus in the Clouds
Of Heaven Fourfold among the Visions of God in Eternity

[Plate 97]

Awake, Awake Jerusalem! O lovely Emanation of Albion
Awake and overspread all Nations as in Ancient Time
For lo the Night of Death is past and the Eternal Day
Appears upon our Hills: Awake, Jerusalem, and come away

So spake the Vision of Albion & in him so spake in my hearing   5
The Universal Father Then Albion stretchd his hand into
                                                        Infinitude.
And took his Bow, Fourfold the Vision for bright beaming Urizen
Layd his hand on the South & took a breathing Bow of carved
                                                        Gold
Luvah his hand stretch'd to the East & bore a Silver Bow bright
                                                        shining
Tharmas Westward a Bow of Brass pure flaming richly wrought   10
Urthona Northward in thick storms a Bow of Iron terrible
                                                        thundering.

And the Bow is a Male & Female & the Quiver of the Arrows of
                                                        Love.
Are the Children of this Bow: a Bow of Mercy & Loving-
                                                        kindness: laying
Open the hidden Heart in Wars of mutual Benevolence Wars of
                                                        Love
And the Hand of Man grasps firm between the Male & Female   15
                                                        Loves
And he Clothed himself in Bow & Arrows in awful state
                                                        Fourfold
In the midst of his Twenty-eight Cities each with his Bow
                                                        breathing

[Plate 98]

Then each an Arrow flaming from his Quiver fitted carefully
They drew fourfold the unreprovable String. bending thro the
                                                        wide Heavens
The horned Bow Fourfold, loud sounding flew the flaming Arrow
                                                        fourfold

Murmuring the Bow-string breathes with ardor. Clouds roll round
the horns

Of the wide Bow. loud sounding Winds sport on the Mountains 5
brows:

The Druid Spectre was Annihilate, loud thundring rejoicing
terrific vanishing

Fourfold Annihilation; & at the clangor of the Arrows of Intellect
The innumerable Chariots of the Almighty appeard in Heaven
And Bacon & Newton & Locke. & Milton & Shakspear & Chaucer*
A Sun of blood red wrath surrounding heaven, on all sides around 10
Glorious, incomprehsible by Mortal Man & each Chariot was
Sexual Threefold

And every Man stood Fourfold. each Four Faces had. One to
the West*

One toward the East One to the South One to the North. the
Horses Fourfold

And the dim Chaos brightend beneath, above, around! Eyed as
the Peacock

According to the Human Nerves of Sensation, the Four Rivers of 15
the Water of Life

South stood the Nerves of the Eye. East in Rivers of bliss the
Nerves of the

Expansive Nostrils West. flowd the Parent Sense the Tongue.
North stood

The labyrinthine Ear. Circumscribing & Circumcising the
excrementitious

Husk & Covering into Vacuum evaporating revealing the
lineaments of Man

Driving outward the Body of Death in an Eternal Death & 20
Resurrection

Awaking it to Life among the Flowers of Beulah rejoicing in
Unity

In the Four Senses in the Outline the Circumference & Form,
for ever

In Forgiveness of Sins which is Self Annihilation. it is the
Covenant of Jehovah

The Four Living Creatures Chariots of Humanity Divine
Incomprehensible

In beautiful Paradises expand These are the Four Rivers of 25
Paradise

And the Four Faces of Humanity fronting the Four Cardinal
                                                    Points
Of Heaven going forward, forward irresistible from Eternity to
                                                    Eternity

And they conversed together in Visionary forms dramatic which
                                                    bright
Redounded from their Tongues in thunderous majesty, in Visions
In new Expanses, creating exemplars of Memory and of Intellect,   30
Creating Space, Creating Time, according to the wonders Divine
Of Human Imagination. throughout all the Three Regions
                                                    immense
Of Childhood, Manhood & Old Age & the all tremendous
                                        unfathomable NonEns*
Of Death was seen in regenerations terrific or complacent
                                                    varying
According to the subject of discourse & every Word & Every   35
                                                    Character
Was Human according to the Expansion or Contraction. the
                                        Translucence or
Opakeness of Nervous fibres such was the variation of Time
                                                    & Space
Which vary according as the Organs of Perception vary & they
                                                    walked
To & fro in Eternity as One Man, reflecting each in each &
                                                    clearly seen
And seeing: according to fitness & order. And I heard Jehovah   40
                                                    speak
Terrific from his Holy Place & saw the Words of the Mutual
                                        Covenant Divine
On Chariots of gold & jewels with Living Creatures starry &
                                                    flaming
With every Colour. Lion. Tyger. Horse. Elephant. Eagle Dove.
                                                    Fly. Worm.
And the all wondrous Serpent clothed in gems & rich array
                                                    Humanize
In the Forgiveness of Sins according to thy Covenant, Jehovah.   45
                                                    They Cry

Where is the Covenant of Priam. the Moral Virtues of the
                                                    Heathen*
Where is the Tree of Good & Evil that rooted beneath the cruel heel

Of Albions Spectre the Patriarch Druid! where are all his Human
                                                              Sacrifice
For Sin in War & in the Druid Temples of the Accuser of
                                                       Sin: beneath
The Oak Groves of Albion that coverd the whole Earth beneath   50
                                                        his Spectre
Where are the Kingdoms of the World & all their glory that grew
                                                     on Desolation
The Fruit of Albions Poverty Tree*, when the Triple Headed Gog-
                                                     Magog Giant*
Of Albion Taxed the Nations into Desolation & then gave the
                                                  Spectrous Oath

Such is the Cry from all the Earth from the Living Creatures of
                                                        the Earth
And from the great City of Golgonooza in the Shadowy Generation   55

And from the Thirty-two Nations of the Earth among the Living
                                                      Creatures*

[Plate 99]

All Human Forms identified even Tree Metal Earth & Stone. all
Human Forms identified. living going forth & returning wearied
Into the Planetary lives of Years Months Days & Hours reposing
And then Awaking into his Bosom in the Life of Immortality.

And I heard the Name of their Emanations they are named Jerusalem   5

THE END OF THE SONG OF JERUSALEM.

EXPLANATORY NOTES

These notes are built on foundations laid by many previous scholars and scholarly annotators, especially G. E. Bentley, Jr, Martin Butlin, S. Foster Damon, D. W. Dörrbecker, Morris Eaves, David Erdman, Robert N. Essick, Mary Lynn Johnson & John E. Grant, Geoffrey Keynes, Andrew Lincoln, Michael Mason, Alicia Ostriker, Morton D. Paley, Michael Phillips, W. H. Stevenson, Joseph Viscomi, and David Worrall: *plurimi pertransibunt et multiplex erit scientia* (Daniel 12.4). Except for that citation of the Vulgate, references to the Bible are to the Authorized King James Version; references to Shakespeare are to the text and lineation established by Stanley Wells and Gary Taylor for the *Oxford* (1988) and *Norton* (1997) editions; references to Milton are to Helen Darbishire, ed., *The Poetical Works of John Milton* (London: Oxford University Press, 1958); definitions are derived from the *Oxford English Dictionary*.

LYRICS

LYRICS FROM *POETICAL SKETCHES*

3 *Poetical Sketches. By W.B.* (London, 1783) was privately published, in conventional typography for the Reverend A. S. Mathew and John Flaxman; the copies (some of which survive with marginal corrections) were 'given to Blake, to sell to friends, or publish' (*BR* 606). Mathew was Minister of the (Anglican) Percy Chapel, Charlotte Street. His wife Harriet held 'conversazioni' at their home in Rathbone Place at which J. T. Smith 'often heard [Blake] read and sing . . . his poems' (*BR* 30). Smith met the Mathews in 1784; Blake was attending the salon by 1780 and the poems were written between his 'twelfth' and 'twentieth year': 1769–77 ('Advertisement' to *Poetical Sketches*). There have been several facsimiles, most recently the photographic reproduction of Copy Q (Preston Blake Collection, City of Westminster Archives Centre; Tate Publishing, 2007).

Song ('How sweet I roam'd from field to field'): Malkin (1806) noted that this poem was 'written before the age of fourteen' (*BR* 569) and suggested that it was 'in the spirit' of Ben Jonson's masque *The Hue and Cry after Cupid* (1608), though he was probably thinking only of the song 'Beauties, have ye seen this toy', reprinted as 'A Hue and Cry after Cupid' in Percy's *Reliques* (Third Series). Blake's speaker is both a bird and a human lover, or possibly the winged Cupid of Jonson's poem (in which case 'the prince of love' is Eros).

10 *Phœbus*: Apollo, the god of light, music and prophecy.

Song ('My silks and fine array'): an Elizabethan pastiche which Swinburne compared to the songs of Beaumont and Fletcher; the 'axe and spade' and 'winding sheet' echo the 'pikeax and a spade | And eke a shrowding sheet' of Thomas Vaux's 'I loathe that I did love' (1557), printed as 'The

Aged Lover Renounceth Love' in Percy's *Reliques* and sung by the grave-digger in *Hamlet* 5.1.

Song ('Love and harmony combine')

4 12 *turtle*: turtledove ('the voice of the turtle is heard in our land', Song of Solomon, 2.12, also echoed in Bunyan's account of Beulah in *The Pilgrim's Progress*).

16 *his*: printed 'her', corrected in two copies.

Song ('I love the jocund dance')

5 13–16 *I love the oaken seat . . . sports to see*: an early version of the second stanza of 'The Ecchoing Green'.

Song ('Memory, hither come')

8 *watery glass*: 'when Phoebe doth behold | Her silver visage in the wat'ry glass', *A Midsummer Night's Dream*, 1.1.209–10.

6 *Mad Song*: the best known mad songs are Ophelia's in *Hamlet* 4.5 but Percy includes six examples in his *Reliques* (noting that 'the English have more songs and ballads on the subject of madness than any of their neighbours') including 'Old Tom of Bedlam' which, like Blake's 'night . . . a-cold', suggests a link to the fragments sung on the heath by Edgar (as 'Poor Tom') in *King Lear* 3.4 though these are actually sane verses sung by a (pretended) madman.

4 *infold*: printed 'unfold', corrected in six copies.

7 *birds*: printed 'beds', corrected in seven copies.

10 *paved heaven*: 'the street of the city was pure gold', Revelation 21.21.

Song ('Fresh from the dewy hill, the merry year'): this and the following poem are written in heroic couplets and in the manner of the eighteenth-century sensibility cult (see note to *The First Book of Urizen* 13.51, p. 393).

2 *flaming car*: Phoebus's 'burning car' (*3 Henry VI*, 2.6.11) was already a stock image for Shakespeare though Blake here uses it of the year rather than the sun.

7 *Song ('When early morn walks forth in sober grey')*

1 'While the still morn went out with Sandals gray', Milton, *Lycidas*, 187.

10 *pleasing woe*: 'If these best passions prompt the pleasing woe, | Indulge it freely', Prologue ('By a Friend') to James Thomson, *Edward and Eleonora, A Tragedy* (1739).

8 *To the Muses*

1 *Ida*: mountain in Crete where Zeus is said to have been born (though also the mountain in Phrygia where Paris made the judgement which led to the Trojan War).

2 *the East*: probably Greece, as in Gray's 'The Progress of Poesy' (1754), though Ritson's 'Historical Essay on the Origin and Progress of National Song' (prefixed to his *Select Collection of English Songs*, 1783, for which

Blake had engraved illustrations after Stothard) notes that 'the Egyptians, the Hebrews, the Arabians, the Persians, the Asiatic Indians' and 'the Chinese' had songs from 'time immemorial'; Ritson concludes by regretting 'the loss of melody and song, which . . . are fallen to rise no more!!'

12 *Nine*: the nine Muses were the goddesses of the arts.

MANUSCRIPT POEMS FROM ANN FLAXMAN'S COPY
OF *POETICAL SKETCHES*

Three additional poems were recorded (not in Blake's hand) on extra leaves added before binding to Copy F (Turnbull Library, Wellington, NZ) of *Poetical Sketches* (inscribed 'from Mrs Flaxman May 15, 1784'). The second poem is an early draft of the 'Laughing Song' of *Innocence*; all three are in a mode closer to pastoral than to the children's hymn.

9 *Song 3ʳᵈ by an old shepherd*: compare Winter's verses ('When icicles hang by the wall') in Shakespeare's *Love's Labour's Lost*, 5.2.

SONGS OF INNOCENCE AND OF EXPERIENCE SHEWING
THE TWO CONTRARY STATES OF THE HUMAN SOUL

This volume, first published as such in 1794, is a rare and remarkable example of a collection of poems uttered in the author's voice, and sincerely, yet from two profoundly different points of view (see Introduction). Blake started to write the *Innocence* songs in the early 1780s: one is partially anticipated in a poem printed in *Poetical Sketches* (1783), three appear in 'An Island in the Moon' (*c*.1782–5), and an early draft of another is found as a manuscript addition to a copy of *Poetical Sketches*. He engraved, printed, and self-published 23 poems, on the model of a book of children's hymns (see Introduction) as *Songs of Innocence* in 1789. There was then a change of mind, probably because of the revolution in France that summer, and over the next three years he made drafts in his Notebook for a volume which would be advertised as *Songs of Experience* in October 1793. This was printed in 1794, initially as a group of 24 poems (three of which had been transferred from *Innocence*, in one case inadvertently). The two volumes were often sold together and, either later in 1794 or early in the following year, Blake engraved a joint title-page for them: *Songs of Innocence and of Experience Shewing the Two Contrary States of the Human Soul*.

Copies B, C, D are the earliest known examples of the combined book, made up from sheets of *Innocence* printed in 1789 and sheets of *Experience* printed in 1794. The joint title-page is first found in Copy B. But since that survives in an odd and probably non-authorial order, the arrangement found in Copy C (Library of Congress) is (with one alteration) followed here. The alteration is the amendment of the obvious error of placing 'A Dream' in *Experience* (caused by the fact that it was printed on the other side of the sheet containing 'The Little Girl Lost', and was thus accidentally carried into the other volume when 'The Little Girl Lost' and 'The Little Girl Found' were deliberately transferred). Blake reprinted

'A Dream' separately and placed it at the end of the *Innocence* poems in Copy E; that correction is followed here. One advantage of this early arrangement is that the volume ends with 'The Clod & the Pebble', a poem in which the voices of both Innocence and Experience are heard.

SONGS OF INNOCENCE

Some of these poems are straightforward expressions of pleasure whose significance is the negative one that they do *not* contain the didactic moralizing customary in children's hymns. In a marginal note to Night 7b of *The Four Zoas*, Blake will observe, 'Innocence dwells with Wisdom, but never with Ignorance'; the wisdom of innocence is endorsed by Jesus's prayer in Matthew 11.25: 'I thank thee, O Father, Lord of heaven and earth, because thou hast hid these things from the wise and prudent, and hast revealed them unto babes'.

Introduction

9 2 *Piping songs*: the speaker moves from piping to singing to writing his songs, rather as Blake is known to have sung his poems at Harriet Mathew's salon before they were printed in *Poetical Sketches*.

10 5 *a Lamb*: both a real or pastoral lamb and Jesus as the Lamb of God ('Behold the Lamb of God, which taketh away the sin of the world', John 1.29).

18 *stain'd the water*: sometimes read as a suggestion that the Innocence poems are tainted or morally flawed; in fact simply the Edenic or pre-industrial form of writing.

11 *The Shepherd*: both literal or pastoral and, by extension, the Jesus of John 10.14: 'I am the good shepherd, and know my sheep, and am known of mine'.

A Cradle Song: a reaction to Isaac Watts's 'Cradle Hymn' (1715); 'A cradle song' (N114) is a draft for a possible Experience contrary but was not engraved.

12 24 *wept for me*: reversing the customary children's-hymn format of an adult teaching children, here the adult is herself instructed by her recollection of the Christ child.

The Lamb: a contrary to 'The Tyger' in *Experience*.

14 *calls himself a Lamb*: John 1.29.

16 *a little child*: compare the third verse of Charles Wesley's 'Gentle Jesus, meek and mild' (*Hymns and Sacred Poems*, 1742, though originally the first verse of a separate poem): 'Thou art gentle, meek, and mild; | Thou wast once a little child'. Both Wesley and Blake are drawing on Matthew 11.29 ('I am meek and lowly in heart'); thirty years later, in 'The Everlasting Gospel', Blake would instead, through the mouth of Joseph of Arimathea, deny Jesus's 'Humility' and assert his 'honest, triumphant Pride' (p. 84).

13 *The Blossom*: there is a possible contrary in 'The Sick Rose'.

10 *sobbing sobbing*: a robin buries the dead children in leaves in the popular ballad 'The Children in the Wood' (see note to 'The Little Boy Lost', p. 355).

Nurses Song: originally sung by Mrs Nannicantipot in 'An Island in the Moon'; a contrary to the 'Nurse's Song' of *Experience*. Here the nurse is persuaded to neglect her customary duty (established by what 'experience' teaches us about over-tired children) to enforce bed-time.

14 *Holy Thursday*: originally sung by Obtuse Angle in 'An Island in the Moon'; a contrary to the 'Holy Thursday' of *Experience*. An annual service of thanksgiving (and fund raising) for charity-school children had been held in London since 1704, moving from Christ Church, Newgate Street, to St Paul's Cathedral in 1782. It was held on a Thursday, usually in May, though never actually on Ascension Day or Maundy Thursday (the two 'holy' Thursdays of the church calendar); by the 1780s as many as 6,000 children were involved. Blake's family supplied haberdashery to the Parish School of Industry in King Street, Golden Square, from 1782 to 1785; see note to *Milton* 42.12 (p. 408).

2 *red & blue & green*: charity schools were often referred to by the distinctive colour of their uniforms, such as the Redcoat School in St Botolphe-without-Aldgate (now in Stepney), the Bluecoat School (Christ's Hospital, then in Newgate Street), and the Green Coat School in Westminster (now Westminster City School). Pupils from Christ's Hospital still process through the City of London, in their blue Tudor uniforms, on St Matthew's Day.

9 *a mighty wind*: 'And suddenly there came a sound from heaven as of a rushing mighty wind' (Acts 2.2), when the Holy Ghost fills the apostles at Pentecost.

12 *angel from your door*: 'Be not forgetful to entertain strangers: for thereby some have entertained angels unawares' (Hebrews 13.2).

The Ecchoing Green: there is a partial first draft in the third stanza of 'I love the jocund dance' (*Poetical Sketches*).

On Anothers Sorrow

15 13 *smiles on all*: 'Are not two sparrows sold for a farthing? and one of them shall not fall on the ground without your Father' (Matthew 10.29).

16 22 *Wiping all our tears away*: 'God shall wipe away all tears from their eyes' (Revelation 7.17).

27 *man of woe*: 'He is despised and rejected of men; a man of sorrows, and acquainted with grief' (Isaiah 53.3).

33 *gives to us his joy*: 'your sorrow shall be turned into joy' (John 16.20).

Spring: compare 'Hymn 2' ('Come let us go forth into the fields') in Anna Laetitia Barbauld's *Hymns in Prose for Children*, Joseph Johnson, 1781).

The School Boy: moved to *Experience* in Copy L, perhaps because it is an account of 'experience' even though its purpose is to denounce it.

18 *The Divine Image*: 'The Human Abstract' is the contrary in *Experience*; another contrary, entitled 'A Divine Image', is found only in Copy BB (sold to Robert Balmanno in 1816). C. A. Tulk was supposedly told by Blake that the poem was written in the New Jerusalem Church, Hatton Garden (*BR* 599). Though the Swedenborgians did not occupy that chapel until 1797, the poem's sense of 'the Divine Humanity' has a Swedenborgian flavour and the poem would be reprinted (together with 'On Anothers Sorrow') in the Swedenborgian *Dawn of Light and Theological Inspector* in April 1825.

11 *human form divine*: Pope's translation of Homer's *Odyssey*, 10.278; Milton, 'human face divine' (*Paradise Lost*, 3.44).

18 *heathen, turk or jew*: contrast 'Lord, I ascribe it to thy grace . . . That I was born of Christian race, | And not a Heathen, or a Jew', Watts, 'Praise for the Gospel' (*Divine Songs*, 1715).

The Chimney Sweeper: the crooked chimneys of old houses were swept by small boys, apprenticed (in effect, sold) to Master Sweeps at the age of 6, who climbed to dislodge the soot; cancer of the scrotum, unique to chimney sweeps, was the first industrially related cancer to be identified, in 1775. The campaign to end the practice began with Jonas Hanway's *The State of Chimney Sweepers' Young Apprentices* (1773) and continued until 1875 (previous Chimney Sweepers Acts in 1788, 1834, 1840, and 1864 had been widely evaded, though mechanical alternatives to the use of climbing boys began to be developed from 1803). Blake's (*Innocence*) poem would be reprinted in James Montgomery's campaigning volume, *The Chimney-Sweeper's Friend* (1824). The contrary in *Experience* is also called 'The Chimney Sweeper'.

3 *weep weep*: a bitter pun on the street cry 'Sweep, sweep', used to advertise the service.

19 5 *Tom Dacre*: possibly an orphan from Lady Dacre's Emanuel charity school in Westminster (a 'Browncoat' school, now in Battersea) since nameless foundlings could be given the school's name as a surname.

16 *shine in the Sun*: Raine (*Blake and Tradition* 1.25–6) suggests a parallel with a passage in Swedenborg's *Concerning the Earths in our Solar System* in which spirits from 'Jupiter, whom they call Sweepers of Chimneys' are 'stripped of their own Garments and are clothed with new shining Raiment, and become Angels' (1758, translated by Richard Hindmarsh (London, 1787), 88–9).

Laughing Song: there is a first version in the 'Song 2nd by a Young Shepherd' in the manuscript additions to the Flaxman copy of *Poetical Sketches* (see p. 351), where the names in the second stanza are the more conventionally pastoral 'Edessa', 'Lyca', and 'Emilie'.

20 *The Little Black Boy*: Quakers petitioned Parliament to abolish the slave trade in 1783 and the Society for Effecting the Abolition of the Slave Trade was founded in 1787. Wilberforce petitioned Parliament to debate it in 1788; it was debated but rejected in 1791 (the Slave Trade

would be banned in 1807, and slavery in the British Empire abolished in 1833). Wedgwood's 1787 'Slave Medallion' ('Am I not a man and a brother?') was used as a symbol of the campaign; the boy in Blake's first illustration slightly resembles it.

14 *to bear the beams of love*: 'Nor is my soul refin'd enough | To bear the beaming of his love', Watts, 'Grace Shining and Nature Fainting' (*Horae Lyricae*, 1709).

The Voice of the Ancient Bard: originally in *Innocence*; in both volumes in Copy O (bought by Flaxman); in *Experience* in late copies (Copy T and later) as the final poem. It is an inspired, bardic statement (and thus innocent) but, like 'The Schoolboy' (also moved), it consists chiefly of a denunciation of the 'Doubt' and 'reason' of experience.

21 *Night*: compare 'Hymn 4' ('The glorious sun is set in the west; the night-dews fall') in Anna Laetitia Barbauld's *Hymns in Prose for Children* (Joseph Johnson, 1781).

22 29 *if they rush dreadful*: Blake breaches the convention whereby children's hymns promise safety during the night ('You may sleep, for he never sleeps: you may close your eyes in safety, for his eye is always open to protect you', Barbauld, *Hymns in Prose*, 33–4) by insisting that the protection consists only of taking your soul to heaven if the 'wolves and tygers' kill you.

42 *lie down and sleep*: it is actually the 'wolf' which 'shall dwell with the lamb' in Isaiah 11.6–7 (and 'the leopard shall lie down with the kid . . . And the lion shall eat straw like the ox') but the passage is usually misremembered.

45 *life's river*: 'And he shewed me a pure river of water of life' (Revelation 22.1).

The Little Boy lost: a first version is sung by Quid in 'An Island in the Moon'. Addison praised 'The Children in the Wood' in the third of his influential essays on ballads (*Spectator* 8) in 1711 and Percy printed it as 'this very popular ballad' in his *Reliques* (1765); Blake would use the motif of the lost child in six of his *Songs* (though the 'loss' is metaphorical, rather than literal, in 'A Little Boy Lost' and 'A Little Girl Lost').

8 *vapour*: a will-o'-the-wisp.

23 *The Little Boy found*: there is no prior version in 'An Island in the Moon', either because the page has been lost, or because Quid the Cynic does not wish to follow 'The Little Boy Lost' with this religious reassurance.

A Dream: originally in *Innocence*; moved (by accident) to *Experience* in Copies A, B, C, and D; moved back to *Innocence* in Copy E and thereafter. There are precedents for the topic in Bunyan's 'Upon the Pismire' and Watts's 'The Ant or Emmet'.

SONGS OF EXPERIENCE

There are drafts of all but three of these poems ('Introduction', 'A Little Girl Lost', 'Ah! Sun-Flower') in the Notebook. This is a more complex volume than *Innocence* in the sense that there are several poems in which the contrary voice of Innocence can be heard, either wholly or partially.

24 *Introduction*: an innocent statement, by the visionary 'Bard', positioned here so that its views can be rejected in the following poem.

4 *Holy Word*: 'In the beginning was the Word, and the Word was with God, and the Word was God' (John 1.1); 'and his name is called The Word of God' (Revelation 19.13); 'the Word' is also a key term for Swedenborg: see *The True Christian Religion* (1771) paras. 189–276.

5 *among the ancient trees*: 'And they heard the voice of the Lord God walking in the garden in the cool of the day: and Adam and his wife hid themselves . . . amongst the trees of the garden' (Genesis 3.8). In Milton, they hear the Son, rather than the Father, when, 'in | The Eevning coole . . . | . . . the voice of God they heard | Now walking in the Garden' (*Paradise Lost* 10.94–8) and Christ's purpose is to 'mitigate thir doom' (10.76).

9 *starry pole*: 'starry sky' is a Homeric formula (*Iliad* 4.44, etc.) which Pope translates as 'starry Poles'; Blake may be remembering Pope's 'Who shall the sovereign of the skies control? | Not all the gods that crown the starry pole' *(Iliad* 8.472-3).

11 *O Earth O Earth*: 'O earth, earth, earth, hear the word of the Lord' (Jeremiah 22.29).

18 *starry floor*: the sky is the floor of Heaven, though the ceiling of Earth.

20 *till the break of day*: that is, *only* until the break of day, when the better world of Eternity will replace the mundane sea and sky.

Earth's Answer: this is the voice of Experience (or the Enlightenment) which sees the physical universe as the only reality, and religion as repressive rather than redemptive. The contrary is the 'Introduction' to *Experience*.

25 *Infant Sorrow*: a cynical contrary to 'Infant Joy'.

26 *A Little Girl Lost*: a statement of the free love doctrine also found in 'Earth's Answer', *Visions of the Daughters of Albion*, and many of the Notebook poems of the early 1790s.

5 *Age of Gold*: the Golden Age of pagan myth, a concept found in Hesiod's *Works and Days* and Plato's *Cratylus*, though also used by Swedenborg: 'The most ancient people who lived before the flood, and whose age was called the golden age, had immediate revelation . . . But that Word is lost' (*New Jerusalem and its Heavenly Doctrine*, 1758, para. 255).

27 *Nurses Song*: the contrary to the 'Nurse's Song' of *Innocence*; for a more symbolic treatment of the topic see 'The Little Girl Lost' and 'The Little Girl Found'.

4 *green and pale*: 'O beware, my lord, of jealousy; | It is the green-ey'd monster' (*Othello*, 3.3.165-6).

The Angel: Stevenson compares 'An old maid early' (see p. 43).

28 *The Sick Rose*: the image is taken from the account of Philander's tuberculosis in Young's *Night Thoughts* (1.355): 'Death's subtle seed . . . beckon'd

the Worm to riot on that Rose so red'. Like tigers, malign bacteria are difficult to reconcile with the concept of a loving God.

The Garden of Love

6 *writ over the door*: 'And thou shalt love the Lord thy God with all thine heart . . . And these words, which I commend thee this day, shall be in thine heart . . . And thou shalt write them upon the posts of thy house' (Deuteronomy 6.5–9), though the words written here are the 'Thou shalt not' of the Ten Commandments (Exodus 20).

The Little Vagabond: the Muggletonian sect (with which E. P. Thompson tried to link the Blake family) held their meetings in pubs until 1869, when they acquired a London meeting room, though the statement here may be more straightforwardly secular.

29 *The Human Abstract*: a contrary to 'The Divine Image'; another contrary to that poem, entitled 'A Divine Image', is found only in Copy BB, sold to Robert Balmanno in 1816 (see note to 'A Divine Image', p. 361).

14 *Mystery*: on the Tree of Mystery see note to *The Book of Ahania*, 5.6 (p. 395). 'Mystery' is the name written on the forehead of 'Babylon the Great, the Mother of Harlots and Abominations of the Earth' (Revelation 17.5) and 'the mystery of iniquity' (2 Thessalonians 2.7) is a false version or distortion of the gospel which Jesus will destroy.

19 *Raven*: for 'the Priests of the Raven' see the Chorus to 'A Song of Liberty' (p. 41). In ancient Germanic or Norse religion, Odin is attended by two ravens; Thomas Percy had translated Paul Henri Mallet's *Monuments de la mythologie . . . des anciens Scandinaves* (1756) as *Northern Antiquities* in 1770.

30 *The Little Girl Lost* and *The Little Girl Found*: these two poems, originally in *Innocence*, were moved to *Experience* in the very first copies (1794) and thereafter. The first two stanzas are spoken in the visionary, Bardic voice of Innocence, and Lyca's behaviour is innocent, but her parents' anxious response (like that of the Nurse in the *Experience* 'Nurse's Song') is experienced.

33 *A Little Boy Lost*: here, unusually, the childish view is associated, not with a visionary, religious perspective, but with the sceptical rationalism of the Enlightenment ('who sets reason up for judge'). This was Blake's view in the early 1790s and the poem may be an irreligious reaction to Watts's 'Obedience to Parents': 'Have you not heard what dreadful plagues | Are threaten'd by the Lord, | To him that breaks his father's law, | Or mocks his mother's word? | What heavy guilt upon him lies! | How cursed is his name! | The ravens shall pick out his eyes, | And eagles eat the same' (*Divine Songs*, 1715).

4 *A greater than itself to know*: this closely resembles a phrase in Blake's sympathetic annotation of Swedenborg's *Divine Love and Divine Wisdom* (1788): 'Man can have no idea of anything greater than Man as a cup cannot contain more than its capaciousness' (*E* 603). But the phrase is

there linked to the Swedenborgian conception of 'the Divine Humanity' (so that God is not 'greater' than man), whereas here it seems to be a more fundamental attack on religion.

33　16 *Mystery*: see note to 'The Human Abstract' (p. 357).

34　22 *burn'd him in a holy place*: a metaphorical, rather than literal account of the repression of sympathizers with the French Revolution, though Joseph Priestley's house in Birmingham was destroyed by arson in July 1791.

The Chimney Sweeper: the contrary to 'The Chimney Sweeper' of *Innocence* (see note, p. 354).

5 *happy upon the heath*: the London climbing boys had a holiday on the first of May, when they paraded through the streets (sometimes to Hampstead Heath), led by the dancing figures of Jack in the Green and the Lord and Lady of the May.

11 *God & his Priest & King*: the monarch is the Supreme Governor of the Church of England.

The Fly: sometimes linked to Shakespeare's 'As flies to wanton boys are we to th' gods; | They kill us for their sport' (*King Lear* 4.1.37–8) and Gray's 'Poor moralist! And what art thou? | A solitary fly!' ('Ode on the Spring', 1748, ll. 43–4) but closer to Uncle Toby's meditation on a fly in Sterne's *Tristram Shandy* (1759–67), Book 2, Chapter 12. The point is that, in a materialist conception, human beings are no more (or less) important than flies.

35　*A Poison Tree*: titled 'Christian Forbearance' in the Notebook draft. The belief that the Javanese Upas tree exhaled a poisonous vapour (it secretes a poisonous juice but its aroma is actually harmless) derived from an article by George Steevens in the *London Magazine* (December 1783) and was repeated by Erasmus Darwin in his *Loves of the Plants* (1789).

London: possibly a response to Watts's 'Praise for Mercies, Spiritual and Temporal': 'Whene'er I take my walks abroad, | How many poor I see . . . How many children in the street | Half naked I behold . . . While others early learn to swear, | And curse, and lye, and steal; Lord, I am taught thy name to fear, | And do thy holy will' (*Divine Songs*, 1715). In Blake's later work, London is seen as a place which is, in practice, Babylon but should be Jerusalem (*Jerusalem* 74.16–17); see note to *Jerusalem* 84.11 (p. 424).

1 *charter'd*: an ironic reference to the fact that the City of London (the world's oldest continuously elected public authority) has charters which guarantee the rights and privileges of its citizens (the first dates from 1067; *Magna Carta* confirms that the City 'shall enjoy its ancient liberties'); removed by Charles II in 1683, they were restored in 1690. Though his examples are Bath and towns in Cornwall, rather than London, Tom Paine, in *The Rights of Man* (1791), argued that 'William the Conqueror and his descendants parcelled out the country . . . and bribed some parts of it by what they called Charters, to hold the other parts of it the better

subjected to their will . . . Every chartered town is an aristocratical monopoly.'

36 7 *ban*: prohibition, though also the 'marriage banns' or prior notice required before an Anglican wedding.

8 *mind-forg'd manacles*: in one version of the Notebook draft, 'german forged': a reference to the Hanoverian origins of the British royal family. Watts's 'Free Philosophy' has: 'I hate these shackles of the mind | Forg'd by the haughty wise' (*Horae Lyricae*, 1709); Blake's phrase gives a stronger sense of self-imposed restriction.

12 *in blood down Palace walls*: Blake had seen soldiers defending public buildings against a mob during the Gordon Riots (1780) though the reference here may be a more metaphorical account of royal responsibility for deaths in battle after the start of the war with France in February 1793.

16 *plagues*: Johnson and Grant suggest gonorrhoea which can cause blindness at birth.

The Tyger: in Blake's lifetime, tigers were seen, not as a precious endangered species, but as a dangerous pest: the modern equivalent would be a cancer cell or a malignant virus. The reference in 'An Island in the Moon' to 'that noble beast the tyger' is clearly identified as a stupid remark (*E* 465) and the 'tygers of wrath' in *The Marriage of Heaven and Hell* (*E* 37), like Fuzon's revolutionary 'tygers' in *The Book of Ahania* 4.36, are useful because they are dangerous: in the Notebook drafts (N108–9) Blake has 'The cruel fire of thine eyes'. The poem works with its contraries ('The Lamb', 'The Shepherd') as an articulation of theodicy (see Introduction). Paul Miner has noted parallels between the phrasing of the poem and passages in James Hervey's *Contemplations on the Starry Heavens* (1748), *Notes & Queries*, 7 October 2008; see note to *Jerusalem* 72.51 (p. 422).

4 *fearful*: something we should be afraid of and dislike.

17 *stars threw down their spears*: in Job 38.7 we are told how the stars reacted to the original act of creation ('When the morning stars sang together, and all the sons of God shouted for joy') but this is an account of their response to the Fall, for which there is no biblical precedent. In Milton the moment is marked, not by stars, but by an earthquake and a thunder storm (*Paradise Lost* 9.1000–3). Blake will use the phrase again in *The Four Zoas* 5.224 for Urizen's fall: 'The stars threw down their spears and fled naked away' (*E* 344).

37 *Ah! Sun-Flower*: an *Experience* poem because the Youth and Virgin only 'aspire' to (hope for) an afterlife.

2 *countest the steps of the Sun*: the old belief that sunflowers turn to follow the movement of the sun across the sky had been questioned as early as Gerard's *Herball* (1597), though it is true of the immature flower buds.

The Lilly: an *Experience* poem because it identifies the majority of beings as selfishly defensive. In Song of Solomon 2.2 the lover is 'As the lily among thorns', though there is also an allusive link to 'Consider the lilies of the field, how they grow; they toil not, neither do they spin' (Matthew 6.28).

38 *Holy Thursday*: the contrary to the 'Holy Thursday' of *Innocence* (see note to p. 353). Here the eye (of experience) is on the frequent scandals about the mistreatment of children in eighteenth-century charity schools, though the statement is ultimately an innocent one: the claim in the final stanza that 'hunger' and 'poverty' are inconceivable in any country which has normal quantities of 'sun' and 'rain' flies in the face of experience (which is all too familiar with relative deprivation in otherwise prosperous countries). The moral intuition which rejects such inequality is visionary rather than experiential.

The Clod & the Pebble: again, a poem which combines Innocence and Experience. The Clod (like the Chimney Sweeper of *Innocence*) recommends self-sacrifice, in the spirit of 1 Corinthians 13.4–7: 'Charity suffereth long, and is kind; charity envieth not . . . Beareth all things, believeth all things, hopeth all things, endureth all things'. The hard Pebble responds with the secular worldly wisdom of Experience.

POEMS ADDED TO LATER COPIES OF *SONGS OF INNOCENCE AND OF EXPERIENCE*

39 *To Tirzah*: Tirzah is one of the daughters of Zelophehad (Numbers 27.1–7) who are allowed to inherit his property because he had no son (see *Jerusalem* 68.53–61). The name also appears in Song of Solomon 6.4: 'Thou art beautiful, O my love, as Tirzah, comely as Jerusalem'. For Blake she is the dangerously attractive embodiment of the Female Will or Nature (the opposite, that is, of Jerusalem who represents the spiritual or ideal). For a different, later use of the name see note to *Jerusalem* 5.40. The illustration contains a quotation: 'It is Raised a Spiritual Body' (1 Corinthians 15.44) which alludes to St Paul's distinction between the 'natural' and 'spiritual' body and his insistence that the physical world is of merely temporary importance: the body 'is sown in corruption; it is raised in incorruption' (15.42).

The poem was not present in the early copies and was thought to date from after 1800 until Viscomi (1993) noted that it 'was printed with *Experience* in an edition of *Songs* ca. 1795' (p. 239 and p. 274). Three copies from this 'edition' are known. In one of them, Copy R, 'To Tirzah' seems 'to have been inserted late', probably after 1808 (p. 291). But it does appear in Copy E (assembled, from plates printed earlier, for sale to Butts in 1806), where it is the penultimate poem, immediately preceding 'The Clod & the Pebble', and in Copy L (Yale) which has a pencilled ownership inscription '1799/JS'. Bentley suggested composition 'perhaps in 1797' (Bentley 1978, p. 682) but it seems to have been even earlier. This confirms Blake's return to a religious understanding of the world several years before the Felpham conversion experiences with which the poem was once linked.

3 *Generation*: the reproductive process of the fallen, physical world, or Nature, associated with the 'Female Will' (see note to 'The Mental Traveller,' p. 365).

4 *what have I to do with thee?*: 'Jesus saith unto her, Woman, what have I to do with thee?' (John 2.4).

A Divine Image: an *Experience* poem found only in posthumous printings and in Copy BB sold in 1816 to the critic and collector Robert Balmanno; Viscomi (1993, p. 91) suggests that the page was 'executed' in 1795 but not 'used' until much later. See notes to 'The Divine Image' (p. 354) and 'The Human Abstract' (p. 357).

LYRICS FROM *THE MARRIAGE OF HEAVEN AND HELL*

The Marriage of Heaven and Hell is undated, except for its advertisement in the 1793 *Prospectus* and a marginal note of '1790' to the words 'it is now thirty-three years since [1757]' on Plate 3 of Copy F. It was probably written and first printed (Copies A, B, C, H) in 1790, very soon after the French Revolution, with publication delayed by Blake's heavy burden of work as a reproductive engraver in 1790–2. Though sometimes identified as a 'prose poem', it is better understood as a compilation of short pieces of parodic and satirical prose (aimed at Emmanuel Swedenborg), with passages of verse at the beginning and the end. These two poems are early examples of Blake's imitation of the Hebrew verse of the prophetic books of the Old Testament and, as such, pioneering specimens of English free verse, though (paradoxically) their argument is for a rejection of religious authority and a celebration of the physical energy of political revolution.

40 *The Argument*: a preliminary summary (usually in prose for a verse text, here in verse for prose) suggesting that the true Christian (such as Bunyan's hero on his meek pilgrimage through 'the Valley of the Shadow of Death'; *The Pilgrim's Progress*, echoing Psalm 23) has been superseded by the false religion of the established Churches. Contemporary clergymen (including Swedenborgian ministers) are 'sneaking serpents' who have to be challenged by the revolutionary anger of Rintrah.

1 *Rintrah*: here an embodiment of rebellious anger; for the later uses of the name see note to *Europe* 8.4.

2 *swag*: hang.

12 *bleached bones*: in Ezekiel 37.1–14, the prophet finds himself in a valley full of the 'dry bones' of 'the whole house of Israel' and revivifies them (as a symbol of the restoration of the Israelites from their exile).

13 *Red clay*: in the Bible, Adam is created from *adamah* (Hebrew: earth); here the creation is of a comfortable world in which Churches have joined the establishment.

A Song of Liberty: though written after the Fall of the Bastille on 14 July 1789 ('France rend down thy dungeon'), the 'Song' is spoken at the time of the American Revolution and is 'prophetic' in the vulgar sense when it calls for that later event. The body of the 'Song' is a celebration of the American uprising; the 'Chorus' returns to the topic of 'The Argument' and denounces established religious and quasi-religious authority.

40 Verse 1. *The Eternal Female*: Nature, or the material forces of the fallen world, later named Vala.

Verse 2. *Albion*: here simply a traditional poetic name for Britain (originally the Celtic *Alban*).

41 Verse 3. *dungeon*: the Bastille, a medieval fortress on the east of Paris used as a prison. A symbol of royal power, it was stormed by a Paris mob on 14 July 1789.

Verses 4–5. *old Rome . . . thy keys*: Jesus tells Peter 'I will give unto thee the keys of the kingdom of heaven' (Matthew 16.19); keys symbolize the authority of the Pope.

Verse 6. *And weep*: the additional words 'and bow thy reverend locks' were erased from the plate to imitate the Bible's shortest verse, 'Jesus wept' (John 11.35).

Verse 7. *new born terror*: the embodiment of the revolutionary energy of the American uprising, later named Orc.

Verse 8. *mountains . . . atlantic sea*: the lost continent of Atlantis, supposedly located where the Atlantic Ocean is now, was described in Plato's dialogues *Timaeus* and *Critias*; James Barry, in his lectures as Professor of Painting to the RA, first given in 1784 (Blake's last year as a student), claimed that art originated with 'the Atlantides, those Titanic descendants of Ouranos'.

Verse 8. *starry king*: the ruler of the Newtonian universe, later to be named Urizen, though also the British Crown (or Church and State), and Satan or Lucifer: 'How art thou fallen from heaven, O Lucifer, son of the morning [literally 'morning star'] . . . For thou hast said in thine heart . . . I will exalt my throne above the stars of God' (Isaiah 13.12–13). In Revelation 12.4 Satan's fallen angels are 'the third part of the stars of heaven'.

Verse 14. *hoary element . . . fled away*: 'And I saw a new heaven and a new earth: for the first heaven and the first earth were passed away; and there was no more sea' (Revelation 21.1).

Verse 16. *Urthona*: here simply an embodiment of mundane power ('Earth owner'), though later developed as one of the four Zoas.

Verse 18. *leading his starry hosts . . . ten commands*: a disturbing combination of George III leading his armies, Satan leading his fallen angels to Hell, and Moses leading the Israelites to the Promised Land and receiving the ten commandments on tablets of stone ('the stony law') as he does so.

Verse 20. *loosing the eternal horses*: the revolution is identified with a classical, rather than biblical, myth: Phaethon commandeering the horse-drawn chariot with which his father, Helios, drew the sun through the sky; see note to *Milton* 5.18–19 (p. 400).

lion & wolf shall cease: 'The wolf also shall dwell with the lamb . . . and the calf and the young lion . . . together' (Isaiah 11.6); the line recurs in *America* 8.15.

Chorus. *accepted brethren*: possibly a reference to the Freemasons.

LYRICS FROM THE 'NOTEBOOK'

42 *'Silent Silent Night'*: (N113 rev).

The Wild Flowers Song: also known as 'I slept in the dark' because the first stanza was a later addition (N107 rev and N109 rev). In line 5 'slept' replaced the deleted words 'was fond'.

43 *'Love to faults is always blind'*: (N107 rev and N106 rev). There is a deleted title: 'How to know Love from Deceit'.

'Are not the joys of morning sweeter': (N109 rev).

'An old maid early eer I knew': (N100 rev).

Morning: (N 8) written in the Notebook pages used in 1802–3 and possibly a lyrical response to the Peace of Amiens which appeared, between October 1801 and May 1803, to have ended the war with France.

BALLADS

Addison's essays on ballads in 1711 (*Spectator*, 70, 74, and 85) created a sophisticated taste for 'the great force which lies in a natural simplicity of thought' found in these 'vulgar pieces' (*Spectator* 409); Percy's *Reliques* (1765) made examples readily available. Percy's prefatory essay acknowledged the derivation of the word from the very different French *ballade* but tried to claim 'an earlier origin' for it: for him this is the characteristic medium of 'the ancient Bards'. By the late eighteenth century there was a widespread enthusiasm for what Ritson, in 1783, called 'modern and sentimental ballads', to which both Wordsworth and Coleridge, in some of their *Lyrical Ballads* (1798), and Blake responded. Ritson referred to ballads as 'narrative compositions'; they are here identified as poems which combine narrative content with the ballad stanza (four lines of alternate iambic tetrameters and trimeters, rhymed abcb) or something close to it. The 'Pickering Manuscript' (a fair copy of ten poems made *c*.1805, later owned by the publisher B. M. Pickering) is sometimes called 'The Ballads Manuscript' (because it is written on paper salvaged from Blake's work on Hayley's *Designs to a Series of Ballads*, 1802). But not all the poems contained in it are ballads and the conventional title remains the least bad alternative. There is a facsimile in Charles Ryskamp, *The Pickering Manuscript* (New York, Pierpont Morgan Library, 1972).

45 *Gwin, King of Norway*: from *Poetical Sketches*. The Norwegian setting may have been suggested by 'Hardyknute. A Scottish Fragment' in Percy's *Reliques*, where Scotland is invaded by 'The King of Norse', after whose defeat 'On Norways coast the widowit dame | May wash the rocks with tears', though Blake's story of a popular uprising against an oppressive

monarch probably reflects his feelings about the American Revolution: Gordred has been seen as an early version of Orc.

45 13 *Gordred*: the name was probably taken from Chatterton's 'Godred Crovan' (1769).

48 *[Quid the Cynic's First Song]* '*When old corruption first begun*': an attack on the medical profession from 'An Island in the Moon' (a Menippean satire written *c*.1782–5 which survives as an incomplete MS fair copy; with Anne Gilchrist in 1863; first fully published 1907). The song was originally for a different character, 'Sipsong' (deleted in MS).

49 '*Fayette beheld the King & Queen*': these are the uncancelled stanzas in the Notebook (N99 rev and N98 rev) in the order in which they there appear. Gilbert du Motier, Marquis de Lafayette (1757–1834) fought in the American Revolutionary War, was a member of the Estates General in 1789, and became commander of the National Guard after the French Revolution. In that capacity he was responsible for the safety (that is, imprisonment) of the royal family in the Tuileries. After his speech in the Assembly denouncing the Jacobins in June 1792 he was declared a traitor; in August the royal family was moved to the Temple and a warrant issued for Lafayette's arrest; he escaped abroad. The discovery of the King's correspondence with potential supporters in a secret cupboard (the 'Armoire de fer') in the Tuileries in November 1792 raised fears of a counter-revolution, suggested in Blake's description of the King and Queen.

50 '*I asked a thief to steal me a peach*': (N114 rev). There is a manuscript copy (Princeton, with no verbal changes from the Notebook) which is dated '1796'.

    '*Never pain to tell thy Love*': (N115 rev). In the first draft, the first line read 'Never seek to tell thy love', and the last, 'He took her with a sigh'.

51 '*I laid me down upon a bank*': (N115 rev).

    '*I saw a chapel all of gold*': (N115 rev).

    '*I fear'd the fury of my wind*': (N113 rev).

    In a mirtle shade: (N111 rev).

52 *The Mental Traveller*: from the Pickering Manuscript. The first commentary on this poem, by Dante Gabriel Rossetti in 1863, is in some ways still the best: 'The mental phaenomenon here symbolized seems to be the career of any great Idea or intellectual movement . . . represented as going through the stages of—1. birth, 2. adversity and persecution, 3. triumph and maturity, 4. decadence and over-ripeness, 5. gradual transformation . . . into another renovated Idea, which again has to pass through all the same stages' (*Gilchrist* 2.98). Another way of putting this would be to say that the poem enacts the futile circularity of life in the material world. For a later statement of the religious alternative to this view see *For the Sexes: The Gates of Paradise* (probably written in 1818, and with a final section in ballad stanza) where Blake regrets that he had once 'clipd the Wings | Of all Sublunary Things' and celebrates his rediscovery of 'The Immortal Man' to whom 'The Door of Death' is 'open' as an escape into Eternity (p. 93).

8 *tears did sow*: 'They that sow in tears shall reap in joy' (Psalm 126.5), though Blake is using this celebration of Israel's escape from Babylonian captivity to reverse the usual experience of conception and childbirth.

10 *Woman Old*: Blake's hatred of the 'Female Will' (deplored as misogynist by feminist critics) is most clearly expressed in *Jerusalem* 30.25–8 and 56.3–10, though it is found in many places in his work, such as the 'shadowy female' and Enitharmon's dream in *Europe* (Plates 4 and 12–16), and the character of Vala; see also note to 'To Tirzah' (p. 360). Matthews (2011) argues that it is based on a pre-feminist construction of the female and in that sense is compatible with feminist argument.

54 57 *freezing Age*: in 1 Kings 1.2 the aged King David's servants bring 'a young virgin' to 'lie in [his] bosom, that my lord the king may get heat'.

55 *The Land of Dreams*: from the Pickering Manuscript.

56 *Mary*: from the Pickering Manuscript. Blake uses l. 21, with reference to himself, in his verse letter to Butts of 16 August 1803 (p. 108).

57 *The Crystal Cabinet*: from the Pickering Manuscript.

8 *Moony Night*: as in 'Beulahs moony shades' (*Milton* 30.5); Beulah (from Isaiah 62.4) is Blake's name for the fallen world mitigated by love; see note to *Milton* 3.1.

58 *The Grey Monk*: from the Pickering Manuscript. There is a draft in the Notebook (N8) and stanzas 2 and 8 would be re-used in 'I saw a Monk of Charlemaine', the poem in the preface to Chapter 3 ('To the Deists') of *Jerusalem*.

59 *Long John Brown & Little Mary Bell*: from the Pickering Manuscript.
William Bond: from the Pickering Manuscript.

61 46 *Moony light*: see note to 'The Crystal Cabinet' (p. 365).

NARRATIVE POEMS

62 *Fair Elenor*: from *Poetical Sketches* (1783) where it is divided (by the printer or editor) into quatrains, though it is not rhymed as a ballad and should probably have been printed as continuous blank verse. An exercise in the fashionable Gothick mode.

63 61 *husband's head*: changed to 'O Elenor, behold thy husband's head' in a manuscript correction to some copies.
Blind-Man's Buff: from *Poetical Sketches* (1783).

64 2 *shepherds nose*: compare Winter's verses ('When icicles hang by the wall') in Shakespeare's *Love's Labour's Lost*, 5.2, and 'Song 3ʳᵈ by an old shepherd' (p. 9).

65 63 *wholesome laws*: no sign here of Blake's later scepticism, sometimes linked to Antinomianism, about laws in general or the 'Old Law' of the Ten Commandments.

66 *The Golden Net*: from the Pickering Manuscript; there is a draft in the Notebook.

DESCRIPTIVE AND DISCURSIVE POETRY

67 *To Spring*: the first of a sequence of seasonal poems in *Poetical Sketches* on the model of Pope's *Pastorals* (1709) and James Thompson's *The Seasons* (1716–30), though written in blank verse in the manner (Stevenson suggests) of Mark Akenside (1721–70).

13–16 *pour . . . tresses*: 'While Spring shall pour his showers . . . | And bathe thy breathing tresses, meekest Eve', Collins, 'Ode to Evening' (1746).

15 *languish'd head*: 'like a neglected rose | It withers on the stalk with languish't head', Milton, *Comus*, 743–4.

To Summer: from *Poetical Sketches*.

68 *To Autumn*: from *Poetical Sketches*.

To Winter: from *Poetical Sketches*.

69 16 *Hecla*: 'And Hecla flaming thro' a waste of snow', James Thomson, 'Winter'; Mount Hecla is an active volcano in Iceland, traditionally seen as a gate of Hell.

To the Evening Star: from *Poetical Sketches*.

3 *torch of love*: the evening star is actually the planet Venus.

To Morning: from *Poetical Sketches*.

70 4 *chambers of the east*: Stevenson compares Spenser's *Epithalamion* 148–51: 'Lo where she comes . . . | Like Phoebe from her chamber of the East | . . . Clad all in white, that seems a virgin best'.

[Obtuse Angle's Song] 'To be or not to be': from 'An Island in the Moon'.

4 *Doctor South*: Robert South (1634–1716), Anglican High Churchman, wit, and fierce critic of Nonconformists who clashed with William Sherlock (see next note) over the doctrine of the Trinity (despite their sympathy on other matters) during the Socinian Controversy of the 1690s.

5 *Sherlock*: William Sherlock (1641–1707), Anglican High Clergyman, Dean of St Paul's; his *Practical Discourse Concerning Death* was published in 1689.

6 *Sutton*: Thomas Sutton (1532–1611), civil servant, coal-owner, and money-lender who left most of his enormous fortune to found the Charterhouse, an almshouse and school in London. In 1612 his other heirs contested the will but, in a key legal case, it was upheld (in the prose text of 'An Island in the Moon', Steelyard the Lawgiver is 'very attentive' to this poem). Sutton was a Protestant hero because his benefaction could be cited in response to charges that the Reformation had destroyed Catholic charities without replacing them.

71 *A fairy skipd upon my knee*: written on the back of a drawing of *The Infant Hercules* (Rosenwald Collection, Library of Congress).

Soft Snow: (N107 rev). The fourth line replaces the deleted 'Ah that sweet love should be thought a crime'.

An ancient Proverb: (N107 rev). There is a fair copy (N99 rev) with 'man' omitted in l. 4, and under the general title 'Several Questions Answerd'.

'Why should I care for the men of thames': (N113 rev).

2 *charterd*: see note to 'London' (p. 358).

72 7 *The Ohio*: Ohio (which takes its name from its river) only began to be settled in 1788, having previously been guaranteed to its Native American inhabitants by the Royal Proclamation of 1763. The government of the new American Republic claimed not to be bound by previous treaties and allowed settlement west of the Appalachians. Ironically (but unconsciously) Blake uses this land grab as an image of liberty.

8 *go to be free*: slavery was not permitted in the new 'Northwestern Territory' (of which Ohio was part) when it was legally established in 1787.

'I heard an Angel singing': (N114 rev).

'O lapwing thou fliest around the heath': (N113 rev). a pencil note on N101 says that this and the following four poems should be engraved 'On 1 Plate' (no such plate is known); Erdman argues that 'Thou hast a lap full of seed' is the poem referred to in this note as 'Experiment'.

An answer to the parson: (N103 rev). Parsons were clergymen of the established, Anglican Church.

'Thou hast a lap full of seed': (N111 rev). Probably the poem entitled 'Experiment' on N101 (see note to 'O lapwing thou fliest around the heath').

73 *Riches*: (N103 rev).

1 *a merry heart*: a familiar ballad phrase found, for example, in Autolycus's song in *Winter's Tale* 4.3.115.

'If you trap the moment before its ripe': (N105 rev).

Eternity: (N105 rev); fair copy N99 rev under the general title 'Several Questions Answerd'.

'The sword sung on the barren heath': (N105 rev).

'Abstinence sows sand all over': (N105 rev).

74 *'In a wife I would desire'*: (N105 rev).

The Question Answerd: (N103 rev; fair copy N99 rev).

Merlins prophecy: (N106 rev). The prophecies of Merlin (the bard and magician of King Arthur's court) are found in Chapter 7 of Geoffrey of Monmouth's *History of the Kings of Britain* (*c*.1136); most of them are very obscure and the Fool makes a joke about them in *King Lear*: 'This prophecy shall Merlin make; for I live before his time' (3.2.94).

Lacedemonian Instruction: (N103 rev). Lacedaemonian means Spartan (Sparta was the chief city of Laconia). The educational reforms of Lycurgus, the legendary law-giver of ancient Sparta, meant that 'youths . . . were taught early to think, to answer in a short and laconic manner, and to excel in sharp repartee' (Lemprière's *Classical Dictionary*, 1788).

74 *Motto to the Songs of Innocence & of Experience*: (N101 rev). The decision not to print this motto in the combined volume, and to use the sub-title instead, marks a significant change of mind from Blake's irreligious stance in the early 1790s; see Introduction.

75 *On the Virginity of the Virgin Mary & Johanna Southcott*: (N2). Joanna Southcott (1750–1814), a self-styled prophetess brought to London by the engraver William Sharp, announced in October 1802 that she was the 'woman clothed with the sun' (Revelation 12.1) who would give birth to the Messiah. Often described as a 'squib', this seems in fact to be a tolerant, if unconvinced, response to her claim.

'Mock on Mock on Voltaire Rousseau': (N9). Blake's most brilliant brief attack on the Enlightenment, using ballad stanza (for polemic, not narrative), and combining modern scientific and philosophical reference with a setting taken from Exodus, where the Israelites escape from Egypt across the Red Sea.

1 *Mock on*: Job replies to his friends, 'Suffer me that I may speak; and after that I have spoken, mock on' (Job 21.3).

8 *Israels paths they shine*: the Israelites are led by 'a pillar of cloud' by day and 'a pillar of fire' by night (Exodus 13.21); when the Egyptians pursue them to the shore of the Red Sea, 'the angel of God' moves the pillar 'behind them . . . and it was a cloud and darkness' to the Egyptians but 'gave light by night' to the Israelites (Exodus 14.19–20); compare also 'we will walk in his paths: for the law shall go forth of Zion, and the word of the Lord from Jerusalem' (Micah 4.2).

9 *Atoms of Democritus*: the Greek pre-Socratic philosopher of the 5th century BC who adapted the atomistic doctrines of Leucippus into what is usually seen as the first account of the universe as a body of atoms in motion.

10 *Newtons Particles of Light*: Newton's *Opticks* (1704) proposed a corpuscular theory of light (in which 'all material things seem to have been composed of . . . hard and solid particles', p. 403) which replaced the wave theory of Christiaan Huygens and Robert Hooke (wave theory was reasserted in the nineteenth century; the predominant modern view is a combined wave–particle theory). See note to *Europe* 16.5, p. 389.

'My Spectre around me night & day': (N13 and N12). In the Notebook there are twenty-two stanzas, some cancelled or unnumbered, the others arranged by repeated renumbering into this final order. There is a pencilled stanza also numbered '1' which, if used as the opening of the poem, would make it more obviously domestic and autobiographical: 'Oer my Sins Thou sit & moan | Hast thou no Sins of thy own | Oer my Sins thou sit & weep | And lull thy own Sins fast asleep'. Even when re-cast into the less explicit terms of 'Spectre' (the rational, male self) and 'Emanation' (the pitying, suffering female self), the poem remains an account of a clash between a husband's ideological belief in free love and a wife's jealous rejection of it which ends with an acceptance of conventional Christian morality; see note to *Jerusalem* 69.15, p. 422.

77 '*Grown old in Love from Seven till Seven times Seven*': (N54). Blake was 49 in November 1806.

The Smile: (Pickering MS).

Auguries of Innocence: (Pickering MS). This poem looks back to the 1780s in its concern with Innocence but forward to Blake's later work in its use of iambic tetrameter couplets, also found in *For the Sexes: The Gates of Paradise* and 'The Everlasting Gospel' (both *c*.1818–19). An augury is a divination or discovery of divine purpose; folk-lore parallels have been suggested for some of the gnomic assertions, especially those about animals and birds. The background to Blake's criticism of cruelty to animals is Sir William Pulteney's unsuccessful attempt to get Parliament to ban bull-baiting in April 1800 and the growing body of opinion which led to the (unsuccessful) anti-cruelty bill proposed in 1809 by Lord Erskine (a Whitefieldian Methodist who had defended Paine, Hardy, Horne Tooke, and Thelwall in the seditious libel and treason trials of the 1790s), the passage of the Cruel Treatment of Cattle Act (1822), the foundation of the Society for the Prevention of Cruelty to Animals in 1824, and the Cruelty to Animals Act (1835).

78 17 *Game Cock*: a fighting cock: cockfighting was legal in England and Wales until 1835 (and in Scotland until 1895).

35 *Chafers*: beetles.

42 *pass the Polar Bar*: enter Eternity; compare 'The eternal gates' terrific porter lifted the northern bar', *The Book of Thel*, 6.1, perhaps suggested by the Neoplatonic interest in the entrance (for humans) to the Cave of the Nymphs in *Odyssey* 13.127 which faces north (though it has no 'bar').

80 126 *see*: 'with' deleted in MS, probably for metrical reasons as the sense is unchanged.

81 127 *perish in a Night*: in Jonah 4, the prophet questions God's merciful treatment of Nineveh. God responds by creating a gourd, which shelters Jonah from the sun, and then causing it to wither. When Jonah is angry, 'Then said the Lord, Thou hast had pity on the gourd . . . which came up in a night, and perished in a night: And should I not spare Nineveh' (Jonah 4.10–11).

131 *Human Form*: the Swedenborgian 'Divine Humanity' or belief that God is best understood as Jesus in his human incarnation.

'*You don't believe I won't attempt to make ye*': (N21).

'*The Angel that presided oer my birth*': (N32).

3 *King*: possibly emended from 'Thing'.

'*All Pictures thats Painted with Sense & with Thought*': (N40).

5 *Rafael . . . Fuseli*: Raffaello Sanzio da Urbino (1483–1520), the painter known as Raphael; Reynolds's *Discourses* (1769–90) saw him as 'foremost of the first' among painters though inferior to Michelangelo in the sublime (see note to 'Sir Joshua Praises Michael Angelo', p. 98 and note);

Henry Fuseli (1741–1825), painter and friend of Blake; see note to 'To my Dearest Friend John Flaxman', p. 378.

81 7 *[begin]*: the word is heavily overscored and hard to determine.

'*You say their Pictures well Painted be*': (N42).

82 *William Cowper Esqre*: (N50). William Cowper (1731–1800), poet, author of the *Olney Hymns* (1779) and *The Task* (1785). A pious Calvinistic Anglican, he suffered from acute depression (believing that he was predestined to damnation; see note to *Milton* 5.2–3). William Hayley took a sympathetic interest in him (too late, in Blake's view) and wrote a biography of him (1803–4) for which Blake engraved illustrations.

'*I rose up at the dawn of day*': (N89).

83 '*Was I angry with Hayley who usd me so ill*': (N23).

1 *Hayley*: see note to 'Of Hs birth this was the happy lot', p. 375.

3 *Stothard*: Thomas Stothard (1755–1834), painter and illustrator; a long-standing friend of Blake (who frequently engraved his designs); they fell out over the *Pilgrimage to Canterbury* painting commissioned by Cromek (see note to 'A Petty sneaking Knave I knew', p. 376).

4 *Schiavonetti*: Louis (or Luigi) Schiavonetti, whom Cromek used to engrave Blake's illustrations for Blair's *The Grave* and Stothard's *Pilgrimage to Canterbury*, died on 7 June 1810.

5 *Macklin . . . Boydel . . . Bowyer*: Thomas Macklin (1752–1800), print dealer and collector; John Boydell (1720–1804), print dealer and publisher; Robert Bowyer (1758–1834), painter and print dealer. Macklin and Boydell commissioned engraving work from Blake (though less than he expected); Bowyer named Blake in the prospectus for his illustrated edition of Hume's *History of England* (1793–1806) but may not, in practice, have used him.

[The Everlasting Gospel]: this text survives as a number of draft passages scattered through the Notebook, probably written *c.*1818–19, and first identified as 'a Fragmentary Poem, entitled "The Everlasting Gospel"' by D. G. Rossetti in 1863. The sequence adopted here is the one established by David Erdman in 1965, together with the 'Preface' which he added in 1981, though two passages which Erdman appended as marginalia are fully included and his suggestion of an 'Epilogue' is more explicitly indicated. According to the 'Preface' the poem is spoken by Joseph of Arimathea (who, in turn, sometimes voices the views of his irreligious opponents), while the 'Preface', 'Epilogue', and first marginal passage are spoken in Blake's own voice; the second marginal passage is spoken by Blake's Spectre. The personal voice (excluded from the main body of the text) is also found in what appears to be some other work on the poem on a separate sheet of paper, watermarked 1818 (Rosenbach Foundation Library). This includes summaries of the argument in both prose ('There is not one Moral Virtue that Jesus Inculcated but Plato & Cicero did Inculcate before him what then did Christ Inculcate. Forgiveness of Sins This alone is the Gospel & this is the Life & Immortality brought to

light by Jesus') and verse ('If Moral Virtue was Christianity | Christs Pretensions were all Vanity | And Caiphas & Pilate Men | Praise Worthy & the Lions Den | And not the Sheepfold Allegories | Of God & Heaven & their Glories').

The phrase 'The Everlasting Gospel' (actually a title for the fragment on N52, though also used in the *Descriptive Catalogue*, E 543) has been used to link Blake to seventeenth-century Antinomian groups, such as the Ranters, and to a tradition stemming from Joachim of Flora (1145–1202) who taught that the 'age of Law' would give way, first, to 'the age of the Gospel' and, then, to 'the age of love and spiritual liberty' (see Morton, 1958, and Hirst, 1964, p. 102). It is, however, first found in Revelation 14.6 ('And I saw another angel fly in the midst of heaven, having the everlasting gospel to preach unto them that dwell on the earth, and to every nation and kindred, and tongue, and people'), from where Blake could have taken it independently. In the *Descriptive Catalogue* (1809), Blake used the phrase to argue, like the syncretic mythographers of his era (he cites Jacob Bryant), that 'the religion of Jesus, the everlasting Gospel' predated all other faiths and philosophies. Here he associates it with a depiction of Jesus as an outspoken rebel, rather than a meek and mild 'man of sorrows' (see note to 'The Lamb', p. 352, and 'Africa' 3.23, p. 391).

1 *Joseph of Arimathea*: a 'rich man' (Matthew 27.57) from Arimathaea (probably modern Ramleh) who retrieved the body of Jesus and placed it in a 'new sepulchre' in 'a garden' (John 19.38–42). The claim that he then brought Christianity to Britain originates in later interpolations made by Glastonbury monks to William of Malmesbury's *On the Antiquity of the Church of Glastonbury* (c.1125) but was sufficiently established for Elizabeth I to use it in her letter to the English bishops in 1559 ('Gildas . . . testifieth Joseph of Arimathea to be the first preacher of the word of God within our realms'; Gildas, in his *De Excidio et Conquestu Britanniae*, c.520, stated that Christianity reached Britain by AD 37 but did not mention Joseph). Blake reworked (c.1810) an earlier engraving as *Joseph of Arimathea Among the Rocks of Albion* and seems also to have known the legend that Joseph visited Britain before, as well as after, the death of Christ (see note to *Milton* 2.2, p. 398).

3 *Pliny & Trajan*: Pliny the Younger (AD 61–113), while Governor of Bithynia (in modern Turkey), corresponded with the Emperor Trajan, c.AD 112, about how Christians should be treated (*Epistulae* 10.96). Pliny's view was that Christians were guilty only of 'excessive superstition', not subversion; Trajan's reply was that they should not be sought out but, if accused and found guilty, should be executed. The letter was well known as the first pagan account of Christianity.

84 15 *he ran away*: at the age of 12, Jesus went to Jerusalem with his parents for Passover. When they returned, 'the child Jesus tarried behind in Jerusalem' and, after 'seeking him' for 'three days', they 'found him in the temple, sitting in the midst of the doctors, both hearing them, and asking them questions' (Luke 2.41–6).

84 20 *I am doing my Fathers business*: 'And he said unto them, How is it that
ye sought me? Wist ye not that I must be about my Father's business?'
(Luke 2.49).

21 *Pharisee*: Pharisees (literally 'the separated' or 'set apart') were a pious
Jewish sect depicted in the New Testament as legalistic and self-righteous.
The 'rich learned Pharisee' is Nicodemus who 'came to Jesus by night' to
question him: 'Jesus answered and said unto him, Verily, verily, I say unto
thee, Except a man be born again, he cannot see the kingdom of God'
(John 3.3).

26 *Scribe*: in the New Testament, scribes (originally copyists) are 'doctors
of the law' (Luke 5.17) who dispute with Jesus: 'Who is this which speak-
eth blasphemies? Who can forgive sins, but God alone?' (Luke 5.21).
Jesus, however, 'taught . . . as one having authority, and not as the scribes'
(Matthew 7.29).

39 *Caiphas*: Caiaphas was the Jewish high priest (AD 18–37) at the time of
the Crucifixion (Matthew 26.3).

45 *Caesars Elf:* a Spenserian usage, applied to knights in *The Faerie Queen*
('Which when the valiant Elfe perceiv'd', 1.1.17), so here a subordinate
officer of a Roman emperor.

47 *dr Priestly*: Joseph Priestley (1733–1804), scientist, Unitarian minister,
political theorist, sympathizer with the French Revolution, member of
the Joseph Johnson circle; Blake rejects him as a representative of rational
or 'Natural' religion.

85 49–50 *Sir Isaac . . . Attributes*: Sir Isaac Newton (1642–1727), mathematician and scientist whose work encouraged Natural Theology, or the
discovery of God's *Attributes* in the natural world, rather than through
revelation.

51 *Indwelling*: the doctrine of the Inner Light (particularly associated
with the Quakers though originally Calvin's 'testimonium spiritus sancti
internum', *Institutes of the Christian Religion*, 1536, 1.7) allowed direct
access to knowledge of the divine and understanding of the scriptures,
without the intervening authority of the Church.

65 *Creeping Jesus*: slang term for an obsequious or ingratiating person.

72 *ancient Elf*: Satan (one of God's 'knights' before his fall; see note to l. 45).

81 *God is no more*: this is the Swedenborgian doctrine of the Divine
Humanity, or belief that God is most essentially manifested in Christ's
human incarnation.

86 93 *the Garden*: the Garden of Gethsemane (Matthew 26.36), where Jesus
prayed during the night before his crucifixion: 'Saying, Father, if thou be
willing, remove this cup from me: nevertheless, not my will, but thine, be
done' (Luke 22.42).

110 *not thro the Eye*: compare 'A Vision of the Last Judgement' *E* 565–6
and Introduction, p. xxii.

87 122 *Adulterous bed*: the episode of Jesus's response to the 'woman taken in adultery' (often confused with Mary Magdalen) occurs in John 8.3–11: 'Now Moses in the law commanded us, that such should be stoned: but what sayest thou? . . . he . . . said unto them, He that is without sin among you, let him first cast a stone at her . . . and Jesus was left alone . . . and saw none but the woman, he said unto her, Woman, where are those thine accusers? hath no man condemned thee? She said, No man, Lord. And Jesus said unto her, Neither do I condemn thee: go, and sin no more'. See note to *Jerusalem* 62.14, p. 419.

125 *Moses Chair*: the episode with the woman taken in adultery takes place in 'the temple' (John 8.2) so Jesus's statements about what 'Moses in the law commanded' are, symbolically, made ex cathedra, or from the high priest's chair.

135 *Sinai*: Mount Sinai, where Moses received the Ten Commandments (Exodus 20) which the gospel of Jesus replaces.

156 *Covenant*: the Old Covenants between God and Noah (Genesis 9.1–17) and God and Moses (Exodus 6 and 20) were, for St Paul, replaced by the New Covenant (or 'testament') of the Gospel (see 2 Corinthians 3.4–11, Galatians 3.6–11, and Jeremiah 31.31).

88 179 *Covet*: envy.

89 211 *three Nights*: 'After three days I will rise again' (Matthew 27.63). Christ's 'harrowing of hell' in the three days between his crucifixion and resurrection is alluded to in 1 Peter 3.19–20 but better known from the Apostles' Creed ('who . . . was crucified, died, and was buried; he descended to the dead. On the third day he rose again') and the Lutheran Augsburg Confession: 'The Word also went down into hell, and truly rose again the third day' (Article 4).

229 *Come said Satan*: the temptation of Christ in the wilderness (Luke 4.1–13; Matthew 4.1–11; Mark 1.12–13) which is also the subject of Milton's *Paradise Regained*.

90 236 *Herod*: Herod Antipas, Tetrarch of Galilee 4 BC–AD 39, a client ruler under the Romans who interrogated and mocked Jesus (Luke 23.11) before returning him to Pontius Pilate (Governor of Judea) for judgement.

262 *Merchant Canaanite*: the driving of the moneychangers and merchants from the Temple (John 2.13–16, Matthew 21.12–13, Mark 11.15–19, Luke 19.45–8). They would have been Jewish (Roman money had to be changed because it had graven images on it, so could not be used in the Temple) not 'Canaanite', so calling them that is an insult.

91 280 *Melitus*: Meletus (probably the son of the tragic poet of the same name) was one of the accusers of Socrates, in 399 BC, accusing him of impiety and corrupting the young.

For the Sexes: The Gates of Paradise: an extended version of Blake's emblem book *For Children: The Gates of Paradise* (1793) which contained 17 uncoloured prints with brief captions (one of them a quotation from Dryden). At some point after 1818 he changed the title, expanded some captions, and added a verse prologue (engraved onto the previous title-page plate) and three new plates of verse at the end. The new plates contain 'The Keys/of the Gates' (numbered to refer back to the frontispiece and sixteen emblems) and an epilogue, 'To The Accuser who is The God of This World'.

91 5–6 *Jehovahs Finger . . . Then Wept*: God wrote the prohibitive laws of the Old Testament (thereby creating the Doctrine of Works, or belief that one is saved by doing or not doing things) but then replaced them with the Doctrine of Faith (see note to *Milton* 11.27–34). Unfortunately, in Blake's account, the established Churches have retained the previous view.

92 13 *Eternal Man*: Albion; see note to *Jerusalem* Plate 27 (p. 413).

16 *Mandrake*: see note to *Jerusalem* 11.22 (p. 411).

23 *Two Horn'd Reasoning*: Daniel has a vision of 'a ram which had two horns' (8.3) which is interpreted as 'the kings of Media and Persia' (8.20) but the reference here is probably to the horned figure of Satan.

25 *Hermaphrodite*: see note to *Milton* 12.36 (p. 402).

93 62 *My Satan . . . Dunce*: 'Satan, thy master, I dare call a dunce' (Young, *Night Thoughts*, 8.1417).

COMIC AND SATIRICAL POETRY

An Anthem: from 'An Island in the Moon'.

94 1 *Bat with Leathern wing*: 'where the weak-eyed bat | . . . flits by on leathern wing', Collins, 'Ode to Evening' (1746).

2 *Winking & blinking*: Samuel Johnson (1709–84) was short sighted and one of his portraits by Reynolds was known as *Blinking Sam* (1775).

9 *kick your Roman Anus*: Dr Johnson's kick would seem to refer to his now famous kicking of a stone, in 1763, to refute Berkeley's (supposed) claim that the universe was immaterial, though that incident would not become well known until its appearance in Boswell's *Life of Johnson* (1791).

11 *Scipio Africanus*: Scipio Africanus the Younger (185–129 BC), Roman general, statesman, and patron of philosophers, best remembered for his appearance in Cicero's *Somnium Scipionis* (*c*.54–51 BC) where, in a dream, he hears the music of the spheres and gives a geocentric and religious account of the structure of the universe.

14 *Cellar goes down*: possibly a reference to Act 3 of Shadwell's *The Virtuoso* where Sir Formal Trifle falls through a trapdoor into the cellar.

[Quid the Cynic's Second Song] 'Hail Matrimony, made of Love!': from 'An Island in the Moon'. A parodic echo of Milton's 'Hail wedded Love, mysterious Law, true sourse | Of human offspring', *Paradise Lost* 4.750–1; originally attributed to a different character: 'Sing a Mathematical Song Obtuse Angle then he sung' (deleted in MS).

95 *[Tilly Lally's Song] 'O I say you Joe'*: from 'An Island in the Moon'. An authentically childish voice (as distinguished from the more sophisticated

version of 'innocent' consciousness found in the *Songs*) and of interest as an early poem about cricket; one of the boys in the illustration to the second plate of 'The Ecchoing Green' is holding a cricket bat.

6 *tansey*: originally 'turd' (deleted in MS); tansey is silverweed, a strongly scented herb.

96 *To Nobodaddy*: (N109 rev). The fallen god of the fallen world; 'Nobody's daddy' (Foster Damon) or 'Daddy Nobody' (Ostriker), similar to Urizen as the 'Father of Jealousy' (*Visions* 10.12), with the 'No' pointing to the 'Thou shalt not' of the old Law or Ten Commandments.

'Her whole Life is an Epigram': (N100 rev).

'When Klopstock England defied': (N1). Friedrich Klopstock (1724–1803), poet known as 'the German Milton' after the appearance of his sublime epic *Der Messias* (1748–73). Blake would paint a head of Klopstock for Hayley's library but this poem is set 'at Lambeth', before the move to Felpham in September 1800, and was probably prompted by accounts from Fuseli of Klopstock's critical view of English poetry, expressed in poems such as 'Die bieden Musen' ('The Two Muses', 1752, in which the British and German muses compete, with the latter expecting to be 'first to gain the wreath'). It has been suggested that the scatological quality of Blake's poem is a response to Klopstock's claim, in a letter to Herder in 1797, that English poetic diction had a Swiftian coarseness but it is not clear how Blake could have known of it.

97 *'The Hebrew Nation did not write it'*: (N39). Written in pencil at a different date from the other (ink) writing on this page.

'When a Man has Married a Wife': (N14).

'The Sussex Men are Noted Fools' (N24). 'H—' is probably William Haines (1778–1848), painter and engraver who, like Blake, engraved for the Boydell Shakespeare Gallery (1790–1803) and Hayley's *Life of Romney* (1809). Though born in Hampshire, he grew up in Chichester (Sussex). After working in South Africa and America 1800–5, he returned to London where he became a successful portrait painter.

To H (*'You think Fuselui is not a Great Painter'*): (N25). 'H' is Robert Hunt who criticized both Fuseli ('a frantic') and Blake in *The Examiner* on 7 August 1808.

To F— (*'I mock thee not'*): (N26). 'F—' is John Flaxman, RA (1755–1826), sculptor and generous friend of Blake.

To Nancy F— (*'How can I help thy Husbands copying me'*): (N27). 'Nancy F' is Flaxman's wife Ann Denman (1760–1820) for whom Flaxman had commissioned Blake to illuminate a copy of Gray's *Poems* (1797–8); she would write to her husband in 1816 about 'being oblig'd to put up with B's odd humours'.

98 *'Of Hs birth this was the happy lot'*: (N27). 'H' is William Hayley (1745–1820), critic, poet, and Blake's patron at Felpham. Hayley's father died

when he was 3, and he was brought up by his mother, Mary Yates, though Blake is commenting metaphorically on Hayley's links to the cult of sensibility (see note to *The First Book of Urizen* 13.51, p. 393).

98 '*Sir Joshua Praises Michael Angelo*': (N28). In the long-standing dispute between the relative merits of the art of Florence (with its stress on *disegno*, or drawing and linear design) and of Venice (with its stress on *colore*, or colour and atmosphere) Blake sided strongly with Florence. He thought that the Royal Academy favoured the Venetian manner, so saw Sir Joshua Reynolds's praise of the Florentine Michelangelo as hypocritical; see *Jerusalem* 74.24–5 and note to 'All Pictures that's Painted with Sense & with Thought', p. 369).

Advice of the Popes who succeeded the Age of Rafael: annotations to *The Works of Sir Joshua Reynolds* (title-page); Blake annotated a copy of Vol. 1 of *The Works of Sir Joshua Reynolds* (2nd edition, London 1798) probably at various times between 1798 and 1809.

'*Some look. To see the sweet Outlines*': annotations to *The Works of Sir Joshua Reynolds* (p. xv).

'*When France got free Europe 'twixt Fools & Knaves*': annotations to *The Works of Sir Joshua Reynolds* (p. ciii).

'*When Sr Joshua Reynolds died*': annotations to *The Works of Sir Joshua Reynolds* (p. cix).

'*When Nations grow Old*': annotations to *The Works of Sir Joshua Reynolds* (Discourse 1, p. 4).

99 '*Hes a Blockhead who wants a proof*': (N28).

'*A Petty sneaking Knave I knew*': (N29). Robert Hartley Cromek (1770–1812) was an engraver, print seller, and publisher who commissioned illustrations from Blake for Blair's *The Grave* (1808), but then had them engraved by Schiavonetti, and (in Blake's account) stole the idea of a painting and engraving of Chaucer's Canterbury pilgrims and had it executed instead by Thomas Stothard.

'*He has observd the Golden Rule*': (N30). The Golden Rule (or Ratio or Section or Mean) is a proposition about satisfactory proportion in works of art which claims that the ideal is a ratio of 1.618 to 1 (or a+b is to a as a is to b): thus a rectangle with a length of 1.618 and a width of 1.

To the Royal Academy: (N33).

'*P— loved me not as he lovd his Friends*': (N34). 'P' is probably Thomas Phillips, RA (1770–1845) whose portrait of Blake, painted in the winter of 1806–7, was exhibited in the RA exhibition of 1807 and engraved by Schiavonetti as the frontispiece to Cromek's 1808 edition of Blair's *The Grave*. A prolific portrait painter, Phillips succeeded Fuseli as Professor of Painting at the RA in 1825; much favoured by Lord Egremont, his *The Archangel Michael leaving Adam and Eve, after having conducted them out of Paradise* (1816) is, like Blake's *Last Judgement* (1808), at Petworth.

On H—ys Friendship: (N35) 'H—y' is William Hayley; there may be a paranoid suggestion here that Hayley had deliberately arranged Scolfield's intrusion into Blake's garden at Felpham; the last line is repeated from 'Fair Elenor', l. 68.

100 *Another [Epitaph] ('I was buried near this Dike')*: (N37).

A Pretty Epigram for the Entertainment of those Who have Paid Great Sums in the Venetian & Flemish Ooze: (N38).

'Rafael Sublime Majestic Graceful Wise': (N39).

'If I eer Grow to Mans Estate': (N39).

Blakes apology for his Catalogue: (N65, with drafts and the title on N62–3).

2 Bartolloze: Francesco Bartolozzi (1717–1815), engraver, whose stippled engraving style had become more popular than the harder, linear manner taught to Blake by Basire; the 'Prose' is the *Descriptive Catalogue* for Blake's 1809 exhibition.

5 Milton only plannd: Dryden's verse play (or libretto) *The State of Innocence* (1677) rearranged Milton's *Paradise Lost* and recast it into heroic couplets; Dryden had actually obtained Milton's consent for this adaptation but Blake interprets it as an implicit criticism.

7 Tom Cooke: Thomas Cooke (1744–1818), engraver, who copied Hogarth's original engravings to make fresh plates, published in 1806 as *Hogarth Restored*.

101 *10 Homer . . . Pope*: Pope's translation of Homer into English heroic couplets (1715–26).

19 Schiavonetti: Luigi Schiavonetti died in June 1810 while at work (for Cromek) on the engraving of Stothard's *Canterbury Pilgrimage*.

VERSE EPISTLES AND DEDICATIONS

The verse letter was a popular form in the eighteenth century, modelled on Horace's *Epistulae* and Boileau's *Épîtres* (1674–83), and used with great distinction in Pope's *Epistles to Several Persons* (1731–5) and *Epistle to Dr Arbuthnot* (1735). The more relaxed, familiar epistle was particularly favoured by women poets and poets from lower-middle- and working-class backgrounds.

102 *To Mrs Ann Flaxman [c.1798]*: written on the last blank page (after the 'Elegy written in a Country Churchyard') of the copy of the 1790 edition of Gray's *Poems* (Yale Center for British Art) which Flaxman had commissioned Blake to 'Illuminate' with 116 watercolours as a present for his wife.

To George Cumberland [1 September 1800]: collection of Robert N. Essick; first published in *Blake Quarterly* 32.1 (1998) where there is a photographic reproduction); George Cumberland (1754–1848), writer, collector, and amateur artist; a friend of Blake from c.1780 to 1827.

7 stands the City in fear: French victories at Marengo (14 June 1800) and Höchstädt (19 June 1800) led to the Austrian withdrawal from the War of the Second Coalition (1798–1800), leaving Britain alone in the conflict with post-Revolutionary France.

103 *To John Flaxman* [12 September 1800]: Pierpont Morgan Library; John Flaxman RA (1755–1826), sculptor, Swedenborgian, and a generous and long-standing friend of Blake.

4 *Fuseli*: Henry Fuseli (1741–1825), painter, born in Zurich, settled in England 1779, RA 1790, Keeper of the RA 1810–25, who became a friend of Blake during Flaxman's absence in Italy 1787–94.

5 *Hayley*: William Hayley (1745–1820), poet, biographer, theorist of epic poetry, Sussex landowner who in 1800 sold his estate at Eartham and moved to a seaside villa at Felpham, where he invited Blake to settle with a promise of artistic patronage. Initially exciting, the relationship became irksome and in 1803 Blake returned to London, though he made further designs for Hayley and would write to express his 'Particular Gratitude' to him in December 1805 (*E* 767).

7 *Ezra*: biblical prophetic writer who describes the return of the Israelites to Jerusalem and the construction of the Temple.

8 *Paracelsus & Behmen*: Theophrast Bombast von Hohenheim (1493–1541), known as Paracelsus, was a Swiss physician, alchemist, astrologer, and mystic whose *Astronomia Magna* was published in 1571; Blake's use of 'gnomes' and 'salamanders' may reflect his theories (see notes to *Milton* 31.20 and *Jerusalem* 13.43); his motto may be echoed in *Jerusalem* 10.20. *Behmen* is Jacob Boehme (1575–1624), shoemaker and mystical writer. English translations of his works began to appear in 1645 and were popular during the Civil War; a new edition edited by William Law (see Introduction) was published 1764–81 and Blake admired it (*BR* 423–4). Law's own *The Way to Divine Knowledge* (1752) states that 'Jabob Behmen may be considered . . . As a Discoverer of the false Antichristian Church, from its first Rise in Cain, through every Age of the World, to its present State in all and every Sect of the present divided Christendom' (1893 edition, p. 195).

To My dear Friend Mrs Anna Flaxman [14 September 1800]: the letter is signed by Catherine Blake but written in Blake's hand (Pierpont Morgan Library; photographic reproduction in Keynes, *The Letters of William Blake*, 3rd edition, 1980, Plates V–VI).

7 *the Turret*: Hayley's villa at Felpham.

104 11 *My Brother*: Robert Blake, who had died in 1787, but was there in spirit (see *Milton* Plate 33).

To Thomas Butts [2 October 1800]: Thomas Butts (1757–1845) was a civil servant in what would now be called the Ministry of Defence and Blake's most loyal patron (Preston Blake Collection, City of Westminster Archives Centre).

105 40 *My Shadow*: Blake's wife Catherine Boucher (or Butcher), 1762–1831; Blake himself is correspondingly his 'wifes shadow' in l. 40.

42 *Sister:* Blake's sister, also called Catherine (1764–1841), lived with her brother and sister-in-law at Felpham.

63 *Ram hornd with gold*: possibly an echo of 'the horns of the righteous shall be exalted' (Psalm 75.10). For Swedenborg 'a sheep' means 'innocence' (*The True Christian Religion*, para. 200) but he does not specify rams and biblical rams' horns are not gilded. The reference is probably a private one between Blake and Butts: Blake made a tempera painting of *Abraham and Isaac* for Butts *c.*1799–1800 (Yale Center for British Art) which shows the ram in the thicket, though the ram's horns do not appear to be painted gold.

106 *To Mrs Butts* [2 October 1800]: in the same letter as the previous poem); Elizabeth (Betsy) Butts, wife of Thomas, ran a boarding school for girls in their house at 9 Great Marlborough Street.

To Thomas Butts [22 November 1802]: Preston Blake Collection, City of Westminster Archives Centre.

15 *Brother John the evil one*: John Blake (b. 1760) was the favourite son who became a baker but failed in business and, in 1793, enlisted as a soldier; he may have died not long thereafter (*BR* 663–4).

107 33–5 *Theotormon . . . Enitharmon . . . Los*: figures introduced into Blake's mythic narrative in the early 1790s and developing during his work on *The Four Zoas* at Felpham.

108 86–8 *Beulahs . . . Single vision*: for Beulah see note to *Milton* 3.1 (p. 398); on *Single vision* see note to 'The Everlasting Gospel', l. 110 (p. 372) and (on 'fourfold vision') notes to *Milton* 17.18 (p. 403) and *Jerusalem* 98.12 (p. 426). The Newtonian view of the universe (that of empirical science) is, in Blake's account, narrow or 'single'; *Jerusalem* will be about the awakening of mankind from such 'sleep'.

To Thomas Butts [16 August 1803]: Preston Blake Collection, City of Westminster Archives Centre.

109 *To the Queen*: a dedication to the edition of Robert Blair's *The Grave* (London, 1808), with illustrations designed by Blake but engraved by Louis Schiavonetti. Curiously, given Blake's reputation as a republican, this flattering address to Queen Charlotte (consort of George III) is the only poem he published in conventional typography: *The French Revolution* did not get beyond the proof stage and both *Poetical Sketches* and the few poems reprinted in magazines and conventional books or pamphlets were published by other people.

'*The Caverns of the Grave Ive seen*': N87; apparently written as a dedication of one of the paintings (either *The Vision of the Last Judgement*, 1808, or *Satan Calling Up His Legions*) made for Elizabeth Ilive (Countess of Egremont since 1801, though subsequently estranged and collecting pictures for her house in London; Blake's paintings were moved to Petworth after her death in 1822).

110 18 *Great Atlantic Mountains*: see note to 'A Song of Liberty', verse 8
(p. 362). In one of Blake's various accounts of the matter, Eden was set on
the mountains of Atlantis and sank into the ocean at the time of the Fall.

BRIEF EPIC

111 *Visions of the Daughters of Albion*: dated 1793, the poem has been seen as
a creative rewriting of both MacPherson's Ossianic 'Oithona: a Poem'
(where Oithona, betrothed to Gaul, is raped and concealed in a sea cave by
Dunrommath; *Fingal and Other Poems*, 1762) and, by Ostriker, of Milton's
masque *Comus* (a discussion of chastity from the opposite point of view).
The structure, as a series of long dramatic speeches, would fit either model,
though the verse is closer to Ossian's rhythmic prose. The topic reflects the
recent upsurge of feminist argument in Olympe de Gouges's *Declaration
of the Rights of Woman and the Female Citizen* (1791; de Gouges would be
guillotined during the Terror in November 1793) and Mary Wollstonecraft's
Vindication of the Rights of Woman (1792). Blake had illustrated the second
edition of Wollstonecraft's *Original Stories from Real Life* in 1791, though
his poem is concerned with the sexual liberation of women, rather than the
social, legal, political, and educational liberation which de Gouges and
Wollstonecraft also advocated. In philosophical terms, the poem develops
into a debate between uniformity and variety. It can also be read as a political allegory in which the Daughters of Albion (British women, not yet the
wicked daughters of *Jerusalem* Plate 5) echo Oothoon's complaint that, for
all its talk of the 'unalienable' quality of human rights, the new American
republic has, in practice, liberated neither slaves nor women. There are
sixteen known copies, with no significant variants.

Plate 3

1–5 *Theotormon . . . Leutha's flower*: Theotormon is an inhibited and moralistic figure (perhaps a New England Puritan) who will reappear in
'Africa' to give Christianity its repressive quality. Foster Damon suggested that the name might be a combination of *theo* (god) and *torah*
(law), though it will be used in later texts for a very different character:
a son of Los who labours at the forge to create 'the instruments | Of
Harvest' (*Milton* 4.12–13). *Leutha* appears to be a version of Venus, goddess of love, so plucking her 'flower' signifies the loss of virginity (compare 'An old maid early eer I knew', l. 8, p. 43).

Plate 4

112 16 *Bromion*: here an authoritarian but uninhibited Southern slave-owner
who rapes, or deceitfully seduces, Oothoon and then tries, unsuccessfully,
to pass her on to her puritanical Yankee boyfriend; in later texts the name,
like Theotormon, will be used for a son of Los who labours at his forge.

19 *jealous dolphins*: in the myth of Acis and Galatea, dolphins save the
sea-nymph Galatea from rape by Polyphemus; the story, from Ovid's
Metamorphoses, had been made familiar by Handel's pastoral opera (1718,
with a libretto by John Gay).

21 *swarthy children of the sun*: Bromion's slaves, 'Stampt' with his 'signet' or brand.

Plate 5

5 *Bound back to back*: either as master and slave or, in the eyes of conventional morality, as locked into an enduring guilt for their sexual transgression.

13 *Theotormon's Eagles*: Zeus punished the rebel Prometheus by binding him on a mountain where an eagle ate his liver (which grew back and was re-eaten every day); the bald eagle was used on the seal of the USA from 1782 and adopted as the national emblem in 1787 (Benjamin Franklin disapproved, preferring the turkey).

20 *eccho back her sighs*: an ironic use of Spenser's marriage poems 'Prothalamion' ('I chanced to espy, | [the] lovely daughters of the flood . . . Sweet Thames run softly, till I end my song') and 'Epithalamion' ('The woods shall to me answer and my Eccho ring'); the wicked Daughters of Albion will 'reply' to Los's song in *Jerusalem* Plate 56.

Plate 7

114 22 *one law for both the lion and the ox*: Oothoon has argued for moral rules which are various and contingent (or adapted to individual identities and circumstances); Bromion argues, more conventionally, for moral and legal codes which are uniform and consistent. Compare 'One Law for the Lion & Ox is Oppression' (*Marriage of Heaven and Hell*, Plate 24; *E* 44).

Plate 8

115 14 *fat fed hireling*: a recruiting sergeant, taking labourers from farms to the army.

17 *parson claim the labour*: Nonconformists fiercely opposed the system of tithes, whereby a tenth of the produce of the land was taken to fund the established Church; Blake had engraved Collings's cartoon 'Tythe in Kind, or the Sow's Revenge' for *The Wit's Magazine* in 1784.

Plate 10

116 1 *copulation*: here between the eye and its object.

5–7 *youth . . . silent pillow*: masturbation.

117 24–6 *catch for thee . . . lovely copulation*: here copulation is sex and the (much debated) lines can be seen as either a generous celebration of free love or a deplorable objectification of women; see note to *Jerusalem* 69.15 (p. 422).

THE CONTINENTAL POEMS: *AMERICA*, *EUROPE*, *THE SONG OF LOS*

Tom Paine, encouraging the rebellious Americans in 1776, lamented that, 'Freedom hath been hunted round the globe. Asia, and Africa, have long expelled her.—Europe regards her like a stranger, and England hath given her warning to depart', going on to observe that 'A situation, similar to the present [in America], hath not happened since the days of Noah until now' (*Common Sense* (Philadelphia, 1776), p. 58 and p. 87). Blake may have had this passage in mind when writing a series of poems on the loss and recovery of freedom in Asia, Africa (jointly published as *The Song of Los* in 1795), Europe (1794), and America (1793). It is clearly a sequence, since the last line of 'Africa' is also the first line of the main text of *America*, and *The Song of Los* might be a general title for all four sections. George Cumberland's bound volume of *America* (F), *Europe* (C), and *The Song of Los* (D) (though also *Visions of the Daughters of Albion*, B) is, however, the only evidence that Blake ever sold the poems as a group and the incongruous order of publication (*America*, *Europe*, 'Africa', 'Asia', when the story runs Africa, America, Europe, Asia) enacts the disruption of 'chronologic order' which Thomas Howes had identified as a characteristic of the prophetic books of the Old Testament (see Introduction). That disrupted order is retained in this edition. The verse is a mixture of Lowth's 'Longer' and 'Shorter' lines (see Introduction): 'longer' in *America*, 'shorter' in 'Africa' (mostly) and 'Asia', with a mixture of the two in *Europe*.

118 *America A Prophecy*: in narrative terms, *America* (1793) is a transitional text. It retains some of the historical specificity of Blake's unfinished *The French Revolution* (a first section of which was printed as page proofs, though not issued, by Joseph Johnson in 1791). But it takes a significant step towards the visionary manner of his later epics, presenting the events of the American Revolution (1775–83) in 'correspondences' between natural and supernatural phenomena (an idea found in Swedenborg and in Milton's 'lik'ning spiritual to corporal forms' in *Paradise Lost*, Book 5). It is also the poem in which Blake's idiosyncratic mythology begins to take shape. The 'new born terror' of 'A Song of Liberty' acquires a name, Orc, and a new role, not only as the prisoner who seduces the jailer's daughter, but also as a sacrilegious version of the Holy Ghost: impregnating the virgin 'female' (or Nature) so that she will give birth to revolution. The 'starry king' is, similarly, now named ('Urizen', as he is in *Visions of the Daughters of Albion*, also published in 1793), while Urthona, mentioned in 'A Song of Liberty', returns as the father of the 'shadowy' female who is first the jailer and then the lover of Orc. The poem is complicated by the use of the word 'angel' (echoing the loyal and rebel angels of Milton's *Paradise Lost*) to refer not only to George III and his colonial governors but also to the leaders of the American rebellion. Two of the governors changed sides, but the others did not, and the terminology becomes confusing. Copy E (Library of Congress) is the model here. Proofs survive of three cancelled plates; the only significant variant is the passage at the end of Plate 4 which was erased or masked in all but two of the copies.

Plate 3

2 *fourteen suns*: sometimes read as the interval between Rousseau's *Social Contract* (1762) and the Declaration of Independence (1776) but probably simply puberty.

3 *His food she brought*: the motif of the jailer's daughter who falls in love with a prisoner is best known from Shakespeare and Fletcher's *The Two Noble Kinsmen*.

17 *Canadian*: the British colony of the Province of Quebec was renamed Upper and Lower Canada in 1791.

Plate 4

3 *siez'd*: though it is not explicit, this is often described as a rape—in which case it frees the American rebels from the charge of acting improperly, since rebellion was (metaphorically) forced on them.

119 17 *foretold*: four additional lines, engraved on the plate, were erased from the page after printing in Copy G (1793) and masked during printing in all copies except A (*c.*1795) and O (sold to John Linnell in 1821):

> The stern Bard ceas'd, asham'd of his own song; enrag'd he swung
> His harp aloft sounding, then dash'd its shining frame against
> A ruin'd pillar in glittring fragments; silent he turn'd away,
> And wander'd down the vales of Kent in sick & drear lamentings.

The passage is usually seen as an expression of disillusionment with the progress of the French Revolution, or anger at British policy towards it, though it could also reflect disappointment at the retention of slavery in the new American republic or regret for the irreligious tone of the poem. Its presence on the plate suggests that the Preludium was written and engraved after the main body of the text.

Plate 5

1 *Guardian Prince of Albion*: the British Church and State, or George III in his dual capacity as King and Supreme Governor of the Church of England; also referred to as 'Albion's Angel'.

4 *Washington . . . Green*: George Washington (1732–99): Commander of the Continental Army 1775–83, first President of the United States 1789–97; Benjamin Franklin (1706–90): printer, writer, scientist, diplomat, member of the Continental Congress and co-author of the Declaration of Independence (1776); Tom Paine (1737–1809): British-born and a rope-maker by trade, he moved to America (on Franklin's recommendation) in 1774, where he wrote *Common Sense* and *The American Crisis* (both 1776); Joseph Warren (1741–75): Boston physician and revolutionary leader, killed at Bunker Hill (1775); Horatio Gates (1728–1806): British by birth (he was Horace Walpole's godson), he settled in America after serving there with the British army, beat Burgoyne at Saratoga (1788), but was beaten by Cornwallis at Camden (1780); John Hancock (1737–93): Boston businessman and member of the Continental Congress; Nathanael Greene (1742–86): Quaker by birth but a talented soldier, he successfully assumed command of the Southern Department after Gates's defeat at Camden.

5 *Meet on the coast*: the meeting is fictitious though Washington, Franklin, and Hancock attended meetings of the Continental Congress in 1774–6

in Philadelphia and Baltimore. *glowing with blood*: the Boston Massacre, in March 1770, a clash between British troops and a crowd in which five people were killed, was stressed in Patriot propaganda.

119 10 *work-bruis'd*: though the depiction of white Americans as slaves may seem tactless from the mouth of the slave-owning Washington, the passage resembles Joel Barlow's *The Vision of Columbus* (1787): 'When Albion's Prince . . . | Shall stretch . . . the sovereign hand | To bind in slavery's chains the peaceful host' (Book 5).

15 *dragon form*: Pharaoh is 'the great dragon' in Ezekiel 29.3.

Plate 7

120 1 *Stone of night*: the altar of the established Church. Jacob, in Genesis 28.18–22, 'took the stone that he had put for his pillows, and set it up for a pillar . . . And this stone . . . shall be God's house'. Protestants substituted a wooden communion table for the stone altar of the Catholic tradition, which they saw as having pagan precedents, both Roman and Druidic.

4 *Mars thou wast our center*: Mars, the planet named after the god of war, symbolically replaces the Sun as the centre of the galaxy to reflect a time of conflict.

6 *The Spectre*: Orc (the term does not yet have the more complex meaning it will have in Blake's later work). *the temple long*: following William Stukeley's *Abury, a Temple of the British Druids* (1743), Blake identified the fallen religion of the Urizenic age with the 'Patriarchal Christianity' of the Druids, whose (supposed) temple at Avebury was said to have an extended, serpentine form; see note to *Milton* 4.20.

Plate 8

2 *linen wrapped up*: revolution announced in the language of the Gospel accounts of the Resurrection (Luke 24.1–12).

6 *slave grinding at the mill*: echoing Milton, *Samson Agonistes*, l. 41 ('Eyeless in Gaza at the Mill with slaves') and Judges 16.21 (where Samson is made to 'grind in the prison house').

15 *Lion & Wolf shall cease*: the line is also found in verse 20 of 'A Song of Liberty' (see note to p. 363).

Plate 10

121 1 *the accursed tree*: a combination of the Liberty Tree (an elm on Boston Common which was a rallying point for rebels from 1765 until its destruction by British troops in 1775) and the tree of the knowledge of good and evil in Eden (Genesis 2.16–3.7). In an antinomian spirit, Orc presents himself as the serpent, encouraging the breach of God's prohibitions; a serpent wreathed around a rod is also the symbol of Asclepius, the Greek god of healing, and Moses has a healing pole with a 'serpent of brass' (Numbers 21.9).

3 *ten commands*: God speaks the ten commandments to Moses on Mount Sinai (Exodus 20.1–17) as the Israelites are making their way through the

'wilderness' and they are later inscribed on tablets of stone; St Paul will insist that 'the epistle of Christ' is written 'not in tables of stone, but in fleshy tables of the heart' (2 Corinthians 3.3).

12 *undefil'd tho' ravish'd*: echoing the free love doctrine of *Visions of the Daughters of Albion.*

17 *head like gold*: alluding to Daniel's survival in the fiery furnace and Nebuchadnezzar's dream of an image with metal limbs (Daniel 3.25–7 and 2.31–5).

Plate 11

1 *my Thirteen Angels!*: here the British governors of the thirteen rebellious colonies. George III issued his Proclamation for Suppressing Rebellion and Sedition on 23 August 1775 and refused to consider the Olive Branch Petition, proposing a peaceful settlement, which the Continental Congress had sent to London in July.

Plate 12

122 10 *Ariston*: in Plato's *Critias*, Poseidon, ruler of the lost continent of Atlantis, steals a human bride; Blake appears to confuse, or mingle, this with Herodotus's account of Ariston, King of Sparta, who steals the wife of a friend (*History*, 2.61). The ideal world of Atlantis serves as a symbolic equivalent to the meeting places (actually Philadelphia and Baltimore) used by the 'angels' (here the political leaders of the American rebels, rather than the colonial Governors) for their illegal Continental Congress.

Plate 13

3 *Bostons Angel*: the Governor of Massachusetts in 1774–5 was a British general, Thomas Gage, and the 'angel' is either Samuel Adams, a member of the Massachusetts provincial assembly who attended the first Continental Congress, or John Hancock, President of the second Congress and the first Governor of Massachusetts after independence.

Plate 14

123 2 *all the thirteen Angels*: in fact, the only colonial Governors to take up the rebel cause were Jonathan Trumbull, Governor of Connecticut, and Nicholas Cooke, Deputy Governor of Rhode Island.

Plate 15

2 *Bernards house*: Sir Francis Bernard had stepped down as Governor of Massachusetts in 1769. The meeting could, in theory, have been held in his former official residence in Boston (Province House in Marlborough Street, demolished 1922) but is, in fact, fictitious.

124 16 *forty millions*: both the number of British troops and the rapidity with which they were defeated are exaggerated. General Howe's army in 1776 had 22,000 men and the fighting continued for almost seven years.

Plate 16

2 *Allen . . . Lee*: Ethan Allen (1748–89) led the forces which took Fort Ticonderoga in May 1775 but was himself captured four months later;

Lee is either 'Light-Horse Harry' Lee (1756–1818), a successful cavalry
commander (and father of General Robert E. Lee), or Richard Henry
Lee (1732–94), the Virginian politician who proposed the motion for
independence to the second Continental Congress in 1776.

124 4 *His plagues*: possibly a literal reference to the epidemics during the siege
of Boston in 1775–6 but also an echo of the plagues which Jehovah inflicts
on Egypt (Exodus 7–12) and those used against Satan's forces in *Paradise
Lost* 6.834–9.

17 *o'erwhelm'd by the Atlantic*: like Atlantis.

Plate 17

3 *Leprosy*: the diseases are metaphors for war-weariness, not literal epidemics: George III's first prolonged period of illness would not be until
1788. The merchants of London and Bristol had not been much incon-
venienced by the fighting in America but were worried about the war with
France and Spain which began when those countries allied themselves
with the Americans in 1778–9.

125 9 *Londons Guardian . . . miter'd York*: again, the sickness is metaphorical:
Robert Hay Drummond, Archbishop of York ('a sensible, worldly man . . .
much addicted to his bottle' in Horace Walpole's view) died in December
1776 but neither the Bishop of London, Robert Lowth (1710–87), nor the
Archbishop of Canterbury, Frederick Cornwallis (1713–83; sometimes
suggested to be 'London's Guardian' because of his official residence at
Lambeth Palace), was seriously ill during the American war.

16 *Bard of Albion*: probably the Poet Laureate, William Whitehead
(1715–85).

26 *tender grape*: 'the vines with the tender grape give a good smell. Arise,
my love, my fair one, and come away', Song of Solomon 2.13.

Plate 18

126 14 *twelve years*: from the British defeat at Saratoga (1777) to the French
Revolution (1789).

19 *five gates*: the five senses.

20 *mildews of despair*: 'The Lord shall smite thee . . . with blasting, and
with mildew', Deuteronomy 28.22.

127 *Europe A Prophecy* (1794) is not an account of the French Revolution
(1789): Orc appears 'in the vineyards of red France' (Plate 18) only at the
very end of the poem. Instead, it describes what (in Blake's view) caused
the revolution to happen and (Plates 12–15) sketches political life in
Britain between the end of the American war and the dismissal of Lord
Chancellor Thurlow in 1792. Enitharmon here functions as a Marie-
Antoinette-like, representative European queen who irresponsibly dreams
(Plates 12–16) for the 'Eighteen hundred years' of the Christian era.
Before and after this period, she and her court indulge in luxurious fri-
volity, treating Orc (here the representative of the radical thought of the

eighteenth century, French as well as Anglo-American) as an intellectual curiosity rather than a political threat. During the dream it is actually the fallen religion of Urizen which flourishes. The imitation of Milton's 'Ode on the Morning of Christ's Nativity' in Plate 6 makes it (shockingly) clear that it was the birth of Christ which initiated this period of decadence and, in the Preludium, the 'shadowy female' (Nature) who was impregnated by the Holy-Ghost-like Orc in the Preludium to *America* explains the matter. She has brought forth 'howling terrors' on other occasions—including, it would seem, Christ, when impregnated by the actual Holy Ghost—but they have all been stamped with Enitharmon's 'signet' and rendered ineffectual. Jesus, in other words, was a failed revolutionary and it will be 'terrible Orc' who redeems the world. Copy B (Glasgow University Library) is the model here. The only significant variant is that Blake added a prefatory address to the reader in two late copies (H and K) in which 'a Fairy mocking as he sat on a streak'd Tulip . . . dictated EUROPE').

Plate 4

6 *travel*: travail or labour (child birth).

Plate 6

128 4 *their abodes*: a close imitation, in both form and content, of Milton's 'On the Morning of Christ's Nativity' (1629), ll. 29–31 and 45–52.

6 *crystal house*: suggesting the Salon des Glaces, or Hall of Mirrors, at Versailles.

7 *Los, possessor of the moon*: though the primary significance of Los's name is the pun on 'loss' (of our unfallen state), it is sometimes seen also as an anagram of 'Sol' (the Sun), in which case he appears here in a diminished or secondary role as the indulgent consort of a decadent queen (who is the Earth as well as Marie-Antoinette).

Plate 8

129 3 *Woman, lovely Woman!*: 'O Woman! Lovely Woman! Nature made thee | To temper Man', Thomas Otway, *Venice Preserv'd* (1682), 1.1.

4 *Rintrah . . . Palamabron*: though Rintrah has previously appeared in 'The Argument' of *The Marriage of Heaven and Hell*, and both Rintrah and Palamabron will later have a more specific significance (as loyal sons of Los who are closely identified with the religious enthusiasm of Whitefield and Wesley), they are here, like Elynittria and Ocalythron, simply members of Enitharmon's extensive royal family.

Plate 11

11 *ramping*: a lion 'came ramping forth', Spenser, *Faerie Queene*, 1.8.12.

Plate 12

130 2 *Eighteen hundred years*: from the birth of Christ to the 1780s.

8 *Albions Angel . . . fled with his bands*: the British surrender in North America after Yorktown (October 1781).

130 14 *ruins of that hall*: Erdman sees this as a metaphorical account of the fall of Lord North's government in March 1782; in more literal terms, the lead roof of Westminster Hall, deemed dangerous and supported by scaffolding since 1740, was removed and replaced with slates in 1782. There is a parallel with Samson's pulling down the roof of the Philistine council chamber 'Upon the heads of all who sate beneath' (Milton, *Samson Agonistes*, l. 1652).

Plate 13

2 *temple serpent-form'd*: see note to America 7.6. The *island white* is Britain or Albion, a name derived either from Celtic *alban* or Latin *albus* (white).

5 *Verulam*: Verulamium, the Roman city now called St Albans where Francis Bacon lived and from which he took his title as Lord Verulam. Though there is no evidence for Blake's suggestion of a Stonehenge or Avebury-like structure at St Albans (the ruins are Romano-British), it enables him to link the Urizenic religion of the Druids with the empirical philosophy of Bacon. Druid temples were *surrounded* with oak trees.

15 *petrify'd against the infinite*: the Fall involves a deterioration of human consciousness, with the skull forming as a bony barrier between the mind and the divine.

131 26 *Stone of Night*: altar (see note to *America* 7.1).

Plate 15

8–9 *vast rock . . . overshadows London city*: the stone keep (or White Tower) of the Tower of London, a royal fortress incorporating a Norman chapel, set, like the Bastille, on the east of the city, so *shadowing* it from the rising sun.

132 15 *Guardian of the secret codes*: the scene shifts from the east to the west of London and the *Guardian* (of the laws) is probably Edward Thurlow (1731–1806), Tory lawyer and politician, Lord Chancellor 1778–92, who fell out with Pitt over policies for repaying the national debt and was dismissed in June 1792. Wearing the *robes* (actually ornamented with gold braid, rather than fur) and wig of the Lord Chancellor, he flees from the Palace of Westminster, along *Great George Street* (built in the 1750s to link the new Westminster Bridge to St James's Park) into the political *wilderness* or, more literally, via the area of St James's Park known as 'the wilderness' to his home in Queen Square, Great Ormond Street. Blake optimistically over-interprets this dismissal as a symptom of a failing government; in fact, Pitt was glad to get rid of the difficult Thurlow, and to replace him with Alexander Wedderburn (a defector from the Foxite Whigs) in January 1793. Pitt's first government would continue until his resignation, over the King's refusal to enfranchise Roman Catholics, in 1801.

26 *a den*: a gaol. 'As I walked through the wilderness of this world, I lighted on a certain place where was a den, and laid me down in that place to sleep: and as I slept I dreamed a dream' (Bunyan, *The Pilgrim's Progress*, with the marginal note 'The gaol').

Plate 16

1 *red limb'd Angel*: Albion's Angel (the King) whose soldiers wore 'redcoats'.

2 *Trump of the last doom*: 'at the last trump . . . the trumpet shall sound, and the dead shall be raised incorruptible', 1 Corinthians 15.52.

5 *Newton*: Sir Isaac Newton (1642–1727), mathematician and scientist, whose identification of gravity as the force which controls the movements of the planets, without any divine intervention, was a triumph of scientific rationalism and a key argument for Deism and 'Natural Religion'; compare *Jerusalem* 93.21–6 where Newton's denial of 'a Conscience in Man' and condemnation of 'the Divine Vision' is a 'Signal of the Morning'. Blake seems to have been unaware of the religious nature of Newton's later work—even his *Opticks* (1704; see note to 'Mock on Mock on Voltaire Rousseau', p. 368) ends with an assertion that Blake might have agreed with: instead of worshipping 'dead Heroes', the pagan philosophers would have done better had they 'taught us to worship our true Author and Benefactor, as their Ancestors did under the government of Noah and his Sons before they corrupted themselves' (p. 406).

133 16 *Erinthus*: like Manathu-Vorcyon, Leutha, Antamon, Oothoon, Theotormon, Sotha, and Thiralatha in the following plate, Erinthus is here simply a name for a figure at the court of the newly awakened Enitharmon.

Plate 18

134 2 *vineyards of red France . . . fury*: in order to align Orc's appearance in France with the English political material of Plate 15, Erdman suggests that this represents the trial and execution of King Louis XVI in 1792–3. As the conclusion of Enitharmon's self-indulgence, however, it seems more natural to identify it with the beginning of the French Revolution in 1789.

135 *The Song of Los* (1795) provides the beginning (in Africa) and end (potentially, in Asia) of the story of the loss and recovery of 'freedom' in the four continents named by Paine in *Common Sense*: the last line of 'Africa' is the first line of the main section of *America*, and at the beginning of 'Asia' the oriental monarchs hear the 'howl' uttered in Plate 15 of *Europe*. Los's status had been ambiguous in *Europe*. Apparently a complacent consort of the decadent Enitharmon, his calling 'all his sons to the strife of blood' at the end of the poem could be either a summons to revolution or a gathering of reactionary forces to resist it. Now, at the beginning of 'Africa', his identity as 'the Eternal Prophet' is made clear (as it is in *Urizen*). His significance in Blake's mythology will continue to grow and there will be another 'Song of Los' in *Jerusalem*, Plates 85–6. The five known copies were colour-printed in 1795 (Blake seems not to have reprinted or sold the poem after its first appearance) and there are no significant variants.

Plate 3

135 *AFRICA*: if inspired Prophets could write the Bible, inspired prophetic
poets (Blake believed) could and should rewrite it. In 'Africa' and *The First
Book of Urizen* he makes his first attempts at rewriting the Fall, here moving it back from the first commission of sin (Eve eating the apple) to the
invention of sin in the first place (God's prohibition of eating the apple).
He combines this with material from the new field of comparative religion
to suggest that all creeds, not just Christianity, have been guilty of creating
codes of prohibitive doctrine ('Thou shalt not'). This, in turn, has made
possible the loss of political liberty which Orc will challenge in *America*.
Though this might seem Antinomian, the criticism of the 'Gospel' of
'Jesus' in Plate 3 means that it is not (the Antinomian rejection of the 'Old
Law' requires its supersession by the Gospel of the New Testament) and,
in the final plate, Blake outlines a more distinctive position. Here he
attacks the figures usually associated with both the Empiricist philosophy
and the revolutionary movements of the eighteenth century (Locke,
Rousseau, Voltaire) and suggests the view (found in Boehme: see note to
'To my Dearest Friend, John Flaxman', l. 8, p. 378) that a true religion
could be distinguished from the fallen religion of the Churches.
Meanwhile, in *The First Book of Urizen*, he was developing a Gnostic
argument that the Fall had taken place still earlier, in the act of Creation.

6–7 *Adam . . . Ararat*: Adam receives God's moral laws in Eden and
they are given again to Noah (Genesis 9), after the flood, when the
Ark grounds on Mount Ararat, though they are seen here as the Urizenic
laws of a fallen religion. Blake's sequence of poems begins in Africa,
either because the Garden of Eden was thought to have been there, or
because recorded history began in the African country of Egypt (see
Urizen 28.10).

9 *By the hands of the children of Los*: Los is now established in Blake's myth
as 'the Eternal Prophet' so his children are the poet-prophets (Isaiah,
Ezekiel, Milton) who transmit divine knowledge, whether true or fallen.

10 *African*: Noah's curse of his grandson Canaan ('A servant . . . He shall
be to his brethren', Genesis 9.25) was held to be the origin of the black
races and was used as a justification of slavery.

11 *Brama in the East*: the Hindu god Brahma; Blake's picture *The
Bramins.—A Drawing* was shown in his 1809 exhibition; his *Descriptive
Catalogue* says that the subject was 'Mr Wilkin translating the Geeta'
(Charles Wilkins's translation of the *Bhagvat Geeta*, 1785).

16 *Abram . . . Chaldea*: the Hebrew patriarch Abraham came from 'Ur of
the Chaldees' (Genesis 11.31) and was told by God to 'Get thee out of thy
country' (Genesis 12.1).

17 *Moses . . . Mount Sinai*: Moses receives the Ten Commandments on
Mount Sinai (Exodus 19–20).

18–19 *Trismegistus . . . Pythagoras Socrates & Plato*: the mythical alchemist
and mystic Hermes Trismegistus (believed during the Renaissance to

have been a pagan anticipator of Christianity, though subsequently shown to have been a 3rd-century AD fabrication) is included with Pythagoras, Socrates, and Plato as a representative of Ancient Greek philosophy; Los's Spectre will invoke his *Smaragdine Table* in *Jerusalem* 91.35.

20 *sons of Har*: human beings: 'Har' and 'Heva' (previously mentioned in *Tiriel*) are a version of the fallen Adam and Eve.

21 *Orc on Mount Atlas*: the Atlas Mountains are in North Africa; Orc is bound there, as Prometheus was on the Caucasus Mountains in Greek myth.

23–4 *Jesus . . . Theotormon*: in *Visions of the Daughters of Albion* Theotormon is an inhibited and moralistic Puritan.

29 *a loose Bible*: the title of the Koran, the sacred text of Islam, is an Arabic word once thought (Stevenson suggests) to mean 'a collection of loose pages' though properly understood as 'the recitation' or 'reading'. From quite early in the text's history there was debate about the order in which the 114 *surahs* (chapters) should be arranged: the conventional pattern seems to be roughly in descending order of length, rather than chronological or thematic.

136 30 *Odin*: the Norse or Germanic god of pre-Christian northern Europe; see notes to 'The Human Abstract' (p. 357) and *Milton* 25.53 (p. 406).

Plate 4

17–18 *Newton . . . Voltaire*: Isaac Newton (1642–1727), John Locke (1632–1704), Jean-Jacques Rousseau (1712–78), Voltaire (François-Marie Arouet, 1694–1778), key figures in the scientific, political, and philosophical life of the Enlightenment, here linked with the Judaeo-Christian, Greek, Christian, Muslim, and Germanic religious traditions as another expression of the fallen doctrines of Urizen.

ASIA: this poem is prophecy in the vulgar sense of predicting the future: having moved from West to East through America and Europe, revolution will continue into the Orient (the failure of this prediction may be one reason why Blake seems not to have reprinted *The Song of Los* after 1795).

Plate 6

137 9 *call for Famine*: the measures proposed by the Kings and Priests of Asia have been compared with the steps taken by the British government to maintain social control in the 1790s. There was an acute shortage of grain in 1795 and widespread rioting over food prices. Though there is no reason to suppose that the government deliberately caused the shortage, military force was used to suppress the riots and relief, under the Old Poor Law, was limited.

18 *allegoric riches*: nominal money (entries in ledgers rather than tangible goods).

Plate 7

138 20–2 *Adam . . . Noah*: rewriting lines 6–9 of 'Africa'.

38 *glandous*: a word coined by Blake to suggest a bodily fluid exuded by the glands, probably semen.

139 *The First Book of Urizen*: this poem, dated 1794, is Blake's revision of, or radical alternative to, the account of the Fall given in the book known in the Bible as 'The First Book of Moses, called Genesis'. Blake removed the word 'First' on some, but not all, pages of copies A (probably the fourth to be printed, in 1795) and G (*c*.1815). This may be because he had abandoned an original plan to write a full Pentateuch (the second, third, fourth, and fifth Books of Moses are Exodus, Leviticus, Numbers, and Deuteronomy), on the lines of the 'Bible of Hell' promised in *The Marriage of Heaven and Hell*. But the presence of the word 'First' makes the link to Genesis clear, in a way which the revised title fails to do, and Copy C (Yale Center for British Art), probably the first to be printed, is followed here (though not the double-column format, common to all copies, which, like the division into chapters, imitates the layout of printed Bibles). The eight known copies differ widely, suggesting that Blake wrestled with the poem over an extended period: Plates 7 and 8 (with its duplicate Chapter 4) were added in later copies. Plate 4 was omitted in Copies D, E, F, and G.

Plate 3

6 *Urizen*: 'Your reason' though also possibly the Greek word 'horizon' (meaning 'limit'). The character will later be developed into one of the Four Zoas, representing the rational aspect of a split human consciousness. Urizen brings himself into being by separation from the 'Eternals', thereby creating the material universe. This creation does not precede the Fall (as in the Bible) but is itself the Fall.

140 36 *globes of attraction*: the Newtonian universe in which bodies are moved by the attractive pull of gravity.

44 *the trumpet*: as Moses is given the Ten Commandments on Mount Sinai there is cloud and 'the voice of the trumpet exceeding loud' (Exodus 19.16).

Plate 4

141 24 *books formd of metals*: sometimes seen as a reference to the fact that Blake's illuminated books were relief-etched into sheets of metal, but all books have, since the 1450s, been formed of metal, whether solid plates or moveable type.

30 *Seven deadly Sins*: the seven deadly or cardinal sins were codified by Pope Gregory I in the late 6th century.

40 *One King, one God, one Law*: a negative version of 'One Lord, one faith, one baptism, One God and Father of all', Ephesians 4.5–6.

Plate 5

143 38 *Los*: previously Enitharmon's consort in *Europe*, Los is now identified as 'the eternal Prophet' (Plate 10.7 and *The Song of Los* 3.1) and is sent by

the Eternals to 'confine' the fallen Urizen, a task which he performs by giving shape to the chaotic matter which Urizen has created. He thereby becomes complicit in the Fall (artists must work with fallen materials, whether words, paints, or metals, even when they are making visionary statements) and is exiled from Eternity. In later texts he will be further characterized as the Zoa who represents the imagination.

38 *dark globe*: in Milton, Satan, on his journey to the Garden of Eden, passes the 'dark globe' of Limbo or 'Paradise of Fools' (*Paradise Lost* 3.498).

Plate 10

9 *sodor*: solder (a metal alloy used to bond other metals). Los's identity as a blacksmith is here first established.

144 23 *White as the snow*: Ostriker suggests a parallel with Locke's white page, or *tabula rasa*, as a model of the human mind.

42 *a first Age*: the seven ages parody the Bible's seven days of creation.

Plate 13

147 51 *Pity*: Blake's scepticism about pity, an emotion cherished by the Sensibility Cult, is best expressed in 'The Human Abstract': 'Pity would be no more, | If we did not make somebody Poor' (p. 29). The cult of Sentiment or Sensibility was a belief, derived from Shaftesbury's *Characteristics* (1711), that the moral sense arose from human feelings rather than from divine revelation.

Plate 15

1 *divided*: the process of division and separation from the primal unity begun by Urizen continues and Los divides into a male and female self (later to be termed an 'Emanation'). The female is identified with 'Pity' (19.1) and then given the name 'Enitharmon' (19.19), also used for a similar but not identical figure in *Europe*: both Los and Enitharmon are changing as Blake's mythic system gradually develops.

Plate 19

149 43 *Human shadow*: Blake will use the word 'shadow' very variously: to mean spouse, or the earthly form of a divine ideal (for both of these see 'To Thomas Butts, 2 October 1800', p. 105), or an individual's suppressed desires; here, more simply, an inferior or diminished version of the true (unfallen) human identity.

Plate 20

150 21 *They took Orc to the top of a mountain*: Orc, the embodiment of revolutionary energy in *America* and *Europe*, is here more fully identified as the child of Los and Enitharmon. He is chained to a rock, like Prometheus, though the fact that this is done by his parents under 'Urizen's dreadful shadow' has some of the qualities of Abraham's binding and (near) sacrifice of Isaac (Genesis 22); Christian commentators saw the binding of Isaac as a type of the Crucifixion. The symbol of the frustration of revolution by established authorities is clear and there are parallels with

Blake's account of the futile circularity of life in the material world in his ballad 'The Mental Traveller'.

Plate 25

152 1–2 *The Ox . . . wintry door*: this brilliant encapsulation of the pain of life in the fallen world will be expanded into the lament of Enion at the end of 'Night the Second' of *The Four Zoas*.

153 37 *seven feet stature*: 'There were giants in the earth in those days' (Genesis 6.4).

41 *the seventh day*: another parody of the biblical seven days of creation.

43 *thirty cities*: Jair's sons had 'thirty cities . . . in the land of Gilead' where they 'did evil again in the sight of the Lord, and served Baalim and Ashtaroth . . . and forsook the Lord and served not him' (Judges 10.4–6), though the parallel here is with the Israelite exile in Egypt.

Plate 28

22 *called it Egypt, & left it*: at the end of Blake's version of Genesis, Fuzon (as Moses) leads an incipient Exodus.

154 *The Book of Ahania*: though it takes its title from Ahania's lament in Chapter 5 (Plates 5–6), this poem, dated 1795, is Blake's rewriting of Exodus as a failed venture in which the escape from Urizen's world (Egypt) led by Fuzon (Moses) ends, not in the Promised Land, but in defeat. It can be read as an account of the failure of the French Revolution: after the self-destructive Terror in 1793, the revolutionary Committee of Public Safety had been replaced, first by the Convention, and then, in 1795, by the Directory. As Blake would put it in his ballad 'The Grey Monk', 'The iron hand crushd the Tyrants head | And became a Tyrant in his Stead' (p. 59). Like *The First Book of Urizen* and *The Book of Los* (another version of the creation myth of *Urizen*), *The Book of Ahania* is divided into chapters and arranged in double columns, to resemble a printed Bible. The books of *Ahania* and *Los* are, however, conventionally etched, rather than relief etched. There is only one known copy of *The Book of Ahania* (Library of Congress).

Plate 3

1 *Fuzon*: in the parody of Exodus, Fuzon is Moses; in the political allegory, he is the embodiment of the French Revolution, though he is sometimes more specifically identified with Maximilien Robespierre (1758–94) who coined the slogan 'Liberté, égalité, fraternité' in 1789 but in 1793 was a member of the Committee of Public Safety which ruthlessly executed its more moderate fellow revolutionaries. After the Convention had overthrown the Committee, Robespierre would himself be guillotined in July 1794. Unlike Orc, who is a son of Los (the Imagination), Fuzon is a son of Urizen (the Reason).

155 32 *Ahania*: Fuzon's assault on Urizen causes him to split into male and female selves; the female self, or 'parted soul' (later to be termed an

Emanation), is identified with 'Sin' (by Urizen, in an echo of Sin's birth from Satan's head, *Paradise Lost* 2.754–8) and named Ahania. Her lament in Chapter 5 is a statement of the ideal condition which would be possible if reason (and, by extension, the Revolution) had not separated itself from a more instinctual human wisdom.

46 *Five hundred years*: a dramatic exaggeration of the forty years which the Israelites spent in the wilderness, following their pillar of fire (Exodus 13.21) towards the Promised Land; a more conventional 'Forty years' will be used in Plate 5 for the period in which human beings shrink from their original state.

Plate 4

16 *Oak*: Druids worshipped in oak groves.

156 38 *I am God*: Robespierre was a Deist who supported the abolition of the French Catholic Church and its replacement by the Cult of the Supreme Being. As President of the Committee of Public Safety, he delivered the oration at the Festival of the Supreme Being in the Champ de Mars on 8 June 1794 (coincidentally the day of Pentecost), after which Jacques-Alexis Thuriot remarked, 'it's not enough for him to be master, he has to be God', and the self-declared prophetess Catherine Théot (1716–94) identified him as the new John the Baptist.

46 *Mount Sinai*: Urizen (established order) slays Fuzon (rebellion) with the Ten Commandments, delivered to Moses on Mount Sinai.

Plate 5

157 6 *Tree of Mystery*: Fuzon's paradoxically 'living' corpse (5.10) is hung, or crucified, on a tree which is a combination of the Cross, the tree from which Eve takes the apple in the Garden of Eden, the poisonous upas tree, and the 'fig' or banyan tree of *Paradise Lost* 9.1101–20, from which Adam and Eve take leaves to cover (or make mysterious) their nakedness after the Fall. It is the crucifix, or key symbol, of Urizenic religion. See note to 'The Human Abstract' (p. 357).

Plate 6

160 41 *selfish fear*: a version of the third stanza of 'Earth's Answer' (p. 24).

DIFFUSE EPIC

These two poems are sometimes felt to require a quasi-biblical level of minute exegesis. They are here given substantial headnotes but are otherwise lightly annotated to encourage a more direct response to the verse: obscurity is a characteristic of the sublime.

161 *Milton*: like Wordsworth's poem *The Prelude* (largely written 1798–1805), Blake's *Milton* (1804–11) is a preface to another work. In Wordsworth's case this was the uncompleted 'philosophical Poem' known as 'The Recluse' (of which only *The Excursion* would be published). In Blake's case it would be *Jerusalem* (1804–20). Both preludes sought to clear the ground

for the major poem which would follow. For Wordsworth this required an autobiographical exploration of what was involved in the 'growth of a poet's mind' at a time when poetry was being redefined by Romanticism. Blake's similar wish to explain the newness of his work could be met, more straightforwardly, by showing how he differed from his great predecessor as a prophetic poet, John Milton. If Blake was to assume Milton's mantle, he had to alter it. *Milton a Poem* is therefore both a personal account of how Blake was inspired to write *Jerusalem* and a statement of what had come to seem wrong about *Paradise Lost* and *Paradise Regained*. This is done, dramatically rather than literally, by making Milton come back, after his death, from Heaven to Earth to purge his errors.

Milton's faults, in Blake's eyes, were theological, intellectual, personal, and literary. He was a Calvinistic Puritan (*De Doctrina Christiana*, with its revelation that Milton's views were less orthodox than had been thought, would not be published until 1825) whose stress on 'right Reason' (*Paradise Lost* 12.84) made him, like Bacon and Locke, a source of Enlightenment rationalism. He was also an official of the government which crushed the Levellers in 1649 and allowed the English Revolution of the 1640s to lapse back into monarchy. At a personal level, he had a series of unsatisfactory relationships with women (his first wife, Mary, and then his daughters). In formal terms, his epics were based on Classical rather than biblical models, and he failed to provide an Apocalypse: his *Paradise Regained* is merely a debate, in which Christ (unlike Eve) defeats the tempting arguments of Satan.

At the beginning of Blake's poem, Milton is in Heaven. But 'a Bard's prophetic Song' (Plates 4–11) reveals that this is the Heaven of a flawed religion ruled by Satan, and Milton resolves to leave it (Plate 12; the Bard's Song can also be read as an encoded account of Blake's quarrel with William Hayley, his patron at Felpham). He descends (Plate 14) towards the material world. Urizen wrestles with him and Tirzah and Rahab tempt him (Plates 17–18) to try to check his progress. He persists and Albion stirs upon his couch (Plate 18). Milton, however, moves on through 'Chaos' into Ulro (Hell). Meanwhile, in Heaven, Ololon (Milton's 'Emanation', the neglected female side of his identity, who is sixfold to represent his three wives and three daughters) resolves to share his fall (Plate 19). Here the narrative is interrupted for the rest of the First Book. Instead, in Plate 20, Los appears to Blake 'in the Vale | Of Lambeth' and leads him to Golgonooza, the city which represents art, where there is a discussion of the significance of Milton's return (Los's sons fear that 'Milton's religion' will undermine the work of Whitefield and Wesley; Plates 20–2). There is then an extended description (Plates 23–8) of the world of Los (the material world with its fallen characteristics mitigated by art).

The story resumes at the beginning of 'Book the Second' (Plate 30), where Ololon leaves Heaven. She descends into Beulah (the fallen world mitigated by love), where she is greeted by a series of songs (Plates 31–2). In Plate 34 Ololon arrives at the gates of Ulro, and in Plate 35 enters it, where she examines 'the Couches of the Dead'. Though her fall might seem to be disastrous, it has in fact opened a route by which humanity can re-ascend to Eden, a process symbolically enacted by the flight of the lark and the rising odours of wild thyme (Plate 35). Ololon herself rises from Ulro and appears in Blake's garden at Felpham (Plate 36) to ask where Milton can be found (Plate 37). Milton promptly appears (Plate 37) but so does Satan (Plate 39). Milton defeats Satan by identifying him as his own 'Spectre' (or rational self), which he now rejects, and the Seven Eyes of God (or Angels of the Presence) celebrate the victory by calling on Albion to awake. But he is still too weak to do so (Plate 40) and in Plate 42 Ololon asks Milton how 'Natural Religion' can be eliminated. He replies (Plates 42–3) with a climactic statement of the principles of the eighteenth-century evangelical revival: the need to 'cast off Rational Demonstration by Faith in the Saviour' and to annihilate 'Selfhood' (the delusive belief that human beings are unfallen or naturally good). In Plate 44 the division, characteristic of the Fall, is reversed, as Ololon ceases to be 'Sixfold' and the Eyes of God become 'One Man, Jesus the Saviour'. In this form they set off to conduct (in Chapter 4 of *Jerusalem*) the apocalyptic awakening of Albion and (Plate 45) 'the Great Harvest & Vintage of the Nations'.

There are four known copies: Copies A and B (1811) have 45 plates (38 of text and 8 full-page designs). Copy C (1818) has 49 plates, omitting the Preface (and thus 'And did those feet in ancient time') but adding five additional plates of text. Copy D (1818) adds another plate of text (50 plates). The arrangement in Copies A (British Museum) and B (Huntingdon Library) is followed here.

Plate 1

161   2 *2 Books*: Blake etched the number '12' but the '1' can be clearly seen on the printed page only in Copies C and D and the word 'Finis' appears at the end of Book the Second (Plate 45). He may have begun with, but abandoned, an intention to replicate the structure of Milton's *Paradise Lost. A Poem in Twelve Books.*

4 *Ways of God to Men*: John Milton's purpose was to 'assert Eternal Providence, | And justifie the ways of God to men' (*Paradise Lost* 1.25–6).

Plate 2

slaves of the Sword: the poems which were the usual models for epic, Homer's *Iliad* and Virgil's *Aeneid*, were much concerned with battles and the destruction (Troy) or creation (Rome) of nation states.

1 *'And did those feet in ancient time'*: though now so well known, this poem was dropped by Blake in 1818 and not reprinted until 1863, when Gilchrist quoted it in Chapter 21 of his biography. It appeared as a separate poem in William Michael Rossetti's Aldine edition of *Blake's Poetical Works* (1875). Robert Bridges included it in his anthology *The Spirit of Man* in 1916 and persuaded Sir Hubert Parry to set it to music for the patriotic Fight for Right campaign. Parry later gave the song to the Women

Voters' Movement; it acquired the title 'Jerusalem' when performed at a Suffrage Demonstration concert in March 1918.

161　2 *upon England's mountains green*: a Cornish legend collected by Sabine Baring-Gould (*A Book of the West*, 1899) had apparently claimed that Joseph of Arimathea was a tin merchant who brought Jesus, as a boy, with him on one of his business trips to the mines in Cornwall. Like the similar legend that Joseph brought Christianity to Britain after Christ's death (see note to 'The Everlasting Gospel', p. 371), this was important, both to the Church of England and to Protestant Nonconformists like Blake, because it enabled them to believe that English Christianity was more ancient than Roman Catholicism.

162　8 *dark Satanic Mills*: not, as is often assumed, a reference to the Industrial Revolution. Blake would have known the Albion flour mill in Southwark (burnt down in 1791) but London was not a manufacturing city and, even in Lancashire (which Blake never visited), steam power began to replace water wheels only in the late 1780s. Rather, he is thinking of the Newtonian model of the universe as a system of planets revolving like mill wheels and of Milton's Samson, 'Eyeless in Gaza at the Mill with slaves' (*Samson Agonistes* 41); see *Jerusalem* 15.14–16.

12 *Chariot of fire*: Elijah and Elisha are parted by 'a chariot of fire, and horses of fire' and Elijah is then taken 'up by a whirlwind into heaven' (2 Kings 2.11).

14 *my Sword*: 'And take the helmet of salvation, and the sword of the Spirit, which is the word of God' (Ephesians 6.17).

15 *Jerusalem*: see note to 3.15.

Plate 3

1 *Beulah*: following Isaiah 62.4 ('Thou shalt no more be termed Forsaken; neither shall thy land any more be termed Desolate: but thou shalt be called Hephzi-bah, and thy land Beulah: for the Lord delighteth in thee, and thy land shall be married') both Bunyan and Blake see Beulah as a space intermediate between earth and heaven; in Blake's case it is the fallen world mitigated by love. Its 'Daughters', while not quite the 'Heav'nly Muse' of Milton (*Paradise Lost* 6), are superior to the pagan Muses of Greek poetry.

13 *atonement*: though Blake may have grown up with a concept of the atonement as a blood-sacrifice, debt payment, or ransom (Mark 10.45; also held by Milton, *Paradise Lost* 3.210–12), he moved in his mature religious thought to more recent ideas of Christ's death as a 'propitiation' (based on Romans 3.25) or reconciliation between God and man. Here he attacks the old concept of penal substitution.

14–15 *Albion . . . Jerusalem his Emanation*: Albion is both the British Isles and humanity (or the universal man); *Jerusalem* is both the capital of the British Isles (London) in its ideal, rather than fallen, state, and the *Emanation*, or alienated female aspect, of the universal man's split self. Jerusalem's symbolic significance derives from Isaiah 52.1: 'Awake, awake; put on thy strength, O Zion; put on thy beautiful garments, O Jerusalem, the holy city' and Psalm 137: 'By the rivers of Babylon, there we sat down, yea, we wept, when we remembered Zion . . . If I forget thee, O Jerusalem, let my right hand forget her cunning. If I do not remember thee, let my tongue cleave to the roof of my mouth; if I prefer not Jerusalem above my chief joy' (verses 1–6). As 'the holy city' it embodies the spiritual ideal from which human beings have been exiled to a symbolic Babylon.

163 17 *One hundred years*: Milton died in 1674, so Blake by 1804 is rounding down.

19 *Sixfold Emanation*: Milton's Emanation (or female self) is sixfold because he had three wives (successively) and three daughters.

Plate 4

1 *Golgonooza*: a symbolic city, constantly rebuilt by Los, which represents art as a barrier against the pain and evil of the fallen, Urizenic world.

4 *London Stone*: a standing stone in Cannon Street in the City of London; probably a fragment of the palace of the Roman governor. Camden's *Britannia* (1586) claimed (without evidence) that it was a central milestone from which distances in Roman Britain were measured. See note to 'The fields from Islington to Marybone', l. 33 (*Jerusalem* Plate 27, p. 414).

6 *Enitharmons Loom*: elsewhere called Cathedron, where Enitharmon constantly weaves to create a physical body for spectres (see note to l. 24). Different characters weave on different occasions, and the moral status of their work varies. In *Jerusalem* Plate 12, the 'pitying looms' of Lambeth weave 'the secret furniture of Jerusalems chamber' (12.38–40). In *Jerusalem* Plate 59 it is the daughters of Los (and Enitharmon) who weave, benignly but with regret because they (like him) are giving form to the fallen world: in *Jerusalem* Plate 92 Enitharmon states that her 'Looms will be no more' when Albion wakes. In *Jerusalem* Plate 83 it is the Daughters of Beulah who weave and Enitharmon 'Joy'd in the many weaving threads' because they are 'Weaving the Web of life for Jerusalem'. In the following plate, however, the 'Daughters' (unspecified) seem to merge with the wicked Daughters of Albion because they unite 'With Rahab as she turnd the iron Spindle of destruction' (*Jerusalem* 84.26–7). In *Milton* 23.33, 'Cathedrons Looms weave only Death'. Blake probably has mixed feelings about Cathedron because it is a female space; see note to 22.17–18 (p. 405).

14 *Lambeths Vale*: Blake lived at 13 Hercules Buildings, Lambeth, from 1790 to 1800; it is a *Vale* in the sense that it is so low-lying that parts of it were known as Lambeth Marsh. The Surrey hills rise to the south towards Brixton and Norwood.

20 *Druid Temples*: William Stukeley, in his *Stonehenge, a Temple restored to the British Druids* (1740) and *Abury, A Temple of the British Druids* (1743),

claimed that the Druids (the Celtic priests mentioned by Caesar and Tacitus) had come to Britain as part of a Phoenician colony 'soon after Noah's flood'. They were 'of Abraham's religion intirely', built Stonehenge and Avebury, and preserved an authentic version of the patriarchal faith or 'true religion' (Stuart Piggott, *William Stukeley: An Eighteenth-Century Antiquary* (1950), 119). Blake accepted this though he saw the 'patriarchal faith' as a false or fallen religion. Stonehenge and Avebury are now thought to have been built in the Early Bronze Age while the historical Druids belonged to a much later, Iron Age culture.

164 24 *Spectre*: though it retains something of its conventional sense of 'ghost' or 'phantom', Blake uses the word to mean the rational aspect of human consciousness when it is separated from physical sensation, emotion, and imagination. The 'Spectre of Albion' is also the calculating, rationally-self-interested identity of Britain—whose military and commercial aggression Blake, like the Foxite Whigs, deplores.

25 *Druid rocky shore*: this line will be repeated in *Jerusalem* Plates 27 and 46. Other contemporary suggestions that the British Isles were the original setting of divine revelation included Francis Wilford's claim to have found in Sanskrit texts (exposed as a forgery in 1805) an account of ancient Hindu veneration of the 'White Islands'.

Plate 5

2–3 *Elect . . . Reprobate*: the first and last of these terms are best known from John Calvin (1509–64) whose doctrine of double and absolute predestination held that an omniscient God must have predestined some beings (the Elect) to salvation and others (the Reprobate) to eternal punishment (*Institutes*, 3.21–4). For Calvin, however, the Redeemed are synonymous with the Elect (as they are for Milton), so that their separation as a third class sounds more Arminian (or Wesleyan): they are sinners who by an act of will accept Christ's saving grace and persevere in faith and works. Blake is here, of course, satirically inverting the normal usage by putting Satan into the category of the Elect and celebrating the Reprobate as rebels (see 25.31–7 and 11.27–34).

18–19 *horses . . . fury*: Satan's inappropriate use of Palamabron's horses is a version of the classical myth of Phaethon who appropriates the chariot and horses with which his father Helios pulled the Sun through the sky, with disastrous consequences. Satan here appears to replace Urizen as the chief villain in Blake's myth though the dispute can also be read as an autobiographical allegory of the falling-out between Hayley (Satan) and Blake (Palamabron) during his three years in Felpham.

165 20 *Gnomes*: see note to 31.20 (p. 406).

Plate 6

166 11 *left sandal*: obscure, though perhaps a version of an ancient Hebrew practice: 'to confirm all things; a man plucked off his shoe, and gave it to his neighbor: and this was a testimony in Israel' (Ruth 4.7). Milton, as

a 'falling star', lands on Blake's 'left foot' in 14.47–9 and will enter Blake's 'Foot' in 19.4, whereupon the 'Vegetable World' appears on Blake's 'left Foot | As a bright sandal' which he binds on 'to walk forward thro Eternity' (19.12–14). The 'angel of the Lord' tells the imprisoned Peter to 'Gird thyself, and bind on thy sandals . . . Cast thy garment about thee, and follow me' (Acts 12.7–8) but the precise significance of 'left' remains unclear. In the pictorial Plates 29 and 33, the falling star lands on Blake's left foot and his brother Robert's right foot, so the purpose might be simply to achieve a visual symmetry.

33 *Thulloh*: not biblical; perhaps, like Michael, a pseudonym for a friend of Hayley.

Plate 7

168 51 *Covering Cherub*: the angel who prevents a human return to paradise: 'So he drove out the man; and he placed at the east of the garden of Eden Cherubims, and a flaming sword which turned every way, to keep the way of the tree of life' (Genesis 3.24).

Plate 9

1 *Eon:* Emanation.

169 16 *condemn'd for the Guilty*: a discussion of the Atonement (see note to 3.13) and the mystery of Christ's death to redeem Man's sin; here Rintrah (the angry rebel) is to be punished for Satan's fault.

Plate 11

171 17 *Six Thousand years*: from creation in 4004 BC (as calculated by Archbishop Ussher in 1650) to an apocalypse in the near future.

172 27–34 *died as a Reprobate . . . and Election . . . Our Virtues*: Christ died as a Reprobate (see note to 5.2–3, p. 400) because he was executed as a criminal, crucified between two thieves. The statement by the Elect to the Redeemed seems to be an Arminian acceptance that salvation is not simply a matter of predestination but a conscious acceptance of Christ's 'Free Gift' of grace. It is this, rather than 'Our Virtues' (or good works), which saves us; compare Article 4 of the Lutheran Augsburg Confession (1530): 'humans cannot be justified before God by their own power, merits, or deeds. Rather they are freely justified for Christ's sake through faith' and Ephesians 2.8–9: 'For by grace are ye saved through faith; and that not of yourselves: it is the gift of God: Not of works.'

Plate 12

3 *Amen*: the end of the Bard's song.

173 15 *Gods of Priam*: Priam was King of Troy (supposedly founded by Dardanus, son of Zeus) so these are the gods of Ancient Greece.

29 *daughters of memory*: memory is a key faculty for Empiricist and Associationist philosophers because the sense data which is, in their view, the sole source of knowledge is held in the mind to be arranged or

'associated' into ideas; Blake believes in intuitive or visionary access to knowledge, acquired by 'inspiration', and sees memory as the enemy of originality.

173 36–7. *Shadow . . . hermaphroditic*: Milton's Shadow is the ghost as which he will return from the dead; by 'hermaphroditic' Blake appears to mean an unsatisfactory mixture of male and female, rather than the profound integration created by reunion with one's Emanation; see *Jerusalem* 58.19–20.

42 *Seven Angels*: 'And I beheld . . . seven eyes, which are the seven Spirits of God sent forth into all the earth' (Revelation 5.6) and 'In all their afflic-tion . . . the angel of his presence saved them' (Isaiah 63.9). In 15.5 Milton becomes an 'Eighth' angel and in 44.10–11 they will coalesce into 'One Man Jesus the Saviour'.

Plate 14

174 8 *Polypus*: a sea creature with tentacles, such as a jellyfish, octopus, or sea anemone, later used by Blake as a symbol of the way in which 'Generation' or physical Nature clutches the fallen universe.

22 *Vortex*: a term found in the *Traité du monde et de la lumière* (written 1629–33, first fully published 1677) by René Descartes which developed a theory of planetary motion based on the model of a universe made up of swirling vortices (circling bands of material particles). A planet comes to rest when its centrifugal tendency is counterbalanced by an equal tendency in the particles in its vortex, otherwise it will either ascend or descend to the next vortex. Allowed by the Catholic Church because, though heliocentric, it suggested the Earth did not move, the theory was widely accepted until the mid–eighteenth century.

36 *Rock of Ages*: the phrase was made familiar by the hymn 'Rock of Ages, cleft for me' published in 1775 by Augustus Toplady (a Whitefieldian Anglican clergyman) though it had been used in one of Wesley's hymns in 1738. Blake uses it to suggest a supernatural funeral couch, a Druid sacrificial altar, and the British Isles. The image originates in Exodus, when God tells Moses that 'I will put thee in a clift of the rock, and will cover thee with my hand while I pass by' (Exodus 33.22). God is himself 'the rock of thy strength' in Isaiah 17.10 and Toplady combined the allusions to depict the crucified Christ as a cleft rock.

175 47 *falling star*: 'And the fifth angel sounded, and I saw a star fall from heaven unto the earth: and to him was given the key of the bottomless pit' (Revelation 9.1).

49 *tarsus*: the small bones of the ankle; see note to 6.11.

52 *sixty years*: an approximation: Milton was born in December 1608 and died in November 1674.

Plate 16

11 *Rahab . . . Hoglah*: not literally the names of Milton's wives and daughters: Rahab's name is taken from the Jericho harlot who sheltered

the Hebrew spies (Joshua 2.1–21), the others are the daughters of Zelophehad (see note to 'To Tirzah', p. 360).

14 *His dictate*: Milton's daughters are said to have resented taking dictation from their blind father.

176 21 *Mundane Shell*: the dome, or sky, of the physical universe.

Plate 17

5 *Arnon*: a river which flows into the Dead Sea. When fighting their way to the Promised Land, the Israelites destroy the Canaanites, survive thirst and disease, and then pitch their tents 'on the other side of Arnon, which is in the wilderness . . . Wherefore it is said in the book of the wars of the Lord, What he did in the Red sea, and in the brooks of Arnon' (Numbers 21.13–14).

177 18 *Four Zoa's*: Zoa is the plural form of the Greek word ζωον (zo-on, meaning living being or animal), used by Blake as a singular; it is translated in Revelation 4.6 as 'beasts', where it seems to be an equivalent of the Hebrew 'Chayot Hakodesh' (translated as 'living creatures') in Ezekiel 1.5–28, where the four creatures stand below the throne on which there is a figure who is 'the likeness of the glory of the Lord'. Blake introduced the term when he re-titled *Vala* (the unpublished poem on which he worked from *c*.1795 to *c*.1805) as *The Four Zoas* (they are still referred to as 'Gods', not Zoas, in Night 9, line 357, *E* 395; Blake began to learn Greek, and thus have access to the Greek text of the New Testament, in 1801). Two of them, Urizen and Urthona, had appeared (as names) in previous poems; two more, Luvah and Tharmas were added to make up the quartet. They represent the four components of human consciousness: physical sensation (Tharmas), emotion (Luvah), reason (Urizen), and imagination (Urthona, usually seen in his earthly form as Los). The Fall involves their separation, producing a disintegrated human condition in which Urizen comes to dominate. Each Zoa has a female self or Emanation: Tharmas/Enion, Luvah/Vala, Urizen/Ahania, Urthona (Los)/Enitharmon.

54 *Natural Religion*: the belief that knowledge of God can be derived from observation of the natural world, as well as, or instead of, revelation (the Bible). Its currency in early eighteenth-century England was accompanied by a Latitudinarian stress on the doctrine of works: a claim that religion was best understood as a system of moral guidance and social control, usually associated with John Tillotson, Archbishop of Canterbury 1691–4, who had edited and completed John Wilkins's *Principles and Duties of Natural Religion* in 1675. Both Tillotson (who married Cromwell's niece) and Wilkins (who married Cromwell's sister) had close links to the Cromwellian regime, which may have encouraged Blake's tendency to associate Milton's Puritanism with Natural Religion in his rogue's gallery of rejected doctrines; see note to 20.39–62 (p. 404).

178 58–9 *Hand . . . Hyle & Coban . . . Scofield*: some of Blake's enemies (who will become more prominent in *Jerusalem*): *Hand* is the three Hunt

brothers (Robert, Leigh, and John) who attacked both Blake and Methodist 'enthusiasm' in their journal, the *Examiner*, 1808–9, using the image of a hand as their editorial signature; *Hyle* (the Greek word ὕλη, 'matter') is probably William Hayley (1745–1820), Blake's patron at Felpham; *Coban* is unidentified though he might be the publisher Henry Colburn (1784–1855) whose arrangement to pay Hayley an annuity for the rights to his *Memoirs* (begun 1808, published 1823) caused much amusement; *Scofield* is the soldier, John Scolfield, whose accusation led to Blake's trial for sedition and assault in 1804.

178 59 *Reubens Gate*: Reuben is Jacob's eldest son, by Leah (Genesis 29.32); Jacob later disowns him: 'Unstable as water, thou shalt not excel' (Genesis 49.4), and Joseph, a younger son by Rachel, ultimately inherits. The Gates of the New Jerusalem are prophetically named after the twelve tribes descended from Jacob's sons: 'northward; one gate of Reuben', Ezekiel 48.31. Blake seems to use Reuben as a representative *homme moyen sensuel*. See *Jerusalem* 67.23.

Plate 18

179 33 *Og & Anak*: Old Testament giants (Numbers 13.33; Deuteronomy 3.11).

60 *Felpham*: the seaside village in Sussex where Blake lived from 1800 to 1803.

Plate 19

1 *Udan-Adan*: the lake of Ulro (Hell).

4 *entering my Foot*: see note to 6.11 (p. 400).

180 16 *Ololon*: Milton's Emanation, or female self, in its heavenly form.

Plate 20

182 15 *Six Thousand Years*: see note to 11.17 (p. 401).

39–62 *Miltons Religion . . . Miracles*: Blake's potted history of religion in the late seventeenth and eighteenth centuries: Puritanism was followed by Natural Religion (see note to 17.54, p. 403) which gave rise to the Deism and Atheism of Rousseau and Voltaire. Swedenborg's visionary writings appeared to check this but he was 'shorn by the Churches' (like Samson, shorn of his strength-giving hair by Delilah, Judges 16) and his creed too became a merely moral one, like the philosophy of Ancient Greece. Matters were 'then' redeemed (in a breach of chronology) by the Methodist Revival, led by Wesley and Whitefield (actually from the 1730s), which reasserted Luther's Solifidian doctrine that we are saved, not by our merits, but by 'the Saviours blood'.

42 *Self-righteousness*: the belief held by, for example, Rousseau (see his *Premier Discours*, 1750, and *Jerusalem* Plate 52) that human beings are naturally good and are only corrupted by circumstances (as opposed to the Judaeo-Christian view that we are born as fallen, or morally imperfect, beings who require correction and redemption).

183 55 *Whitefield . . . Westley*: George Whitefield (1714–70) and John Wesley (1703–91), the leaders, respectively, of the Calvinist and Arminian branches of Methodism. Whitefield is associated with the angry and indignant Rintrah, Wesley with the mild and gentle Palamabron to suggest the movement's double nature: both denouncing sin and announcing forgiveness. Rintrah and Palamabron are now sons of Los, so Methodism is the product of visionary art and imagination.

Plate 22

17–18. *bring him chained . . . Bowlahoola*: Rintrah and Palamabron fear that the return of 'Miltons Religion' will undermine the Methodist Revival; *Bowlahoola* is the workshop where Los's forge is located. Like Allamanda, the farm, it is a department of Golgonooza: the city of art, constantly built and rebuilt in the fallen world to resist the incursions of 'Generation' or materialism. Bowlahoola can be understood as the unfallen form of 'Law' (23.48), Allamanda as 'Commerce' (24.43), and Los's unnamed press (for both wine and printing; 24.8) as 'War'. On the apparently similar but more ambiguous Cathedron see note to 4.6 (p. 399).

184 47 *Calvin and Luther*: the Protestant revival of Christianity in the sixteenth century led to wars of religion; Rintrah (like Blake) hopes that the same will not be true of Methodism.

Plate 23

185 12 *Theotormon . . . Bromion*: names previously used for very different characters in *Visions of the Daughters of Albion*.

32 *Paul . . . Luther*: four men who gave doctrinal or institutional rules to the Christian church: St Paul (in his Epistles), Constantine (who made Christianity legal in the Roman Empire and founded Constantinople, the capital of the Greek Orthodox Church), Charlemagne (founder of the Holy Roman Empire), and Luther (the effective founder of the Protestant Churches). Blake senses a forbidding, or no-saying quality in such rules and systems which he associates with the Covering Cherub (the angel stationed to keep human beings out of Paradise). Both Paul and Luther will elsewhere be treated very sympathetically by Blake and 'a Monk of Charlemaine' ('Constantine' in the first version of the Notebook draft, N8) will be the hero of the poem included in the introduction to Chapter 3 of *Jerusalem*.

35 *Cathedrons Looms*: see note to 4.6 (p. 399).

Plate 25

189 3 *Wine-press on the Rhine*: though the fighting did not literally take place 'on the Rhine', the French occupation of the Kingdom of Prussia, after Napoleon's victory at Jena in 1806, lasted until 1812.

18 *whole extent of the Globe*: Blake sees the completion of the European exploration of the Earth (except for Antarctica, not found until 1820) as a sign that the era of life in the fallen world may be coming to an end.

190 42 *Mundane Egg*: see note to 16.21 (p. 403).

48–9 *Lambeth . . . Asylum*: Blake had lived at Lambeth from 1790 to 1800; here he notes that his visionary work there was surrounded by inappropriately classical references. His own address was 13 Hercules Buildings (named after the old Hercules' Pillars Tavern). The Apollo Gardens (an amusement park opened in 1788) was nearby, as was the Asylum for Female Orphans (built on the site of the Hercules Tavern) where the inmates were taught to sew. By the time *Milton* was finished, the area had changed: the *Monthly Magazine* in August 1812 noted that 'The Apollo Gardens . . . and other places in this neighbourhood, formerly the resort of the gay and the vicious, are now scarcely remembered'. Instead, Lambeth was known for its philanthropic institutions and the 'conventicle' in which 'Mr Carpenter, the . . . visionary preacher', promulgated 'the extraordinary doctrines of Johanna Southcott' (Vol. 34 (1812), 4–5).

53 *Thor & cruel Odin*: in 1789 George Steevens (see note to 'A Poison Tree', p. 358) fabricated the tombstone of the Danish and English King Hardicanute, which he claimed to have dug up in Lambeth, and exhibited it in a local shop window; it was engraved for the Society of Antiquaries before Steevens exposed his own forgery. Hardicanute did, in fact, die (of drink, at a wedding) in Lambeth in 1042 and (as Chatterton observed in 'Godred Crovan'; see note to 'Gwin, King of Norway', p. 363) Anglo-Saxon kings claimed descent from Odin (or Woden).

61 *Lamb & his Bride*: 'And I John saw the holy city, new Jerusalem, coming down from God out of heaven, prepared as a bride adorned for her husband', Revelation 21.2.

Plate 26

191 24–5 *Luban . . . Entuthon Benython*: Luban is the north gate of Golgonooza; Entuthon Benython is the forest to the east of it.

Plate 27

192 3 *Giving to airy nothing*: from Theseus's dismissive account of the imagination which 'gives to airy nothing | A local habitation and a name', *A Midsummer Night's Dream*, 5.1.16–17.

Plate 28

195 58 *Zelophehads Daughters*: see note to 'To Tirzah' (p. 360).

63 *Erythrean*: the Indian Ocean.

Plate 29: a pictorial plate depicting the star descending on Blake's left foot; see note to 6.11 (p. 400).

Plate 30

196 2 *Beulah*: see note to 'The Crystal Cabinet' (p. 365).

Plate 31

197 20 *Four Elements*: Paracelsus (see note to 'To My Dearest Friend John Flaxman', l. 7, p. 378) retained Aristotle's concept of the four elements

but believed that each was inhabited by spirits: air by sylphs, water by nymphs, earth by gnomes, and fire by salamanders.

Plate 33

199 *ROBERT*: Blake's brother Robert Blake (1762–87); a pictorial plate to mirror Plate 29; see note to 6.11 (p. 400).

Plate 34

200 31 *Storge*: the Greek word for 'love', especially the mutual affection of parents and children.

Plate 35

201 2 *War & Hunting*: rather unexpectedly war and hunting are the chief activities in Eternity though they are, of course, 'mental strife' or intellectual conflict.

202 49 *Wild Thyme*: after the allusion to *A Midsummer Night's Dream* in 27.3, this flower was perhaps suggested by Oberon's 'I know a bank where the wild thyme blows' in the same play (2.1.249) though the magic flower is there 'love-in-idleness', or pansy (2.1.168).

62–3 *First Heaven named Luther . . . Twenty-seven Churches*: the Lutheran Church is the twenty-seventh, and most recent, in succession from Adam (see 37.35–42) but the 'First' if we are to reverse the process and work our way back to Adam and thus re-enter Paradise. Twenty-seven is used by Blake as an incomplete number, one short of the perfect twenty-eight (4 × 7). *The Lark*: 'Hark, hark, the lark at heaven gate sings', *Cymbeline* 2.3.17.

Plate 36

203 10 *my Garden*: Blake's cottage garden in Felpham.

24 *three years*: Blake lived at Felpham from 1800 to 1803; he may have conceived *Milton* and *Jerusalem* there (or extracted material for them from his work on *The Four Zoas*) but he did not literally 'write' them there.

31 *my Shadow of Delight*: Blake's wife, Catherine, who 'has had Agues & Rheumatisms almost ever since she has been here' (letter to his brother James, 30 January 1803, *E* 725).

Plate 37

204 11 *Wicker Man of Scandinavia*: Caesar stated that the Druids enclosed human victims in a wicker case, shaped like a man, and ignited them as sacrifices (*De Bello Gallico* 6.16); Blake links this to the 'Scandinavian' religion of Thor and Odin.

205 43 *a Dragon red*: 'And there appeared another wonder in heaven . . . a great red dragon', Revelation 12.3.

Plate 39

206 27 *Jerusalem . . . in the Dens of Babylon*: the prophetic literature of the Old Testament is much concerned with Israel's exile in Babylon and the wish to return to Jerusalem.

206 48 *Self annihilation*: the rejection of 'self-righteousness' (the belief that
human beings are unfallen and capable of justification by their own merits
or good works).

Plate 40

208 35 *Legions*: a city mentioned in Geoffrey of Monmouth's *History of the
Kings of Britain* and supposedly the third most important in Roman
Britain after London and York. Holinshed thought it was Isca (Caerleon,
near Newport in South Wales).

49 *Bognor*: a seaside town in Sussex, close to the village of Felpham. In the
late eighteenth century it was being developed into a resort by Sir Richard
Hotham (1722–99), a process satirized in Jane Austen's unfinished novel
Sanditon. It is not notable for 'Rocks': it is an area of London Clay with
silty muds and sands.

Plate 42

209 12 *Hume & Gibbon & Bolingbroke*: David Hume (philosopher and historian, 1711–76), Edward Gibbon (historian, 1737–94), and Henry
St John, Viscount Bolingbroke (politician and political philosopher, 1678–
1751) were leading figures of the Scottish and English Enlightenment
(see Introduction). Beilby Porteus, Bishop of Chester (Bishop of London
from 1787), denounced 'the works of Bolingbroke, of D'Alembert, of
Hume' in his sermon to the Charity School service in St Paul's Cathedral
in 1782 (see note to 'Holy Thursday', p. 353).

22 *John in Patmos*: St John the Divine had the vision recorded as the Book
of Revelation on the island of Patmos.

Plate 43

210 26 *Ark & Curtains*: God commands Moses to make 'an ark' to contain 'the
testimony' (of the law) and to enclose 'the tabernacle with ten curtains of
fine twined linen' (Genesis 25.10–16 and 26.1). These are precisely the
kind of ritual regulations (or 'Old Law') which Christians believed had
been overthrown by the Gospel.

213 *Jerusalem The Emanation of The Giant Albion*: this is Blake's rewriting of
Paradise Regained in the spirit of The Revelation of St John the Divine,
though a good deal of it is, in practice, concerned with the Fall, so is closer
to *Paradise Lost*. The apocalyptic reawakening of Albion (both humanity
in general and Britain in particular), his reintegration with Britannia
('England'), and reconciliation with Jerusalem (the spiritual ideal; see
note to *Milton* 3.15) occur in the fourth and final chapter, addressed
'To the Christians'. Before that, there are three chapters, addressed
'To the Public', 'To the Jews', and 'To the Deists'. The first begins by
describing Los's heroic attempts to resist the evil consequences of the Fall,
despite which a despairing Albion (Plates 19–25) decides to die. Chapter 2
consists of a series of death-bed speeches and attempts to dissuade him.
Chapter 3 is an extended description of the world after Albion's death, as
Los struggles to keep it from chaos. For Blake's summary of his mythic

scheme see Plate 27; there is also an intermittent political allegory in which Albion and Luvah are the Britain and France of the Napoleonic Wars.

The poem has the date 1804 on its title-page and Blake states in Plate 38 that, 'I write in South Molton Street', where he lived from 1803 to 1821. Sixty plates had been etched by 1807; the remaining forty were made between then and 1819. Some 'Detached Specimens' (or coloured proof sheets) were exhibited at the Water Colour Society's exhibition in 1812. The references to 'Hand' (or the three Hunt brothers) cannot have been made before 1808 and Plate 63 is (in part) about the Allied victory over France in 1814–15. The most notable later development was the introduction into Blake's myth of the figure of Brittannia, first mentioned in the notes on *The Last Judgement* in 1810 as 'the Wife of Albion Jerusalem is their daughter' (*E* 558), and shown in Plate 32 as a figure who is 'divided into Jerusalem & Vala'. The uncertainty over whether it is Brittannia or Jerusalem who is Albion's Emanation (see note to 32.28, p. 415) suggests that Blake may have conceived the beginning and end of the text before writing the middle. The poem began to be assembled as a book in 1819 and there was no complete copy before 1820. There are six known lifetime copies. The most significant variant is the order of the plates in Chapter 2. The conventional numbering of the plates, from 1 to 100, is that of Copies D and E (both printed on paper watermarked 1820). But in copies A and C (printed on paper watermarked 1818, 1819, and 1820) Plates 42 and 29–32 are placed between Plates 46 and 47 and Blake returned to this earlier order in Copy F (*c*.1826). That earlier order is followed here.

Plate 3: the erasures from the plate (here restored in italic) seem to reflect Blake's disillusionment with his 'Public' after the failure of his 1809 exhibition.

After my three years slumber: Blake lived in Felpham, a seaside village in Sussex, 1800–3.

The '*last words of Jesus*' (erased from the plate) are Matthew 28.18, quoted from the Greek New Testament ('All power is given unto me in heaven and in earth'); they are part of the risen Christ's address to his disciples after his death.

Plate 4: the epigraph ('Only Jesus') is from the Gospel accounts of the Transfiguration ('And when they had lifted up their eyes, they saw no man, save Jesus only', Matthew 17.8); Blake had learnt some Greek from Hayley but not enough to avoid using epsilon and the terminal form of sigma in what should read Ιησους.

214   1 *Ulro*: Hell.

5 *dictating the words*: in *Milton* Blake had modestly claimed to be inspired by the 'Daughters of Beulah'; here he claims to be taking dictation from Jesus himself.

215   27 *demonstration*: the experimental method of empirical science.

Plate 5

215   10–12 *Udan-Adan . . . Entuthon-Benython*: the lake and forest of Ulro.

216   25–7 *Hand . . . Bowen*: for Hand, Hyle, and Coban see note to *Milton* 17.58–9
(p. 403). John Quantock, John Peachey, and William Brereton were Sussex
magistrates involved in Blake's trial for sedition in 1803–4 (*BR* 167). 'Slayd'
is unidentified; Lieutenant George Hulton of the First Royal Dragoon
Guards acted for his (probably illiterate) subordinates who had made the
charges. John Scolfield was the soldier who claimed to have been assaulted,
John Cock was a fellow soldier and witness; 'Kotope' and 'Bowen' are
unidentified though there was a lawyer called Bowen on the Sussex circuit.

40 *Tirzah and her Sisters*: no longer the five daughters of Zelophehad
(Numbers 27.1; see note to 'To Tirzah', p. 360) but twelve sisters of a figure who now seems to be the other 'Tirzah' of the Bible: the Canaanite
city captured by Joshua (Joshua 12.24) which became a rival to Jerusalem
as capital of Israel (1 Kings 15.33–4, 2 Kings 14.13–20). Her sisters have
names taken from the legendary history of Britain (two of them, Cordella
and Gonorill, familiar from Shakespeare's use of the same material in
King Lear), except for the Welsh martyr Gwinefred, the Scots 'Cambel'
(Campbell), and the biblical Mehetabel (possibly Geoffrey of Monmouth's
'Methahel').

Plate 6

217   1 *His Spectre*: this is Los's rational self ('The Spectre is the Reasoning
Power in Man', 74.10), here best understood as the sceptical, empirical,
and secular side of Blake that had written the *Songs of Experience* ('Thou
art my Pride & Self-righteousness', 8.30). For a different view see Paley
(1967–8) which argued that Los's Spectre was a portrait of William Cowper
(see 'William Cowper Esqre', p. 82).

Plate 7

218   10 *deceitful Friendship*: with Albion.

26 *Edom*: the people of Edom were long-standing enemies of Israel.

30 *Luvah*: Luvah is both the Zoa who represents emotion and (in the
political allegory) France (see 63.5–6 and 66.15).

219   70 *Abomination of Desolation*: a detestable sacrilege (originally a heathen
idol set in a holy place). Jesus quotes the phrase from Daniel 11.31 in
Matthew 24.15–16.

Plate 8

1–3 *Albions River . . . The place of wounded Soldiers*: Ranelagh Gardens
(1741–1803; now part of the grounds of Chelsea Hospital) and Strombolo
Gardens (1762–*c*.1810) were fashionable pleasure grounds in Chelsea.
Cromwell (later Florida) Gardens (1762–97) were actually in Brompton,
slightly further north. *Albions River*: the Thames which flows past Chelsea,
where the Royal Hospital (founded by Charles II) is a home for old soldiers.

220   20 *Babel & Shinar*: Babel is the Hebrew word for Babylon, set in the
plain of Shinar (where Noah's descendants built the tower).

Plate 9

221 18 *Furnaces . . . spiritual sword*: Los compels his rational self to help him forge the dismaying experiences of the contemporary world into a sword; compare 'And did those feet', l. 14, *Milton*, Plate 2.

222 34 *Erin*: Ireland, which had become part of Great Britain by the Acts of Union of 1800–1 (having previously been in a merely 'personal union' because of a shared monarch). Blake may simply be responding to its status as a new component of 'Albion', though some critics link Erin's role in the poem to the Irish Rebellion of 1798 and Robert Emmet's rebellion of 1803; see note to 74.54–5 (p. 422).

Plate 10

10 *Negation*: see 17.33–41.

20 *System . . . by another Mans*: a famous self-definition by Blake but possibly a version of Paracelsus's motto, 'Alterius non sit qui suus esse potest' ('Let no man be another's who can be his own'; *Astronomia Magna*, 1537, published 1571).

223 32 *Spectre of Urthona*: Los is the earthly form of Urthona, so Urthona's Spectre is also Los's Spectre.

42 *Enitharmon*: the Emanation, or female self, of Urthona (and thus of Los); just as Milton was reunited with his Emanation, Ololon, in *Milton*, so Los must be reunited with Enitharmon.

47 *he is Righteous*: Los's Spectre offers an example of severely rational Calvinist logic (see note to *Milton* 5.2–3, p. 400).

Plate 11

224 22 *mandrake . . . Reubens gate*: see note to *Milton* 17.59 (p. 404). In Genesis 30.14–17 Reuben gathers mandrake plants (the toxic *mandragora officinarum*, supposedly an aid to female fertility) for his mother Leah. Her sister, the barren Rachel, asks for some in return for letting Leah sleep with her husband Jacob.

Plate 12

225 28 *Ever weeping Paddington*: Paddington, just west of central London, was a rural district until the late 1820s. It is 'mournful' because the Tyburn gallows, on which criminals were publicly executed, had stood there until 1783, though 'Ever weeping' may also reflect the fact that the Tyburn Brook was an important source of London's water. The *golden builders* are artists creating Golgonooza, not literal construction workers.

38 *Lambeth . . . looms*: Blake had lived and worked in Lambeth in the 1790s; see notes to *Milton* 4.6 and 25.48–9. Why it should still be seen as a source of spiritual regeneration is not clear unless Blake believes that Lambeth Palace, the London home of the Anglican Archbishop of Canterbury, is the symbolic repository of a spiritual truth, currently hidden by Druidism and Natural Religion, which will eventually be discovered and released; see note to 34.45–7 (p. 415).

226 46 *The great City of Golgonooza*: the extended description is modelled on
the accounts of the Temple in Ezekiel 40–3 and of the new Jerusalem in
Revelation 21. Bunyan had published *The Holy Citie or the New-Jerusalem:
wherein its goodly light Walls. Gates, Angels and the Manner of their Standing
are expounded* in 1669.

58 *Ezekiel . . . Chebars flood*: 'Now it came to pass . . . as I was among the
captives by the river of Chebar, that the heavens were opened, and I saw
visions of God . . . and, behold, a whirlwind came out of the north . . . out
of the midst thereof came the likeness of four living creatures' (Ezekiel
1.1–5). This is the Hebrew precedent for the Greek 'beasts' or zoa of
Revelation. The *Chebar* was a river in Babylonia, probably a branch of
the Euphrates.

Plate 13

227 32 *Twenty-seven Heavens*: see note to *Milton* 35.62–3 (p. 407).

43 *Salamandrine men*: salamanders are lizard-like amphibians which were
thought to be able to survive in fire ('so cold that it puts out fire on contact', Pliny, *Natural History*, 10.86); Paracelsus thought that the element
of fire was inhabited by spirits in the form of salamanders (see note to
Milton 31.20, p. 406).

228 59 *six thousand years*: see note to *Milton* 11.17 (p. 401).

Plate 14

2 *Cherub at the Tree of Life*: see note to *Milton* 7.51 (p. 401).

4 *Vegetated Tongue*: Tharmas is the Zoa of sensation, here the 'vegetated'
physical senses of the fallen world of Generation.

Plate 15

229 15–16 *Loom . . . Water-wheels*: looms and mills ('water-wheels') are
now directly associated with the key philosopher and scientist of the
Enlightenment.

230 25 *narrow Canaanite*: that is, narrowly in Canaan rather than in the whole
of (spiritual) Israel.

Plate 16

231 35 *Reuben in Carmarthenshire*: Stevenson makes the point that 'before the
Fall, Albion was the Holy Land', so the counties of Britain are also the
territories of the twelve tribes of Israel; the literary model is the listing of
districts in Joshua 12–13.

Plate 17

234 59 *Bath . . . Canterbury*: Blake disapproves of Canterbury (the diocese
of the Anglican Archbishop) but approves of Bath, partly because of its
healing waters, but probably also because of Richard Warner (1763–1857),
curate at St James's Church, Bath, who preached a sermon in May 1804,
to a military congregation, on 'War Inconsistent with Christianity'
(Erdman, 1977, 476–7). Warner was an antiquary, an Evangelical, and an

outspoken Foxite Whig. If this is the reference, Blake's point is that the official Church supports the government's war policy (bishops have seats in the House of Lords) but one of its clergymen (in Bath) opposes it.

Plate 18

235 32 *Potters field*: when Judas repents and returns to the chief priests the thirty pieces of silver he had been paid for betraying Christ, 'they took counsel, and bought with them the potter's field, to bury strangers in' (Matthew 27.7).

40 *Polypus*: see note to *Milton* 14.8 (p. 402).

46 *his*: Albion's.

Plate 19

16 *Eon*: Emanation.

236 42 *Lilly of Havilah*: 'And a river went out of Eden to water the garden . . . and became four heads . . . the first . . . compasseth the whole land of Havilah, where there is gold' (Genesis 2.10–11).

Plate 20

237 11 *Vala replied*: Vala's speeches are, of course, deceptive.

Plate 21

239 45 *Arks of Oak*: the Ark of the Covenant was made of 'shittim (acacia) wood' (Exodus 25.10); Blake is here punning on 'Ark' as a ship (as in HMS *Ark Royal*), the fact that warships were made of oak, and the song 'Hearts of Oak' (1760, with words by David Garrick).

Plate 24

242 46–7 *Atlantic . . . Erythean . . . Hesperia*: the Fall caused the disappearance of Atlantis and a similar continent in the Indian Ocean; *Hesperia* was the Ancient Greek term for Italy but is here probably the Garden of the Hesperides, where the Mediterranean meets the Atlantic.

Plate 27

244 *Albion was the Parent of the Druids . . . Created by the Elohim*: a summary of Blake's myth in its later form. The name 'Albion' comes from Holinshed's *Chronicles* (1577), where he is the giant who first conquered Britain. Blake uses it in *The Four Zoas*, *Milton*, and *Jerusalem* to refer to a giant figure (sometimes compared with Swedenborg's 'Grand Man' or the 'Adam Kadmon' of the Kabbala) who contains 'in his mighty limbs all things in heaven & Earth'. His fall precedes the historical narrative of the Hebrew Bible, since it is in 'his Chaotic State of Sleep' that God ('the Elohim') creates 'Satan & Adam & the whole World' (in the 1809 *Descriptive Catalogue* he is compared to the Greek 'Titans' who preceded the Olympian gods, *E* 543). Albion is thus, in a sense, the parent of Adam and the ancestor of Adam's children, the antediluvian patriarchs through whom the line of descent passed to Noah. Those patriarchs were the priests of that early era of human history and, in Blake's account, the original Druids. Their ancient temples survive at Stonehenge and Avebury but the direct

knowledge of the divine brought from Eden by Adam deteriorated in their hands into the fallen religions of the postdiluvian world. Though Jesus came to redeem mankind, his message has been suppressed by the enduring power of the druidic establishment and will not be heard until Albion awakes and is reunited with his Emanation, Jerusalem.

244   13–15 *Jew's-harp-house . . . Green Man . . . Willans farm*: the Jew's Harp was an eighteenth-century tavern and tea garden, and the Green Man a pub, standing in the five hundred acres of farmland north of the New (now Marylebone) Road, of which Willans Farm was part. Blake would have known the area as a boy. The farm leases expired in 1811 and the freeholder (the Crown) decided to redevelop the land as the elegant estate called Regent's Park. The Jew's Harp was demolished in 1812 but development was gradual, chiefly between 1817 and 1828. Blake is still describing the area as open country (in the present tense: 'to bathe delight') in which an ideal, or spiritual Jerusalem is imaginatively created.

245   22 *Og*: the giant King of Bashan conquered by the Israelites in Deuteronomy 3.1–11.

24 *Satans Synagogue*: a phrase used in Revelation (2.9 and 3.9) of 'them which say they are Jews, and are not'.

26 *Paddington*: see note to 12.28 (p. 411).

33 *London Stone*: set, in Blake's day, against the wall of St Swithin, London Stone (demolished 1962), which may have encouraged his belief that it was a relic of a Stonehenge-like Druidic temple; John Strype's *Survey of London* (1720) had suggested that it may have been 'an Object or Monument of Heathen Worship', noting that 'the Druids had Pillars of Stone in Veneration' (p. 194). See note to *Milton* 4.4 (p. 399).

45–6 *Rhine . . . Danube*: for *Rhine* see note to *Milton* 25.3 (p. 405); Napoleon crossed the Danube in July 1809 and defeated the Austrians at the Battle of Wagram, an unprecedentedly bloody battle, with more than 70,000 casualties.

246   66 *in my dark self-righteous pride*: see note to *Milton* 20.42 (p. 404).

Plate 28

247   15 *deadly Tree*: this is both 'Moral Virtue and the Law' (the belief that you are saved by good works rather than by Christ's free gift of grace) and, more literally, the gallows-tree or scaffold which stood by Tyburn Brook until 1783; see notes to 12.28 (p. 411) and 82.60 (p. 424).

Plate 29

248   28 *Hermaphroditic*: see note to *Milton* 12.36 (p. 402).

Plate 30

250   31 *Female Will*: see note to 'The Mental Traveller', l. 10, p. 365.

41 *Mam-Tor*: a mountain in the Derbyshire Peak District, with a Bronze Age hill fort.

Plate 32

252 28 *Brittannia*: Brittannia is first mentioned in the notes on *The Last Judgement* (1810) as 'the Wife of Albion Jerusalem is their daughter' (*E* 558). The account of her here as a figure who is 'divided into Jerusalem & Vala' might seem to suggest that she, rather than Jerusalem, is Albion's Emanation (thus contradicting the 1804 title-page). Her repentance is key to Albion's awakening in Plate 94 and she unites with him when she 'enter[s] Albions bosom' in Plate 96; Jerusalem, correspondingly, is the bride of 'The Lamb of God', not Albion, in Plate 27. Elsewhere in Plate 94, however, Brittannia is described as 'a Female Shadow' (though Jerusalem is also a 'Shadow' in 85.29) and Jerusalem's status as the 'Emanation of Albion' is reasserted in Plate 97. This uncertainty may reflect the poem's dual function as political and spiritual allegory (in political terms Albion's Emanation is Brittannia, in spiritual terms Jerusalem) though it also suggests that Blake may have conceived and drafted the beginning and end of the poem before he wrote the middle.

31 *Four Zoa's*: see note to *Milton* 17.18 (p. 403).

Plate 34

254 17 *infinite senses*: compare the 'flexible senses' of 'the Immortal' in *The First Book of Urizen* 3.38.

42 *South Molton Street*: Blake lived at 17 South Molton Street from 1803 to 1821.

45 *Verulam! Canterbury!*: Blake links Canterbury (the diocese of the Anglican Archbishop) with Verulam (St Albans, the home of Francis Bacon, father of empirical science) to identify the creed of the established Church as Natural Religion (see note to *Milton* 17.54, p. 403). But he also sees it as a 'Generous immortal Guardian golden clad!', suggesting that it is capable of redemption and of being, thereafter, an 'immortal Guardian': the cathedral cities will play a leading role, in the rest of this chapter, in the attempt to save Albion. Blake would be buried with his family in the Nonconformist Bunhill Fields but asked for an Anglican burial service. See note to 12.38 (p. 411).

255 55–8 *a Gate . . . Tyburns*: Blake's imagined or visionary 'Gate' is on the site now occupied by Marble Arch, stretching from Hyde Park to Tyburn (where, until 1783, public executions were held). The physical gate which has stood there since 1851 is, ironically, the triumphal arch designed in 1827 as a formal entrance to Buckingham Palace.

Plate 35

12 *Cambridgeshire*: Los's association with Cambridge is usually thought to reflect the fact that Milton was a graduate of that university.

Plate 36

256 3 *Friends of Albion*: the cathedral cities of England, Wales, the Isle of Man, and (just) Scotland (Edinburgh), perhaps with a suggestion that they resemble the 'friends', or comforters, of Job.

256 21 *The Twenty-four*: the minor cathedral cities, rising to twenty-eight
(37.23) when Canterbury/Verulam, York, London, and Edinburgh are
added; see note to 38.55 (p. 416).

257 48 *Selsey*: the original site, on the Manhood Peninsula, of Chichester
Cathedral, abandoned in 1075 after it was made inaccessible by the sea.

57 *Bowlahoola & Allamanda*: see note to *Milton* 22.17–18 (p. 405).

Plate 37

1 *Bath who is Legions*: on *Bath* (the diocese of Bath and Wells) see note to
17.59; on *Legions*, which Blake now seems to identify with Bath, see note
to *Milton* 40.35 (p. 408).

258 23 *The Twenty-eight*: see notes to 36.21 (p. 416) and 38.55 (p. 416).

Plate 38

5 *Four Complexions*: the four 'Humours' of medieval medicine or the four
components of human consciousness represented by the Four Zoas.

259 37 *Oshea . . . Peor*: Oshea (Joshua) and Caleb were part of the team sent
by Moses 'to spy out the land of Canaan'. They returned after 'forty
days', reporting that, 'it floweth with milk and honey' but struggled to
convince the Israelites to go there (Number 13.7–27 and 14.10). In Peor
the Israelites 'began to commit whoredom with the daughters of Moab'
(Numbers 25.1) and, after a subsequent plague, a headcount revealed that
Joshua and Caleb were the only surviving men of fighting age who had
originally left Egypt with Moses.

260 55 *Bristol & Bath . . . ye Seventeen*: Blake refers to 'Seventeen' (of the
cathedral cities) again in 40.37, where he also mentions 'the other Ten',
but then immediately adds 'And these the names of the Eighteen combining with those Ten' (with Bath appearing in both lists) to get to his
declared total of twenty-eight.

65 *Wicker Idol*: see note to *Milton* 37.11 (p. 407).

Plate 39

261 31 *Elijah*: 'Behold, I will send you Elijah the prophet before the coming
of the great and dreadful day of the Lord' (Malachi 4.5).

Plate 40

262 1 *healing City!*: see note to 17.59 (p. 412).

30 *Oxford*: Oxford will be referred to again as 'immortal Bard!' in 41.7.
That phrase suggests Shakespeare (the Bard of Avon), who was often
linked anecdotally to Oxford, a city on his route between Stratford and
London (see 98.9); 41.6 contains a similarly imprecise reference to Milton
(it is thought) as 'Ely, Scribe of Los'. Another possibility would be the
Methodist hymn writer Charles Wesley, a graduate of Oxford as Milton
was of Cambridge, and an appropriate communicator of 'leaves of the
Tree of Life'. If the injunction 'take thou these leaves' is addressed to
a living person, however, the most likely candidate is Edward Marsh
of Oriel College (who would publish a volume of hymns in 1837): Blake

refers to 'my much admired and respected Edward the Bard of Oxford' in a letter to Hayley, 27 January 1804 (*E* 741).

Plate 41

263 4 *mountain palaces of Eden*: in 66.1–2 Blake will state that Stonehenge was built from 'the precious unhewn stones of Eden', so appears here to be suggesting that they were taken from previous buildings in the mountains of Wales, thus anticipating some much more recent theories about the origins of the bluestone sections of Stonehenge. Geoffrey of Monmouth believed the stones had come (by magic) from Ireland but Stukeley insisted that they came from a nearby quarry 'upon Marlborough Downs' (*Stonehenge, A Temple Restored to the British Druids*, 1740).

Plate 43

266 9 *The Reactor*: probably a reference to Newton's Third Law ('To every action there is always opposed an equal reaction'; *Mathematical Principles of Natural Philosophy*, 1687). Here Albion's spectre: the Satanic power of scientific materialism and legalistic morality.

18 *City of the Woods . . . Ephratah*: Bethlehem, the 'City of David', originally known as Ephrath ('fruitful land') and later called Bethlehem Ephratah. In Psalm 132.5–6 David seeks 'a place for the Lord' and hears of it 'at Ephratah: we found it in the fields of the wood'.

267 28 *locks*: sometimes emended to 'rocks' following l. 2.

268 59 *Enion*: the Emanation of Tharmas.

61 *Luvah strove to gain dominion*: in the political allegory, 'Luvah is France' (66.15).

Plate 45

270 15–16 *Isle | Of Leuthas Dogs*: the Isle of Dogs (so called because a royal kennels was once there) is a peninsula on the north bank of the Thames to the east of London. Why they should be Leutha's dogs is not clear, except that Leutha resembles the goddess Venus (see *Visions of the Daughters of Albion* 3.1–4), the West India Docks opened on the Isle of Dogs in 1802, and prostitutes are associated with sailors.

25 *Bethlehem*: not here the village in Palestine (though there is an allusion to its Hebrew meaning: 'house of bread') but the Bethlehem Hospital (or Bedlam), a psychiatric hospital, founded in 1377 and in Moorfields from 1676 to 1815, when it was moved to Lambeth.

Plate 47

272 6 *Wicker Man*: see note to Milton 37.11 (p. 407).

Plate 48

273 9–11 *Decalogue . . . Revelations*: this is the Swedenborgian canon of the Bible: the books identified in *Arcana Coelestia* (1749–56), *The New Jerusalem* (1758), and *The White Horse* (1758), as having 'the internal sense'. To get his 'Sixteen pillars' (on which Albion's funeral couch rests)

Blake combines the seventeen prophetic books individually listed by Swedenborg into the single category of 'Prophets'. Swedenborg did not reject the other books of the Bible but saw them as historical and didactic rather than divinely inspired. The Book of Job and the Pauline Epistles are the most striking exclusions, especially for Blake who made such extensive use of them.

273 28 *pensive Woman*: Stevenson and Ostriker suggest Erin, though she does not speak until l. 53 and this is actually a combination of the Emanations of Albion's 'Friends': the cathedral cities (36.3), who are English, Welsh, and Scottish but not Irish.

Plate 49

276 66 *State*: a state is a moral condition or category; Blake distinguishes it from an individual human being so that we can hate the sin but love the sinner.

Plate 50

3 *Twelve Gods of Asia*: see *Milton* 37.17–35. They are all biblical and Classical pagan deities from the Near East.

Plate 52

278 *Vegetated Spectre*: a merely material conception of the human, as body and mind without soul.

Foote: Samuel Foote (1720–77) mocked Whitefield in his play *The Minor* (1760).

Alexanders . . . Fredericks: military leaders: Alexander the Great, Julius Caesar, Frederick the Great, successive Kings Louis of France.

279 '*I saw a Monk of Charlemaine*': previous versions are found both in the Notebook (N8) and in the Pickering Manuscript (see 'The Grey Monk', p. 58).

21 *Titus!*: Roman Emperor AD 79–81 who had captured Jerusalem and destroyed the Temple in AD 70.

Plate 53

280 15 *Golgonooza*: the imaginary city which symbolizes art's role, in the fallen world, as a barrier against Urizenic materialism; see notes to 12.46 (p. 412) and *Milton* 22.17–18 (p. 405).

Plate 54

281 25 *Arthur*: the legendary king who led the British against the Saxons after the fall of the Roman Empire; Blake sees him as a prototype or representative of later military rulers; see 64.15–16. In his *Descriptive Catalogue* (1809) Blake refers to 'Arthur's conquest of the whole world' (*E* 542).

Plate 55

282 32–3 *Lucifer . . . Eighth*: Milton was the eighth Eye of God or Angel of the Presence in *Milton* (see note to *Milton* 12.42, p. 402).

Plate 56

283 4 *power over Man*: on Blake's view of female see note to 'The Mental Traveller', l. 10 (p. 365).

Plate 57

285 6–7 *Stone-henge . . . Rosamonds Bower*: Druid temples, though it is hard to credit the Druidic status of some of them: Rosamund's Bower was supposedly built at Woodstock in Oxfordshire by King Henry II as a hiding place for his mistress Rosamund Clifford and destroyed when Blenheim Palace was built in 1705–30. Maldon and Colchester were Roman settlements in Essex; Aylett Sammes's *Britannia Antiqua Illustrata* (1676) claimed (wrongly: the site was a fort not a temple) that Maldon had been a 'British religious centre' where heathen gods were worshipped (Worrall, 1977) and Philip Morant's *History of Essex* (1789, 1810, 1816) suggested there had been Druidic oak groves at Colchester (Lindsay and Locherbie-Cameron, ' "Malden" in Blake's *Jerusalem*', *Blake*, 22.4 (1989) 136–9).

Plate 58

286 20 *Hermaphroditic*: see note to *Milton* 12.36 (p. 402).

Plate 59

287 7 *Mundane Shell*: see note to *Milton* 16.21 (p. 403).

Plate 60

288 2 *Albions Spectre who is Luvah*: in the political allegory Luvah (otherwise a Zoa) is France; see 43.61 and 66.15.

Plate 61

290 6 *Marry a Harlot & an Adulteress*: though the primary reference here is to the Bible, Charles James Fox, leader of the anti-war, radical Whigs, married Elizabeth Armistead (1750–1842), a courtesan who had been the kept mistress of the Prince of Wales and several of his own political colleagues, in 1795; they lived together very happily until his death in 1806.

Plate 62

292 14 *thy Magdalen*: Blake shares the common confusion of Mary Magdalen (Luke 8.2 and John 20.1–17) with the 'woman . . . which was a sinner' (Luke 7.37) or the 'woman taken in adultery' of John 8.3–11 (see note to 'The Everlasting Gospel', l. 122, p. 373). Jerusalem is a fallen woman 'A Harlot I am calld') in the sense that the ideal human condition of Eternity has become the Babylon of the modern world. Believing that the fallen woman of Luke is the Mary to whom Jesus appears after his death (John 20.1–17), Blake can argue that a repentant prostitute or adulteress is superior to the chaste biblical matriarchs listed in ll. 9–12: the Rahab of l. 10 is not the harlot of Jericho (Joshua 2.1) but Rachab, the wife of Salmon, an ancestor of Christ (Matthew 1.5). See next note.

18 *& the Life*: 'Jesus said unto her, I am the resurrection, and the life: he that believeth in me, though he were dead, yet shall he live', John 11.25. Jesus actually says this to another biblical Mary, the sister of Martha, after the death of their brother Lazarus (see previous note).

Plate 63

293 1 *Annandale*: the valley of Annandale in the Scottish Borders has a hollow
known as the Devil's Beef Tub and oak woods, so counts (for Blake) as
Druidic.

6 *Paris*: as an episode in the political allegory, this says that Napoleonic
France (Luvah) destroyed freedom or free speech ('the Angel of the
Tongue') and that Britain (Albion) then brought France (or Napoleon)
'To Justice' in Paris. The Parisian authorities surrendered to the British,
Russian, Austrian, and Prussian Coalition in March 1814 and by the Treaty
of Fontainebleau (April 1814) Napoleon was exiled to Elba. He escaped
and returned to Paris for his 'hundred days' in March 1815. After defeat
at Waterloo in June, he returned briefly to Paris but then fled to Rochefort,
from where he was taken to St Helena. Coalition forces entered Paris on
29 June 1815. The phrase 'denying the Resurrection' could be a reference
either to the defeat of Napoleon's return (or resurrection) from Elba or
to the irreligious character of Imperial France; if only the latter, then
'Justice' would be the Treaty of Fontainebleau. Blake's concern in the rest
of the plate is with the inappropriate triumphalism of the response to
victory in Britain and the rest of the world ('from | Ireland to Japan',
ll. 33–4); see note to 73.15 (p. 422).

Plate 64

295 15 *Arthur*: see note to 54.25 (p. 418).

296 34 *Taxing the Nations*: the phrase echoes the Bible ('there went out
a decree from Caesar Augustus, that all the world should be taxed', Luke
2.1), but the reference seems to be to Britain's (or Albion's) emergence
from the Napoleonic Wars as a global imperial power; see note to 98.52
(p. 427).

38 *Rephaim . . . Machpelah*: though the Hebrew word *Rephaim* can be
used in the sense of 'ghosts of the dead', the valley, south of Jerusalem, is
not particularly associated with graves; *Machpelah* is the cave in which
Abraham and his family were buried (Genesis 23.19–20).

Plate 65

5–56: *For in the depths . . . Stone of Trial*: this passage about industrial
labour is, with slight alteration, taken from *The Four Zoas*, Night 7.

297 24 *polish brass & iron*: reminiscent of Adam Smith's account of pin-making,
as an example of the 'division of labour' which makes nations prosperous
(*The Wealth of Nations*, 1776, 1.1).

33 *carried away in thousands*: a reference to the press gangs which took men,
by force, to serve in the wartime Royal Navy. Since crews, other than
officers, were discharged at the end of every voyage this usually meant
recovering them, but it was, none the less, bitterly resented.

Plate 66

298 2 *Building*: Stonehenge; see note to 41.4 (p. 417).

299 13 *Cove*: the horseshoe-shaped group of stones around the so-called altar stone at Stonehenge.

300 45 *Six months . . . a winter*: possibly suggested by the bitter winter of 1795–6, or by 'the year without a summer' in 1816, if this plate was written at so late a stage of the poem's history.

301 75 *Cheselden hills*: Chiseldon, in Wiltshire, is on the Marlborough Downs, eight miles from Avebury; Blake's spelling may be a confused recollection of the name of the surgeon William Cheselden (1688–1752) whose *Anatomy of the Human Body* (1713) and *Osteographia* (1733) were used by art students as well as doctors (see 89.29 and *Milton* 14.49).

Plate 67

302 23 *Josephs Coat*: in Genesis 37 Joseph's brothers envy him; Reuben says they should not kill him but leave him in a 'pit that is in the wilderness', Judah says they should sell him to the Ishmaelites. They do, and then take his 'coat of many colours' and 'killed a kid of the goats, and dipped the coat in the blood' to suggest that he had been killed by a wild animal (Genesis 37.18–32). See note to *Milton* 17.59 (p. 404).

Plate 68

304 41 *Twelve Stones of Power*: 'And Elijah took twelve stones, according to the number of the tribes of the sons of Jacob . . . And with the stones he built an altar in the name of the Lord . . . and cut the bullock in pieces, and laid him on the wood' (1 Kings 18.31–3); Blake associates this with the sacrificial altars of Molech and of the Druids: see l. 24.

51–2 *Uzzah . . . Great Tartary*: Uzzah drives the cart carrying the 'ark of God' but 'when they came to Nachon's threshing floor, Uzzah put forth his hand to the ark of God, and took hold of it; for the oxen shook it. And the anger of the Lord was kindled against Uzzah; and God smote him there for his errors; and there he died by the ark of God' (2 Samuel 6.3–7); *Great Tartary* is central Asia; Swedenborg believed that 'an ancient Word existed in the world . . . previous to the Israelitish Word . . . this Word is preserved in heaven . . . and exists at the present day among the nations of Great Tartary', *The True Christian Religion*, 1771, para. 266.

60–1 *Spies from Egypt . . . Meribah Kadesh*: 'And Moses sent them to spy out the land of Canaan . . . So they went up, and searched the land from the wilderness of Zin unto Rehob, as men come to Hamath . . . And they returned . . . to all the congregation of the children of Israel, unto the wilderness of Paran, to Kadesh' (Numbers 13.17–26). The Israelites resist the spies' recommendation and God tells Moses, 'ye rebelled against my commandment in the desert of Zin . . . to sanctify me at the water . . . that is the water of Meribah in Kadesh' (Numbers 27.14); this is the chapter in which the daughters of Zelophehad demand a female right to inheritance: see note to 'To Tirzah', p. 360).

Plate 69

305 15 *to give her maiden to her husband*: an echo of the controversial lines in
Visions of the Daughters of Albion 10.24–6, repeating the suggestion that
wives should make their maidservants sexually available to their husbands,
and probably suggested by Genesis 30.4 where Rachel, finding that she is
barren, gives her husband 'Bilhah her handmaid to wife', by whom Jacob
gets a son. William and Catherine Blake had no children.

Plate 70

306 4 *Three . . . Heads*: Hand represents the three Hunt brothers who edited,
the *Examiner* (see note to *Milton* 17.58–9 (p. 403).

Plate 72

310 50–1 *Fenelon . . . Hervey*: Pietist Christians from both Protestant and
Roman Catholic backgrounds. Francois Fénelon (1651–1715), Archbishop
of Cambrai but condemned by the Pope in 1699 for his defence of the
mystical, Quietist doctrines of Madame Guyon (Jeanne-Marie Bouvier
de la Motte-Guyon, 1648–1717; Cowper's translation of her poems was
published in 1801, while Blake was at work on illustrations for Hayley's
Life of Cowper); St Teresa of Avila (1515–82), Spanish nun and mystic
whose spiritual guide, *The Interior Castle*, 1577, was first published in
English in 1675; George Whitefield (1714–70), charismatic leader of the
Calvinist branch of the Methodist movement; see notes to *Milton* Plate
20; James Hervey (1714–58), Methodistical and Calvinist Anglican clergyman whose writings Blake had referred to in 'An Island in the Moon',
c.1784, and whose prose poem *Meditations among the Tombs*, 1746, he would
illustrate in a painting of *c*.1820; see note to 'The Tyger', p. 359.

Plate 73

311 15 *Fourfold Monarchy*: either Albion, since the British Crown was four-
fold at this date (England, Ireland, Scotland, and Hanover), or possibly
a reference to the Quadruple Alliance of Britain, Austria, Prussia, and
Russia (all monarchies) established in 1815 to maintain peace in Europe
after the end of the Napoleonic Wars; see note to 63.6 (p. 420).

312 43 *States*: see note to 49.66 (p. 418).

Plate 74

313 24–5 *Harmonies . . . Outline*: on Blake's commitment to Florentine linear
outline, rather than the 'Lights & Shades' of Venetian *colore* and chiaro-
scuro, see note to 'Sir Joshua Praises Michael Angelo', p. 376.

44 *divided Simeon*: Blake is describing the way in which the twelve sons of
Jacob (or tribes of Israel) were divided, or separated, a process which he
sees as part of the Fall. Jacob curses Simeon and Levi for their cruelty:
'I will divide them . . . and scatter them in Israel' (Genesis 49.7; see
next note). Simeon's descendants occupied Amalek territory: 'the sons of
Simeon . . . smote the rest of the Amalekites that were escaped, and dwelt
there unto this day' (1 Chronicles 4.42–3).

54–5 *Shechem . . . Dinah . . . Stratford place*: Shechem, a Hivite (from
Lebanon), 'ravishes' Jacob's daughter Dinah but then falls in love and

wishes to marry her. Dinah's brothers deceitfully say that if the Hivites agree to be circumcised they will agree to this merging of the tribes. But 'on the third day, when they were sore' they are attacked, killed, and despoiled by Simeon and Levi (Genesis 34; see previous note). *Erin* is Ireland; the 'Wound' may be an allusion to the failure to deliver the Catholic Emancipation which Ireland had been promised, after the Act of Union in 1801; Blake lived in South Molton Street from 1803 to 1821, on the other side of Oxford Street from *Stratford Place*, where No. 7 was refurbished in 1815, by Blake's acquaintance the architect C. H. Tatham, to serve as a residence for the Archdukes of Austria and Prince Nicholas of Russia during their post-Waterloo state visits to London; the painter Richard Cosway lived in the street from 1792 to 1821.

57 *Land of Cabul*: Cabul was a border city near Carmel and actually part of the inheritance of the tribe of Asher (Joshua 20.24–31), not 'Joseph & Benjamin'; it was one of the twenty cities given by Solomon to Hiram, King of Tyre, in return for building materials used for the Temple, who punningly called them 'the land of Cabul' (Hebrew: 'worthless'), 1 Kings 9.11–13.

Plate 75

314 2 *Bladud*: legendary British king, supposed founder of Bath and father of King Lear.

Plate 77

'*Saul Saul*' '*Why persecutest thou me*: Acts 9.4.

316 '*I stood among my valleys of the south*': compare 'in the land of the Chaldeans . . . I looked, and, behold, a whirlwind came out of the north, a great cloud, and a fire . . . out of the midst thereof came the likeness of four living creatures' (Ezekiel 1.3–5).

31 *Publicans and Harlots*: 'the scribes and Pharisees . . . said unto his disciples, How is it that he eateth and drinketh with publicans and sinners?' (Mark 2.16); Blake may be thinking of the willingness of Methodists to preach outdoors to unrespectable audiences.

Plate 78

317 12 *Forty-two*: probably a mistake: there are 'Thirty-two Counties of Ireland' in 72.15 (as there were in reality until 1838).

318 26 *Giants causeway*: a natural rock formation of basalt columns on the sea shore in County Antrim, Northern Ireland.

30 *Philisthea*: the land of the Philistines (Palestine).

Plate 80

320 16–18 *My Father . . . battles fierce*: Vala is speaking; she is usually the Emanation of Luvah but here seems also to be his daughter. In the political allegory Albion (Britain) has conquered Luvah (France) in 'battles' but then been overcome by French scepticism and rationalism.

321 42–6 *them . . . They . . . they*: not clear but probably the 'Children of Jerusalem' of l. 33.

322 57 *Skiddaws top*: mountain in the Lake District, near the Castlerigg stone circle, and probably chosen because Blake's enemies are seizing the high ground. But also near Keswick, where Coleridge lived 1800–4, Southey 1803–43, Shelley 1811–12, and not far from Wordsworth's Grasmere and Rydal, so Blake may possibly be enlarging the composite figure of Hand to include other contemporary writers.

323 Plate 82: this plate appears to have been hastily inscribed: there are two sets of deleted half-lines (here restored in italics) and several obvious copying errors (also here corrected): 'hands' (corrected to 'feet', line 43); 'Defomity' (69); 'sistes' (72); 'softeng' (77); 'Furnaes' (78–9).

324 59 *Billingsgate*: a Ward of the City of London, between London Bridge and the Tower, best known for its fish market, conducted on a wharf in Lower Thames Street from the Middle Ages to 1982.

60 *Albions fatal Tree*: public executions were held at Tyburn until 1783 (see notes to 12.28 and 28.13) but from 1783 to 1868 at Newgate Prison (named after an ancient gate in the west wall of the City of London).

Plate 83

325 10 *stone in orderd forms*: possibly the round Martello Towers (1805–8) and prison-like barracks built in southern counties during the Napoleonic Wars, resembling in shape the 'Druidic' temples of Stonehenge and Avebury.

326 14 *Saxon*: Stevenson suggests the German Saxons, parted from their Anglo-Saxon brethren.

51 *old Parent*: Ostriker suggests Old Father Thames.

327 52 *eight thousand and five hundred years*: Los is even older than the 5,800 years suggested by Archbishop Ussher's calculation of the biblical date of creation (see note to *Milton* 11.17), unless Blake has got his numbers the wrong way round.

72 *Cathedrons Dome*: see note to *Milton* 4.6 (p. 399).

Plate 84

328 11 *London*: this is a description of the image which accompanies the poem 'London' in *Songs of Experience*; seen unthinkingly London is London, seen through the eyes of Experience London is Babylon (l. 12), while seen through the eyes of Innocence it is potentially Jerusalem.

15–16 *Broad Street . . . Lincolns Inn*: a catalogue of places in London where Blake had lived: the corner of Broad(wick) Street and Marshall Street (1757–72, 1779–82), Poland Street (1785–90), Great Queen Street near Lincolns Inn (1772–9).

27 *Spindle*: see note to *Milton* 4.6 (p. 399).

Plate 86

329 3 *Reins:* kidneys, loins, the seat of the affections: 'I am he which searcheth the reins and hearts' (Revelation 2.23).

330 19 *New Jerusalem:* 'And I John saw the holy city, new Jerusalem, coming down from God out of heaven, prepared as a bride adorned for her husband' (Revelation 21.2).

Plate 89

334 6–7 *Pharisaion . . . Saddusaion:* Greek words for Pharisees, Scribes (see note to 'The Everlasting Gospel', l. 26, p. 372), Elders, High Priest, Priests, Sadducees (rivals of the Pharisees, holding a more conservative doctrine); compare 'the elders of the people and the chief priests and scribes came together' (Luke 22.66).

17–18 *brick-kilns | Disorganizd:* during their captivity in Egypt, the Israelites' lives are 'made bitter with hard bondage, in morter, and in brick' (Exodus 1.14). When Moses asks Pharaoh to grant them a holiday, he responds by saying that they must, additionally, gather their own straw for brick-making and they are 'scattered abroad throughout all the land of Egypt to gather stubble' (Exodus 5.12).

21 *ridges of Stone:* these may be mountain ranges but see note to 68.41 (p. 421).

29 *Scapulæ & Os Humeri:* shoulder blades and upper arm bone; see note to 66.75 (p. 421).

335 53 *Religion hid in War:* repeating 75.20.

Plate 90

336 23 *his Furnace:* this is a plate of reversals in which Hand, rather than Los, has a 'Furnace' (on 'Highgates heights', not Lambeth's vale) and Blake's enemies 'appropriate | The Divine Names'; Los is accordingly 'Terrified' in l. 53.

24 *Boadicea:* Boudica, Queen of the Iceni (in modern Norfolk), who led a British revolt against the Romans in AD 60, destroying Colchester, London, and Verulam, before being defeated at the Battle of Watling Street. Blake sees her as a cruel embodiment of the Female Will.

337 56 *a God of mercy:* so called.

59 *rocking Stones:* seen as Druidic monuments rather than natural phenomena.

Plate 91

1 *forgive a Friend:* Los has long been Blake's hero, now he becomes a mouthpiece through which Blake himself speaks (how can a Zoa have friends, or worry, l. 15, about whether or not to give them things?). This sense of direct, authorial presence will be confirmed in the next plate when we are told that 'The Poets Song draws to its period' (92.8) and in 97.5.

338 34 *Smaragdine Table:* the Tabula Smaragdina or Emerald Tablet is a brief hermetic treatise supposedly by Hermes Trismegistus (see note to 'Africa', *Song of Los* 3.18–19).

Plate 93

340 8 *Reuben found Mandrakes*: see note to 11.22 (p. 411).

10 *Rintrahs Plow*: see the Bard's Song in *Milton* Plates 5–6, though it is
Palamabron's harrow, not the plough (of Los and Rintrah), that Satan
there appropriates.

Plate 94

341 7 *white Rock*: Britain (see note to *Europe* 13.2, p. 388).

20 *England who is Brittannia*: see note to 32.28 (p. 415).

Plate 95

342 16–18 *Urizen . . . Anvil*: the Four Zoas return to their proper roles,
both in their symbolic functions as ploughman, shepherd, weaver, and
blacksmith, and to a proper balance of reason, sensation, emotion, and
imagination in human consciousness. Los (imagination) is praised because
he alone 'kept the Divine Vision' at a time when Rationalists, Empiricists
(see Introduction), and Sentimentalists (see note to *The First Book of
Urizen*, Plate 13) rejected it.

Plate 96

343 14 *thou canst not live*: see 'because I live, ye shall live also' (John 14.19)
and 'Now if we be dead with Christ, we believe that we shall also live with
him (Romans 6.8). Blake is stressing the Solifidian idea that it is faith
in Christ's redemptive self-sacrifice, not our own merits or good works,
which saves us.

37 *Living Waters*: 'I will give unto him that is athirst of the fountain of the
water of life freely' (Revelation 21.6).

Plate 98

345 9 *Chaucer*: in the apocalyptic resurrection, the empiricist villains of the
Enlightenment are united with the imaginative artists Milton, Shakespeare
(see notes to 40.30 (p. 416) and *Milton* 27.3 and 35.49, pp. 406, 407), and
Chaucer. Blake had made a painting and engraving of *Sir Jeffrey Chaucer
and the . . . Pilgrims on Their Journey to Canterbury* in 1808–10 and
described them in his *Descriptive Catalogue*, a *Prospectus*, and the so-called
'Public Address' (*E* 532–40, *E* 567–70, *E* 571–82).

12 *Fourfold*: once the Four Zoas (imagination, reason, sensation, emotion)
are back in balance, human consciousness is properly fourfold rather than
narrowly single.

346 33 *NonEns*: not being (following Late Latin 'ens', being; used by Boehme,
'the Ens or Essence of the Divine Light', in the ninth of his *Theosophic
Epistles*, 1618–24, translated 1649, and by Milton, 'At a Vacation Exercise',
1627).

46 *Covenant of Priam*: the pagan gods of Greece (see note to *Milton* 12.15)
are given their own 'covenant', like those between God and Noah and
Moses (see note to 'The Everlasting Gospel', l. 156, p. 373).

347 52 *Albions Poverty Tree*: the tree (previously Urizenic religion and the Tyburn or Newgate gallows; see note to 28.15) acquires an additional meaning as empire, here seen as an excuse for oppressive tax collection: the East India Company earned a large part of its revenues by collecting taxes (on commission) for local rulers and the American Revolution had been provoked by the imposition of taxes on sugar and tea; see note to 64.34. *Gog-Magog*: 'Gog, the land of Magog' is an enemy of Israel in Ezekiel 38–9; Gog and Magog are referred to in Revelation 20.8 as figures who will be unleashed by Satan in the last days; Geoffrey of Monmouth combined the names as 'Gogmagog' for a giant killed in the settlement of Britain by Brutus and his Trojans; separate statues of Gog and Magog stand in the Guildhall of the City of London. Like Geoffrey of Monmouth, Blake combines the names but gives the figure a triple head like Hand (see note to *Milton* 17.58–9).

56 *Thirty-two Nations*: see 72.38–42 where there are also thirty-two 'islands in the ocean' plus Britain (Albion) of which they will all (initially in an imperial sense but, after the reawakening, in a spiritual sense) become part.

INDEX OF TITLES AND FIRST LINES

MORE ABOUT **OXFORD WORLD'S CLASSICS**

American Literature

British and Irish Literature

Children's Literature

Classics and Ancient Literature

Colonial Literature

Eastern Literature

European Literature

Gothic Literature

History

Medieval Literature

Oxford English Drama

Philosophy

Poetry

Politics

Religion

The Oxford Shakespeare

A complete list of Oxford World's Classics, including Authors in Context, Oxford English Drama, and the Oxford Shakespeare, is available in the UK from the Marketing Services Department, Oxford University Press, Great Clarendon Street, Oxford OX2 6DP, or visit the website at www.oup.com/uk/worldsclassics.

In the USA, visit www.oup.com/us/owc for a complete title list.

Oxford World's Classics are available from all good bookshops. In case of difficulty, customers in the UK should contact Oxford University Press Bookshop, 116 High Street, Oxford OX1 4BR.

Late Victorian Gothic Tales
Literature and Science in the
　Nineteenth Century

JANE AUSTEN
Emma
Mansfield Park
Persuasion
Pride and Prejudice
Selected Letters
Sense and Sensibility

MRS BEETON
Book of Household Management

MARY ELIZABETH BRADDON
Lady Audley's Secret

ANNE BRONTË
The Tenant of Wildfell Hall

CHARLOTTE BRONTË
Jane Eyre
Shirley
Villette

EMILY BRONTË
Wuthering Heights

ROBERT BROWNING
The Major Works

JOHN CLARE
The Major Works

SAMUEL TAYLOR COLERIDGE
The Major Works

WILKIE COLLINS
The Moonstone
No Name
The Woman in White

CHARLES DARWIN
The Origin of Species

THOMAS DE QUINCEY
The Confessions of an English
　Opium-Eater
On Murder

CHARLES DICKENS
The Adventures of Oliver Twist
Barnaby Rudge
Bleak House
David Copperfield
Great Expectations
Nicholas Nickleby

A SELECTION OF   OXFORD WORLD'S CLASSICS

WILLIAM MORRIS	**News from Nowhere**
JOHN RUSKIN	**Praeterita**
	Selected Writings
WALTER SCOTT	**Ivanhoe**
	Rob Roy
	Waverley
MARY SHELLEY	**Frankenstein**
	The Last Man
ROBERT LOUIS STEVENSON	**Strange Case of Dr Jekyll and Mr Hyde and Other Tales**
	Treasure Island
BRAM STOKER	**Dracula**
W. M. THACKERAY	**Vanity Fair**
FRANCES TROLLOPE	**Domestic Manners of the Americans**
OSCAR WILDE	**The Importance of Being Earnest and Other Plays**
	The Major Works
	The Picture of Dorian Gray
ELLEN WOOD	**East Lynne**
DOROTHY WORDSWORTH	**The Grasmere and Alfoxden Journals**
WILLIAM WORDSWORTH	**The Major Works**
WORDSWORTH and COLERIDGE	**Lyrical Ballads**